PROTECTIONISM AND THE FUTURE OF INTERNATIONAL SHIPPING

DR ADEMUNI-ODEKE
Faculty of Law,
University of Aberdeen

Protectionism and the Future of International Shipping

The Nature, Development and Role of Flag Discriminations and Preferences, Cargo Reservations and Cabotage Restrictions, State Intervention and Maritime Subsidies

1984 **MARTINUS NIJHOFF PUBLISHERS**
a member of the KLUWER ACADEMIC PUBLISHERS GROUP
DORDRECHT / BOSTON / LANCASTER

Distributors

for the United States and Canada: Kluwer Academic Publishers, 190 Old Derby Street, Hingham, MA 02043, USA
for the UK and Ireland: Kluwer Academic Publishers, MTP Press Limited, Falcon House, Queen Square, Lancaster LA1 1RN, England
for all other countries: Kluwer Academic Publishers Group, Distribution Center, P.O. Box 322, 3300 AH Dordrecht, The Netherlands

Library of Congress Cataloging in Publication Data

Ademuni-Odeke, Dr.
Protectionism and the future of international shipping.

Bibliography: p.
Includes index.
1. Merchant marine--Government policy. 2. Shipping--Government policy. 3. Maritime law. I. Title.
HE736.A34 1984 387.5'068 83-25055

ISBN 90-247-2918-1

PRINTED IN THE NETHERLANDS

To Helmy and my Mother

Contents

PART TWO
TRADITIONAL METHODS OF ESTABLISHING NATIONAL FLEETS

PART FIVE
RESOLVING THE PROBLEM: RECOMMENDATIONS

PART SIX
OVERALL CONCLUSION AND BIBLIOGRAPHY

Foreword

Dr. Ademuni-Odeke has undertaken an ambitious project in seeking to assess the future prospects for the development of the world's merchant shipping industry. Starting from the premise that the majority of states which have achieved independence since the Second World War inevitably regard the establishment of a national merchant fleet of their own as a mark of their political and economic vitility, he proceeds to examine the methods they have employed to achieve this objective and gives a critical assessment of their chance of success. In such a situation it is perhaps not surprising to discover that developing states have initially resorted to the well tried and traditional methods adopted by their predecessors to reach this goal, namely, flag preference, flag discrimination, maritime subsidies and state intervention. The author expresses some doubt as to the legality of many of these traditional methods of support when viewed from the standpoint of customary international law and the various international conventions and agreements in the economic sphere. There is, however, considerable force in the central thrust of his argument that such traditional approaches to the problem no longer make economic sense – it is no longer practical to attempt to defeat well-established maritime regimes at their own game. In the absence of an expanding market it is the author's view that the answer is to be found not in increased competition, but in the development of joint ventures and other forms of cooperation between developing and developed maritime nations. Ultimately he envisages such cooperation being monitored by an International Shipping Authority directly responsible to the United Nations General Assembly.

Dr. Ademuni-Odeke makes a forceful and persuasive case which gains additional strength when advanced during a period of widespread depression in the industry. The author is to be congratulated on the admirable grasp he displays of the wealth of material at his disposal and, while he relies heavily on US experience for examples to bolster his central theme, he nevertheless draws illustrations from a wide variety of shipping regimes ranging from Indonesia to Peru.

The concept is original and intriguing, the approach is balanced and persuasive, and the study as a whole provides a valuable contribution to an understanding of the problems facing the world's shipping industry at the present day.

Institute of Maritime Law,
University of Southampton

Prof. J. F. Wilson

Preface

Protectionism is a practice that has dominated issues in international shipping in the past, and will continue to do so for decades to come. Currently, hardly any maritime conference or convention transpires without its mention; drums of ink and roles of paper have, no doubt, been used for this purpose. It was the subject of the GATT Ministerial Conference held at the beginning of 1983 and of the UNCTAD VI Conference at Belgrade, Yugoslavia, in May-June of that year. It is bound to occupy many more minds, with more urgency, for the rest of this decade now that the UN Code of Conduct for Linear Conferences has come into effect (October 6 1983).

In international trade, protectionism means the advocacy of protective tariffs as a means of developing national wealth and power. The chief arguments in support of this policy have been: encouragement of infant industry; opportunity for the employment of a variety of individual talents through industrial diversification; savings in the cost of transportation; conservation of national resources for home use; and national power, in the form of a self-reliant economy. The prevailing economic conditions, world-wide, have meant that very few nations indeed have been able to resist the temptation to resort to the protectionist lever in maritime transport.

This has led to wide-spread use in international shipping relations of such restrictive measures as flag discrimination, flag preference, cargo-reservation, cabotage restrictions, state intervention, maritime subsidies and other forms of state aid. But what exactly are these terms? What is their origin, history and/or development? What functions do they perform or are they designed to perform? How effective have they been? And what have been the consequences of their use for the economy, or in the area of international customary, and economic laws, as well as in international shipping itself? How could these affect the future prospects for the development of national and international maritime fleets? Where does the way forward lie?

These, and many other related matters, are the questions which this survey covers and to which it attempts to offer solutions. In the past, these rather crucial issues have only been treated piecemeal and not as a whole and in comprehensive depth. In this respect, this book was long overdue and fills a large gap that has existed for some time. I believe its strength is its pragmatic and multi-disciplinary approach: it covers issues ranging from history to law, politics, trade and commerce, international law, international relations, economics, transportation, development studies, finance, accounting, international trade, and, of course, shipping itself. Indeed, the very international nature of shipping demands nothing less than such a method.

In choosing this approach, I have attempted to combine and draw into the research my practical experience and training in law and the shipping industry, both in the DMNS and TMNS; that is, my long residence in the TMNS and my upbringing in the DMNS. The book will be an *invaluable companion* to all involved, in one way or another, with maritime transport and transport economics; it will be a suitable *ready reference* for shipping executives and administrators, lawyers, civil servants, policy decision-makers, port administrators, etc.; it will be a *guide* for researchers and academics involved in maritime economics, transport studies, politics, science, economic history, international law/relations, and so on. It will also be *a useful textbook* for law students and students of maritime law, navigation, nautical studies, and especially of the Institute of Shipbrokers, Chartered Insurance Institute, Chartered Institute of Transport, etc. Lastly, I hope it might constitute a valuable addition to the library shelves of some research institutes, reference libraries, public libraries, universities, polytechnics, institutes, academies, national libraries, depositories, etc. Although the book has taken about five years to research and prepare, facts and figures have been revised and updated twice, including immediately before going to press.

University of Aberdeen
Scotland, October 1983

Dr Ademuni-Odeke

Acknowledgements

This book is the final product of the efforts of many colleagues and friends, and of help from almost every continent – a fact which, in itself, testifies to the comprehensiveness and thoroughness of the survey. It has not been possible to thank every person and organisation who helped, both directly and from behind the scenes, to make this project a success; that would have been an awesome task. But I remain grateful and indebted to them all. I would like to draw the readers' attention to the list of some of these individuals and organisations below.

In addition, I would like to express my special gratitude to Professor John F. Wilson for reading through the draft and writing the foreword; to Dr Ralph Beddard for reading through the first draft and making useful comments; to my former colleagues Dr Amil Vitharana of the Sri Lankan Bureau of Freights (Colombo) and Dr Maria Dotsika Papavisilou of the Prime Minister's Office, Athens, Greece, for their encouragements and provision of materials; to Mrs Julia O'Sullivan for reading through the final draft; to Mrs Jacqueline G. Betteridge, for her forbearance and her patient secretarial assistance over those five years; and above all to Helmy for the graphics, and for her encouragement, support and understanding.

However, the final responsibility for any shortcomings, or errors, and for the views expressed in this text, lies with me.

Organisations and institutions

African E. Enterprises, London
African Educational Trust, London
Bremen Institute of Shipping Economics, Bremen
Canadian Transport Commission, Ottawa
College of Nautical Studies, Southampton
Dalhousie Ocean Studies Programme, Halifax
European Economic Community, Brussels
Federal Maritime Commission, Washington DC
General Council of British Shipping, London
Inter-Library Loan Services, Southampton University

International Chamber of Commerce, Paris
International Chamber of Shipping, London
International Labour Organisation, Geneva
International Maritime Organisation (IMO), London
International Monetary Fund, New York
International University Exchange Fund, Geneva
Institute of Maritime Law, Law Faculty, Southampton University
Lloyds List, London
Lloyds Register of Shipping, London
Maritime Administration, Washington DC
National Library of Economic and Political Science, L.S.E., London
National Library of Scotland, Edinburgh
Nautical Institute, London
Netherlands Maritime Research Institute, Rotterdam
Organisation for Economic Cooperation and Development, Paris
Seatrade Academy, Cambridge
Seatrade, Colchester
University of Aberdeen, Old Aberdeen, Scotland
United Nations Conference on Trade and Development, Geneva
University of Southampton, Southampton
University of Wales, Institute of Science and Technology, Cardiff
World Bank, (IBRD), Washington
World University Service (UK), London

Individuals

Dr Ralph Beddard, Institute of Maritime Law, Southampton University
Dr Auni Benham, Shipping Division UNCTAD
Dr Omar Franco, Caracas, Venezuela
Mr Richard Gage, MARAD Representative US Embassy, London
Messrs Rosa Greaves, Faculty of Law, Southampton University
Miss Joan Hoyle, Law and Social Sciences Department, Southampton University Library
Mr Magnus Johns, Open University, Milton Keynes, England
Dr Costa R. Mahalu, Hamburg, West Germany
Miss Diana Marshalsay, Inter-Library Loan Department, Southampton University Library
Mr Angus N. Nicholson, ICC Caracas Project, Southampton Docks
Mr Eric Pollock, Associated British Ports (formerly The British Transport Docks Board)
Mr D.E. Ross, British Library of Political and Economic Sciences
Mr D. Petropoulos, EEC Transport Directorate
Mr Frederick Korswargen, Lima, Peru
Professor S.G. Sturmey, Abidjan, Ivory Coast
Mr Geoff Fanning, Librarian, College of Nautical Studies, Warsash, Southampton
Miss Fiona Cooper, Library Assistant, College of Nautical Studies, Warsash, Southampton

List of abbreviations used

ACP	African, Caribbean and Pacific Countries (Lome Convention)
AID	Agency for International Development (USA)
ANCAP	National Fuels, Alcoholic and Portland Cement Administration (Uruguay)
ASEAN	Association of South East Asian Nations
ASTINAVE	Venezuelan Shipyard Company at Los Tecques
ATDAA	Agricultural Trade Development and Assistance Act (USA)
BIMCO	Baltic and International Maritime Conference
BISPCO	British and Irish Steam Packet Company Limited (Irish)
BMLA	British Maritime Law Association
BOP	Balance of Payments (Problems)
BP	British Petroleum
BR	British Rail
BSC	British Shipbuilders Corporation
BSF	British Shippers' Federation (Association)
CAACE	Comité des Associations D'Armateurs des Communautés Européennes
CARGO-nos	Cargo Not Otherwise Stated
CAVN	Compañia Anónima Venezuelana de Navegación
CCF	Capital Construction Fund (USA)
CEN(J)SA	Council of European and Japanese National Shipowners' Association
CENSA	Committee of European Shipowners' Association (*see* CES)
CES	Committee of European Shipowners (*see* CENSA)
CIF	'Cost Insurance Freight'
CIFE	Comitato Interministeriale per la Programmazione Economica (Italian)
CGM	Campagnie Générale Maritime (French)
COMANAN	Compagnie Morocain de Navigation
CMEA	Council for Mutual Economic Assistance (*see* COMECON)
COMECON	Commission for Economic Cooperation (*see* CMEA)
CMI	Comitée Maritime Internationale
COMPSA	Compañia Arrendataria Monopolis de Petroleons SA (Colombia)

CONG	Congress (The US House of Representatives)
CPSA	Corporacion Naviera Peruana Sudamericana (Peru)
CPV	Compania Panana de Vapores (Chile)
CRF	Construction Reserve Fund (USA)
CSAV	Compania Sudamericana de Vapores (Chile)
CSG	Consultative Shipping Group
CTM	Compania Portuguese de Transporto Maritimas
CUP	Cambridge University Press
DESS	Department of Education and Sciences (UK)
DHSS	Department of Health and Social Services (UK)
DBP	Development Bank of the Phillipines
DMNS	Developing Maritime Nations
DOA	Department of Agriculture (USA)
DOC	Department of Commerce (USA)
DOCENAVE	Vale de Rio Doce Navegaco SS (Brazil)
DOJ	Department of Justice (USA) (The Judiciary)
DOT	Department of Transport (USA)
dwt	Deadweight tons (*see* grt)
EAC	East African Community (former)
EANSL	Eastern African National Shipping Line (former)
ECA	Economic Commission for Africa (UN)
ECAFE	Economic Commission for Asia and the Far East (UN)
ECE	Economic Commission for Europe (UN)
ECLA	Economic Commission for Latin America (UN)
ECOSOC	Economic and Social Council (of the UN)
ECOWAS	Economic Organisation of West African States
EEC	European Economic Community
EFTA	European Free Trade Area
ELCANO	Empressa Nacionale (Spain)
ELMA	Empressa Lineas Maritimas Argentinas
EMPREMAR	Empressa Maritimas del Estado (Brazil)
ERP	European Recovery Programme (under Marshall Plan)
EXIMBANK	Export-Import Bank (USA, Japan)
FAO	Food and Agricultural Programme (UN) (Rome)
FINCANTIERI	Finanziaria Cantieri Navali (Italian)
FINMARE	Financia Maritima
FMB	Federal Maritime Board (USA; *see* FMC)
FMC	Federal Maritime Commission (USA; successor of FMB)
FMG	Flota Mercante Grancolombiana (Colombia)
FOA	Foreign Operations Administration (USA)
FOB	Free on Board
FOC	Flags of Convenience
FRG	Federal Republic of Germany (West Germany)
FRONAPE	Flota Nacionale de Petroleiros (Brazil)
GATT	General Agreements on Tariffs and Trade
GCBS	General Council of British Shipping
GDP	Gross Domestic Product (*see* GNP)
GDR	German Democratic Republic (DDR; East Germany)

GNP	Gross National Product (*see* GDP)
grt	Gross registered tons (*see* dwt)
GSP	General Schemes of Preferences
GAZOCEAN	Moroccan-French Gas Company
HATRICS	Hampshire Technical Research Industrial Commercial Series
IBRD	International Bank for Reconstruction and Development (World Bank)
ICA	International Cooperation Administration (USA)
ICAO	International Civil Aviation Authority
IAC	International Admiralty Court (Appellate) (*see* IDC)
ICJ	International Court of Justice
ICC	International Chamber of Commerce
ICNT	Incomposite Negotiating Text (of UNCLOSS)
ICS	International Chamber of Shipping
IDA	International Development Association
IDC	International Admiralty Court (*see* IAC)
IFC	International Finance Corporation
ILO	International Labour Organisation
IMF	International Monetary Fund
IMMA	International Merchant Marine Authority
IMMB	International Merchant Marine Bank
IMCO	Inter-Governmental Maritime Consultative Organisation (*see* IMO)
IME	International Maritime Exchange
IMO	International Maritime Organisation (successor of IMCO)
IMS	International Monetary System
INI	Industriale Nacionale Italia
INTERTANKO	International Association of Independent Tanker Owners
IRI	Instituto per la Ricostruziane Industriale (Italian)
ISA	International Seabed Authority
ISC	Irish Shipping Company
ISF	International Shipping Federation
ITO	International Trade Organisation (forerunner of GATT)
ITWF	International Transport Workers' Federation
LAFTA	Latin American Free Trade Area
LAMCO	Liberian Mining Corporation
LASH	Lighters Aboard Ship
LDCS	Less Developed Countries
LNG	Liquified Natural Gas (Carriers)
LSC	Liberian Shipping Corporation
LSE	London School of Economics and Political Science
MARAD	Maritime Administration (USA)
MFN(c)	Most Favoured Nation (Clause)
MARPHOCEAN	Marocain Phosphate Ocean
MMDF	Merchant Marine Development Fund
MMAO	Merchant Navy and Airline Officers (Association)
MMSA	Merchant Marine Service Association
MIT	Massachusetts Institute of Technology

MNCS	Multinational Corporations
MSE	Multinational Shipping Enterprises;
NATO	North Atlantic Treaty Organisation
NIC	National Industrial Commission (Peru)
NICS	Newly Industrialised Nations
NIEO	New International Economic Order
NILI	National Italian Line
NIMO	New International Maritime Order
NUS	National Union of Seamen
NY	New York
OAU	Organisation for African Unity
OBO	Oil-Bulk-Ore (Combine Carriers)
OCP	L'Office Chirifione de Phosphate (Moroccan)
OEEC	Organisation for European Economic Cooperation (*see* OECD)
OECD	Organisation for Economic Cooperation and Development (successor of OEEC)
OPEC	Organisation of Petroleum Exporting Countries
OUP	Oxford University Press
PANLIBHO	Panamanian, Liberian and Honduras (*see* FOC)
PCL	Polytechnic of Central London
PEMBEX	Petrolens Mexicanex
PERNI	Indonesian National Shipping Line
PSC	Provident Shipping Company (Liberia)
RBPCS	Restrictive Business Practices
R & D	Research and Design (Department of British Ship Research Association)
RNSA	Royal Netherlands Shipowners' Association
ROC	Republic of China (Nationalist) (Taiwan, Formosa)
RORO(s)	Roll-on Roll-off(s)
SAFMARINE	South African Marine
SAS	Scandinavian Airline Services
SCINDIA	Shipping Corporation of India
SCS	Socialist Countries
SEA	South East Asia
SEATO	South East Asian Treaty Organisation (*see* ASEAN)
SIMA	Peruvian National Shipyards
SUNAMAM	Superintendancy of the National Merchant Marine (Brazil)
STNS	State Trading Nations (Planned Economics)
TDB	Trade and Development Board (of UNCTAD)
TCM	Export Development Corporation (Portugal)
TISC	Total Investment Shipping Company (Liberia)
TMN(S)	Traditional Maritime Nation(s)
TW	Third World
UAE	United Arab Emirates
UAR	United Arab Republic (Egypt)
UDI	Unilateral Declaration of Independence
UK	United Kingdom (England, Ulster, Wales, Scotland, Isle of Man, Channel Isles)

UN(O)	United Nations Organisation
UNCLOSS	United Nations' Conference on the Law of the Sea
UNCTAD	United Nations Conference on Trade and Development
UNDP	United Nations Development Programme
UNESCO	United Nations Educational Scientific and Cultural Organisation
UNIDO	United Nations Industrial Development Organisation
USC	United States Codes
US CONG	United States Congress
US SEN	United States Senate
VAT	Value Added Tax
VCD	Verolme Cork Dockyard (Irish)
WHO	World Health Organisation
YPE	Yacimientos Petroliteros Fiscales (Argentine Oil Co.)
ZIM Lines	Israeli National Shipping Line

Flag abbreviations

Abbreviation	*Country*	*Abbreviation*	*Country*
Ag	Algeria	DD	East Germany (Democratic Republic)
Al	Albania		
Am	USA		
An	Angola	Do	Dominican Republic
Ar	Argentina		
As	Austria	Du	Netherlands
Au	Australia	Ec	Ecuador
Ba	Bahrain	Eg	Egypt
Bb	Barbados	ES	El Salvador
Be	Belgium	Et	Ethiopia
Bh	Bangladesh	Fa	Faroes
Bm	Burma	Fi	Finland
Bn	Benin	Fj	Fiji
Bo	Bolivia	Fr	France
Br	United Kingdom and Colonies	Ga	Gabon
		Ge	West Germany (Federal Republic)
Bs	Bahamas		
Bu	Bulgaria	Gh	Ghana
Bz	Brazil	Gm	Gambia
Ca	Canada	Gn	Guinea
Ce	Sri Lanka (Ceylon)	Gr	Greece
		Gu	Guatemala
Ch	Chile	Ha	Haiti
Cm	Comoros	Ho	Honduras
Cn	Cameroun	Hu	Hungary
Co	Colombia	Ia	Indonesia
CR	Costa Rica	Ic	Iceland
Cu	Cuba	Ih	Irish Republic
CV	Cape Verde	In	India
Cy	Cyprus	Iq	Iraq
Cz	Czechoslovakia	Ir	Iran
Da	Denmark	Is	Israel

Abbreviation	*Country*
It	Italy
Iv	Ivory Coast
Ja	Japan
Jm	Jamaica
Jo	Jordan
Ke	Kenya
Ko	South Korea
Ku	Kuwait
Le	Lebanon
Li	Liberia
Ly	Libya
Ma	Malta
Mb	Mozambique
Me	Mexico
Mg	Madagascar
Mn	Monaco
Mo	Morocco
Ms	Mauritius
Mt	Mauritania
Mv	Maldives
My	Malaysia
NA	Netherlands Antilles
Ne	Nepal
Ng	Nigeria
Ni	Nicaragua
No	Norway
Nu	Nauru
NZ	New Zealand
Om	Oman
Pa	Panama
PG	Papua New Guinea
Ph	Poland
Pi	Philippines
Pk	Pakistan
Po	Portugal
PP	Philippines
Pv	Peru
Py	Paraguay
Qt	Qatar
RC	Peoples Republic of China
RK	North Korea
Rm	Romania
Ru	USSR
SA	South Africa
Sc	Seychelles
Se	Senegal
Sg	Singapore
Si	Saudi Arabia
SL	Sierra Leone
Sn	Suriname
SO	Somalia
Sp	Spain
Ss	Switzerland
Su	Sudan
SV	St Vincent and Grenadines
Sw	Sweden
Sy	Syria
Ta	Tanzania
Tg	Togo
Th	Thailand
Tn	Tunisia
To	Tonga
Tr	Trinidad and Tobago
Tu	Turkey
Tw	Taiwan
UA	United Arab Emirates
Ug	Uganda
Ur	Uruquay
Va	Vanuatu
Ve	Venezuela
Vn	Vietnam
WS	Western Samoa
Ye	Yemen (Democratic Republic)
Ys	Yugoslavia
Za	Zambia
Zr	Zaire

Part One

Protectionism and the quest for national fleets

Introduction to Part One

The general trend in international shipping is that of an industry in decline. Its proximity to international trade means the decline is in line with the general recession world-wide. Among the TMNS (Traditional Maritime Nations) the story of the industry is characterized by lay-ups, overtonnaging and dwindling activities at the repair and building yards.[1] Sufficient trade exists among these countries and the necessary resources are available to sustain a viable industry. Yet it is a case of the 'big boys' attempting to streamline trade or seeking to get out altogether.

Surprisingly, however, the pessimism and decline of the TMNS is matched by the enthusiasm and slow, but steady increase of the fleets of the DMNS (Developing Maritime Nations) and the SCS (Socialists Countries).[2] Most striking are the fleets of the Far-Eastern DMNS, such as the Philippines, South Korea, Singapore, Malaysia, Indonesia and Hong Kong, that have not only expanded greatly in the recent past but have also developed repair and building yards that now compete effectively with those of the TMNS.[3]

Why do we find this paradox of the former giants seeking every opportunity to exit and the newcomers clammering to enter? Could it be that the DMNS and SCS could manage better and more cheaply, but have always been unfairly kept out? Could this defy the general classical theory of the doctrine of comparative advantage?[4] Does this paradoxic trend reveal anything previously unknown,[5] or is the development merely caused by the owners in the TMNS, weary of their dwindling profits due to labour demands and recession, selling off or transferring them to the DMNS where the costs of operations are relatively lower? If so, what effects will this have on the flags of convenience and the liner conference systems that had emerged for this very reason?[6]

Surely, with centuries of experience behind them and endowed with all the prerequisite resources, the 'big boys' must know best and have now decided this is the time to quit![7] Why then are the DMNS, with all their handicaps and in the face of this overwhelming evidence against them, clammering to get in? What is so 'holy' or 'magical' about shipping that attracts the DMNS to risk their badly needed and scarce resources? In other words, what makes shipping tick? These are some of the issues raised and discussed in this opening part of the survey.[8]

Table 1. The world merchant fleet by flags as of April 1st, 1983 (ships of 300 grt and dwt, and over).[a]

Flag[b]	No. of ships	grt[c]	nrt	dwt
Liberia[d]	2 061	66 847 753	51 116 064	131 215 631
Japan	4 193	38 023 877	23 929 521	63 041 212
Greece	2 694	35 178 067	23 348 303	61 046 572
Panama[d]	3 834	31 838 388	21 202 029	53 978 325
UK	1 212	18 939 847	12 803 070	30 520 541
Norway	744	18 929 225	13 516 584	34 572 073
USSR	3 007	18 162 449	9 515 495	24 450 575
US	1 046	16 518 917	11 758 526	25 921 309
France	392	10 029 250	7 169 330	17 467 008
Italy	922	9 167 787	5 945 275	15 369 775
PR of China	910	7 679 467	4 577 338	11 690 742
Spain	713	7 065 378	4 985 909	13 488 308
Singapore	620	6 704 047	4 478 407	11 391 238
FR of Germany	1 063	6 527 893	4 573 131	10 682 841
India	425	6 089 056	3 951 771	9 951 594
Brazil	424	5 656 871	3 979 049	9 398 355
South Korea	625	5 473 363	3 494 158	9 294 089
Saudi Arabia	279	4 965 024	3 517 075	8 885 967
Denmark[e]	567	4 852 358	3 183 537	7 977 410
Netherlands[f]	668	4 573 548	2 993 711	7 262 439
Hong Kong	191	4 152 506	2 751 514	6 839 514
Sweden	346	3 787 035	2 462 259	6 043 377
Poland	336	3 265 204	1 990 563	4 768 152
Philippines	384	2 596 899	1 686 531	4 244 638
Yugoslavia	316	2 519 835	1 561 398	3 848 575
Taiwan	167	2 484 065	1 619 367	4 017 355
Turkey	397	2 282 276	1 456 462	3 780 148
Romania	243	2 271 730	1 359 808	3 527 576
Cyprus	519	2 248 322	1 398 337	3 592 924
Finland	213	2 154 416	1 318 793	3 280 159
Argentina	204	2 087 688	1 239 441	3 136 066
Belgium	93	1 984 490	1 477 591	3 402 632
Kuwait	86	1 943 234	1 306 970	3 242 598
Australia	95	1 736 765	1 076 270	2 771 235
Indonesia	644	1 582 610	960 470	2 347 783
Iran	108	1 438 578	1 012 078	2 509 983
Iraq	58	1 403 065	994 828	2 551 737
GDR	190	1 284 394	705 780	1 716 696
Algeria	77	1 265 338	838 165	1 907 335
Mexico	103	1 239 876	774 278	1 979 166
Malaysia	204	1 206 128	799 951	1 709 951
Portugal	93	1 174 473	833 344	2 002 015
Canada	196	1 172 287	775 187	1 803 982
Bulgaria	115	1 156 617	645 762	1 734 251
Libya	38	878 139	638 229	1 588 138
Cuba	108	759 296	445 045	1 035 415
Venezuela	92	748 241	445 994	1 086 098
Malta	105	708 331	429 898	1 057 353
Israel	62	666 667	381 414	888 354
South Africa	38	648 990	397 589	839 031

Table 1. (cont.)

Flag[b]	No. of ships	grt[c]	nrt	dwt
Peru	79	641 319	395 804	955 616
Bermuda	48	616 622	373 360	932 838
Pakistan	69	602 484	354 904	868 172
Bahamas	61	593 815	367 824	827 158
Egypt	132	522 766	298 269	707 427
Nigeria	42	431 429	263 018	627 509
Thailand	140	426 560	248 852	636 964
Chile	53	414 157	270 786	704 942
Lebanon	218	377 039	207 834	552 772
North Korea	38	360 427	229 655	624 718
Bangladesh	119	357 572	207 790	521 778
Colombia	49	339 600	193 435	434 784
Ecuador	48	335 832	199 173	505 515
Morocco	60	319 777	190 257	525 830
Switzerland	34	318 515	194 791	473 460
Cayman Islands	131	283 285	170 504	461 029
Qatar	22	238 301	151 303	384 001
Maldives	42	236 070	136 162	350 272
Honduras	131	235 346	134 623	321 348
Ireland	71	232 593	135 097	296 633
UAE	83	230 842	140 711	364 970
Vietnam	72	228 618	137 601	351 030
New Zealand	35	221 947	123 573	258 090
Uraguay	26	189 843	121 829	304 505
Czechoslovakia	19	184 265	115 355	276 870
Ghana	28	177 462	104 224	240 266
Sri Lanka	31	170 965	96 986	251 506
Tunisia	27	162 524	90 036	229 721
Ivory Coast	13	130 927	70 782	174 176
Austria	18	103 776	66 422	179 159
Sudan	11	93 237	55 473	126 612
Iceland	51	87 182	54 526	145 191
Angola	23	82 227	52 492	127 017
Hungary	20	78 975	40 427	109 348
Zaire	9	77 951	51 222	118 514
Gabon	4	75 866	56 557	142 182
Madagascar	21	71 536	41 156	101 346
Burma	24	68 175	41 447	93 059
Naura	5	56 406	37 842	81 537
Albania	15	51 770	30 332	76 448
Tanzania	14	45 647	26 914	65 890
Syria	37	43 925	24 122	63 010
Gibraltar	26	41 010	24 401	644566
Barbados	2	40 460	29 120	71 540
Dominican Republic	26	37 636	23 006	64 529
Cameroon	4	37 052	24 059	59 458
Togo	4	36 732	23 211	53 520
Mauretania	7	34 989	21 684	49 862
St. Vincent	18	31 904	17 228	46 225
Paraguay	28	30 048	17 947	38 308
Ethiopia	14	29 787	16 475	45 506
Guatemala	6	27 786	16 530	39 616

Table 1. (cont.)

Flag[b]	No. of ships	grt[c]	nrt	dwt
Nicaragua	9	24 714	14 636	37 226
Mozambique	11	21 411	12 369	32 154
Jordan	4	20 727	11 112	30 328
Monaco	3	18 143	10 503	29 046
Fiji Islands	14	18 084	9 599	24 928
Papua New Guinea	27	18 017	10 109	22 134
Costa Rica	14	17 071	8 251	23 218
Bolivia	2	14 913	7 694	19 150
Tonga	11	13 664	6 904	19 174
Senegal	7	12 712	7 462	18 383
Surinam	8	12 162	7 117	17 392
Bahrain	11	10 458	5 943	16 411
Trinidad & Tobago	8	9 207	4 932	7 943
Cape Verde	6	9 000	5 969	16 724
Jamaica	5	8 284	5 156	13 983
Guyana	17	7 870	3 928	9 166
Somalia	3	7 035	3 171	1 759
Equatorial Guinea	2	6 412	3 583	6 648
Vanuatu	7	5 415	2 802	7 546
Republic of Yemen	5	5 093	2 525	7 943
St. Lucia	5	4 968	2 704	7 144
Virgin Islands	9	3 891	1 921	4 700
West Samoa	1	3 838	1 748	5 536
Benin	1	2 999	1 894	4 400
Oman	4	2 603	1 452	3 883
Kiribati	3	2 054	1 027	2 074
Gambia	1	1 597	977	2 900
Anguilla	4	1 524	857	2 138
Turks & Caicos Islands	3	1 430	915	2 195
Arabic Republic of Yemen	3	1 260	685	1 340
Kenya	1	1 168	692	1 590
Cambodia	1	998	557	1 458
Montserrat	1	711	334	1 000
Comora Islands	1	649	342	1 358
Seychelles	1	505	260	521
Soloman Islands	1	499	279	742
Republic of Guinea	1	387	178	510
All flags	34 733	387 226 512	260 499 317	657 389 329
April 1st, 1982	34 562	388 991 968	262 425 606	662 148 581
April 1st, 1981	33 969	385 225 364	260 489 725	658 253 968
April 1st, 1980	33 606	382 368 871	258 823 847	655 495 419

Source: Institute of Shipping Economies, Bremen. For detailed figures concerning the World Merchant Fleet compare the June issue of this periodical.

[a] In the strict sense, i.e. sea-going cargo and/or passenger carrying vessels and tonnage for commercial purposes only (incl. US Reserve Fleet of about 1.3 mill grt).

[b] Flags in italics are the DMNS among the top 100.

[c] In case of double measurements the tonnage figures refer to full scantling vessels as opposed to shelterdeckers; other measurement techniques are not considered.

[d] Open registry countries.

[e] Including Faroe Island.

[f] Including Netherlands Antilles.

CHAPTER 1

Protectionism and international shipping

1. Introduction

This book is a review and a detailed comparative study of the role played by flag discrimination, flag preference, cargo reservation, state intervention and maritime subsidies, with specific reference to the practice of the US and the developing maritime nations (DMNS).[9] Shipping has hitherto been the exclusive preserve of the advanced or industrialised nations and has been run on liberal principles. The end of the war resulted in the emergence from colonialism, of the so-called underdeveloped countries – herein referred to as the developing maritime nations, and designated as the DMNS.[10] The end of the war also saw the emergence of the planned economies or socialist countries (SCS). These latter countries brought to the scene a conflicting political and economic philosophy, and advocated individual national fleets.[11]

This challenge to the original international cross-trade fleets coupled with the technological revolution, marked a change away from the TMNS' *laissez-faire*.[12] The DMNS were further dissatisfied with the effects of flags of convenience, liner conferences, the incidence of rising freight rates and the emergence of synthetics which undermined their international trade positions as suppliers of raw materials. Considering the close link between international shipping and international trade, the improvement of a country's balance of payments' position is, therefore, a major rationale for shipping.[13] However, the DMNS lack the prerequisites for the establishment and development of economically viable national fleets, hence their resort to the use of restrictive practices. Ironically, they are joined in this by the US.

Conflicts arise when the use of these methods is aided by state protectionism and when the rationale for their employment is extended to include political and security reasons.[14] Contravention of international customary law, international economic laws and possible economic disruptions threaten to wreck the very fabric of national and international maritime fleets. This survey sets out to outline what constitutes these *protectionist* or restrictive practices, or traditional methods.[15] It also examines the ensuing consequences of the said approach and seeks remedies which might assist in transforming the inevitable *confrontations* to *consultation.* It is proposed that *cooperation* in the form of joint ventures, *inter alia,* will be the way out in the future for the development of national and international fleets.[16]

Table 2. Container traffic in selected ports of developing countries, 1978 and 1979

Country or territory	Port	Container traffic 1979 in TEU's	Container traffic 1978 in TEU's	Per cent change 1978 over 1979
Hong Kong	Hong Kong	1 303 923	1 226 256	6
Singapore	Singapore	698 506	539 379	30
Republic of Korea	Busan	632 835	506 556	25
Saudi Arabia	Jeddah	496 390	340 537	46
Philippines	Manila	322 050	209 976	53
Saudi Arabia	Damman	211 250	158 445	33
United Arab Emirates (UAE)	Dubai	169 825	136 046	25
Jamaica	Kingston	153 280	143 297	7
Thailand	Bangkok	146 432	106 964	37
Kuwait	Shuwaikh	122 256	91 246	34
Malaysia	Port Kelang	117 281	98 913	19
Ivory Coast	Abidjan	116 385	19 466	498
Nigeria	Lagos/Apapa	98 086	143 964	– 32
India	Bombay	77 832	13 599	472
Morocco	Casablanca	57 825	52 000	11
Trinidad	Port of Spain	51 346	36 384	·41
UAE	Sharjah (PK)	50 836	54 205	– 6
Argentina	Buenos Aires	49 862	25 573	95
Cyprus	Limassol	48 846	31 309	56
Egypt	Alexandria	45 605	12 411	267
Panama	Cristobal	42 672	32 402	32
Bahrain	Mina Sulman	42 569	38 953	9
Panama	Balbao	39 546	30 765	29
Malaysia	Penang	35 179	23 998	47
Honduras	Puerto Cortes	32 539	31 277	4
Philippines	Cebu	32 191	8 821	265
Haiti	Port-au-Prince	29 267	23 023	27
UAE	Jebel Ali	29 267	–	–
Lebanon	Beirut	25 422	21 391	19
Cameroon	Doula	25 097	21 584	16
Papua New Guinea (PNG)	Lae	22 810	19 521	17
Chile	Valparaiso	22 118	13 214	67
Brazil	Rio de Janeiro	21 030	17 648	19
Mexico	Tuxpan	19 639	18 700	5
Jordan	Agaba	16 742	11 587	44
Kenya	Mambasa	15 146	8 643	75
India	Cochin	13 829	4 326	220
Panama	Bahia las Minas	13 265	10 807	23
PNG	Port Moresby	12 480	12 433	0
Ecuador	Guayaquil	12 438	9 566	30
El Salvador	Acajutla	11 051	–	–
Benin	Cotonou	8 525	5 865	45
Others		50 319	16 720	201
Total		5 544 136	4 327 770	28
(Per cent of world traffic		18.7	16.3)	

Source: UNCTAD, *Review of Maritime Transport*, 1981 TD/B/C14/222, p. 16.

2. Importance of transportation for development

Transport is an integral part of the production process and, therefore, has a direct bearing on a country's economy and development.[17] The very survival of a nation depends fundamentally on the movement of the goods it produces and receives in exchange from other nations. This dependence is felt in all the varied activities that characterise a nation's life. Transport is, therefore, of vital concern to a country's preservation of permanent national objectives in every field.[18] There is an intimate relationship between national security, broadly defined, and economic and social development, in that the former requires the fullest and most profitable commitment of national potential in all fields of endeavour – social, economic, political and military.[19]

If without security there can be no development, the reverse is also true. The relationship between these two factors – security and development – provides the precise forms and proper perspective for an analysis of the problem of transport in all its intricate and multifold aspects.[20] Although transportation, generally speaking, is vital to every nation, the relative importance of each of the several modes of transport may vary from one nation to another. This variance depends on the interplay of a multiplicity of physical and economic factors, such as geographic location, territorial arrangements and topography, extent of navigable inland waterways,[21] economic and technological advances, size of the domestic market, direction of the main stream of trade, or even entirely subjective factors, such as the national inclination or disposition of its people.[22]

A particularly important link between transport and development is in international interactions. The mode of transportation is maritime and the development is international trade.[23] This is more pronounced in the case of the TMNS. Maritime transport is, in general, of paramount importance for the DMNS that have yet to build important commercial exchanges with their continental neighbours as well as the TMNS, and are largely dependent[24] on what is still recognisable as a colonial or semi-colonial pattern of trade with more or less distant TMNS. However, not all countries have the same social, political and economic systems. Neither are all countries at the same level of economic development.[25]

3. Importance of maritime transport in international trade

Not all the DMNS necessarily approach specific maritime transport problems from the same angle. The countries that already have, or aspire to have, merchant marine fleets of their own, tend to look at these problems from the carriers' point of view, as well as from the perspective of transport users.[26] Other countries which have not yet taken a decision on the issue of whether or not they should build a merchant marine, tend to approach maritime transport problems from the users' point of view.[27] Whatever their approach may be, there is no doubt that all the DMNS are now unanimous in acknowledging the importance of the merchant marine to their national security, international trade and overall economic development.[28]

Table 3. Distribution of world fleet and TEU capacity of fully cellular container-ships by groups of countries, mid-1980

Flags of registration in groups of countries	Number of ships	TEU capacity and percentage shares (in brackets)
1. Developed market-economy countries (TMNS)	415	380 595 (76.0)
2. Open-registry countries	120	55 864 (11.1)
Total 1 and 2	535	436 459 (87.1)
3. Socialist countries of Eastern Europe and Asia (SCS)	42	15 329 (3.1)
In Eastern Europe	41	15 059 (3.06)
In Asia	1	270 (0.04)
4. Developing countries (DMNS)	68	37 991 (7.6)
In Africa	1	48 (–)
In America	15	1 484 (0.3)
In Asia	52	36 459 (7.3)
In Europe	–	–
In Oceania	–	–
5. Other – unallocated	17	11 180 (2.2)
World total	662	500 959 (100.0)

Source: UNCTAD, *Review of Maritime Transport*, 1981, TD/B/C.4/222, p. 19.

What is also undisputed is that maritime transport is one of the few genuinely international, if not supranational, industries that exist in the world today. This is due to its strong link with international trade.[29] In no other industry would it be possible to set up a transaction that involves so many different national entities as those that can be lumped together in one shipping deal. Imagine a modern super tanker, which may be owned by a Greek national through a Liberian company. The ship may well have been built in Japan, but powered by Danish engines.[30] It will no doubt be manned by a crew of mixed nationality, including, for example, some Italian officers and Philippino crew. It may have been financed through a New York bank and insured in London, time chartered to an oil multinational corporation (MNC) for three years to carry Saudi Arabian crude oil from the Gulf to Rotterdam via the Cape.[31]

However, this kind of arrangement and calm could exist and continue only so long as shipping remained under the monopoly of the TMNS. This was so because only the relatively wealthy TMNS could afford such a capital-intensive industry: basically privately run and very slow to change.[32] This is not to suggest there were no problems. The first set of major problems involved those related to flags of convenience, liner conference systems and the rising freight rates.[33] The second set were those related to technological development as exemplified by computerisation and containerisation of the industry.[34] But these were the kinds of problems that the industry could handle so long as the orthodox economic methods, based on supply and demand, were adhered to in the establishment and development of national fleets.[35]

4. *Laissez-faire* in international shipping

There was, at this stage, little or no state interference in national and international shipping. The principle of *laissez-faire* negated the existence of nationalised or state-established and state-aided national fleets as we know them today.[36] It would follow that the new set of problems could no longer be contained by the industry. The twentieth century, and in particular the 1960's and 1970's, has seen a steady erosion of the freedom of the high seas, a principle much supported by the independent shipowners in the TMNS but far from being universally accepted.[37] The move towards the limitation of the freedom of action on the part of those who own and operate ships has taken a number of different forms. The most controversial of these is, undoubtedly, the move towards *protectionism* in maritime transport. However, as will be evident shortly, maritime protectionism is not a twentieth century concept.[38]

In fact Britain, as the major opponent of the notion in the last century, has been rightly identified as the initiator of protectionism in the seventeenth century. It will be remembered that this is when *Oliver Cromwell's Navigation Acts* reserved portions of English seaborne trade to domestic flag ships, in order to guard against encroachment from the Dutch.[39] Protectionism in shipping takes many forms and it is by no means exclusively practised in any one economic or political bloc of countries.[40] *Cabotage* and the principle of reserving a country's coastal trade to its own ships and its own seamen is widespread. The US *Jones Act* of 1919 is a case in point, requiring US-built and US-manned vessels to perform all coastal trade, including, of course, the attractive market of transporting Alaskan oil to the other 49 states.[41]

5. Protectionism in international shipping

France and Japan are two major importers of foreign oil that operate a *de facto* policy of reserving this coastal trade for their own flag ships.[42] Yet it is in fact the Latin American DMNS which have earned their continent the distinction of being known as the *cradle of protectionism*, by their policies of cargo reservation since World War II.[43] It is also among the group of 77 DMNS that the impetus lies for further extensions of flag discriminations and preferences, a philosophy threatening to tear international shipping apart. It will be demonstrated in the next chapter how the emergence from colonial bondage and the ensuing nationalism of the former colonies (now the DMNS) led to the demand for national fleets.[44] This politicisation of shipping prefers national to inter-

Table 4. Comparison between total cargo turnover and fleet ownership by groups of countries, 1970, 1975, 1977 and 1978

Country group	Year	Goods loaded and unloaded (million tons)		Total of goods loaded and unloaded (million tons)	Deadweight tonnage of merchant fleet (million tons)	Percentage of world total of goods loaded and unloaded	Percentage of world total of merchant fleet (owned (dwt))
		Loaded	Unloaded				
Developed marked-economy and open-registry countries (TMNS)	1970	802.7	2 010.4	2 813.1	282.2	54.8	86.5
	1975	1 008.8	2 342.3	3 351.1	477.5	54.7	87.4
	1977	1 159.6	2 634.9	3 794.5	548.8	54.9	85.6
	1978	1 206.6	2 558.5	3 765.1	560.4	53.2	84.5
Socialist countries of Eastern Europe and Asia (SCS)	1970	158.8	87.6	264.4	21.7	4.8	6.7
	1975	188.4	123.6	312.0	33.0	5.1	6.0
	1977	245.2	180.7	425.9	39.8	6.2	6.2
	1978	243.7	201.2	444.9	43.0	6.3	6.5
Developing countries (DMNS)	1970	1 643.3	431.6	2 074.9	20.5	40.4	6.3
	1975	1 875.0	588.9	2 463.9	33.3	40.2	6.1
	1977	2 063.4	626.9	2 690.3	50.4	38.9	7.9
	1978	2 099.8	765.5	2 865.3	56.9	40.5	8.6
World total	1970	2 604.8	2 529.6	5 134.4	326.1	100.0	100.0
	1975	3 072.2	3 054.8	6 127.0	546.3	100.0	100.0
	1977	3 468.2	3 442.5	6 910.7	641.3	100.0	100.0
	1978	3 550.1	3 525.2	7 075.3	662.8	100.0	100.0

Source: UNCTAD, *Review of Maritime Transport*, 1981, TD/B/C.4/222, p. 22.

Table 5. Total world merchant fleet: summary of quarterly figures 1981–1983 (ships of 300 grt and dwt, and over).[a]

Year/month	No. of ships	grt	nrt	dwt
1981				
January 1st				
All flags	33 867	384 005 111	259 744 427	657 027 133
Dry cargo tonnage	26 443	207 515 092	129 816 750	320 695 545
Tanker tonnage	7 424	176 490 019	129 927 677	336 331 588
April 1st				
All flags	33 969	385 225 364	260 489 725	658 253 968
Dry cargo tonnage	26 487	208 622 830	130 539 504	322 162 055
Tanker tonnage	7 482	176 602 534	129 950 221	336 091 913
July 1st				
All flags	34 145	385 741 752	260 617 920	658 365 872
Dry cargo tonnage	26 617	210 290 030	131 602 738	324 455 524
Tanker tonnag	7 528	175 451 722	129 015 182	333 910 348
October 1st				
All flags	34 303	386 654 672	261 053 218	659 230 496
Dry cargo tonnage	26 732	211 780 600	132 558 397	326 570 259
Tanker tonnage	7 571	174 874 072	128 494 821	332 550 237
1982				
January 1st				
All flags	34 360	388 168 313	262 195 524	661 944 093
Dry cargo tonnage	26 793	213 591 952	133 944 210	329 720 554
Tanker tonnage	7 567	174 576 361	128 251 314	332 223 539
April 1st				
All flags	34 562	388 991 968	262 425 606	662 148 581
Dry cargo tonnage	26 964	216 140 502	135 639 579	334 059 483
Tanker tonnage	7 598	172 851 466	126 786 027	328 089 098
July 1st				
All flags	34 684	389 094 988	262 259 914	661 444 575
Dry cargo tonnage	27 040	218 059 455	136 914 602	337 366 104
Tanker tonnage	7 644	171 035 533	125 345 312	324 078 471
October 1st				
All flags	34 723	389 175 660	262 197 115	661 586 860
Dry cargo tonnage	27 088	219 749 953	138 115 433	340 778 063
Tanker tonnage	7 635	169 425 707	124 081 682	320 808 797
1983				
January 1st				
All flags	34 732	387 979 163	261 252 363	659 303 198
Dry cargo tonnage	27 091	220 425 405	138 637 316	342 251 866
Tanker tonnage	7 641	167 553 758	122 615 047	317 051 332
April 1st				
All flags	34 733	387 226 512	260 499 317	657 389 329
Dry cargo tonnage	27 125	222 156 218	139 806 609	345 364 236
Tanker tonnage	7 608	165 070 294	120 692 708	312 025 093

Source: Institute of Shipping Economics, Bremen.
[a] See footnotes to Table 1.

national fleets. It has been pointed out further that because they lack the necessary skilled manpower, capital, technical know-how, established ports and the prerequisite infrastructure, these countries have resorted to protectionism as a method of establishing and/or developing their own national fleets.[45]

These restrictive approaches, to the building of national fleets, led to legal as well as economic problems. Apart from radically changing the established fabric of international shipping they threaten to tear it apart.[46] The overall aim and objectives of this book could thus be described as an analysis of the factors that led to the demand and/or rise of the concept of national fleets as opposed to the original mainly international fleets.[47] In other words, it is an analysis of the traditional methods of establishing and/or developing national fleets, including the ensuing problems and the future prospects of replacing international with national fleets.[48] Put another way, it is an inquiry into the nature, history, function and consequences to the future of international shipping of: flag discrimination, flag preference, cargo reservation, state intervention and maritime subsidies, to mention but a few.[49]

6. The approach or methodology

The purpose of the analysis is to arrive at a conflict-resolving mechanism which could reverse the current climate of *confrontation* and substitute *co-operation* between the DMNS and the TMNS, on the one hand, and among DMNS themselves on the other.[50] The pros and cons of protectionism are considered and a suggestion is made for a more rational attitude. The survey takes a pragmatic approach and acknowledges the conflicting interests that come into play.[51] There are as many converging interests as there are diverging ones – positive and negative contradictions. What is not disputed, however, is that continued confrontation is bound to drastically affect the future prospects for the development of national fleets and, thereby, severely disrupt international trade and international relations, as well as world peace.[52]

Such confrontations and/or disruptions cannot be in the long-term and overall interests of any of the parties involved, especially as the legal framework is but a mere expression of wider economic and political demands.[53] This multidisciplinary approach to the survey is also rendered necessary because shipping encompasses not only international law, but also international trade, economics, politics, etc. It is also for this reason that the rationale for the establishment and/or development of national fleets is bound by political, economic and security factors.[54] Throughout the survey attempts have been made to include definitions and explanations, to simplify economic and legal principles, in an attempt to put the study in a proper perspective: shipping is part of and is influenced by trends in the international systems, and should always be considered within that context.[55]

There has been an attempt to insert short sub-introductions between parts and chapters in addition to this (main) introduction and overall conclusions. There is little mention of statutory law except for the first of the main provisions in which the general spirit of the legislations are referred to;[56] nor is there much emphasis on case law. However, some cases are discussed and many others are mentioned in the footnotes. A full list of cases, statutes, regulations and other bye laws are provided in the comprehensive bibliography for the interests and benefits of the readers.[57] It goes without saying that this has been a comparative, rather than an exhaustive study with specific reference to the DMNS and the TMNS. The US functions as the main example of TMNS practices. Mention is also made of the third actors, the STNS (State Trading Nations).[58]

7. Definition problems

As indicated in the list of abbreviations used, the term Traditional Maritime Nations (TMNS) is applied, for the purposes of this survey, to the western, Capitalist, market economy, or industrially advanced nations;[58] the term State Trading Nations (STNS)[59] refers to the communist or socialist countries, mainly of Eastern Europe, sometimes known simply as the Socialist Nations/Countries (SCS);[60] while the term Developing Maritime Nations (DMNS) designates the former colonies of Africa, Asia and Latin America.[61] The normally popular use of 'underdeveloped' countries is avoided because of the confusing-derogatory meaning it may convey.[62] Let us assume that the DMNS are those countries which, on average, offer their inhabitants a level of consumer products and material well-being appreciably inferior to that provided by the economies of the TMNS and STNS.[63] The former are mainly the *South* and the latter the *North* as in the *North–South* dialogue.[64]

Attempts were also made to avoid the use of 'poor' or 'poorer' countries both of which are relative terms, if not controversial ones. To designate a country as a DMNS also raises implications as to its present economic performance – as evidenced by the average consumption and material well-being which could be improved by means which are known and understood.[65] The abbreviation DMNS might elsewhere be used interchangeably with 'developing countries', 'less developed countries' (LDCS), 'the Third World' or 'the South'.[66] The word 'poorer' nations may also be used but not the word 'underdeveloped' as this classification is intended for this study only and does not imply any judgment regarding the stage of development of any country or territory.[67]

Some of the DMNS may well fall into other categories such as the STNS of Eastern Asia, but that is for political references only. At the same time the leading open registry countries are normally removed from the DMNS and recorded with the TMNS or as separate groups.[68] The TMNS, on the other hand, refers to the industrialised countries of Europe, North America, Japan, Australia and New Zealand.[69] Some of the DMNS have larger fleets and more facilities than some of the TMNS but that is another matter.[70] However, for the purposes of the major confrontation the argument is between the DMNS and TMNS; the STNS came into the picture only rarely, supposedly, because they had no colonial relations with the now DMNS.[71]

8. Outline

The survey is divided into six parts each of on average two chapters, including Chapter 1 which is the introduction and the concluding remarks. Part I deals with the reasons for the breakdown of international shipping, as we know, and its replacement with national fleets. Chapter 1, *Protectionism in international shipping*, traces the background analysis of the importance of transportation to national economic development – social, political and economic. It also analyses the linkage between maritime transport and international trade and the role of the former in the development of the latter. But the internationality and peaceful development of shipping that had previously existed was shattered by changed circumstances – the rise of protectionism and the concept of the national fleet. The traditional methods (restrictive practices) are introduced.

Chapter 2, *The quest for national fleets*, develops the background of the study in further detail by discussing the reasons and supposed rationale behind the emergence of demands by the DMNS for national fleets of their own – separate from the previous international fleets. These include changed material conditions, resulting from their emergence from colonial domination; the problems caused by the liberalism of the TMNS, resulting in concepts such as the freedom of the high seas, flags of convenience and the liner conference systems; and other factors, such as inequalities prevailing in maritime transport, the soaring maritime transport costs to the DMNS and the encouragement given to the DMNS by the work of the UN in this field. The connection between the rising freight rates and the balance of payments of the DMNS ranks highly in their growing concern.

Where Part I establishes the reasons for the transformation from international to national fleets, Part II concentrates on the first of the traditional mechanisms for establishing national fleets. This is basically an analysis of the focus on the national flag – a comparative approach based on the practices of selected DMNS and TMNS. Chapter 3, *Flag preference*, tackles the first category of this mechanism. Despite its size and influence in international trade, the US merchant marine, like those of the DMNS, is still too small to carry a significant portion of the nation's trade. To develop its fleet the US has adopted the same method as that applied by the DMNS – protectionism. For this reason the examples in this chapter are drawn largely from the DMNS and the US.

The advantages and disadvantages of the major elements, such as cargo reservation, bilateralism, cabotage and state financed cargoes, are outlined briefly. The relationship between these restrictive mechanisms and the general trade policies of the countries in question is also highlighted. Chapter 4 continues with the analysis of the second facet of the focus on the flag – *Flag discrimination*. Indeed, unless otherwise stated, flag discrimination means and includes flag preference. However, an attempt is made to distinguish between the two. But the relationship between them is imminent, hence the apparent overlap and repetition. Worth noting is the countervailing flag discrimination – i.e. the pros and cons of the rise of this particular method.

Once the concept of the national fleet is established in Part II, the next stage is its development. For this, additional methods are necessary. These turn out to be maritime subsidies and state intervention treated together here as state aid and assistance. On this occasion, the examples of the practice are not restricted to the US and the DMNS. For, after the destruction caused by World War II and in view of the ensuing competition from the newly established fleets of the DMNS, the TMNS too found themselves in need of re-developing their national fleets.

Chapter 5 narrows the discussion down to *Maritime subsidies* – one of the most effective mechanisms of state aid to the national fleet. Having further divided maritime subsidies into indirect and direct subsidies, attention is then focused in this section on the distinction between fiscal and financial assistance. Justification for this mechanism is based on the fact that subsidies are not restricted to the merchant marines but apply to industry generally. To strengthen the effects of these methods of establishing and developing national fleets these policies are inevitably linked with the financial and trade administrations. Chapter 6, *State intervention*, is devoted to the development purposes and mechanisms of this method. The natural result of state intervention is state participation and nationalised shipping. The strong link with export/import and balance of payments' policies should also be noted.

Part IV concentrates on the problems caused by protectionism as a method of establishing and developing national fleets. Whereas previously international shipping was run on economic principles and customs and traditions established over time, the restrictive practices do not necessarily take these principles into account. This poses both legal and economic problems. These are some of the problems discussed in this part of the survey. It has been pointed out that one of the problems facing shipping and international trade is that customs and traditions established centuries ago face challenges from changes that have occurred. Customary international law in particular has come under increasing pressure. The other doctrine under challenge is free trade.

Chapter 7, *Customary international law*, is devoted to such problems as equality of treatment in international law, especially the equality of flags, the freedom of the high seas (especially the freedom of maritime transport), the freedom of navigation, the doctrine of national treatment and the most favoured nation clause. Chapter 8, *International economic laws*, examines the provisions of the IMO Convention, the GATT provisions, the OECD Code, the EEC Treaty, the proposed UN code on Restrictive Business Practices, and the Conventions and treaties regarding navigable waterways of international concern. Chapter 9, *Economic consequences of protectionism*, presupposes that the ensuing inefficiency and rising freight rates, as well as disruptions of international trade and maritime transport, are problems that cannot easily be ignored.

Part V, *Conflict resolution*, discusses the future prospects for the development of national and international maritime fleets. A combination of economic and legal problems leads to confrontation and, if left unchallenged, threatens to radically change the nature of the national fleet and have disastrous effects on international trade. Recommendations aimed at finding solutions are put forward. The concluding section of the survey, therefore, forecasts the future and the prospects for the development of national fleets. The final section, Part VI, contains the *Concluding remarks*, the *Conclusion*, *Footnotes*, *Bibliography* and *Annexes*.

Appendix 1

Classification of countries and territories

Code 1	Canada	United States of America
Code 2	Japan	

Code 3		Australia	New Zealand
Code 4		Austria (L)	Italy
		Belgium	Monaco
		Denmark	Netherlands
		Faeroe Islands	Norway
		Finland	Portugal
		France	Spain
		Germany, Federal Republic of	Sweden
		Gibraltar	Switzerland (L)
		Greece	Turkey
		Iceland	United Kingdom of Great Britain and Northern Ireland
		Ireland	Yugoslavia
		Israel	
Code 5		South Africa	
Code 6		Albania	Hungary (L)
		Bulgaria	Poland
		Czechoslovakia (L)	Romania
		Germany, Democratic Republic of	Union of Soviet Socialist Republics
Code 7		China	Vietnam
		Democratic People's Republic of Korea	
Code 8	8.1	*Northern Africa*	
		Algeria	Morocco
		Egypt	Tunisia
		Libyan Arab Jamahiriya	
	8.2	*Western Africa*	
		Angola	Liberia
		Benin	Mali
		Cape Verde	Mauritania
		Congo	Nigeria
		Equatorial Guinea	St. Helena
		Gabon	Sao Tome and Principe
		Gambia	Senegal
		Ghana	Sierra Leone
		Guinea	Togo
		Guinea-Bissau	United Republic of Cameroon
		Ivory Coast	Western Sahara
			Zaire
	8.3	*Eastern Africa*	
		Burundi (L)	Mozambique
		Comoros	Reunion
		Djibouti	Seychelles
		Ethiopia	Somalia
		Kenya	Sudan
		Madagascar	Uganda (L)
		Mauritius	United Republic of Tanzania
			Zambia (L)
Code 9	9.1	*Caribbean and North America*	
		Antigua	Guadeloupe
		Bahamas	Haiti
		Barbados	Jamaica

		Bermuda	Martinique
		British Virgin Islands	Monserrat
		Cayman Islands	Saint Pierre and Miquelon
		Cuba	Saint Kitts-Nevis-Anguilla
		Dominica	Saint Lucia
		Dominican Republic	Saint Vincent and the Grenadines
		Greenland	Turks and Caicos Islands
		Grenada	United States Virgin Islands
	9.2	*Central America*	
		Belize	Honduras
		Costa Rica	Mexico
		El Salvador	Nicaragua
		Guatemala	Panama
	9.3	*South America – Northern seaboard*	
		Guyana	Suriname
		French Guyana	Trinidad and Tobago
		Netherlands Antilles	Venezuela
	9.4	*South America – Western seaboard*	
		Chile	Ecuador
		Colombia	Peru
	9.5	*South America – Eastern seaboard*	
		Argentina	Falkland Islands (Malvinas)
		Bolivia (L)	Paraguay (L)
		Brazil	Uruguay
Code 10	10.1	*Western Asia*	
		Bahrain	Lebanon
		Cyprus	Oman
		Democratic Yemen	Qatar
		Iran	Saudi Arabia
		Iraq	Syrian Arab Republic
		Jordan	United Arab Emirates
		Kuwait	Yemen
	10.2	*Southern and Eastern Asia*	
		Bangladesh	Macau
		Bhuten	Malaysia
		Brunei	Maldives
		Burma	Pakistan
		Democratic Kampuchea	Philippines
		East Timor	Republic of Korea
		Hong Kong	Singapore
		India	Sri Lanka
		Indonesia	Thailand
Code 11		Malta	
Code 12		America Samoa	Papua New Guinea
		Christmas Island (British)	Solomon Islands
		Fiji	Tonga
		French Polynesia	Tuvalu
		Kiribati	Vanuatu
		Guam	Wake Island
		Nauru	
		New Caledonia	

Source: UNCTAD, *Review of Maritime Transport 1980*, TD/B/C.4/222, Annex 1, pp. 1–3.

Notes

1. See, for example, Rowe, Philip J., 'Depression brings problems to Greek owners employing Asian seamen (government policy to protect jobs of own nationals)'. *Asian Shipping,* July 1983, pp. 29–31.
2. E.g., 'Taiwanese maritime industries'. (special report) *Lloyd's List,* 27 July 1983, pp. 5–11.
3. Seaward, Nick, 'ASEAN report. The quest for unity. Indonesia, Malaysia, the Philippines, Singapore, Thailand'. *Seatrade,* Vol. 12, No. 6, June 1982, pp. 97–103.
4. See, for example, Sohmen, Helmut, 'The world and shipping. The new maritime order'. *Lloyd's Shipping Economist,* Vol. 5 No. 6, 1983, pp. 6–8.
5. The DMNS have argued for a long time that given equal opportunities they could do better than the TMNS due to their cheap labour and generally lower costs.
6. The flags of convenience and the liner conferences developed as a means of cutting down the then soaring costs of running merchant fleets.
7. 'Small shipping. Restructuring necessary to counter diminishing size and competitiveness'. *Nor. Shipping News,* Vol. 39, No. 9, 15 July 1983, pp. 13–16.
8. Cf. Leshem, Z., 'The status and contribution of Israel shipping in the Israeli economy'. *Sapanut,* Vol. 12, Nos. 2–3, Autumn–Winter 1982/83, pp. 22–25.
9. Gonzales, Avelino, 'Bilateralism: the solution to an antiquated international shipping policy'. *Journal of International Affairs,* No. 36, 1983, pp. 329–339.
10. For details see the definitional problems ahead; also Appendix I, pp. 18–19 and Chapter 2.
11. The SCS introduced planned economies and state trading while the DMNS introduced shipping nationalism.
12. Such as Buckingham, Lisa (ed.), 'European protest at Libya cargo sharing plan'. *Lloyd's List,* no. 52269, Thursday 20 January 1983, front page.
13. Abrahamson, B., *International Ocean Shipping: Current Concepts and Principles.* Westview, 1980, introductory chapter.
14. Ariyoshi, Yoshiya, 'Marine transportation and the security of the West'. In: Miles, Edward, L. and Allen, Scott (eds.), *The Law of the Sea and Ocean Development Issues in the Pacific Basin.* Honolulu, 1983, pp. 451–65. Note: Commentary, pp. 466–70.
15. 'Traditional methods' would normally be the "sound economic principles", but in this book this term is used to mean the reverse, i.e., protectionism.
16. Krzyzanowski, M. T., 'International cooperation in shipping'. In: Ryden, Inger (ed.) *Shipping and Ships for the 1990's.* Stockholm School of Economics, 1980.
17. Brown, Robert T., *Transport and the Economic Integration of Latin America.* The Brookings Institution, 1966; Moseley, M. J., *Accessibility, the Rural Challenge.* Methuen, 1979.
18. *Ibid.,* Chapter III, 'Intra-South-American trade and transport'. pp. 31–48; see also Jacobs, F., *Fire Snake: the Railroad that Changed East Africa,* 1980.
19. *Ibid.,* Chapter VII, 'Ocean transport and economic integration', pp. 114–61.
20. Black, W. C. and Black, T. A., 'Deriving areas for mass transit systems', *Trans. Res. News,* Vol. 16A, No. 3, May 1982, pp. 185–98.
21. See also Black, John A. and Rimmer, P. J., 'Japanese highway planning: a Western interpretation'. *Transportation,* Vol. 11 No. 1, March 1982, pp. 20–49.
22. Bannister, David, 'Transport needs in rural areas – a review and proposal'. *Transport Reviews,* Vol. 3, No. 1, January–March 1983, pp. 35–48.
23. See, for instance, Chapter 1, "The development of international seabourne trade'. In: UNCTAD *Review of Maritime Transport 1980,* TD/B/C.4/222, pp. 3–8.
24. In the case of Africa see Hoyle B. S. and Hilling, D. (ed.), *Seaports and Development in Tropical Africa.* Macmillan, 1970.
25. This is true of even the DMNS hence such expressions as 'the poorest 25', 'the geographically disadvantaged', 'the landlocked', etc.
26. Especially the Newly Industrialised Nations (NICS), such as Korea, Singapore, Brazil, the Philippines, Hong Kong, Taiwan, etc.
27. These are mainly the land-locked, the poorest, the geographically disadvantaged, etc;

see Campbell, Thomas C., 'Transport and its impact on developing countries'. *Transportation Journal,* Fall 1972.

28. This probably explains why these countries are clammering to enter shipping when the TMNS might want exit.
29. See again UNCTAD Doc. No. TD/B/C.4/222, Chapter 2, 'Development of the world merchant fleet'. pp. 9–22, and compare with Chapter 1, *supra.*
30. This is especially true of Flag of Necessity vessels; see US Congress, House, Committee on Merchant Marine and Fisheries, Third Flag: Hearings before the Sub-Committee on the Merchant Marine, 94th Congress, 1st and 2nd Sess., Nos. 94–35, 1976.
31. The only other means of transportation other than rival shipping is air aviation, see O'Connor, W. E., *An Introduction to Airline Economics.* Praeger, 1978.
32. 'Ship management in the North of Britain', *Lloyd's Shipping Manager,* Vol. 4, No. 2, June 1983, pp. 61–64.
33. See 'An economic analysis of freight rate disparities in US liner trade'. *Applied Economics,* Vol. 15, No. 3, June 1983, pp. 403–409.
34. Frankel, Ernst, 'Shipping: choice of technology'. *Maritime Policy and Management,* 10, 1983, pp. 1–10.
35. But this is no longer the case necessarily; see, for instance, Thuong Le T., 'The impact of US regulatory practices on the productivity of ocean liner services: a comment', *Maritime Policy and Management,* 10, 1983, pp. 61–65.
36. E.g. Caras, C. G., 'US Maritime administration financing procedures available for new ship construction'. *Business Lawyer,* 36, 1981, pp. 1887–97.
37. See the discussions in Chapter 7 on the problems relating to protectionism in international customary law.
38. See the next few paragraphs; see also, generally, the discussion on the development of flag preference and discriminations in Chapters 3 and 4.
39. See Gold, Edgar, *Maritime Transport: The Evolution of International Marine Policy and Shipping.* Lexington, 1981.
40. See, for instance, Mott, David, 'Owners seek UK protectionism move'. In: *Lloyd's List,* No. 52350, Wednesday 27 April 1983, p. 3.
41. Cf. William, Steven, 'DOT promises maritime reform policy in the next few months". *Practitioners Journal,* 49 I.C.C., (1982) pp. 199–200.
42. Teltsch, G., 'Shipping aid policy in Britain, France'. *Sapanut,* Vol. 12, Nos. 2–3, Autumn–Winter 1982/83, p. 10.
43. 'Latin American warning on cargo-reservation'. *Lloyd's List,* No. 52362, Thursday 12 May 1983, p. 4.
44. See Chapter 2, section 3 and Sturmey, S. G., 'The shipping policy of developing countries'. In: *Shipping and Ships for the 1990's. Supra,* pp. 71–80.
45. See Pavaskar, M., *Second India Studies: Transport.* Verry, 1979.
46. Probably into the small and big league, as happened in aviation; see Chapter 10, section 1; see also Altshuler, A. (ed.), *Current Issues in Transportation Policy.* Lexington, 1979, p. 189.
47. There will be very few cross-traders as a result of this; see Levine, H. A., *National Transportation Policy.* Lexington, 1978.
48. See also Chapter 10, and O'Sullivan, P., *Transport Policy: Geographic, Economic and Planning Aspects.* Barnes and Noble, 1980.
49. See generally Olson, 'Cargo preference and the American merchant marine'. *Law and Contemporary Problems.* Vol. 80, 1960, p. 82.
50. See also Voss, B., 'International cooperation in shipping'. In: *Shipping and Ships for the 1990's. Infra.*
51. Between the shippers and shipowners, the DMNS and TMNS, and the SCS and TMNS. See, generally, Ames, M., *Science and the Political Process.* Communications, 1978.
52. Shipping cannot be seen outside the global context of international relations and peace; see, again, O'Sullivan, P. *Transport Policy: An Interdisciplinary Approach. Infra.*
53. 'International shipping – today and tomorrow'. *Hansa,* Vol. 120, No. 13, July 1983, pp. 1171–1174.
54. WAMS (Wartime Adaptation of Merchant Ships), *Shipbuilding & Mar. Eng. Int.* Vol. 106, No. 1266, March 1983, pp. 131–33.

55. O'Sullivan, P., *Transport Policy: An Interdisciplinary Approach.* Barnes and Noble, 1980.
56. The aim has been to write a simple textbook on international shipping rather than one on maritime law; see O'Sullivan, P., *supra.*
57. Interested readers will be most encouraged to look these up; for details see the appendixes of the *Annual Proceedings of the Fordham Corporate Law Institute 1977 – International Regulation of Maritime Transportation.* pp. 523–647.
58. See Table 1; see also Averin, I., 'International shipping and the Soviet merchant marine'. In: *Shipping and Ships for the 1990's. Supra,* pp. 58–64.
59. See Table 1 and Burke, R. J., 'International shipping policy: a view of Western Europe'. In: *Shipping and Ships for the 1990's.* Supra, pp. 48–57.
60. See Table 1; see also North, R. N., *Transport in Western Siberia: Tsarist and Soviet Development.* University of British Colombia Press, 1979.
61. See Table 1; see also Patankar, P. G., *Urban Mobility in Developing Countries.* Verry, 1979, p. 10.
62. The usage does not necessarily have an economic definition: Bennathan, E. and Walters, A. A., *Pricing and Investment Policies for Developing Countries.* Oxford, 1979, p. 200.
63. Adopting consumer approach; see also Bhatt, V., *Development Perspectives: Problems, Strategies and Policies.* Pergammon, 1980.
64. See North–South dialogue; see also Silvers, A. and Grosson, P., *Rural Development and Urban-Bound Migration in Mexico.* Johns Hopkins, 1980, p. 100.
65. See, generally, Hall, D., *A Spatial Analysis of Urban Community Development Policy in India.* Wiley, 1981.
66. See Table 1; see also 'Innovation for Third World Trade'. *Lloyd's List,* No. 52397, Thursday 23 June 1983, p. 18.
67. Ordinarily 'develop' implies to progress to a more advanced state or condition – *Rabin* v *Central Businessmen's Association* 116 Kan. 280, 226P, 764, at 706, 38 A.L.R. 26.
68. See Tables 6 and 7 on management and beneficial ownership of open registry.
69. These are mainly the EEC and OECD; see again Burke, R. J., 'International shipping policy: a view of Western Europe'. *Supra.*
70. See Table 1.
71. See Chapter 2, section 3.

CHAPTER 2

The quest for national fleets

1. Introduction: International shipping after the war

This chapter reviews the reasons and developments that led to the demand, by the DMNS, for national fleets. These are, mainly, the changing material conditions in the international system and the DMNS' dissatisfaction with the then prevailing shipping liberalism.[1] The work of the United Nations, especially the Development Decade and International Development Strategy, including the New International Economic Order, has added more impetus to this demand.[2]

In the quarter century since 1957, the volume of world seaborne trade has grown more than 200%. During the same period, world shipping tonnage has trebled to an estimated 300 m.grt. While shipping tonnage has not increased quite as rapidly as seaborne trade, it has exhibited a marked tendency towards an accelerated rate of growth. The world merchant fleet grew at the rate of 7.5% between mid-1967 and mid-1968. This rate increased to 9.8% in the following years[3] (see Tables 15–17).

Although the rate of growth declined during mid-1969 to mid-1970 (7.9%), more than one third (37%) of the total increase in world shipping tonnage in the 26-year period occurred during 1967–1972. This growth in tonnage occured mainly in the tanker and bulk fleet.[4] As against an overall increase of 65% in world shipping during the 18 years since 1964, tanker and bulk carrier tonnage registered increases of 80% and 200%, respectively. The rate of growth in the remaining categories, such as cargo liners, has remained minimal (about 16%).[5] The interesting thing to note is that very little of the said expansion occurred in the DMNS. The last figure is pertinent because of the emphasis the DMNS currently place on the liner trade in discussions on world shipping. Thus a limited number of flags (the TMNS) have accounted for the major part of the growth in world shipping tonnage since 1957.[6]

Historically, the organisation and development of shipping services to meet the demand for world-wide ocean transport has been left to the uncoordinated efforts of private entrepreneurs in the conditions of free market.[7] As a result, the shipping trade has been characterised, until recently, by abrupt and uneven fluctuations in the demand for shipping services, thereby causing considerable variations in the price of transport, which often bore no relation to actual transport costs.[8]

But this marked structure, in which market factors, such as demand and supply, are the major determinants of transport prices, is gradually changing. In the first place, the activities of several governments which can or do assist their national merchant marines or otherwise intervene in their maritime industry, exert an influence unrelated to free market factors or freight rate setting.[9] Secondly, shipping in the TMNS belongs to vertically integrated enterprises and forms a large part of the world's tonnage. This sector of the shipping industry generally operates outside the preview of free market. Petroleum companies are the major operators in integrated fleets, but many other industrial enterprises, engaged in the production or processing of basic material such as iron ore, bauxite, sulphur, grain, sugar and LNG have also followed suit.[10] They do not necessarily own all the ships under their control, but do have ships on long term time charter and then operate them as integrated fleets. Thirdly, the liner trades, often organised in conferences of one kind or another, are less susceptible to open market conditions. Liner conferences are designed to absorb the effect of short term market fluctuations, thereby nullifying the effect of free market factors on the determination of freight rates.[11]

As a result of these three factors, free competition operated directly and unhampered only in a diminishing sector. Under- and over-supply may be even more accentuated than has been the case in the past. Free competition might not have been ideal but at least could be tolerated by the colonial powers (TMNS). It could have worked as between equals.[12] But something happened that was to challenge and transform free competition. This occurrence was the emergence, as a result of changed material conditions, of the DMNS from colonial domination.

2. Changed material conditions: Emergence from colonial domination of the developing countries

At the end of World War II, international shipping was controlled almost exclusively by a few maritime powers (TMNS). International trade was also dominated by these countries. For the nations that have emerged from colonial or semi-colonial status since 1945, economic growth is virtually linked with an increasing share in international trade since, in general, a large proportion of their GNP is composed of exports.[13] The DMNS have not, however, been fortunate in their commercial and financial relationships with the outside world. The prices of their major exports, largely primary products, have been generally stagnant or declining. On the other hand, prices of manufactured goods, which are their main imports, have been rising.[14] The impact of these divergent price trends on the economies of the DMNS has been intensified by an increasing demand for imported capital goods and industrial input for the economic infrastructure, and for agricultural and industrial development.[15]

The resulting decline in terms of trade of the DMNS has been further aggravated by the heavy impact of rising freight rates that these countries have experienced as net buyers of shipping services. It is no surprise, therefore, that in a deteriorating balance of payments situation, the DMNS have become very conscious of the adverse impact on their balance of payments of the outflow of foreign exchange in payment of shipping services and other invisible transactions.[16] Hence the strong link between shipping, the balance of payments and international trade. According to an estimate made sometime ago, the total freight charges in the trade of the DMNS with the TMNS in 1961 were approximately 4.7 billion US \$.[17] The relative importance of this figure can be appreciated by comparing it with the total imports and exports of the DMNS in the same year – approximately 23.6 billion US \$ and 23.0 billion US \$, respectively. Since 1961 (the year chosen was when most of the DMNS gained independence), the value of the trade of these countries has increased by more than 100%.[18]

Freight rates have also increased appreciably during this period, and it can safely be assumed that total freight charges paid by the DMNS have increased considerably since 1961.[19] These considerations suggest that there is an underlying disequilibrium in the present distribution of the world shipping fleet that needs to be carefully examined. The DMNS wish to establish their own national fleets to balance this inequality and reduce the external flow of foreign exchange.[20] The desire of the TMNS (spurred by strong domestic pressure groups) to preserve the *status quo* monopoly, initially based on colonial exploitation and strategic considerations, was an important factor in the development of the present disequilibrium in the distribution of shipping in the world. However, the distribution of the world fleet was never really founded on purely economic considerations, as the TMNS would have us believe.[21] For the same reasons the basis for the establishment of national fleets by the DMNS is only partly economic.

The situation is in fact changing, but exceedingly slowly. International support for a more dynamic change is still lacking, or is at best half-hearted. The DMNS have long pleaded for more active cooperation in this area by the TMNS, asking in particular for assistance in the form of loans or concessionary terms to acquire the tonnage they need.[22] As early as the 1950's, several of the then newly independent DMNS began to pay increasing attention to shipping and allied trade problems and evolve their own policies. Shipping problems and policies were also brought up in the regional commissions of the UN and especially ECOSOC, ECAFE, ECA and ECLA.[23] But the first global effort to formulate a common approach to shipping and related matters, from the point of view of the DMNS, was not made until UNCTAD I, held in Geneva in 1964. Then a comprehensive response to shipping questions, by these countries, crystallized at the Algiers conference.[24]

This conference was held in October 1967 in preparation for UNCTAD II. The *Charter of Algiers* adopted at this preliminary session includes a statement of the aspirations and goals of the DMNS in the field of shipping.[25] Technical and managerial training of personnel was considered another possible method of establishing and/or developing national fleets. It is interesting to note that despite all the existing barriers to the expansion of the role of the DMNS in world shipping, an increasing number of the DMNS, including some of the more economically advanced among them (the Newly Industrialised Nations, NICS), have already made up their minds to enter the field, and many more are following suit.[26] They have established national fleets. And despite serious difficulties, conference membership has been gained on a number of routes. But it has not been easy for the DMNS.

The difficult process of gaining access to more conferences, including way-port conferences, and of obtaining a greater share of the traffic, still continues.[27] Where the DMNS have encountered problems in strengthening their national merchant fleets, they have not hesitated to imitate the TMNS in supporting their own fleets through cargo reservations, flag discriminations, maritime subsidies and state intervention. These traditional methods of establishing and developing national fleets have their advantages and disadvantages.[28] The essential point, however, is to recognise the conflicting interests inherent in the present system. These conflicts, which led to the DMNS establishing and/or developing their own national fleets, began with conflicting schools of thought regarding shipping. The new school of thought, the protectionists, advocated nationalism in shipping and the right of every nation to establish and/or develop its own national fleets if it so wished.[29]

3. The problems of internationalism in shipping: The shipping liberalism of the advanced shipping nations

Thus, since World War II, two distinct schools of thought on the operation of the merchant marine industry have emerged. One school of thought, the free market school, wishes to retain the *status quo*, and holds that shipping services should be provided by private enterprise on the basis of free competition and that the choice of ship, whatever its flag, should be the prerogative of the shipper.[30] This school also believes that shipping should be as international as possible in that only the few countries which are able to do so should be allowed to run shipping services. The other school maintains that governments must take the ultimate responsibility for the provision of shipping services under the national flag, and that this responsibility should be fulfilled, if necessary, by such means as cargo preference, flag discriminations, maritime subsidies, bilateralism, fiscal incentives and many other visible and invisible incentives.[31]

It is in liner shipping that the controversy between these two schools has become most obvious. The advocates of a free market are to be found mainly among the shipowners of the so-called TMNS, often supported by the governments of these countries.[32] Never before had shipowners' associations in the TMNS felt the need so strongly for governmental support on an issue. Many owners who had equated government interference, of any kind, with flagrant restriction of their freedom of action were now to be seen in animated conversation with civil servants whose help they sought for protection from a threat that had never manifested itself in such a form before.[33] However, their main aim is to maintain their dominant position in the maritime traffic between other countries and their own, and to continue their influence in cross-trades between other countries. The leading followers of protectionism are the USSR and, ironically, the US – the two super powers, for whom this policy is part of a global security policy.[34] They are joined by the newcomers to the merchant marine industry – whether they are developing or developed nations. It is not surprising that the DMNS belong to the second category which also includes the STNS. Whereas about 65% of the volume of seaborne trade is generated by production in the DMNS, these countries' fleets amount to only 7–8% of the total world tonnage and they account for an even smaller share (about 6%) of tonnage on order.[35] Sixty per cent of the world's tonnage is registered under only six flags, namely those of Liberia, Japan, the UK, Norway, the US and the USSR. Whether the free market concept – which is possibly more rationalistic than realistic – is right or wrong, it is a fact that its advocates have not succeeded in stopping or containing the escalation of the practices they reject.[36]

As to the second school of thought, it seems futile to discuss its merits and demerits at this point, since, as will be shown later, the whole controversy may fade away in the wake of every country getting involved in it.[37] Following these differing schools of thought, one of the problems the DMNS have had to contend with is the so called *laissez-faire* attitude of the TMNS. In response to the emergence of the national fleets of the DMNS, some TMNS, particularly those engaged in cross-trades, have pleaded frequently for a return to the more orthodox *laissez-faire* system of running international merchant marines.[38] The latest expression by these countries of their conviction that cargo reservation leads to increased transport costs and lower standards of service, is to be found in the decision taken by the ministers of the TMNS in Tokyo in February 1971.[39]

3.1 Laissez-faire, *the freedom of the high seas and national fleets*

The TMNS' pleas for *laissez-faire* are not likely to be very convincing as long as many of these same countries benefit from such a system. This apparent departure has added fuel to the DMNS' demands for the right to establish and/or develop national fleets of their own.[40] It would seem to be in the interest of all parties concerned to resolve the situation in a rational manner before further mutual misunderstanding, suspicions and retaliatory measures bring about a fully-fledged classical trade war.[41] One of the fundamental maritime doctrines of the *laissez-faire* system is the so-called *freedom of the high seas.* The detailed aspects of this freedom are dealt with at a later stage where it is considered as one of the problems caused by the traditional methods of establishing and/or developing national fleets.[42] It will also be evident in the latter chapters that freedom of the high seas is one of the stumbling blocks to state intervention in the merchant marine.

For the moment it will be remembered that this doctrine is an invention of the post-mercantilist period in Europe and will always be associated with the name of Grotius.[43] During the mercantilist period a number of European TMNS established such a stranglehold in the merchant marine industry and trade, that the continued adherence to the doctrine which gave them strength would have limited their further growth; whereas the doctrine of free trade and freedom of the seas, which Grotius enunciated, opened the prospect of continuous growth, if the same doctrine could be sold to their competitors whose growth it would surely stunt.[44] The national fleets of the DMNS and STNS were, therefore, a response to this affront, *inter alia.* It will further be remembered that at this time Holland was ready to preach the doctrine of the high seas and to put the principle into practice because the Dutch had the most powerful fleet in the world.[45]

The British, on the other hand, from the last years of the 16th century, would have none of such doctrines. Britain rigorously applied a protectionist policy to the merchant marines which guarded the commerce of the Empire strictly for the British merchant fleets and those of her trading partners.[46] By mid-century, however, with 52% of the world's commercial tonnage, Britain was in a strong position to abandon control and espouse liberty. For the same reason the DMNS will have none of the freedom of the high seas till such time that their national fleets are well established and developed. Besides, there is more to the doctrine than at first appears.[47] It was often thought to encompass within itself liberalism in commercial relations, so that any departure from commercial liberalism was a breach of this doctine.[48]

It would be useful to pause for a moment to examine the relationship between the doctrine and *laissez-faire.* Freedom of the high seas in this post-mercantilist sense is one facet of the doctrine of free trade.[49] It is a commercial doctrine and its application produces satisfactory results for all parties only to the extent that the buyers and the sellers in the market have roughly equal bargaining power.[50] That can hardly be said of the current international atmosphere prevailing between the buyers and sellers of the TMNS and the DMNS: on the contrary, the doctrine was developed by the strong in buying and selling, to whom the advantages of free trade were overwhelming.[51]

In the political sense the doctrine of the freedom of the high seas is quite different. The real freedom of the seas is the right of all commercial vessels, pursuing their lawful and peaceful endeavours, to sail the high seas and to enter territorial waters[52] without let or hindrance, and to find a safe harbour in case of trouble. Taken to its natural conclusion the doctrine means perfect conditions of equality and includes the rights of all nations, developed or developing, to establish and/or develop, national merchant marine fleets of their own irrespective of their means.[53] Thus, freedom of the high seas in the political sense is related to questions fundamental to the rights of man and the sovereignty of all nations to do what they want when and as they wish.[54]

Whereas the use of the same expression in the TMNS' and the commercial sense is a mere statement in a maritime context of the economic doctrine of *laissez-faire*[55], political freedom of the sea is a real freedom; commercially it is nothing more than the freedom to exploit.

The second facet of *laissez-faire* is shipping liberalism. The liberalists soon tired of the results of the application of the doctrine while continuing to enjoy the intellectual pleasures of arguing in its support.[56] Only 25 years after the British Shipowners gained the freedom of competition which they ardently craved for, they created the conference system to prevent the very competition they had supported. Adam Smith, one of the few really wise British economists, understood. He observed that when two or more people in the same commerce come together, even for social reasons, they would soon begin to talk of ways in which they could collectively improve their positions vis-à-vis the market, that is, to consider what we now call restrictive practices.[57]

In practice the cost of the competition to which the application of the doctrine of liberalism led, had nothing to do with the doctrine as it is usually understood today.[58] This is true not merely because technology has expanded the scale of so many activities that competition is impossible – although this is an important factor – but because of the market size limitations. Even where competition remains possible, the competitors do not want it.[59] They do not feel invigorated and strengthened by the presence of competition, but insecure and uncertain. The thrusting competitive entrepreneur enjoys the game of course, as does the tennis player, but the objective is victory, and victory is attained only when the position reached is unassailable; that is, competition is at an end because the rivals are either subjugated or eliminated.[60] Rather than face either consequence, and in order to avoid them, the DMNS decided to establish and/or develop national merchant marine fleets of their own.

3.2 Liberalism, flags of convenience and national fleets

This is the other aspect which will occupy our attention in relation to liberalism. No doubt the establishment and development of national fleets by the DMNS was in part a response to, and the direct consequence of, the resentment of *flags of necessity*, as they are sometimes known.[61] Liberalism in shipping has led to liner conferences (post); it has also led to periodic catastrophic surpluses of shipping, in which liberal principles are immediately abandoned in a spate of lay-up, subsidy and scrapping schemes. It has led to a shabby compromise of the flag of convenience, the ship with its body in Famagusta, its money in Monaco and its sail entrusted to a group of mercenaries.[62] Shipping is in a mess. The TMNS would have us believe it is the industry's own fault, and that they could do nothing about it. One may not agree with them when one discovers that the major part of world tonnage is under flags of convenience or the control of a small group of countries.[63] In fact, about 72% of world deadweight tonnage in 1976 (60% gross) was owned by interests in France, Greece, Italy, Japan, Norway, UK and US – all Liberian and Panamanian tonnage included (Table 6).

One is aware that these seven countries do not own all Liberian and Panamanian tonnage, but they do own the major part and since none of the tonnage of the other *flag of convenience* fleets which they assuredly own, or part own, is attributed to them not much injustice has been done.[64] The DMNS, therefore, wished to establish their genuine national fleets rather than the flags of convenience which they would have to hold in proxy for the TMNS. Thus, the rise of national fleets among the DMNS was both a response to and a result of dissatisfaction with the flags of convenience.[65] We see that the seven TMNS preaching liberalism in merchant marines control about two-thirds of the world supply of shipping. How can they blame others for their mess? Yet they themselves are not to blame in that within the system as it works, there is little or nothing they can do.[66]

Within a national economy the contradictions inherent in the attempt to practice liberalism in a non-liberal framework (or be illiberal in a liberal framework) can be more or less easily resolved.[67] National enterprises operating in an international environment do not have this capacity and so have been unable to resolve the conflicts between the liberal principles and their pragmatic operations.

Besides freedom of the seas, conferences and liberalism, the fourth facet of *laisse-faire* is, therefore, flags of convenience or open registry.[68] In addition to seeking state support, the merchant marine industry in the TMNS has long been exploring ways of cutting down its costs by gaining access to certain

Table 6. True management[a] of open-registry fleets, 1980 (number of vessels and thousands of dwt).

Country or territory of true managers	Country or territory of registration													
	Liberia		Panama		Singapore		Cyprus		Bermuda		Bahamas		Total	
	Nb	Dwt	Nb	Dwt	Nb	Dwt	Nb	Dwt	Nb	Dwt	Nb	Dwt	Nb	Dwt
United States of America	515	50 734	227	3 608	3	30	1	3	17	172	6	30	769	54 577
Hong Kong	584	36 063	587	10 318	32	388	3	18	9	63	–	–	1 215	46 850
Japan	220	10 215	579	7 331	58	3 861	1	30	–	–	–	–	858	21 437
United Kingdom	180	13 671	72	685	52	829	25	135	51	2482	–	–	380	17 802
Greece	125	11 902	185	2 158	7	55	319	1 694	–	–	1	16	637	15 825
Monaco	76	7 185	35	3 101	–	–	1	5	–	–	–	–	112	10 291
UK-based Greek shipowners	85	6 131	36	872	4	70	22	237	1	31	–	–	148	7 341
Germany, Fed. Rep. of	53	2 247	127	1 876	155	2 162	46	223	3	21	–	–	384	6 529
Singapore	22	641	93	596	373	4 133	1	12	–	–	–	–	489	5 382
Unspecified	59	2 078	187	2 136	4	28	1	13	–	–	–	–	251	4 255
Switzerland	55	3 116	63	841	7	129	1	9	–	–	–	–	126	4 095
Norway	81	2 544	14	190	13	253	7	14	3	52	–	–	118	3 053
Italy	23	1 650	60	603	1	3	5	43	2	6	1	25	92	2 330
Israel	22	1 656	7	283	–	–	–	–	–	–	–	–	29	1 939
Netherlands	22	816	84	940	12	37	6	19	–	–	–	–	124	1 812
France	24	1 314	23	106	3	61	–	–	–	–	–	–	50	1 481
Republic of Korea	10	729	114	695	–	–	–	–	–	–	–	–	124	1 424
Canada	11	957	7	23	4	307	–	–	4	41	2	2	28	1 330
Indonesia	28	507	43	592	1	2	1	10	–	–	–	–	73	1 111
US-based Greek shipowners	24	994	10	79	–	–	1	1	–	–	–	–	35	1 074
66 countries, entities or territories each managing less than 1 million dwt	89	2 675	446	2 377	33	314	90	443	25	244	8	17	691	6 070
Unidentified	10	360	184	749	12	169	43	187	6	21	3	2	258	1 488

Source: UNCTAD, *Review of Maritime Transport*, 1981, TD/B/C.4/222, p. 12.

[a] The 'true manager' is the person, company or organization responsible for day-to-day husbandry of the ship concerned (as distinct from the manager of the company nominally owning the vessel). The country of management has been assumed to be the country of domicile of the true manager.

advantages available in the DMNS. Chief among these has been the endeavour to seek refuge in registering ships under flags of convenience – which happen to be in the DMNS.[69]

Even more significant is their widespread tapping of the DMNS for their labour supply; the special significance of such practices is that they are tantamount to depriving the DMNS of their major advantage in shipping.[70] Moreover, a large number of ports in the DMNS are subsidized by governments and the users of such ports – mainly the TMNS fleets – naturally benefit from such subsidies. Finally, shipowners in the TMNS have set up companies in the DMNS with nominal or minority local participation.[71] One objective of such ventures is to benefit from the privileges granted by the governments of these countries to indigenous national fleets. A flag of convenience operator using world liberalism probably comes nearer to the original usage of the word than others.[72] He is running his ship as far as possible to suit himself, untroubled by national fiscal or social legislation, by international safety conventions, or by trade unions.

The people who turned to flags of convenience after World War II saw themselves as following the old tradition of the tough, risk-taking entrepreneurs opening up new frontiers for the benefit of world trade in the fashion of the pioneer American settlers in the mid-West.[73] But they could also be seen as men looking for the soft option, limiting their risks, bound by neither loyalty nor kinship to a country, concerned only with personal profit and the protection of that from taxation and the social rules imposed in their own countries to safeguard objectives (equally the product of liberalism) related to human dignity and equity.[74] That, then is liberalism and internationalism in shipping at its absurd extremes: quite the opposite of the national fleets that the DMNS wish to establish. The present generation of flag of convenience owners cannot even plead service to world transport as the justification for their activities[75] (Tables 6 and 7).

As for liberalism, perhaps only Norway, and to a certain extent Greece, can claim some credit among the TMNS for having developed their national merchant fleets largely unaided by the state. None of our other seven liberal DMNS could give such a liberal answer as Greece.[76] France, Italy and Japan have never made any secret about the importance they attach to shipping and their willingness to assist their respective industries. At government level, in terms of direct assistance, the British might return a Norwegian answer and, give or take a few investment allowances – which the Norwegians also enjoyed – and flag preference during the infancy of the industry some 250 years ago, this would not be a bad answer.[77] But the British were the inventors, have always been the main proponents, and remain almost the only supporters of an illiberal system designed to negate whatever competitive consequences might follow from the practice of liberalism.[78]

We are now referring to the other of our themes of liberalism, liner conferences, which, however necessary they may be, are the very paradigm of the conflict between the liberal principles and pragmatic operations noted earlier.[79] The sour relationship between the liner conferences and the DMNS accounted for the desire, on the part of the latter, to establish and/or develop national fleets of their own.[80] The detailed account of the development, function and effects of liner conference systems is either not necessary or beyond the scope

Table 7. Beneficial ownership[a] of open-registry fleets, 1980 (number of vessels and thousands of dwt).

Country or territory of beneficial owners	Liberia Nb	Liberia Dwt	Panama Nb	Panama Dwt	Singapore Nb	Singapore Dwt	Cyprus Nb	Cyprus Dwt	Bermuda Nb	Bermuda Dwt	Bahamas Nb	Bahamas Dwt	Total Nb	Total Dwt
United States of America	572	57 128	263	6 996	13	218	5	28	29	145	6	30	888	64 545
Hong Kong	550	34 770	412	7 670	32	366	3	18	2	49	–	–	999	42 873
Greece	276	23 919	217	2 304	14	425	343	1 923	–	–	1	16	851	28 587
Japan	225	11 512	641	7 946	58	3 861	1	30	–	–	–	–	925	23 349
Germany, Fed. Rep. of	55	2 521	134	1 990	162	2 275	69	359	3	21	–	–	423	7 166
Norway	122	5 187	20	366	22	601	4	9	4	78	–	–	172	6 241
Unspecified	83	2 941	199	2 257	4	28	1	13	–	–	–	–	287	5 239
Singapore	5	126	81	485	322	3 405	1	12	–	–	–	–	409	4 028
Switzerland	61	2 999	47	687	6	141	1	9	–	–	–	–	115	3 836
United Kingdom	41	2 754	55	235	24	93	13	83	5	316	–	–	138	3 481
Netherlands	31	1 802	84	938	10	35	6	19	–	–	–	–	131	2 794
Italy	29	1 901	70	667	1	3	5	43	3	9	1	25	109	2 648
Canada	12	384	7	23	–	–	–	–	47	2239	2	2	68	2 648
Israel	30	1 856	7	283	15	335	1	16	–	–	–	–	53	2 490
China	1	11	100	1 630	–	–	–	–	–	–	–	–	101	1 641
Monaco	26	1 345	12	229	–	–	–	–	–	–	–	–	38	1 574
France	21	1 245	24	108	3	61	–	–	–	–	–	–	48	1 414
Indonesia	33	569	40	570	1	2	1	10	–	–	–	–	75	1 151
67 countries, entities or territories each benefically owning less than 0.5 per cent	135	4 855	586	4 026	75	813	77	337	22	255	8	17	903	10 303
Unidentified	10	360	184	749	12	169	43	187	6	21	3	2	6 991	217 496
Total	2 318	158 185	3 183	40 159	774	12 831	574	3 096	121	3 133	21	92	6 991	217 496
Share in total open-registry fleets	33.1	72.7	45.5	18.5	11.1	5.9	8.2	1.4	1.7	1.5	0.3	–	100.0	100.0

Source: UNCTAD, *Review of Maritime Transport*, 1981, TD/B/C.4/222, p. 3

[a] The beneficial owner is the person, company or organization which gains the pecuniary benefits from the shipping operations.

of our intentions. However, suffice it to say that, at this stage, the cornerstone of the DMNS' criticism of internationalism and liberalism in shipping concerns the liner conferences.[81]

3.3 Internationalism, liner conference systems and the rise of national fleets

The liner conferences are such a crucial issue in the shipping industry that they, more than any other factors, led to the urgent response from the DMNS to establish and/or develop their own national fleets.[82] The bulk of the international trade of most of the DMNS (in terms of value) is carried by conferences that regulate the liner trade in shipping. Naturally, the structural mechanisms and functioning of liner conferences have attracted considerable attention in the DMNS.[83] Liner conferences were initially established to organise and control trade between colonial powers and their overseas possessions. Since the TMNS also own the bulk of world shipping tonnage, it is not surprising that the shipping lines of the TMNS normally have a dominant position within the liner conferences.[84] For instance, the membership composition of some of the important liner conferences operating in India's international trade from the TMNS, STNS and flags of convenience countries involves only five Indian flags.[85] A similar situation usually prevails with respect to the other DMNS. It was reported in 1968 that of the then 118 regular shipping lines serving the Latin American region, only 17 operated under Latin American flags. Surely no region or country can stand this disparity any longer.[86] Moreover, the headquarters of the liner conferences are generally located in the TMNS. These features of the liner conference system have an important bearing on the shipping needs and trade requirements of the DMNS. The views of these countries have not been fully reflected in the decisions of the liner conferences because even where their national shipping lines participate in the conferences, they are generally in a minority.[87]

This is not to say that the lines do not exercise any influence, or that they would necessarily place national interest above their own self-interest.[88] However, the location of the headquarters of the liner conferences in the TMNS and their consequent lack of high level local representation in the DMNS can lead to an inadequate appreciation of the problems and special needs of these countries by conferences – or, at least, to a time lag in communication and the consideration and solution of these special problems (see Appendix 2).[89] This partly explains the fact that cargo n.o.s. freight rates are applied to a large number of non-traditional exports of the DMNS and that there is a delay in the fixing of specific freight rates for such goods. Liner shipping of the DMNS, if any, can expand and remain economically viable only if these countries secure liner conference membership for their national shipping lines;[90] they have to establish and develop their own national fleets where they are still non-existent.

The initial resistance of the established shipping lines of the TMNS has given way to a growing appreciation of the claim of the national shipping lines of the DMNS to membership in liner conferences serving their national trades. But the same cannot be said of liner conferences serving way-port trades.[91] It was only after considerable effort that a resolution was adopted at the fourth session of the committee on shipping of UNCTAD in April/May 1970 recommending that governments of member states of UNCTAD invite liner conferences in related way-port trades to consider favourably, fairly and on equal terms, applications of the national flag lines,[92] in particular of the DMNS, for admission as full members, subject to the rights and obligations of conference membership. In some instances, requests from national fleets of the DMNS, for membership in way-port conferences had been refused for apparently no adequate reasons.[93] (For conference malpractices, see Appendix 2, p. 58.)

In other cases the national fleets of the DMNS had not applied for membership because they were not certain that they had a reasonable chance of being granted membership. The carriage of cargoes from way-ports adds flexibility to shipping operators, and can be an important factor in improving the economics of operation on some liner routes.[94] The denial of this facility to national shipping lines of the DMNS not only frustrates their attempts to improve the economics of their operations, but also amounts to discrimination against them. Yet these liner conferences, we are supposed to believe, represent liberalism at its highest in international shipping.[95] While arguing that liberalism is not what it says, one recognises several characteristic features. For these we need to go beyond the rhetoric as it is applied in international shipping.[96]

The question is a more fundamental one; for instance, we find that the societies which use the expression 'liberalism' and the economies which use the term 'competitive', to describe themselves are also marked by extensive private ownership and control of means of production, by government accountability to a parliament elected on a broad,[97] but not necessarily universal suffrage, by a broad concern with human liberty and human rights, including the rights to employment and economic and social security, by freedom of association among working people, entrepreneurs and political groups and by the acceptance of the principle that the role of government[98] is limited to keeping the ring clear and leaving the competitive, economic and social groups to fight it out. The politico-juridical outlook of the DMNS and STNS is not the same, hence the latters' reliance on the state to establish, develop and protect[99] an industry – including national fleets.

Even with this broad statement of the basic elements of such societies, we already find a contradiction emerging. The right of free association creates restrictive business practices inimical to the attainment of social objectives;[100] the pursuit of private profit is not necessarily compatible with the maintenance of employment. This latter observation has been proved true by the current mass unemployment as the direct consequence of the monetarist experiment by the present Conservative government in Britain.[101] So the task of the government to keep the ring clear has become more and more extensive and, as it has grown, so have the inherent contradictions in the system. The shipping industry, like any societal infrastructure gets caught in this inevitable contradiction. Indeed, it would be absurd to see the shipping industry outside the socio-political and economic-juridical philosophy.[102]

Returning to shipping, we wish to argue that shipowners acting in an international environment form a national base, with a political and economic philosophy which gives little help in the determination of day-to-day practices, have been ill-adapted to meet the challenge coming from within their own group, or from groups outside, even though these outside groups own a minority of tonnage of world shipping.[102] In 1976, for instance, the breakdown in terms of DWT, was:

Seven big liberal states	72%
Twenty-one small liberal states	14%
State trading nations	6%
Developing countries	8%

In concluding this section on the problems caused by liberalism in international shipping, we would like to say that the system of carrying on in a more or less liberal way, then resorting to government or restrictive action to patch up or start the pump when the ship gets into trouble, does not constitute a coherent doctrine and, hence, provides no base from which to assess the coherence and relevance of the emergency measures adopted.[103] In particular because hindsight is easier than foresight, the solution applied today is more likely to be relevant to yesterday's than today's problems. Besides the obstructive *laissez-faire* policies of the TMNS, what the DMNS have had to contend with is an almost non-existent share in oceanborne trade and shipping. These inequalities are attributed to the previous prevailing conditions. One of the ways to redress this imbalance is for these countries to establish and develop their own national fleets.[104]

4. The inequalities between the advanced and the developing nations in maritime transport

The DMNS' concern for their insignificant share in world shipping, their huge freight bill, and the nationalism of emergent countries were the immediate factors that led to the establishment and development of national fleets by these countries.[105] The anxieties of the DMNS about the development of their national fleets, in relation to the requirements of their trade, can best be understood against the background of their participation in international seaborne trade and world shipping. Their share in the volume (weight) of international seaborne trade in the years 1959, 1965 and 1969 was 22.9%, 18.6% and 18½% for goods unloaded.[106] Their overall share of total goods unloaded and loaded fluctuated between 41% and 48% in these years.

The share of the DMNS stands out in sharp contrast to their level of participation in world trade. While their share in goods loaded and unloaded averaged 41.4% in 1969, the latest available figures indicate that these countries, excluding Liberia and Panama (flags of convenience), owned only 8.0% of the total world shipping tonnage.[107] On the other hand, the flags of the TMNS (including Southern Europe) and the flags of convenience together accounted for 83.5% of world tonnage. The ownership of shipping tonnage registered under flags of convenience is not difficult to ascertain as they are largely controlled by the TMNS.[108] According to the *Rochdale Report* no less than half is beneficially owned by US companies or individuals and a considerable part of the remainder by persons who have, or once had, Greek nationality.[109]

Even more disheartening from the point of view of the DMNS is the declining trend in the portion of world shipping tonnage owned by them, which even at

Table 8. Summary of straightforward increases in freight tariffs announced in 1975, 1976 and 1977.[a]

	1975		1976		1977	
Size of increase (percentage)	Number of increases	Percentage of total	Number of increases	Percentage of total	Number of increases	Percentage of total
Under 5	1	0.8	9	0.6	4	2.5
5 and less than 7.5	5	3.8	22	14.8	32	20.0
7.5 and less than 10	8	6.1	27	18.1	38	23.7
10 and less than 12.5	30	23.1	31	20.8	31	19.4
12.5 and less than 15	24	18.5	26	17.4	27	16.9
15 and less than 20	49	37.7	19	12.8	22	13.8
20 and over	13	10.0	15	10.1	6	3.7
Total	130	100.0	149	100.0	160	100.0

[a] Excluding announcements which (i) referred to a flat increase in terms of an absolute amount per unit of cargo (4 in 1977 as against 11 in 1976 and 4 in 1975); (ii) did not specify the percentage amount of the increase (13 such announcements in 1977 as against 5 in 1976 and 1 in 1975).

Source: TD/B/C4/178/Rev.1 (ibid), p. 22, below Table 25.

its peak in 1964 was only 8.1% and in 1970 was reduced to 7.0%.[110] Tables 9–12 show the distribution of world tonnage among the different groups of countries and the share of these groups in the growth of the world merchant fleet since 1964. The composition of the merchant fleets of the DMNS is also imbalanced in relation to the commodity composition of their international trade.[111] Currently, the DMNS are the source of 90% of the world export of crude petroleum and petroleum products, yet their share in world tanker tonnage is only about 4%. In 1968, the DMNS exported 60% of world iron-ore exports and 58% of rock phosphate, 80.4% of bauxite and aluminium, 10.9% of coal, and 31.9% of grain.[112]

These commodities are usually carried in specialised bulk carriers. But the share of the DMNS in the world bulk carrier tonnage (including combination vessels such as ore-oil-grain carriers or ore-oil carriers) in 1970 was only about 5%.[113] The analysis of the world tonnage on order as of October 1970 revealed that the comparative position of the DMNS was to deteriorate further in the following years. As mentioned above, although these countries then owned 7.6% of world shipping tonnage, their share in tonnage on order was only 4.5%.[114] Moreover, tonnage on order statistics suggested that the DMNS, in sharp contrast to the TMNS, were perpetuating the sectional imbalance in the composition of their fleets.

4.1 The imbalance in international shipping: The share of the developing countries in oceanborne trade and world shipping

In 1970 ships other than bulk carriers and tankers accounted for 39% of the total world tonnage (excluding the US Reserve Fleet and the US and Canadian Great Lakes tonnage); but in the case of the DMNS they accounted for 62.9%. In the same year, ships other than bulk carriers and tankers accounted for only 10.6%.[115] of world tonnage on order, yet such ships represented 32% of the tonnage ordered by the DMNS. Although no precise data was available on the total gross earnings of the world merchant marine industry, one analysis estimated them to be about US 11.4 billion dollars in 1964.[116] In view of the great increase in total world tonnage as well as rising freight rates, between 1964 and 1970, the current output of the shipping industry (two decades later) must be appreciably higher than the 1964 estimate. Of the 1964 estimated total gross earnings, roughly 40% was attibuted to liner trades.[117]

Since then, tanker and bulk carrier tonnage has increased by 90% and 200%, respectively. The tonnage of other ships, however, rose by only 11%. On the basis of these figures, it can safely be assumed that since 1964 the proportion of gross earnings contributed by the tanker and the bulk carrier sectors[118] to the total earnings of the merchant marine industry have increased while that of the liner sector has declined. The share of the DMNS, however, in the gross earnings of the shipping (world) industry was estimated to be less than 5% in 1964.[119] By 1970, their percentage share of ship earnings was smaller since their share, not only of world tonnage, but also in the most profitable sectors of the industry (the bulk carrier and tanker trades) had been declining.[120]

As indicated above, one of the discoveries of the investigation of maritime

Table 9. World tonnage on order as of 30 September 1977 (thousands of dwt).[a]

Country grouping	All ships	Tankers 150 000 dwt and over	Tankers under 150 000 dwt	Ore/oil and OBO carriers	Other bulk carriers	Full container ships	Part container ships	RO/RO cargo ships	Lash ships	Other ships
1. Western countries	37 232	11 419	4 422	912	5 707	1 272	204	1 170	–	9 130
2. Open registeries	14 123	4 525	1 898	345	4 283	418	31	57	24	2 541
Total 1 plus 2	51 358	15 944	6 320	–	12 990	1 690	235	1 227	24	11 671
3. Socialist countries	2 890	–	632	–	800	25	16	283	72	608
In Eastern Europe	2 752	–	612	–	755	25	16	283	–	527
In Asia	138	–	11	–	45	–	–	–	–	82
4. Developing countries[b]	10 644	1 287	348	–	3 496	117	48	56	–	3 812
In Africa	956	–	2	–	153	–	–	10	–	791
In America	6 300	1 132	317	–	2 447	31	48	29	–	1 064
In Asia	3 357	155	29	–	896	86	–	17	1	1 958
In Oceania	0.1	–	–	–	–	–	–	–	–	0.3
5. Other unallocated	862	–	102	–	265	22	–	37	–	437
World total	65 755	17 231	7 394	3 198	17 551	1 855	299	1 602	96	16 259

[a] World tonnage on order as of 30th September 1980 (Table 10) indicates a drop of 30%.
[b] Developing countries in Europe had no tonnage on order.

Table 10. World tonnage on order as of 30 September 1980[a] (thousand dwt).

Countries of registry	All ships	Tankers 150 000 dwt and over	Tankers under 150 000 dwt	Ore/oil and OBO carriers	Other bulk carriers	Full container ships	Part container ships	Ro/Ro cargo ships	Other ships
1. Developed market-economy countries (TMNS)	23 875	1 430	5 859	2 142	8 769	729	110	491	4 345
2. Open-registry countries	16 933	594	6 654	890	7 325	136	–	10	1 324
Total 1 plus 2	40 808	2 024	12 513	3 031	16 094	865	110	501	5 669
3. Socialist countries (SCS)	1 264	150	172	–	79	–	–	334	529
In Eastern Europe	1 003	150	46	–	79	–	–	310	418
In Asia	261	–	126	–	–	–	–	24	111
4. Developing countries total[a] (DMNS)	8 331	581	1 474	280	3 738	74	–	70	2 114
In Africa	347	–	5	–	63	–	–	–	279
In America	3 716	–	652	280	2 035	–	–	70	679
In Asia	4 267	581	817	–	1 640	74	–	–	1 155
5. Other unallocated	514	210	–	–	111	132	–	16	45
World total[b]	50 917	2 965	14 159	3 311	20 022	1 071	110	921	8 357

[a] Developing countries in Europe and in Oceania had no tonnage on order.
[b] Owing to rounding off, the totals do not always add up.

Source: UNCTAD, *Review of Maritime Transport* 1981, TD/B/C.4/222, p. 33.

Table 11. Distribution of world tonnage[a] (grt and dwt) by groups of countries of registration in 1965, 1970, 1976 and 1977 (mid-year figures).

Flags of registration in groups of countries	Tonnage and percentage (in parenthesis) (millions of grt) 1965	1970	1976	1977	(millions of dwt) 1970	1976	1977	Increase in tonnage (grt): Share of increase (%) 1965–1977	1976–1977	Index 1977 (1965 = 100)
1. Western countries	102.2	141.1	207.3	211.0	210.9	337.0	345.1	45.0	17.3	206
(TMNS)	(69.6)	(64.8)	(56.5)	(56.5)	(64.7)	(56.1)	(53.8)			
2. Open-registry countries[b]	22.1	40.9	99.5	109.2	70.3	184.2	203.2	36.0	45.3	493
	(15.1)	(18.8)	(27.1)	(28.1)	(21.6)	(30.6)	(31.7)			
Total 1 and 2	124.3	182.0	306.8	320.2	281.2	521.2	548.3	81.0	62.6	258
	(84.7)	(83.6)	(83.6)	(82.4)	(86.3)	(86.7)	(85.5)			
3. Socialist countries	10.9	19.5	31.4	33.3	21.7	37.0	39.8	9.2	8.9	306
(SCS)	(7.4)	(8.9)	(8.5)	(8.6)	(6.6)	(6.1)	(6.2)			
In Eastern Europe	10.3	18.6	27.6	28.8	20.5	31.5	33.3	7.6	5.6	280
	(7.0)	(8.5)	(7.5)	(7.4)	(6.2)	(5.2)	(5.2)			
In Asia	0.6	0.9	3.8	4.5	1.2	5.5	6.5	1.6	3.3	750
	(0.4)	(0.4)	(1.0)	(1.2)	(0.4)	(0.9)	(1.0)			
4. Developing countries	10.9	15.2	27.4	33.4	21.5	40.8	50.9	9.3	28.0	306
(DMNS) total	(7.4)	(7.0)	(7.5)	(8.6)	(6.6)	(6.8)	(7.9)			
In Africa	0.6	0.8	2.5	3.8	1.1	3.6	5.7	1.3	6.1	633
In America	4.8	6.4	9.8	10.8	8.7	14.3	15.9	2.5	4.7	225
In Asia	5.5	8.0	15.0	18.6	11.7	22.8	29.1	5.4	16.8	338
In Europe	–	–	–	0.1	–	–	0.1	–	0.4	–
In Oceania	–	–	0.1	0.1	–	0.1	0.1	0.1	–	–
5. Other unallocated	0.7	1.2	1.5	1.6	1.7	2.2	2.3	0.4	0.4	229
	(0.5)	(0.5)	(0.4)	(0.4)	(0.4)	(0.4)	(0.4)			
World total	146.8	217.9	367.1	388.5	326.1	601.2	641.3	100	100	265
	(100.0)	(100.0)	(100.0)	(100.0)	(100.0)	(100.0)	(100.0)			

[a] Excluding the USA reserve fleet and the United States and Canadian Great Lakes fleets, which in 1977 amounted, resp., to 1.7, 1.7, 1.8 million.

[b] The composition of this group of countries differs from that adopted in the report 'Economic consequences of the existence or lack of genuine link between vessel and flag of registry'. Report by the Secretariat of UNCTAD (TD/B/C4/168 and Corr. 1). However, for the sake of statistical consistency, the classification of countries in this table has not been changed.

Note: Compare the 1980 figures in Table 12.

Source: UNCTAD, *Review of Maritime Transport,* 1977, TD/B/C.4/178/Rev.1; indicated as Table 4 on p. 4, New York 1979, sales no.

Table 12. Distribution of world tonnage[a] (grt and dwt) by groups of countries of registration, 1965, 1970, 1979 and 1980 (mid-year figures).

Flags of registration in groups of countries	Tonnage and percentage (in parenthesis) (millions of grt) 1965	1970	1979	1980	(millions of dwt) 1970	1979	1980	Increase in tonnage (grt): Share of increase (%) 1965–1980	1979–1980	Index 1980 (1965 = 100)
1. Developed market-economy countries (TMNS)	102.7 (70.0)	141.8 (65.1)	212.1 (52.0)	214.3 (51.7)	211.9 (65.0)	348.0 (51.6)	350.1 (51.3)	41.7	31.9	209
2. Open-registry countries	22.1 (15.1)	40.9 (18.8)	114.1 (28.0)	114.2 (27.5)	70.3 (21.6)	212.3 (31.5)	212.6 (31.1)	34.4	1.5	517
Total 1 and 2	124.8 (85.1)	182.0 (83.9)	326.2 (80.0)	328.5 (79.2)	282.2 (86.6)	560.3 (83.1)	562.7 (82.4)	76.1	33.4	263
3. Socialist countries (SCS)	10.9 (7.4)	19.5 (8.9)	38.0 (9.3)	39.3 (9.5)	21.7 (6.6)	46.9 (7.0)	48.7 (7.1)	10.6	18.8	361
In Eastern Europe	10.3 (7.0)	18.6 (8.5)	31.3 (7.7)	32.0 (7.7)	20.5 (6.2)	36.9 (5.5)	37.8 (5.5)	8.1	10.1	311
In Asia	0.6 (0.4)	0.9 (0.4)	6.7 (1.6)	7.3 (1.8)	1.2 (0.4)	10.0 (1.5)	10.9 (1.6)	2.5	8.7	1 217
4. Developing countries (DMNS)	10.4 (7.0)	14.5 (6.7)	41.4 (10.2)	44.7 (10.8)	20.5 (6.3)	63.4 (9.4)	68.4 (10.0)	12.8	47.8	430
In Africa	0.6	0.8	4.7	4.9	1.1	6.9	7.2	1.6	2.9	817
In America	4.8	6.4	13.4	14.5	8.7	20.0	21.8	3.6	15.9	302
In Asia	5.0	7.3	23.1	25.0	10.7	36.2	39.1	7.5	27.5	500
In Europe	–	–	0.1	0.1	–	0.1	0.2	–	–	–
In Oceania	–	–	0.1	0.1	–	0.2	0.1	–	–	–
5. Other unallocated	0.7 (0.5)	1.2 (0.5)	2.0 (0.5)	2.0 (0.5)	1.7 (0.5)	3.1 (0.5)	3.0 (0.5)	0.5	–	286
World total	146.8 (100.0)	217.9 (100.0)	407.6 (100.0)	414.5 (100.0)	326.1 (100.0)	637.7 (100.0)	682.8 (100.0)	100	100	282

[a] Excluding United States reserve fleet and United States and Canadian Great Lakes fleet, which in 1980 amounted, respectively, to 1.7, 1.7, 2.0 million grt.

Source: UNCTAD, *Review of Maritime Transport,* 1981, TD/B/C.4/222, p. 10.

Table 13. Age distribution of world merchant fleet by type of vessel as of 1 July, 1980 (percentage of total in terms of grt).

	Type of vessel	Total	0–4 years	5–9 years	10–14 years	15 years and over	Average[b] age July 1980	Average age July 1979
1. Developed market-economy countries (TMNS)	All ships	100	25.4	36.5	19.0	19.1	9.55	9.09
	Tankers	100	25.6	42.9	17.3	14.2	8.72	8.00
	Bulk carriers[a]	100	23.7	39.3	22.5	14.5	9.11	8.45
	General cargo	100	25.1	16.8	19.2	38.9	12.54	12.74
2. Open-registry countries	All ships	100	21.8	41.6	18.2	18.4	9.58	8.85
	Tankers	100	20.6	51.9	15.9	11.6	8.50	7.42
	Bulk carriers[a]	100	22.8	38.7	25.8	12.7	9.05	8.61
	General cargo	100	15.5	17.9	14.0	52.6	14.81	14.74
Total 1 plus 2	All ships	100	24.1	38.3	18.7	18.9	9.56	9.00
	Tankers	100	23.6	46.4	16.8	13.2	8.64	7.77
	Bulk carriers[a]	100	23.4	39.1	23.6	13.9	9.09	8.50
	General cargo	100	22.0	17.2	17.6	43.2	13.26	13.37
3. Socialist countries of Eastern Europe and Asia (SCS)	All ships	100	18.9	22.2	24.5	34.4	12.44	11.81
	Tankers	100	16.2	20.2	21.6	42.0	13.57	11.95
	Bulk carriers[a]	100	33.2	28.0	21.7	17.1	8.99	8.76
	General cargo	100	14.3	21.2	25.4	39.1	13.42	12.93
4. Developing countries (excluding open-registry countries) (DMNS)	All ships	100	29.1	25.2	20.6	25.1	10.34	9.90
	Tankers	100	28.9	32.2	21.9	17.0	9.20	8.24
	Bulk carriers[a]	100	30.6	28.4	27.7	13.3	8.85	8.03
	General cargo	100	24.7	18.2	16.5	40.6	12.68	12.91
World total	All ships	100	24.2	35.2	19.5	21.1	9.93	9.38
	Tankers	100	23.8	44.0	17.5	14.7	8.89	8.00
	Bulk carriers[a]	100	24.6	37.5	23.8	14.1	9.07	8.50
	General cargo	100	21.2	18.0	18.8	42.0	13.18	13.20

[a] Including combined carriers.
[b] To calculate average age it has been assumed that the ages of vessels are distributed evenly between the lower and upper limit of each age group. For the 15 years and over age group, the mid-point has been assumed to be 22 years.

Source: UNCTAD, *Review of Maritime Transport,* 1981, TD/B/C.4/222, p. 21.

Table 14. Distribution of tonnage on order by groups of countries of build, 1970 and 1978–1980 (thousand grt; in brackets, percentage of world total).

	As at end of third quarter of each year			
Country grouping	1970	1978	1979	1980
Developed market-economy	67 063	20 810	18 843	24 959
countries (TMNS)	(96.2)	(74.0)	(70.7)	(75.7)
Developing countries	884	4 657	4 681	5 026
(DMNS)	(1.3)	(16.6)	(17.5)	(15.3)
Socialist countries	1 592	2 146	2 604	2 110
(SCS)	(2.3)	(7.6)	(9.8)	(6.4)
Other – unallocated	175	511	527	869
	(0.2)	(1.8)	(2.0)	(2.6)
World total (100.0)	69 714	28 124	26 655	32 964

Source: UNCTAD, *Review of Maritime Transport,* 1981, TD/B/C.4/222, p. 34.

transport initiated by UNCTAD I was that maritime transport costs account for a substantial part of the balance of payments deficits of the DMNS.[121] The investigation (elaborated in the next chapter) exposed the striking imbalance between the volumes of the seaborne cargoes originating in the DMNS and the cargo carrying capacity of these countries. These are the trade flows to which the DMNS must first look in seeking to participate in the carriage of maritime cargoes.[122] Yet the present carrying capacity of the merchant fleets of the DMNS is utterly inadequate to claim any significant share in the cargoes originating from their territory.

The fall in the DMNS' share may be insignificant, but the fact remains that the share of the DMNS in world shipping is very small, especially when compared with their share in the volume of world trade.[123] As far as one can discern future trends, this imbalance between the DMNS' trade and their shipping is likely to become more and more acute in the next few years. World shipping will, therefore, continue to be dominated in the near future by the TMNS.[124] The only chink in the armour of the TMNS is the growth of the fleets of the STNS, which have been gradually increasing their share in world shipping. A new picture of world shipping may gradually emerge. This changed picture will still be imbalanced if the part that the DMNS plays in it is not consistent with their own importance in world trade.[125]

Since few DMNS are in a position to provide the considerable amount of resources needed to bring about a change in the shipping pattern, international support for their individual efforts is urgently needed from the rest of the international maritime community.[126] Otherwise the DMNS have a reason for concern. To reverse this imbalanced trend they have had to establish and/or develop national merchant marine fleets of their own.[127] Short of support from the international shipping community they had to go it alone. That has meant the use of traditional methods, namely, flag preference and discrimination (for establishment) on the one hand, and state intervention, maritime subsidies and state aid (for development), on the other.[128]

4.2 The growing concern of the developing maritime nations

In the case of most DMNS, international trade is even more closely related to national economic growth than is the case with most TMNS. This relationship can be expected to continue and to remain crucial in the years to come.[129] Hence the vital importance to the DMNS of maritime transport, on which they rely for exporting their products and importing their essential requirements. There are, therefore, compelling objective reasons to take the views of the DMNS, on merchant marine matters, very seriously. In 1969, for instance, the DMNS generated about 65% (by volume) of all cargo loaded in the oceanborne trade of the world.[130] The control and operation of shipping, however, continue to be in the hands of a certain number of the TMNS. Certainly, there is nothing inherently wrong with a single country or a group of countries relying wholly, or almost wholly, upon transport provided by a foreign country or a group of countries.[131] But the continuation of their present dependence on shipping services controlled by the TMNS is unacceptable to the DMNS for a number of reasons, as will be elaborated in subsequent chapters. Briefly, these are as follows. Firstly, the reliance on foreign operators has certain unfavourable implications for the already serious balance of payments' problems of most DMNS.[132] The foreign exchange constraint on these countries is so severe that they are understandably anxious to save as much foreign exchange as possible.

Secondly, the group of countries that control shipping do so mainly because it is a profitable activity. Hence the decisions of their enterprises are more closely linked to profits than to those of service to trade. From the point of view of users,[133] this arrangement – despite its numerous favourable considerations – leads to a high degree of uncertainty. The DMNS feel (and rightly so) that a vital part of their national product should not depend upon the profit motive of a group of foreign private enterprises.[134] These are areas best served by national fleets – service-rather than profit-oriented. The experience of both the TMNS and the DMNS during the last two world wars and other periods of international tension has convinced many governments that it is imprudent in the long run to rely too heavily on a situation in which foreign shipowners determine shipping policies.[135]

Thirdly, the fact that the shipping industry is controlled by a number of the TMNS is only partially the result of some basic advantages that these countries possess (such as the relative abundance of capital for a relatively capital intensive activity);[136] to a large extent, the position of these countries is the result of their international shipping policies and of historical and traditional factors coupled with geographical accidents.[137]

It is no coincidence that several TMNS have also been major colonial powers. In many cases, the fleets of these countries were originally established for not entirely 'economic' reasons, and many continue to exist partly as a result of generous subsidies or other forms of assistance from their governments.[138] There is an *a priori* reason why an economic activity should not be subsidized by national governments. In an international industry like the merchant marine, however, subsidization by a few countries or a grcup of countries leads to consequences of far-reaching importance for the policies of other countries.[139] Moreover, nations that practice such policies themselves are on very weak ground indeed when they object to similar assistance policies on the part of other countries, insisting, at the same time, that industries in these other countries be founded on sound economic criteria.[140]

Yet such an insistence has been consistently made by the TMNS in recent years. This dichotomy in standards is not acceptable to the DMNS. The DMNS have been contending for many years with a general decline or instability in the prices of primary products (their principle exports) and with a continued rise in the price of manufactured goods (their principle imports).[141] The resulting deterioration in their terms of trade has adversely affected their real import capacity. Two other factors further intensify the foreign exchange constraint of the DMNS. First, a large number of primary commodities are threatened today by the development of various synthetic substitutes in the TMNS.[142] Rubber and jute may be cited as examples. Second, an increasing number of the DMNS have been directing their efforts to producing and exporting semi-manufactured and manufactured goods.[143]

In addition to the tariff and non-tariff barriers that they have to surmount in the TMNS, these goods face stiff competition from established industries in the TMNS. Against this background one can fully appreciate the concern of the DMNS about the regular upward trend in freight rates charged for the carriage of their exports and imports by foreign shipowners.[144] Rising freight rates, of course, affect both the DMNS and the TMNS. But the relative elasticity of demand and supply of goods traded by the DMNS and the TMNS are such that the DMNS probably bear the brunt of rising freight. Thus, the desire to cut down the freight bills is another of the DMNS' motives to establish and/or develop national fleets of their own.[145] Moreover, these freight bills are payable in the badly needed foreign exchange.

5. Maritime transport costs to the developing countries' national fleets, international trade and the balance of payments

The trade position of the DMNS is further handicapped by the nature and value of their export commodities, the level of their industrial development, and the structure and evolution of freight rates. There is, however, still another factor that increases the vulnerability of their exports in competitive foreign markets and affects the total foreign bill that they have to bear.[146] This is the incidence of the cost of transport (the question of who bears the transport costs in a trading transaction) which depends, essentially, on the relative elasticities of many agricultural products that are important in the export trade of the DMNS. These are generally low, especially in the short run. Although the demand elasticities for the same products are also generally low, they are nevertheless higher relative to supply elasticities.[147]

Most primary commodities are produced in a number of countries that compete with each other as suppliers in the world market, and synthetic substitutes are now available for many primary products.[148] As such the demand elasticities of these products are generally higher (for an individual country) because the buyer country can switch either to another supplier or to synthetic substitutes. In such a situation, the suppliers in the DMNS have to bear the major part of

Table 15. The ratio of liner freight rates to prices of selected commodities, 1970 and 1976–1979

		Freight rate as a percentage of price [ab]				
Commodity	Route	1970	1976[c]	1977[c]	1978[c]	1979[c]
Rubber	Singapore/Malaysia–Europe	10.5	11.9	11.9	12.1	9.7
Tin	Singapore/Malaysia–Europe	1.2	1.4	1.0	1.0	0.9
Jute	Bangladesh–Europe	12.1	19.1	15.8	11.9	16.1
Sisal hemp	East Africa–Europe	19.5	17.2	15.9	17.4	15.7
Cocoa beans	Ghana–Europe	2.4	1.7	1.0	1.7	2.0
Coconut oil	Sri Lanka–Europe	8.9	8.3	10.1	9.7	8.0
Tea	Sri Lanka–Europe	9.5	9.6	6.0	6.4	8.8
Coffee	Brazil–Europe	5.2	4.4	3.1	5.6	5.1
Palm kernels	Nigeria–Europe	8.8	28.4	23.6	15.1	1.9
Coffee	Colombia (Atlantic ports)–Europe	4.2	3.0	1.8	2.4	3.0
Cocoa beans	Brazil–Europe	7.4	6.4	3.2	5.0	6.1
Coffee	Colombia (Pacific ports)–Europe	4.5	3.2	2.0	3.2	4.6

[a] CIF prices were quoted for rubber (London–RSS), tin, jute (UK-pwc grade), sisal hemp, cocoa beans (Ghana–Europe), and palm kernels. For cocoa beans (Brazil–Europe), and coffee (Colombia–Europe and Brazil–Europe), unit values of exports were quoted. Prices of the remaining commodities are quoted on FOB terms.

[b] Freight rates include Suez Canal varying surcharges, when applicable, bunker and currency adjustment factors, and, for coconut oil only, a 'tank cleaning surcharge'. Whenever a conversion of freight rates to other currencies has been necessary for 1979, this was based on currency parities as given in *International Financial Statistics* published by the International Monetary Fund (November 1980) and valid as at the end of 1979. Annual freight rates were calculated by taking a weighted average of various freight rates quoted during the year, weighted by their period of duration.

[c] In 1976, the prices of sisal hemp and coconut oil were taken from UNCTAD, *Monthly Commodity Price Bulletin*, *Special Supplement 1960–1976*, September 1977. In 1977 the price of coconut oil was taken from UNCTAD, *Monthly Commodity Price Bulletin*, September 1978. In 1978 the prices of coconut oil and sisal hemp were taken from UNCTAD, *Monthly Commodity Price Bulletin*, revised *Special Supplement 1960–1978*, April 1979. In 1979, the prices for coconut oil and sisal hemp were taken from UNCTAD, *Monthly Commodity Price Bulletin*, November 1980.

Source: UNCTAD, *Review of Maritime Transport,* 1981, p. 39.

transport costs, and the escalation of these costs results in a decline in the FOB value of goods exported.[149] At the same time the supply elasticities of manufactured goods (which comprise most of the imports of the DMNS from the TMNS) are generally higher than the elasticities of demands for these products in the DMNS.[150]

Although on a world-wide basis the elasticity of demand for manufactured goods may be relatively higher than the elasticity of supply, this situation does not necessarily apply in the case of the DMNS since their manufactured imports may be financed largely by credits,[151] grants or loans which have tended to restrict the choice of supplier to the aid-giving countries. As a result, a considerable part – perhaps a major portion – of the transport costs of manufactured goods produced in the TMNS is passed on to importers in the DMNS.[152]

Table 16. Estimate of total freight costs in world trade in 1970, 1977, 1978 and 1979

Year	Country group	Estimate of total freight costs on imports (in mil. US $)	Value of imports (CIF) (in mil. US $)	Freight cost as percentage of value of imports
1970	World total	22 626	292 070	7.75
	Developed market-economy countries	17 483	240 847	7.26
	Developing countries	5 143	51 223	10.04
	In Africa	1 144	10 510	10.88
	In America	1 819	17 358	10.48
	In Asia	2 098	22 552	9.30
	In Europe	–	–	–
	In Oceania	82	803	10.21
1977	World total	68 520	1 036 955	6.61
	Developed market economy countries	45 365	808 615	5.61
	Developing countries	23 155	228 340	10.14
	In Africa	5 234	48 371	10.82
	In America	6 074	63 514	9.56
	In Asia	11 681	114 952	10.16
	In Europe	–	–	–
	In Oceania	166	1 503	11.04
1978	World total	79 142	1 207 887	6.55
	Developed market-economy countries	51 403	933 204	5.51
	Developing countries	27 739	274 683	10.10
	In Africa	6 303	57 874	10.89
	In America	6 672	71 924	9.28
	In Asia	14 569	143 130	10.18
	In Europe	–	–	–
	In Oceania	195	1 755	11.11
1979	World total	99 765	1 522 773	6.55
	Developed market-economy countries	66 761	1 193 850	5.60
	Developing countries	33 004	328 923	10.03
	In Africa	7 113	65 015	10.94
	In America	8 489	93 110	9.12
	In Asia	17 174	168 694	10.18
	In Europe	–	–	–
	In Oceania	228	2 104	10.84

Source: UNCTAD, *Review of Maritime Transport,* 1981, TD/B/C.4/222, p. 40.

This trend could have been eliminated, or at least reduced, were the importing DMNS to have their own national fleets carrying this inward trade. Thus, the DMNS bear a major share of the costs of transporting both their exports and their imports.[153] This situation only increases their already great sensitivity to rising freight rates and the resultant desire for their own national fleets.[154]

The exports of the DMNS consist mainly of primary commodities or semi-manufactured goods. The per-unit value of these commodities is generally low. Consequently, freight rates constitute a large component of the CIF costs in the case of primary commodities and semi-manufactured goods than they do in the case of the manufactured goods.[155] According to the *UNCTAD Commodity Survey* of 1968 which provides information about the price trends of primary commodities that are important in the export trades of the DMNS, the unit values of commodity exports, barring a few exceptions, have shown a declining trend.[156] Most primary commodities and semi-manufactured goods are shipped from the DMNS in liner ships. Freight rates for liner transport in general have been rising steadily. For example, a reliable freight rate index of cargo handled in the Antwerp/Hamburg range of ports rose from 100 to 153 between 1954–1967.[157] This rise has continued in the 70's and 80's.

Similar increases have been experienced elsewhere. In some cases, the rise in freight rates has been even steeper, particularly since 1967. Moreover, available data indicated that voyage charter rates have also gone up for bulk commodities exported from the DMNS, such as raw sugar and copra, as well as for bulk commodities imported by them, such as grains, flour and fertilisers.[158] At the same time, the prices of commodities in which the DMNS, as suppliers, generally have a predominant interest have been declining. Only the prices of raw jute and tobacco increased marginally over the period 1957–1967. Studies carried out for some specific commodities clearly establish the adverse correlation between liner freight rates and commodity prices.[159] For instance, an analysis of variations in the prices of natural rubber in Singapore and of freight rates charged for its liner transport to the UK and Western Europe (which constitutes the principal market for Malaysia/Singapore rubber) reveals a steep decline in the unit value of exports and an increase in the liner freight rates.[160]

According to this analysis, freight costs expressed as a percentage of the price of rubber, increased from 3.55% in 1960 to 9.6% in February 1968. For one variety of logs exported from West Africa, the ratio of estimated freight costs to CIF prices (at Bremen, West Germany) rose from 29.6% to 34.1%[161] The price index for sawn-timber exported from Malaysia and Singapore showed a marginal increase from 100 to 102, between 1960 and 1968, while freight rates indices increased from 100 to 112 for timber exported to Europe and 100 to 148 to the US (Atlantic Coast).[162] Similar correlations between prices and freight rates are evident from data compiled by the UNCTAD Secretariat for the period 1963 to 1967 regarding the export of hemp to Europe from East Africa and the Phillipines, jute from Bangladesh, palm kernels from Nigeria, cocoa beans from Brazil and tea from Sri Lanka and India. The examples could go on and on, but the point to be made here is that, whatever the circumstances, the DMNS bear the brunt of rises in freight rates.[163]

5.1 International trade, freight rates and the drive for national fleets by the developing countries

Another study carried out to show the relationship between freight rates and FOB prices of commodities important in India's export trade revealed that between 1960–1961 and 1969–1970 liner freight rates continued to rise steadily while prices of goods either declined or increased at a much slower rate than freight rates.[164] Freight rates expressed as a percentage of the FOB value of goods exported to the UK, US, West Europe and Australia did increase for a large number of commodities, including tea, hessian-cloth, iron and steel goods, pepper, coffee, oil cakes and raw tobacco.[165] The DMNS also find themselves in a disadvantageous position in regard to non-traditional exports, mostly manufactured goods. As such goods have only recently become export items, they generally have not been assigned specific freight rate tariffs.[166] Consequently, the DMNS are charged a rate prescribed for cargo n.o.s. (not otherwise specified) for exporting such goods.[167] The average freight rate for a particular liner trade route, likewise a detailed 1968 survey of maritime freight rates in the foreign trade of Latin American countries showed that in the case of simple manufactures, the proportion of commodities requiring the application of n.o.s. rates[168] on the various routes was 28.5%, while in that of highly processed manufactures it reached 45.8%. An even steeper increase in liner freight rates may be expected in the near future as a result of inflationary trends around the world, especially in the TMNS.[169]

Primary commodities exported by the DMNS, many of them facing stiff competition from synthetics, cannot absorb the increasing freight components in the bonded price of these goods.[170] Increases in the prices of ships and fuel oil, repair costs, and insurance charges are all bound to be reflected in freight rates. While the escalation of these expenses is nearly universal, the same cannot be said of the rising level of stevedoring costs incurred in the loading and unloading of cargoes.[171] The rising standard of living in the TMNS has caused a continuous demand for higher wages and other benefits for dock labour, leading to increasing stevedoring expenses which have a significant impact on total transport costs. For example, on some of the liner routes serving India, stevedoring expenses in foreign ports represented about 18% to 39% of total gross earnings in 1968–1969,[172] and about 45% in the late 70's.

To a certain extent the TMNS have attempted to insulate freight rates from the costs of dock labour by resorting to containerisation.[173] Container traffic has expanded rapidly in recent years, but container ships were originally confined to shipping lanes between the TMNS. To date, the few known routes involving the DMNS are:

(1) A service between the US, Brazil and Argentina;[174] and
(2) A service between Europe and the Far East, aimed at Japan which will only, incidentally, serve the DMNS *en route*.[175]

It appears that for some time to come the liner trades of the DMNS will continue to depend on the conventional ships and break-bulks (not bulk or unitized) cargoes. The DMNS still have to grapple with the primary problems of establishing and/or developing national fleets let along taking on the problems of containerisation.[176]

For these reasons the liner freight rates in the trade of the DMNS will continue to be highly sensitive to the escalation of stevedoring costs in the TMNS. The effect of rising stevedoring costs is perhaps the most difficult and, thus far, intractable problem facing the shipping and trade of the DMNS. Although these countries are in no way responsible for rising labour costs in the TMNS,[177] their economies ultimately bear the burdens of these costs mainly because they do not have national fleets of their own. In some cases the DMNS have tried to counter-balance the effects of higher freight rates on their exports by increasing direct or indirect export incentives (post).[178] But this process cannot be continued beyond a certain point without causing serious distortions in the economies of the exporting countries. The export potential of the DMNS, particularly for primary commodities, may be seriously affected unless some method can be evolved to protect their trade from the impact of increasing stevedoring costs in the ports of the TMNS.[179]

5.2 Freight rates, national fleets and the balance of payments' problems (BOP) of the developing countries

Paradoxically, the paramount importance of shipping, self-evident as it may seem through an *ex post facto* rationalisation, was not detected at once by the DMNS. It was only dimly perceived when the first round of discussions on the challenge of under-development[180] took place in the early 1950's. At that time, economists and planners pondering over the social economic and technological disparity between the TMNS and the DMNS, placed little emphasis on the behaviour of science in trade relations between the TMNS and the DMNS. The debate on ways and means of reducing the gap between the TMNS and the DMNS centred on increasing productivity, industrialisation,[181] and expansion and diversification of invisible exports. Little, if any, attention was paid either at the national or international level, to the question of the foreign exchange deficits incurred by the DMNS in invisible transactions in shipping and in insurance services.[182]

Statistical information on these transactions was lacking and the shipping and insurance industries, which accrued large amounts of foreign exchange from their operations, propagated the myth that invisible exports were unimportant and unprofitable, and their techniques mysteriously complex.[183] Such matters, it was suggested, should be left to those who know best. However, statistical data on shipping transactions collected by some DMNS since the UNCTAD I session revealed the horrifying picture.[184] For example, according to the statistical data gathered by the Brazilian government since 1967, Brazil's foreign trade in 1968 generated a freight cost of 541.3 million US $ on exports and imports. In that year, Brazilian flag vessels earned only 69.3 million US $ in freight revenue, or 13% of the total.[185] Foreign vessels chartered by Brazilian shipowners and nationals accounted for a further 116.2 million US $, or 21% of the total freight costs. Vessels of foreign flags earned the remaining 358.8 million US $, or 66% of the total.[186] The share of foreign shipping of the overall freight revenue was, in fact, even greater than this figure suggests, since a large part of the revenue earned by chartered ships is utilised by the chartering foreign countries.[187] If Brazil's position (a supposedly more affluent DMNS) could be as bad as this, that regarding the poorer DMNS was appalling, while that of the developing countries without national fleets of their own is likely to be even worse.[188]

The published figures on service transactions, however, do not reveal the full impact of freight costs on the balance of payments of the DMNS. An examination of the real incidence of freight costs will show that the one who pays the freights is not necessarily the one who actually bears the cost of transportation.[189] As will be evident later, when goods are sold on a CIF basis the exporter or his agent is responsible for the payment of the freight. Inversely, when the commercial operations are made on FOB basis the importer pays the freight. But it is neither the exporter in the first case, nor the importer in the

Table 17. Freight rate indices, 1978–1980 (monthly or quarterly figures).

	Liner freight rates[a] (1965 = 100)			Dry cargo tramp time charter[b] (1976 = 100)			Dry cargo tramp trip charter[c] (July 1965– June 1966 = 100)			Tanker freight indices[c] VLCC/ULCC			Medium size crude carriers			Small crude and product carriers			Handy size (dirty)			Handy size (clean)		
	1978	1979	1980	1978	1979	1980	1978	1979	1980	1978	1979	1980	1978	1979	1980	1978	1979	1980	1978	1979	1980	1978	1979	1980
January	237	247	283				134	144	194	20	31	50	47	97	121	74	185	203	121	278	285	126	304	309
February	241	250	284	87	138	254	133	146	210	21	22	34	43	95	89	80	174	153	110	296	268	123	279	257
March	241	254	285				134	158	209	19	44	34	42	119	96	76	204	167	122	307	298	126	258	286
April	242	259	285				135	156	217	19	39	33	46	84	85	80	146	144	121	226	259	120	300	262
May	242	265	285	115	194	297	148	168	221	20	38	33	49	101	81	79	181	142	114	249	267	121	275	263
June	241	269	284				138	178	226	21	44	40	46	127	84	81	243	127	107	326	250	120	351	274
July	241	274	283				137	196	203	26	71	32	49	150	65	88	233	107	127	329	177	133	363	196
August	241	277	285	112	206	252	139	190	207	31	54	29	65	126	59	104	206	109	148	345	187	172	365	161
September	241	278	286				141	201	201	36	55	40	64	122	60	103	236	98	157	366	193	186	373	197
October	242	277	287				142	203	204	45	54	33	92	124	67	136	222	115	149	402	170	205	408	188
November	242	278	289	133	237	261	149	206	227	50	54	42	128	135	93	212	265	178	282	431	211	275	398	208
December	242	276	292				150	203	241	40	62	45	97	134	115	181	304	207	270	424	219	239	375	243
Annual average	241	267	286	112	194	266	140	179	213	29	47	37	64	118	85	108	217	146	152	332	232	162	337	237

[a] Liner index compiled by the Ministry of Transport of the Federal Republic of Germany. Monthly weighted assessments of freight rates on cargoes loaded or discharged by liners of all flags at ports in the Antwerp/Hamburg range.
[b] Compiled and published on a quarterly basis by the General Council of British Shipping.
[c] Compiled and published by *Norwegian Shipping News* (Oslo). Worldscale = 100, as effective in each year.

Source: Review of Maritime Transport, 1981, TD/B/C.4/222 p. 37.

latter, who will necessarily bear the actual costs of the freight.[190] In practice, the relative supply and demand elasticities of a product determine who bears the major part of the transport costs. Since a situation of complete inelastic demand or supply usually does not prevail, the burden of transportation will be shared between importer and exporter.[191]

But this sharing is, more often than not, unbalanced to the detriment of one party or the other. An UNCTAD Secretariat Report, analysing the incidence of transport costs concluded that for many of the world's agricultural products,[192] on which the DMNS rely for much of their export earnings, supply elasticities are low in the short run. Although overall demand elasticites for most of these commodities are also low, the elasticity of demand facing the individual supplier or the whole group of suppliers in a single country is likely to be relatively high unless that country is the only source of supply and there are no ready substitutes for the commodity.[193] The supplier in these cases, therefore, normally bears the bulk of the transport costs and any increase in these costs is matched by an almost equal decline in his net receipts per unit sold.[194]

Although the elasticity of demand for many manufactured products tend to be relatively high in the DMNS, they remain lower than the elasticities of their supply to the countries concerned.[195] Thus, the major part of the freight rates is borne by the importers. It can be deduced from these conclusions that when it comes to freight costs, the TMNS are playing a game governed by the rule of *heads I win – tails you lose,* and the DMNS are always the losers. And losers indeed they are and will remain so for some time to come.[196] The alternative to being condemned to the unpalatable position of permanent losers is for them to establish and/or develop national fleets of their own. That would, in fact, be in line with the Charter of the UN.[197]

6. The United Nations and national fleets of the developing countries – Development Decades: The development strategy and the new international maritime order

The right of the DMNS and the urgent need to establish and/or develop national fleets of their own was given impetus by the series of the *UN Development Decades* for the 1960's, 1970's and 1980's.[198] The *Second Development Decade* had as its objective to promote, by national and international action, the earning of the DMNS from invisible trade and to maximise the net outflow of foreign exchange from those countries arising from invisible transactions, including shipping.[199] Of particular concern was, firstly, the principle that the national shipping lines of the DMNS, when established, be admitted as full members of liner conferences operating in their national maritime trade and have an increasing and substantial participation in the carriage of cargoes generated by their foreign trade.[200]

Secondly, that the TMNS governments should encourage liner conferences to consider favourably, fairly, and on equal terms, applications of the national shipping lines of the DMNS when established, for admission as full members to way-port conference trades related to these countries' own foreign trade, subject to the rights and obligations of conference membership.[201] In order

Table 18. Deliveries of new buildings, 1978–1980[a] (number of ships and thousand grt/dwt).

Type of ship	1978	1979	1980
Tankers			
Number	152	147	164
grt	3 510	2 592	2 875
dwt	6 799	4 732	4 839
Bulk/oil carriers			
Number	8	7	8
grt	418	297	326
dwt	757	514	554
Ore and bulk carriers			
Number	173	82	87
grt	3 634	1 803	1 852
dwt	6 255	3 029	3 210
General cargo ships[b]			
Number	299	264	184
grt	2 584	2 171	1 365
dwt	3 801	3 034	1 949
Other ships			
Number	1 139	1 150	1 266
grt	3 255	3 258	2 981
dwt	3 561	3 653	3 128
Total			
Number	1 751	1 650	1 709
grt	13 401	10 121	9 399
dwt	21 173	14 962	13 680

[a] This table has been completely revised. The figures refer to the period January to September for each year.
[b] Vessels of 2 000 grt and over.

Table 19. Distribution of deliveries of new buildings by groups of countries of build, 1978–1980[a] (thousand grt and in brackets percentage of world total).

Country grouping	1978	1979	1980
Developed market-economy countries (TMNS)	10 948 (83.8)	8 036 (82.0)	7 392 (81.6)
Developing countries (DMNS)	797 (6.1)	930 (9.5)	993 (10.9)
Socialist countries (SCS)	995 (7.6)	664 (6.8)	478 (5.3)
Other, unallocated	324 (2.5)	164 (1.7)	197 (2.2)
World total	13 064 (100.0)	9 794 (100.0)	9 059 (100.0)

[a] This table has been completely revised and based on January to September information. However, the total tonnages are not exactly the same as in Table 21 because of possibly incomplete figures given in the quarterly returns.

Source: UNCTAD, *Review of Maritime Transport,* 1981, TD/B/C.4/222, p. 35.

Table 20. Distribution of tonnage on order by type of vessel and by country of registry as of 30 September 1978, 1979 and 1980 (in percentage).

Countries of registry	Year	All ships	Tankers 150 000 dwt and over	Tankers under 150 000 dwt	Bulk/oil carriers (incl. ore/oil)	Ore and bulk carriers	Full container ships	Part container ships	Ro/ro cargo ships	General cargo ships	Other ships
1. Developed market-economy countries (TMNS)	1978	53.6	69.2	55.6	28.6	45.3	42.2	93.4	66.8	50.5	57.2
	1979	51.2	71.4	44.9	58.8	42.9	67.0	87.4	55.8	44.1	56.4
	1980	46.9	48.2	41.4	64.7	43.8	68.0	100.0	53.3	45.6	56.6
2. Open registry countries	1978	14.8	16.5	27.9	4.1	11.7	24.0	–	5.2	13.7	8.7
	1979	22.0	11.1	44.8	7.7	21.2	19.3	–	3.3	8.9	13.9
	1980	33.2	20.1	47.0	26.8	36.6	12.8	–	1.1	10.4	19.7
Total 1 and 2	1978	68.4	85.7	83.5	32.7	57.0	66.4	93.4	72.0	64.0	65.9
	1979	73.2	82.5	89.7	66.5	64.1	86.3	87.4	59.1	53.0	70.3
	1980	80.1	68.3	88.4	91.5	80.4	80.8	100.0	54.4	56.0	76.3
3. Socialist countries (SCS)	1978	6.7	–	5.6	18.0	10.0	2.3	–	15.1	7.0	6.8
	1979	5.9	2.9	0.9	5.8	8.4	1.4	–	32.7	9.2	6.9
	1980	2.5	5.0	1.2	–	0.4	–	–	36.3	7.0	5.9
In Eastern Europe	1978	6.4	–	5.6	18.0	10.0	2.3	–	15.1	5.6	6.8
	1979	5.2	2.9	0.7	5.8	8.4	1.4	–	26.3	6.5	5.8
	1980	2.0	5.0	0.3	–	0.4	–	–	33.7	3.8	5.9
In Asia	1978	0.3	–	–	–	–	–	–	–	1.4	–
	1979	0.7	–	0.2	–	–	–	–	6.4	2.7	1.1
	1980	0.5	–	0.9	–	–	–	–	2.6	3.2	–

4. Developing countries[a] (DMNS)	1978	22.0	14.3	9.2	42.5	31.3	17.1	6.6	9.7	24.4	24.5
	1979	19.5	10.6	9.4	27.7	27.2	1.5	12.6	8.0	36.3	21.9
	1980	16.4	19.6	10.4	8.5	18.7	6.9	–	7.6	36.5	17.2
In Africa	1978	2.4	–	0.2	–	0.5	–	–	5.6	7.3	7.1
	1979	2.0	–	–	–	1.0	–	–	0.6	7.2	6.9
	1980	0.7	–	–	–	0.3	–	–	–	2.7	3.8
In America	1978	13.4	14.3	7.2	42.5	21.6	1.2	6.6	3.9	10.4	0.7
	1979	11.2	10.6	7.2	27.7	19.1	–	12.6	6.4	10.7	1.0
	1980	7.3	–	4.6	8.5	10.2	–	–	7.6	15.0	3.2
In Asia	1978	6.2	–	1.8	–	9.2	15.9	–	0.2	6.7	16.7
	1979	6.3	–	2.2	–	7.1	1.5	–	0.1	18.3	14.0
	1980	8.4	19.6	5.8	–	8.2	6.9	–	–	18.8	10.2
In Oceania	1979	–	–	–	–	–	–	–	0.9	–	–
5. Other unallocated	1978	2.9	–	1.7	6.8	1.7	14.2	–	3.2	4.6	2.8
	1979	1.4	4.0	–	–	0.3	10.8	–	0.2	1.5	0.9
	1980	1.0	7.1	–	–	0.5	12.3	–	1.7	0.5	0.6
World total Million dwt	1978	41.0	7.9	5.6	1.9	10.2	1.8	0.2	1.4	7.7	4.2
	1979	38.2	5.2	9.7	2.0	9.3	1.7	0.1	1.0	5.4	3.7
	1980	50.9	3.0	14.2	3.3	20.0	1.1	0.1	0.9	3.5	4.8
% share by type of vessel	1978	100.0	19.3	13.7	4.7	24.9	4.4	0.6	3.4	18.8	10.2
	1979	100.0	13.7	25.4	5.2	24.3	4.5	0.3	2.7	14.1	9.8
	1980	100.0	5.8	27.8	6.5	39.3	2.1	0.2	1.8	6.9	9.6

[a] Developing countries in Europe had no tonnage on order for the whole period and in Oceania for 1978 and for 1980.

Source: UNCTAD, *Review of Maritime Transport*, 1981, TD/B/C4/222, p. 32.

that the DMNS may have an increasing and substantial participation in the carriage of maritime cargoes, and recognizing the need to reverse the existing trend, whereby the share of the DMNS in the world merchant fleet has been declining instead of increasing, the DMNS were to be enabled to expand their national and multinational merchant marines[202] through the adoption of such measures as may be appropriate to permit their shipowners to compete in the international freight market and thus contribute to a sound development of shipping. These are the measures outlined in Parts II and III ahead.[203]

Finally, it was also felt necessary that further improvements be made in the liner conference system, and all unfair practices and discrimination, where they exist in liner conferences, be eliminated.[204] However, in the determination and adjustment of liner freight rates, due consideration should be given, as far as is commercially possible and/or appropriate, to:

(1) The needs of developing countries, in particular their efforts to promote non-traditional exports; and[205]

(2) The special problems of the least developed among the developing countries, in order to encourage and promote the export and import interests in these countries.[206]

To achieve these objectives, governments of TMNS and members of UNCTAD were urged, upon request by the DMNS, within the framework of the then overall development priorities, to duly consider extending, directly or through international institutions, financial and technical assistance; including training[207] to the DMNS to establish and expand their national and multinational merchant marines, including tanker and bulk carrier fleets, and to develop and improve their port facilities. And, within assistance programmes, special attention was to be paid to projects, including training projects[208] for developing the shipping and ports of the least developed of the DMNS and for reducing their maritime transport costs. It will be remembered that all these broad objectives are directly in line with and designed to redress the kinds of imbalances that have been outlined earlier in this chapter.[209]

It will also be observed that considerably more progress seems to have been made, along these lines, in the *International Development Strategy*[210] of the Second UN Development Decade than had been made in the first decade, when the objectives had been concluded in more radical terms. The establishment of UNCTAD in 1964, and its committee on shipping in 1965, was a landmark for the efforts of the DMNS to establish and/or develop their own national merchant marine fleets. Notably the *UNCTAD Memorandum of Understanding on Shipping*[211] was to have a far-reaching effect on international shipping and radically change the future prospects of the national fleets. The DMNS' case was further strengthened by the demand for a *New International Maritime Order* (NIMO),[212] the maritime aspects of the New International Economic Order 1974. The UNCTAD *Code of Conduct for Liner Conferences*, the UN *Multimodal Transport Convention* and the call for *cargo sharing* in the bulk trade are to be seen as facets of NIMO.[213]

The New International Economic Order was bolstered by the *Programme of Action* in its establishment, the *Charter of the Duties and Rights of States*[214] and the *Rights of Peoples and States to their Natural Resources*.[215] The DMNS have also cited in support of their case the propagation by some academics and intellectuals, including those in the TMNS, of the *Right of Development*[216] for their rights to establish and/or develop their national merchant marine fleets. More recently, to add to their many claims, the *UN General Assembly Resolution* was passed as an *International Development Strategy* for the *Third UN Development Decade*,[217] which, with regard to maritime transport, declared that in the transport sector, national and international action will promote the development of seaborne trade and other transport systems.[218] The increase in participation by the DMNS in world transport connected with international trade is noted in particular, as well as the fact that appropriate structural changes must be carried out where necessary to further this development.[219] The Declaration calls upon the International Community, whatever that means, to continue to take the necessary steps to enable the DMNS to compete more efficiently and to expand their national and multinational merchant fleets so as to increase this substantially with a view to reaching, as close as possible, 20% of the DWT of the world merchant fleet by 1990.[220] That figure at one time stood at 8% and has been dropping steadily ever since.

The Resolution expects the *UN Code of Conduct for Liner Conferences* to have been implemented by its signatories.[221] It also expects early in the decade the *Convention on International Multimodal Transport* to have come into force, which will facilitate the development of multimodal transport operations by the DMNS.[222]

In this chapter, I hope I have indicated the unequal relationship that exists in international shipping, and have established the justification for nations to establish national fleets of their own, mainly, as a means of attempting to rectify this disequilibrium.[223] The next two sections will outline the traditional methods that these nations use to establish and/or develop national merchant marine fleets of their own.[224]

Appendix 2

Summary of grievances of African countries to the conferences serving the region

Conferences	Admission requirements	Malpractices: Definition	Malpractices: Policing	Rates: General	Rates: Contract	Conference administrative expenses
American West African Freight Exports Imports East Coast Canada/ United States	must provide regular service to trade route admission fee is U.S. $5 000 security deposit is U.S. $25 000	payment of agency fees in excess of 5% and $2\frac{1}{2}$% at loading and discharge port respectively employment of more than one agent at either port payment of *unreasonable* agent/husbanding fees, entertainment, souvenirs, and/or holiday gifts	neutral body reviews all complaints complaints referred to screening committee by the Chairman of the neutral body screening committee consists of 3 member lines elected on rotating basis for 1 year neutral body investigates upon decision of Screening Committee 1st offense (a) max. U.S. $10 000 or (b) equivalent to freight money, whichever is the greatest sum 2nd offense (a) max. U.S. $15 000 or (b) same as above 3rd offense (a) max. U.S. $20 000 or (b) same as above 4th offense (a) max. U.S. $25 000 or (b) same as above damages liquidated on prorata basis with members	reserve the right to declare rates on certain commodities open establishment of agreed minimum rate	the spread between the contract and non-contract rate is 15% of the contract rate in the Westbound group the contract rate is offered for only specific commodities	each segment inbound, outbound) of the conference shall bear 50% of all expenses and each member shall be charged equally for expense
Canada-South Africa Rate Association	requires a letter to the conference outlining the corporate and trade name, the	absorption by lines of wharfage storage or other charges accrued against cargo	Chairman/Chief Executive shall refer complaints to a committee of 3, one of who shall be himself acting as Chairman with the other 2	reserve the right to declare rates on specific commodities to be open provided there exists	No contract rate	50% of the total operating expenses shall be shared equally, remaining

Conferences	Admission requirements	Malpractices		Rates		Conference administrative expenses
		Definition	Policing	General	Contract	
Exports East Coast Canada	service contemplated and such *other* information as the conference may request acceptance based on at least 3/4 majority admission fee is Cdn. $10 000 security deposit is Cdn. $5 000		appointed by him from representative lines Committee investigate the allegations in a way they deem appropriate 1st offense max. Cdn. $2 500 2nd offense max. Cdn. $3 000 3rd offense max. Cdn. $25 000	*unanimous* consent of members establishment of agreed minimum rates		50% shall be prorated between the members on the basis of the number of sailings made by their respective ships
Canada East Africa Rate Association Exports East Coast Canada	must provide regular service to trade route acceptance based on at least 3/4 majority of existing members admission fee is Cdn. $10 000 security deposit is Cdn. $4 000	a member permitting any vessel owned, chartered, controlled, or operated by him to be used in this trade which does not fully adhere to all rates, charges & practices an agent of the signatories to this agreement performing the ship's husbanding of tramp vessels carrying full unpacked homogeneous cargoes in bulk, where the Agent is connected with the fixing of the vessel control of the cargo or is in any manner interested in the vessel or cargo	Chairman needs unanimous vote of conference members to determine what action should be taken for the violation of tariff- sum equal to 10 times the freight and other monies which said member would have received had applicable tariff been assessed for the violation of agreement 1st offense max. Cdn. $2 500 2nd offense max. Cdn. $5 000	reserve the right to declare rates open establishment of agreed minimum rates	No contract rate	50% of the total operating expenses shall be shared equally by all members, remaining 50% shall be prorated between the members on the basis of the number of sailings made by respective ships during the whole calendar year
South Africa Canada Rate Association Imports	must provide regular service to trade route acceptance based on at least 2/3 majority of existing members	member engaging either directly or indirectly in the transportation of cargoes at rates other than what was agreed upon	Secretary has the authority to investigate any allegations as he/she deems necessary 1st offense max. Cdn. $2 500 2nd offense max. Cdn. $5 000 3rd offense max. Cdn. $25 000	reserve the right to declare rates on particular commodities to be open establishment of agreed minimum rates	No contract rate	50% of the total operating expenses shared equally, the remaining 50% shall be prorated among the members on the basis of the

Appendix 2 (*Continued*)

Conferences	Admission requirements	Malpractices		Rates		Conference administrative expenses
		Definition	Policing	General	Contract	
East Coast Canada	admission fee is Cdn. $10 000 security deposit is Cdn. $5 000	all vessels owned or operated by a number not adhereing to all rates and regulations an agent of the signatories to the agreement performing the ship's husbandry of tramp vessels carrying full unpacked homogeneous cargoes in bulk, where the agent is interested in the vessel or cargo	the above fines for non-observance of Agreement for non-observance of Tariffs sum equal to 10 times the freight which said member would have received had the applicable tariff been assessed			number of sailings made by their respective vessels during the whole calendar year
East Africa Canada Rate Association Imports East Coast Canada	same as above (South Africa Canada Rate Association)	same as above	same as above	same as above	same as above	same as above
United States Great Lakes & St. Lawrence Ports/West African Agreement Exports Imports East Coast Canada United States	must provide regular service to trade route all application for membership will be acted upon immediately	no information	neutral body which has complete authority to conduct an investigation as warranted penalty for damages max. U.S. $10 000 for each violation	reserve the right to declare rates on specific commodities to be open establishment of agreed minimum rates	the spread between the contract and non-contract rate is 15% of the contract rate	no information

Source: Canadian Transport Commission, *International Liner Shipping* and Canada, pp. 107–109.

Notes

1. Zamora, S., 'Rate regulation in ocean transport: developing countries confront the liner conference system'. *Cal. L. Rev.*, Vol. 59, p. 1299.
2. Ogley, R. C. 'The Law of the Sea Draft Convention and the New International Economic Order', *Marine Policy*, July 1981, p. 240.
3. UNCTAD *Review of Maritime Transport*, 1969, p. 10.
4. Sodersten, B., *International Economics*, 1970, pp. 113–118.
5. See also 'Towards a new trade policy for development', *Proceedings of UNCTAD*, pp. 5–64.
6. *Ibid.*
7. UN. DOC. E/CONF. 46/41, 1964.
8. 1 Statistical Office of the UN 1968, *World Trade Annual* XI, 1968.
9. Myint, 'The classical theory of international trade and the underdeveloped countries', 68 *Econ. J.* 317, 1958.
10. Marx, D., *International Shipping Cartels* 3, 1953, pp. 223–29.
11. E.g., liners carried approximately 25% of total seaborne trade in 1964.
12. *Shipping and the World Economy* 5, UN. Doc. TD/B/C.4/17, 1966.
13. In 1968 the DMNS exported 32 427 4 million dollars worth of trade to the TMNS.
14. See note 13; compared to 6 752.8 million dollars worth of trade among themselves.
15. But imports from the TMNS to the DMNS totalled 32 802.1 million dollars for the same year.
16. See note 15.
17. IMF *Direction of Trade* 32 (Annual 1964–1968).
18. Under present trade patterns the DMNS export primary products and raw materials to the TMNS (25 370 million dollars in 1968).
19. See note 18; they import chemicals, machinery and other manufactures needed for industrial development (28 800 million dollars in 1968).
20. For footnotes 18–20 see 2, Statistical Office of the UN, 1968 Supp.
21. *Ibid.*; *Supplement to the World Trade Annual* XI, 1969.
22. The quantity of world exports by sea more than doubled between 1959–1968, increasing to a total of 2 050 metric tons.
23. UNCTAD *Review of Maritime Transport*, 1969, at 3–4.
24. See UN Doc. No. MM. 77/1/20, October 30, 1967.
25. For the text see 7 ILM, pp. 177–90.
26. The 63.5% DMNS' share of this total in 1968 represents an increase from the 1959 share of 61.4%.
27. UNCTAD Doc. No. TD/B/C.4/66, 1969.
28. See end of Chapter 3 and Chapter 8 for details.
29. Chrzanowski, I., 'Governments and shipping' *Fairplay*, vol. 274, no. 5050, 12th June 1980, p. 18.
30. See, for instance, Roscoe Pound 'Liberty of contract', *Yale Law Journal*, Vol. XViii, New Haven, Conn., 1908–1909, pp. 454–487.
31. Bain, J., *Industrial Organisation*, N.Y., 1959, p. 100.
32. Cf. (same author) *Barriers to New Competition*, Harvard University Press, Camb. Mass., 1956, p. 50.
33. Note. 'Who will run shipping?', *Norwegian News*, No. 9, 14/5/76, p. 5.
34. *Ibid.*
35. See Al-Jadir, A., 'Developing a fairer share', *Seatrade*, Sept. 1980, p. 152.
36. *Economist Intelligence Unit*, 'Ocean shipping and freight rates and developing countries', 1964.
37. See also *UN Monthly Bulletin of Statistics* for same year (1964).
38. Hawkins, R. *et al.*, UNCTAD: "Reprieve for cross-traders", *Seatrade*, May 1972, p. 3.
39. Farndon, R., 'Developed Nations "falling into a political trap on cargo sharing"', *Lloyd's List*, Thursday 24/4/80.
40. See Adler, M. J., *The Capitalist Manifesto*, N.Y., 1958.
41. Cf. US National Association of Manufacturers, Economic Principles' Commission, N.Y, 1958.

42. *Ibid., The American Individual Enterprise System,* N.Y., 1946.
43. This doctrine was first fully developed by Graphics in his *Mare Liberam* (1609).
44. See also Dimock, M., *Free Enterprise and the Administrative State,* University of Alabama Press, 1951.
45. Heilbroner, R. L., *The Making of Economic Society,* N.J., 1962.
46. Cf. Samuelson, P., *Economics,* 5th ed., N.Y., 1961.
47. Smith, A., *The Wealth of Nations,* N.Y., 1937.
48. See also *The End of Laissez-Faire,* London, 1926.
49. *Ibid.*
50. Dimock, M., *supra.*
51. Note 48 above.
52. *Ibid.*
53. Simons, H., *A Positive Program for Laissez-Faire,* Chicago, 1948.
54. *Ibid.*
55. Simons, H., *Economic Policy for free society,* Chicago, 1948.
56. *Ibid.*
57. But see Hayek, *The Road to Serfdom,* Chicago, 1944.
58. *Ibid.*
59. See US *Sherman Anti-trust Act.*
60. And the *Clayton Anti-trust Act.*
61. Samuelson, P., *supra,* Chap. 24.
62. *Ibid.,* Chap. 25.
63. Carlisle, R., *Sovereignty for Sale,* Naval Institute Press, 1981.
64. Zeis, P. M., *American Shipping Policy,* Princeton, N.J., 1938.
65. US Cong. Investigation: *Transfers of Ships to Foreign Registry,* 81st Cong., 1950.
66. US. Doc. Ships Registered under PANLIBHO, 1968.
67. Machlup, F., *The Economics of Sellers' Competition,* Baltimore, 1952.
68. *Ibid.*
69. US. Doc. *Foreign Flag Merchant Ships owned by US Parent Companies as of June 30, 1947,* 1975.
70. *Ibid.,* as of December 31, 1976 (Washington G.P.O.), 1978.
71. Watts, A. D., 'The protection of merchant ships', Byil, vol. 33, 1957, p. 52.
72. Witig, E., 'Tanker fleets and flags of convenience . . . ' Tex. In: L. J. Winter, 1979.
73. Woolsely, C. H., 'New treaties between the US and Panama', *AJIL,* Vol. 31, 1937, p. 297.
74. Singh, N., *Maritime Flag and International Law,* Leiden, Sijthoff, 1978.
75. OECD, *Maritime Transport,* 1971.
76. Sampson, A., *The Seven Sisters,* N.Y., Viking, 1975.
77. Naess, E., *The Great Panlibho Controversy,* Gower Press, 1972.
78. Chamberlain, E. H., *The Theory of Monopolistic Competition,* Harvard U.P., 1931.
79. Sturmey, S. G., *Ocean Freight Rates and Economic Research,* Geneva, 1966.
80. Richards, P. J., 'Shipping problems of underdeveloped countries', *Bulletin of Oxford Institute of Economics and Statistics,* Aug. 1967, pp. 265–80.
81. Zamora, *supra.*
82. *Hearings before the Anti-trust Sub-committee of the Committee on the Judiciary,* 86th Cong., Part 1.
83. *Ibid,* Vol. 1, p. 690.
84. Clark, J. M., *Competition as a Dynamic Process,* The Brookings Institution, Washington D.C.O., 1961.
85. Shils *et al.,* 'Foreign flags on US ships: Convenience or necessity?' *Industrial Relations.*
86. UN Doc. E/CN. 12/812, 1969.
87. *Ibid.,* p. 13.
88. Marx, D., *supra,* 3.
89. UNCTAD Doc. No. TD/B/C.4/62/Rev.1., 1970.
90. *Ibid.,* pp. 3–6.
91. See 'Report of the working party on shipping', in 1 *Proceedings, supra,* pp. 219, at 221.
92. UNCTAD Doc. No. TD/B/C./38/Rev.1, 1969.
93. See note 89, *supra.*

94. Marx, D., *supra,* pp. 260–262.
95. Marx, D., *supra,* pp. 45–67.
96. Report of the *Royal Commission on Shipping Rings,* CMND No. 4668, 1909.
97. H. R. Doc. No. 805.
98. *Ibid,* 63rd Cong., 2nd Sess., 1914.
99. *Ibid,* at 416–17.
100. Report of the *Royal Commission on Shipping Rings, Supra,* at 78.
101. See generally Marx, *supra,* pp. 50–67.
102. Note that the British Report produced no restrictions on conference practices.
103. But cf. the *Alexander Committee* whose recommendations resulted in the *Shipping Act of 1916,* Chap. 451, 39 Stat.
104. *Ibid,* at 728, as amended, 46 USC para 801–42, Supp. V., 1970.
105. UNCTAD, *Level and Structure of Freight Rates,* p. 5.
106. Locklin, D., *Economies of Transportation* 744, 6th edn. 1966.
107. See Tables 3–5 in Chapter 1.
108. McGee, 'Ocean freight rate, conferences and the American merchant marine' 27 U.Ch.L.Rev. 191, 1960.
109. *Ibid,* pp. 272–79, 1960.
110. Locklin, *supra,* pp. 130–57.
111. UNCTAD, 'The Liner Conference System', p. 10.
112. McGee, *supra,* pp. 205–57.
113. 'Ocean shipping and freight rates and developing countries' in 5 *Proceedings* 212.
114. *Ibid.,* p. 219.
115. Be Viev, 'Ratemaking in international shipping conferences', 4 *Stan. J. Int. Studies,* 1969, p. 84.
116. *The Liner Conference System, supra,* p. 29.
117. See also, 'Problems of shipping and ocean freight rates in the ECAFE Region' in 5 *Proceedings* 311.
118. *Ibid.* at 324–30.
119. UNCTAD *Shipping and the World Economy* at 5.
120. 'Progress report on the study of conference practices and adequacy of shipping services', *ibid.,* p. 7.
121. *Ibid.,* pp. 9–11.
122. *Ibid.,* UNCTAD Doc. No. TD/B/C.4/39 1968.
123. Marx, *supra,* p. 307.
124. Locklin, *supra,* p. 135.
125. Marx, pp. 307–10.
126. Locklin, pp. 143–149.
127. See UNCTAD, *Maritime Freight Rates in the Foreign Trade of Latin America, supra,* p. 10.
128. Locklin, pp. 139–40.
129. Bennathan, E., *et al., The Economics of Ocean Freight Rates,* 1969, pp. 30–34.
130. Marx, pp. 223–38.
131. *Ibid.,* pp. 186–200.
132. *Ibid.,* pp. 201–22.
133. UNCTAD, *The Liner Conference System, supra,* pp. 17–23.
134. Cf. Section 14 of US *Shipping Act 1916,* 46 USC para 812, 1964.
135. UNCTAD, *Level and Structure of Freight Rates, supra,* p. 22.
136. Cf. Report of the *Royal Commission on Shipping Rings, supra.* pp. 38–39.
137. *Ibid.,* pp. 48–50.
138. Note 135, *supra,* p. 22.
139. See also *The Liner Conference System, supra,* pp. 36–37.
140. 'Report of the working Party on Shipping', *supra,* at 221.
141. UNCTAD Doc. No. TD/B/C.4/76 Nov. 1970, 'The impact on world seaborne trade of changes in shipping costs', especially the annex.
142. 'Innovations for third world trade', *Lloyd's List,* No. 52397, Thursday 23rd June, 1983, p. 18.

143. *Ibid.;* see also 'Liner shipping and the developing countries', *Norwegian News,* Vol. 7, No. 39, 3rd June, 1983, pp. 79–82.
144. See 'Third world drops finance demands', *Lloyd's List,* No. 52395, 21st June, 1983, Thursday, front page; and Al-Jadir, A., 'Participation of the developing world in maritime transport', *Greenwich Forum VI* (World Shipping in the 1990s') 1980, pp. 149–156.
145. Institute of Shipping Economics: shipping statistics (monthly figures of shipping, freight markets, etc.), Bremen, August 1983, Vol. 27, No. 8, tables.
146. de Vries, H., 'The passing of risks in international sales under the Vienna Sales Convention 1980 as compared with traditional terms', *Eur. Trans. Law,* Vol. XVII, No. 5, 1982, pp. 495–528; and Brewer, J., 'Third world operators interest buoying prices', *Lloyd's List,* No. 52366, Thursday, 17th May, 1983, p. 2.
147. '*Problems of Shipping and Ocean Freight Rates in the ECAFE Region*', *supra,* p. 311.
148. *Ibid.,* at pp. 324–27.
149. *Alexander Committee Report, supra,* at p. 416.
150. *Ocean Shipping and Freight Rates and Developing Countries, supra,* p. 219.
151. *Ibid,* at p. 268.
152. McGee at p. 289.
153. Marx, at pp. 301–302.
154. *Level and Structure of Freight Rates, supra,* p. 5.
155. *Review of Developments in World Shipping,* p. 11.
156. *Ibid.,* UNCTAD Doc. No. TD/B/C.4/25, 1967.
157. Cf. 12 FMC, 1968, p. 34.
158. *Ibid,* pp. 40–41.
159. McGee, *supra,* pp. 198–200.
160. 'Report of the Working Party on Shipping', *supra,* p. 219.
161. *Ibid.,* at 220–23.
162. *Ibid.,* at p. 219.
163. *Ibid.,* at p. 220.
164. Singh, N., *Achievements of UNCTAD I (1964) and II* (1968) *in the Field of Shipping and Invisibles,* 1969, at p. 11.
165. See *International Transoceanic Transport and Economic Development,* p. 4.
166. *Ibid.,* at p. 10.
167. *Ibid.,* UNCTAD Doc. No. TD/B/C.4/46, 1969.
168. UNCTAD *Review of Maritime Transport,* 1969, p. 8.
169. *Maritime Freight Rates in the Foreign Trade of Latin America, supra,* at p. 16.
170. *Ibid.,* at p. 17.
171. *The Liner Conference System, supra,* pp. 27–28.
172. *Ibid.,* at p. 30.
173. World Trade Annual 2, *supra,* at XII.
174. 21 IMF *Balance of Payments Yearbook* 2, 1970.
175. *Review of Development in World Shipping, supra,* pp. 15–26.
176. *Ibid.,* UNCTAD Doc. No. TD/B/C.4/25, 1967.
177. Sodersten, *Supra,* at pp. 233–40.
178. Koch, A., *Current Pricing Behaviour in Liner Shipping,* 1968, pp. 17–29.
179. See *The Maritime Transport of National Rubber* pp. 68–77.
180. *Ibid.,* UNCTAD Doc. No. TD/B/C.4/BO/Rev.1, 1970.
181. Kindgeberger, C., *International Economics,* 4th ed., 1968, pp. 86–101.
182. *Ibid.,* at pp. 105–29.
183. Thommen, *International Legislation on Shipping,* pp. 25–29.
184. *Ibid.,* UN Doc. No. TD/32/Rev.1, 1968.
185. *UN Maritime Conference, Final Act and Related Documents* 29, 1948.
186. *Review of Studies and Activities in the Field of Shipping and Ports* 23.
187. *Ibid.,* UNCTAD Doc. No. TD/B/C.4/26, 1967.
188. Marx, *supra,* pp. 272–79.
189. *Ibid,* at p. 277.
190. Gosovic, UNCTAD *North Sea Encounter* 568 International Conciliation, 1968, p. 5.

191. *Ibid.*, p. 6.
192. *Ibid.*, p. 10.
193. Gardner, UNCTAD 22 *International Organisation* 99, 1968.
194. *Ibid.*, at p. 100.
195. G.A. Res. 1707.
196. 16 UN GAOR Supp. 17.
197. *Ibid.*, at p. 17.
198. *Ibid.*, UN Doc. No. A/5100, 1961.
199. ECOSOC Res. 917.
200. 34 UN ECOSOC, Supp. 1, at 7.
201. UN Doc. No. E/3671, 1962.
202. *The Liner Conference System, supra,* p. 220.
203. That is flag preference, flag discrimination, maritime subsidies and state intervention.
204. 'Level and Structure of Conference Freight Rates', *supra,* pp. 225.
205. G.A. Res. 1785.
206. *Ibid.*, 17 UN GAOR, Supp. 17, at 14.
207. *Ibid.*, UN Doc. No. A/5217, 1963.
208. See generally the report of the conference in 1 *Proceedings, supra,* at p. 101.
209. *Ibid.*, at p. 105. This item had been stressed in the earlier *Joint Declaration of the Developing Countries Made at the Eighteenth Session of the General Assembly* G.A. Res. 1897.
210. See the GA Res No. 2626 (XXV), *Shipping,* para 74.
211. UN GAOR, Supp. 15, at 24.
212. See UN GA Res. A/Res/3201 (S-VI) 9 May 1974; 13 ILM.
213. NIMO is a relatively new doctrine, see Sturmey.
214. For the *Declaration and the Programme of Action on the Establishment of the New International Economic Order,* see G.A. Res. 3202 (S-VI), 1 May 1974, 13 ILM 715 (1974).

    For the *Charter of Economic Rights and Duties of States* see the G.A. Res. 3281 (XXIX) 12 Dec. 1974, 14 ILM 251 (1975).
215. For the *Resolution on Permanent Sovereignty over Natural Resources.* See G.A. Res. 88 (XII), 19 Oct. 1972.
216. For the *Right of Development* see 1979 *Hague Requel,* Special Supplement.
217. For the *International Development Strategy for the Third UN Development Decade;* see G.A. Res. A/Res. 35756 of 20 January 1981.
218. *Ibid.*, para 128–33.
219. *Ibid.*, para 128.
220. *Ibid.*
221. *Ibid.*, the Code comes into force on 6th October 1983.
222. For the *UN Convention on an International Multinodal Transport* see TD/MT/CONF./16.
223. The imbalance between the TMNS and DMNS in the *Share of International Shipping.*
224. These are flag preference, flag discrimination, maritime subsidies, etc.

Part Two

Traditional methods of establishing national fleets

Introduction to Part Two

Part I considered, in their historical context, the reasons that led to many nations breaking away from international shipping and seeking to establish and/or develop national fleets of their own. This Part starts by looking at the traditional methods of establishing national fleets. While these methods tend to be unorthodox they are ironically referred to as 'traditional'. For the reasons outlined therein, the DMNS were unable to follow the usual methods, based on the sound economic principles of establishing economic enterprises. In practice, they achieved their objectives by buying second-hand ships from the TMNS and developing or establishing ports in their own countries.

The two main examples used throughout Part II are those of the US and the DMNS. In this respect the word 'establish' is used not only to denote starting afresh, as in the case of the DMNS, but also diversifying as in the case of the US. In each case, only the leading examples are discussed. Otherwise the main mechanisms, purposes and objectives of the various aspects of this method are as outlined in the main body of the discussion. The rest of the examples are to be found in summary form in the appendices at the end of Chapter 3. Further examples are provided in the detailed notes and annexes.

The advantages and disadvantages relating to this Part in particular are also discussed. The problems relating to the methods generally are to be found in Part IV. Otherwise the term 'flag discrimination' is used here to mean and include 'flag preference' and all the mechanisms included therein. The analysis in this part is mainly narrative in order to lay the foundations for later discussions. There is heavy reliance on descriptions, historical analysis and definitions of the various concepts used. This is to facilitate proper appreciation of this rather complex field.

CHAPTER 3

Flag preference

1. Introduction

The first of the mechanisms used to aid and protect merchant shipping is *flag preference.* However, this mechanism is similar to, and has the same characteristics as, the others. No suitable definition of flag preference exists yet but the nearest is that of the OECD Maritime Transport Committee.[1]

> '. . . By various measures, discrimination is practised in favour of ships of the national flag and against ships of other countries flags. Such measures are, for example:
> (a) Measures in the field of exchange control.[2]
> (b) Legislative provisions in favour of the national flag.
> (c) Arrangements made by governmental or semi-governmental organisations giving preferential treatment to national flags.[3]
> (d) Preferential shipping clauses in trade agreements.[4]
> (e) The operation of import and export licencing systems so as to influence the flag of the carrying ship.
> (f) Port regulations.[5]
> (g) Taxation measures'[6]

However, flag preference, like the other major forms of restrictive shipping practices, is a:

> 'State shipping policy that discriminates between different flags in giving cargo by preferring or giving priority to the domestic flag in giving cargoes and/or granting privileges.'[7]

There are a dozen or more categories of flag preference practised by some or all the TMNS, DMNS and the STNS. For our purposes these can be grouped into four major categories:

(a) Type 1: *Cargo reservation*
- (i) Cargo sharing
- (ii) Cargo preference
- (iii) Cargo reservation

(b) Type 2: *Exclusions and trade arrangements*
- (i) Cabotage restrictions
- (ii) Bilateralism
- (iii) Multilateralism

(c) Type 3: *State-financed cargoes*
  (i) Foreign aid cargoes
  (ii) Agricultural relief cargoes
  (iii) State-financed cargoes
(d) Type 4: *Miscellaneous flag preferences*
  (i) Foreign-parity flag preference
  (ii) Inland-parity flag preference
  (iii) Miscellaneous flag preference

These are only broad categories and the list is by no means exhaustive.[8] We shall now proceed to discuss, briefly, a selection of these (with the various state practices in the subsequent table at the end of the chapter).

2. Cargo reservation

Cargo Reservation is the most popularly known of the flag preference mechanisms. This too is only a generic term encompassing cargo sharing and cargo preference.

2.1 Cargo sharing

Cargo sharing was the original idea at the inception of restrictive shipping practices and although it has since crystallized into a distinct practice it is still, by and large, often confused with flag discriminations (post). Authors tend to juggle with these terms whenever it suits them yet they convey different concepts. In the first place, cargo sharing is not, or at least is not intended to be, discriminatory; it is possibly the oldest known and most acceptable of the restrictive shipping practices.[9] Secondly, it may only be preferential in the sense that State A may prefer, for various reasons, to share her cargoes with flags of State B rather than with those of State C. Thirdly, cargo sharing may contain an element of cargo reservation but this is only in so far as it applies to that state's portion of a given cargo; in other words, a state could reserve, say, 50% of the cargoes for her national flag and yet still participate in (cargo) sharing of the remaining 50% unreserved portion.[10]

Normally, the verb to 'share' connotes the principle of partaking or parity. As will be evident in the succeeding chapters, cargo sharing is the most fair of the restrictive shipping practices and the one akin to the liberal principles of reciprocity, most favoured nation treatment, foreign parity standards and, indeed, national treatment and flag equality.[11] Cargo sharing means literally 'sharing' whereas cargo preference, cargo reservation and flag discrimination may import the element of 'winner takes all'. The principles behind cargo sharing may involve a number of parties, for example two (on a 50–50 basis), and a variety of other different portions, such as that proposed by the *UN Code of Conduct for liner Conferences* of, 40–40–20[12] as a guideline.

Cargo sharing, like all the other mechanisms, is used for establishing and developing national merchant marines. The idea behind it is that it guarantees automatic supply of cargoes, which generates demand for national flag carriers and so on. As the OECD Maritime Transport Committee was, correctly, to point out: 'Since the war the principle of shipping freedom is being increasingly threatened by administrative and other measures taken by the governments of various countries to protect their national fleets or even to create such fleets.'[13]

Thus, as is evident from the tables in this chapter, it would appear that it is the general rule, rather than the exception, that the less restrictive countries prefer cargo sharing to either cargo preference or cargo reservation and flag discriminations. This is particularly true when it comes to the TMNS. It may denote a position of superiority and confidence in competitiveness in the sense that the most restrictive countries are the STNS and DMNS whose merchant fleets are either still non-existant or, when they do exist, are disadvantaged one way or another:[14]

'In most cases, these countries are newcomers to the maritime world and have built up their fleets for reasons of prestige or in the belief a lifeline in times of war is thereby assured. . .'[15]

Cargo preference, on the other hand, is a bit more restrictive than cargo sharing as a flag preferential method of establishing and developing national fleets.

2.2 Cargo preference

The similarities and distinctions between cargo preference and flag discrimination will be sufficiently outlined in the subsequent chapter. Suffice it to say at this stage, however, that the distinctions may appear cosmetic if not theoretical. Be that as it may, the term 'cargo preference' is used interchangeably with cargo sharing and cargo reservation.[16] There does not appear to be an appropriate definition of cargo preference, distinct from flag discrimination, as most authors generally tend to combine or use the two interchangeably. But the underlying principles are different; in our view, both cargo sharing, and cargo preference constitute a governmental intervention in the structure of the existing maritime system, subdividing the freight market by adopting legislation or concluding treaties that set up an order for carrier preference.[17]

In other words, such cargo preference seeks to reserve a portion of the volume of cargo flowing between the trading partners, with the object of directly favouring certain ship owners, usually – but not always – adopting the flag as the operative criterion. The principle involved in cargo preference is that there is cargo available its distribution is not left to market forces, but rather the state intervenes and allocates that cargo, giving priority first to the domestic flag, or where domestic tonnage is not available or incapable of meeting the demands required, then to foreign flag carriers. And even among foreign flags, friendly flags (by treaty or otherwise) will be preferred to ordinary third party flags.[18]

Another method of effecting cargo preference is to award high (freight) quality cargoes to domestic flag carriers with the bulky, low quality, cargoes to the others. However, both flag discrimination and flag preference, as controls over a portion of the demand for maritime transport, are formidable instruments that may be employed to foster the establishment and development of certain merchant marine industries for economic or political purposes.[19] Without singling out one country in particular, it would be fair to point out that cargo preference as a method of fostering national fleets is common to the United States and the DMNS, especially those of Latin America:

> 'In some cases such practices are resorted to by countries with limited resources and little or no experience in ship management, who find that they cannot attract business except by the imposition of discriminatory measures.'[20]

Otherwise, cargo preference is a subdivision of flag preference, which is in turn a type of or a sub-division of flag discrimination, but a discrimination which applies only to cargoes. Cargo preference may – and often does – take the form of giving preferences to the national flag, then to flags enjoying national treatment, flags of most favoured nations, flags of trading partners, and finally other flags; whereas flag discrimination may – but does not have to – take these degrees of priority into consideration.[21] Finally, the last of these methods in the first type of flag preference is cargo reservation.

2.3 Cargo reservation

Without further analysis it can safely be summarised that cargo reservation is a form or a sub-division of flag preference, itself a form of flag discrimination. It's principles, characteristics, criteria and other features are nonetheless similar to those of cargo sharing and cargo preference. Even at the level of semantics, the term 'preference' comes from the verb to 'prefer' or 'preferred', meaning possessing or accorded priority, advantage or privilege, and generally denoting a prior or superior claim or a right of payment as against another thing of the same kind.[22] 'Reservation', on the other hand, comes from the verb to 'reserve' or 'reserved', meaning to keep back, set aside, to retain or to keep in store for a future time.[23] Thus, bearing in mind the aforementioned, and relating it to maritime transport, cargo reservation would likewise denote state action aimed at reserving a certain portion of exports and/or imports for vessels flying the national flag. In other words, cargo reservation is an admission (or guarantee) by the state to her national lines that:

> 'We shall put aside cargo for you no matter whether you are inefficient or late or what. . .'[24]

Like all the other mechanisms, cargo reservation is resorted to for the same reasons – to enable speedy establishment and development of national merchant marine fleets. However, though a practice known predominantly among the DMNS, it is not quite unknown among some TMNS such as the US, and (as was to be expected) among the STNS, some of which are fairly sophisticated.[25]

> 'In other cases, however, the countries practising discrimination are larger and more highly developed. In many of them either the whole or part of the merchant fleet is owned by the state and in some much of the export and import trade is in the hands of the state as well.'[26]

It also goes without saying that all the countries noted in Appendices 3 and 4 as practising some form of cargo sharing, cargo preference and flag discrimination inevitably do practice cargo reservation as well, for the simple reason that one would have to reserve cargoes away from flag A, for example, before assigning the same cargo to the preferred flag B.[27] Both cargo preference and cargo reservation may take the form of percentages (e.g. 40%), fractions (e.g. $\frac{1}{3}$), quality (e.g. all electronic goods), freights or tonnage of cargoes. In the final analysis it should be observed that it would be quite reasonable for a country to reserve a certain portion of cargo sufficient to maintain her flag as a commercial entity, particularly if her fleet cannot be assured of cargo in the open market or on the homeward journey.[28]

The legitimacy of the wishes of these countries is recognised by the OECD. The only objections are the methods used to advance and achieve this objective:

> 'At their meeting in Tokyo in February 1971 (– – – – – –), ministers of the Consultative Shipping Group adopted a resolution on flag discrimination. This resolution expressed concern at the increasing application of such measures by governments. Ministers did, however, recognize the legitimate wishes of the developing countries to build up and expand their merchant fleets.[29] They agreed that these aspirations would be best realised if developing countries aimed at establishing and operating their shipping on a competitive, economically viable basis, and they agreed to consider requests for financial and technical assistance for this purpose sympathetically. . .'[30]

Further discussions on cargo reservations appear at the end of this chapter.

The second type of flag preference is exclusions and trade arrangements.

3. Exclusions: Bilateralism and multilateralism

This type of exclusion consists of three main categories. The first is total exclusion of foreign flags from a particular area, the best example being restrictions in coastal waters known alternatively as cabotage restrictions. The other two result from trade arrangements, either through the home country and another country (bilateral), or through or by a group of countries (multilateral). But first cabotage restrictions.

3.1 Cabotage restrictions or unilateralism

The term 'cabotage' is a nautical term derived from Spanish, literally denoting navigating from cape to cape along the coast without going out into the open sea – i.e., in nautical waters. Thus, in international law generally, and maritime trade in particular, cabotage is identified with coastal trade so that it means navigating and trading along the coast between the ports thereof.[31] Since they are relatively new concepts, there are no suitable definitions of this kind of restrictive shipping practice. The nearest we can get to a definition are descriptions and/or explanations. In that sense cabotage is discriminatory, being the practice of keeping foreign flags out of coastal waters. Since coastal waters are regarded as internal waters, cabotage trade is therefore regarded as internal trade.[32] By totally excluding foreign flags and, therefore, foreign competition, the idea behind cabotage restrictions is the same as outlined above, i.e. to promote the establishment and development of national merchant marines in a particular trade area through guaranteed supply and demand.[33]

In this case, state intervention negates competition and replaces the market forces of demand and supply. In that respect cabotage restrictions are a form of flag preference but with as far-reaching effects as flag discrimination; whereas cargo preference refers to preferential treatment, cabotage does not allow for that kind of comparison.[34] In that respect, cabotage can be likened to cargo reservation in as far as coastal trade is reserved for the national flag. But that is as far as the analogy goes; cabotage differs from reservation in that, in the former, reservation is normally 100% (i.e. total) and not just a portion of the cargo as would normally be the case with cargo reservation and cargo sharing.[35]

The only limitations on cabotage are where the coastal waters form part of an international waterway, for example, the Suez and the Panama Canals, or the international strait; although in these areas the coastal state has jurisdictional sovereignty similar to that on international rivers and landmasses.[36] Apart from the coastal states' obligations under international trade law, most states adopt a protectionist approach for various reasons, and cabotage restrictions are no different.[37] In other words, the rationales are more than economic, but it is not our intention to go into these details here. We would like to limit ourselves to the economic rationale, i.e., that cabotage restrictions are resorted to as a means of establishing and developing national merchant marines.[38]

The second type of flag preference mechanism used for this purpose is trade agreement or arrangement, and is a bilateral as opposed to the unilateral approach characteristic of cabotage restrictions. Secondly, bilateralism is not a total exclusion of foreign or third party flags as is cabotage. Finally, although bilateralism may have as its prior aims the development of national fleets it is also part of the practice of international commerce.

3.2 Bilateralism

As indicated above bilateralism, in maritime commerce is borrowed from the international trade practice of bilateral negotiations and agreements – 'bi' implying transactions and negotiations between two parties. The term is generally used to refer to trade agreements between two countries. For instance, there are bilateral clearing agreements, bilateral payments' agreements and, of course, bilateral trade agreements. Bilateral trade and payments' agreements are substitutes for more efficient and economic multilateral trade.[39] However, except for limited advantages in periods of disturbances, bilateral agreements are usually harmful to world trade and to countries participating in them and as such shipping arrangements are no exceptions. This may be noted as one of the disadvantages of bilateralism in shipping. When trade between any two countries is conducted through bilateral agreements, it tends to be reduced to the level at which the value of goods moving in one direction exactly equals the value of goods moving in the other direction.[40]

It is this fact which appeals to the maritime nations that practice bilateralism. However, as a result, less effective use might be made of the world's resources, since there are fewer opportunities to take advantage of international specialisation. Moreover, trade is directed from its normal channels into channels that are determined by the central system and not by market forces.[41] Many countries lacking foreign exchange seek bilateral agreements to overcome this shortage. It is not difficult to see why this appeals to shipping where the balance of payments' argument ranks very high. It is also not difficult to realise why the DMNS, especially, resort to bilateralism in both oceanborne and ordinary international trade.[42] A further disadvantage of this kind of approach is that once it begins it has a tendency to spread; when, for instance, nations placed at a disadvantage, because of exchange controls, adopt controls themselves as a means of striking back at other countries – hence countervailing-flag discriminations (post).

Applying this analogy to maritime commerce, a kind of picture emerges. Two countries conclude a trade agreement with a maritime clause, or alternatively a purely maritime agreement, between them, that seeks to divide cargo, involved in the trade between them, between their two respective national flag fleets. This is fast becoming the most common and acceptable practice in international maritime commerce. Normally it is in the ratio of 50–50 and may be embodied in a treaty, an understanding or, indeed, a convention.[43] Originally, the 50–50 division restricted the shares between only the two parties to the treaty and/or understanding, excluding any other third parties. Although bilateralism is now almost universally recognized and accepted, the interests of third parties who might have customarily plied that trade were not entirely forgotten.[44] This formula or guideline has now been extended from 50–50 to 40–40–20, or some other similar arrangements that might be worked out by the parties.

Our first example is, therefore, that of the *UN Code of Conduct for Liner Conferences*, which embodies the spirit of this guideline. Nothing could have better suited the aspirations of the DMNS in their endeavour to establish and develop their own national fleets. This code is, therefore, the first application of the use of bilateralism as a mechanism to achieve this objective.[45] This was the underlying objective of the DMNS when they piloted this code, as a tool of development, into an international convention. It will be remembered the spirit of the code is that:

> 'The group of national shipping lines, if any, of two countries, the foreign trade between which is carried by the conference, shall have equal rights to participate in the freight and volume of traffic generated by their mutual foreign trade carried by the Conference.'[46]

Although this applies only to the liner conference portion of oceanborne trade, and although the 40–40–20 split is not explicit or rigid in the porposed convention, nevertheless it is useful, and a recognition of the rights of states to partake in the cargoes generated by their trade.[47] The DMNS have further interpreted this as the international recognition of their legitimate right to use bilateralism as a mechanism to establish and develop their own national merchant marines. It is yet to be seen how this will become a practical reality.[48]

Our second example of bilateralism in international shipping is that involving the USSR and the US which we shall discuss *in extenso*, not simply because it involves the leading TMN and STN and, also the world's largest trading partners, but because of the light it sheds on bilateralism in oceanborne commerce. No doubt the two countries have bilateral maritime arrangements with other countries but of immediate concern is the *US–USSR Maritime Agreement of 1972*,[49] as amended and updated from time to time. At the same time that the two countries completed a general trade agreement, they also entered into the said maritime agreement. Although its objective appears to be to foster US–

Soviet maritime commerce (by opening commercial ports and affording both the US-flag vessels and Soviet-flag vessels the opportunity to participate equally, and substantially, in the carriage of all cargoes moving by sea between the two nations), which objective is typical of maritime bilateral treaties anyway, the underlying objective must surely be to enable both countries to expand their merchant marines generally and on this route in particular.[50]

In the said treaty this equal and substantial share is defined as not less than one third ($\frac{1}{3}$ or $33\frac{1}{3}\%$) of the bilateral government-controlled trade. Secondly, any inequality in the division of the uncontrolled cargoes between the flag fleets of the two states is to be adjusted through the allocation of controlled cargoes. The definition of controlled cargoes applied to the US conforms with that used in prior domestic US legislation.[51] The Soviet definition of controlled cargoes, however, is much more expansive and includes all bilateral cargoes imported into or exported from the territory of the USSR where a commercial body or other authority or entity of the USSR has, or would have, the power at any time to designate the carrier. It would appear that the effect of this inclusive language is to expand the coverage of the agreement's cargo preference provisions to a substantial portion of the US–USSR bilateral trade.[52] However, in the case of the US this agreement only covers government controlled cargoes, whereas in the USSR, a STN, such division is superfluous.

This agreement marks a landmark in maritime jurisprudence. In the first place, it created a shipping trade where none existed before, which must have (one way or the other) aided the expansion of the merchant marine of the two parties; a hypothesis quite consistent with our contention.[53] Secondly, although there are no statistics relating to US growth there are, however, indications that the Soviet merchant marine has almost doubled over this decade. Though this cannot be attributed entirely to such bilateral arrangements as the one in question, since there is no statistical evidence, some part of the expansion must be attributed to it.[54] Thirdly, as the first known of such major treaties between a STN and a TMN, it could easily be interpreted as a free trade recognition of restrictive practices as a means of development and expansion of national fleets through trade expansion.[55] Fourthly, the importance of the participation of third flag vessels was recognized, emphasizing the absence of any conflict with any treaty obligations to other TMNS and other maritime states. This refutes the jurisprudence prevalent among the liberal TMNS that there is an irreconcilable conflict of laws in the trade between market and planned economies.[56] Finally, this maritime agreement has become a firmly established part of the trade policies of the US and the USSR. In addition, the US and the USSR recently reaffirmed their commitment to foster bilateral trade through preferential regulation by renewing the maritime agreement.[57] All this must surely lead, indirectly, to further expansion of the merchant marines of the two parties.

The third mechanism of the second type of flag preference is exclusion of other flags through a multilateral trade agreement. This kind of arrangement is sometimes known simply as multilateralism.

3.3 Multilateralism

This is yet another of the principles derived from international trade, meaning trade between more than two nations. In the free trade sense it is supposed to be the means of extracting the maximum gains from international trade and the division of labour.[58] It contrasts with bilateralism, in which one country makes an agreement to trade with another. Bilateralism places limits upon consumers' freedom to buy goods in the cheapest market and prevents the realisation of full international specialisation with each country producing, for export, the products in which it has the largest comparative advantage.

A further disadvantage is that if, on the other hand, a country adopts bilateralism when the rest of the world is trading multilaterally, and there are no serious problems of unemployment at home, it cuts itself off from the advantages of free trade and lowers the standard of living of its inhabitants.[59] It is also worth remembering, however, that multilateral trading may be difficult to maintain if a major currency becomes scarce. For example, the dollar was scarce after the war because the rest of the world was anxious to buy from the US and ran into deficits with her. This is thought to have resulted in protectionism in international trade generally, and maritime commerce in particular.[60] This situation was aggravated by the fact that some countries discriminated in their commerce not only against the hard currency area, but also against other countries that insisted on trade deficits being settled in gold or dollars. A case in point was when France tried to cut down her imports from Germany in order to keep her gold and dollars to pay for imports from the US.[61]

Governments and international institutions, such as the GATT and the IMF, have tried to restore free multilateral trade. They have been helped by the gradual disappearance of the dollar problem, the successful reconstruction of Europe after the war, the relative stability, until recently, of the US economy, an increase in the world liquidity through the media of the IMF, EPU and the policies of the US Export–Import Bank (post).[62] Thus, international shipping has to learn and borrow from international trade by adopting these principles and practices through treaties, agreements and conventions or merely memoranda of understanding. The *UN Code of Conduct for Liner Conferences* is yet another example of international efforts at both bilateral and multilateral approaches; bilateral, when it seeks the 50–50 basis, and multilateral, when it adopts the 40–40–20 approach.[63] The other examples of multilateralism in international shipping are the maritime clauses of regional groupings, free trade areas and economic communities, such as COMECON, EEC, LOME Convention, etc.

What must constantly be borne in mind is that the motive behind multilateralism in oceanborne commerce is the desire to develop and expand the national merchant fleets of the parties involved, individually or severally. Apart from the above-listed examples, one of the earliest known attempts by the TMNS is the *British Commonwealth Merchant shipping Agreement*.[64] At the other end of the spectrum – probably one of the finest examples of multilateralism among the DMNS in particular and international shipping in general – is the solution chosen by the Latin American countries. It will be remembered that one of the first outcomes of the *Latin American Free Trade Association* was the *Convention on Water Transport* of May 1966,[65] providing for a flag preferential system, though by then national preference legislation and cargo-sharing treaties were already common, covering both regional and international trade.[66] Of specific relevance is Article 4 of the convention which reserves the carriage of the seaborne trade between the contracting parties to their national vessels, in equality of treatment and other conditions established in the convention and its associated regulations.[67]

Needless to say, the preferential regime thus envisaged is multilateral, and its implementation gradual in time and volume, following the growth of the transport capacity of the contracting parties. However, vessels of non-contracting parties, operating regular and traditional services, will be allowed to participate in transportation between the contracting parties if they fulfil the following requirements:[68]

(a) Their participation does not constitute an obstacle to free trade between the contracting parties and the stable expansion of their merchant marines; (the emphasis clearly conveying the development objective of the multilateral convention);[69]

(b) Their normal schedule is between ports of their own country and those of the contracting parties:[70]

(c) Their countries do not implement restrictive measures on traffic with, or against, vessels belonging to the contracting parties (a clause forestalling countervailing actions);[71]

(d) They must abide by trade tariffs established by the Conference or similar bodies set up by the treaty.[72]

Though multilateralism in shipping may have its advantages, it also has its disadvantages as a departure from freedom of shipping. Although departure from the traditional patterns has evident advantages from the point of view of the operation of vessels, its implementation is difficult. The basic sources of disagreement are the criteria adopted for the distribution of reserved shipments.[73] Countries controlling a large volume of trade will still aspire to reserve a substantial part for their own carriers.[73] On the other hand, members whose foreign trade is insufficient to sustain the development of the viable merchant marine industry will favour an integrated multilateral approach expecting to obtain a share in the carriage of trade between their bigger partners.[74] Herein lies the root cause and the problems of shipping preferences and discriminations; those who have nothing to contribute and, therefore, nothing to share will quickly advocate sharing, on the failure of which they resort to the restrictive lever; those who have and, therefore, have everything to lose, advocate free trade. On a global scale, the DMNS represent the former while the TMNS represent the latter.[75]

In quite a different context, this analysis of the inherent conflict of interests may explain the long delay in the ratification of the *LAFTA Convention on Water Transport*; only the fifth ratification was deposited in 1975, no less than a whole decade after the signing of the treaty.[76] It is also significant that, as of then, the two major trading countries of the continent – Argentina and Brazil – had not ratified it. The convention eventually did not take off, and even if it had there would probably be no evidence to suggest it would have achieved its objective – expansion of the national merchant marines of the contracting parties. It was a brave attempt at multilateralism in shipping though.[78] It is true that most of the restrictive shipping practices of the DMNS are implemented by the Latin Americans. It is also true that the fleets of these countries have grown a great deal since the inception of these restrictive practices. Restrictive shipping practices might have achieved their desired aims – that of aiding the establishment and development of national merchant marine fleets.[79]

While this could have been true it could also have been a coincidence since these countries also generate sufficiently substantial trade to maintain viable national merchant marine fleets in any event.[80] Assuming that the metaphor 'trade follows the flag' is true it is difficult to envisage a country with insufficient oceanborne trade of its own being able to establish, develop and sustain a national merchant marine fleet purely on the basis of restrictive practices.[81] Otherwise the principle behind multilateralism in shipping in general, and the lesson of the *LAFTA Convention* in particular, is that it would be possible for a group of countries to agree to pool their reciprocal oceanborne commerce in order to create a wider freight market to be shared, at least in principle, by their national flag vessels with equality of conditions.[82] Their multilateral preferences may be introduced in isolation or in the context of a wider process of economic integration as was the case with the *LAFTA Convention on Water Transport*.[83] Whereas these are actions that several governments can take jointly, there are still many actions they take unilaterally, one of these is our third type of flag preference, that pertaining to state-financed cargoes.

4. State-financed cargoes

State-financed cargoes are a type of flag preference practised mainly by the (aid giving) wealthier nations.[84] Although it is probable that most TMNS include such maritime clauses in trade agreements with the recipient DMNS, notable among them is the US. In June 1954, for instance, the then OEEC Maritime Transport Committee noted with concern that preferential shipping regulations applicable under *Public Law no. 17* of the 26th March, 1934, to the carriage of all cargo financed by loans made by instrumentalities of the US government were also being applied to cargo financed by US private banking institutions against guarantee by US government banking agencies.[85] These regulations were being applied to shipments of cotton from the U.S. to Japan under a loan financed by 14 private banks which had been guaranteed by the Export–Import Bank of Washington. The Maritime Transport Committee considered that the application of *Public Resolution no. 17* in the circumstances represented an unjustified extension of the preferential measures at present in force which would affect all the maritime transport countries if the ruling was to pass unchallenged.[86] *State-financed-cargo-flag-preference* represents the sophistication that has been reached in using all the means available to a state to establish and/or expand her national fleet.[87] State financed cargo is really a broad category which includes foreign aid cargo preference, surplus agricultural commodities and relief aid, and government-financed cargo preferences. The other rationale and motives for resort to this particular mechanism will be apparent in the ensuing discussion. For US practice see Table 21 and Appendix 4.

4.1 'Foreign aid cargoes' preference

Foreign aid shipments, as a type of preference, is a brain child of the US,

Table 21. US Government-sponsored cargoes–calendar year 1980.

Public Law 664 Cargoes

Shipper	U.S.-flag Revenue ($1 000)	Total (metric tons)	U.S.-flag (metric tons)	Percentage U.S.-flag tonnage
Action	12	12	9	75
Board of International Broadcasting	47	150	128	85
Agency for International Development:				
Loans and Grants	57 272	1 421 225	688 857	48[2]
P.L. 480–Title II	127 797	1 595 504	861 404	54
Department of Agriculture:				
P.L. 480–Title I	119 842	3 544 373	1 452 217	41[2]
Other Agriculture Programs	24	35	29	83
Department of Commerce:				
Industry and Trade Administration	525	987	966	98
Maritime Administration	90	219	219	100
Other Agencies	50	252	98	39[3]
Department of Defense:				
Military Assistance Program				
Foreign Military Sales Credit	21 936	81 689	55 667	68[3]
Corps of Engineers–NEGEV	7 810	30 349	14 187	47[4]
Department of Energy:				
Bonneville Power Administration	216	5 789	2 780	48[2]
Strategic Petroleum Reserve	15 270	2 540 037	210 693	8[5]
Department of Health and Human Services	30	52	34	65
Department of the Interior:				
Bureau of Reclamation	200	2 384	1 019	43[2]
Other Agencies	23	48	24	50
Department of Justice	29	51	47	92
National Aeronautics and Space Administration	145	230	214	93
Tennessee Valley Authority	1 285	6 804	4 690	69
Department of the Treasury:				
Chrysler Corporation	2 549	30 957	12 070	39[2]
Other Agencies	9	8	8	100
Department of Transportation:				
Federal Highway Administration	1 393	11 529	4 877	42[2]
Urban Mass Transportation Administration	404	811	591	73
Other Agencies	36	61	48	79
International Communications Agency	1 033	1 827	1 384	76
Department of State:				
Sinai Support Mission	14	27	17	63
Foreign Building Office	309	862	797	92
Other Agencies (does not include AID)	5 442	6 729	4 912	73
Other Agencies	137	140	116	83

Public Resolution 17 Cargoes

Shipper	Total freight revenue	U.S.-flag freight revenue	Percentage U.S.-flag
Export-Import Bank	$87 039 758	$65 270 107	75

1. Civilian agencies plus Department of Defense Foreign Military Sales Credit Program, Military Assistance Program, and U.S. Army Corps of Engineers, NEGEV. Other Department of Defense cargoes not included.
2. These agencies were below the required 50% participation due to the non-availability of U.S. flag service as provided in P.L.664.
3. A substantial number of bill of lading equivalents for MAP and FMS cargoes were not processed from DOD tape reels.
4. U.S. flag participation in the NEGEV is calculated on a revenue ton basis in accordance with an agreement between MARAD and DOD and was 54% in CY80.
5. DOE/SPR had minimal U.S. flag participation due partly to an oil exchange agreement, but primarily because DOE/SPR included shipments of Alaskan North Slope oil covered under the Jones Act as U.S. flag participation and in foreign source oil acquisitions failed to provide adequate opportunities for U.S. flag participation.

Source: MARAD 1981, pp. 31–32

which is hardly surprising; the US is the biggest aid-donor country in the world and although many other aid-donors, now and then, resort to this restrictive practice, our leading example will inevitably be that of the US. The main operative legislation in this respect is *Public Law no. 664*[88] – the *Cargo pre-*

ference Act, 1954,[89] which amended Section 901 of the *Merchant Marine Act*, 1936.[90] It will be remembered that the former legislation codified various references in existing American foreign aid programmes, for example, the original *Economic Co-operation Act, 1948.*[91] The principles and objectives behind cargo preference in foreign aid cargoes is that the act applies where American aid is furnished *without provisions for reimbursements*, which presumably means and includes aid cargoes which although technically *sold* by the US, are, in reality, given away for a purely nominal or token sales price.

It would appear that this reimbursement provision was intended to exclude from the coverage of the legislation instances where the US government acts simply as an agent, on a reimbursable basis for the foreign aid recipient nation.[92] The *Cargo Preference Act, 1954*, came in to fill a *lacuna* as, before it, there had been many instances where, for example, fertilisers and other economic-aid commodities were purchased from a European country for delivery to the Far East on a laid-down cost basis under which American flag vessels were effectively frozen out because of the lower rates quoted by low-cost foreign competitors.[92a] Here is another classic example of a restrictive practice being used first to negate or displace market forces and secondly, to support a high cost, and probably an inefficient, merchant marine.

There are few agencies involved in the administration of the aid programme. The statute is applicable principally to shipments financed by loans or grants of the Agency for International Development (AID).[93] There is some indication that the use of this particular preference is beginning to pay-off. The fact that AID will not finance delivery services aboard foreign flag vessels has resulted in the use of the US flag vessels considerably in excess of the minimum 50% requirements. This is coupled with an orchestrated 'Ship American' campaign waged by the Federal Maritime Commission (FMC), Department of Commerce (DOC), Department of Trade (DOT), American Shipowners and other vested shipping interests in the US.[94] This success would not have been possible without these flag preference requirements since – as indicated above – American vessels would be very uncompetitive; their freight rates quotations being higher due to higher running costs. Thus, therein lie the motives and/or rationale behind flag preference.[95]

This type of flag preference has, moreover, been given a boost. The US Foreign Operations Administration (FOA), was frequently thought to be the main agency shipping offshore procurement cargo in foreign bottoms. But the *Cargo Preference Act, 1954*, applies whether cargoes are produced within or without the US; this extra-territoriality, if we may call it such, guarantees the US flag vessels a wider market in addition to guaranteeing them the domestic market.[96] Otherwise the cargo preference requirement of offshore procurement applies to given supplies as well (post). Lastly, the responsibility for the enforcement of the applicable 50–50 provisions in placed on the cooperating countries by the ICA (FOA's successor) regulation; if the 50–50 requirement is not met by geographical areas[97] for any three month period, the recipient country has to refund ICA reimbursements for commodities, insurance and freight as the ICA Director, in his discretion, shall consider necessary to effect a compliance by the cooperating country with the foreign requirement for the period of time.[98]

In conclusion, therefore, the *Merchant Marine Act, 1936*, the *Cargo Preference Act, 1954* and the *Economic Cooperation Act, 1948, ejusdem generis*, place an obligation on AID, ICA, etc.[99] These statutes require that whenever the US purchases, donates or finances any equipment, materials, or commodities, or merely guarantees the convertibility of foreign currencies in any of these transactions, the appropriate Federal Agency must ensure that, if ocean transportation is required, at least 50% of the gross tonnage of such cargo moves aboard privately owned US commercial flag vessels to the extent that such vessels are available at fair and reasonable rates.[100] If the US flag vessels can be guaranteed 50%, where under normal circumstances they would probably have competed for 10% or so, then this is consistent with the presumption that the merchant marine fleet would expand to meet this guaranteed demand. These statutes are applicable principally to shipments financed by loans or grants of AID but also apply to surplus agricultural commodities.

4.2 'Surplus agricultural commodities and relief aid' preferences

This is really part of foreign aid cargo flag preference; however, its importance merits a separate discussion and lengthy emphasis. It, too, is a creation of the US, from where, naturally, the highlights come. However, this time the operative legislation is *Public Law No. 17*,[101] as amended. Briefly, this legislation states that exports of agricultural or other products fostered by government loans are to be carried *exclusively* in vessels of US registry unless it is determined by MARAD that such vessels are not available in sufficient numbers, or in sufficient tonnage capacity, or on necessary sailing schedules, or at reasonable rates. It would be worth noting a short history of this piece of legislation in order to appreciate its role in the development and expansion of the US merchant marine. What initiated this particular flag preference programme was that agricultural exports, which hit new heights during the Korean War, fell off rapidly from late 1952, thus the surplus built up to alarming proportions.[102] In Congress emphasis centred on measures to overcome the farm surplus situation and stimulate the export of agricultural commodities, which measures involved the sale of prince support stocks to commercial firms, donations for relief use, and the inclusion of sales for foreign currencies in Mutual Security Programmes.[103]

Since the merchant marine is the twin arm of international trade, this stimulation of exports of agricultural commodities had to go hand-in-hand with the promotion of the use of US flag vessels through this cargo preference clause. This, *inter alia*, was the string attached to this aid programme. In 1954, therefore, the 83rd Congress confirmed substantial authorisation for this purpose and established an additional programme of sales for foreign currency under Title 1 of the *Agricultural Trade Development and Assistance Act* (ATDAA). Housed under *Public Law no. 480*,[104] this programme seems to have paid off. This particular flag preference example underlines the fact that maritime trade and practice not only serves but follows international trade policies. For instance, in the first five years of the programme it is estimated that agreements totalling some US $5 000 000 000 were signed with foreign countries, including over US $40 000 000 for ocean freight to be paid by the Department of Agriculture,[105] which boasted, then, that the 50–50 cargo preference provision had added at least US $12 000 000 to reducing the cost of the farm subsidies.

However, it is the Department of State which negotiates surplus agricultural agreements with foreign countries. Thus, as far as the US was concerned the idea was 'we give you the food, but on our plates', giving the recipients no choice. In any case, it would be very generous for the US to allow the benefits of their enormous surplus agricultural aid and foreign trade to foreign – though cheaper and much more efficient – vessels, who had done nothing to earn it.[106] Apart from certain limited exemptions the tendency is to apply the Act whenever cargo is 'touched anywhere along the line by the hand of the government'.[107] The stress on government benefit in disposing of products at the highest price obtainable would tend to ignore legislative history that the reimbursement exception to the Act's coverage was intended to take care of situations where the Government only acted as *agent* rather than selling the products itself.[108] Be that as it may, this particular flag preference legislative scheme has been one of the most effective in keeping the US merchant marine afloat.[109] However, the greatest objection to this pedigree of flag preference has been that relating to government-financed cargoes.

4.3 'Government-financed cargo' preferences

This category is in many ways similar to the cargo preferences attached to foreign aid and surplus agricultural and relief supplies. However, in some cases it also differs from the two as herein outlined. In principle these are cargoes arising from purchases or transactions using government loans, or other assistance to the buyer, in a foreign country or to that foreign country itself.[110] In many countries restrictions are imposed on the shipment of this type of cargo preference, in part or in whole, being given to national flag carriers. One would normally expect this sort of relationship in a trade agreement between a developed and developing country – hence, the label 'aid with strings'. Once again, a TMN that practices this kind of flag preference is the US.[111] The operative legislation is *Public Law no. 17*, which stipulates that shipments financed by the Export–Import Bank (EXIMBANK) of Washington will include in their credit agreements a requirement that cargo shipment be made in US flag vessels, unless the requirements are waived by MARD (later FMC).[112] In certain circumstances, notwithstanding the availability of US flag vessels, vessels of the recipient nation may be allowed to share up to 50% of the EXIMBANK-financed cargoes under general waivers of P.R. 17 which are usually good for the life of a particular credit.

Otherwise, general waivers are granted only when the FMC is satisfied that parity of treatment is extended to US flag-vessels in the trade of the foreign nation as in the *National Treatment Preference* (post).[113] And even if a general waiver is granted, it applies only to vessels of the recipient nation's registry to the extent of their capacity to carry the cargo, based on normal flow of traffic from the interior through ports of shipments and not in excess of 50% of the total movement of cargo under the credit. Suppose that the aid recipient is, for example, Uganda, a land-locked country with no merchant marine of her own; what this means is that such cargoes would have to be carried 100% in American flag vessels.[114] As expected, third flag vessels (i.e., of the countries other than the US or the recipient) are barred from competing for EXIMBANK cargoes unless the US flag vessels are not available, and if so, at reasonable rates.[115]

In the operation of this scheme, in addition to its own banking operations, the EXIMBANK conducts special leading operations for other agencies involved in the game. For example, it funds loans for the Office of Defence Mobilisation under the *Defence Production Act, 1950,*[116] and it performs several functions for ICA: credits under the *Mutual Security Act, 1954*;[117] emergency wheat loans; or, for example, the US$ 100 000 000 credit to the former European Steel and Coal Community under the *Mutal Security Act, 1951*;[118] and ICA investment guarantees (currency transfer and loss by war or confiscation).[119] As noted above, the last category is not covered by the Cargo Preference Scheme, nor is the Bank's insuring, for example, of consignment of cotton bales against war risk and expropriation.[120] However, ICA regulations, apparently, subject the remaining cargoes to cargo preferences. It is this kind of use of flag preference by the US and other countries, to establish and expand their national merchant marine fleets, irrespective of the sound economic criteria, which has infuriated the other OECD members, among others.[121] At the inception of this programme, and on the proposal of the then-OEEC Maritime Transport Committee, the Council of the OEEC adopted a resolution requesting the US government to reconsider the practice of applying the provisions of this *Public Resolution no.. 17* to transactions which, but for the existance of guarantee from the EXIMBANK, would be of an ordinary commercial character.[122]

5. Miscellaneous flag preferences

There are many other forms of flag preference, all of them designed to improve the position of the national fleet. We shall combine them under three broad categories: foreign parity, inland parity and miscellaneous flag preferences;

5.1 Foreign parity flag preferences

In purely international trade terminology, *foreign parity* is alternatively known as the conditional *Most Favoured Nation Clause* (MFNC); the supposedly non-discriminatory aspect of the principle of *National Treatment*. In a way this is related to the already discussed bilateralism and multilateralism.[123] The MFNC is employed in international commercial agreements, which are treaties in which tariff privileges accorded by a country to any other countries are automatically extended to all other countries with which it has treaties, awarding MFN or national treatment; for example, a MFNC in a treaty between Country A and B might state that B's goods entering A's ports would not be subject to duty higher than that levied on similar goods from any other country, and vice-versa.[124] The two countries thus receive in principle an assurance of treatment in tariffs at least as good as that enjoyed by any other country and a safeguard against tariff discrimination and consequently flag preference.[125]

This, however, is only true of the unconditional MFNC which automatically extends the benefits of tariff and maritime concessions to all countries enjoying foreign parity status with the tariff reducing country, whether the concessions are given freely, or reciprocally, that is in return for counter concessions.[126] Of late, however, many countries, especially the DMNS, have made departures from the classical theory of unconditional MFNC, in favour of the conditional MFNC; the latter makes extentions of the privilege dependent upon the grant of similar concessions by the country benefiting from them.[127] It will be remembered that before 1914 the unconditional MFNC in bilateral trade agreements was thought to be influential in promoting free trade (although in practice the automatic extension of the benefits was often nullified by administrative devices such as tariff descriptions designed to confine concessions to one country).

It will also be remembered that between the wars the effectiveness of the concession was weakened by the use of the conditional form and, more importantly, by the growth of quotas.[128] It would, therefore, appear that maritime flag preferences and flag discriminations found their roots in the conditional MFNC, which now forms the basis of bilateralism. There were also doubts about the efficiency of isolated bilateral negotiations based on the MFNC principle. The unconditional clause could deter tariff concessions whenever a bilateral agreement, to reduce tariffs, threatened to result in both parties giving other countries more benefits than they received themselves.[129] After World War II, the search for a way out of this difficulty, while preserving the benefits of the MFNC, led to the GATT.

This provided for simultaneous bilateral tariff agreements between pairs of countries, the concessions being generated by the use of the MFNC and incorporated into a single multilateral agreement. Thus originated the bilateral and multilateral maritime preferences as we know them today.[130] Probably the best examples of these in maritime treaties are those of the US – the details of which are given in the appendices at the back.

All the examples of the bilateral and multilateral approaches already discussed can also be attributed to the foreign-parity flag preference.[131] The other aim of the principle of national treatment, which relates it more to maritime practices, is the inland parity flag preference.

5.2 Inland parity flag preferences

The standard of *national treatment* or *inland parity* means that the parties accord to each other's nationals the same treatment as they accord their own nationals. This is sometimes known as equality of treatment or the standard of reciprocity which means that one party accords the other exactly the same rights and advantages that the other accords in return.[132] *National treatment* has been the standard predominantly applied to shipping since the beginning of the free trade era.[133] It will be remembered that the authoritative pattern had been set by the *Cobden Treaty of 1860* which was concluded between France and Great Britain, and which in general provided for MFN treatment, but with respect to merchant marines, granted national treatment or reciprocity or equality or inland parity preferences.[134]

The example of the Cobden Treaty was followed by a great number of commercial treaties of this period. The view that national treatment was the most equitable standard for shipping has, indeed, been accepted not only on a bilateral but also on a multilateral basis, as evidenced above.[135] The outstanding treaty in this respect (post) is the *Convention and Statute on the International Regime of Maritime Ports* of December 9, 1923. This provides, *inter alia*, that as regards the access to, and the use of, ports, every contracting state undertakes to grant the vessels of every other contracting states equality of treatment with its own vessels.[136] We shall return to this convention, but as much as this convention, which has been ratified by 23 states, has done to facilitate the commercial operations of ships in ports, it does not lend itself to be applied to the participation of ships in maritime transport as such.

The application of *national treatment* also to this field has, therefore, been frequently advocated. It is accepted that national treatment represents the highest standard that could be granted because it can be assumed no state treats its own nationals on a less favourable basis than foreigners.[137] If, however, this standard is to be made the basis of a reciprocal agreement, the state expected to grant this standard must ask itself what benefit it will get in return for its own nationals, i.e., what is the status enjoyed by the nationals of the other contracting party. Obviously certain differences in the material status of the nationals of both states will always be found. But if these differences exceed a certain measure it is plain that the agreement on national treatment would create unwarranted restrictions for the nationals of the one and unjustified benefits for the nationals of the other state.[138]

This, then, is the natural limit for the application of this standard. One can then understand the reluctance and the predicament of the STNS. It is precisely for this reason that there has been a marked departure from this principle in international trade generally, and maritime trade in particular; hence all the discriminatory and preferential maritime policies.[139] It may not be safe to assume that because of the above factors, this principle of national treatment in public international law and trade has, therefore, been abandoned; but it may be true to say this constitutes an exception to the practice even though not a total abandonment.

In order to extend the applicability of *inland parity,* the attempt has been made to add to an agreement on national treatment a clause providing that neither party could claim inland parity in order to receive rights which reach further than those it is granting its own nationals.[140] This means, however, that a combination of two standards is sought which are quite different and which, therefore, amounts to a contradiction in terms. If a combination of such types could be held valid at all, it would impart a mere exception rather than a general rule. For an example of this combination-exception in particular, and the modern practice of inland parity in oceanborne trade generally, see the American illustrations in Appendices 3 and 4.[141]

5.3 Miscellaneous flag preferences

The flag preference headings discussed above are but only broad generalisations. It has not been, and, indeed, it would not be, possible to deal with all the various types of preferences that may be open to states.[142] The above list is further supplemented, and complimented, by the discussion of such similar topics in the next chapter (flag discrimination) and the subsequent section (maritime subsidies and state intervention).[143] Nevertheless, the discussion would not be complete without considering some, but not all, of the miscellaneous categories which pertain particularly to the US.[144] For instance, even though there seems to be no regulation or policy statement on the subject, it would appear that in returns under the *Mutual Defence Assistance Act of* 1949, certain equipment, for example from the UK,[145] would still be subject to cargo preference,[146] since the UK makes delivery alongside the ship at the point of origin. Similarly, transportation to Italy, for instance, of surplus Defence Department property for sale there,[147] would be subject to the same requirement as that relating to surplus agricultural commodities and relief aid. However, the opposite result should obtain when transportation follows purchase, about stipulations in the contract of sale.[148]

Equally applicable are student exchange programmes for which the government provides funds, including transportation of effects.[149] But these would seem not to be subject to cargo preference.[150] Furthermore, the *Cargo Preference Act of* 1974 expressly exempts from its requirements cargoes carried in the three ships of the Panama Canal Company, a government-owned corporation which primarily serves the needs of the Panama Canal and its workers.[151] The list could be endless but we must stop somewhere. The contributions of flag preferences towards the establishment and/or expansion of national fleets may be indirect rather than direct, largely political rather than purely commercial, but they are nevertheless there. They may be gradual and not easily compatible.

6. Advantages and disadvantages of flag preferences

It is in this light that the advantages and disadvantages of flag preference can now be assessed, with particular reference to the role of cargo-sharing as stipulated in the *UNCTAD Code of Conduct for Liner Conferences.*[152] The Emphasis lies on the advantages; the discussion on the disadvantages is continued in Chapter 9.

6.1 Development aspects of the Code of Conduct

This section-heading makes reference to the most notable – and notorious – provision in the Code: Article 2(4), concerning the sharing of conference trade amongst member lines. There are two basic provisions:[153] first, that in the liner trade between any two states, the national shipping lines of those states shall have equal rights; and, second, that third-party lines shall have the right to acquire a significant portion of the foreign trade:

> 'Third-country shipping lines, if any, shall have the right to acquire a significant part, such as 20 per cent in the freight and volume of traffic generated by that trade.'[154]

There are two issues to be discarded. First, there are the expectations of the DMNS that the Code will aid them in promoting their foreign trade – hence the expansion of their national fleets – by the automatic guarantee of, say, 40% of cargo whichever way. It may not, of course, be as clear-cut as that.[155]

Notwithstanding all the doubts, however, these countries interpret the cargo-reservation regime of Article 2(4) as authority to effect a major change in the world liner shipping industry in their favour. Theoretically, as the national shipping lines of the DMNS come to be more and more firmly established, their share of the relevant conference trades will undoubtedly increase;[156] and the significant share allowed to cross-traders will correspondingly diminish. Whether this result (assuming it comes to pass) is a desirable one or not, from the economic and political standpoint of world trade and development, is the subject of the third part of this inquiry.[157]

The second issue is that the DMNS hope that the Code will yield improvements in their balance of payments and, therefore, promote their foreign trade.[158] After all, the Code resulted from prolonged efforts by them to terminate the domination of the merchant marine industry by the TMNS, and to eliminate the perceived economic disadvantages of the existing liner conference system for them (DMNS). They (the DMNS) take the view that the conference systems creates monopoly power enabling the lines of the TMNS to charge excess rates and to dominate international shipping and international trade.[159] Therefore, by assuring membership and sufficient cargo to the national lines of the DMNS, the Code was designed to enable them (the DMNS) to become dominant forces and, hence, ensure that reasonable conference cargo rates are set for their notion's foreign trade.[160]

It is in this light that we must envisage the rationale behind these countries' attempts to use flag preference in particular, and flag discrimination generally, for development purposes.[161] There may be doubts as to the use of flag preference for such purposes. There may be further doubts as to its effectiveness and success for the said purposes. But none can question the wisdom regarding its justification.

6.2 Advantages of flag preference

State intervention in this respect must have some advantage. Let us being with cargo-sharing as stipulated in the Code.[162] There can hardly be any doubt that without some kind of international agreement for liner shipping, for instance, all countries would sooner or later have to introduce legislation in one form or another in order to protect the interests of their oceanborne trade or their shipowners.[163] This would lead to controversial and contradictory legislation, with the shipowners wedged in between, having to choose to obey either their own law or that of other countries.[164] In this respect the cargo-reservation stipulation in the *UNCTAD Code Convention* could have a harmonising effect and contribute to the elimination of excessive unilateral legislation in shipping.[165]

Even if cargo-reservation does not significantly aid the establishment and expansion of national fleets, at least this harmony is badly needed by international shipping.[166] Though far from being a perfect solution, the stipulation (particularly if its guidelines were somewhat improved and were used in a reasonable way) could help shipowners, shippers and governments to enhance their relations and possibly even open the door to national deregulation on a universal basis.[167] The outcry against the cargo-reservation in the Code was only to a limited extent directed against the Code as such, which, apparently, is more liberal than many critics are prepared to admit. The objections were particularly raised against the cargo-sharing clause in that document.[168]

The 40–40–20 formula, to be used merely as an indication for a possible division of shares, could eventually have a negative effect for the merchant marines of countries with only a small cargo potential of their own.[169] If one, therefore, looks at those who vigorously oppose cargo-sharing, one finds that most of them are either cross-traders or lines which by national legislation or tradition already carry more than 40% of their own trade. The British are no exception; they fall into both categories.[170] Due to the technical revolution, inflation, recession and the rise of nationalism, the situation was such that unless practical solutions were found quickly the assumptions, following, would not all be unrealistic:[171] there would be a steady expansion of multilateral legislation eventually affecting all countries with national merchant marine fleets.

There would be more and more bilateral arrangements; more and more outside influence on tariff making, be it from governments or shippers' associations where liberal trade still existed, there would be the playground for the fleets of STNS, and fly-by-night operators, causing yet more cut throat competition and instability.[172] Furthermore, lines would not be able to earn sufficient return on their capital; they might not even cover their operating costs. Since modern ships are mostly tailor-made and require large specialised equipment, lines cannot easily withdraw from trades and sell their ships but might simply have to go bankrupt.[173] In the end, governments would have had to step in anyway and introduce protective laws where such do not already exist.

The consequences, in the final analysis, can only be that the merchant marine industry becomes a public utility world-wide which might entail higher costs and inefficiency.[174] In our view, there is only one solution to maintain a free, healthy and viable merchant marine service and that is through cargo-sharing. It would have to go hand in hand with improved conference organisation, as advocated by the *UNCTAD Code of Conduct for Liner Conferences,*[175] and would require the backing of the respective governments. Cargo-sharing would, first and foremost, allow a coordinated and orderly supply of modern tonnage in line with the requirements of the respective trade.[176]

6.3 Flag preference and development

This is the most fundamental reason for commercial operation of merchant marines in the future. Hundreds of millions of dollars could have been saved by the shipowners in the US, for instance, over the past 12 years,[177] if such an approach had been made possible as a matter of international, rather than national concern. Taking all these factors into account, one might now appreciate a number of positive elements in the cargo-reservation stipulations of the *UNCTAD Code of Conduct for Liner Conferences.*[178] In our view, it gives the liner shipping the chance to improve the conference system and go to cargo-sharing arrangements, where possible, on a commercial basis.[179] We would be the last to deny cross-traders the right to continue serving trades in which they have an historical tradition and merit.

We realise that for some of them, particularly the Norwegians, the offering of world-wide shipping services is still the major national industry and source of income, next to fishing and oil.[180] On the other hand, it should be borne in mind that equally no-one can deny the merchant fleets of the cargo-sharing countries a substantial share of cargo generated by their trade.[181] Four examples could be cited to illustrate the point: the Federal Republic of Germany is a typical example of a country with about 10% of the oceanborne world trade and not even 3% of the world's merchant marine tonnage strength.[182] The US is the other example of a country generating about 30% of oceanborne world trade but whose merchant marine accounts for only about 5% of the world's merchant fleets.[183] Besides Japan, all the other leading maritime nations are cross-traders whose share of world trade is nowhere near that of their oceanborne world trade. Surely not even free trade can deny these nations the legitimate, inalienable right to reserve a large proportion of the cargoes they contribute to the well-being of international trade.[184]

This explains why the US pursues flag preference with such vigour. Sharply contrasting with this situation is the UK with hardly 5% of world oceanborne trade, yet at one point she had virtually over 50% of the world's merchant marine fleets.[185] But it is probably not because of the 40–40–20 formula that West Germany's liner shipowners support the Code. In some trades they could certainly gain, but they probably realised – and rightly so[186] – some time ago that it would be better to make money carrying, say, 38% rather than lose money with 42% of a given trade; it is not the exact percentage but the principle that matters.[187] Cargo-sharing agreements have already been made where a happy medium has been found and where both the national lines and the cross-traders cooperate in harmony.[188] In such trades the shares of the individual lines always apply to the ranges or areas, and go hand in hand with a sensible realisation programme leading to the best possible use of the highly expensive ship space.[189]

6.4 Flag preference and the future of international shipping

Naturally, this realisation must not be overemphasized the merchant marine industry must offer first class service to international trade in terms of frequency, coverage of ports and availability of space.[190] For this purpose, appropriate committees must be established between merchants and shipowners in order to safeguard satisfactory operation. Concluding this chapter on flag preference we would like to recapitulate the advantages we see in a efficient cargo-sharing system;[191] the merchant marine industry would essentially remain a commercially-oriented business; government involvement or intervention would probably be limited; the merchant marine industry, worldwide, would achieve a reasonable profit which should, however, never be allowed to get out of hand; the industry, especially its liner segments, could collectively pursue long term fleet planning,[192] enabling them to provide shippers with optimal ships and avoiding overtonnaging in the trades.

Shippers would have the guarantee of a good service at reasonable rates because optimal utilisation of ships' space means reduced costs and consequently less need for higher rates.[193] Furthermore, irregularities in the trade, caused by rate-wars would be largely eliminated; although they would have to gradually reduce their overall share, there would be a guaranteed position for traditional cross-traders which have served the respective trades for decades;[194] such principles, being in line with the basic principles of the *UNCTAD Code of Conduct for Liner Conferences*, would no doubt appeal to the DMNS and could replace their strictly bilateral cargo-sharing ideas.[195] It is our firm conviction, therefore, that cargo-sharing, especially in liner shipping, is not only a practical solution, but a necessity.

The initiative has had to be taken by the DMNS[196] and the US, but successful results will depend entirely on close cooperation between shipowners and shippers, on the one hand, and on coordinated assistance from governments of both the TMNS nad the DMNS, on the other.[197] This must be designed to ensure the orderly development of both the private and public commercial merchant marines in the interests of international trade and to the benefits of all parties concerned.[198] Such a solution is inevitable, otherwise the DMNS will claim total national sovereignty which entitles their governments to the take-over of all properties (post) inside national boundaries; and to the consideration of national security and independence which require that complete ownership and control of the merchant marine sector be in state hands.[199]

7. Conclusion

For the merchant marine sector to be in state hands would be tantamount to *eminent domain* rules, on the basis of which national takeovers of merchant marine facilities and tasks would be better assured and in which the needs of the government and those of the domestic producers and shippers would be met.[200] As has been noted, the infant industry argument can be used in support of excluding foreign flags from transport markets; under the pretence that domestic transport companies (whether private or public) are too inexperienced or under-capitalised to compete efficiently and effectively with the seasoned and well-financed foreign-based flags, they could turn, as many TMNS indeed do, to the use of preferential treatment in favour of their national merchant marine flags when choosing carriers for the management of export and import cargoes.[202]

Thus, through practice rather than legislation or the exercise of government power, foreign flags could be permanenetly excluded from the transport market or at least discriminated against; they may continue to unilaterally implement cargo-reservation rules, a privilege which (we repeat) can hardly be denied to any country.[203] They could, then, continue allocating cargoes to their own merchant marine flags up to its maximum practical carrying capacities and only allow foreign flags a part of the merchant marine business when additional carrying capacity is needed. The options facing international shipping are either to formalise cargo reservation or face these undesirable consequences.[204] It may be negotiating pistol to head, but that is the reality of the situation.

Appendix 3

Summary of the practices by selected developing maritime countries[a]

Country[b]	Preferences											
	Cargo preference	Cargo reservation	Cargo sharing	Cabotage restrictions	Bilateralism	Multilateralism	Foreign aid shipments	Surplus agricultural commodities and felief aid	Government-financed cargoes	Foreign parity preferences	Inland parity preferences	Miscellaneous
Algeria		X		X	X	0	0		X			X
Argentina	X			X	X	X	0		X			X
Brazil	X		X	X	X	X	0		X			X
Chile				X	X	X	0		X			X
China[1]	X		X	X	X	0	0		0			X
Colombia		X		X	X	X	0		X			X
Cyprus[2]				X	0	0	0		0			X
Ecuador	X	X		X	X	0	0		X			X
Egypt[3]	X	X		X	X	X	0		0			X
Gabon			X	X	X	0	0		X			X
Ghana				X	X	X	0		X			X
India				X	X	0	0		X			X
Indonesia	X	X	X	X	X	0	0		X			X
Iran				X	X	0	0		0			X
Iraq				X	X	0	0		X			X
Israel	X			X	X	0	0		0			X
Korea[4]				X	X	0	0		0			X
Kuwait	X			X	X	0	0		0			X
Lebanon[5]				X	X	0	0		0			X
Liberia[6]				X	X	X	0		0			X
Libya				X	X	0	0		X			X
Malaysia				X	X	0	0		0			X
Mexico			X	X	X	X	0		0			X
Morrocco[7]				X	X	0	0		0			X
Nigeria	X			X	X	X	0		X			X
Pakistan				X	0	0	0		0			X
Panama				X	X	X	0		X			X
Peru	X	X		X	X	X	0		X			X
Phillipines			X	X	X	X	0		0			X
Saudi Arabia[8]				X	X	0	0		0			X
Singapore			X	X	X	0	0		0			X
South Africa[9]				X	0	0	0		X			X
Thailand				X	X	0	0		0			X
Turkey[10]					X							X
UAE[11,2]					X							X
Uruguay				X	X	X	X	X				X
Venezuela			X		X	X	X	X				X
Zaire					X			X				X

[1] Republic of China sometimes known as Nationalist China or Taiwan or Formosa.

[2] Member of the developing countries of Western Asia: Code 10(1) of UNCTAD categorisation.

[3] Arab republic of, formally United Arab Republic (UAR).

[4] South, or The Republic of, as opposed to North.

[5] Flag of convenience developing country.

[6] Leading (flag of convenience) tonnage in Africa and world.

[7] Arab Kingdom of.

[8] Arab Kingdom of.

[9] Sometimes categorised as a developed market economy country (only one in Africa): codes of UNCTAD categorisations.

[10] Sometimes categorised as an OECD/developed market economy country of Western Europe: Code 4 of The UNCTAD categorisations.

[11] United Arab Emirates.

X: Evidence of the practice.

0: Either no practice or no known evidence of.

[a] Selection based on fleet statistics as of December 31, 1976, and of vessels over 1 000 dwt only, derived from merchant fleets of the world, issued by US Maritime Administration's Division of Trade Studies and Statistics.

[b] These are but about 3/5 of all the developing countries. The position could have changed ever since with more developing countries meeting the 1 000 dwt ships mark. Socialist developing countries are not included.

[c] It is interesting to note that whereas (almost) all landlocked developed maritime countries own merchant marines; this is not necessarily the case with developing countries.

Source: Compiled from sources and information from *Maritime Subsidies* 1978 (US Maritime Administration Publication), various books, journals and periodicals on cargo preferences.

Appendix 4

Summary of the preferential practices by the traditional maritime nations[a]

Country	Cargo preference	Cargo reservation	Cargo sharing	Cabotage restrictions	Bilateralism	Multilateralism	Foreign aid shipments	Surplus agricultural commodities and relief aid	Government-financed cargoes	Foreign parity preferences	Inland parity preferences	Miscellaneous
Australia	X			X								X
Austria[b]												X
Belgium												X
Canada	X			X	X							X
Denmark				X								X
Finland[1]	X			X								X
France	X			X	X							X
Germany[c]	X		X	X	X							X
Greece[2]	X		X	X	X						X	X
Iceland[1]				X								X
Ireland												
Italy	X			X								X
Japan	X			X								X
Liechtenstein												X
Luxemburg[b]												X
Netherlands				X								X
New Zealand				X								X
Norway[1]				X								X
Portugal[1]			X	X					X			X
Spain[1]	X			X	X							X
Sweden[1]				X								X
Switzerland[b]				X								X
United Kingdom	X										X	X
United States	X	X	X	X	X	X	X	X	X X	X	X	X

[1] European but not yet members of the EEC, though considering membership.
[2] Recently joined the EEC.
[3] Developed maritime countries of Eastern Europe are not included either in the discussion or table.
[a] Based on list of mainly member countries of the OECD and the EEC.
[b] Landlocked but owns merchant marine fleets of their own.
[c] Federal Republic of (West Germany).

Source: Compiled from various books, journals, etc.

Notes

1. OECD, *Maritime Transport*, 1960, p. 10.
2. See Chapter 5.
3. (a) and (b).
4. E.g. bilateralism.
5. E.g. berth and port discriminations.
6. For fiscal and financial relief see Chapter 4.
7. Malinowski, W. R., 'Towards a change in the international distribution of shipping', *International Conciliation*, Publication No. 582, March 1972.
8. UNCTAD Secretariat, Report by, Doc. No. TD/B/C.4/63., 4 Nov. 1970, 1 of 3.
9. Metaxas, *Economics of Tramp Shipping*, 1971, pp. 24–26.
10. Rochdale, paras 136–140, p. 40.
11. Black, *Law Dictionary, op. cit.*, p. 1542; and Chambers, *Twentieth Century Dictionary*, p. 1244.
12. *UNCTAD Code of Conduct*, Article 4(2); *UNCTAD Conference of Plenipontentiaries on the Code*, Vol. II, TD/Code/13/Add.1.
13. OECD, *Maritime Transport*, 1961, p. 53.
14. US Dept. of Commerce, MARAD, *Maritime Subsidies*, 1978, p. 52.
15. OECD, *Maritime Subsidies*, 1961, Chapter 1.
16. O'Loughlin, *Economics of Sea Transport* (1st edn.), pp. 149, 156–59, 163.
17. Hearns G. H., 'Cargo preference and control' *J. Mar. L. & Comm., Vol. 2*, No. 3, pp. 481–82.
18. Cufley, C. F. E., *Ocean Freights and Chartering*, 1974 (reprint), Chapter 10.
19. *Ibid.*, pp. 316, 317–18.
20. OECD, *Maritime Transport*, 1962, p. 18.
21. Cufley, *supra, The Movements and the Development of World Merchant Shipping*, pp. 309–36, at 319–20.
22. Macdonald A. M., OBE, *Chambers' Twentieth Century Dictionary*, 1977 Rev., p. 1057.
23. *Ibid.*, p. 1148.
24. Olof, H., *Flag Discriminations Purposes, Motives, and Economic Consequences*, Publication of the Swedish School of Economics, No. 3, 1956, p. 39.
25. Gorter, W., *United States Shipping Policy*, for Council of Foreign Relations, by Hemper & Brothers, NY, 1956.
26. OEEC, *Maritime Transport*, 1953, p. 42.
27. Cufley, *Flag Discriminations and Trade Reservations, op. cit.*, pp. 318–319.
28. UNCTAD Doc. No. TD/B/C.4/38/Rev. 1, paras 337–40, p. 91.
29. See also *Advantages of Cargo Reservation* at the end of this chapter.
30. OECD, *Maritime Transport*, 1964, p. 39.
31. Goss, R. O, (Preferences, peoples' expressions of) *Advances in Maritime Economics*, CUP, 1979 (1st edn.); in Introduction especially at p. 14.
32. Rochdale Report, paras 141, at 41.
33. *Ibid.*, Chapter 5, *Coastal and Short Sea Trades*, paras 296–320, pp. 60–62.
34. *Ibid.*, paras 220(1) and 222(1).
35. *Ibid.*, para 220(1), p. 60.
36. E. g. *Treaty Between the Argentine Republic and Chile* defining the boundaries between the two countries (Tierra del Fuego, Neutrality of Straits of Magellan, etc.) signed at Buenos Aires July 23, 1881, *British and Foreign State Papers*, pp. 1104–05.
37. UNCTAD TD/B/B.C/4/63-3 of 3.
38. *Ibid.*
39. Raymond, F. M., *Foreign Exchange in the Postwar World*, Twentieth Century Fund, NY, 1954.
40. See also text under *Multilateralism*.
41. As to its advantages/disadvantages see end of Part I and also Part III to this survey.
42. Chalmers, H., *World Trade Policies*, University of California Press, Berkeley, Calif., 1953.
43. Friedman, W., *The Changing Structure of International Law*, Feffer & Simons, NY

1964, Chapter 5, pp. 51–59.

44. *Ibid.*, pp. 196–201 i.e. 'Less developed countries and the universality of international law'.
45. *Ibid.*, 'Conflicts of ideology and universality of international law', pp. 202 to the end.
46. Article 4(2) (a) of *Code of Conduct for Liner Conferences*.
47. *Ibid.*, Article 4(2) (b).
48. See *Advantages of Cargo Reservation* at end of this chapter.
49. US Department of State Bulletin: *Agreement Regarding Trade Act*, October 18 1972, No. 595, 1972.
50. Fitzerpatrick, 'Soviet-American Trade 1972–74; a summary', 15 *Virg. J. Int. L.*, 1974, p. 39.
51. *US–USSR Maritime Agreement*, 1972, Annex 111(a).
52. *Ibid.*, 'White House Fact Sheet'.
53. US Department of State Bulletin, No. 661, 1972, Annex 111(1) (c) (iii).
54. Though this agreement was interrupted by US Embargo following the Afghan crisis.
55. This treaty is in line with Soviet (& STNS) concepts of international trade relations and law being concluded only through treaties.
56. US Acpt. of State Bulletin, No. 96, 1976; *Agreement Regarding Certain Maritime Matters*, Dec. 29 1975.
57. The six-year agreement, which went into effect January 1 1976, was signed on December 19 1975 and expired on December 29 1981.
58. See again Munkesell R. F. and Chaimers H., *supra*.
59. Hufbanner, G.C. *et al., The GATT Codes and the Unconditional MFN Principle* pp. 59–95, 3rd Article in the Symposium on the Multilateral Trade Agreements II, ILJ Geon. Wash. Un. Vol. 12, No. 1, 1980.
60. Rubin, A. P., 'The international legal aspects of unilateral declarations AJIL, Vol. 71, 1977, pp. 1–30.
61. Hardy, M., 'The UN and General Multilateral Treaties concluded under the auspices of the League of Nations' *Brit. Yearbook Int. L.*, Vol. 39., 1963, pp. 425–40.
62. Anderson, D. R., 'Reservations to multilateral conventions: A re-examination' *Int. 4 Contemp. LQ*, Vol. 13, 1964, pp. 450–81.
63. Sturmey, S. G., 'The development of the Code of Conduct for Liner Conferences', *Marit L & Man.*, Vol. 3, No. 2, April 1979, pp. 133–148.
64. *Commonwealth Shipping Agreement of 1931*.
65. Buss, W. D., 'The basic international structure of LAFTa and the proposals for its modifications: Intergovernmentalism v regionalism' *Case WRJ Int. L*, Vol. 2, 1969, pp. 34–57.
66. Stemmer, O. J., 'Flag discrimination in Latin America', *J. Marit L. & Comm.*, Vol. 10, No. 1, p. 129.
67. Brown, R. B., *Transport and the Economic Integration of Latin America*, pp. 153–54.
68. *Ibid*, Chapter 6, i.e. 'Latin American Shipping Policies and the LAFTA Maritime Convention', pp. 88–94.
69. *Ibid*, pp. 153–54, i.e. 'Shipping Rates and Service and Draft LAFTA Treaty'.
70. Simmonds, K. R., 'The Central American Common Market: An experiment in regional integration', *Int. & Comp. LQ*, Vol. 16., 1967, pp. 911–45.
71. Garcia, A. FV. *et al*, 'Institutional and economic perspectives on Latin American integration, *Proc. Am. Soc. Int. L.* Vol. 61, 1967, pp. 167–86.
72. Brown, *supra*, pp. 107–13, i.e. 'Latin American Shipping Policies'.
73. Article 4 of LAFTA Water Convention.
74. Stemmer, O. J. *supra.*
75. Brown, *supra, pp. 124–31*, i.e. 'Present Maritime Service within LAFTA Water Convention Area'.
76. W. R. P. 'Resource Allocation and Integration in the Central American Common Market', *NUJ Int. L & Polit.*, Vol. 3, 1970, pp. 107–35.
77. Brown, *Supra*, pp. 154–56 'Effect of Imbalances of Trade Flows, Other Views of the Rate Problem, and the Reservation of Cargo for LAFTA Ships'.

78. *Ibid.*, pp. 138, 145–49. In fact this bold attempt did not take off due to lack of sufficient ratifications.
79. Brazil, Argentina, Venezuela and Mexico account for about half of the LAFTA Economic Country Trade.
80. LAFTA Water Convention was terminated and replaced by a new and hopefully more viable Maritime Economic Country.
81. Brown, *supra*, Chapter IX, pp. 216–7.
82. *Ibid.*, 'Transport Policy', pp. 218–20.
83. *Ibid.*, 'Conclusion relating to LAFTA', pp. 221–24.
84. Rubin, S. J., *The Conscience of the Rich Nations, The Development Assistance Committee and the Common Aids Efforts*, NY, Harper & Row, 1966.
85. Note that Japan too has an EXIMBANK.
86. OEEC, *Maritime Transport*, 1954, para 68.
87. Hence State Intervention (post), *ibid*, p. 54.
88. 68 State. 832, 1954.
89. 46 USC 1241 (b), 1964.
90. 49 Stat. 2015.
91. 1954 House Hearings 92.
92. S. Rep. No. 1584, at 2.
92A. 'Contribution of federal aid to trade', Appendix 2, at 15 of *Public Law 480.*
93. *Agricultural Trade Development and Assistance Act*, 68 St stat. 445, 1954, as amended, 7 USC paras 17–19, 1721–24, 1964 (Titles 1, 11).
94. See also 73 Stat. 610, 1959, as amended, 7 USC para 1731–36, 1964 (Title IX).
95. Foighel, I., 'Aid to developing countries – A legal analysis', *Novdisk Tid. Int. Ref.*, Vol. 40, 1970, pp. 87–175.
96. Perry, M. W. *et al.*, 'US foreign policy and emerging legal policy issues of technology transfer', *Proc. Am. Soc. Int. L.*, Vol. 70, 1976, pp. 1–10.
97. S. Rep. No. 2286, 87th Cong. 2nd. Sess. 44, 1962.
98. 68 Stat. 832, 1954, as amended, 46 USC para 1241 (b), 1964.
99. *Ibid.*
100. See also *Rochdale Report*, para. 150, p. 43.
101. *US Maritime Research Committee*, 'An analysis of the application of *Public Law 664* (50–50) to the disposal of Agricultural surplus under *Title 1 Public Law 480*', reprinted in Senate Hearings', 108.
102. Hyde, J. N. 'Economic development agreements', *Hague Recueil*, Vol. 105, 1962, pp. 267–74.
102. Triffin, R., *The World Money Maze: National Currencies in International Payments*, Yale University Press, New Haven, 1966.
103. 48 Stat. 500, 1934, 15 USC para 616 (a), 1964.
104. H. C. on Merchant Marine and Fisheries, 'Cargo Preference and its Relation to the Farm Surplus Disposal Program', H. R. Rep., No. 1818, 84th Cong, 2nd Sess., 6, 1956.
105. *Ibid.*, June 5, 1956, 7 UST DIA 7071 TIAS, No. 3588 (effective June 5, 1956).
106. See also TIAS, No. 3989 (effective Feb. 3, 1958).
107. US Dept of Agric. 'Export Credit Programs for Financing Dollar Sales of US Agricultural Commodities', 1959.
108. 1954, *Senate Hearings*, H. R. Rep. 2329, at 2.
109. *Ibid.* at 97; see generally *International Co-operation Administration, Investment Guarantee Handbook*, 1957, (GPO) Washington D.C.
110. 12 CRF, para 402 3(a), 1963.
111. Greiger, R., 'The unilateral change of economic development agreements', *Int. & Comp. LQ*, Vol. 23, 1974, pp. 73–104.
112. US Dept of Commerce, MARAD, Statement on *Public Resolution No. 17*, July 24, 1959, reprinted in *Alcoa SS Co. V Cia Anomima Venezuela de Navegacion*, 7 FMC 345, 737, 1962; affirmed sub-nom Alcoa SS Co. V FMC 321 F. 2d 756 (DC Cir. 1963).
113. See Annex on *MFN and National Treatment*.

114. The US was a major donor to the Eastern African Disaster Relief, 1979–81.
115. Cf. Scwarzenberger, G. *et al.*, 'Equality and discrimination in international economic law', *Yearbook WA*, Vol. 25, 1971, pp. 163–81.
116. 1956 *Senate Hearings* 125.
117. Contra, the 151 Act.
118. 1954 *Senate hearings*: 'Defence Department Directives on Mutual Defence Shipments'.
119. 68 Stat. 832, 1954.
120. 46 USC para. 1241 (Suppl. V 1958).
121. *Rochdale Report*, para. 151, p. 43.
122. *Ibid.*
123. Viner, J., *International Economics*, The Free Press, Glencoe, N.Y., 1951.
124. Jahnkel, L. G., 'The EEC & the MFNC', *Can. Yearbook Int. L.* Vol. 1, pp. 252–71.
125. Sturmey, S.G., *supra*, pp. 102, 114 i.e. 'Flag Discrimination and Import Tariff'.
126. Murase, S., 'The MFN in Japan's treaty practice during the period 1854–1905', *Am. J. Int. L.*, Vol. 70, 1976, pp. 273–97.
127. Verbit, G. P., *Trade Agreements for Developing Countries*, N.Y. 1969.
128. Timberg *et al.*, 'Control of International Restrictive Business Practices', *Proc. Am. Soc. Int. L.*, Vol. 69, 1975, pp. 170–92, at 180.
129. Anon 'Tariff surcharges and article II of GATT', NY, *U. J. Int. L. & Polit.*, Vol. 5, 1972, pp. 341–56, at 349 and 351.
130. Sturmey S. G., *supra*, pp. 194–8, 206–7, 405, 409–10, i.e. 'Flag discrimination in bilateral trade agreements and the 50–50 Rule'.
131. Hudec, R. E., *The GATT Legal System and World Trade Diplomacy*, NY, 1975.
132. US Dept. of Trade, *Memo submitted to the President's Advisory Committee*, Aug. 1965.
133. Rohreke, H. G., *The Formula and Material Concept of Flag Equality*, p. 1.
134. *Treaty of Friendship, Commerce and Navigation Between the US and West Germany*, Article IV (1), TIAS, No. 3593.
135. For this Convention see Great Britain *Treaty Series* No. 24, 1925.
136. Singh, N., *British Shipping Laws,* Vol. 8, *International Conventions on Merchant Shipping*, pp. 1558–68.
137. Note 134 above, Article IV (2).
138. Hackworth, *International Law*, Vol. 5, 1943, p. 272.
139. *John T. Bill Co.* v. *US 104 F. 2d 67 (CCPA 1939)* in Bishop W. W., *International Law Cases & Materials*, pp. 160–64.
140. Article 1(1), *US–West German Treaty; Bill Co.* v *US*, p. 161.
141. *Ibid.*, proclaimed Oct. 14, 1925, 44 Stat. 2132, Article VII.
142. UNCTAD Doc. No. TD/B/C.4/63 1, 2, 3. *Corigenda and Addenda* 1–2.
143. Article XII, *US–Belgium Treaty*, 1875, (19 Stat. 628, 1 *Mallay Treaties* 90).
144. Indeed most examples are from the US, e.g. House Hearings, No. 2329, at 2.
145. *US–UK Agreement*, May 13, 1957, para 3, 1957, 8 UST & OIA 835 TIAS., No. 3843.
146. Presumably to the 100% American Flag Shipping requirements of 32 CFR para 1.309(b) (2) (Supp. 1958).
147. *US–Italy Agreement*, June 22, 1957, 8 UST & DIA 881, TIAS, No. 3850.
148. 1954 *House Hearings* 63.
149. See text under *Surplus Agricultural Commodities and Relief Aid.*
150. See *Commission for Education Exchange Agreement between US and Paraguay*, April 1957, 1957 SUST & DIA 946, TIAS, No. 3856.
151. *Cargo Preference Act 1954* as amended by *Cargo Preference Act 1974.*
152. UNCTAD Doc. No. TD/105 1972, and Corr. 1.
153. UNCTAD Doc. Sales No. E. 78.11.D.7.
154. Sanklecha, S. N.., 'Need for fiscal relief and loan assistance', *Indian Shipping*, No. 6.
155. Prof. Tinbergen, Rotterdam Lecture, Delta Conference 1976 on Cooperation in Maritime Transport.
156. Franklin, P., *The Economic Impact of Flag Discrimination in Ocean Transportation,* 1968, p. 79.

157. See also Benham A., *A Study of the Value of National Fleets and Shipping Policies in Developing Countries* MSC UWIST, 1974, p. 143.
158. Wijkman, 'Effects of cargo reservation. A review of UNCTAD'S Code of Conduct for Liner Conferences', *Marine Policy*, Vol. 4, No. 4, Oct. 1980, pp. 271–90.
159. *Ibid*.
160. Frankel *et al*., 'Impact of cargo sharing on US liner trade', *Marine Policy*, Vol. 5, Jan. 1981, pp. 23–39, at 25.
161. *The Future of Liner Shipping, op. cit*., chapter on cargo reservation.
162. Rojis, E., *The Future of Liner Shipping* – one view from a developing country in the Future of Liner Shipping, *op. cit*.
163. Bast G. H. and Kelift, M. C., 'Cost consequences of cargo reservation – a case study', in *The Future of Liner Shipping, op. cit*.
164. This was the underlying assumption in the DMNS' acceptance of Article 2(4) of the *UN Code of Conduct for Liner Conferences*.
165. Hudson, L. G., 'Tools in liner shipping – present and future impact', in *The Future of Liner Shipping*.
166. Some cargo sharing agreements stipulate unequal share of allocation to the participants in either direction.
167. *Code of Conduct for Liner Conferences*, Vol. 1 and II, UNCTAD, 1975.
168. Note that the *USSR–US Agreement* calls for 33–33–33 split while the *Brazil–US Agreements* call for 50–50.
169. Sager, K. H., 'The UNCTAD Code and its consequences', *Norwegian News*, Vol. 9, 1966, pp. 18–20.
170. Laing, E. T., 'The rationality on conference pricing and output policies, Part II', Marit Stu. Man., Vol. 3, 1976, pp. 141–52.
171. GATT, Geneva, *International Trade* (annual).
172. Clearly, F. F., 'The future of sea lines companies', *2nd International Maritime and Technology Conference* Papers 76, Vol. 2, pp. 1–16.
173. Zerby, J. A., 'On the practicality of the UNCTAD 40–40–20 Code for Liner Conferences', Marit Pol. Man., Vol. 6, No. 4, 1979, pp. 241–52.
174. Cf. Harbridge House Inc., *US Merchant Marine in National Perspectives* D.C. Heath, Lexington, MA, 1979.
175. *Ibid., The International Conference System*, Report for US Dept. of Commerce (Doc.) 609.
176. Ramsy, R. A., 'The world trade versus the supply of shipping and ships', *Marine Policy*, Vol. 5, No. 1, Jan. 1980, p. 62.
177. Tresselt, D., *The Controversy Over the Division of Labour in International Seaborne Transport*, Bergen, p. 6.
178. UNCTAD Doc. No. E/Con. 46/C.3/5, 1964.
179. Corden W. M., *The Theory of Protection*. Oxford, 1971, Chap. 9.
180. Corden, *Trade Policy and Economic Welfare*, Oxford, 1974, Chap. 8.
181. UNCTAD Doc. No. TD/103, 1971.
182. UNCTAD Doc. No. TD/111/C.4/1.14.
183. Turvey R., 'A simple analysis of optimal fares on scheduled transport services', *The Economic Journal*, March 1975.
184. UNGA Resolution A/Res. 3201 (S-VI), 1 May 1974.
185. UNCTAD Doc. No. UNCTAD/Ship/127 p. 23, 23 Oct. 1978.
186. UNCTAD Doc. Sales No. E. 69. 11.D.1.
187. Valente, M. G., 'Shipping and developing countries', *International Conciliation*, March 1971, No. 582.
188. *Protection of Shippers' Interests*, 1978, UN, N.Y., E.78.11.D.7.
189. *Promotion Freight Rates on Non-traditional Exports of Developing Countries*, UN Doc. TD/105, corr. 11.
190. UNCTAD Secretariat, Report by, *The Nature and Extent of Cargo Reservation*, 170.
191. *Ibid*.
192. UNCTAD Secretariat, Report by, *Balance of Payments Aspects of Cargo Liner Freights and Expenditures*, 1964.

193. *Ibid.*
194. UNCTAD Secretariat, Report by, *Implementation of International Development Strategy in Shipping and Ports*, 1971.
195. *Ibid.*
196. Cf. UNCTAD Secretariat, Report by, *Development of Merchant Marines* (resolutions adopted at UNCTAD III), Santiago de Chile.
197. *Ibid.*
198. See also UNCTAD Secretariat, Report by, *Merchant Fleet Development*, 23 Oct. 1978.
199. *Ibid.*
200. Cf. *The Programme of Action on the Establishment of a New International Economic Order*, UN General Assembly, 1974.
201. *Ibid*; resolutions adopted by the UN General Assembly, 1 May 1974, A/Res. 320 (S-VI).
203. UNCTAD Secretariat, Report by, *Merchant Fleet Development*, 1978, UN, NY.
204. But see particularly UNCTAD Secretariat, Report by, *Establishment or Expansion of Merchant Marines in Developing Countries*, UN Pub. Sales, No. E.69.11.D.1.

CHAPTER 4

Flag discrimination as a method of establishing national fleets

1. Introduction

Flag discrimination is a development from flag preference; it is a less liberal mechanism designed to strengthen development and protective measures. In many respects it has all the characteristics of flag preference, being its continuation and having the experience of flag preference behind it. Discrimination is a noun derived from the verb to 'discriminate', meaning: ' To note the difference of or between: to select from others: treat differently because of prejudice'.[1]

Flag discrimination has its roots in the US, where, with reference to common carriers, especially railroads, it involves a breach of the carrier's duty to treat all shippers alike, and afford them equal opportunity to market their products. Although originating as an interstate and non-discriminatory concept of a carrier's failure to treat all alike under similar conditions, flag discrimination was developed in the US and used as a protective and expansionist device directed against foreign flags in export and import trade.[2]

Thus, in merchant marine terms, discrimination and the criteria of flag discrimination were outlined in the preceding chapter and will be developed more fully in the succeeding chapters. As noted earlier, no suitable definition as yet exists for this term, except that it is a generic term for a series of activities directed mainly at a foreign flag with regard to access to cargoes, ports or services with the objective of making it less competitive.[3] Therefore, for the purposes of this discussion, the actions in question may be described and explained thus:

> 'Flag Discrimination is a measure employed by a state which interferes with international maritime transport and provides less favourable treatment for other flags than for the national flag.'[4]

Though sometimes mistaken for, and used interchangeably with, flag preference, flag discrimination can frequently be distinguished. Whereas there is an element of discrimination in flag preference, flag discrimination covers a wider area than flag preference which, in most cases, is a restrictive discrimination regarding cargoes. It will be apparent from the examples in both cases that flag preference is more common and, probably, more tolerated than flag discrimination.[5] The varied categories of flag discrimination practices can be grouped under four major headings thus:

(a) *Type 1: Port surcharges*
  (i) Berth and port discrimination
  (ii) Fees and surcharges
(b) *Type 2: Scheduled cargoes*
  (i) Itemised cargoes
  (ii) Energy transportation
  (iii) Defence transportation
  (iv) Government supplies
(c) *Type 3: Essential trade routes and others*
(d) *Type 4: CIF/FOB and miscellaneous discriminations*

However, these are only broad categories and the list is by no means complete.[6] In addition, some of these categories might overlap with examples listed under flag preference and state intervention, respectively. For example, scheduled cargoes have many characteristics in common with state-financed cargoes. Although there are also many basic differences, the two concepts share the same principles and objectives, namely: first, to protect national fleets from external competition, and, secondly, to aid their development or expansion. This is probably true despite the occasional denial by the practising countries that this is not the case.[7] Indeed, in an elaborate questionnaire sent to all maritime nations, by the UNCTAD Secretariat requesting them to list the types of flag discrimination, flag preference, maritime subsides and state intervention practised by them, very few, if any, bothered to reply. And even the few who did reply largely denied imposing any restrictions in favour of their national flags against foreign flags.[8]

2. Port surcharges and discriminatory fees

The point of contact between a nation and the outside world regarding international commercial exchanges is at international airports and seaports.[9] Such intercourse communication can also take place at road and rail border posts. Discrimination is therefore bound to occur at any of the latter three points, since only an insignificant amount of trade is airlifted. We shall concern ourselves with seaports, since the concept of flag is more associated with ships and aircraft than railroads or road transport.

2.1 Port discrimination

From a purely commercial point of view this is perhaps the least subtle and, probably most obvious flag discrimination; not to mention that it is probably one of the most unfair and least tolerated. In many ways this discrimination is related to the subsequent example of discriminatory fees. However, as in all other restrictive shipping practices, the idea behind port and berth discrimination is, in many ways, to give preference to national carriers and at the same time discriminate against foreign flag vessels so that it has double effect.[10] The first instance is the treatment of ships in port. This practice can take the form of hindering the activities of the ships of countries one wishes to place in a worse position than the ships of one's own country. As such it sometimes happens that the handling of the said ships in the port is deliberately delayed in their unloading and loading, for instance.[11] Through these delays the affected ships are prevented from obtaining freight incomes as a consequence of *demurrage* and other surcharges. It is also known for a country to have higher tariffs for foreign ships and lower (or none at all) for their own flag-vessels.[12]

The same discriminatory principles are repeated as regards access to berths, so that permission to berth is not granted on a first-come-first-served basis as would normally be the case. A domestic liner that comes in later would have a berth clearance before a foreign flag-vessel which might have arrived much earlier.[13] Or indeed, a certain sector of modern, well-equipped and efficient berths may be reserved for domestic vessels only, with foreign flag-vessels being directed to wait or to proceed to outmoded, less sheltered and probably inefficient ports or berths at some distance away.[14] We have seen that where the ports are not seaports, but inland river ports, cabotage restrictions could be another argument for discriminating against foreign flags. Consequently, in terms of giving the home flags an unfair lead or economic advantage, port and/or berth flag discrimination may be totally unjustified.[15] Especially where it ranges from allocating cargo, 'to national flags first', to all sorts of absurd practices.

However, besides the justification of having to ensure some trade for the national flag, one can see other advantages accruing to the interests of ocean-borne commerce from port regulations and planning which may often be labelled flag discrimination. In case of port congestion, there is good reason to want to re-route other vessels to other berths or even other ports. This is more so as regards lucrative ports and/or central-popular berths.[16] Unfortunately, the vessels re-routed may happen to be mainly foreign flags. Another reason could be that the particular port is government-controlled, for example, where government supplies (post) and, at times, urgently required emergency relief cargo is loaded and unloaded. Such discrimination might be unpopular but should be understandable. Moreover, it is not entirely without precedent in other forms of transportation, for example, air transport.[17] Just as the national airlines might enjoy priority at national airports where the national headquarters are located, it may be only fair that similar treatment is accorded or extended to national merchant marine vessels in national seaports, a place they should, after all, regard as home.[18]

Not all port discrimination is practised for commercial reasons or with the aim of protecting and expanding national merchant fleets. There are those which function merely in support of a principle. For example, most, if not all, socialist countries do not allow flags of convenience into their ports as a policy which constitutes their contribution to the UNCTAD efforts to discourage and eventually phase out open registry.[19] That would, no doubt, form a valid rationale, in some circles, for port discrimination. Yet other forms of flag discrimination may result from a country's commitment to fulfil an international obligation. As in the case of sanctions' discrimination, mentioned earlier, in aid of UN embargoes, certain countries discriminate against South African or Israeli flag-vessels by total exclusion from their sea ports, or air ports and air space in case of aircrafts.[20] Beyond isolating this as a form of flag discrimination, its merits and demerits are beyond our scope to question.

We have also consistently maintained the defence and security aspects of flag discrimination. The full impact and examples of this will be dealt with later.[21] Suffice it to say, at this stage, however, that some ports with, or near naval, military or other similar installations vital to a country's national interest may be completely out of bounds, as against foreign flags and what would normally be regarded as hostile or not-too-friendly states. The reasons behind policy may be economic as well as security, i.e., fear of espionage and sabotage.[22] This is particularly so if the same principles are applied to berths or ports within proximity of economic and research installations, for example, oil terminals or rigs, space research stations and other offshore activities. This is particularly common in the TMNS. This discussion confirms our argument that flag discriminination arises partly from states' mistrust of each other as well as in the belief that restrictions can be used for advancing economic, political and security objectives.[23]

Another example of this kind of discrimination is expenditure that particularly affects foreign vessels and cargo carried by foreign vessels – commonly known as discriminatory fees and surcharges.

2.2 Discriminatory fees and surcharges

The object of this kind of flag discrimination is to institute some kind of resource transfer from foreign vessels to the home governments, which resources would hopefully be re-deployed in the establishment, development and expansion of national fleets, with some part being applied to improve the domestic port systems and other maritime-related infrastructures. But it is an abhorrent type of resource transfer, being mandatorily applied.[24] The other objection to this taxation-type transfer is that it is penal. The first category, therefore, involves tonnage measurement, where the fleets of different countries are classified in different ways, by means of which discrimination is exercised. Fees based on such classifications are also varied, to the benefit of the fleet of the home country.[25] The second category is discrimination relating to consular fees which affect the ships of different nations to different degrees. Such measures can be of significance when the consular fees are very high. For instance, the charges for small quantities of cargo can be almost as high as the freight itself.[26] Thirdly, there are discriminations in charging pilot fees which points to the hardships and extra costs to foreign flag vessels.[27]

Then there are taxes on the freight incomes of foreign shipping companies. On the one hand, expenditure that affects cargo carried by foreign vessels is more of an inland or internal measure. On the other hand, there is discrimination with respect to railway tariff rates, whereby goods that have been brought into the country by the country's own ships are allowed lower railway freight rates.[28] Paradoxically, the freights of the home-flag vessels can, as a consequence, be charged at a higher rate than those of the foreign flag vessels – *higher* (not lower), in order to make it lucrative for the internal railway system to pick up first.[29] Then there is discrimination concerning duties, whereby cargoes which arrive by ships of foreign countries are taxed with a higher duty, which is discriminatory against foreign shipping companies.[30]

The list is endless. Among the few advantages of this type of flag discrimination is that it enhances the competitiveness of the home flag and raises revenue which in some cases may be badly needed. As to whether a significant amount can be raised to be ploughed back into port investments is another matter.[31] Apart from being penal there is the danger that foreign flags could be driven away by prohibitive charges thereby defeating the whole purpose of the scheme. O'Loughlin noted correctly that:

> 'In practice there have been cases of these taxes being so penal as to constitute virtual prohibition of the foreign flag vessel.'[32]

The other point worth noting is that such taxes are always passed onto the customers, thereby making the goods, passing through a discriminating port, very expensive. There is also the question whether ports ought to be making excessive profits, or any at all, as opposed to providing a service and only charging enough to cover their operational costs.[33] One would tend to agree with the *Rochdale Report* that:

> 'In principle, we consider that the charge payable should be related to the length of time for which a ship uses the port facilities and the nature of the facilities required. In this way the charges paid by a ship using them would be related to the costs incurred by the port. authority in providing them. . .'[34]

and that these proposals are consistent with the policy, for the long term, set out in paragraph 18 of the White Paper, Nationalised Industries, *A Review of Economic and Financial Objectives*, which states that:

> '. . . pricing policies should be devised with reference to the costs of the particular goods and services provided. . . The aim of pricing policy should be that the consumer should pay the true costs of providing the goods and services he consumes, in every case where these can be sensibly identified.'[35]

Where surcharges are not the criteria, scheduled cargoes may be the yardstick for flag discriminations.

3. Scheduled cargoes

Flag discrimination implies that a country's national flag has to carry most, if not all, of the export and import cargoes generated by that country's international trade.[36] Nowhere is this better illustrated than in relation to that cargo which the country is best able to produce, by virtue of the law of comparative advantage, or which that country considers to be of vital priority and in the national interest.[37] It is presumed that in most cases such cargoes, if artificially directed to the home flag, would alone manage to sustain a viable national fleet. These fall under four major headings. The first is itemised or designated cargoes.

3.1 Itemised or designated cargoes

Known alternatively as essential commodities, this discriminatory scheme is used to exclude foreign merchant marines altogether from certain selected cargoes. The scheme refers to both exports and imports.[38] Briefly, there are certain cargoes that are of crucial or strategic importance to particular nations for various reasons, with the result that such cargoes are recommended to be carried only, or as much as possible, in national flag vessels. They could comprise a particular country's major exports and, therefore, the largest foreign exchange earner; this would be the case especially with a single-crop country.[39] Such a country would wish freight from its transportation to go to the national flag. As in the case of Japan, the scheme could be directed specifically at less bulky, but high-valued freight, especially compact computers, HiFis and other valuable electronic, or communications equipment.[40]

But a classic example of the use of scheduled cargo discrimination as a means of developing a country's national fleet is when a country wishes to diversify its fleet by developing a particular type of vessel regarded as crucial but not already forming part of its fleet.[41] The argument normally advanced by the country concerned is that necessity is the mother of invention. Demand generates supply: make the cargo scheduled and you will obtain the type of vessel that carries it.[42] It is conceivable that this is how modern prestigious ships such as RO/ROS, LASH, LNG's, OBO's, supertankers, etc., were acquired in the first place by the flags who own them.[43] Spain, presumably for this reason, restricts many scheduled imports, such as petroleum, tobacco, cotton, etc., to national vessels through state monopolies.[44] But the absurd way in which such a development objective can be stubbornly pursued, regardless of any notions of sound economic principle, is well illustrated by the American case.

It will be remembered how the experience of the Pacific Coast Apple Industry illustrated this callous disregard of commercial considerations, and the administrative rigidity that has characterised the requirement for the US to diversify her fleet by the use of scheduled cargo processes.[45] The case in point arose when the required refrigerator tonnage off the West Coast for sales to Europe was virtually non-existant in 1952–53 even though there was a 'reefer' tonnage available on the East Coast.[46] The FMB insisted on a protracted delay until a refrigerator was built, and refused application for waiver under the 50–50 cargo preference provision which, *inter alia*, could have meant using the already available reefer tonnage lying idle on the East Coast.[47] Thus, despite these difficulties, the importance of the time involved and the fact that the Government would have suffered no loss (these being surplus agricultural commodities and relief shipments), the Department of Agriculture persisted in applying the *Cargo Preference Act, 1954*,[48] to the letter on a commodity by commodity basis.

So the apple sellers could not rely on the possibility of commodity waivers as these would be offset in shipments of some other commodity. The December, Christmas 1954 trade with Britain, for example, was lost as a result, even though there was never any question that the waiver would have been in order. The same situation held for the sales of surplus fresh fruits products as well as animal products.[49] The FMB might have ended with a diversified merchant marine, with the addition of the refrigerated vessels, but with no cargo to carry that year since the crop was lost. About thirty years later the development argument was still fanatically being pursued by the Americans, this time in the form of energy transportation.

3.2 Energy transportation

This time the use of flag discrimination for development purposes manifested itself in the controversial *Energy Transportation Security Act of* 1974[50] which requires a minimum of 20% cargo reservation for American flag vessels.[51] But at its initial stages the bill surmounted stiff opposition in both Houses, to get its development provisions accepted. President Ford at first vetoed it, stating that the development requirements would have had an adverse impact on foreign relations, and would have created serious inflationary pressures by increasing oil costs.[52] However, because of the consequences of the Arab-Israeli war (which the bill was out to remedy in the first place) and intense lobbying[53] it was eventually passed by Congress on the basis of:

(i) National security;
(ii) Recent administrative action Supportive of flag discrimination: and
(iii) Increased domination of foreign trade by flag-fleets of foreign states.[54]

To emphasize further the security reasons for the use of flag discrimination it was asserted that the US must be able to supply its armed forces and domestic consumers with fuel and supplies in times of crisis. It was pointed out by the pro-development lobby group that at that time there was a reliance upon large numbers of tankers and ships which sailed under foreign flags,[55] but which were owned by US citizens or corporations. Such vessels were subject to requisitioning by the Secretary of Commerce:

> 'whenever the President shall proclaim that the security of the national defence makes it advisable, or during any national emergency declared by proclamation of the President.'[56]

The use of flag discrimination for development purposes seems to grow from strength to strength whenever the merchant marine industry finds itself playing a leading role in national defence. For instance, in the American case an incident that added urgency and necessity to the energy transportation flag discrimination concerned the Arab-Israeli war.[56A] Despite the fact that the PANLIBHO fleets are entitled to US war-risk insurance in return for being US 'effective control fleets', the Liberian restrictions on the use of these vessels, by the US for military purposes, questioned the legal basis of the US requisition claim in the event of the flag state opposition. And reports, at the time, that oil shipments to US armed forces were withheld by oil companies during the 1973 Arab-Israeli war,[57] alarmed the Americans and encouraged the initiation of this legislation.

For this reason, Representative Frank Clark, reflecting the position of many of the bill's supporters argued that:

> 'Today we are engaged in a worldwide conflict for oil. For the good of our country, we must never forget that in this conflict foreign flag tankers are manned by mercenaries. . .'[58]

Thus, in this context energy transportation flag discrimination had economic as well as defence and security elements. No doubt, after the crucial role that the merchant navy has played in the Falklands crisis, the Development School, on both sides of the Atlantic, will be in greater ascendency regarding both energy transportation and the defence transportation itself.

3.3 Defence and security transportation

Defence and national security, in addition to politics and economics, are fast emerging as the major motives for flag discrimination and flag preference.[59]

Supposedly for fear of espionage and sabotage, various countries are keen not to allow what they schedule as security shipments to fall into enemy hands through the use of foreign and, often unfriendly flag-vessels. For this purpose, defence and security means and includes, shipments for a country's own or for allied defence (as, for example, in the NATO and Warsaw Pact), and shipments of defence aid to other friendly countries.[60] Although this type of cargo could be airlifted (where urgently required) or shipped in existing normal vessels, including those belonging to allies and other friendly nations, countries have often ignored these alternatives and insisted on establishing and/or developing their national merchant fleets for the purpose.[61] The argument being that it would be very unwise to entrust supplies for immediate combat use to foreigners. And this argument includes not only the cargoes in question but encompasses a wider jurisprudential meaning, as well as for the military itself, military intelligence, political, diplomatic, economic and almost all confidential and top security shipments.[62]

To get an idea of what this means, a few examples can be given, especially from the TMNS. In Portugal, for instance, without prejudice to bilateral agreements, all Portuguese cargoes shipped to the military or scientific research bases existing or to be established in Portuguese territory are to be carried exclusively in the national bottoms.[63] However, the most noteworthy example of this flag discrimination comes from the US. It will be recalled that the first cargo preference statute of that country provided that ocean transportation for the Army, Navy coal, fodder supplies and provisions must be carried on US flag vessels.[64] This statute is still operative, though in an amended form.[65] Secondly, exclusive use of US flag vessels is required for shipments owned by the government and in possession of the Military Department, and which are intended for the use of the military department – whatever all that elaboration means.[66]

The discrimination extends beyond the usual exclusion coverage, for instance, with respect to:

> 'Supplies for the use of the United States which are contracted for and require subsequent delivery to a military department but are not owned by the government at the time of shipment. . .'[67]

Private US vessels (if available at fair and reasonable rates) must be employed to transport at least 50% of the aggregate gross tonnage per annum, computed separately for dry bulk carriers, dry cargo liners and tankers.[68] There are no statistics available to show that this type of flag discrimination has aided the expansion of the US flag fleets despite the fact that since 1904 these items have included enormous shipments of coal, provisions, fodder or supplies.[69]

This is the case despite the fact that the list has been lengthened to include federal officers and employee travel,[70] as well as transportation of effects and automobiles.[71] At the other end of the spectrum, in the DMNS, a random example is provided by the Phillipine practice. Inevitably, however, this is all tied in with the American example. The Phillipines[72], like most of the other ASEAN members with a mutual defence pact with the US through SEATO, is another of these security-conscious nations. For example, all imports of US agricultural commodities under S. 402, of the US Government's *Mutual Defence Security Act (Public Law no. 480)*[73] which are in excess of the 50% required to be carried on US flag vessels, must be shipped in Phillipine flag vessels when available. One can understand the advantage of a nation having a merchant marine capable of coping with wars, hostilities and emergencies; but its economic opportunity cost must be enormous.[74]

One must be aware that wars are not fought all the time and that there is the danger of establishing and expanding a large war-footing merchant navy which would be expensive to maintain but idle most of the time.[75] This is so because such a merchant navy would have to be larger than was necessary for the trade requirements of a nation at any given time. Even if that were not the case, as the Falklands crisis has shown, its application to defence seriously interrupts the normal economic activities of a merchant navy.[76] On the other hand, rather than have an economically useless standing naval reserve, disruption of economic life is the price the community would have to pay, whenever the merchant marine is diverted to fight wars. One problem that remains, however, is the difficulty of distinguishing defence and security shipments from purely government shipments.[77]

3.4 Government supplies

We should note that government supplies are not necessarily the same as the state-financed cargoes discussed above.[78] Although there is a great deal of similarity between the two,[79] government supplies should be understood to mean supplies intended for use by the central government and its departments, including the public sector.[80] Alternatively known as government-controlled cargoes, they are mainly imports intended for government use or exports intended for diplomatic and consular use.[81] In this latter aspect, they include vehicles, stationery, diplomatic bags, provisions and even food rations. Government supplies would not normally include military hardware and provisions – these would belong to the categories of defence and security – but modern requirements imply that the bulk of government supplies is based on military considerations.[82]

Another factor that adds importance to this scheme of flag discrimination is that currently there are so many foreign troops from the powerful nations stationed abroad, normally in the less developed and deprived world, that enormous shipments are continuously being made from home ports to support them and their dependants.[83] Among the TMNS, only one other example, apart from the US, is worth mentioning. We mentioned earlier that in Portugal, all cargoes shipped by the public sector entities must be carried in Portuguese flag vessels or foreign flag ships chartered by Portuguese shipowners, except in the case of reciprocal or international agreements providing for other arrangements.[84] Up to 50% of such cargoes can be carried on ships of the importing or exporting country, if the laws of that country concede equal treatment for Portuguese flag vessels.

However, as indicated above, by far the most outstanding illustration remains that of the US. In addition to examples given above, supplies for research purposes (e.g., space programmes or for outposts in the Arctic and the Antarctic) and to those countries heavily dependant on US foreign aid fall under this category.[85] Undoubtedly, the Department of Defense is the largest shipper of government supplies and, further, categorises its supplies into two main types for purposes of flag discrimination: government-owned supplies in its possession or that of a contractor; and government supplies, including those for foreign aid, contracted for but not owned by the government at the time of the shipment.[86] For instance, supplies of the first category, when for the use of the military departments, are subject to the 100% American flag preference, unless American flag vessels are not available at fair and reasonable rates. Both the motives for and the sophistication of the application of modern flag discrimination is further provided by this American illustration.[87] For instance, enforcement of the Defence Department regulations with respect to flag discrimination, is ensured by requiring insertion of one of three clauses in any contract which may involve ocean transportation.[88] First, if the contract involves government-owned property in possession of the contractor or any contract under which title to property may pass to the government prior to shipment – a clause is inserted in the contract requiring the shipment only as directed by the contracting officer who is guided by the regulations and applicable departmental procedures.[89] The shipment must be made only by American flag vessels in the circumstances discussed above.[89A] Secondly, when the supplies are contracted for, but not government-owned at the time of shipment, a clause is inserted in the contract allowing the contractor to choose his own method of transportation, but requiring him to furnish to the contracting officer one copy of the applicable ocean shipping documents indicating for each shipment under the contract the name and the nationality of the vessel and the measurement tonnage shipped on such a vessel.[90] Thirdly, the defence regulations also provide that additional provisions concerning vessels to be used may be inserted in accordance with departmental procedures.[91] Accordingly, Navy procurements directives permit additional provisions allowing the contracting officer to determine, where possible, in large shipments, when and how compliance with the 50% requirement is to be achieved.[92] However, none of these Defence Department regulations applies to shipments of classified supplies where the classification prohibits the use of non-governmental vessels.[93] Furthermore, the use of government vessels in encouraged to meet essential military requirements involving special transportation services which cannot be performed by the privately owned and operated merchant fleet; such a category may include peacetime troop transport which was taken over by private American shipowners.[94]

As regards flag discrimination of government supplies' in the DMNS, one example that immediately comes to mind is that of Ecuador.[95] In this latter case all imports and exports which are the property of the government or its enterprises, or of public entities or private institutions which are intended for social or public purposes, as well as cargo belonging to mixed companies in which the government owns more than 50% of the capital, are obliged to be transported in vessels owned by national shipping companies or by those which cargo reservation laws consider as such. However, 59% of the cargo may be transported on vessels belonging to the importing or exporting country provided this is done on the basis of reciprocity.[96] There is not much emphasis on defence-related cargoes in the DMNS as regards government supplies. However, in modern times the distinction between government supplies and defence shipments may be very thin indeed or even non-existent.[97]

The merits of state supplies as a motive for flag discrimination cannot be over-emphasized. Security compels states to restrict defence shipments to their own national flags or to those of military allies.[98] However, this kind of flag discrimination is practised more for policy than development reasons. Even if it were for the latter reasons these cargoes normally constitute a very small proportion of any country's shipments. Not only are they insignificant, therefore, but they are also normally referred to as non-commercial cargoes.[99] They are only available for ordinary private merchant vessels where military or government-owned vessels are unavailable. Figures are not available to indicate the extent to which this type of flag discrimination might have contributed towards the expansion of the merchant marines of those countries that practice it.[100] A mechanism most likely to influence such expansion is essential routes' flag discriminations.

4. Essential trade routes' discriminations

As in most, of the other forms of discrimination, the essential trade routes' doctrine has its origins in American jurisprudence. Resorted to for both policy and development motives, there appear to be two categories of essential trade routes; those that are not commercially viable and, therefore, need subsidies and the protective measures of flag discrimination, and those that are both not commercially viable or geo-politically strategic.[101] The strategic importance of the latter militates their being set aside, exclusively, for the domestic flags. To the former category belong sea routes leading to remote and normally underdeveloped regions within the country itself, the neglect of which may lead to the stagnation or lagging behind of the affected districts.[102] These routes are normally commercially unprofitable but politics dictate their maintenance nevertheless.

In the first place, these routes are declared designated or simply essential routes.[103] Secondly, services to these areas are maintained or only made possible through maritime transportation subsidies. The next step is that the said routes become sheltered from competition through flag discrimination and other preferential means. In the case of the United Kingdom such essential trade routes may be those serving the outlying islands, like the Shetlands and the Hebrides in the North of Scotland.[104] In the case of the DMNS, such as the archipelagic countries of South-East Asia, the routes may be to one of the deprived islands.[105] The second category normally consists of militarily strategic and/or economically lucrative routes, such as the North Atlantic serving North America and Western Europe. It carries the largest volume of trade linking the world's most industrialised regions. And from the security point of view it is the mainstay of NATO.

Since the doctrine is essentially an American creation, and although many other countries have since adopted the practice in designating their own essential trade routes, it is, nonetheless, to the US that we shall turn for the definition, descriptions, principles and motives involved.[106] It will be remembered that there are links with the condition attached to the recipients of foreign aid. For example, to qualify for maritime subsidy (post), shipping companies must, *inter alia*, operate vessels on what are designated as essential trade routes. But what exactly are essential trade routes? MARAD has defined an essential trade route as:

'A route between ports of the United States coast area or areas to foreign markets which has been determined by the Maritime Administration to be essential for the *promotion, development, expansion*, and maintenance of the foreign commerce of the United States.'[107]

(Emphasis added to indicate the development element of the flag discrimination.)

Thirty-one essential trade routes had been designated, by 1952, on the basis of considerations involving economic, geopolitic, national defence and steamship economics. Emphasizing its economic role, the *Murray Report*, for instance declared that:

'The essential trade route concept is sound and has contributed to the economic stability of the liner segment of our merchant fleet in the foreign trades. However, constant scrutiny of all trades should be given in order to ensure that the granting of subsidy aid is in keeping with the traffic needs of essential trade routes.'[108]

The link between maritime subsidies and flag discriminations and the policy issues involved in both perhaps comes out most clearly in the operation of essential trade routes.

Operating differential subsidies, for instance, are granted only to companies that schedule sailings on one or more of the then 31 essential trade routes of the US. It may be interesting to note that those routes were designated essential by the FMC on May 20, 1946, and were found to be, in the words of the *Merchant Marine Act*, 1936, also:

'essential for the promotion, development, expansion and maintenance of the foreign commerce of the United States.'[109]

Further, under Section 211 of the Act, the FMC was instructed to:

'give due weight to the cost of maintaining each of such steam ship lines on essential trade routes, the probability that any such line cannot be maintained except at heavy losses disproportionate to the benefit accruing to foreign trade, the number of sailings and types of vessels that should be employed in such lines and any other facts and conditions that a prudent businessman would consider when dealing with his own business, with the added consideration, however, of the *intangible* benefits the maintenance of any such line may afford to the foreign commerce of the United States and to the national defence.'[110]

The proponents of maritime subsidies and flag discriminations have always justified them on the grounds that they have been recognised by this piece of legislation. For instance, in reviewing the essential trade routes, as early as 1953, the FMC noted that:

'present day influences in the world are different from those influences which exerted force in 1936 when the initial concepts regarding trade routes existed.'[111]

It then continued:

'As a result of recent world events other factors. . . must be considered, for the reason that their influence is, of increased importance to the national welfare of the United States.'[111a]

Therein lie the origins, purposes, characteristics, and importance of flag discriminations and maritime subsidies, in general, and the essential trade route doctrine in particular, seen, at least, from the US point of view. As mentioned above, MARAD also listed four basic areas of consideration as paramount in the determination of essential trade routes. Under the first category of *economics*, the factors considered in designating and operating a subsidized essential trade route, by and large, underline the said objectives. These are:

(1) Comparison of the trade area with total trade as to exports, imports, dollar balance exchange, and post-war and pre-war trends in these items;
(2) The significance of the trade to the economy of the US as measured by such factors as the importance of exports and imports to the US economy, the competition between American and foreign goods, and raw materials and resource potentials;
(3) Domestic industrial relocation and development as they are related to trade;
(4) Trade inhibitions – tariffs, currency restrictions, quantitative restrictions and licencing systems.[112]

These criteria are quite in line with the general purposes of the establishment and development of national merchant marines. This is a conclusive and self-explanatory list of these objectives. Neither is there anything unusual about the *geopolitical* factors, which include:

(1) Climate, geographical position and strategic position;
(2) Aid programme;
(3) United States and its defence;
(4) Political effects of US flag shipping on the routes;
(5) Influence of the trade route on so-called fringe nations;
(6) Development of trade and of trade possibilities because of political factors;
(7) The competitive position of the products of the changed political status of foreign areas.[113]

And, as expected, *military* considerations include such factors as:

(1) Direction of movement of military cargoes;
(2) Stock-piling activities; and
(3) The advantages of increased exports to areas near trade routes essential to the national defence.[114]

These objectives would seem to cover almost every other aspect of the national economy especially those pertaining to trade. And, finally, *steam ship economics* encompasses judgments about many matters, among them:

(1) Delimiting the trade areas to conform to economic ship-operating practices;
(2) The service requirements of the areas, and the characteristics of the vessels to be employed; and
(3) The type of foreign competition to be encountered.[115]

As in all the other aspects of the use of flag discrimination as a tool for development, it is not possible to determine with acceptable accuracy the effects of the policy of fixing essential trade routes upon the US or, indeed, any national merchant marine and its foreign competitors. MARAD will not release data that would reveal the percentage of cargoes carried by subsidized operators on each trade route for fear of competition and, probably, the figures would not be particularly encouraging. However, in 1952, liners of all flags lifted about 35 million long tons of dry cargo on essential trade routes of the US alone, with the US flag vessels managing only 35% of that. These do not appear to be encouraging statistics but then essential trade route flag discriminations had just come into operation. Although subsequent figures have not been available from which to appraise the scheme, at least for that year, subsidized liners were overwhelmingly important in carrying the US share of liner-lifted dry cargoes on *essential trade routes*.[116] It would appear that the US-flag vessels' share of dry-cargo tonnage on essential trade routes was far higher than on other unprotected routes though, again, the data do not permit the inference that the establishment of certain routes as essential has attracted US liners to them.

There may be indications that the designation of a trade route as essential, plus the presence of subsidized operators, does not necessarily lead to US shipping companies and, indeed, shipping companies of any other nations, gaining a large share of available dry cargoes so as to enable their expansion. It also appears that the mere designation of a route as essential by MARAD does not necessarily adversely affect foreign shipping lines.[117] Only indirectly does essential trade route designation affect foreigners or the discriminated flag. Non-subsidized American as well as foreign flags are also affected. Finally, the granting of operating differential subsidies only to the liner operators on *essential trade routes* leaves a substantial area of shipping open to private competition free from direct governmental assistance.[118] This seems to be the case whether the discriminating country is the TMN or DMN.

At the other end of the spectrum, an example of essential trade route flag discrimination from a DMN is that of the Republic of South Korea, which in many respects is almost identical with the US policy. In South Korea, too, the government may order any maritime transportation businessman receiving subsidy or loan, under applicable loan, to operate his ship on a specific dometic or international essential trade route for a fixed period.[119] Any loss from this service will be compensated in a manner prescribed by a Presidential Decree. When the ship concerned in the subsidized essential trade route is considered too old for the public interest, the government may order the substitution or improvement of the ship itself bearing the loss caused by such substitution or improvement. However, there is an element of internal flag discrimination as well.[120] Government substitution and improvement is not confined to operators on essential trade routes but the difference is that those related to essential trade routes take precedence over others in the domestic construction of ships. Likewise, when a maritime transportation businessman operates his ship on a regular international and/or essential trade route for the promotion of foreign trade and to earn foreign currency the government may subsidise any loss he sustains, as prescribed by the said Presidential Decree.[121]

South Korea is one of the emerging NICS with a good economic performance. She is also one of the many DMNS relying heavily on maritime subsidies and flag discrimination. She has had marked expansion in her foreign trade with corresponding expansion of her merchant marine and shipbuilding to match that trade boom. It is not clear how much of that establishment and expansion of her national merchant marine is attributable to maritime subsidies and flag discrimination, generally, and essential trade routes designation in particular.[122] Despite this, most other DMNS, who are not also NICS, have not had similar expansion in their merchant marines, despite heavy dependence on maritime subsidies and flag discrimination. Although Korea's expansion in the maritime sector can be linked directly to her better overall economic performance, yet there might be some correlation between the flag discrimination, trade performance and expansion of the merchant marine sector.[123] It could be the case of the flag following trade rather than vice versa.

5. CIF, FOB and miscellaneous discriminations

There are many other flag discriminatory mechanisms operated by various countries in an effort to develop and expand their national merchant fleets. We are unable to discuss all of them for reasons of time and space. Even if that were not the case we do not think the said mechanisms would markedly aid the merchant marines to any significant level. One or two are, however, worth mentioning. The first of these are *CIF shipments*. The letters CIF when used in a mercantile agreement for the sale of goods involving shipment, denote that the sum named in the agreement includes the cost of the goods, insurance during the transit to the purchaser and freight: CIF (cost insurance freight) for short.[124] Under CIF contracts, therefore, the seller's duties are:

(1) To ship at the port of shipment, within the period specified in the contract, goods of the contract description;[125]
(2) To procure on shipment, a contract of affreightment under which the goods will be delivered to the destination contemplated by the contract;[126]
(3) To insure the goods on terms current in the trade so that the insurance will be available for the benefit of the buyer;[127]
(4) To make out an invoice of the goods;[128] and
(5) To tender to the buyer the bill of lading, the invoice and the policy of insurance.[129]

It is the duty of the buyer to take up the documents and pay for them, and this is so whether or not the goods arrive, for if they are lost he will have the benefit of insurance.[130] The *FOB contract*, on the other hand, means 'Free on Board.' Under an ordinary FOB contract the seller puts the goods safely on board,[131] pays the charges of doing so, and for the buyer's protection – but not under a mandate to do so except, only upon terms of a reasonable and ordinary bill of lading or other contract of carriage[132] – gives up possession of the documents to the ship. There is no further contractual liability on the seller as soon as he delivers the goods to the carrier; his obligations cease there and then as far as he is concerned. The buyer under an FOB contract cannot claim delivery of the goods before shipment.[133] So much for the purely legal position of the parties. The relevance of CIF and FOB shipments, regarding trade policies, lies especially in the way they affect the preferential and discriminatory status of various flag vessels in relation to access to cargoes and other related treatments.[134]

There are certain loopholes and mechanisms of the CIF and FOB contracts that have been exploited by national entities for discriminatory purposes. The disadvantage of the CIF, for instance, is that the consignor or seller has the right to choose the carrier and that could mean any carrier other than the flag carrier of the consignee's nationality or choice; where, therefore, flag discrimination exists in the consignor's country he would be duty bound to use his national carrier for such exports. Where discrimination exists it is probable that the consignee's country would have preferred otherwise; this in effect involves loss to the consignee's national flag vessels not only of the freights but also of insurance premiums and the consequential loss of the foreign currency that would be involved.[135] On the FOB contracts, however, the situation is reversed; it is the consignee or buyer who chooses the carrier, and the assumptions are that he would prefer or be compelled to choose his national carrier. That being the case freight and premiums will be earned by the consignee's national flag carrier and local insurance firms, respectively.[136]

In previous cases we saw how policy decisions interfere with or replace market forces. In this respect we see how policy decisions utilise the loopholes in the operation of market forces. In both cases, the sum total of the effects is that the choice and competition element is negated. There is an element of consideration in return for the consignor/consignee's undertaking to ship with the national flag.[137] It will be apparent in the second part of this inquiry that in return for subsidies, incentives, inducements and benefits, the consignors and consignees enter contracted undertakings with their governments to use domestic flags to make earnings and savings of foreign currency that would have been spent on foreign flags. It is assumed that national sentiment can also provide sufficient inducements to opt for the national flag.[138] We have had to discuss this at length not because it makes a large contribution to the expansion of national fleets, but because of the light it sheds upon the complex mechanism that now constitutes modern flag discrimination.

Another example of this type of flag discrimination is where it is stipulated that imported goods are to be quoted FOB after which currency is allotted with preference for cargoes shipped on the country's own keels, where a bilateral maritime agreement exists between the consignee and the consignor's countries.[139] Examples of this exist in the DMNS. In the Republic of Korea, for instance, the Government encourages the use of Korean flag vessels by awarding some government procurement contracts on an FOB, rather than a CIF basis, thereby enabling these ships to compete on a more equal basis with the established fleets of the TMNS.[140] The extent to which this policy is successful is indicated by the relatively large ratio of cargoes carried by its oceangoing merchant fleet. During 1975, for instance, South Korean vessels carried about 33% of Korean oceanborne foreign trade. Furthermore, it was expected that South Korean flag-vessels would be handling approximately 44% of the country's trade by 1978; that is an excellent ratio by any international standard, let alone by a DMN one.

Of course, the result could not entirely be attributed to the CIF/FOB policy, or indeed flag discrimination in general.[141] As noted above, the difficulty in making any inference is compounded by the fact that, South Korea being a NIC, its economy was expanding rapidly at the time. Nevertheless, it would be fairly safe to assume that the expansion of the South Korean merchant fleet is due, to a certain extent, to the operation of flag discrimination in general, and CIF/FOB mechanisms in particular.

Our final illustration is also from a DMN, another Far Eastern NIC nation, the Phillipines.[142] The *Phillipine Presidential Order No. 37*, provides that all purchases of Phillipino imports be made on an FOB basis; that all freight payments be made in pesos in the Phillipines; and that preference on the carriage of imports be given to Phillipine flag vessles. As in the case of South Korea, the Phillipine CIF/FOB policy also seems to have aided the expansion of the national merchant fleet.[143] Though the Phillipine record on this is not as impressive as that of her South Korean neighbour, it is nevertheless quite good. For example, largely due to the CIF/FOB policy, Phillipine flag vessels carried an average close to 22% of Phillipine foreign trade in 1970 (24.3% of imports and 19.4% of exports). Figures for 1978 onwards are not yet available, but on this basis they would be good, if not better than the South Korean ones.[144] That being the case, just as in the South Korean example, the Phillipine CIF/FOB policy would seem to have paid off.

Finally, there are the types of discrimination which may not have direct bearing on the developments of national fleets. One of these consists of *sanctions' discriminations*[145] which, though affected by a state, nonetheless support political and international obligations. The other type involves *discrimination by private individuals*[146] or private institutions (like conference discriminations) which might aid national shipping but are not actively encouraged by the state.[147]

6. Advantages and disadvantages of flag discrimination

As noted in the previous chapter, there may be some justification for flag discrimination. However, although it guarantees the national flag a monopoly, through artificial direction of cargoes, this advantage is only a short term solution and may not last long. The purely economic disadvantages of flag discriminations are the subject of the next part of this inquiry.[148] Here we shall concentrate on the legal consequences. The major problem is that of countervailing actions from the discriminated countries. For instance, the OECD countries pledged to continue to give special consideration to the problems created by flag discrimination by govenments; and will also keep a close watch on the situation resulting from the policy of creating or developing national merchant fleets without economic justification.[149]

6.1 The OECD counter measures

The OECD governments have continued to take action to resist the growth of these discriminatory practices and to show that they are contrary to the best interests of international trade. In particular, the Committee on Maritime Transport has welcomed the successful action taken by a number of the member countries to include a non-discriminatory shipping clause in trade agreements with other countries.[150] In view of the serious situation with which they have been faced some governments have been forced to consider the question of possible counter-measures to deal with flag discrimination. As will be evident, the government of the Federal Republic of Germany has in fact obtained powers which would enable restrictions to be imposed on the employment of ships belonging to countries which practice discrimination against German ships.[151]

In certain areas these threats did bear fruit. An event which was noted with pleasure by the OEEC Maritime Transport Committee in 1960 was the decision of the Government of Turkey to withdraw virtually the whole of the restrictions on the use of foreign shipping which had been in force for many years for reasons connected with the balance of payments.[152] Some European governments, which had no adequate legal powers to defend their shipowners against discrimination, had to examine the circumstances under which such legislation might be produced. In this connection, the Italian government passed a law in March 1963 which provided for the setting up of a Commission whose function it would be in certain circumstances to propose a system of control on the shipments of good in the ships of offending countries.[153]

These Italian powers are similar to those adopted by the Federal Republic of Germany in September 1961. Other countries simply widened the powers of their already existing measures against restrictions in international trade generally.[154] Finally, and inevitably, flag discrimination invited retaliation in return, which in itself became a type of flag discrimination as the discriminated tried to defend themselves. Alternatively known as countervailing actions, retaliatory flag discrimination is neither a flag preference nor is it intended to be such.[155]

6.2 Retaliatory flag discrimination

To retaliate is to hit back, and has the same meaning as to countervail:

> 'To counterbalance; to avail against with equal force or virtue; to compensate for or serve as an equivalent of or substitute for';[156]

hence *countervailing duty*, as it is termed in international trade. Unfortunately, international maritime trade is bound to experience this type of restrictive practice, as the discriminated against seek to balance the score. The characteristics, principles and objectives of retaliatory flag discrimination will become clearer in the examples discussed in detail below.[157]

In the Federal Republic of Germany (FRG), for instance, this type of flag discrimination is justified as *Measures Against Detrimental Shipping Policies of Foreign Countries*. To effect it the government can restrict the conclusion of freight contracts and charters between residents of countries which exclude West German flag vessels from free competition.[158] As regards freight contracts in liner services (general cargo with freight exceeding US$400 000), all such contracts concluded with carriers which are residents of, for instance, Brazil, Burma, Indonesia, Uruguay, Venezuela, etc, must be licenced by the Wasser and Schiffahorts Direcktionen-Bremen of Hamburg offices, which are acting on behalf of the West German Maritime Authority.[159]

The Japanese law on *Special Measures Against Unfavourable Treatment of Japanese Ocean-Going Ship Operators by Foreign Governments and Others*,[160] has the same application and effect as the German one, and entered into force on the 20th July, 1977. Under this piece of legislation, the Minister of Transport, when the interests of Japanese oceangoing ship operators are significantly harmed by unfavourable treatment by any foreign governments and others, may order, against the oceangoing ship operators of such countries, the restriction of or prohibition on port access, and loading or unloading of cargo in Japanese ports.[161] The penalties for non-observance are quite severe; anyone who acts against any such order, when prosecuted, is subject to penal servitude for a period not exceeding twelve months or a fine not exceeding 5 000 000 yen.

But before any restrictions are enforced the Minister for Transport must notify the oceangoing operators of the foreign country concerned that he may order any countermeasures unless the harmful situation ceases to exist within a period not shorter than six months.[162]

The retaliatory flag discrimination is almost exclusively the privilege of the TMNS aimed at the DMNS. The UK joined the race by enacting the *Protection of Trading Interests Act, 1980*,[163] the purpose of which is to provide protection for requirements, prohibitions and judgements imposed or given under the laws of the countries outside the UK, but affecting the trading or other interests of persons in the UK. The Act goes much further than the *Shipping Contracts and Commercial Documents Act, 1964*, which it repeals and replaces, and the *Merchant Shipping Act, 1974*, a modern English statute designed to reintroduce flag discrimination.[164] In introducing the 1980 Act in the House of Commons, the Secretary of State for Trade described its aims as:

> 'to reassert and reinforce the defences of the United Kingdom against attempts by other countries to enforce their economic and commercial policies unilaterally on us.'[165]

From the history of this legislation, as the Parliamentary debates shown, however, it is the United States against which the Act is primarily directed. It will be remembered that the object, *inter alia*, is to curb the purported extraterritoriality of US flag discrimination and cargo preference legislation.[166] This is a form of countervailing action.

6.3 Countervailing flag discrimination

Countervailing flag discrimination is linked to the formulation of general countervailing duties in international trade, i.e:

> 'An import tax levied on a commodity on which exporters have been paid a subsidy or an export bounty. The main purpose of countervailing duty is to offset the special advantage of subsidized exports, placing them on an equal footing with imports and with domestic products. The amount of the countervailing duty usually equals the amount of the subsidy. The use of the countervailing duty is a method of counteracting subsidized dumping operations by foreign countries.'[167]

Naturally, the US itself could hardly be kept out of the countervailing flag discrimination scene. Here again the US has assumed the leading role with a variation on the big stick policy.[168] The US means of combating flag discrimination in international shipping has had a varied history. Initially, relief from alleged discrimination against US flag vessels is sought through diplomatic negotiations. If the discriminating government participates in the EXIMBANK credits, however, general waivers of *Public Resolution No. 17* may be denied pending restoration of parity of treatment to US flag vessels.[169] Failing solution at the conference table, and if the denial of *Public Resolution No. 17* waivers has no remedial effect, the US, through the FMC, may resort to powers granted by Section 19(1)(b) of the *Merchant Marine Act, 1920.*[170]

The FMC and its predecessors have issued regulations pursuant to the Statute only twice since the date of its enactment. In 1960, for instance, the then FMB (now FMC) first adopted general regulations dealing with foreign governments' discrimination against US flag vessels.[171] To the extent that discriminatory fees and charges are imposed on US flag vessels by a foreign government, the US will impose offsetting fees and charges on the vessels favoured by the discriminating foreign government. Also if other discriminatory practices exist against US flag vessels, appropriate offsetting regulations will be imposed.[172] As one of the results of the 1964 shake-up catalyzed by the then-Senator Paul Douglas and the Joint Economic Committee, the FMC did promise to play an active role in ferreting out and eliminating foreign discriminations against US flag vessels.

It would appear that the FMC's new-found boldness derives from years of congressional investigations and criticisms that concluded that the FMC's predecessors had not discharged their statutory responsibilities.[173] This explains why the new FMC is trying very hard to remove this stigma and is assuming a militant pose for the benefit of its critics at the expense of criticism from this side of the Atlantic. A detailed statement approved by the FMC on 9th March, 1964 announced the establishment of an Office of Internal Affairs charged with keeping an eye on foreign flag discrimination[174] that might call for remedial action pursuant to Section 19(1) of the *Merchant Marine Act, 1920*. But it would appear that as a practical matter, no action has or is likely to be taken under Section 19(1)(b) in response to discrimination unless the FMC receives a complaint from an American flag carrier.[175]

Singled out as the most harmful types of flag discrimination are those which artificially direct changes to national flag carriers and prevent US flag carriers from fully participating in the carriage of goods[176] – a somewhat paradoxical statement since the effect of the US cargo preference law is to artificially divert cargoes to US national flag carriers and to prevent non-US flag carriers from fully participating in the carriage of the diverted cargoes.[177] The point is often stressed that reservation of cargoes to vessels of the US flag applies only to non-commercial cargoes that would not exist except as purchases for an account of the US or as an aid or US-financed cargoes, with financing of times approaching the outright gift category.[178]

However, AID pointed out in its Cargo Preference Report for fiscal year 1963 that long shipments then represented the largest portion of the US foreign assistance programme.[179] Moreover, as we have seen, the US has extended the application of the 50–50 cargo preferences rule to commercial wheat sales to the Soviet Union and to other Eastern Socialist Countries.[180] This concession was granted long ago by the late President Kennedy under pressure from maritime labour groups and has, ever since, been a source of irritation to US wheat dealers who claim the high cost of shipping wheat via the US flag vessels has precluded them from supplying this market.[181]

Notes

1. Black, *Law Dictionary*, (Rev. ed.), 1968.
2. OECD, *Maritime Transport*, 1969, p. 59.
3. *Ibid.*
4. Rohreke, H. G., *The Formula and the Material Concept of Flag Equality, op. cit.*
5. *Ibid.*
6. *Rochdale Report*, para. 147, pp. 42–43.

7. UNCTAD Doc. No. TD/B/C.4/63.
8. OECD, *Maritime Transport*, 1967, p. 41.
9. For Seaports/Airports.
10. UNCTAD Doc. No. TD/B/C.4/38 Rev., para 333, at p. 91.
11. *Ibid*., para 333.
12. UNCTAD Doc. No. TD/B/C.4/63, *op. cit.*
13. House Report No. 1419, 87th Cong., 1st Sess. *The Ocean Freight Industry* (GPO), Washington DC, 1962, pp. 110–25.
14. UNCTAD Doc. No. TD/B/C.4/38 Rev., *op. cit*., paras 335, at p. 91.
15. *US Federal Maritime Commission*, Docket No. 65-34.
16. UNCTAD Doc. No. TD/B/C.4/38/Rev 1, *op. cit*., para. 335, at p. 91.
17. *Ibid*.
18. Sturmey, S. G., pp. 102, 199, 220.
19. *US Federal Maritime Commission*, Docket No. 65-45 'Investigation of ocean freight rate structures in the trade between the US North Atlantic Ports and ports in the UK and Eire – Agreement Nos. 7100 and 5850.'
20. US Congress: Joint Economic committee, Hearings before the Sub-Committee on Federal Procurement and Regulation, *Discriminatory Ocean Freight Rates and the Balance of Payments*, Part 1, (GPO) Washington DC, April 1965, p. 1.
21. Sturmey, S. G., 'Flag discrimination against panlibho', op. cit., pp. 220–21
22. Se also *Sanctions Discriminations* (post).
23. UNCTAD Doc. No. TD/B/C.4/38/Rev, Chapter X, section 3, paras 336, p. 91.
24. Olof, H., *op. cit*., pp. 44–45, i.e. 'Expenditures that affects foreign vessels'.
25. *US Federal Maritime Commission*, Docket No. 66-49 Nov. 1967: 'North Atlantic Mediterranean Freight Conferences – Rates on Household Goods' (GPO), Washington DC, p. 10.
26. UNCTAD Doc. No. TD/B/C.4/63.
27. O'Loughlin, C., *op. cit*., pp. 94, 115 & 178.
28. Sturmey, S. G., *op. cit.*, pp. 18, 30, 33.
29. House Report No. 1419, Cong., 1st Sess. 'The Ocean Freight Industry' (GPO), Washington DC, 1962, pp. 123 & 124.
30. UNCTAD Doc. No. TD/B/C.4/38 Rev. paras 323, p. 89.
31. *Ibid*., para 324, p. 59.
32. O'Loughlin, C., *op. cit*.
33. OECD, *Maritime Transport*, 1965, p. 50.
34. *Rochdale Report, op. cit*.
35. *Nationalised Industries*: 'A review of Economic and Financial Objectives 1967' (Cmnd. 3437), HMSO.
36. Hence the spirit of Article 4(2)(a) of the *UNCTAD Code of Conduct for Liner Conferences*.
37. *National Interest* is a lucid term; but see also the *Energy Security Transportation* (post).
38. *Lloyd's List* and *Shipping Gazette*, London, 20 Aug. 1968, 'Report on United States Department of Transportation Research Study'.
39. UNCTAD Doc. No. TD/B/C.4/38/Rev, *op. cit*., para 341.
40. Apart from the said American efforts to develop the refrigerated carriers in 1954, the other is the Algerian one to develop the LNG.
41. Diversification and self reliance are strong motivations for the establishment/development of national fleets.
42. US Dept. of Commerce, MARAD, *Maritime Subsidies, op. cit*, pp. 149–252.
44. UNCTAD Doc. No. TD/B/C.4/38/Rev, *op. cit*., Chapter 10, i.e. 'Discriminations between products and shippers'.
45. *Ibid*., para. 348, i.e. 'Limits to overall discrimination versus individual product discrimination'.
46. H. R. Rep. No. 1818, at 12.
47. *Hearings on Operation and Administration of Cargo Preference Act before the House on Merchant Marine and Fisheries, ibid*.
48. *Ibid*.; See also 84th Cong., 2nd Sess., 2, 1956.

49. Senate Committee on Agricultural and Forestry, Amendments to *Public Law* 480, 83rd Cong., S. Rep., No. 2290.
50. Kilgour, 'The energy transportation security act 1974', *J. Mar. L. & Comm.* 1976, Vol. 7, p. 557.
51. *Senate Hearings* on S. 2089 & HR8193, *supra*, note 21, at 7.
52. *Washington Post*: Dec. 17, 1974, para A, at 2, and 1974 Pub. Papers 786.
53. *Washington Post*; Jan. 1 1975, para A, at 12 Col. 1.
54. H. R. Rep. No. 1003, 93rd Cong., 2nd Sess. 2, 1974.
55. Joyner, C. C., 'Latin America's communal response to the energy crisis. The Latin American Energy Organisation (OLADE)', *Lawyer of Americas*, Vol. 6, 1974, pp. 637–661.
56. Note: 'The American merchant marine, flags of convenience and International law', *Virg. J. Int. L.*, Vol. 3, 1963, p. 121.
57. Naess E., *The Great Panlibho Controversy*, 1972.
57A. Exec. Order No. IV, Nov. 2, 1973, reprinted in Senate Hearings on S.2089 and HR.8193, *supra*, note 21, at 210.
58. H.R.8193, 93rd Cong., 2nd Sess., 1974; reprinted in Senate Hearings S.2189 and H.R.8193, *supra*, note 21, at 7, 93rd Cong., 2nd Sess. (1974); reprinted in id., at 5.
59. See also *Rochdale Report* – last sentence of para 147 and opening sentence of para 150 both at p. 43.
60. Henkin, L. *et. al*, 'The social scientist looks at international law of conflict management', *Proc. Am. Soc. Int. L.*, Vol. 65, 1971, pp. 96–106.
61. *Rochdale Report*, Chapter 21, 'National security', paras 1400–15, pp. 371–74.
62. US Dept of Commerce, MARAD, *Maritime Subsidies*, 1978, pp. 137–39 with 'Flag discrimination' at p. 138.
63. 33 Stat. 518, 1904.
64. 70A Stat. 146, 1956; 10 USC para. 2631, 1964.
65. *Armed Services Procurement Regulations* 1–1402(1)(A)(II), 1960.
66. *Ibid.*, (1)(B) 1963.
67. Stat 2051, 1936; 46 USC para. 1241, 1952.
68. 33 Stat. 518, 1964; 10 USC para. 2631 (Supp. V, 1958).
69. 70 Stat. 187, 1956; 36 USC para. 1241 (C).
70. 10 USC para. 4748, 6157, 19748, (Supp. V. 1958) (Army, Navy and Airforce, respectively).
71. 17 Stat. 405, 1932; 5 USC, para. 173(C), 1952.
72. US Dept. of Commerce, MARAD, *Maritime Studies*, 1978.
73. 'The best congress money can buy', *CBS New Reports*, (Dan Rather – Correspondent), Jan. 31 1975.
74. *Washington Post*, Aug. 10 1976, at para A3, col. 1.
75. 46 USC para. 1742 and 1283, 1970.
76. Trade Act 1974 (*Public Law* No. 93–618).
77. See also 88 Stat. 1978 (Codified in large at USC, para 2101–2487, Supp. V. 1975).
78. *Ibid.*
79. *Ibid.*
80. *Rochdale Report*, paras. 150–151.
81. See further for definitions of government supplies.
82. Sturmey, S. G., *op. cit.*, pp. 33, 124–5, 202–4, 206–8, 226, 375, 385.
83. E.g. Nato troops in Europe, Cuban/Soviets in Angola, French troops in Francophone Africa, etc.
84. *Maritime Subsidies*, 1978, pp. 137–39, at. 138.
85. Such outposts are in Greenland, Iceland, etc.
86. 32 CFR para 1.309 (Supp. 1958).
87. *Ibid.*, para 1.309(b)(2).
88. See *US–Spanish Agrt.*, July 30 1954, para 2(9)(ii), 1954, UST & DIA 2328 TIAS, No. 3094.
89. 32 CFR para 1.309(d)(1) (Supp. 1958).
90. *Ibid.*, para 1.309(d)(2).
91. 'Military sea transportation service', by 32 CFR para 1.309(e)(1)(ii) (Supp. 1958).
92. *Navy Procurement Directive* 1–307(e)(1).

93. 32 CFR para 1.309(c)(2)(v) (Supp. 1954).
94. H.R. Dep., No. 2329, at 3.
95. *Maritime Subsidies*, 1978, pp. 38–39.
96. *Ibid.*, at p. 39.
97. *Merchant Marine Bulletin of American Legion*, March. 1958, p. 4.
98. *US–West German Agrt.*, April 4 1954, para 2(a)(111).
99. *Ibid.*, 1957, 8 UST & DIA 497, TIAS, No. 3804 (effective Feb. 7 1957).
100. See also final paragraphs of last chapter.
101. UNCTAD Doc. No. TD/B/C.4/38/Rev. 1, para 337.
102. Gorters, W., *The United States Shipping Policy, op. cit.*, pp. 162–168.
103. UNCTAD Doc. No. TD/B/C.4/38/Rev. 1, paras 337–340, Table 49 at p. 92.
104. HMSO *Report of the Committee of Inquiry into the Major Ports of Great Britain*, London, Sept. 1962, CMND 1824.
105. *Ibid.*, Chapters 40, pp. 196–198; some of these islands (300 mls apart) are urgently in need of such schemes.
106. Section 714 *Merchant Marine Act, 1936*.
107. Gorter, *supra*, Chapter IV, at p. 131.
108. *Ibid.*, p. 121.
109. US Dept. of Commerce, *Review of Essential US Foreign Trade Routes* (GPO), Washington DC, 1953, p. 4.
110. *Ibid.*, at p. 6.
111. Gorter, *op. cit.*, Chapter VIII p. 163.
112. *Ibid.*, p. 163.
113. *Ibid.*, p. 164.
114. *Ibid.*, p. 164.
115. *Ibid.*, p. 164.
116. US Dept of Commerce, *Review of Essential Trade Routes, op. cit.*, pp. 6–7.
117. US Dept. of Commerce, MARAD, *US Oceanborne Foreign Trade Route Traffic Carried by Dry Cargo Ships*, Calender Year 1948, 1950 & 1953, Washington DC, 1953 (GPO), part 2, p. 5.
118. US Dept of Commerce, Bureau of the Census, *US Waterborne Trade*, Washington DC, June 24 1955 (GPO), p. 10.
119. Drewery Shipping Consultants, *The Emergence of Third World Shipping*, No. 6, 1978, para 2.1, p. 12.
120. *Ibid.*, para 2.1.1, p. 13.
121. *Maritime Subsidies* 1978, pp. 95–98, at 98, para. H.
122. Probably a large portion.
123. As are indeed for most of the other NICS in SEA.
124. Sassoon, D. M., *British Shipping Laws*, Vol. 5, 2nd edn., 1975.
125. *Renter* v *Sala* 1979 4 CPD 239.
126. *Biddel Bros.* v *E. Clements Horst Co.*, 1911. IKB 214, at 220.
127. *Wilson Holgate & Co.* v *Belgian Grain Produce Co.*, 1920, 2KB at 1.
128. *Diamond Alkali Export Corporation* v *F. L. Burgeors*, 1921, 3KB 443.
129. *Re Keighley Maxted & Co. and Bryan, Durant & Co.*, 1894, 70 LT 155.
130. *Weis* v *Produce Brokers Co.*, 1921 7 LLLR211.
131. Per Lord Porter in *Comptoir d' Achat et de Neute du Boerenbond Belge S.A.* v *Louis de Ridder Linitada* (The Julia) 1949, AC 293 at 309; 1949 1A11 ER. 269, at 274.
132. *Olearia Tirvena S. P. A.* v *N. V. Algenieene Oliehandele*, 1972, 1 LL.R.341.
133. In *Wimble* v *Rosenberg*, 1913 3KB 743.
134. Section 32(3) *Sale of Goods Act, 1893*.
135. 'Preferential treatment: A new standard for international economic relations', *Harv. Int. L.J.*, Vol. 18, pp. 109–135 (Winter 1977).
136. Guest A. G., *Benjamin's Sale of Goods*, 1st ed., 1974, pp. 687–910.
137. Learning Resources Centre, Plymouth Polytechnic, *Maritime Studies, Current Awareness Bulletin* No. 369, 19th June 1981.
138. Lebuhn J., 'Practising CIF and FOB today', *Eur. Trans. L.*, Vol. 16, No. 1, 1981, pp. 24–36.
139. *United Baltic Corporation* v *Burgett and Newsman*, 1921, 8 LLLR190.

140. *Emergence of Third World Shipbuilding, op. cit*., p. 13.
141. *Maritime Subsidies*, 1978, *op. cit*., p. 96.
142. *Rochdale Report*, p. 437.
143. *Ibid*., p. 439.
144. *Maritime Subsidies*, 1978, p. 97.
145. Shah, M. J., 'International conventions applicable to FOB and CIF sales and to multi-modal transport of goods sales', *Eur. Trans. L*., Vol. 16, No. 1, 1981, pp. 67–90.
146. Friedhem, R. L., *The Political, Economic and Legal Ocean Managing Ocean Resources*, 1979, pp. 91–103.
147. *Ibid*., p. 101.
148. Chapter on *Economic Consequences*.
149. This has been the case since the OEEC days.
150. We shall deal with this in Part III of this survey.
151. See also *Countervailing Flag Discriminations* below.
152. OECD, *Maritime Transport*, 1961, p. 20.
153. See also *Retaliatory Flag Discriminations* below.
154. See the German practice ahead.
155. Both a form and response to Flag Discriminations.
156. Chambers, *Twentieth Century Advanced Learners' Dictionary*.
157. Allison D. G., 'Non-tariff trade barrier challenge: development and distortion in the age of interdependence', *Tul. LJ* Vol. 12, 1976, pp. 1–64.
158. *Maritime Subsidies*, 1978, pp. 53–59, at 58.
159. Stigler, G. J., 'The Economist plays with blocs', Papers and Proceedings, 66th Annual Meeting of the American Economic Association, *American Economic Review*, Evanston III, 1954.
160. *Maritime Subsidies*, 1978, pp. 90–94, at 93/94.
161. Taji, Y., 'Japanese shipbuilding and shipping', *Shipping and Shipbuilding Record*, 14 April 1932, p. 423.
162. HMSO, Imperial Shipping Committee, *British Shipping in the Orient*, London, para 198, p. 62.
163. Marston G., 'United Kingdom Protection of Trading Interests Act 1980', *JWTL* Vol. 14, No. 5, Sept/Oct. 1980, pp. 461–65.
164. See also Cadwallader, F. J. J. (The Merchant Marine Act 1974) 'Flag discrimination or something More?', 1976, *Current Legal Prob*., Vol. 29, pp. 99–111.
165. House of Commons Debate, Vol. 973, p. 1533 15 Nov. 1979.
166. E.g. *The Export Administration Act 1979*; see also the *UK-Merchant Shipping (Liner Conferences) Act 1982*, ss. 1–2.
167. Galbraith, T. K., *American Capitalism: The Theory of Countervailing Power*, 1952, p. 100.
168. Barcello, T. J., 'Subsidies and countervailing – analysis and a proposal', *Law & Pol. Int. Bus*. Vol. 9, 1977, pp. 853–877.
169. See also *Rio Tinto Zinc Corporation V Westinghouse Electric Corporation*, 1978, AC 547, at 617.
170. 41 Stat. 995, 1920; as amended, 46 USC. para 876, 1964.
171. See also para 26 of the *Shipping Act 1916*, 39 Stat. 737; as amended 46 USC para 825, 1964.
172. 46 CFR paras 506.1–506.3 (Supp. 1965).
173. See *Chilean Merchant Marine Law No. 12,041*, June 22 1956.
174. and *Columbian Decree 994* April 29 1966 and 1028 July 21 1969.
175. *Douglas Report*, p. 20.
176. *Cellar Report*, pp. 359–60.
177. Agrts. No. 9847–8 Revenue Pools US/Brazil Trade FMC, 1970.
178. Cargo Pooling Agrts Nos. 9682–4 FMC, Sept. 4, 1970.
179. AID *Cargo Preference Report* 1, 1964.
180. H.R.S. 89th Cong., 1st Sess., 1965, pp. 43–50.
181. H.R. Senate 89th Cong., 1st Sess., 1965, 51–52.

Appendix 5

Details of main provisions involving flag discrimination in force or contemplated by certain countries at 31st October, 1983.

Country	Cargo reserved to national fleets	Other measures and trade agreements
Algeria	The government requires export contracts for both oil and LNG to contain a 50% cargo clause giving preference to Algerian flag vessels.	Algeria and Brazil have a maritime, navigation and transportation agreement covering all traffic between their ports; it excludes petroleum and bulk cargo shipments. Traffic between French and Algerian ports is reserved for French and Algerian flag ships. Algeria has bilateral agreements with the USSR, Bulgaria, the German Democratic Republic, Guinea, China and the Republic of Cape Verde that divide cargo on a 50–50 or 40–40–20 basis.
Argentina	The 1973 Merchant Marine Law reaffirmed the 1969 law establishing the 'right' of Argentine flag vessels to carry 50% of all goods exported or imported by state and municipal governments, companies in which the state has a holding of at least 50% and non-official imports and exports financed by any state credit institution or enjoying any form of import duty reduction, tax concession or exchange control relief. It also requires a minimum of 50%. Argentine flag carriage of all goods under any international commercial trade agreement.	Argentine flag vessels are exempt from consular and similar fees. The government reserves the right to deny port facilities to foreign ships which do not operate under approved agreements. Under the 1973 law the government has the power of approval over all freight conference agreements involving Argentine overseas commerce. Any freight conference which appears to place limitations on Argentine ships (below 50 per cent carriage) will not be recognized. Argentina has 50–50 bilateral agreements with Uruguay, Peru, Brazil, Chile, Colombia and the USSR. In the event of a shortage of national flag ships it is necessary to obtain a waiver for transport in the third flag carriers. Three US companies have equal access agreements with Argentina covering the southbound movement of government-controlled cargoes.
Australia	Trade between New Zealand and Australia must be carried in New Zealand or Australian flag ships.	
Bolivia	(i) 30% (rising to 50%) of all cargoes in trades regularly served by the newly-established Bolivian shipping line, once it is in operation. (ii) Government and official imports and exports, and imports of basic foodstuffs. (At present not enforced).	The Bolivia/Uruguay trade agreement contains a discriminatory shipping clause.

Appendix 5 (*Continued*)

Country	Cargo reserved to national fleets	Other measures and trade agreements
Brazil	All goods imported or exported by federal, state, municipal or public administration departments, public enterprises and mixed-economy firms and all imports and exports enjoying tariff concessions, preferential internal fiscal treatment, national finance or international loans must be carried in Brazilian flag ships. The same applies to all ordinary paper (excluding special paper and pulp) unless special arrangements are made. The government has a monopoly on the transport of petroleum and petroleum products; small companies existing before the law was passed are exempt. Provision is made for a waiver of cargo preference under the following circumstances: Up to 50% of the total weight of import or export cargoes obligatorily linked to transportation in Brazilian flag ships can be liberated in favour of the flag of the exporting or importing country provided the buying or selling nation concedes at least equal treatment to Brazilian flag ships. When exportation or importation of merchandise subjects to liberation is made to or from a country that is not served by ships of both the countries involved, the Brazilian Superintendency of Merchant Marine will effect prior liberation of cargoes covered by Decree Law 666, designating the transporter. Should no ship of the Brazilian flag or the flag of the importing or exporting country be in a position to take the cargo, the Brazilian Superintendency of Merchant Marine can, at its discretion, permit the cargo to be transported by a third flag ship specifically designated.	Brazil has advantageous rates of exchange for carriage costs on national lines. Foreign shipping companies cannot operate from Brazil unless they are members of a conference to which a Brazilian company belongs. An exporter who ships aboard a Brazilian vessel has taxes on production and circulation credited to him for the purpose of buying raw materials for his product. SUNAMAN (National Merchant Marine Superintendancy) 1970 provides for 50–50 US–Brazillian carriage of coffee and cocoa. Brazil has 50–50 cargo-sharing agreements with Argentina, Chile, Peru, Uruguay and Nigeria when flag vessels are available. All trade between Brazil and Mexico must be carried in national flag ships on a 40–40 basis; each nation is allowed to code 10% to third flag vessels, with preference given to countries of Latin American Free Trade Association; vessels chartered by Mexico or Brazil enjoy the same status. Brazil and Algeria have a maritime, navigation and transportation agreement covering all traffic between their ports; it excludes petroleum and bulk cargo shipments. Brazil regulates the conferences in which it participates to ensure increased carriage for its own flag. Three US lines have sailing, pooling and equal access agreements with Brazilian lines. Brazil issues shippers an 8% tax credit, based upon cost of merchandise plus freight, on frozen orange juice if the shipper uses Brazilian flag vessels. If the shipper uses foreign flag vessels, the credit is based upon the cost of merchandise only. The US has negotiated equal access with Brazilian lines under this law.
Burma		Nationalised shipping agencies favour national flag ships.

Canada	Effective from 1st January, 1966, traffic between ports located within the Great Lakes, their connecting tributory waters and the St. Lawrence River and its tributory waters as far seaward as a straight line drawn from Cap des Rosiers to Westpoint, Anticosti Island, to the North Shore of the St. Lawrence River along the meridian of longitude 63° west (Havre St. Pierre), was restricted to Canadian Registered vessels, for which duty has been fully paid.	Withdrawn from certain clauses of the British Commonwealth Merchant Shipping Agreement in 1975 freed Canada from the obligation to continue to give preference to Commonwealth built and registered.
Cameroon	Cameroon Shipping Lines enjoy the exclusive right to transport all imports for the government, public collectives and state-owned companies. All importers and exporters who do not present at customs a Cameroon Shipping Lines bill of lading or a certificate of dispensation are fined 15% of the value of the merchandise: CIF for imports and FOB for exports.	All contracts for private imports and exports must give priority to Cameroon Shipping Lines or obtain a waiver from the company for any shipping it cannot handle.
Chile	Since 1969 all cargoes of the state, state-owned enterprises and bodies in which the state has an interest or part interest have had to be carried in state-owned vessels; the same applies to 50% of imports and exports other than nitrate and most ores, bulk cargoes and oil. If a state-owned vessel is not available, the goods may be carried in a Chilean-owned ship. If none are available, exceptions will be made. If a trading partner grants 50% carriage between the nations, exceptions will be made. Provision was made in 1975 for 50% of export cargoes to be carried on flag ships of the country of destination provided that the country recognized the equal rights of Chilean vessels. For five years ships will be considered Chilean if operated by Chilean lines. The Ministry of Transport has issued new procedures on cargo allocation whereby 50% of export cargo, whether US bound or way-port, will be reserved for Chilean flag shipping, and 50% will be open to shippers' free choice. If space on a Chilean flag ship is not available within a set period of time cargo can be transported by a foreign flag ship without having to request a waiver from Chilean flag companies.	Foreign lines by obtain status as 'associated' carriers and acquire the right to participate in transport and compete for cargo on the same basis as Compania Sudamericana de Vapores, the shipping line with minority state interest. (Two US companies have such pooling agreements.) Chile has 50–50 cargo-sharing agreements with Argentina and Brazil, subject to availability of national flag ships.

Appendix 5 (*Continued*)

Country	Cargo reserved to national fleets	Other measures and trade agreements
China		Self-reliance in shipping is a government policy. No details of cargo reservation laws, as such, are available outside China. However, the Chinese maritime authorities have directed that at least half of the country's seaborne foreign trade should move in Chinese flag ships, all of which are operated by the China Ocean Shipping Company, a state-owned and controlled monopoly. Special taxes are imposed on exports and passengers departing from Chinese ports on foreign flag ships unless exempted for specific national flag ships by a maritime agreement. Preference is given to Chinese subsidiary companies operating ships under Panamanian and Hong Kong flags. Exports are shipped on a CIF and CF basis, imports on an FOB basis. In each instance this allows China to control the flag under which goods are shipped. In 1975, 71 per cent of China's overseas commerce was carried in its own ships.
Colombia	The 1969 cargo preference law requires not less than 50% of general import and export cargoes on routes served by Colombian ships to be hauled on such ships, providing that the requirements of Article 2 of Decree No. 1208 are met. Decree No. 1208 reserves no more than 50% of bulk, liquid and refrigerated import and export cargo to Colombian flag vessels. Reserved cargoes are stipulated only when they do not conflict with previous government agreements and foreign loans. Decree No. 1670 orders that shipments to all government entities (autonomous, semi-autonomous and of mixed private and public nature) must comply with the 50% reservation law above. Latin American shipowners registered in the Latin American Association of Shipowners can participate in transportation of reserved cargoes on the same terms as Colombian vessels provided that equal treatment is given to Colombian ships in those countries.	Imports are on an FOB basis; freight and insurance are to be paid in Colombian currency, of which a proportion in non-transferable. Colombia has 50–50 bilateral shipping agreements with Argentina and Uruguay

Denmark	Effective from July 31, 1973, any sea transport of goods from Denmark to greenland requires a permit from the Minister of Greenland. Exempt from this requirement are Danish Government institution ships, and transport by sea of goods required for the operation of the Danish-American defense areas.	
Dominican Republic	Legislation has been passed reserving the national ships 40% of general import and export freight, 50% of import freight privileged with fiscal exoneration by the Incentive and Industrial Protection law, 50% of all Cargo exported by state enterprises and 60% of liquid, bulk and general cargo imported by government-controlled institutes, state-owned enterprises and those enterprises in which the state is the main stockholder.	
Ecuador	In 1974 the National Council of the Merchant Marine and Ports raised the percentage of Ecuadorian general cargo reserved for national flag ships from 30 to 50%. The Hydrocarbons Law of 1971 reserves 50% of all oil cargo to national flag vessels. All government cargo, as well as cargo shipped by organizations in which the government has more than a 50% capital investment, must be carried aboard national flag ships.	
Egypt	30% of imports and exports must be carried in Egyptian vessels.	In 1976 the Council of State decreed that all seaborne shipments entering or leaving Egypt that pertain to state business, public institutions, public organizations and their affiliates must be arranged and supervised by the Egyptian Company for Maritime Transport or the foreign agents of that company. Egypt has a 50–50 bilateral agreement with India.
France	A Decree of April 1931, as amended in August 1970, requires that two-thirds of French oil imports be carried in French flag vessels or in ships of which the charter parties have been approved by the Ministry of Fuel and the Ministry of Transport (Merchant Marine). Legislation of 1935 and 1936 states that 50% of coal imports	French lines do not compete against each other in any one conference; joint companies have been established with the shipping lines of other EEC countries to ensure orderly markets. The government has statutory authority to restrict freedom of French ship-owners to charter vessels; the chartering of all ships over

Appendix 5 (*Continued*)

Country	Cargo reserved to national fleets	Other measures and trade agreements
	destined for the public services or subsidized enterprises and 40% of imports not destined for the above cited services or enterprises should be carried by French registered vessels.	500 gross tons must be reported to the government, which may offer opposition on the grounds of national interest. France and the Ivory Coast have a maritime cooperation agreement providing for reciprocity between the two nations regarding cargo sharing, tariffs, freight forwarding and freight handling. Traffic between French and Tunisian ports is restricted to French and Tunisian flag ships. Traffic between French and Algerian ports is reserved for French and Algerian flag ships.
Gabon	The government reserves 50% of refined petroleum product exports for vessels of the state-owned shipping company Sonatran.	A Government Decree signed on September 7, 1978 confirms the division of cargo using UNCTAD's 40–40–20 formulas, expressly reserved for Gabonese flag vessels.
Federal Republic of Germany		Shipowners and operators may claim a 50% reduction in the corporate tax on income earned from shipping services in foreign trades. German flag vessels receive tax-free fuel. The government is empowered to restrict the conclusion of freights contracts and charters between residents and carriers that are residents of countries which exclude German ships from free competition. Germany has 50–50 cargo-sharing agreement with South Korea, and ratified the UNCTAD's 40–40–20 code.
Ghana	All imports and exports of industrial and commercial goods are reserved for the state-owned shipping company.	All cargoes ordered by the Ghana Supply Commission (government purchasing organization) are handled by Black Star Line as shipping agent. Cargoes go on the first available conference ship. Discriminatory shipping and insurance clauses annexed to import licences require importers to use vessels of state-owned lines.
Greece	Coastal trade is reserved to Greek flag ships.	Greece and the USSR, Poland, and the People's Republic of China have signed a shipping agreement which provides for the devleopment of bilateral relations.

Guatemala	Legislation of 1971 reserves all import cargoes to Guatemalan national flag lines and fixes a penalty of 50% of the total freight charges for violation.	In 1971 tax exemption was granted for import cargoes carried by national carriers under the Industrialization Promotion Act, exports of timber and certain other goods to the US, goods imported duty-free under the Industrial Development Law and government imports. Guatemala has a 100% surcharge on imports from certain countries with which it has an adverse balance of payments unless carried on national flag ships or associated lines.
India	Shipments for government account must be carried in Indian flag ships. The government is exerting cargo preference pressure on the oil import trade. National refineries give preference to Indian flag lines, which are to transport 90% of all crude as compared with 30% in April 1976. Export-Import Bank cargoes not conveyed on US flag ships must be carried on Indian flag ships.	Trade agreements with the German Democratic Republic, Iran, Poland, Peru and Rumania contain a 'best endeavour' clause to allocate bilateral cargoes to flags of either country on the basis of equality of tonnage and earnings. India has a 50–50 bilateral agreement with Egypt and the USSR. India and Bulgaria have initialled a cargo-sharing agreement allocating equal quantities of cargo to their respective flag vessels; no income tax will be levied by either country upon the freight earnings from cargo moving between ports of their countries. The India, Pakistan and Bangladesh conference observes 40–40–20 cargo sharing.
Indonesia	45% of European cargoes are allocated to Indonesian flag vessels. The Indonesian Freight Board has unlimited authority to discriminate in favour of national flag carriage at any time in the future. The Minister of Sea Communications has ruled that transhipment of goods for Indonesia must be in Indonesian-owned ships using only Indonesian transhipment ports. Indonesian-owned coasters will be used for transhipment from Bangkok, Thailand, and Kompong Som, Kampuchea. If national vessels are unavailable, third-flag carriers may be licensed to carry transhipments.	In 1971 a tax was imposed on foreign shipping at a rate of 4% of the gross revenue from sales made anywhere in the world for transport of passengers and freight within or from, but not to, Indonesia. A law of 1964 provides that all requests for shipping space for export of Indonesian commodities be channelled through Indonesian shipping boards. This is designed to give national shipping companies priority. Indonesia has a bilateral agreement with the USSR. Indonesia and Singapore have a cargo-sharing agreement whereby 55% of cargo from Indonesia must go on Indonesian vessels and 45% on Singapore ships.
Iran	All government imports must move on Iranian ships. Iranian Decree No. 25510 of 23 August, 1976 created a bureau at the Ministry of Commerce for the purpose of planning a programming the importation and shipment of government goods. All ministries	Iranian Line ships have preferential berthing in Iran.

Appendix 5 (*Continued*)

Country	Cargo reserved to national fleets	Other measures and trade agreements
	and government enterprises and organisations (excluding the War Ministry and the Armed Forces which are covered by their own regulations) are responsible for arranging for the shipment of their own goods, whether by sea or by air, through the Ministry of Commerce. The Ministry of Commerce arranges with the Iranian Merchant Marine for the shipment of such goods.	
Iraq	First preference is given to Iraqi flag ships.	An Iraqi-Soviet agreement provides for the transport of Soviet goods exported to Iraq on Iraq bottoms, and the assignment of Soviet crews to some Iraqi vessels.
Israel	Financial Regulations of October 1972 require the issuance of import licences on an FOB basis, thereby giving the Government of Israel control over the choice of vessel and the placement of cargo insurance. In November 1977 this regulation was changed, and many items no longer need an import licence.	Requirements for the use of Israeli vessles to carry meat to Israel have been negotiated in a series of bilateral agreements between Zim Israeli Navigation Lines and foreign exporting nations.
Italy	Italy, in defense from cargo preference, may restrict the use of ships of countries which discriminate against Italian-flag ships. Shipments on such vessels are subject to government authorisation. The navigation code excludes all foreign flag ships from domestic trade.	Italy and the Soviet Union have signed a bilateral shipping pact which provides for the setting up of a jointly operated liner service to promote trade between them. It also stipulates that Italian ships should carry all raw materials while Soviet ships should carry general cargo.
Ivory Coast		Legislation passed in 1975 regulates maritime transport on the 40–40–20 cargo-sharing principle. Only freight rates negotiated and ratified by the government are applicable in the Ivory Coast. A maritime cooperation agreement between the Ivory Coast and France provides for reciprocity between the two nations regarding cargo-sharing, tariffs, freight forwarding and freight handling.
Japan	The Law on Special Measures Against Unfavourable Treatment to Japanese Ocean-Going Ship Operators by Foreign Governments	Japanese operators are granted tax credits against earnings in the foreign trades.

	and Others entered into force on 20 July 1977. The Minister for Transport, when the interests of Japanese oceangoing ship operators are significantly harmed by unfavourable treatments by any foregoing governments and others, may order, against the oceangoing ship operators of such a country, the restriction or prohibition of access, and loading or unloading of cargo in Japan. Anyone who acts against any such order shall be subject to penal servitude for a period not exceeding one year or a penalty not exceeding 5 million yen. Before any restrictions are enforced the Ministry for Transport may notify the ocean-going operators of such foreign country that he may order any countermeasures unless the harmful situation ceases to exist within a specified period not shorter than six months.	All industries are eligible for tax exemption on 1.5% of the total export sales of shipping services or 40% of net export income earned by selling shipping services, whichever is lower. This applies to invisible exports only; under the GATT, Japan cannot offer tax benefits or monetary incentives on visible exports. Japan has bilateral agreements with China, Taiwan and South Korea. Utilization of government financing or licensing services often results in the direction of commercial cargoes to Japanese flag carriers; e.g. for years tobacco cargoes from the US have been shipped exclusively in Japanese flag ships. The close relations between government and industry necessarily result in a shipping policy that is essentially a 'ship Japanese' programme.
Korea	Korean flag vessels must be used for the transportation of such cargoes as major designated cargoes and liner cargoes, except to the extent that a waiver is obtained from the Authorities concerned.	When a foreign operator of vessels is deemed to have committed acts hindering the development of marine transportation of Korea, or to have confused the order of trade, routes, the Korean government may take the necessary countermeasures.
Kuwait	According to the Middle East Economic Digest (16th September, 1977) Kuwait has decreed that 100% of its natural gas exports to the US and 50% to Japan must be shipped in Kuwait vessels. (At the time of the report, however, Kuwait had no LNG carriers.)	Crude oil sales contracts include a clause requiring that Kuwaiti tankers or those owned in part by Kuwaiti interests receive preference.
Libya	All shipping activities in Libya are controlled by the General Maritime Transport Company, a Government owned concern which in turn owns virtually the entire Libyan fleet.	The entirely state-owned, Universal Shipping Company, Benghazi, is the sole agent of tanker shipping in all Libya. The Turkish and Libyan governments have established maritime transport stock company.
Malaysia	On January 1, 1980 the Malaysian government instituted a policy whereby all coastal traffic is restricted to ships that are registered in Malaysia and priority is to be given to ships owned by Malaysians. In 1979 only about 40% of the vessels participating in coastal shipping were Malaysian registered.	Malaysia has adopted the UNCTAD Code of Conduct for Liner Conferences' cargo carriage ratio of 40–40–20.
Mexico	Traffic of PEMEX (the state petroleum company) is reserved for national flag vessels.	In 1963 an export tax was imposed on bee honey at a rate of 1 per cent if shipped by Mexican flag vessels and 3% if shipped otherwise. A decree of 1st January 1966 provides subsidies for products intended

Appendix 5 (*Continued*)

Country	Cargo reserved to national fleets	Other measures and trade agreements
		for export if shipped in Mexican flag vessels or foreign flag vessels under charter to Mexican shipping companies. Subsidies of 50% of the freight rate are granted for manufactured products intended for export and subsidies of 25% of the freight rate are granted for semi-manufactured products or manufactured products not for end consumption. The government subsidizes the cost of its vessels' fuel to the extent of 50% of the total cost. Legislation of 1966 grants and subsidy of 25% of the freight rate to Mexican producers who ship their products to areas bording the US, Guatemala and Belize by rail, ship or air. Legislation of 1967 encourages exports of cotton by granting a 97.7% reduction in the export tax to shippers who use Mexican flag vessels or vessels chartered by national shipping companies. Mexico has a 40–40–20 bilateral agreement with Brazil; preference is given to Latin flag lines. Preferential treatment in orther areas is given on the basis of administrative action rather than law: Approval of applications for import licences subject to provisi that goods in question be imported in Mexican flag vessels. Where goods are restricted by currency quotas, the cost of sea transportation is not charged against the quota if the goods are imported on national flag vessels. Many state-owned agencies insist that their imports be carried on national flag ships.
Morocco	40% of impo⁻ts and 30% of exports must be shipped on national flag vessels.	On November 5, 1979, Morocco and France reached an agreement to split maritime cargo 50–50 on a case by case basis.
Nicaragua	Under legislation of 1972 cargoes bought or sold by the state shall be transported exclusively by Nicaraguan shipping enterprises. 50%	

	of commercial cargoes shall be carried in Nicaraguan flag ships and 50% in those of its trading partner; should the other party not provide shipping services, the Nicaraguan share may rise to 80%	
Nigeria	Legislation of 1972 reserves 50% of all foreign trade to national flag vessels. All importers and exporters whose business is registered in Nigeria grant priority of their sea freight to the Nigerian National Shipping Line (NNSL) in order to give the national line effective cargo control.	Nigeria has a 50–50 bilateral agreement with Brazil. Nigeria's National Policy on liner shipping follows the cargo-sharing principles of the UNCTAD Code. The NNSL is responsible for carbing up the cargo on the 40–40–20 basis retaining 75% of the total Nigerian allocation for itself and apportioning the remaining 25% amongst the other Nigerian lines.
Pakistan	50% of all US-aid and World Bank aid cargoes must be shipped on national flag vessels. Coastal shipping is restricted to the national flag vessels. Coastal shipping is restricted to the national flag when available.	Cargo preference is practised among participants in international shipping conferences which reserve a portion of the conference trade to Pakistani ships. Pakistan has a 50–50 bilateral shipping agreement with Poland. Pakistan participates in a conference with India and Bangladesh which observes 40–40–20 cargo sharing.
Panama	Cabinet Decree No. 15 of January 27, 1972 provides that foreign vessels that dock at ports which are not government approved or operated or that carry out commercial activities in the navigable waters of the Republic, may obtain from the General Directorate of Shipping and Consular Affairs a permit allowing them to take part in coastal shipping, provided there has been a previous designation of fiscal agents and payment of a tax which will not exceed US dollars 150 per trip or operation.	While there is no restriction on the operation of foreign ships in Panama's territorial waters, coastal shipping is restricted to Panamanian flag vessels. A fishing licence is required for all vessels fishing for commercial purposes in the navigable waters of the Republic of Panama. Failure to obtain the licence will result in a fine from ten thousand dollars to a hundred thousand dollars.
Peru	Legislation of 1970 reserves 30–50 per cent of Peruvian exports and imports (calculated on a monthly basis) for Peruvian flag ships. Imports exempt from customs dury must be carried in national flag ships when available. Legislation of 1974 gives Corporacion Peruana de Vapores, a national line, the preferential right to transport imports and exports, of the Peruvian government, public corporations or corporations in which the government has a major interest; it requires lines of other nations to have loading contracts with CPV for any portion of such cargoes which CPV cannot carry.	Under legislation of 1969 preference in the carriage of cargoes enjoying important duty exemption shall be given firstly to Peruvian flag vessels, secondly to foreign flag vessels chartered to Peruvian companies and finally to foreign flag vessels associated with Peruvian companies. Legislation of 1957 provides that national flag ships shall pay 50% of regular fees for ship clearances and for certification of consular invoices and bills of lading. Dry docking fees are 5 cents per ton for Peruvian ships and 15 cents per ton for foreign ships. Peruvian flag ships pay about 40% less than foreign flag ships in

Appendix 5 (*Continued*)

Country	Cargo reserved to national fleets	Other measures and trade agreements
	Legislation of 1976 guarantees that CPV shall receive preference in the carriage of all government cargoes, national and local.	Callao' and 50% less in other ports for mooring and unmooring. Wharf demurrage, charges for repair, docking and fuelling are less for Peruvian flag ships than for foreign flag vessels. Peru has 50–50 bilateral agreements with Argentina, India and Brazil whereby the two parties have a right on equal terms to transport the cargoes and share the freight receipts derived from their bilateral trade.
The Philippines	Legislation of 1976 requires any company which receives any subsidy, tax concession, assistance, contract or subcontract from the government to use Philippine flag vessels for all import and export cargo and personnel transport to the maximum extent service by such ships is available. Overall preference on the carriage of imports is given to Philippine flag vessels. All imports under control of government agencies and corporations must be shipped on national flag vessels unless they are not readily available. Import licences will be issued for government cargo only when it is imported on national flag ships, unless none are available. Legislation of 1975 provides that the government will take all steps necessary, including provision of direct incentives, to enable Philippine flag vessels to carry a substantial and increasing share of foreign trade. It states that Philippine flag vessels and those owned, controlled or chartered by Philippine nationals shall carry a share of cargo at least equal to that carried by its trading partners. All imports of US agricultural commodities under Section 402 of the US Mutual Security Act and US PL 480 which are in excess of the 50% required to be carried in US flag ships must be shipped in Philippine flag ships when available.	All purchases of Philippine imports must be made on an FOB basis and all freight paymernts must be made in pesos. Exporters will be able to deduct from their taxable income an amount equivalent to 150% of overseas freight expenses and charges in Phillippine ports incurred in shipping export products, provided they use Philippine flag carriers. Enterprises registered with the Board of Investments will be allowed to deduct from their taxable income 200% os shipment costs incurred in transport of their products and raw materials to and from foreign ports provided that they use Philippine flag vessels for their shipments.
Portugal	The Merchant Marine Secretariat has prepared a draft law stipulating that:	Portugal and the USSR have a 50–50 cargo-sharing agreement. The 'right' of other countries' ships to participate in trade between the ports

	1. Where no bilateral agreement exists all imports and exports exceeding 10 tons by entities owned or partly owned by the government must be carried on Portuguese flag ships; 2. Where a bilateral agreement exists, as much of the cargo as possible should be reserved for Portuguese flag ships; 3. All imports exceeding 10 tons financed by bank credits or guarantees must be carried on Portuguese ships. 4. In all the above provisions, FOB terms must be obtained for imports and CIF terms for exports.	of Portugal and the USSR will not be affected, however. Portugal and Mozambique have agreed that all trade between the two countries shall be reserved for Portuguese flag ships.
Saudi Arabia	Legislation of 1975 requires that 5 per cent of Saudi exports (primarily oil) be carried in Saudi vessels, rising to 50% by 1980. Overall, 25% of trade is reserved for national flag vessels when financial and other terms are competitive.	Saudi vessels have a lower bunkering rate that foreign flag vessels.
Singapore	There does not appear to be direct flag discrimination in Korea except that foreign-owned ships of less than 1 600 grt. cannot be registered in Singapore. Ships 1 600 grt. or above must be less than 15 years old to be registered.	The Singapore Shipping Association and Indonesian Shipowners' Association signed an agreement in 1975 which provided for a 50–50 cargo sharing by association members in the trade between the two countries. Singapore-Soviet Shipping Company (SinSov) is a 50–50 venture between Soviet and Singapore interests.
South Africa	All government cargo from Europe to South Africa must move on South and Southeast African conference lines, of which SAFMARINE is a member.	
South Korea	Under the shipping Promotion Law it is mandatory for exporters and importers to use Korean flag ships exclusively. Waivers are allowed only if no Korean vessels is available. With completion of its first container ships, Korea demanded that container cargo move in Korean flag vessels. If no suitable Korean flag vessel is available in three days, cargo may move on foreign flag vessel. Legislation of 1976 states that imports of crude oil, iron ore, lumber, grain and fertilizer will be carried in national flag ships, subject to availability.	The government encourages the use of Korean flag ships by awarding some government procurement contracts on an FOB basis rather than a CIF basis. A preferential interest rate for importing raw materials for export production is extended to cover freight costs when imports are carried on Korean flag ships. South Korea has bilateral agreements with the USA, the Federal Republic of Germany and Japan.
Spain	All imports of crude oil, tobacco and cotton for domestic consumption must be shipped in Spanish vessels if capacity is available.	When Spanish flag ships are subjected by another country to measures contrary to free competition they have the right to apply similar measures in return. Coastwise trade is reserved to Spanish flag ships.

Appendix 5 (*Continued*)

Country	Cargo reserved to national fleets	Other measures and trade agreements
Sri Lanka	The Ceylon Shipping Corporation has a monopoly on all cargo imports for government and state-owned corporations.	In 1972 Sri Lanka and China signed a joint shipping agreement, which included the provision that 'both countries will have a fair and equal opportunity in the carriage of commodities'.
Taiwan		It has been agreed that 50% of total trade between Taiwan and Japan shall be carried in national flag ships.
Tanzania		Since 1976 income tax has been levied on the gross receipts of foreign shipping lines accuring from outbound shipping freight and passengers. The tax does not apply to transhipment traffic. Tanzania and China have a joint shipping agreement.
Thailand	Legislation of 1972 provides that double dury must be paid on certain types of imported goods unless they are carried in ships licensed by a special interdepartmental committee. Government agencies are encouraged to use the government-owned forwarding agent (the Express Transport Organisation) vessels belonging to the Thai Maritime Navigation (TMN) and The United Thai Shipping Corporation (UNITHAI).	In December 1978, the Mercantile Marine Promotion Act B.E.2521 was passed which aims at promoting Thai-flag vessels though fiscal and other measures, including cargo preference and prevention of dumping by foreign flag vessels. The Law empowers the government to permit a deduction amounting to no more than 50% of the costs of carriage, when using Thai flag vessels for the carriage of exports and imports, from the shippers' net income prior to income tax calculation. It also empowers the government to make mandatory the use of Thai flag vessels for the transportation of seaborne cargoes ordered by governmental agencies and enterprises.
Turkey	A public-sector cargo must be carried in national flag ships. Legislation of 1975 states that all imports should be carried by national flag ships whenever possible. When none are available, any other line may ship the goods after obtaining a nomination certificate'.	The Maritime Bank exerts pressure on exporters and importsers to ship commercial cargoes on Turkish ships when available.
UAE	A decree of 1951 provides that 30% of exports and imports be carried in national vessels.	A number of bilateral agreements contain discriminatory shipping clauses including those with the USSR, India and Rumania.
UK	The UK will ratify the UNCTAD Code of Conduct for Liner Conferences but without the operations of its cargo-reservation provisions, subject to the EEC Brussels' Package 1979.	The repealed Shipping Contracts and Commercial Contracts Act 1964, The Merchant Shipping Act 1974, The Protection of Trading Interests Act 1980 and the Merchant Shipping (Liner Conferences) Act 1982 provides for countervailing powers against persons, agents, and organi-

		sations whose governments discriminate against the UK (or any other foreign-flag) vessels.
USA	These categories of cargo are subject to the 50–50 cargo sharing or preferences: 1. Government owned cargoes 2. Government controlled cargoes 3. Essential trade routes' cargoes 4. Defence and military cargoes 5. AID cargoes 6. EXIMBANK or government financial cargoes 7. Certain Department of Agriculture cargoes 8. ETC	Coastwise and intercoastal trade is restricted to US flag vessels. The US/People's Republic of China and the US/USSR maritime agreements provide that each country shall carry a 'substantial share', (not less than one third), of the total number of weight tons of bilateral cargo carried in the trade between them. Agreements between the US and the Latin American countries give the respective national flag carriers equal access to the government controlled cargoes traded between them.
USSR and COMECON	The USSR, the COMECON and the STNS or SCS sell goods on CIF basis and buy on FOB basis.	All trades including oceanborne trade between these countries and the rest of the world is conducted on the basis of bilateral trade agreements. Most of these countries have or are about to ratify the UNCTAD Code of Conduct's 40–40–20 cargo sharing.
Uruguay	Legislation of 1977 reserves a minimum of 50% of export cargo Uruguayan flag vessels. Import cargo must be carried on national flag lines whenever available; availability will be determined by the Executive in consultation with the Ministry of Transport and Public Works. Import registrations must indicate the means of transport. Vessels registered elsewhere may be used only with authority from the Ministry of Transport and Public Works and on the following conclusions; 1. That they are included in international commercial agreements with Uruguay; 2. Tat they are included in agreements or freight conferences in which Uruguay participates. Preference will be granted to foreign vessels which realize equal conference traffic with Uruguayan flag lines, provided that the rates quoted do not exceed those offered by non-conference lines on the same route. The Executive can extend preference to exports of merchandise, assets or products which benefit from fiscal exemption and to those	The Executive has authority to establish rebates to be granted for cargo exported in national flag vessels. The exporter may deduct the corresponding freight rebates from his taxes. The government reserves the right to decide upon the validity of all conference agreements involving import and export cargo. The Executive can disqualify national and foreign enterprises from operating in Uruguayan ports if the conferences in which they participate have not been duly approved. All general merchandise is subject to an important surcharge; cargoes arriving on Uruguayan ships receive a 10% rebate. Goods shipped from US Gulf ports where Uruguayan flag vessels call pay an extra 5% surcharge; shipments from US East Coast ports where no Uruguayan ships call do not pay a surcharge. Merchandise arriving in Uruguay for use by state entities, as well as certain exports, is entitled to 'fiscal exemptions' only when shipped in Uruguayan flag ships. Trade with LAFTA countries is considered as coastal trade; cargoes from LAFTA countries are exempt from the consular fee if they arrive in Uruguayan vessels.

Appendix 5 (*Continued*)

Country	Cargo reserved to national fleets	Other measures and trade agreements
	whose financing or guarantee is cannelled through institutions forming part of the national banking system. Uruguayan vessels are defined as those 51% or more owned by Uruguayan citizens. On routes in which Uruguayan flag vessels do not participate, waivers will be granted, provided reciprocity of cargo is agreed. Infringement carries a penalty of from 10 to 100% of the freight value generated by the shipment in questionl	Uruguay has 50–50 cargo-sharing agreements with Argentina, Brazil and Colombia; an agreement with Bolivia contains a discriminatory clause.
Venezuela	The Law for the Protection and Development of the National Merchant Marine requires that 50% of all exports and imports, including oil, be carried in national vessels, which are defined as ships at least 75% owned by Venezuelan nationals. The government hopes to reach this goal by 1985. The transport of not less than 10% of exports and imports of petroleum and its derivatives is currently reserved for Venezuelan flag ships; the proportion will gradually rise to 50%. Transport of ore, wheat and other free-flowing cargo shall be treated likewise, both as imports and exports. The government has suggested that preference should be given to state-owned Compania Anonima Venezolana de Navigacion (CAVN) in the shipment of cargoes controlled or contracted by the government.	The Venezuelan Pilotage Law allows the Executive to grant Venezuelan ships exemptions of up to 50% of the charges established by the Law. In addition, national flag ships pay 50% charges set by the pilotage regulations of individual ports. CAVN operates joint shipping services with several 'associated' lines from Europe and Japan; imports partially or totally exempt from import duties must move on CAVN or 'associated' line ships, thereby assuring CAVN of a definite share of the cargo in areas where it maintains a service.
Yugoslavia		The Yugoslav National Bank grants exporters and export premium of 20% on ocean freight to US North Atlantic ports and 30% on that to other ports if shipment is made via a Yugoslav port on a Yugoslav flag ship. If no Yugoslav flag ship is available a certificate to that effect must by obtained from the Association of Yugoslav Shipowners.
Zaire	The Compagnie Maritime Zairoise has the monopoly of export shipping from Zaire and the monopoly of all imports purchased with the assistance of the Bank of Zaire. It may bestow a portion of this operation on other companies of its choice.	

Part Three

Traditional methods of developing national fleets

Introduction to Part Three

Once a national fleet is established, the task does not end there. There is need for constant replenishing to avoid stagnation. In this section, therefore, attention is devoted to the traditional methods of developing national fleets. The line of demarcation between *establishment* and *development* can be very fine. Indeed, establishment continues into development. The same mechanism can be applicable in both areas, hence the overlap with and repetition of some of the earlier references.

This time both the DMNS and the TMNS need and use these *traditional* methods in their efforts to develop their fleets. There is an attempt, at this stage, to link the development of national fleets to the control and promotion of export and import trade generally and foreign exchange controls in particular. Although treated here as part of state intervention, maritime subsidies are really more an aspect of state assistance and are not resented as much or as damaging in their effects as the other types. Apart from subsidies, all the mechanisms outlined in Parts II and III can be referred to as forms of flag discrimination.

CHAPTER 5

Maritime subsidies as a method of developing national fleets

1. Introduction

The acceptable face of state intervention has taken the form of maritime subsidies which, as the title implies, consist mainly of financial aid and fiscal relief to shipping and shipbuilding.

1.1 Financial aid and fiscal relief to shipping and shipbuilding

The majority of countries provide significant assistance to shipping, some as an overall assistance to industry generally and others specifically to the merchant marine industry. Some countries on the other hand give little assistance to shipping, or none at all, and originally only a small fraction of the TMNS fleets received operating subsidies.[1] In some cases a considerable share of all assistance is reserved for coastal shipping, whereas in others it is given in exchange for contractual services within the national transportation system. We shall not attempt to measure specific amounts but only seek to review the development effects on the international level of financial aid[2] and fiscal relief to shipping and, discuss the reasons for such assistance and the forms in which it is extended. By their nature, the international effects of such assistance are entirely different from those which may be caused by flag discrimination.[3]

The main reasons for financial aid and fiscal relief to shipping have been the need to establish and develop merchant fleets (by reconstruction or renovation), to remedy financing problems and exceptionally high operating costs, or the need to compensate for special services.[4] The main forms of financial aid are operating subsidies and various financing aid schemes. Fiscal relief is mainly extended in the form of various depreciation privileges. This chapter, therefore, contains a historical account of the reasons which have led a number of countries to grant financial aid, or fiscal relief to their shipping industry, and of the types of aid which have recently been in force.[5] There are distinctions between financial aid and fiscal relief, aid to shipping and to shipbuilding, assistance to coastal shipping and to vessels operating in international ferries. We shall return to that later. The similarities are that they are all a form of subsidy.[6]

1.2 What is a subsidy?

In an economic context a subsidy is a payment to individuals or businesses by a government for which it receives no products or services in return. The purpose of such payments is to maintain a particular service – in this case a maritime transport service – at a price that the public can readily afford but that cannot otherwise be profitably supplied at this price. The particular service or product should be essential to the public welfare and/or national interest. The government would, therefore, find it necessary to subsidize the enterprise in order to keep it operating and producing the service or product.[7] In the US, for instance, federal subsidies are given to airlines to carry mail; to railroads and other means of public transporation of commuters; to farmers under the various agricultural programmes; and last, but not least, to the merchant marine industry to build and operate ships.

In the US the term 'subsidy' has been used to include governmental payments to other governments, now referred to as grants-in-aid.[8] On the other hand, in a legal context, a subsidy is:

> 'Something, usually money, donated or given or appropriated by the government through its proper agencies, in this country by the Congress.'[9]

In American law, therefore, a subsidy is a grant of money made by the government in aid of the promoters of any enterprise, work or improvement in which the government desires to participate, or which is considered a proper subject for state aid because it is likely to be of benefit to the public and/or the national interest.[10] The fact that the merchant marine is subsidized means it is regarded as essential.

What is worth noting is that subsidies are payments by the state to producers or distributors in order to reduce prices, and, secondly, that subsidies are inevitably linked to transportation and international trade. In this respect it will be further remembered that the earliest known subsidies are those on exports in order to encourage their sale abroad. Thirdly, subsidies can be provided indirectly or directly by deliberately running the merchant marine, and any other means of transportation, at a loss between manufacturing centres and ports.[11] Fourthly, and finally, however, subsidies, like tariffs, do interfere with the operation of the principle of comparative costs and so do not benefit the whole world. It is in this context that we focus attention on maritime subsidies; subsidies made to the merchant industries for various reasons and purposes noted earlier and below. Maritime subsidies take different forms and are not limited to the discussion in this chapter. As we noted, there were elements of subsidy in flag preference and discrimination; no doubt there will be more examples in the chapter dealing with state intervention (post).[12]

1.3 Maritime subsidies

Maritime subsidies, *inter alia*, are at the forefront of current controversy in international maritime trade and transportation. Consequently, some knowledge of transport economics and international trade is a prerequisite for a fuller appreciation of maritime subsidies in particular, and state aid to the merchant marine industry generally. The two are interrelated and one affects the other. It would appear one would require some understanding of the structural set-up of the political economy of both the TMNS and DMNS.[13] This might dispel the popular opinion in shipping circles that it is the STNS and DMNS which normally resort to the malpractice of maritime subsidies. The argument continues that these two, with their autocratic political system and planned economies, are encroachments on and a hinderance to established liberal international trade principles and the imbedded market-economy doctrine of free trade.[14]

As this inquiry will, hopefully, show, this belief may be popular but not necessarily true. One may not feel competent to speak for the STNS but one may feel duty bound to do so on behalf of one's origins – the DMNS – in their attempt to establish, develop and/or expand their merchant marine fleets through subsidies. Besides, whatever the prejudices, since World War II there has been a marked shift in the capitalist economies towards mixed enterprises,[15] together with some limited economic planning and outright nationalisation in certain essential sectors. The result is that it is now the general rule rather than the exception that almost all countries are involved, one way or the other, in planning and participation in both national and international economics.[16]

The *laissez-faire* doctrine – at least the classical kind – seems to have eroded. In the final analysis, therefore, government participation in, and government control of, the economy is no longer the exclusive monopoly of the STNS, with their so-called clients, the DMNS. This is true of subsidies to industry in general and maritime subsidies particularly. This inquiry may prove the accuracy or inaccuracy of this preposition.[17] The DMNS have laid themselves open to such accusations by making demands on the established TMNS. But there is ample evidence to show that both camps share responsibility for resorting to maritime subsidies and state intervention in favour of the merchant marine industry, with development objectives in mind. This can be traced from the origins of maritime subsidies. For centuries before the coming into being of the DMNS as national entities, the TMNS already practiced maritime subsidies.[18]

1.4 Origins of maritime subsidies

Subsidies, maritime or otherwise, are neither new concepts nor new practices.[19] In early English law subsidy was already known as:

> 'An aid, tax or tribute granted by parliament to the King for the urgent occasions of the Kingdom, to be levied on every subject of ability according to the value of his lands'.[20]

At about the same time international law also recognised subsidies, albeit for motives far removed from what we know today, as:

> 'The assistance given by one nation to another to enable the latter to carry on a war, when such a nation does not join directly in the war'.[21]

So much for the general outline of the origins of subsidies by parliament and in international law.

Maritime subsidies, too, probably date from the same period. As early as the seventeenth and eighteenth centuries maritime subsidies were already a common feature in British industry and took a variety of forms.[22] Japan, too, gave certain types of subsidies to her merchant marine industry as early as the eighteenth

Table 22. Maritime subsidies before 1914.[a]

Country	Type of maritime subsidy: Postal subvention	Operational subsidy	Construction subsidies	Indirect subsidies	Cargo preference
Austria Hungary[b]	X	X	X	X	
Brazil[c]	X	X		X	
Denmark	X				X
Egypt[d]	X				
France	X	X	X	X	
Germany[e]	X				X
Greece	X				X
Italy	X	X	X		
Japan	X	X	X		
Mexico[c]	X	X			
Netherlands	X				
Portugal	X				
Russia[d]	X	X	X	X	X
Spain	X		X		
Sweden	X				X
United Kingdom	X				
United States	X				
–					X

[a] Excluding cabotage restrictions.
[b] Now Austria and Hungary.
[c] Only developing maritime nations then (DMNS).
[d] Now East and West Germany.
[e] Before the 1917 Revolution; now USSR.
Source: Sturmey Sig. *British Shipping and World Competition.* p. 28.

century, for the purposes of its establishment and expansion.[23] Noting the current strength of the Japanese merchant marine industry one must admit that the effort succeeded. The Japanese example has been imitated by others, notably by the DMNS. The belief is 'if they can do it so can we'. Be that as it may, the US was not left out either, she too entered the race immediately before the nineteenth century and continued through into the twentieth.[24] Thus, maritime subsidies are not a new phenomenon, nor were they started by the DMNS, as we would be led to believe.

It will be apparent from Table 22 that of the 17 examples considered only three (Brazil, Egypt and Mexico) are DMNS. The above examples, however, take the form of indirect subsidies. Although nowadays operational and constructional subsidies would be categorised as direct, and cargo reference as a form of flag discrimination, at that time they were all classified together as subsidies. However, before World War I, shipbuilding subsidies were granted in Austria, Greece, Japan, Italy and Russia. Between the wars almost every major TMN gave subsidies in some form or another in an attempt to halt the contraction in the industry during the slump, or to enable it to contract on a rational basis.[25] Therein lie the other motives for granting maritime subsidies. O'Loughlin, however, notes that direct subsidies have been common since World War II, although there have been a number of minor subsidies, some in the smaller DMNS.

1.5 Postal subvention

This is probably the earliest known form of direct maritime subsidy. At the present time it has been phased out by most, if not all maritime nations, and are only discussed here for historical purposes. Sturmey, notes that, as early as the nineteenth century, aid to shipping predominatly took this form and that Britain took the lead.[26] Thornton, however, points out that there was little to be proud of at the time (1837) in the British merchant marine, hence, presumably the resort to subsidy. However, even he (Thornton) does not doubt the role of this form of subsidy.[27] As to its value, he confirms that the decision to put the carriage of mails out to contract was one the commercial importance of which:

> '. . . cannot be too strongly emphasized. The. . . mail policy of the British government. . . gave the British ocean shipping a start it never lost'.[28]

Unfortunately, and inevitably, the British have lost that lead ever since. Sturmey concurs with Thornton's contention that although the policy was a naval one, intended to expedite the mails and reduce the cost of carrying them by replacing the alarmingly inefficient naval services, the:

> '. . . mail subventions were of profound consequence in bridging the gap between the known high costs of steamship operation and commercial revenue obtainable'.[29]

It would appear that the majority of the TMNS followed the British lead. Sturmey further notes that these early postal subventions may be considered as examples of *infant industry* subsidies which succeeded in their aim precisely because they were working with, and not against the economic tide.[30] And that in their other aim, that of providing ships as reserves for the navies of the countries concerned, the policy was less successful. For example, the large express ships of the North Atlantic in particular were extremely useful in World War I in the unsuspected roles of troopships and hospital ships, but that early in the war the navies of both Britain and Germany became convinced that they had made a mistake in subsidizing mail ships for use as auxiliary cruisers.[31] This realisation seems to have virtually ended the use of mail subventions as subsidies for this purpose. Following World War II, and with further technological advancement, particularly the advent of diesel engines, mail subventions were replaced by more modern and more direct subsidies.[32]

2. Direct subsidies

Direct subsidies are granted to both coastal vessels engaged in domestic trade and to ocean shipping, i.e. vessels operating on international services. In line with the general development objective, assistance to coastal shipping may be necessary to redress structural problems of the coastal fleet, in cases where owners of small coastal vessels have insufficient access to the capital market,[33] or in exchange for certain contractual services in the public interest, which are not attractive to private shipowners. The common characteristics of aid schemes for the reserved sector of coastal shipping are the intimate relations with other fields of national economic policy and the absence of immediate and noticeable effects on international shipping.[34]

Direct aid to vessels operating in international services, on the other hand, is designed to improve the international competitive position of the vessels receiving such aid, or to make possible the construction and operation of vessels which otherwise might not have been able to face international competition.[35] This may, of course, be detrimental to the competitive position of other vessels which do not receive such aid and may introduce distortions into the general international shipping scene. On the other hand, it can also be argued that assistance to ocean shipping may be necessary because of special internal circumstances for which the national shipping industry cannot be held responsible.[36]

Financing problems have been mentioned most frequently as reasons for government assistance. The high proportion of capital costs in the total cost of shipping makes the industry particularly sensitive to conditions in the capital market.[37] New vessels are usually built with a considerable amount of credit and even small differences in credit conditions, and especially in rates of interest, can considerably affect the economics of new building. In countries with an insufficient capital market, shipping investments may thus encounter particular difficulties.[38] High domestic interest rates and tight credit conditions are not only typical for some of the developing OECD member countries, but have been specifically mentioned by the more industrialised TMNS, such as Germany and Japan, as consequences of the war and, therefore, as reason for post-war government assistance to shipping.[39]

2.1 Reasons for direct subsidies

Other countries refer to lack of interest in shipping investments. It appears that the high risks of the industry have led even the more advanced TMNS with more developed capital markets to grant assistance in order to encourage private investments in shipping.[40] Germany, for example, mentions the precarious structure of owners' finances due to war and it appears probable that similar problems existed in the other TMNS. Finland and Sweden at the time did call attention to the special problems of small shipowners who may have insufficient access to the capital market.[41]

A number of different reasons have led the governments of both TMNS and DMNS in recent years to grant aid to their shipping industries. Leaving aside for the moment the question of compensation for special services (which we have touched on briefly and to which we shall return shortly) deemed necessary in the public[42] national interest, governmental assistance to shipping is motivated either by problems of the national shipping sector, or even more frequently, by particular conditions of the national economy outside the shipping sector. The need for reconstruction or renovation of the fleets has also been mentioned by a number of countries as a reason for government assistance.[43]

Certain TMNS, in the course of their industrial development, have granted aid with a view to the modernization of their ocean fleets and their adaptation to present-day competitive conditions. Exceptionally high operating costs can be due to numerous reasons which are more or less beyond the control of the shipowner.[44] A high national wage level, for instance, puts the operation of US vessels at a particular disadvantage; while France has problems with its special maritime system of social security, as an important factor contributing to a higher than average level of operating costs, and has called attention to the considerable impact of the different methods of financing maritime social security in various countries.[45]

The position of the vessel or a shipping company in international competition can be influenced by any of the major cost items. Besides capital costs and operating costs, the fiscal conditions of the country of registration may be a reason for competitive disadvantage.[46] Public assistance is often granted for special services. The public utility aspects of certain remunerative coastal services, especially of passenger services, or services between the mainland and the outlying islands has been mentioned. In some of these cases rates or fares are controlled or subject to governmental approval.[47]

Special service obligations are, however, not confined to such domestic services. All countries giving direct subsidies to international deep sea operations make this aid conditional upon the operation of certain services deemed essential in the national interest.[48] Thus, financial or fiscal aid has been described, in practically all cases, as due to particular conditions within the individual country or its shipping industry. Some TMNS, however, have mentioned that they were obliged, on some occasions, to extend special aid to a number of shipping companies when continuing depressed conditions on the world shipping market made the servicing of certain loans impossible.[49] In the domain of direct financial aid, direct operational and constructional subsidies, allowances or grants constitute the most easily discernible form of assistance.[50]

2.2 Operation subsidies

The operational subsidy in the US probably best exemplifies all the principles and characteristics of this particular category. An operating[51] -differential subsidy is granted to the US ship operators to place the operating costs of US flag vessels on a parity with those of foreign competitors.[52] The subsidy is based on the difference between the fair and reasonable cost of insurance (protection and indemnity and hull and machinery premiums), maintenance, repairs not compensated by insurance, wages of officers and crew, and subsistence of officers and crews on the passenger vessels, and the estimated costs of the same items if the vessels were operated under foreign registry.[53]

Subsidy is paid pursuant to operating subsidy contracts between the government and the operators.[54] Authority for the payment of the subsidy under these contracts is contained in Title VI of the *Merchant Marine Act, 1936,* as amended.[55] In accordance with the government/industry efforts to reduce government expenditures on privately owned merchant shipping, recently executed operating subsidy contracts have not included subsidy for hull and machinery insurance premiums, and maintenance and repair costs, persuant to the provisions of *Section 603* of the Act. The section permits the parties to the operating subsidy contracts to agree to a lesser amount of subsidy than that which is necessary to achieve parity.[56] Under *Title VI,* the operators holding subsidy contracts must be US citizens and must possess certain other qualifications. The Secretary of Commerce must determine that the subsidized vessels are of US construction and that the operation of such vessels in an essential service is required to meet the foreign flag competition and to promote the foreign commerce of the US.[57]

Table 23. US ODS Accruals and outlays – January 1, 1937 to September 30, 1981.

	Accruals			Outlays		
Calender year of operation	Subsidies	Recapture	Subsidy accrual	In FY 1981	Total amount of net accrual paid	Net accrual liability
1937–1955	$682 457 954	$157 632 946	$524 825 008	0	$524 825 008	0
1956–1960	751 430 098	63 755 409	687 674 689	0	687 674 689	0
1961	170 884 261	2 042 748	168 841 513	0	168 841 513	0
1962	179 727 400	4 929 404	174 797 996	0	174 467 393	330 603
1963	189 119 876	(1 451 917)	190 535 793	0	190 535 793	0
1964	220 334 818	674 506	219 660 312	0	219 660 312	0
1965	183 913 236	1 014 005	182 899 231	0	182 899 231	0
1966	202 734 069	3 229 471	199 504 598	0	199 504 598	0
1967	220 579 702	5 162 831	215 416 871	0	215 416 871	0
1968	222 862 970	3 673 790	219 189 180	0	219 189 180	0
1969	233 201 233	2 217 144	230 984 089	0	228 038 947	2 945 142
1970	232 686 761	(1 908 643)	234 595 404	0	234 449 812	145 592
1971	203 401 051	(2 821 259)	206 222 310	0	205 261 360	960 950
1972	192 512 930	0	192 512 930	0	190 732 158	1 780 772
1973	219 569 907	0	219 569 907	0	219 468 476	101 431
1974	220 912 243	0	220 912 243	427 844	218 982 010	1 930 233
1975	261 806 899	0	261 806 899	830 625	259 445 924	2 360 975
1976	281 947 153	0	281 947 153	3 956 444	272 993 888	8 953 265
1977	300 713 310	0	300 713 310	1 227 775	289 593 256	11 120 054
1978	287 579 374	0	287 579 374	624 436	277 404 552	10 174 822
1979	275 253 064	0	275 253 064	2 346 774	264 910 958	10 342 106
1980	393 734 024	0	393 734 024	108 962 332	354 360 169	39 373 855
1981	272 476 455	0	272 476 455	216 161 017	216 161 017	56 315 438
Total regular ODS	$399 838 788	$238 186 435	$6 161 652 353	$334 537 247	$6 014 817 115	$146 835 238
Soviet grain programs	146 444 444	0	146 444 444	316 423	144 058 407	2 386 037
Total ODS	$6 546 238 232	$238 186 435	$6 308 096 797	$334 853 670	$6 158 875 522	$149 221 275

Under certain circumstances, e.g., to passenger vessels, in addition to the liner trades, operating subsidy is also authorised for the cruiser trades. With respect to cargo vessels, prior to the enactment of the *Merchant Marine Act, 1970,* which extensively amended the 1936 Act, operating subsidy was payable only to liner type vessels with scheduled sailings on established trade routes.[58] The 1970 amendments broadened the scope of the term 'essential service' to authorize the payment of operating subsidy to aid in the operation of bulk carrier type vessels, whether or not operating on particular services, routes or lines. Also *Public Law 91–103* enacted December 31, 1970, which further amended Title VI of the 1936 Act, permits the payment of operating subsidy on leased as well as owned vessels.[59] The subsidized operators under the operating-differential subsidy contracts must assume the obligations of a replacement programme. Under this scheme they are contractually required to construct new vessels to replace the existing vessels in their subsidized fleets as the existing fleets becomes obsolete.[60]

The number of vessels to be built under the replacement programme and the vessels' designs are agreed upon after negotiations between the subsidized ship operators and the US Government Department of Shipping.[61] Since the enactment of *Public Law 93–603,* permitting the payment of operating subsidy on leased vessels, many of the ship operators, in order to raise the large amounts of capital necessary for the construction of modern vessels, have taken advantage of the leverage lease financing methods to lower the shipbuilding costs.[62] Under this arrangement, the ownership of the newly constructed vessels is vested in the financial institutions and the vessels leased to the subsidized operators under bareboat charters. This method of financing, however, is not used solely in connection with the construction of vessels by operators who are receiving an operating subsidy.[63] The total amount of subsidy paid under the operating differential subsidy contracts during the fiscal year 1977–1978 was US $344 million. Subsidy paid during the fiscal year 1977 under the special operating-differential subsidy executed in connection with the shipment of grain to the USSR was US $34.3 million.[64]

2.3 Constructional subsidies

Besides direct operating subsidies, several countries do give construction subsidies. Among the TMNS these are tied to construction in domestic yards and are designed to decrease domestic building costs in order to approximate them to those of foreign builders.[65] It can be assumed that these subsidies do not include any element of assistance to the shipowners concerned. Figures of expenditure under this heading are not available, but as in the case of operating subsidies, all these schemes are subject to certain conditions being fulfilled on the part of the beneficiary.[66] It should also be noted that in some countries these schemes are not limited to shipping but that a large range of industries are also eligible for these grants. Construction subsidies, to the extent that they benefit the shipowner, can obviously stimulate the construction of modern vessels and can help to improve productivity and foster the technical progress of a country's fleet – a prerequisite for fleet expansion.[67]

Table 24. US Operating-differential subsidy accruals and outlays by lines – January 1, 1937 to September 30, 1981.

Lines	Accruals				
	ODS	Recapture	Net accrual	ODS paid[i]	Net Accrued liability
Aeron Marine Shipping	18 829 958	0	18 829 958	17 108 704	1 721 254
American Banner Lines[a]	2 626 512	0	2 626 512	2 626 512	0
American Diamond Lines[a]	185 802	28 492	157 310	157 310	0
American Export Lines[b]	701 299 996	10 700 587	690 599 409	683 121 281	1 478 128
American Mail Lines[c]	158 240 739	7 424 902	150 815 837	150 815 837	0
American President Lines[c]	798 275 674	17 676 493	780 599 181	769 681 682	10 917 499
American Shipping	7 052 025	0	7 052 025	6 548 893	503 132
American Steamship	111 751	0	111 751	76 462	35 289
Aquarius Marine Co.	9 063 101	0	9 063 101	7 815 902	1 247 199
Aries Marine Shipping	22 332 947	0	22 332 947	19 399 450	2 933 497
Atlantic & Caribbean S/N[a]	63 209	45 496	17 713	17 713	0
Atlas Marine Co.	7 807 174	0	7 807 174	6 580 666	1 226 508
Baltimore Steamship[a]	416 269	0	416 269	416 269	0
Bloomfield Steamship[a]	15 588 085	2 613 688	12 974 397	12 974 397	0
Chestnut Shipping Co.	16 968 935	0	16 968 935	13 772 172	3 196 763
Delta Steamship Lines	405 618 506	8 185 313	397 433 193	375 318 171	22 115 022
Ecological Shipping Co.	5 132 094	0	5 132 094	4 182 841	949 253
Farrell Lines	471 916 662	1 855 375	470 061 287	455 867 544	14 193 743
Prudential Lines[d]	582 933 194	24 223 564	558 709 630	557 821 250	888 380
Gulf & South American Steamships[e]	34 471 780	5 226 214	29 245 566	29 245 566	0
Lykes Bros. Steamship	977 534 910	52 050 598	925 484 312	888 169 304	37 315 008
Margate Shipping	33 065 115	0	33 065 115	28 906 985	4 158 130
Moore McCormack Bulk Transport	23 576 352	0	23 576 352	23 130 896	445 456
Moore McCormack Lines	598 236 180	17 762 445	580 473 735	570 829 906	9 643 829
N.Y. & Cuba Mail Steamship[a]	8 090 108	1 207 331	6 882 777	6 882 777	0

Oceanic Steamship[e]	114 749 126	1 171 756	113 577 370	112 775 925	801 445
Pacific Argentina Brazil Line[a]	7 963 936	270 701	7 693 238	7 693 238	0
Pacific Far East Line[f]	292 197 331	23 479 204	268 718 127	260 214 752	8 503 375
Pacific Shipping Co.	8 226 796	0	8 226 796	6 710 102	1 516 694
Prudential Steamship[a]	26 098 640	1 680 796	24 417 844	24 417 844	0
Sea Shipping[a]	25 819 800	2 429 102	23 390 698	23 390 698	0
States Steamship	233 796 721	5 110 997	228 685 724	224 703 580	3 982 144
U.S. Line[g]	591 304 289	54 958 689	536 345 700	534 354 832	2 090 868
Waterman Steamship	172 849 054	0	172 849 054	165 127 824	7 721 230
Worth Oil Transport	9 198 117	0	9 198 117	8 030 260	1 167 857
Zapata Products	16 172 141	0	16 172 141	14 673 510	1 498 631
South Atlantic Steamship[a]	96 374	84 692	11 682	11 682	0
Seabulk Transmarine I & II, Inc.	1 189 283	0	1 189 283	885 370	303 913
Equity	740 002	0	740 002	459 006	280 996
Total regular ODS	$6 399 838 788	$238 186 435	$6 161 652 353	$6 014 817 115	$146 835 238
Soviet grain programs[h]	146 444 444		146 444 444	144 058 407	2 386 037
Total ODS	$6 546 283 232	$238 186 435	$6 308 096 797	$6 158 875 522	$149 221 275

[a] No longer subsidized or combined with other subsidized lines.
[b] AEL was acquired by Farrell Lines, March 29, 1978.
[c] APL merged its operations with AML's, October 10, 1973.
[d] Changed from Prudential-Grace Lines, Inc., August 1, 1974.
[e] Purchased by Lykes Bros. Steamship Co.
[f] Went into receivership August 2, 1978.
[g] Ceased to be subsidized line in November 1970.
[h] Included 33 subsidized operators as of September 30, 1979.
[i] Includes prior year adjustments between operators.

Source: MARAD 1981, p. 21.

Table 25. US Construction reserve funds – September 30, 1981.

Company	Balance (dollars)
Cargo Carriers, Inc.	1 675 000
Central Gulf Steamship Corp.	1 000
Gulf Mississippi Marine Corp.	100
Ingram Industries, Inc.	85 000
Joan Turecamo, Inc.	3 876
Lee-Van, Ltd.	650 000
Mobil Oil Corp.	3 283 438
National Marine Service, Inc.	1 145 300
Total, September 30, 1981	6 843 714
Net decrease fiscal year 1981	8 663 628

Source: MARAD 1981, p. 13.

Among the TMNS, the system operated by the Irish Republic is probably a much more elaborate example, where state subsidies, for this purpose, are payable for ships built in Irish yards.[68] The Shipping Financing Corporation, a subsidiary of the Industrial Credit Company, a government investment bank, provides loans at low interest rates towards the cost of ships built domestically so that credit facilities can be extended to shipowners comparable to those available in other countries. The only substantial shipbuilding yard in Ireland, however, is the Verolme Cork Dockyard (VCD) in which there is a substantial state investment by way of loans, grant contributions, and share subscriptions. In addition to its shipbuilding facilities, the yard has extensive ship repair and general engineering units.[69]

There have been two forms of state aid available for shipbuilding at VCD:

(a) Credit facilities and subsidized interests for shipowners (i.e. shipping finance); and

(b) Maximum loss subsidy of 7% of the contract price of a vessel.[70]

Under the Shipping Finance Scheme, which is administered by the shipping Finance Corporation (a subsidiary of the Industrial Credit Co.), credit is provided for shipowners ordering vessels from VCD. The credit terms which comply with OECD and EEC Regulations, are limited to 70% credit over seven years at no less than 8% interest.[71] VCD also had the benefit of a subsidy scheme to offset losses incurred in shipbuilding. The operation, however, expired at the end of 1977. The limit to the subsidy was 7% of the contract price of the vessel[72] or the loss incurred in building the vessel, after depreciation whichever was the lesser.[73]

India, on the other hand, provides the example from the DMNS: the government owns the Hindustan Shipyard at Visakhapatnan, and the Cochin Shipyard.[74] Subsidy is paid directly to the yard and varies according to the cost of construction of a ship. Until March 31, 1976, it was 5% of the international price of the ship which was fixed at the average of the valuation received from reliable foreign ship valuers in three or four leading shipbuilding countries.[75] This assistance by the government to the shipyard will be reduced at the rate of 1% every two years. Shipbuilding is also assisted to the extent of an actual price differential between the indigeneous price and the lowest international price of six vital items of machinery subject to a ceiling of 10% of the international price. This pricing policy is at present under review by the government.[76] Construction subsidy is sometimes known as *modernization*.

2.4 Modernization subsidy (scrap and build and demolition)

We noted earlier that the need for reconstruction or renovation of fleets has been given by a number of countries as a reason for government assistance.[77] It will also be recalled that Germany and Japan, for instance, granted considerable assistance during the post-war years in order to help the reconstruction of the ocean fleet which had been almost entirely lost during the war. Certain countries, in the course of their industrial development, have granted aid with a view to the modernization of their ocean fleets and their adaptation to present-day competitive conditions.[78] Among the TMNS, some, e.g. France and Sweden, have aided the modernization of their coastal fleets and certain others, including the US, have granted assistance to ocean shipping with the specific purpose of promoting the construction of modern vessels.[79]

The first type of modernization is what is known in the trade as *scrap and build.*[80] For instance, the Italian *Law no. 622* of 24 July, 1959, as amended, provides shipowners (who scrap vessels and contract to build new units of a gross tonnage amounting to at least 50% of the scrapped vessels) with a subsidy of 30 000 Italian lira per weight ton of the new vessel.[81] When the gross tonnage of the new vessel exceeds 75% of the crapped vessel's tonnage, the grant is also limited to 75% of the scrapped vessel's gross tonnage.[82] Vessels scrapped must be at least 15 years old and have been registered in Italy for at least five years. However, Law No. 720 of 23 December, 1975 extended this subsidy, with some modifications, until 31 December, 1980.[83]

Japan, on the other hand, introduced the scrap and build system in 1961.[84] In the Japanese case when a shipowner intends to scrap a super-annuated home-trade cargo ship, and build a new one of the same type, he may be granted permission to utilise the measures by which part of the construction if financed by the Maritime Credit Corporation on condition that he shares the ownership of such a ship with the corporation.[85] The terms of such financing vary. The total amount of finance in the fiscal year 1976, for instance, was 12 400 million yen.[86]

The other TMN is the US.[87] It will be remembered that Section 510 of the *Merchant Marine Act, 1936,* authorises MARAD to acquire privately owned obsolete vessels[88] in exchange for an allowance of credit payable to the shipowner or shipbuilder on the construction of new vessels. It also provides for the acquisition of marine class vessels constructed under Title VII of the *Merchant Marine Act, 1936,*[89] and *Public Law 911*, and other suitable vessels constructed in the US, which have never been under foreign documentation, in exchange for obsolete vessels in the National Defence Reserve Fleets.[90] A second category of state aid is known properly as modernization subsidy.

The merchant marine industry has not escaped the effects of technological advance in industry. By modernization we mean the installation of technological advance in industry. By modernization we mean the installation of technologically advanced machinery in place of old machinery.[91] In some cases there

Table 26, US National Defense Reserve Fleet, 1945–1981.

Fiscal year	Ships	Fiscal year	Ships
1945	5	1964	1739
1946	1421	1965	1594
1947	1204	1966	1327
1948	1675	1967	1152
1949	1934	1968	1062
1950	2277	1969	1017
1951	1767	1970	1027
1952	1853	1971	860
1953	1932	1972	673
1954	2067	1973	541
1955	2068	1974	487
1956	2061	1975	419
1957	1889	1976	438
1958	2074	1977	333
1959	2060	1978	306
1960	2000	1979	317
1961	1923	1980	320
1962	1862	1981	317
1963	1819		

Source: MARAD 1981, p. 48.

has been merely substitution. Modernization by the substitution of new machinery for similar but older machinery because of the modren equipment's superiority is attributable to technical improvements rather than to mere newness.[92] However, large amounts of outmoded plant and equipment are still being used by the merchant marine industry. Moreover, the development of new technological improvements is making production techniques introduced only a short time ago obsolete, hence the necessity of state subsidies to keep abreast. A number of the TMNS have definite schemes in this regard.[93]

In Canada, for instance, modernization is known alternatively as *demolition subsidy*.[94] The *Income Tax Act* provides a tax deferral on insurance proceeds arising from the involuntary disposition of a vessel, provided that these funds are reinvested in a replacement vessel. Under a programme instituted in 1976, money spent by shipbuilders on the modernization of equipment will be matched by the government to a limit of 3% of the value of the new construction.[95] In France, on the other hand, investment subsidies are available to owners on certain conditions for the modernization of cargo liners wherever built.[96] Also equipment grants are payable during the period of the Seventh Plan (1976–1980) at rates varying from 2% to 15% of the contract price depending on the type of ship and totalling not more than US $222 million.[97] However, passenger ships and long range tankers do not qualify for these grants.

In Belgium, modernization subsidies fall under the depreciation accounting category. Under this scheme, expenditure for modernization of existing ships or loss of major repairs and alterations on the acquisitions of second-hand ships are subject to the same schedule of depreciation.[98] However, the objective behind modernization subsidies, as in the other cases, is to increase efficiency and competitiveness.[99] The third and final heading of modernization subsidy is a combination of yard conversion and part expansion subsidies. In quite a few countries these are treated as modernization or construction subsidies.[100]

This is not entirely accurate, for, whereas the former relate to the ocean-going vessels themselves, the latter are much more applicable to the shipyards and ports – the fixed structures,[101] the only common denominator being that all are building subsidies. A couple or so of the TMNS have definite programmes regarding yard conversions. In France, for example, the government supports a programme for the conversion of the shipyards and the retraining of shipyard employees for other industrial activities.[102] Investment grants of up to 20% of the cost of equipment have been available for the conversion of small and medium-sized shipyards since the decree of 27 December, 1960.[103]

On the other hand, in Norway, in connection with the restructuring of shipyards, government loans can be granted over 12 years with no interest – or down payment – during the first three years.[104] The loans may cover up to 40% of the coast involved. For the fiscal year 1978, US $7 million were granted for this purpose. This is a follow-up of a parliamentary decision taken in 1977 granting loans, limited to US $91 million, for restructuring and employment purposes. And in Spain, government approval must be obtained for expansion or conversion of shipyards.[105] As to port expansion subsidies, one distinct example is West Germany, where credits are granted to port operators to enlarge facilities. Interest is 5.5% with repayment periods of 12 years.[106]

As to the DMNS, the Chilean charges have been known to be insufficient to cover costs and, therefore, a subsidy from the fiscal budget was found necessary to maintain port operations.[107] Even then, port rates in Chile remain the same for all shipping and there is no evidence of port or berth flag discrimination of the kind we saw earlier operating in some ports. Being an archipelagic country, Indonesia has so many ports, dotted on numerous islands, that they could hardly be developed without some form of assistance.[108] Port expansion is needed and planned for several Indonesian ports. The most important expansion plans are for the port of Jandjung, near Djakarta.[109] At times it is difficult to differentiate between modernization and depreciation subsidies particularly when it comes to accounting systems.

2.5 Actual depreciation subsidies

Actual depreciation is a reduction in the value of fixed assets.[110] The most important causes of depreciation are wear and tear (loss of value caused by the use of an asset), the effects of the element (i.e. decay or corrosion), and gradual obsolescence, which makes it unprofitable to continue using some assets until they have been fully exhausted.[111] The annual amount of depreciation of an asset depends on its original purchase price, its estimated useful life, and its estimated salvage value. A number of different assessing methods of the amount of depreciation have been developed and a number of such various references are made in this chapter.[112] Using the simple *straight line method* (post), which considers depreciation a function of time, the annual depreciation cost is calculated by dividing the cost of the asset (original minus salvage cost) equally over its entire life.

When the life of a fixed asset, like a ship, is a function of use rather than of time, industry employs the *production method*, in which depreciation is calculated in proportion to the use (generally expressed in terms of hours of operation or units produced) which has been made of the asset.[113] There are also a number of decreasing-charge methods, such as the *diminishing-value method* and the *sum-of-the digits method* which allocate higher depreciation costs to the beginning years of the operation of an asset and lower depreciation costs to the latter years. These methods assign the greatest depreciation to the earlier years of the asset's life, when the greatest decrease in resale value normally occurs. Such accelerated depreciation (post) methods can be used in accordance with the tax laws to reduce the overall cost of new capital investments.[114]

These economic bases are used to evaluate maritime direct depreciation subsidies. Take the case of West Germany. In that country the depreciation of ships is based on a regular useful life of 14 years for dry cargo ships, and 12 years for tankers, reefers, special container ships and LASH ships. The 12-year period is also applied to dry cargo ships delivered after December 31, 1972.[115] The ships may be written off in unchanging amounts (straight line method) or in annually decreasing amounts (regressive methods). In the latter case, the percentage of the ships' value used to calculate the depreciation must not amount to more than the double percentage applicable in using the straight line method (for ships chartered after August 31, 1977, 250%). Depreciation must neither exceed the acquisition value nor go below the scrap value of the vessel (US $20 per GRT).[116]

A special depreciation allowance may be requested by German owners for new vessels, either built on demand or purchased from stock. The special depreciation allowance may also be used in the first years of the vessel's life including the year of its construction or purchase. The cumulative amount of special depreciation was originally up to 30% of the acquisition costs.[117] This special depreciation is accorded in addition to the ordinary depreciation and may only be used if the ship is being depreciated according to the straight line method. The special depreciation percentage was raised from 30% of the vessel's constructed or purchased cost from 1975 to 1978. This scheme was extended for four additional years. After five years of the vessel's life, the remaining value is depreciated in a straight line over the rest of the vessel's useful life. Vessels for which this special depreciation is called upon may not be sold within 8 years of construction or purchase.[118]

Still in the German case, special depreciation on ships ordered in or after 1971, may only generate an accounting loss for the owner if no less than 30% of the ship's construction costs have been financed from the owner's capital funds. If this requirement is met, special depreciations are admissible, but any accounting losses resulting therefrom must not exceed 15% of the value of the vessel. This regulation is not applicable to ships of no less than 1 600 gross tons (except tankers, seagoing tugs and special prospecting vessels).[119] But not all depreciations are special and actual, nor are subsidies limited to them only; there is also accelerated or anticipated depreciation. In the economic context this is a faster-than-historical rate of depreciation of fixed assets for income tax purposes. It is a method of depreciation that makes the depreciation allowance, and hence the tax allowance, available earlier in the life of the asset. We shall reserve discussion of fiscal relief for the later treatment of indirect subsidies. Suffice it here to refer to one example, i.e., special allowances for depreciation of more than 100% of the purchase price of a new vessel. A large number of countries grant a certain latitude in respect of depreciation provisions or the formation of tax-free reserves, thus giving verious possibilities to defer tax payment.[120] Numerous different provisions in this respect exist in the various countries, some of them permitting the constitution of tax-free reserves, others allowing depreciation periods of less than the physical life of a ship, or permitting various forms of accelerated depreciation, e.g. higher rates of depreciation during the early life of a vessel.[121] *Accelerated depreciation* either takes the form of constant depreciation percentages (reducing balance method) instead of linear depreciation or of special depreciation allowances during the first years of the vessel's life, the kind discussed above.[22]

2.6 Accelerated depreciation subsidies

Provisions for accelerated depreciation must be considered in view of today's rapid technical progress and the correspondingly early economic obsolescence of assets, typical of the shipping sector. Once free depreciation is permitted a new vessel could be written off entirely during the first year.[123] Although this takes account of the fluctuating character of shipping profits, few companies make enough profit to postpone a significant amount of tax. It seems worth noting, however, that attitudes of the fiscal authorities in different countries with regard to the accounting life of a ship vary considerably, and that normal depreciation periods are between 5 and 25 years.[124] By using the liberalised provisions for computing depreciation in the US, for instance, a business can recapture almost 50% more of its investments in a fixed asset during the first half of the asset's useful life than it could when it was limited to a straight line depreciation as in actual depreciation.[125]

Again in the US, rapid tax amortization certificates issued during World War II and the Korean conflict, in order to stimulate defence and defence-supporting investment, permitted the American shipping companies to write off within 5 years assets that would normally have been depreciated over a longer period.[126] Accelerated depreciation in any form does not increase the total tax free allowances for capital consumption. This applies to the merchant marine as to any other industry.

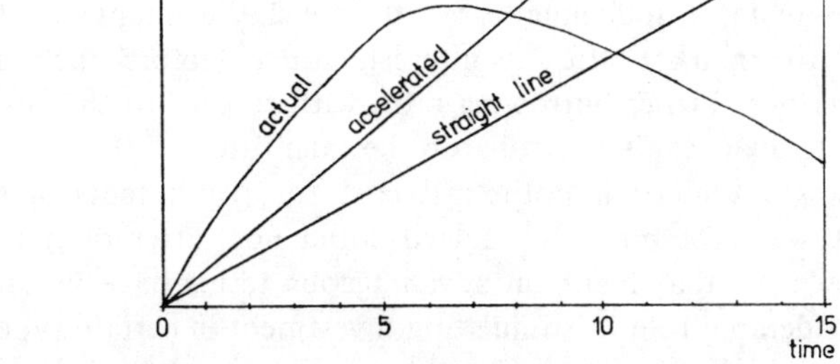

Figure 1. Depreciation subsidies.

In Australia, for instance, this kind of depreciation is allowable in respect of a plant or articles owned by the taxpayer[126A] and:

(a) Used by him during the year of income for the purpose of producing assessable income; or

(b) installed ready for use for that purpose and held in reserve by him.[127]

Thus in Australia, as in the US, the date from which depreciation of a new ship should commence for income tax purposes may vary according to the facts of each individual case. The handover date would be appropriate if at that time the ship required no further fitting out in order to begin service and if the handover point was at a port from which the ship would normally take on passengers or cargoes.[128] For instance, a ship intended for an Australian coastal run would not be regarded as installed ready for use for the purposes of providing assessable income merely upon delivery at a foreign shipyard. It is not considered that the depreciation of such a ship would commence, for income tax purposes, when it reached the first port of its Australian run.[129] The merits and demerits of depreciation subsidies, as development measures, will be considered later as will those for the other categories of direct maritime subsidy – loans and interest subsidies.

2.7 Loan subsidies

Loans by governments or public financing institutions, for new vessel building, purchase or repairs, are given by many countries, making this the category of aid most frequently granted. The conditions under which such loans are given vary from country to country and often between individual loans.[130] In the various examples we came across, interest rates varied between 2.5% and 6.5%, repayment periods between 5 and 25 years, and loans of up to 30% to 80% of the ship's value are granted. All offer some advantage over commercial loans but these advantages are of quite different importance.[131] In limited cases it appears that the loan conditions and terms closely approach those of the open capital market. In these cases, as in the others, lack of access to the normal capital market for certain owners (small or medium-sized firms) seems to be the primary motive for government intervention. As will be apparent, most countries limit loans to building, purchase or conversion of coastal vessels. In a few others, loans are conditional upon building in national yeards and the shipbuilding sector is, in fact, the beneficiary.[132]

The impact of shipbuilding loans on the public purse and the significance of such loans for the individual recipient are difficult to assess. While it may be possible to estimate, in individual cases, the subsidy element of a loan received at less than the market rate of interest, other factors such as prolonged repayment periods, higher borrowing rates with respect to the ship's value and easier access to loan capital, can hardly be quantified.[133] It may be somewhat easier to assess actual or hypothetical cost to governments of special credit schemes, but we have not (and indeed could not) attempt it here. It seems probable, however, that loans on advantageous terms have in some countries played a considerable role in stimulating investment in certain types of shipping and have possibly been effective in this respect at relatively low cost to the government by combining aid with a large element of self-help.[134]

From this point of view, the Swedish Ship's Mortgage Bank presents an interesting example. While the government has contributed the original stock, the institution raises capital on the open market and gives mortgages on commercial terms for vessels under 3 000 grt. This makes it one of the most common types of direct subsidies outside the building subsidies.[135] In addition, the Swedish government provides, within certain limits, for loans obtained by Swedish shipyards from domestic or foreign credit insitutions.[136] We shall risk detailed discussion over this Swedish illustration for the sake of the illuminating examples it provides of this type of subsidy.[137] In Swedish terms, the aim of these subsidies is to help shipyards to refinance part of their outstanding construction credits to Swedish and foreign shipowners. In this respect, it may be similar to construction subsidy, but that is as far as the similarity goes. For the latter subsidies are used primarily as collateral security for loans secured by mortgage.[138]

The Swedish system, in effect since 1936, was continued under the Shipbuilding Act of November 2, 1978. According to the legislation, the actual volume of the guarantees was to be allowed to increase by US $1.1 billion to the extent of US $3.8 billion before the end of 1981[139] Swedish owners, ordering from Swedish yards, are to receive a 'unit-off-loan' of a maximum of 25% of the new-building price. The loans run for 5 years and are free of interest. After 5 years the ship will be assessed and if the value of the ship has increased the gain will be divided equally between the state and the owner.[140] In addition, credit guarantees of a maximum of 70% of the building price can also be obtained. The loans covered by the guarantees may have a maturity period of 12 years maximum. To receive a 'write-off-loan' and/or credit guarantees the order had to be placed with a Swedish yard before the end of 1979 – the ship to be delivered before the end of 1980.[141]

The Swedish Ship's Mortgage Bank grants credits to Swedish shipowners against a mortgage within 50–70% of the estimated value of a new ship. The credit period is 15 years for loans with 50% of the value and 10 years for those between 50% to 70% of the value. The loans are redeemable by annual instalments of 1/15% and 1/10% per annum, respectively.[142] The rate of interest is dependent on the current rate of interest ruling on the bond market at the time of the grant, but remains unchanged during the credit period. Outstanding loans amounted to about US $250 million on December 31, 1977. To meet temporary economic difficulties the Bank has been given facilities to postpone the annual installment payment provided that the risk situation is acceptable.[143]

Since July 31, 1977, the Government can issue guarantees for loans to Swedish shipowners. The aim of this guarantee system is to prevent modern Swedish ships being sold at extremely low prices. The ships must belong to shipping companies with a clear ability to overcome their economic problems and in the future remain profitable companies.[144] The total volume of these guarantees for Swedish owners will amount to US $115 billion. In the Act, resulting from the Bill to Parliament of November 2, 1978, the two major shipping companies of Sweden, the Salen shipping Group and the Brostrom Shipping Group were expected to receive specially designed support by government guarantees and loans for the period 1979–1982 for the Salen Shipping Group, and 1979–1983 for the Bostrom Shipping Group, respectively. The Bostrom Shipping Group is also expected to receive a direct financial contribution of US $18 million.[145]

2.8 Interest subsidies

The last, but not least, significant direct subsidy is *interest subsidy*. Closely related to public loans under advantageious conditions are interest subsidies, usually for commercial loans, reportedly in operation by four TMNS, one of which has since discontinued its cheme.[146] Japan, for instance, had been granting a 3.0% subsidy on private loans and a 2.5% one on Development Bank Loans, while Italy provided up to 3.5% on certain loans. In France, the interest subsidies were designed to bring interest rates for commercial loans down to a minimum of 3% under certain conditions.

Interest, of course, is the price paid for the use of loan monies over a period of time. Inidividuals, businessment and governments buy the use of loan monies to purchase ships[147] and other capital goods, because they can increase production and productivity through the introduction of new plants and new machines. Likewise, consignors and consignees pay interest for the use of loan monies, because they wish to make purchase of goods and services in excess of their current income.[148]

Even governments pay interest for the use of loan monies because their expenditure usually exceeds their receipts. According to the *loanable funds theory of interest* the details of which are now relevant here – the price of monies equals the price paid for the use of loanable funds.[149] The intersection of the supply and demand curves of loanable funds designates the rate of interest. In most economies, therefore, businessmen look to governments not only for loans and loan subsidies, but for interest subsidies as well. Shipowners and shippers are no exceptions; on the contrary they are at the forefront.[150] Most maritime nations resort to some type of interest subsidies. In the Netherlands, for instance, the government grants interest subsidies to Dutch shipbuilders enabling them to furnish credits at reduced rates to both domestic and foreign customers.[151]

However, in conformity with the understanding of the OECD, the Dutch government grants such subsidies for credits of up to 70% of the cost of ships for export, for a maximum duration of 7 years.[152] The interest subsidy consists of the difference between the current market rate of interest, based on the yield of State Bonds, and the minimum net interest rate of 8% mentioned in the *Understanding*. Besides, only those shipyards that are prepared to rationalise their programmes in mutual co-operation and collaborate in research and cost-saving are eligible for this interest subsidy.[153] Most TMNS are member countries of the OECD, so their conditions and terms for granting interest subsidies would be similar, if not identical, to that of the Netherlands. The fact that direct maritime subsidies have become the general rule, rather than the exception, underlines their importance in the protection and development of industries generally and merchant marine industries in particular.[154]

Like any other protective aid measure, direct maritime subsidies have their disadvantages and advantages. These will be dealt with at the end of this chapter. Where direct subsidies are denied or unavailable, they are often substituted by indirect subsidies.[155]

3. Indirect subsidies

At times, however, the difference between direct and indirect subsidies can be very thin or, indeed, non-existant. Direct Subsidies normally fall into the domain of financial aid, whereas Indirect Subsidies are sometimes referred to as fiscal relief. In examples such as the granting of special depreciation allowances exceeding the original cost of the vessel, the two are interrelated.[156] Otherwise indirect subsidies or fiscal relief, is normally granted in the form of permission to carry forward or back losses and various possibilities of deferring tax-payments and credit guarantees, eg, through free or accelerated depreciation to assets or through the formation of tax-free reserves.[157] However, the most commonly recognized example in the investment allowance.

3.1 Investment allowances and grants

Within this category are Investment Pormotion Allowances, Investment grants. One type of fiscal relief is closely related to direct financial assistance to shipping. Investment allowances, i.e. special allowances for depreciation of more than 100% of the purchase price of a new vessel or asset, are granted by many countries, some of which have recently discontinued the scheme and replaced it with investment grants (post) which are assumed to have a similar effect, but are demanding on the public purse.[158] One example that immediately captures one's attention is that of Australia, where, for instance, a plant ordered or contracted for between January 1, 1976 and June 30, 1978 attracted an investment allowance of 40% of the cost of the plant, provided that the plant was first *used* or *installed ready for use* by June 30, 1979. The allowance combined with depreciation allowances, results in total deductions equivalent to 140% of cost.[159]

However, for plant ordered or contracted for before or between July 1, 1978, and June 30, 1985, the investment allowance will be at the rate of 20%, but the plant will need to be first used or installed ready for use by July 1, 1986. The income tax deduction for the investment allowance will become available in the financial year in which the plant is first used or installed ready for use.[160] However, capital expenditure on the purchase of a new ship would attract the investment allowance, provided that the ship was to be used (wholly or exclusively) in Australia for the production of assessable income. A ship that sails between Australia and overseas ports would not meet this requirement.[161] This is rather unusual since most assistance is geared to aiding international trade.

Investment allowances are known by different names and are operated as different schemes in different countries depending on the accounting system in existance. In West Germany, for instance, the same category of subsidy is known as an Industrial Investment Promotion grant. Under this scheme, in the first half of 1975, for instance, the German government introduced a $7\frac{1}{2}\%$ investment promotion grant for all German investors who realized certain investments within a given period of time.[162] Many German shipowners seem to have made use of that opportunity by placing new orders, a great deal of them with foreign yards. However, the programme seems to have ended in mid-1976 to be replaced by grants and guarantees.[163]

The final two types of financial assistance most frequently granted by the TMNS are investment grants and credit guarantees, usually for commercial loans. These were prevalent in Belgium, the US and Denmark, the latter country reserving the guarantee for the building or converting of freighters of 500 grt and less.[164] Such guarantees can lower the rate of interest by the difference between the government and commercial long-term borrowing rates without actually incurring any outlay for the government. The government is thus taking some of the commercial risks involved and may, of course, incur expenditure in case of default of the firms concerned.[165] Thus, unlike the promotional allowances, the guarantees are a kind of government insurance against the risks of inconvertibility or expropriation of foreign shipping investments.

3.2 Investment guarantee and deferred credits

The investment guarantee programme was first undertaken by the US merchant marine to encourage the flow of AID programme to the DMNS.[166] Shipowners making approved direct foreign investments, particularly in the developing countries, had to purchase protection against the risk of being unable to convert foreign shipping earnings into dollars, and the risk of expropriation or confiscation by the government of the country in which the investment was made.[167] This example illustrates yet further how much international shipping is interrelated to international trade and to foreign aid and foreign

Table 27. US Federal ship financing guarantees (Title XI) program summary (Statutory limit 9.5 billion dollars). Principal liability on September 30, 1981.

	Contracts in force		Applications pending	
Vessel types	Vessels covered	Principal amount[a]	Vessels covered	Principal amount[a]
Deepdraft vessels				
Tankers	82	$2 043 643 779	25	$736 136 500
Cargoes	145	1 193 156 750	4	69 987 000
LNGs	16	1 322 350 400	0[b]	
Bulk/OBOs	21	414 064 778	2	71 425 000[b]
Total	264	$4 973 215 707	31	$877 548 500
Other types				
Drill rigs/ships	84	$1 111 602 516		
Tugs/barges/drill service	2 949	1 602 072 935	2 000[b]	1 038 621 313[b]
Miscellaneous	16	170 955 133	11	138 515 125
Total	3 049	$2 844 630 584	2 011	$1 177 136 438
Total vessels	3 313	$7 857 846 291	2 042	$2 054 684 938
Shipboard lighters	2 118	$77 790 684	409	$6 571 000
Total	5 431	$7 935 636 975	2 451	$2 061 255 938

[a] Rounded to the nearest dollar.
[b] The end-of-year backlog also included proposed financing of 8 LNGs and 48 drilling vessels totaling some $2.2 billion. (see test.)
Source: US – MARAD 1981, p. 11.

investments. As we have noticed, foreign investment guarantees were offered by the FOA, as provided for under the Mutual Security Act 1951. However, the guarantees do not protect the investment against ordinary business risks, but only against adverse actions by foreign governments.[168] Besides, the foreign elements have not been used very extensively and have not achieved their aim of significantly expanding the merchant marine fleet or increasing the flow of private merchant marine capital into the developing countries.

The latter objective was only achieved by the encouragement and promotion of flags of convenience, while the former could only be achieved by the alternative method of extending the guarantees to domestic merchant marine investment.[109] The States of Hamburg, Bremen, Niedersachsen (Lower Saxony) and Schleswing-Holstein accord, to a limited extent, guarantees for credits for the purchase of new commercial ships built in local yards, when such credits cannot be covered by usual ship mortgages.[170] These credit guarantees are available to German nationals and, according to the arrangements between the coastal states, they are also available to other nationals of the EEC and OECD countries.[171] The other example is from the Netherlands where government-guaranteed commercial loans may be given, in exceptional cases, to shipping companies for investment purposes.[172] However, unlike West Germany, here no provision is made for any facility with regard to the interest to be paid or to the period of redemption, a characteristic which would tend to assimilate this scheme to deferred credits or outright loans.[173]

The Deferred Credit, as a form of investment allowance subsidy, is sometimes known as loss carrying. In a business, subject to strongly fluctuating trade conditions, such as shipping, the permission to carry forward losses in order to deduct these from future profits or to carry back losses to diminish the taxable profit of a previous year may be of considerable significance.[174] The permission to carry forward losses is given in most countries. It should be noted, however, that these provisions apply, in most cases, not only to shipping but to all industries. In quite a few countries losses may be carried forward for an unlimited number of years; a number of countries allow five years and some permit ten years.[175] In Singapore, where this type of subsidy is predominant, the programme is executed under the scheme: Deferred Credit for Financing Vessels Built in Singapore. This recently announced ship financing scheme is available for the contruction of vessels under 5 000 dwt under the following terms:[176]

Loan quantum	Up to a maximum of 50% of contract value.
Interest rate	Fixed rate of $9\frac{1}{2}\%$ or thereabouts during the tenure of the loan.
Repayment	Up to a maximum of 7 years after delivery.
Disbursements	In accordance with making progress.
Currency	In Singapore Dollars.
Types of vessels	Generally for vessels over 100 grt and tugboats over 500 bhp. Each case will, however, be decided on its own merits. Military craft and all types of drilling equipment are excluded.

The scheme is designed partially to finance deferred credits granted by local shipyards to the owners of the vessels under construction.[177] The vessels to be financed must be completely built in Singapore. In the event that the deferred credit granted by a shipyard exceeds 50% of the contract value, additional financing may be made available to the shipyard on commercial terms, i.e. without subsidy elements. The interest rate would most likely be on a floating basis.[178] Within the scheme deferred credit subsidies is the financing of yard construction expansion and yard equipment under the following terms:[179]

Amount	50% of cost facilities
Interest rate	$9\frac{1}{2}$% or thereabouts
Duration	Up to 8 years

But perhaps the most elaborate indirect subsidy consists of a series of tax exemptions, allowances, deductions, etc, normally considered under the umbrella name of tax benefits.

3.3 Tax benefits

The fiscal system relating to the taxation of shipping may, under certain conditions, have similar beneficial effects for the shipowners as financial assistance. However, fiscal provisions most often apply to income tax liability and consequently will usually be relevant provided that profits are made.[180] For many shipping companies in the TMNS, profitability has in recent years been very poor, so that they may not have been able to exploit fully the opportunities available in the form of fiscal relief. This type of subsidy comprises direct tax benefits and customs' duty exemptions.[181] The US programme is not only the most elaborate and most comprehensive, but is also the one that brings out clearly all the important principles, features, characteristics and motives for and of maritime tax benifits. For this reason it will be dwelt on at some length.[182]

In general, shipping is treated similarly to other industries, except where US citizens owning or leasing eligible vessels may obtain certain tax benefits through the maintenance of the CCF and the CRF. The CCF programme is a method of aiding US vessel operators in accumulating capital necessary for the construction, reconstruction and acquisition of vessels of US registry built in the US.[183] The purpose of the programme is to remove certain competitive disadvantages that US operators encounter relative to foreign flag operators. The CCF extends tax deferral privileges to vessel operators in the US foreign commerce and in the non-contiguous and Great Lakes domestic trades.[184] The CCF programme is authorised by Section 607 of the *Merchant Marine Act, 1936*, as amended, and arose from the 1970 amendments to the Act. Prior to 1970 only subsidized operators had tax deferred funds, under Section 607.[185]

The revised CCF programme under Section 607 is now available to both subsidized and non-subsidized operators, and the old CRF's have been phased out of existence. Briefly, Section 607 allows for deferment of income tax payments on certain deposits of money or other property, if the funds are used to construct vessels in US shipyards.[186] An operator's earnings or gains are realised from the operation of an *agreement* vessel, from the net proceeds arising from the sale or other disposition of the vessel or form insurance or indemnification

Table 28. US capital construction fund holders–September 30, 1981.

A & G Corp.	Hannah Marine Corp.
Aeron Marine Shipping Co.	Houston Natural Gas Corp.
Alaska Aggregate Corp.	Hvide Shipping, Inc.
Alaska Riverways, Inc.	Inland Steel Co.
Amak Towing Co., Inc.	Intercontinental Bulktank Corp.
American Atlantic Shipping, Inc.	Interstate Marine Transport Co.
American President Lines, Ltd.	Interstate Towing Co.
American Shipping, Inc.	Luedtke Engineering Co.
Aquarius Marine Industries, Inc.	Lykes Bros. Steamship Co., Inc.
Ashland Oil, Inc.	Madeline Island Ferry Line, Inc.
Atlantic Marine Industries, Inc.	Marine Leasing Corp.
Atlantic Richfield Co.	Matson Navigation Co.
Atlas Marine Co.	Middle Rock, Inc.
Bankers Trust New York Corp.	Monticello Tanker Co.
Barge Bandon, Inc.	Moore McCormack Resources, Inc.
Bethlehem Steel Corp.	Mount Vernon Tanker Co.
Blue Lines, Inc.	Mount Washington Tanker Co.
Bultema Dock and Dredge Co.	Montpelier Tanker Co.
Bultema Marine Transportation, Inc.	National Gypsum Co.
Cambridge Tankers, Inc.	National Marine Service, Inc.
Campbell Towing Co.	Neuman Boat Line, Inc.
Cement Transit Co./Medusa Corp.	O.L. Schmidt Barge Lines, Inc.
Central Gulf Lines, Inc.	Ogden Corp.
Citimarlease (Burmah I), Inc.	Oglebay Norton Co.
Citimarlease (Burmah LNG Carrier), Inc.	Ohio Barge Line, Inc.
Citimarlease (Burmah Liquegas), Inc.	Overseas Bulktank Corp.
Citimarlease (Fulton), Inc.	Pacific Shipping, Inc.
Citimarlease (Whitney), Inc	Prince William Navigation Co.
Cleveland-Cliffs Iron Co.	Prudential Lines, Inc.
Cook Inlet Tug & Barge Co.	Reynolds Leasing Corp.
Cove Maritime Companies, Inc.	Ritchie Transportation Co.
Crowley Maritime Corp.	River & Gulf Transportation Co.
CSI Hydrostatic Testers, Inc.	S & E Shipping Corp.
Delta Steamship Lines, Inc.	Seabulk Tankers, Inc.
Dillingham Tug & Barge Corp.	Sea Savage, Inc.
Durocher Dock & Dredge, Inc.	Smith Lighterage Co., Inc.
El Paso Arzew Tanker Co.	Sun Company, Inc.
El Paso Howard Boyd Tanker Co.	Tidewater, Inc.
El Paso Southern Tanker Co.	Transway International Corp.
Exxon Corp.	Tug Alaska Mariner, Inc.
Farrell Lines, Inc.	Tug Wasp, Inc.
Ford Motor Co.	Union Oil Co. of California
Foss Alaska Lines, Inc.	United States Cruises, Inc.
Foss Launch and Tug Co.	United States Lines, Inc.
Fred Devine Diving & Salvage, Inc.	United States Steel Corp.
GATX Corp.	Warrior & Gulf Navigation Co.
General Electric Credit and Leasing Corp.	Waterman Steamship Corp.
General Electric Credit Corp. of Delaware	Western Pioneer, Inc.
General Electric Credit Corp. of Georgia	Windjammer Cruises, Inc.
Graham Boats, Inc.	Worth Oil Transport Co.
Great Lakes Towing Co.	Young Brothers, Ltd.
Hannah Brothers	Zidell, Inc.

Source: US – MARAD 1981, p. 12.

for the loss of such a vessel. Also included are earnings from the investment or re-investment of amounts on depositin the CCF. In general taxable income of the operator is reduced to the extent that deposits of money are made into the fund under these categories.[187]

3.4 Construction deposits

An operator may also deposit in a CEF amounts allowable as a depreciation deduction with respect to agreement vessels. Such deposits do not directly reduce taxable income, but the earnings from such funds may be accumulated on a tax deferred basis.[188] By the investment of assets in the CCF, a fundholder may compound the fund benefits and devleop an expanded pool of tax deferred funds. However, the investment of the funds in securities and stocks is subject to certain restrictions which are intended to preserve the integrity of the fund. A fund established pursuant to Section 607,[189] is maintained in three accounts: an ordinary income account, a capital gain account, and a capital account. The manner in which the funds would be taxed if not deposited in the primary determinant of the account to which a deposit is credited.[190]

When qualified withdrawals are made from the fund for the construction, reconstruction or acquisition of vessels, barges or containers certain basic adjustments are made to the assets being acquired depending upon the account from which the monies are withdrawn.[191] Withdrawals from the ordinary income account reduce the tax basis of the acquired vessel by an amount equivalent to the amount withdrawn; withdrawals from the capital gain account result in a partial reduction basis and withdrawals from the capital account do not reduce the tax basis of the acquired vessel.[192] If a withdrawal is made from the fund for other than a qualified purpose, any amounts withdrawn from the ordinary income and capital gains accounts are taxable as earned in the year of withdrawal. Additionally, the tax attributable to the non-qualified withdrawal is subject to an interest charge for the period between the year the account was deposited and the year the withdrawal was made.[193]

Since the tax paid is on non-qualified withdrawals, no adjustments to the basis arise as a result of a non-qualified withdrawal. The CRF authorised by *Section 511 of the Merchant Marine Act, 1936*, as amended, is also a financial assistance programme which provides tax deferral benefits to US shipowners.[194] Through the CRF, shipowners operating vessels in the foreign or domestic commerce of the US can defer the gains attributable to the sale or loss of a vessel.[195] The proceeds deposited must be used to construct, reconstruct or acquire vessels of US state registry built in the US. Although any gains on such transactions are not recognised for income tax purposes, nevertheless, if the deposits are properly expended for a vessel, the basis for determining appreciation of such a vessel is reduced by the amount of any such gains.[196]

The ability to defer gains on certain transactions through deposits to the CRF applies only to vessel owners. Citizens operating a vessel owned by another party cannot benefit from the provisions. Section 511 also permits a vessel owner or operator to deposit in the CRF earnings from the operation of US registry vessels and earnings from the investment of such funds.[197] Such deposits do not exempt the tax-payer from tax liability for the earnings, nor do they

Table 29. US maritime subsidy outlays – 1936–1981.

Fiscal year	CDS	Reconstruction subsidy	Total	ODS	Total ODS & CDS
1936–1955	$248 320 942[a]	$3 286 888	$251 607 830	$431 109 987	$592 717 817
1956–1960	129 806 005	34 881 409	164 687 414	644 115 146	808 802 560
1961	100 145 654	1 215 432	101 361 086	150 142 575	251 503 661
1962	134 552 647	4 160 561	138 713 238	181 918 756	320 631 994
1963	89 235 895	4 181 214	93 417 209	220 676 685	314 093 894
1964	76 608 323	1 665 087	78 273 410	203 036 884	281 310 254
1965	86 096 872	38 138	86 135 010	213 334 409	299 469 419
1966	69 446 510	2 571 566	72 018 076	186 628 357	258 646 433
1967	80 155 452	932 114	81 087 566	175 631 860	256 719 426
1968	95 989 586	96 707	96 086 293	200 129 670	296 215 963
1969	93 952 849	57 329	94 010 178	194 702 569	288 712 747
1970	73 528 904	21 723 343	95 252 247	205 731 711	300 983 958
1971	107 637 353	27 450 968	135 088 321	268 021 097	403 109 418
1972	111 950 430	29 748 076	141 698 479	235 666 830	377 365 310
1973	168 183 937	17 394 604	185 568 541	226 710 926	412 279 427
1974	185 060 501	13 844 951	198 905 452	257 919 080	456 824 532
1975	237 895 092	1 900 571	239 795 663	243 152 340	482 948 003
1976[b]	233 926 424	9 886 024	243 712 448	386 433 994	630 146 442
1977	203 479 571	15 052 072	218 531 643	343 875 521	562 407 164
1978	148 690 842	7 318 705	156 009 547	303 193 575	459 203 122
1979	198 518 437	2 258 492	200 776 929	300 521 683	501 298 612
1980	262 727 122	2 352 744	265 079 866	341 368 236	606 448 102
1981	196 446 214	11 666 978	208 113 192	334 853 670	542 966 862
Total	$3 332 255 535	$213 674 103	$3 545 929 638	$6 158 875 522	$9 704 805 160

[a] Includes $131.5 million CDS adjustments covering the World War II Period, $105.8 million equivalent to CDS allowances which were made in connection with the Mariner Ship Construction Program, and $10.8 million of CDS in fiscal years 1954 to 1955.
[b] Includes totals for FY 1976 and the Transition Quarter ending September 30, 1979.

Source: US – MARAD 1981, p. 61.

postpone the time such earnings are includable in the gross income. However, earnings so deposited are considered to have been accumulated for the reasonable needs of business and are not subject to accumulated earnings tax.[198] This ability to accumulate funds for the construction, reconstruction, or acquisition of a vessel is the only benefit available through the CRF to a non-owner operator of a vessel. Other forms of tax subsidies are customs duties exemption for domestic flag vessels. In that respect they resemble flag discrimination.[199]

3.5 Customs exemptions

Exemptions from customs duties operate on the same principles and, sometimes, in lieu of general tax benefits. Again this is but an umbrella name for numerous, but related subsidies. They are referred to under different titles in different countries.[200] In Australia, for instance, they are known simply as fees and are operated on the principle that machinery and equipment used in the construction of new ships in Australian yards may, in some circumstances, be imported duty-free when equivalent goods are not reasonably available from Australian manufacturers.[201] In Canada, on the other hand, this kind of fiscal relief for the merchant marine industry is known by its traditional name of customs duties, and is not payable on ships imported into Canada to engage exclusively in international trade.[202]

Secondly, vessels constructed and registered in Commonwealth Countries are free to engage in the Canadian coasting trade, with the exception of the coasting trade within the Great Lakes and St. Lawrence River Basin, which is restricted to vessels registered in Canada. Besides, vessels of Commonwealth registry entitled to the MFN tariff treatment, may engage in the coasting trade in Canada upon payment of a duty of 25%.[203] However, vessels of registry other than Commonwealth are not normally entitled to engage in the coasting trade. This is a good example of aid to shipping which is combined with the MFN principle as well as with flag discrimination. There is, however, provision of the temporary use of non-Commonwealth registered ships in the coasting trade when a suitable Canadian vessel is not available.[204] In such circumstances, the vessel is subject to the same duty prorated for each month in service in Canada. Otherwise materials imported for the building of ships for export are duty-free; for ships for the domestic market, duty is payable at the normal rate.[205] This illustrates the fact that more emphasis is placed on aiding ocean going vessels and, therefore, oceanborne commerce.

However, the more *concise* practice among the TMNS is that of Spain, where it is known as customs duty exemption. In this case imported material for incorporation in ships for export is considered as a temporary import and is, therefore, exemption from customs duty.[206] To take account of customs duties paid on imported material and equipment for ships for the domestic market a rebate of 7% is granted which partly offsets these duties; the rebate is reduced to 4.5% in the case of imported propulsion gear and equipment for fishing vessels. In the case of ships for export, the rebate is calculated after deducting from the value of the ship, the value of materials imported under the system governing temporary imports.[207] The DMNS follow similar principles. In Argentina, for instance, the *Expressa Lineas Maritimas Argentinas* (ELMA) is exempt from all taxes and the Income Tax Act establishes promotional regulations for private ship enterprise. Some countries, however, prefer actual direct payment to mere tax exemptions.[208] This is akin to direct assistance and is known as compensation subsidy.

3.6 Compensatory subsidy

Compensatory subsidy to the merchant marine industry is, of course, only part of a wider governmental compensatory fiscal policy[209] towards industry generally. Normally, a government resorts to this kind of indirect aid in the management of government finance to compensate for fluctuations in national income and employment – compensatory fiscal policy, which combines deficit and surplus financing, and attempts to achieve a high level of employment by maintaining a high level of national income.[210] It uses taxation and spending to produce the desired balance. To maintain the desired level of income during a business decline any decrease in private spending or investment must be balanced by a government policy of either increasing government spending (raising total government purchases from private business) or reducing taxes (increasing the income of consumers, business or both).[211] To maintain the desired level of income during a period of expansion and inflation government policy should comprise reduction in expenditure borrowing, a possible increase in taxes, or both. If such government action is timely, and the amounts involved are large enough, substantial fluctuations in national income and employment may be avoided.[212] Thus, in many countries aid to the merchant marine industry has to be viewed in the general context of the national income and employment policy. National merchant marines are gradually becoming integrated into the general national budgetary and economic planning; it was originally largely a private sector in private hands. Generally, private consumption is relatively stable in the short run, while private investment is relatively volatile.[213]

The foregoing analysis is more applicable to the private sector, and more so to the merchant marine industry which is an industry still largely in private hands,[214] in the TMNS at least. It was in recognition of this fact that this kind of fiscal relief or indirect maritime subsidy was devised.[215] There is both the direct compensatory and the inflation/cost escalation subsidy. Both examples are illustrated by the French practice. Describing its action as *Reimbursement of part-cost pursuant to Article 79*,[216] the government decided in 1966 to reimburse shipowners for part of the cost incurred pursuant to Article 79, entitled *Accidents and Illness occuring on Board in course of Embarking* – a rather clumsy heading[217] obscuring the real purpose of the subsidy scheme. Nevertheless, these kinds of costs are peculiar to French shipowners, and constitute one of the elements of their handicap with regard to foreign shipowners,[218] rather than aid in the protection and/or expansion of the national fleet.

3.7 Inflation and insurance subsidies

However, the decision to reimburse part of these costs has the same motivation as the decision concerning the allowance for compensatory subsidies and/or inflation subsidies. Thus, in France, together with compensatory subsidies, the Ministry of Transport administers a programme that guarantees compensation for increases in shipbuilding costs, that exceed a set threshold (currently 7.3%).[219] Note, however, that inflation subsidies are quite different from export credit insurance (post).[220] To illustrate this difference, take the case of Denmark which administers the latter. The Danish export credit insurance is based on purely commercial insurance principles rather than subsidy principles.[221] The scheme is voluntary and no lower limit is set for such insurance; premiums vary between 0.125% and 0.25% p.a. of the outstanding debt and 0.3% p.a. of outstanding debts for political risks. These principles are, however, not applicable to inflation subsidy.[222] In contrast, inflation subsidies are more akin to the credit guarantee subsidies discussed earlier.[223] Perhaps inflation subsidies are more appropriately practised in the UK where they are referred to as cost escalation insurance or simply depletion allowance.[224] The British government operates a temporary scheme of cost escalation insurance on sales by British shipbuilders to both the domestic and export market.[225] Within the development objective the scheme is designed to give shipbuilders a measure of protection against exceptional and unpredictable increases in UK costs.[226] To qualify for cover, however, a prospective contract for the supply of items must reach an individual unit value of about £500 000, have a manufacturing period of at least 2 years, and have a basic contract price of at least £2 000 000.[227] We have so far concentrated on subsidies that involve machinery and services; but have hardly mentioned those relating to labour. Indeed subsidies for machines, without corresponding subsidies for the men who operate the machines, would be an incomplete scheme.[228]

3.8 Seamen's welfare benefits

The list of indirect subsidies, operated by different countries, is endless. There are many varieties, all of them aimed at protecting and expanding the national merchant marines one way or another.[229] We shall, however, limit ourselves, here, to two main types: seamen's welfare benefits, and subsidies to Research and Maritime Academics. With regard to the first of the two examples we have already mentioned the French maritime social insurance. The other illustration from a TMN is that of Greece. It is interesting to note that this is part of the new Greek drive and initiative to attract back to the Greek flag, Greek seamen and vessels currently operating under flags of convenience.[230] Interesting, because whereas the policy of expansion of other countries is directed at new building and protectionism, the Greek initiative is moving in exactly in the opposite direction – to attract back her already existing fleet presently registered under different flags.

Thus, on the basis of legislation recently[231] introduced, persons of Greek descent who have an established permanent residence abroad, Greeks employed abroad and seamen serving on board oceangoing vessels, are exempt from payment of transfer tax (which in other cases ranges from 11% to 13%) on purchase of real property made throught the importation of foreign exchange.[232] More specifically, persons of Greek descent who have resided abroad for at least five years are entitled to the above exemption provided they purchase real property in Greece within a period of five years, at the latest from their return from abroad.[233] In addition, Greeks employed abroad as workers or employees should have completed at least three years of work abroad and receive their wages or salaries in foreign exchange to qualify for the above exemption subsidy.[234] Lastly, Greek seamen employed on board Greek or foreign flag vessels for at least three years and receiving their pay in foreign exchange are also eligible for this tax exemption.

The inducement subsidy acts as an attraction for foreign exchange, in addition to its expansionist motive, hence the strong link between merchant shipping and balance of payments considerations.[235] The Italian approach on the other hand seems to be designed more fot he protection of the seamen themselves. For instance, an Italian law, which became effective in March 1977, makes maritime agents responsible for the social welfare, payment of salaries, and insurance coverage of all new crews employed.[236] However, the maritime agents must produce guarantees from flags of convenience shipowners covering insurance and salaries before taking on new Italian crews.[237] Where their wages do not cover social benefits or are not adequate the Italian government will subsidize the cost of sickness benefits, medical expenses, pensions etc.[238]

In Britain, as in France and West Germany, social benefits are part of the National Health insurance schemes administered by the DHSS.[239] In addition, maritime welfare is part of the general subsidies to the merchant marine industry in general and shipbuilding in particular.[240] Last, but not least, or the indirect maritime subsidies are the grants for research and the nautical maritime academies.[241] The rationale behind this is that unless the government intervenes, these expenses would otherwise be borne by the industry, thereby diverting valuable investments from direct ploughback.[242] It is hoped that money used for research and maritime academies to train both the shore and seagoing officers and crew will improve efficiency and productivity in the industry.[243] It will, of course, also create and/or protect jobs in addition to aiding the general purpose of expanding the national fleet and maintaining a pool of trained and skilled labour.

3.9 Ship research grants

Although the merchant marine industry is still largely in private hands, especially in the TMNS, nevertheless governments retain an overall interest and derive the greatest benefits; Rather than leave the private sector to go it alone, it is only reasonable that governments intervene when ever necessary. Thus in Canada, for instance, research grants are not restricted to the merchant marine industry. All industries are entitled to aid under various general programmes covering as much as 50% of the cost of approved research.[244] State contribution to maritime research and maritime academies in Denmark, on the other hand, is in the form of financial support amounting to about 0.15 million US $ p.a. given by the government to institutions engaged in shipbuilding research. Other governments are, however, more involved in such aid schemes.[245]

Japan, for instance, has a fully established ship Research Institute as well as a University of Mercantile Marine attached to the Ministry of Transport, Science, Education and Industry, both of which had annual running costs of approximately 2 300.00 million yen in the fiscal year 1976.[246] In addition, the Nuclear Ship Development Agency was established with government funds in 1963. The Netherlands Maritime Institute finances part of its maritime research programme with government funds,[247] while in Norway and Sweden various institutes carry out shipbuilding research and receive some public financial support. These institutes work on a task basis and are becoming less dependent on government subsidy.[248]

Research related to shipbuilding, in Britain, is carried out by the state-run National Physical Laboratory.[249] The government also supports selected research and design (R & D) work done by firms or research associations, and gives specific aid to certain projects of the British Ship Research Association.[250] State aid for R & D work averages about £2 000 000.00 p.a.[251] Benefits from such indirect subsidies are also indirect; they accrue over a long period of time and are, therefore, difficult to evaluate. In the way they seem to achieve the objectives of aiding the expansion of national merchant marine fleets. It is no coincidence that the more advanced maritime nations like Japan, UK, US, West Germany and the Scandinavian countries are also the largest investors in maritime subisidies generally, and research and maritime academies in particular.[252] However, the use of maritime subsidies as a means of protecting the aiding the expansion of national merchant marine fleets has its advantages and disadvantages.

4. Advantages and disadvantages of maritime subsidies

Some of the advantages and disadvantages have already been noted above. They are very different from those of flag preference and flag discrimination. However, more elaborate criticism of restrictive shipping practices will be dealt with in Part III.[253] Suffice it to point out here that of all the protectionist shipping measures, maritime subsidies are probably more tolerated and better understood, though not necessarily accepted, than flag discrimination and other forms of state intervention.[254]

4.1 Maritime subsidies and flag discrimination contrasted

In this connection it should, however, be pointed out that the effects of financial aid and fiscal relief at the international level, are different from those which may be caused by flag discrimination, i.e. through discriminating practices of governments which limit the freedom of using ships flying other flags.[255] The latter physically limit or exclude the possibility of other vessels competing with those in favour of which flag discrimination is practiced. Higher rates and inadequate service may result. The burden of flag discrimination falls eventually upon the users of shipping services who, in addition, are denied the right to ship by the vessel of their choice.[256] Whereas flag discrimination is not compatible with, for example, the *OECD Code of Liberalisation* (post), financial and fiscal measures are, to a certain extent, regarded by even the OECD countries as acceptable means of alleviating particular problems of the national shipping sector.[257]

However, as will be apparent in due course, the main advantage and/or argument in favour of maritime subsidies is that of supporting an infant industry. We saw that this argument was used by the TMNS in establishing and/or expanding their national merchant marine fleets. The fact that this policy succeeded has been duly noted by the DMNS. In the case of the latter countries, their merchant marines are still an undeveloped industry which may not be able to weather the initial period of experimentation and financial stress because of strong foreign competition.[258] Many years ago in the US *Report of Manufacturers.* Alexander Hamilton stated that such industries should be protected by tariffs and subsidies until they had a chance to grow out of their infantile stage. The DMNS have seized on this argument that, given such a period of grace, they could be expected to develop economies of scale and technological efficiency so that rates would be reduced and they would be more competitive with foreign flags.[259]

Essentially the argument runs that 'we can produce it cheaper if you give us the chance'. The only problem, as practice has shown, is that once you start giving support you never can stop. *Once an infant always an infant.*[260] The DMNS will also have discovered that the TMNS who originated this form of support still provide it today, almost 2000 years later, at a more sophisticated level and both qualitatively and quantitatively better than do the DMNS. But such minor set-backs should not diminish the overall advantage of using maritime subsidies as a means of both establishing and expanding one's national merchant marines.[261] Such advantages become apparent when we turn to the economics of transportation subsidy.

Recent information on the overall physical and economic characteristics of the maritime transportation system throughout the world indicates that it continues to experience the greatest absolute and relative increases in operating deficits compared to other competing modes of transport.[262] Due to these continued and long-standing deficits, therefore, governments have been forced to increase the level of subsidies to the merchant marine in order to ensure the retention of essential services. It now appears that maritime subsidies, both for the running of the fleets and for shipbuilding are unavoidable.[263] Moreover, in the light of the energy supply uncertainty, increased congestion on land and other problems, governments are making greater efforts to revitalise the system. There is also the growing awareness that revenues generated through shipping freights will not support the upgraded system. Increasingly, then, governments, at all levels, continue to use direct financial support and indirect fiscal relief as the most common tool to aid the system.[264]

Far from enabling its expansion, it is not clear whether the aid given is sufficient to keep the system alive and running at all. However, as we pointed out earlier, this causes other problems. When governments initiate large maritime subsidy programmes to give effect to the allocative decisions of individuals or other governments, the constraints introduced by the subsidy may be difficult to observe.[265] The provisions of the aid payments may prevent an economically optimal allocation of resources resulting in costly distortions from the favourable situation.[266] The primary argument used for government intervention in the transportation market is usually made in terms of economic efficiency and other broad social objectives.[267] This is understandable, for it is established that gross revenues earned by the merchant marine systems seldom cover costs of operation. In cases where the revenues obtained from freights result in a substantial cashflow loss, then governments have to subsidize by paying either part or the entire loss.[268] There are other reasons for justifying maritime subsidies.

4.2 Justifying maritime subsidies

If the criticisms against maritime subsidies are economic, so are those in its defence. Whereas the arguments against are based on economic efficiency, the arguments for, are based on economies of scale.[269] For instance, in a research project they conducted, Mayer, Kain and Wohl note that subsidies for urban transportation, for example, are justified if economies of scale are great. That is, if urban transportation is characterised by significantly increasing returns as the scale of operations increases, then only by subsidization can consumers reap the full benefits of scale effects.[270] This policy is also advocated by Mohring, who concludes in his thesis that transport subsidies are justified in cases where economies of scale are extensive and the price elasticity of demand is high. The economic reasoning for subsidies in industries with returns which increase in proportion to scale – of which transport is foremost – is as follows.

In decreasing cost industries, output can be expanded with a less than proportionate increase in total costs. This means that incremental or marginal costs will be less than average total costs.[271] The consequence is that in order to make it possible to satisfy the requirement that total cost equals total revenue, average cost pricing would have to be imposed.[272] However, in order to ensure the optimum in resource allocation, output should be priced at marginal costs. If this latter rule is followed, total revenues would be less than total costs and a subsidy is required to make up the difference characterised by the discrepancy between marginal and average cost pricing. Hence the economic justification for subsidy.[273] To illustrate the allocative issues which the two pricing schemes raise, consider Figure 2 below. The demand curve is given by DD'. Also shown

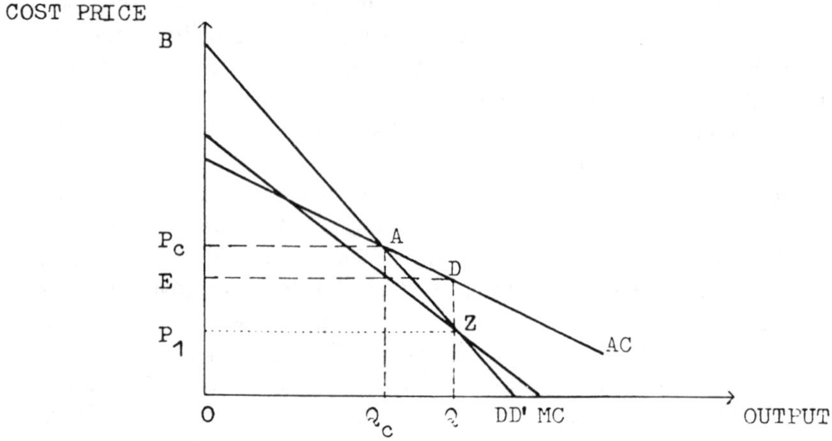

Figure 2. Subsidy curve.

are decreasing marginal and average cost curves: MC and AC. The constraint that total revenue should cover total cost requires that the price should equal average cost. In that case, total output of OQ_c will have to be produced and sold at a unit price OP_c. Inefficiency in the conventional sense results from the fact that consumers are prevented from purchasing output at a price just equal to marginal cost.[274] The consumers' surplus of average cost is ABP_c. Now consider the implications of marginal cost pricing in an effort to avoid welfare losses due to average cost pricing. If price falls to OP_1, consumers purchase output Q at marginal cost. The consumers' surplus increase to P_cAZP_1. It is, therefore, apparent from the figure that this price (P_1) does not cover average cost by the amount DZ, and a tax-financed subsidy in the amount P_1EDZ is required to cover that total.[275] Thus, the economic justification for the subsidy hinges on the result that the increases in consumers' surplus P_cAZP_1 exceed the subsidy payment P_1EDZ.

4.3 Conclusion on maritime subsidies

The foregoing analysis is particularly applicable to maritime transport. Further justification for maritime subsity has already been discussed and will be elaborated on later. What should be borne in mind is that no government will spend tax-payers' money on subsidies unless the project is of vital importance to the public or national interest.[276] In that respect, one can see no other reasons except that a national merchant marine is believed to be of vital *economic, political* and *security* interest by many of the world's governments, and in order to ensure that these interests are upheld, many governments have developed a wide variety of maritime subsidy schemes.[277] The role played by the merchant marine in the Falkland's crisis will no doubt underline its defence role; many more governments might be more prepared to devote large subsidies to protection and consequent expansion.[278]

We noted at the opening of the chapter that the underlying reasons for resumption of maritime subsidies, on a large scale, was to save the merchant marine industries from what would otherwise have been total collapse due to the after effects of the previous two world wars and the ensuing recessions and fierce competition. Shipping enterprises are very expensive ventures; after the war, operational and crew costs, *inter alia*, soared to astronomical levels.[279] In fact, at one point, supply of shipping services was ahead of the demand from international trade; if it were not for subsidies the industry would have faced extinction. There were about four recommended solutions to the problem; one such solution involved transfers to flags of convenience; the second was the development of liner conference systems; the third was outright state nationalisation.[280]

All three suggested solutions have been tried. Yet none of these mechanisms could solve the industry's problems. What, therefore, emerged was a combination of the three, plus provisions for maritime subsidies. Thus, to many countries, the main motives for maritime subsidies were:[281]

(a) The necessity of combating depression and unemployment in the heavy engineering industry, usually the first and hardest hit in a slump;[282]
(b) The strategic necessity of maintaining, at home, the skills and facilities

necessary to build ships in the event of blockade in any war – this has been an important consideration particularly in the US, and finally what we have always maintained in this thesis;[283] and

(c) The need to protect the industry from foreign competition and to aid its establishment (in the case of DMNS) and/or expansion (in the case of TMNS).[284]

In addition to maritime subsidies, and flag discriminations, a further mechanism was found necessary, particularly if the third objective was to be achieved. This additional mechanism was not only supplementary to subsidies and flag discriminations, but was introduced upon the realisation that the two were not achieving the desired objectives quickly enough.[285] This turned out to be direct state intervention – a more discriminatory mechanism. In our next chapter we proceed to deal with this newer and harsher measure.

Notes

1. OECD, *Maritime Transport*, 1971, p. 10.
2. US Dept. of Commerce, MARAD, *Maritime Subsidies*, 1978, p. 20.
3. See the Chapter on *Economic Consequences* (post).
4. Such as Military Services.
5. But this is not exhaustive.
6. See further on for details.
7. US Joint Economic, *Subsidy and Subsidylike Programs of the US Governments* GPO, Washington DC, 1960.
8. These programs cost US 57.3 billion dollars, 19 July 1950–June 30 1961 according to the above report.
9. Black, *Law Dictionary*, pp. 1596–1957.
10. *Kennecott Copper Corporation* v *State Tax Commission*, D.C. Utah, 60. F. Supp. 181, at 182.
11. Utility to the public is an esential pre-requisite for governments to grant subsidies.
12. Farm Subsidies, i.e. 'Agricultural support subsidies' (UK) under *The Agricultural Act 1947*.
13. Kilgour, J. G., 'Double subsidy issue in shipping', *J. Marit. Law Comm.*, Vol. 4, No. 6, 1975, pp. 395–407.
14. Readings in the *Theory of International Trade* (Committee of the American Economic Association).
15. *Rochdale Report*, paras 170–182, pp. 48–57.
16. Note 14 (above) especially the Introduction.
17. Rochdale Report also notes US, UK, Japan, Italy, France and Spain for subsidies, *op. cit*.
18. Lawrence, S. A., *International Shipping: The Years Ahead*, Lexington, Mass: Lexington Books.
19. O'Loughlin, C., *The Economics of Sea Transport*, pp. 82–85 & 84–85.
20. Black, *Law Dictionary, op. cit*., p. 1597.
21. *Ibid*., p. 1597.
22. Sturmey, S. G., *British Shipping and World Competition*, at pp. 28–29.
23. *Ibid*., pp. 19–20, 31–32 & 20–21.
24. *Ibid*., pp. 122–24, 128–36 188–91.
25. *State Aid to the Merchant Marine in Major Maritime Nations before the war, op. cit*.
26. See again *Public Policy in the Ocean Freight Industry In promoting Competition in Regulated Markets*, Phillips (ed.), Washington D.C., Brookings Institution, 1975.
27. Sturmey, S. G., *op. cit*., pp. 30–31.
28. Thornton, R. H., *British Shipping*, Cambridge, 1959, pp. 21–22.
29. Evershem, F., *Effects of Shipping Subsidization*, Bremen, 1958, p. 15.
30. Smith, R., *Influence of the Great War upon Shipping*, NY 1919, p. 135.

31. *Report of the German Control Stations and the Atlantic Emigration Traffic*, Nov. 1916, CMND 9092, 1918.
32. Sanstad J. E., *Shipping and Shipbuilding Subsidies*, US Dept. of Commerce, 1932, p. 326.
33. *Ibid.*, p. 327.
34. *Ibid.*, p. 328.
35. Bennathan, E. and Walters, A. A., *Port Pricing and Investment Policy for Developing Countries*, OUP, 1979.
36. See also Devanney, J. W., *Marine Decisions under Uncertainty* Cambridge, Md: Cornell Maritime Press, 1971.
37. Grossman, W. L., *Ocean Freight Rates* Cambridge Md: Cornell Maritime Press, 1956.
38. See also Hanson, P., 'Soviet Union and world shipping', *Journal of Soviet Studies*, July 1970.
39. Lloyds of London, *Lloyds Calendar and National Yearbook*, (Annual) London: Lloyd's of London Press.
40. Moyer, C., 'A critique of the rationales for present US maritime programmes', *Transportation Journal*, Winter 1974.
41. Pearson, C. S., *International Marine Environment Policy: The Economic Dimension*, Baltimore: Johns Hopkins University Press 1975.
42. Smith, J. R., Ocean Freight Rates *Political Science Quarterly* No. 2 1906.
43. UN *The Application of Modern Transport Technology to Mineral Development in Developing Countries*, NY, 1976.
44. US Dept. of Justice, Antitrust Division. *The Regulated Ocean Shipping Industry, Report, 1977*, (Stock No. 027-000-00474-1).
45. Zannetos, Z., 'Presistent economic misconceptions in the transportation of oil by sea', *Marit. Stud. & Man*., No. 1, 1973.
46. US Congress, Senate Committee on Commerce, Science and Transportation, *Illegal Rebating in the US Ocean Commerce*. Hearings before the Subcommittee on Merchant Marine and Tourism 95th Cong., 1st Sess., serial no. 95-13, 1977.
47. See also US Congress, Joint Economic Committee. *Discriminatory Ocean Freight Rates and the Balance of Payments*, 89th Cong., 1st Sess., Jan. 6, 1965.
48. Thorbun, T., *The Supply and Demand of Water Transport*, Stockholm School of Economics, 1960.
49. Metaxas, B. N., 'Notes on the internationalization process in the martitime sectors', *Marit. Pol. & Man*., Jan. 1978.
50. FMC Fact Finding Investigation No. 6: *The Effect of Steamship Conference Organisation, Rules, Regulations, and Practices upon the Foreign Commerce of the US*, 1965.
51. US Senate *Merchant Marine Study and Investigation* (Govt. Aid to Shipping), Washington GPO, 1980.
52. US Maritime Commission *Economic Survey of the American Merchant Marine*, Washington GPO., 1937.
53. Report to the President on Foreign Economic Policies, Washington GPO., 1980, p. 89.
54. Post-war Planning Committee – Post-war Economic Outlook for American shipping, Washington GPO, 1946, p. 4.
55. Treasury Dept. (Communication from the President) Scope and Effects of Tax Benefits Provided to the Maritime Industry) (Washington GPO, 1953).
56. US Dept. of Commerce, MARAD, *Review of Essential Foreign Trade Routes* (Washington GPO, 1953), p. 14.
57. *Ibid*., p. 6; also Sect. 211 of the 1936 Act.
58. *Ibid*., 'Employment of US Flag Merchant Fleet Seagoing Vessels, 1 000 GRT and over as of 31/12/55', Report # 300.
59. US Cong. *Study of the Operations of MARAD & FMB* Hearings before the Committee on Merchant Marines and Fisheries, 84th Cong., 1st Sess. (Washington GPO, 1955), p. 20.
60. US Dept. of Commerce, MARAD, *US Oceanborne Foreign Trade Route Traffic* (1948, 1950, 1951 & 1952) (Washington GPO), pt. 2.

61. US Dept of Commerce, MARAD, *The Annual Report of MARAD for Fiscal Year 1972* (Washington GPO), para. VII, pp. 84 & 85.
62. *Ibid.*, Fiscal Year 1973, para IV, p. 69.
63. *Rochdale Report*, para 209, pp. 56–57.
64. US Dept. of Commerce, MARAD, *Maritime Subsidies*. 1978 (Washington GPO), pp. 169–170.
65. Fair, M. L. and Williams, E. W., *Economics of Transportation and Logistics*, Business Publications, Dallas, 1973.
66. Pegrum, D. F. *Transportation: Economics and Public Policy*, 3rd edn., Homewood I11.: R. D. Irwin, 1973.
67. Norton, H. S., *Modern Transportation Economics*, 2nd ed., Columbus Ohio: Charles E. Merrill Publishing Co., 1971.
68. 'Irish container industry – tanked up for action' (tanker container manufacture), *Cargo Syst. Int.*, Vol. 7, No. 9, Sept. 1980, p. 43.
69. US Dept. of Commerce, MARAD, *Maritime Subsidies* (Washington GPO), Nov. 1978, p. 80.
70. 'Ireland' (features on Irish Offshore development). *Oilman*, 28 June 1980, pp. 14–17.
71. Legion, R., 'Shipping and the EEC', (EEC Regulations and decisions on Shipping) *Seaways*, Oct. 1980, pp. 13–16.
72. Republic of Ireland (Shipping, Shipbuilding, Ports, Finance, Oil) *Lloyd's List*, 5 April, 1979, pp. 5–11.
73. The other TMNS are Canada, Denmark, Finland, France, Italy, Japan, Netherlands, Norway, Spain, Sweden, UK and US.
74. 'Indian Container Manufacturing plans hot up', *Cargo Syst. Int.*, Vol. 6, No. 7, July 1979, pp. 91–93.
75. '*Nagpas* v. *India* 2: Merchant marine – an evaluation', Navy International, Vol. 83, No. 7, July 1978, pp. 26–28.
76. The DMNS doing this are Argentina, Brazil, Korea (South), Pakistan, Peru, Venezuela, etc.
77. Dept. of State Bulletin, *Diplomatic Adjustments by the Maritime Nations*, Jan. 17, 1966, pp. 78–85.
78. Marx, D. Jr., *International Shipping Cartels*, Princeton N. J., Princeton University Press, 1953.
79. Tresselt, D., *Shipping and Shipping Policy in Latin America*, Smaskrifter, No. 21, Bergen, 1967.
80. Puty, J., 'To scrap or not to scrap', *Nautical Review*, Vol. 3, No. 3, March 1979, pp. 5–7.
81. 'Italian marine industries', (Shipping, roro, liners, shipbuilding, ports, etc.) *Fairplay*, Vol. 270, No. 4990, 19 April, 1979, p. 33.
82. 'Shipbuilding and allied activities in Italy', (shipbuilding, engine building), *Shipbuild & Mar. Eng. Int.*, Vol. 102, No. 1229, June 1979, pp. 233–248.
83. Italy (shipowners, shipbuilding, ship repair, ports) *Norwegian News*, Vol. 6, No. 48, 7 Dec. 1979, pp. 19–23.
84. Sturmey, S. G., *British Shipping and World Competition, op. cit.*, p. 121.
85. Kadoi, T., 'Shipbuilding under reduced facilities' (outlook for shipbuilding in Japan) *Zosen*, Vol. 24, No. 11, Feb. 1980, pp. 17–19.
86. Nakamura, G., Diversification in Japanese shipbuilding industries', *Ibid.*, pp. 24–27.
87. 'US Report' (shipping, trade, shipbuilding, energy, safety, technology) *Seatrade*, Vol. 8, No. 6., June 1978, pp. 113–125.
88. Waitehouse, 'Maritime spring clean', (US shipping policy) *Seatrade*, Vol. 8, No. 5, May 1978, pp. 3–4.
89. US Shipbuilding, *Marine Engineers Review*, July 1978, pp. 1–10.
90. 'Review of the shipbuilding and ship repairing industries in the US east coast', *Shipp. World & Shipbuild.*, No. 3937, Jan. 1978, pp. 55–57.
91. McGraw-Hill Survey 1958 revealed US needed 95 billion dollars to modernise.

92. Keezer, D. M. & associates, *New Forces in American Business*, McGraw-Hill Book Co., N.Y. 1969, 1959.
93. Modernization in a maritime sense.
94. 'Canada Report' (artic development, shipping, commodities, shipbuilding, ports) *Seatrade*, Vol. 9, No. 8, Aug. 1979, pp. 97–107.
95. Canadian marine industries, *Lloyd's List*, Special Report, 30 April, 1981, pp. 5–7.
96. Tinsley, D., 'Seeking greater freedom in *La France Libre*', (French Shipping) *Fairplay*, Vol. 269, No. 4985, 18 March 1979, pp. 23–27.
97. Revel, M. D., 'Financial needs and trends of international shipping', *Maritime Management*, Vol. 2, No. 2, March 1979, pp. 7–10.
98. 'West Germany' (shipping, heavy lift, engines, shipbuilding and ship repairing) *Shipp. World & Shipbuild.*, No. 3955, July 1979, pp. 487–95.
99. 'Belgian marine industries', (shipping, shipbuilding, ports) *Fairplay*, Vol. 269, No. 4984, 8 March 1979, pp. 37–45.
100. The other TMNS are Spain and the US; there is evidence among the DMNS.
101. Normally yard conversion, port development and/or expansion go together.
102. Dobler, J. P., 'Restructuring French shipbuilding industry offers high technology', *Norwegian News*, Vol. 37, No. 6, May 1981, pp. 87–90.
103. 'French shipbuilding and allied insustries', (Survey) *Mot. Ship* (Suppl.), May 1981, pp. 5–15.
104. 'Norway: Land of the entrepeneurs', (shipping and shipbuilding) *Shipp. World & Shipbuild.*, April 1980, pp. 231–34.
105. 'Shipping in the Norwegian national budget', *Norwegian News*, Vol. 10, 17 Nov. 1978, pp. 12–13.
106. 'West German marine industries – a special report', (shipping, shipbuilding, ports) *Fairplay*, Vol. 267, No. 4959, 14 Sept. 1978, pp. 41–62.
107. Clement, A. G. A., 'A promising future for owners and builders', *Latin Am. Shipp.*, 1979, pp. 13.
108. Hornick, R. N., *Indonesian Maritime Law*, Vol. 8, No. 1, Oct. 1976, pp. 73–85.
109. 'Still the world's ship repair bargain basement', (Singapore, Malaysia, Phillipines, Indonesia, Hong Kong) *Shipcare Marit. Man.*, Vol. 12, No. 9, Oct. 1980, p. 35.
110. *N. Y. Life Insurance Co.* v *Anderson*, CCA, NY 263F 527, at 529.
111. *Boston & A.R. Co.* v *New York Cent. R. Co.*, 256 Mass. 600, 166 Wis. 163 NW 652, at 655.
112. *People ex rel. Adwondack Power & Light Co.* v *Public Service* Co., 193, NYS, 186, 191, 200 AD 268.
113. It represents only what observation and experience suggest as likely to happen, with a margin over.
114. *Southern Bell Tele & Bell Tele Co.* v *Rail Commission of South Caroliana* DCSC 5F 2d, 77 at 96.
115. 'HAS Shipbuilding a future in Western Europe?', *Norwegian News*, No. 17, 14 Sept. 1979, pp. 29–31.
116. 'West German marine industries', *Fairplay*, Vol. 272, No. 5014, 4 Oct. 1979, pp. 21–36.
117. Beth, H. L., 'Restructuring of European industries & shipbuilding', *European Shipping and Shipbuilding* (Conference Proceedings), 1978, pp. 99–116.
118. 'West German marine industries', *Fairplay*, Vol. 267, No. 4959, *op. cit.*, pp. 41–62, at 50.
119. The other TMNS are Australia, Belgium, Canada, France, Italy, Japan, the Netherlands, Norway, Sweden and the US; the only other DMNS are Taiwan and India.
120. UNCTAD Secretariat, Report by, *International Transoceanic Transport and Economic Development*.
121. *Ibid.*, in connection with ELOSOC Resolution 1372 (SLV).
122. *Ibid.*, 'Concerning activities of the UN system of organisation in the transport field' (TD/B/C.4/46) Jan 6. 1969.
123. See also UNCTAD, Secretariat Report by, Document No. (TD/B/C.4/36) Dec. 13, 1968.

124. Terborgh, G., *Realistic Depreciation Policy Machinery and Allied Products Institute*, Washington DC, 1954.
125. Grant, E. and Horton, P. Jr., *Depreciation*, The Ronald Press Co., NY, 1949.
126. Finney, H. A. and Miller, H. E., *Principles of Accounting*, 5th edn. Prentice-Hall Inc., Englewood, Cliffs NJ, 1957.
126A. Bierman, H., *Managerial Accounting Introduction*, The Macmillan Co., NY, 1959.
127. US Treasury Dept. Publications 456(7–62) *Depreciation Guidelines and Rules*.
128. Siltor, R. *et al*., Depreciation: A Special Report, *Journal of Taxation*, May 1963.
129. Australia (Shipping, trade unions, container services, shipbuilding) *Marine Week*, Vol. 5, No. 23, 23 June 1978, pp. 9–14.
130. Phillips, F. E., 'The INNOVATIVE national line' (Australia national line) *Containerisation*, Vol. 14, No. 3, March 1980, pp. 26–30.
131. Black, R. M., 'The Australian shipper – his shipping needs', *Australian Symposium on Shipping Management* (Conference Proceedings) Nov. 1977, Vol. 1 pp. 17–20.
132. *Ibid*., Vol. 11, pp. 1–2.
133. *In re-Lallar's Estate*, 362, Ill. 621 1 N.E. 2nd 50, 53.
134. Carter, H. W. and Snaveley, Y. W. P., *Intermediate Economic Analysis*, McGraw-Hill Book Co., NY, pp. 343–47.
135. Conrad, J., *An Introduction to the Theory of Interest*, University of California Press, Berkeley, Calif., 1959.
136. *McLondon* v *Johnson*, 71 GA. App. 424, 31 S.E. 2nd, 89, at 92.
137. 'Combating the loan shark' *Law & Contemp. Prob*., Winter 1941.
138. 'The Swedish shipbuilding bill', *Norwegian News*, Nov. 23 – 8th Dec. 1978, pp. 18 & 21.
139. Wallin, B., 'Sweden, one of the world's great carrying nations' (Survey) *Shipbroker*, Vol. 4, No. 2, March 1978, pp. 21–29.
140. 'Swedish marine industries: first signs of Spring?' *Fairplay* Vol. 278, No. 5101, 4 June 1981, pp. 26–32.
141. 'Scandinavia: Marine industries survey', *Zosen*, Vol. 25, No. 13, March 1981, 50 pp.
142. Banks, J. S., 'Scandinavian liner companies – maintaining a bold front with a massive investment in ro-ro', *Cargo Syst. Int*., Vol. 6, No. 2, Feb. 1979, pp. 28–31.
143. 'Report on Scandinavia' (Shipping, shipbuilding) *Fairplay*, Vo. 270, No. 4992, 3 April 1979, pp. 8–14.
144. Sweden (Special reports on shipping, shipbuilding, ports) *Lloyd's List*, 31 May 1979, pp. 5–13.
145. *Emerging Maritime Loans*, C.1, S.2. The Draco, 7 Feb. Cas. 1, 042.
146. Smith, W. W., 'Monetary theories of the rate of interest: a dynamic analysis', *Review of Economics and statistics*, Vol. XL, pp. 15–21.
147. 'The loan shark problems today', *Law & Contemp. Prob*., Winter 1954.
148. Keynes, J. M., *The General Theory of Employment, Interest and Money*, Harcourt, Brace and World, Inc., NY, 1936.
149. See again Fisher, I., *The Theory of Interest, op. cit*., NY, 1954.
150. 'The case for maritime subsidies', *Tanker Bulker International*, Vol. 4, No. 5, May 1978, pp. 18–19.
151. de Tony, J., 'Netherlands marine industries. . . , '*Fairplay*, Vol. 276, No. 5076, 11 Nov. 1980, pp. 27–33.
152. 'The Netherlands. . . ', *Lloyd's List*, 16 April 1981, pp. 5–15.
153. *Ibid*., p. 16.
154. See again 'The case for maritime subsidies', *op. cit*., p. 20.
155. The other TMNS are Denmark & the US; there is no evidence of the practice among the DMNS.
156. Note that between July 1 1950 to June 30, 1961 the US spent 57.3 billion dollars on this.
157. US Joint Economic Committee, *Subsidy and Subsidylike Programs of the US Government* (GPO, Washington DC, 1960).
158. *Securities & Exchange Commission* v *Wickham*, D.C. Minm. 12F, Supp. 245, at 247.
159. 'Australia – Special report', *Lloyd's List*, 10 Aug. 1978, pp. 4–15.

160. 'East Asia & Australia' (Survey), *Nov. Oil*, Vol. 5, No. 2, Feb. 1978, pp. 63–65.
161. Heaton, P. M., 'In Eastern waters', *Sea Breezes*, Vol. 53, No. 408, Dec. 1979, pp. 761–65.
162. 'West Germany' (Survey), *Marine Weekly*, Vol. 5, No. 32, 1 Sept. 1978, pp. 16–22.
163. The only other TMNS is Japan; there is no evidence of any DMNS.
164. Buchanan, N. and Ellis, H. S., *Approaches to Economic Development*, The Twentieth Century Fund, NY, 1955, Chap. 16.
165. Commission of Foreign Economic Policy, *Staff Papers* (GPO, Washington DC, 1954) pp. 126–34.
166. Venhausser, C. W., 'The US merchant marine at the crossroads', *Port Baltimore Bulletin*, Nov. 1980, p. 22.
167. Kendall, L. C., 'The modern American merchant marine', *US Naval Institute Proceedings*, Oct. 1979, pp. 70–76.
168. See German (Survey), *Asian Shipp.* No 22, Oct. 1980, pp. 19–23.
169. Pearson, J., 'Shipping and the EEC', *Seaways*, July 1981, pp. 11–15.
170. See again 'The Netherlands', *Lloyd's List*, 16 April 1981, pp. 5–15.
171. The other TMNS are the UK and Greece; and the DMNS are China (Taiwan) and Singapore.
172. *Moore* v *Sampson Country*, 220 N. C. 232, 17 S. E. 2d, 22 at 23.
173. *US* v *Marine Co*., C.C.A. ILL., 90F. 2d 549, 551.
174. See also 'Singapore' (Govt. Subsidies), *Asian Shipp*., April 1981, pp. 57–58.
175. See also 'Singapre Report', *Shipcare & Marit. Man*., Vol. 13, No. 18–26.
176. 'Singapore Report', *Zosen*, Vol. 25, No. 2, May 1980, pp. 16–18.
177. 'Ship repair in Singapore', *Asian Shipp*., No. 4, July 1978, pp. 30–32.
178. US Treasury Dept., *Your Federal Income Tax Annually.*
179. Seltzer, L. H., *The Place of the Personal Exemptions in the Present Day Income Tax – Taxation Revision Compendium, Tax Foundation* NY, 1959, Vol. 1, pp. 449–514.
180. US Internal Revenue Code, US Treasury Dept., *Your Federal Tax Annually*.
181. *Ibid*.
182. Kahn, H., 'Personal deductions in the Federal income tax', *National Bureau of Economic Research*, Inc., Princeton University Press, NJ, 1960.
183. Customs Exemptions (post) are also a form of tax relief.
184. Boyes, J. R. C., 'No quick fix for US marine industry', *Containerisation*, Vol. 15, No. 15, No. 6, June 1981, pp. 32–36.
185. Wade, S., 'US shipping policy in the melting pot', *Fairplay*, Vol. 279, No. 6105, 2 July 1981, p. 47.
186. Levy, H., 'US liner shipping policy', *International Container Industry Conference Proceedings*, Nov. 1977, pp. 17–22.
187. Blackwell, R. J., *Implementation of the Merchant Marine Act*, 1970, Vol. 5, No. 2, Jan. 1974, pp. 167–81.
188. Agman, R. S., '*Competition, rationalization and US shipping policy*', *J. Marit. Law & Commerc*, Vol. 7, No. 1, Oct. 1976, pp. 1–50.
189. Maguire, C. J. and McDaniel, R. E., *Proceedings of the Maritime Safety Conference*, Vol. 38, No. 4, June 1981, pp. 43–99.
190. 'Midyear Review', *Fairplay*, Vol. 267, No. 4950, 13 July 1981, pp. 48–89.
191. Madigan, R. E., *Taxation of the Shipping Industry*, Cornell Maritime Press, Cambridge, Maryland, 54 pp.
192. *Rochdale Report*, para 172, p. 49.
193. US Report, *Seatrade*, Vol. 81, No. 6, June 1978, pp. 113–25.
194. Goldman, P., 'Alternative proposal for US maritime policy', *Seatrade*, Vol. 10, No. 1, Jan. 1980, pp. 25–27.
195. 46 USC Title 27 (1976 Ed.) p. 711.
196. 46 USC Title 27 Section 1161.
197. *Ibid*., Section 1151.
198. *Ibid*., Section 1171 (g).
199. *Ibid*., Section 1161(1) on Taxation of Deposits upon failure of conditions.

200. *Ibid*., Section 1161(n).
201. *US* v *Fischo*, D. C. Wash., 262F. 1001, 1005.
202. Ellsworth, P. T., *The International Economy*, The Macmillan Co., NY, 1958.
203. Kindleberger, C. P., *International Economics, op. cit.*
204. Australia (Report), *Marine Week*, Vol. 5, No. 23, 23 June 1978, pp. 9–14.
205. See 'Canadian Restrictive Trade Practices Commission', para. 437, p. 126 of the *Rochdale Report*.
206. O'Connel, D. P., 'The Federal problem concerning the maritime domain in Commonwealth countries', *J. Marit. Law & Commerc*., Vol. 1, No. 1, Oct. 1969–70 pp. 441–42.
207. Hayman, C., 'Canadian shipowners make their feelings known', *Seatrade*, Vol. 8, No. 7, July 1978, p. 15.
208. Shaw, J., 'Empressor Maritimas Lineas, Argentinas SA', *Asian Shipp*., May 1981, pp. 7–9.
209. Musgrave, R. A., *A Theory of Public Finance*, McGraw-Hill Book Co., NY, 1959, part 1.
210. Hansen, A. H., *Fiscal Policy and Business Cycles*, W. W. Norton & Co., Inc., NY, 1941.
211. Engle, W. P., *Economic Stabilization*, Princeton University Press, NJ, 1952.
212. *Strustman* v *Des Meines City Ry. Co*., 180 Iowa, 524, 163, N. W. 580 at 585.
213. Samuelson, P. A., *Economics*, 5th Ed. McGraw-Hill Book Co., NY, 1961, pp. 275–77.
214. Ackley, G., *Macroeconomic Theory*, The Macmillian Co., NY, 1961, pp. 424–39.
215. Slichter, S. H., *Reconciling Expansion with a stable Price Level: Problems of the US Economic Development Committee for Economic Development* NY, 1958, Vol. 1.
216. Tinsley, D., 'Knowing where one's strength lies' (French Report), *Fairplay*, pp. 13–15.
217. France (Survey), *Marine Week*, Vol. 6, No. 30, 27 July 1979, pp. 21–25.
218. The other TMNS are the Netherlands and the US; the DMNS are Brazil and Korea (South).
219. Thorpe, W. L. and Quandt, R. E., *The New Inflation*, McGraw-Hill Book Co., NY, 1959.
220. 'France's Maritime Strategy', *Navy International*, Vol. 85, No. 10, Oct 1980, pp. 588–92.
221. Chamber of Commerce of the US, *An Introduction to Doing Business, op. cit.*
222. Denmark (Survey), *Shipbroker*, Vol. 5, No. 6, Nov. 1979, pp. 21–25.
223. Schimdt, W., 'No reduction in Danish Fleet', *Norwegian News*, No. 5, 9 March 1979, pp. 5–7.
224. US Joint Economic Committee, *Staff Report on Employment Growth & the Price Levels* (GPO, Washington DC), Dec. 1959.
225. British Shipbuilders (Survey Report), *Mot. Ship.*, Vol. 59, No. 704, March 1979, Supp. 18 pp.
226. UK Shipping (Survey), *Shipp. World & Shipbuild*., Vol. 175, No. 3978, July/Aug. 1981, p. 8.
227. 'British shipping: another year of crisis', *Norwegian News*, Vol. 37, No. 1, Jan. 1981, pp. 76–77.
228. See also *Seatrade*, Vol. II, No. 1, Jan. 1981.
229. Richardson, H. J., *The Economics and Financial Aspects of Social Security*, University of Toronto Press, 1960.
230. Burns, E. M., *Social Security and Public Policy*, McGraw-Hill Book Co., NY, 1956.
231. Carlson, V., *Economic Security in the US*, McGraw-Hill Book Co., NY, 1962.
232. Greece (Survey), *Norwegian News*, Vol. 37, No. 1, Jan 1981, pp. 79–81.
233. Greece (Report), *Marine Weekly*, Vol. 6, No. 11, Nov. 1979, pp. 19–24.
234. Greek (Report), *Lloyd's Shipp. Econ*., Vol. 2, No. 9, Sept. 1980, pp. 8–14.
235. 'Greek shipbuilding' *Fairplay*, Vol. 274, No. 5046, 15 May 1980, pp. 51–69.
236. Italian (Report), *Mot. Ship. Special Survey*, 1980, 32 pp.

237. Italy (Survey), *Marine Week*, Vol. 6, No. 4, 26 Jan. 1979, pp. 23–29.
238. Italy (Review), *Shipp. World & Shipbuild.*, Vol. 174, No. 3969, Oct. 1980, pp. 8–14.
239. Press, J., 'The collapse of the contibutory pension scheme', *Transportation History*, Vol. 5, No. 2, Sept. 1979, pp. 91–115.
240. Cf. Greek example, *Lloyd's Ship. Manager*, Vol. 1, No. 2, May 1980, pp. 9–11.
241. Bess, D., 'The maritime academies are all wet', *US Naval Institute Proceedings*, Oct. 1979, pp. 70–76.
242. Rich, G., *The Plymouth Experience, European Shipp. & Shipbuild.* (Conference Proceedings), 1978, pp. 51–74.
243. See 'Canadian Shipping', *Lloyd's List*, 20 April 1978, p. 6.
244. Cf. Wallace, A., Denmark (Report), *Fairplay*, Vol. 266, No. 4941, 11 May 1978, pp. 8–10.
245. 'Training: govts., universities and industry involved', *Offshore,* Eng., Feb., 1978, pp. 23–28.
246. Watt, D. C., *Integrated policy for the Oceans – Teaching in the University World Marine Policy*, Vol. 4, No. 1, Jan. 1980, pp. 67–69.
247. 'The Netherlands' (Special Report), *Lloyd's List*, 17 April 1980, pp. 5–17.
248. 'Dutch government sails in with rescue package', *Seatrade*, Vol. 8, No. 4, April 1978, pp. 16–19.
249. 'Nautical Colleges', *Seaways,* Aug. 1980, pp. 18–22.
250. *Rochdale Report*, paras 683–000, pp. 183–87.
151. *Ibid.*, Chapter 12, paras 649–779, pp. 180–211.
252. Cf. Netherlands (Report), Vol. 268, No. 4967, 9 Nov 1978, pp. 57–63.
253. i.e. economic consequences of.
254. Subsidy is not a discrimination.
255. Patton and Schornhorst, 'Cargo preference and flag discrimination in international law – actions & reactions', 34 *Geo. Wash. Rev.* 257, 1965.
256. Morse, 'A study of American merchant marine legislation', 25 *Law & Contemp. Prob.* 57, 1960.
257. Capone, 'US laws and the UNCTAD Code', 15 *Va. J. Intl. Lt.* 249, 256–58, 1975.
258. Gordon, 'Shipping regulation and the FMC', 37 *U. Ch. L. Rev.* 90, 90–95, 1969.
259. James, 'Some current developments in the US control of international shipping', 7 *International Law*, 541, 1973.
260. 46 USC para. 1101 (Supp. V. 1975).
261. Goss, R. O., *Studies in Maritime Economics* 22–23, 1968; Jones *supra*, Note 9, at 545.
262. Clark, E., Haddock, H. and Volens, S., *The US Merchant Marine Today: Sunrise or Sunset?*, 53, 1970.
263. Olson, 'Cargo preference and the American merchant marine', 25 *Law & Contemp. Prob.* 82, 1960.
264. E.g., *Yugoslav Emergency Relief Assistance Act 1950*, Ch. 1182, 64 Stat. 1122.
265. *Journal of Commerce*, Feb. 25, 1976, at 1, col. 11.
266. Kilgour, 'The Energy Transportation Security Act', 1974, 7 *J. Mar. L. & Com.* 557, 1976.
267. *New York Times*, Jan. 24, 1974, at 1, col. 7.
268. Note: 'The American merchant marine', 3 *Va. J. Int. Lt.* 121, 1963.
269. Mohring, H., *Transport Subsidies and Economic Development of the Atlantic Provinces*, pp. 110–12.
270. Meyer, J. R., Kain, J. F. and Woal, M., *The Urban Transportation Problem*, Harvard University Press, 1965, pp. 343–44.
271. Studnicki-Gizbert (ed.), *Issues in Canadian Transport Policy*, 1974, p. 298.
272. Jones, P. M., 'Defining demands for models of travels', *Transportation*, Vol. 7, 1978, pp. 119–25.
273. See also US Dept. of Transportation 1974, National Transportation Report: *Current Performance and Future Prospects*, Summary Report, July 1975.
274. See also 'Harvard University analysis of investment alternatives in the Colombian

transport system', *Transport Research Programme*, Final Report, Cambridge, Mass., 1968.

275. And Holland, E. P., 'Economic systems models for transport sector studies: a critique of the Harvard Transport Program Multiregional Economic Model and proposal for a more political one', *IBRD Economic Review*.
276. See again Sorrell, L. C., *Government Ownership and Operation of Railways for the US, op. cit*.
277. O'Loughlin, *op. cit*. pp. 84–85.
278. *Report of the Shipbuilding Inquiry Committee* (Gedde's Report) HMSO, 1966, London, p. 146.
279. *Rochdale Report*, paras 180–000, p. 50.
280. See also IBRD *Economic Staff Working Paper*, No. 131, July 1972.
281. See the *Rochdale Report* on flags of convenience and maritime subsidies.
282. Sturmey, S. G., *op. cit*, pp. 104–105, and 119–120.
183. *Rochdale Report*, para 174, p. 49.
284. Sturmey, S. G., *op. cit*., pp. 30–31.
285. Eversheim, E., *Effects of Shipping Subsidization Bremen*, 1958, p. 15.

CHAPTER 6

State intervention as a method of developing national fleets

1. Introduction

Although state intervention is the latest development in restrictive practices in international shipping, it is really both a form and a continuation of flag discrimination. This is because, though like the others it does not have a precise definition, it nevertheless has a description similar to that of flag discrimination. It will be remembered that:

> 'Flag discrimination is more easily recognised than given a comprehensive description. It comprises above all any action by which governments restrict the freedom of traders to choose the ships in which cargo may be carried and thus places impediments in the path of the free flow of international trade. Examples are:
> (a) cargo preference laws;
> (b) measures in the field of exchange control;
> (c) preferential shipping clauses in trade agreements;
> (d) the operation of import and export licencing systems so as to influence the flag of the carrying ship;
> (e) port regulations; and
> (f) taxation measures'.[1]

In some respects items a, c, e and f have already been covered. Whereas flag discrimination and maritime subsidies were mainly internally oriented, state intervention is geared much more to external trade and an integration of the merchant marine fully into the national economy, international trade and tariff operations generally. It has, therefore, both a wider and a deeper application.

1.1 Interference or intervention

By this we mean the nature of the main responsibilities which governments or states have assumed towards the merchant marine industry.[2] Government shipping policies are welcomed in certain sectors and resented in other[3] circumstances. Where these policies are welcome, especially when they provide relief or constitute positive reactions from one's own government, they are referred to as *intervention.*[4] However, when similar policies are adopted by foreign governments or consist of supposedly negative reactions from domestic governments, they are interpreted simply as *interference.*[5] This ability to switch sides has characterised the mixed feelings with which the industry, especially among the TMNS, has responded to bold moves by states towards the industry. Besides the industry being predominantly in private hands in these countries, there is a general belief that the least active governments are the best governments.[6]

Government involvement, however, dates back to the emergence of maritime subsidies. In our view, therefore, both flag discrimination and maritime subsidies are a form of state intervention; negative and positive reactions, respectively, at least from the view of the industry.[7] Whereas the object of subsidies was to save the industry from collapse, flag discrimination and state intervention are designed to avoid the benefits of subsidies extending to foreign flags. In other words, the former two were the beginning of and natural progression to the latter. The general direction of all, however, is to establish, protect and develop national merchant fleets for political, security and economic reasons.[8]

Nevertheless, state intervention takes as many forms as has been broadly indicated.

> 'The Government's responsibilities towards the industry fall into two categories. The first, . . . is a general responsibility concerning the industry's commercial interests both at home and overseas, and promoting its contribution to the national well-being; the second . . . is a more detailed regulatory function, established by statute, for the safety of ships and the welfare of seafarers'.[9]

Under the first category fall the kinds of actions described above; the actions of the second category are either not relevant, or only remotely so, to the establishment and expansion of national fleets. Some of these regulations are, no doubt, common to the general industrial and commercial sector,[10] but quite a few are peculiar to the merchant marine industry. What has provoked an outcry from some, is the fact that in the past, industry in general and shipping in particular were left to the private sector to manage and control. This was no longer the case following the two World Wars.[11] But the main reason for exceptions, especially among the shipowners in the TMNS, was the unfair advantage in which they were put by the massive state support and protection by the DMNS, not to mention the fact that the emerging fleets of the DMNS cut into the previous monopoly-like position of the TMNS fleets.[12] Of late, however, state intervention has assumed international proportions, with the international community adopting a common policy towards shipping as envisaged by the *UNCTAD Code of Conduct for Liner Conferences.*

1.2 Nature and development of intervention

Comparing modern shipping with what it was before World War II, and for some time after 1945, there can be no doubt that the industry has taken a battering and has undergone a major change,[13] the implications of which affected its very existence and in particular the position of the private and commercially operating shipowners. We refer to the steady increase of state intervention.[14] Serious government intervention in the shipping industry commenced after World War II when the DMNS, in an effort to promote their national shipping industries, used unilateral legislation to preserve a good part of their exports and imports for their national flags.[15] The real breakthrough came in the sixties when Brazil, for instance, introduced a law protecting as much as 50% of its trade for its national flag and virtually compelled foreign shipping companies to accept the position.[16] Within a relatively short period of time, almost all Latin American and a number of other DMNS followed this pattern and the traditional carriers in those trades had to cut back considerably their participation, to the benefit of, and in the face of fierce competition from, the newly emerging national lines.[17]

Parallel with this development, many of the said countries tried to use the membership of their lines in the respective liner conferences to influence the level of rates in the tariffs, paying particular attention to their basic export commodities.[18] Since it is normal practice in many conferences that general increases have to be agreed almost unanimously by all members, this indirect government intervention proved to be quite successful, and in fact still is today.

Another type of government intervention is the regulation of conferences through national legislation. As will be apparent later, a typical example is provided by the *US Shipping Act, 1916,* particularly as revised in *1961*.[19] One aspect of the regulation which was resented by the shipping conferences in that country was the requirement that the people running these services spend more than half of their time on bureaucratic red-tape. The other objection was that everyday conferences in the US trades must comply with countless rules and orders of the FMC in order to prove that they are not violating the anti-trust regulations.[20] A further disadvantage of this kind of state intervention, as claimed by the private sector, is that, even with the best of intentions, this is a difficult task and the shipping industry has to employ an army of lawyers to help them interpret legal language in order to avoid possible treble damage suits and other penalties.[21] Hence, the criticism that state intervention and flag discrimination cause inefficiency leading to high costs and higher freight rates. In fact, in the North Atlantic route, the shipping companies came to the conclusion that their lawyers' fees had been considerably higher than the profits the lines had collectively made in one particular year. State intervention through national legislation does take place in a number of the TMNS (other than the US), such as Canada and Australia, as well as in many DMNS.[22] The US example, however, has by far the most far-reaching effect since compliance with its laws can be time consuming and costly; for, even small and accidental violations can be dangerous due to anti-trust implications. The most annoying aspect, to the private operators, is that many commercial plans and objectives are virtually paralyzed by this over-regulation.[23]

Another example of government intervention involves the oceanborne commerce of the STNS.[24] Perhaps the word intervention is inappropriate here – it is rather complete government control.[25] As in flag discrimination, through FOB purchases, CIF sales and the exclusive involvement of state agencies in the export and import trade, the mechanism does not leave the slightest freedom for private operators in these countries. Consequently, national ships are used almost exclusively.[26] Closely related to the practices of STNS, is, of course, bilateralism, i.e. the strictly bilateral shipping arrangements between two countries mostly on a 50–50 basis.

Bilateralism is the common procedure adopted between and amongst STNS and DMNS.[27] As noted earlier, it can safely be assumed that any country, whose shipowners want to participate in its shipments to and from the USSR, for instance, can only achieve this aim if a bilateral shipping agreement is reached on an equal access basis, and tariffs with a viable rate level are accepted. Where this is not the case, USSR ships will carry almost the entire trade in both directions, leaving third flag carriers no chance at all.[28] The shipping agreement signed between the US and USSR in 1972, and renewed in 1976, also follows this plan. This kind of state intervention seems to have become internationally acceptable with the advent of the *UNCTAD Code of Conduct for Liner Conferences*.[29]

However, it is no exaggeration to assert that far more than 50% of all ocean-borne trade in the world was already, to a greater or less degree, affected by government intervention before the discussion about the UNCTAD code even started.[30] To many people this code appeared to be the culmination of state involvement. To others (and the author is one of them) there are a number of positive aspects involved, not only with the UNCTAD code, but with state intervention generally.[31] State intervention takes many forms. We have been able to isolate state control, state participation, state aid and others, and will proceed to discuss them below, starting with state control.

2. State control

We have just noted that the reconstruction of the TMNS' fleets after the war involved a large outlay of capital, the replacement of obsolete uneconomic tonnage demands, and further large investments.[32] A reasonable and relatively stable freight level and a fiscal system which permits owners to accumulate sufficient funds for replacement or expansion, are the two factors requisite for the maintenance, on a commercial basis, of efficient and cheap overseas shipping services.[33] In their turn, these basic factors are essential to the proper functioning and development of international maritime trade generally. However, conditions are no longer ideal for the operation of these market forces. Rather, violently fluctuating freight markets, resulting in periods of unhealthy boom and acute depression, are the order of the day.[34] They are as unwelcome to shipowners and governments, as they are to everyone else, since they increase the difficulties of planning ahead and lead, at times, to laid-up tonnage and periods of unemployment.

This, plus the desire of states to establish, develop and expand national fleets of their own, has led various governments to intervene and control the industry[35] through supervisory planning, directives and approvals, regulatory agencies, domestic registry and control of foreign participation. But first the supervisory planning.

2.1 Supervisory planning

State planning of the economy is no longer the monopoly of STNS and DMNS; it is now widely accepted as a fact of life. Neither is the shipping industry to be viewed outside this government intervention in industry and commerce.[36] What differs, however, is the degree of planning; ranging from total, in the case of STNS, through mixed economies, in the case of DMNS, and semi-control in the case of TMNS.[37] What is generally agreed is that the planned economy is a system in which some or all of the decisions on allocation, production, investment and distribution are made by a central government agency. The collective economic planning used in a typically planned economy is based on the assumption that social welfare can be recognized and pursued more effectively under centralized planning.[38]

The predominantly private shipping concerns among the TMNS are, however, quick to point out that this assumption denies the advantages to which it is said to lead and results in chaotic disharmony between production and consumption.[39] They further point out that in planned shipping, the initiative for economic activities and decisions concerning them do not originate with the shipping entrepreneurs.[40] And, of course, they resent the idea that the government should start with an overall plan of major objectives and then attempt to achieve the fullest possible utilization of available resources in line with the state objectives. Nevertheless, for the reasons stated above, the shipping industry accepts some form of state intervention on the basis that in modern times there is, after all, no single government that does not act as the general overseer of the economy. But that is about all they are prepared to accept.[41]

The shipowners and shipping companies fear the elimination of the market mechanism in price formation and the government undertaking to replace the market functions that exist in completely planned economies. They further fear that the planned shipping agencies (post)[42] created in various countries, to set up production goals, resource allocations and decision-making regarding production and investment, are steps towards totalitarianism. Such systems exist even in such pro-Western DMNS as Taiwan, where shipments are planned under the supervision of the Ministry of Commerce, with first priority being given to, for instance, vessels built under the Measure for the Joint Development of Trading, Shipping and Shipbuilding.[43] In the Taiwanese example, second priority is given to ordinary vessels of Taiwanese nationality and third choice to other vessels. One can detect the discrimination practised in this for development objectives.[44]

The nature, extent and policy underlying merchant marine planning in Taiwan is such that when shipping companies plan to build new vessels, for instance, they must first seek domestic shipbuilding companies.[45] If the latter are unable to undertake the construction, only then can private shipowners place orders with foreign shipyards, even then only after gaining Ministry of Commerce approval.[46] And, as expected, in line with the development objectives of state planning, high priority is given to the building of such vessels as container ships, multipurpose cargo ships and special ships for carrying imported bulk grains and minerals.[47] With the exception of construction for foreign ship owners, it can only be assumed that the types of vessels listed above are those in shortest supply with the national flag or in response to the national flag demands to service international trade, or both.[48]

However, these vessels must carry the Taiwanese flag, sail in lanes pertinent to the international trade of Taiwan, and not be leased out but run by the

Taiwanese owners.[49] Finally, the domestic shipbuilding price under the measure cannot exceed 5% of the international price for similar vessels of the same type and function. The down payment must be 20% of the total price before the ship is handed over to the shipowner; the period for payment of instalments is not less than seven years.[50] There is a subsidy to enable local owners to purchase on credit over longer periods. Thus, the previously predominantly privately owned merchant marine industry now finds itself having to comply with state supervisory planning requirements. These range from external commerce to shipping and shipbuilding, of which the Taiwanese case is but one example.[51] However, sometimes government directives and requirements for government approval are used instead of supervisory planning to control the merchant marine.

2.2 Government directives and approvals

State direction of the merchant marine industry is conducted for precisely the same objectives outlined in state planning above. The principles applied in employing both mechanisms are about the same.[52] It will, no doubt, be clear by now that in the government direction of the economy there are two types of modern approach. One is the partial directive that has evolved under the private enterprise system. It is this with which the shipping industries are acquainted among the TMNS,[53] and this approach on which we shall, therefore, focus our attention. It will also be remembered that under this system government direction may be applied through the general economic policy that is designed to smooth economic fluctuations experienced in the free enterprise system.[54] This may take the shape of actions to offset a recession, the instruction of general shipbuilding projects to provide employment, the reduction of taxes to increase the purchasing power of shipowners and shippers, and the lowering of interest rates to encourage investments.[55] Government policies to prevent inflation and to encourage economic growth are also examples of limited instances where government directives and the requirements for government prior approvals may be necessary.[56]

As in the case of flag discriminations and maritime subsidies, government directives and approvals take many forms, such as proclamations, byelaws, pronouncements, decrees, etc.[57] It is needless to emphasize that these directives and approvals are more common among the STNS and DMNS. A typical example is the case of Israel, where government approval is necessary before foreign ships can be chartered by an Israeli party. Such approval is obtainable only if domestic ships are unavailable on competitive terms, or when special lift ships are required.[58] Secondly, under Israeli law on this point, a ship must have at least 50% Israeli ownership to be registered under the Israeli flag. Perhaps all these stringent requirements are necessary given Israel's volatile position in the Middle East. Besides, as in most DMNS, shipping is of extreme importance to Israel since almost all her foreign trade is seaborne.[59] In fact, shipping has become Israel's second most important foreign exchange earner, after tourism, and is expanding at an accelerated rate. In 1969, for instance, Israeli flag-shipping carried approximately 50% of her foreign trade, that is by far the highest proportion outside the STNS. Not all of this can be attributed to the approval policy, but a large percentage must have been due to it.[60] So, in a way, the government feels vindicated for initiating and continuing the intervention policy, and through it, the control of the merchant marine industry directives and requirements for approvals.[61] Of couse, these approvals and directives were most common in flag discriminations and subsidies. We also noted that these government directives are often initiated and justified as a *quid pro quo* for state subsidies to the merchant marine industry; it is the price the industry has had to pay in return for state aid.[62]

In this respect, we should remember the case of South Korea. The South Korean government may direct any maritime transportation, receiving subsidy or loan, under the applicable law to operate his ship on a specific domestic or international route for a fixed period.[63] Any loss from this service is compensated in a manner prescribed by a *Presidential Decree.*[64] Thus. the government is prepared to offer a double subsidy, as in this case, in return for compliance with its directives. We also noted, furthermore, that when the ship concerned in the above item is considered too old for the promotion of public or national interest, the government may direct that the ship be substituted or improved, itself bearing any loss to the owner caused by such a substitution or by such improvements.[65] Moreover, this process takes precedence over others in the domestic construction of ships. Finally, in 1976, the South Korean government directed that, where possible, all new ships for the Korean merchant fleet would be built at the country's own yards, again with the government undertaking to subsidize owners and yards.[66] Non-compliance with such directives can have very serious consequences, including treating the vessels concerned as foreign for the purposes of flag discrimination and subsidies, and/or outright acquisition. The approval requirement enables the government to plan maritime services not according to market requirements, but rather according to national needs.[67] We do not single out South Korea other than for using this as a typical example of this kind of state intervention. Such intervention is normally effected through a licensing system. However, nowhere is state intervention illustrated better than through regulatory agencies.[68]

2.3 Regulating agencies

As noted in the section on the nature and development of state intervention, regulatory control through state agencies marked the beginning of unilateral actions by various governments aimed at controlling the liner conference sector[69] in particular. Many statutes, commissions and reports were introduced in various countries with varying degrees of success. In the final analysis, regulatory shipping agencies were set up, including associations and councils, aimed at self regulation.[70] Although they may play only a small role, or none at all in aiding the establishment, development and expansion of national fleets, they are nevertheless worth discussing, being the finest example of state intervention in the merchant marine industry through control mechanisms. The best known of these are the GCBS and the FMC.[71]

But it is the US version (FMC) that has raised protests from the world shipping community. The US government as a large shipper, shipowner and operator, and as the agency responsible for the national welfare, is in an anomalous position as regards the adoption of an appropriate policy towards shipping generally and shipping conferences in particular.[72] It wants competition to be free enough to ensure rates at a level approximate to those that would be established in a free competitive market. It also wants stable rates, which can best be obtained by permitting ship operators to form monopolistic combinations.[73] However, the formation of such groups is not ordinarily favoured by the government. The American government and public have a deep traditional anti-trust feeling which can be detected not just in the FMC, but also in the other agencies, such as the DOJ, DOC, DOT, DOA etc. On this matter, the government, as represented by these institutions, and the shipping industry do not see eye to eye.[74] They are as far apart as they can possibly be. The private operators, on the one hand, claim that the overtonnaging of some trades, often a concomitant of the monopolistic combinations reminiscent of what they (private operators) would wish, may, after all, be in the interest of their national defence.[75] The argument of the government, on the other hand, is that the conflicting interests and desires cannot be reconciled in the policy of the US government towards liner conferences in particular, and the merchant marine industry generally. It is because of this that Section 14 of the *Shipping Act, 1916,* prohibits the formation of combinations, the use of fighting ships, retaliation against any shipper for non-compliance with combination agreements, and use of unfair or unjust discriminatory contracts.[76] Section 14(a) provides the means of disciplining foreign lines participating in liner conferences affecting the US for such breaches.[77]

Section 15 requires all liner conference agreements affecting US flag lines in US foreign trade to be filled with the FMC; and Section 16 forbids unreasonable discrimination for or against persons, localities and classes of traffic.[78] Further regulations are provided in the *Merchant Marine Act, 1920* and the *Merchant Marine Act, 1936,* as amended from time to time. It is interesting to note that the US, which prohibits flag discrimination is also the major practitioner of it.[79] However, in reading these laws one must remember that the government cannot directly regulate the rates of services established by international liner shipping conferences. Though the law may appear to give the government the right to regulate rates, this applies only to domestic operations.[80] The American attempt to extend this regulation, in some respects, beyond her borders has met with a stiff response from other countries. So for the moment at least, the US government can exact indirect control over international liner conference agreements only by refusing to approve the participation of US flag vessels, by penalising them if they do so, and by refusing certain port privileges to the foreign flag vessels involved.[81]

The limited power of any national government prevents it from effectively controlling international shipping, and this is true even of the US. For the US, this fact has been particularly vexing because of the said anti-monopoly and anti-control bias of government policy.[82] For the most part, most other TMNS do not share this bias. They accept cartels with little official animosity. The US, on the other hand, accepts liner conferences but it puts restrictions on their US members. In short, the US flag vessel operators are not forbidden to join conferences but they must not engage in certain practices adopted by some conferences.[83] Although this intervention had no bearing on the expansion of the US fleet it has probably retarded it. One area, however, where the US has been successful, and which is relevant to the expansion of its national fleet, is the control of foreign participation in domestic shipping. This will be discussed in a wider context in the section on state participation with respect to the financing and managing of a national fleet (post).[84]

2.4 Control of foreign participation

Permitting foreign investment to participate in one's national economy can lead to expansion, but again it may retard expansion of certain sectors which rely heavily on foreign capital and foreign skills to their detriment. Foreign investment, in this case, would be the acquisition by a government, or its citizens[85] of assets abroad, or by the government or citizens of other states in a given country. Such investments may take the form of bank deposits, foreign government bills, government or industrial securities, or titles to land, buildings, capital equipment, related to the merchant marine industry, or the vessels themselves.[86] Private investment abroad will normally be made in the hope of a higher interest, dividend, or other income than can be obtained at home,[87] or in the expectation of alterations in exchange rates, or out of fear of political or taxation changes at home, as was the case with foreign registry.[88]

Government investments, on the other hand, are undertaken for political, diplomatic, military or other reasons that may pay little attention to the yield of the investment. An example is provided by the TMNS' loans to the DMNS.[89] The problem is to weigh the political and other advantages, which are difficult to judge, against the additional yield the investments would have earned elsewhere. The benefits to a country as a whole from investment abroad, as compared with investment at home, are not confined to the monetary interest or yield received by the investor, because they may affect employment, the productivity of labour, or the terms of trade and state revenue.[90] It does not, however, necessarily follow that foreign investment yields a lower social return than investment at home. It may be higher, for example, where it reduces the price of imports. It also does not follow that foreign investment should be made exclusively by governments, which are able to take indirect social effects into account, because government investment tends to become political investment whereas the errors of individual investors tend to cancel out.[91] From a recipient country's point of view, foreign investment can lead to control of certain sectors, of national economic life, by foreigners. This can be unwise. There is no country in the world which does not have foreign investment on her soil, including the US.[92] Noting the defence importance of shipping, an attempt has been made by various countries to either control or eliminate foreign participation in this sector.

Yet again, the best example is probably that of the US.[93] Section 27 of the *Jones Act, 1952,*[94] for instance, sets out three conditions for foreigners to engage in US domestic cargo trade. The first is the *documentation* requirement which prohibits all but US flag vessels from engaging in this trade. The idea is that such vessels could then be subject to other policies reflected in US domestic laws; requiring documentation under US laws would probably facilitate conforming to these laws.[95] Examples of these laws are those relating to the regulation, expansion and defense role of the national fleets. The second requirement is the *construction* requirement which specifies that vessels engaging in the domestic trade must be built in the US.[96] This requirement, however, neither allows alien investment in the construction industry,[97] nor operations by aliens as domestic carriers. It may negatively affect the possibility of a foreign carrier competing in the domestic trade, because of the likelihood that most of its fleet would have been built outside the US.[98]

The third requirement is that of *ownership* or *management*. Section 27 requires the individual owner to be a citizen and, by reference to section 2 of the *Shipping Act, 1970,* the corporate owner to be domestically organised and owned, to the extent of 75% of the ownership interest, by US citizens.[99] The same ownership interest requirement applies to partnerships.[100] In addition to the Chief Executive Officer, the Chairman of the board of a corporate owner must be a US citizens and the number of alien directors, if any, must be less than the quorum of the board.[101] In addition, aliens who invest in domestic enterprises unrelated to the maritime industries generally[102] must arrange their business so that all water cargo transportation is handled by carriers rather than by the business itself.[103] Even though the business itself could handle the carriage most efficiently, the cost of transport is increased and the potential profitability lowered.[104] Thus, this restraint might prove to be an indirect impediment to foreign investment in other industries as well.[105]

The fourth, and final, requirement relates to *environmental protection,* safety and other regulatory concerns, all of which are served by easing the flow of funds into the merchant marine, especially by aliens. The investment restraint prohibits the entry of new foreign competitors into the field.[106] This control of foreign investments in the US merchant marine serves to prevent foreigners from gaining a foothold in the industry and aids expansion and employment efforts. It may retard rapid expansion, by denying vital foreign investments, but at the same time it ensures that whatever expansion takes place is truly American, which is good for security, political and economic reasons.[107] If this policy results in the development of a truly national fleet then it is that kind of fleet that this inquiry is all about.

Closely related to state control is actual state participation.

3. State participation

All the previous forms of protection and intervention by the state have been from a distance, detached. However, with the benefit of hindsight, many countries discovered that the most effective means of control, and the fastest way to expand, is through direct state participation in the financing, management and direction of the merchant marine industry.[108] In that way, governments are kept in touch with the problems and needs of the industry, etc. They also take part in the daily routine and decision making process; being able to influence these important decisions and being party to them.[109] State participation gives the industry more protection – the necessary stability for expansion. This is true, at least of the STNS and DMNS. State participation in the merchant marine industry is effected through joint ventures and partnerships, state ownership, nationalised industries and through arrangements to award a monopoly to state contracts and state purchases. But first, joint ventures and partnerships.

3.1 Joint ventures and partnerships

Joint ventures initially meant an association of individuals or firms formed to carry out a specific business project.[110] Now, of course, parties may include states and state institutions. Although a joint venture is very similar to a partnership, it differs in that it is limited to the success or failure of the specific project for which it was formed. As in the case of a partnership, a joint venture is formed by a contractual agreement in which each partner assumes unlimited liability for the organization's debts. The other mechanism of state intervention is through partnership.[111] Ordinarily, a partnership is a type of business in which two or more persons (or states in this case) agree on the amount of their contribution (capital and effort), and on the distribution of profits, if any. Partnerships are more common in the retail trade, accounting and law than in expensive and heavy industries like merchant shipping.[112]

Since the partners pool their capital, partnerships, in general, are larger than, say, proprietorships, which also exist in shipping; but they are still relatively small when compared with shipping corporations (post). In many respects, however, shipping partnerships are similar to shipping proprietorships.[113] But the distinct feature is that these are different from ordinary partnerships. They are subject to government regulations and are not characterized by unlimited liability, which means that all the partnership assets are not available as security for their creditors. Thus, one of the most effective ways of state control of the merchant marine industry is through part-participation.[114] This is particularly true of the DMNS. These ventures and partnerships are normally in association with local or foreign business investments. The important point to note, in this respect, is that state participation involves majority shares for the purposes of maintaining control. *Control* is the objective of the exercise or the operative word from the state point of view.[115]

The shipping ventures and partnerships are sometimes regional exercises, as in the case of Colombia. It is understandable why Colombia would, for instance, seek to control her shipping; it is special to Colombia with its two coastlines and its large coffee exports which supply some 50–55% of foreign exchange earnings.[116] The Colombian flag line, *Flota Mercante Grancolombiana,* is such an exercise in regional ownership. Colombia's National Federation of Coffee Growers controls approximately 80% of the ownership, with the remaining 20% controlled by the Development Bank of Ecuador.[117] At one time the Venezuelan Government also participated in *Flota's* ownership. As might have been expected, there were strings attached to this state participation; although there were no legal requirements, in effect, imports for governments or quasi-government agencies were generally carried by *Flota.*[118] There were also benefits: close ties with the Colombian government and publicity for the advantages of shipping via *Flota* account for the shipping line's strong position.

In Egypt, too, joint ventures in the maritime transport industry are encouraged by awarding such ventures tax-free operations for the first five years and other fringe benefits.[119] And in South Korea companies wishing to receive government assistance must have a minimum tonnage of 20 000 grt, and minimum capital of 500 m *won*; joint ventures with overseas interests are permitted, provided that national interests are 51% or more and the Board of Directors is at least 60% South Korean.[120] Liberia, on the other hand, became a partner through the LSC in two shipping companies incorporated in Liberia, the TISC and the

PSC.[121] The LSC owns 50% of TISC, the remainder being shared equally by Dutch and Israeli interests. The PSC is owned jointly by the Liberian government and the Graengesburg Company of Sweden, a large stockholder in LAMCO mines.[122] Finally, the Malaysian Government signed an agreement to establish a major shipyard at Johore Bharn on a joint venture basis with Japanese and other investors. When completed, it will be one of the largest in the SEA.[123]

In some cases these efforts have assisted in the establishment and expansion of national fleets; in others, they have served to hinder that progress. What is not denied is that they have enabled governments to control and direct shipping.[124] Not all governments have been satisfied with part-participation as a method of state intervention. Quite a few governments have opted for total control – nationalisations of at least certain sectors of shipping and shipbuilding – hoping this would speed up the establishment and development of national fleets.

3.2 Nationalised shipping and shipyards

Nationalisation is, of course, an act by which a government takes over the ownership and operation of a shipping company or shipyard which was previously in the hands of foreign or private citizens.[125] These governments argue that such nationalisations increase productive efficiency by permitting the direct investment of public funds, by enlarging the scale of operations, and by co-ordinating operations more effectively.[126] On the other hand, private shipping concerns and other opponents of nationalisations, especially among the TMNS, state that the record of private shipping enterprises is such that government takeovers are unnecessary,[127] and that government ownership is usually characterized by excessive costs because of elaborate, over-centralized organization.[128] However, as will be evident in the succeeding chapters, nationalisation, and other forms of state intervention, have been used by some countries purely as a means of eliminating foreign ownership of their merchant marine industries or as part of a policy of wholesale nationalising of all major industries, as in the UK.[129]

In the latter case, for instance, on July 1, 1977, 19 shipbuilding companies, 5 diesel marine engine manufacturers and 3 training companies were nationalised to form the BSC.[130] Labour, industry and government were represented in a management which planned to use economies of scale to obtain more orders for the industry.[131] The docks, too, were nationalised and operated under the BTDB. The BTDB were returned to private concerns in 1983 under the new name Associated British Ports (ABP). The shipyards, however, remain decentralized so that individual shipyard performance can be measured. The pooling of orders takes place only when required to facilitate the securing of orders.[132] The other example from the TMNS is provided by Portugal, where, by *Decree Laws 205-C/75* and *205-D/75* of 16 July, 1975, the *Companhia Nationale de Navegaco* and the *Companhia Portuguese de Transporto Maritimas,* respectively, were nationalised.[133] The same decree nationalised the shares of *Sociedade Portuguesa de Navios Tanques, Lda Soponate.*

In addition, *Resolution No. 153/77* of May 5, 1977, called for the creation of *Navis-Navega cus de Portugal* to function as a coordinator and supervisor of the public business management of these firms, already established in the field of sea navigation, without prejudice to the anatomy and legal individuality of the latter.[134] The *Law Decree of November 16, 1977* established NAVIS. These nationalised shipping organisations, therefore, became state-owned. State-owned shipping does not normally exist on its own. Many countries have had to start new national fleets where none existed before.[135]

3.3 State-owned shipping

State-owned shipping, which has mushroomed, especially among the DMNS, is not only another alternative method of state intervention in the industry, but is, perhaps, the only true case of states establishing their own national fleets.[136] Often this development exists either side by side with joint ventures, partnerships and nationalised shipping, or is the only form permitted to operate. Whereas such ownerships would have been unthinkable about a century ago, today public ownership of merchant shipping is the general rule rather than the exception.[137] In such cases, then, the industry becomes part of the government ownership and operation generally. The principle involved is that the government replaces private shipowners as the supplier of capital. Thus, the government supplies the capital and determines the maritime facilities to be provided.[138]

In addition, the government chooses the management, assumes the responsibility of paying labour, purchasing supplies, setting the prices for oceanborne trade and maritime services, determining the freight rates, and reaping profits or meeting deficits if they are incurred.[139] This governmental act of removing private ship ownership and assuming the operation of the shipping enterprise is what is called government or public ownership. It may come about through the creation of parastatal shipping bodies or, assuming what was already in existence, through nationalisation. However, as in the case of the STNS and DMNS, perhaps the term 'state intervention' then loses its meaning.[140] Intervention ends with nationalisation and other previously mentioned methods of state control. But when there is a concern created by the government from public funds it would be an anomaly to refer to government direction of it as intervention or even participation. This is true of state shipping and all government holdings.[141]

Sometimes state shipping companies deliberately put pressure on the private sector to conform to state control. The action of the Irish Government is an example of the former; the ISC and the BISPCO seem to have been created because the government was dissatisfied with the way private shipping behaved.[142] By the 31st May, 1978, shortly after coming into being, the ISC, which operates mainly in the deep sea trade on charter and tramping and had only 8 bulk carriers of 142 943 grt, soon became effectively the owner of the St. Patrick and St. Killian car ferries. These ferry companies had previously resisted compliance to and control by the government. But when the government undercut their operations they had no choice but to allow themselves to be taken over.[43]

Otherwise government ownership does not exclude, and often invites, partnership, as in the above-discussed incidents or the cases of FINMARE of Italy.[144] FINMARE is a holding company in which the IRI, an agency of the Ministry of State Holdings, owns 75% of the shares and the public owns 25%.[145] Hence, shareholdings in FINMARE and IRI in shipping companies entitled to government subsidies are shown in Table 30.[145]

Table 30. Ownership of shares.

Company	FINMARE (%)	IRI (%)	Tirrenia (%)
Italia	90	10	
Lloyd Triestino	80	20	
Adriatica	60	40	
Tirrenia	80	20	
Torremar	48.51		51.49
Caremar	48.51		51.49
Siremar	48.51		51.49

In addition, approximately 80% of the shipbuilding in Italy is owned and operated by FINCANTIERI, a holding company in which IRI, owns 100% of the stock.[146] In accordance with the CIPE recommendations of October 7, 1967, the shipyards under FINCANTIERI control were reorganised under a new entity called ITALCANTIERI which now includes the Sestri, Monfalcone and Castellamere shipyards.[147]

The immediate motive behind these forms of state intervention, i.e. participation and control, is to enable the state to integrate shipping into the general industrial, economic and commercial planning programmes. The paramount objective is to enable the swift establishment and expansion of national fleets.[148] The intention may be good, but as to whether these measures 'deliver the goods' is a different matter. We have been able to outline several options open to governments but we have no feedback and, therefore, no way of knowing whether the overall objectives have been or will be achieved through these mechanisms.[149]

The other alternative similar to, but different from, state ownership is state purchase.

3.4 State purchase

State purchase of ships is not a type of ownership but rather a state subsidy with active state participation.[150] The programme involves both credit facilities to the national lines, for the purchase of ships and leaning towards the said lines for any purchases the state makes. The purchase could be of foreign flag vessels or domestic vessels registered aborad.[151] The country where such practice is prominent is Greece, where more often than not the aim of the scheme is:

> 'In order to attract foreign economic interests, including shipping companies which may or may not be controlled by Greek interests, for the purposes of establishing regional or home offices in Greece . . . '[152]

This is perhaps a much clearer and more direct method of attempting to establish and develop a national fleet than most of the others we have touched on. First, for the purchase of foreign flag ships to promote the modernization of Greece's merchant fleet, the Greek government (as we noted) has authorized local banks to issue letters of guarantee covering up to 50% of the total value of vessels flying foreign flags, which are bought in order to be subsequently registered under the Greek flag.[153]

The balance of the cost of these vessels must be provided by the purchaser himself in foreign exchange. Credits to be extended to purchasers, on the basis of the bank letters of guarantee mentioned above, should be repayable in no less than a year in equal annual or semi-annual instalments.[154] This is a type of state subsidy but one with a difference; first, because it involves active state action and, second, because it involves state participation. Vessels to be purchased under the foregoing scheme must be less than 12 years old. In cases where the purchase is of coastline cargo vessels, and coastline passenger vessels (including passenger ferry boat/ships) flying foreign flags are involved, a scheme similar to the one outlined in the previous paragraph is applicable.[155] Under the scheme, bank letters of guarantee may cover up to 80% of the total value of the ships purchased provided, however, that the total value of each vessel does not exceed US $1 000 000 and its age is not less than 8 years.[156]

Insurance of bank letters of guarantee for the purchase of ships whose value is in excess of 1 000 000 US $ shall be contingent upon special approval by the Greek Currency Committee. However, to qualify for the benefits extended under the above schemes, prospective purchasers of foreign flag vessels should undertake a commitment to register such vessels under the Greek flag.[157] The second category is that of purchases of national flag ships registered abroad. Again in the Greek example, for this purpose, local banks are authorised to extend loans for the purchase of ships flying the Greek flag provided that:

(a) The vessel to be purchased is less than 15 years old;[158] and

(b) The amount of the loan does not exceed 50% of the value of the vessel or the maximum of US $ 100 000 for each vessel.[159]

Otherwise the loans are repayable in three years (five equal semi-annual instalments) with a period of grace of one year. And, finally, loans intended to finance purchases of ships in general (Greek flag or foreign flag) bear a minimum interest rate of 14% p.a.[160]

This Greek scheme seems to be achieving its objectives. In fact, there have been indications that the Greek flag has grown ever since. But this is not a point that should be overstressed. This programme lays emphasis on modernization rather than general expansion.[161] Even if that were not the case, Greece is one of those countries with many flags registered abroad and it is these which are returning. That puts Greece in a unique position that cannot be compared with many other countries. At any rate attracting back one's own flags can hardly be called expansion.[162] The fact that the scheme seems to be successful in this case does not warrant a generalisation that state purchase is a viable mechanism for every nation to establish and expand its national fleet.[163] Thus, as it relates to Greece, state purchase as a form of state intervention must be seen in that limited extent. What might, however, justify general application are state contracts.

3.5 State contracts

Originally known as *admiralty contracts,* state contracts are, strictly speaking, a kind of discrimination or preference that favours domestic construction companies with access to government contracts.[164] In a wider sense, however, these contracts involve payment for keeping units of the merchant navy in reserve for the navy's account. Such contracts also have a more cost-motivated form inasmuch as they include a special compensation for armaments.[165] Here we shall restrict ourselves to the non-military aspects of admiralty contracts. Inevitably this type of contract is linked to the construction subsidy.[166] In Argentina, for instance, the benefits of state contracts are applicable only to companies owned or controlled by resident Argentine citizens.[167]

Australia, on the other hand, provides a bounty for the construction of ships built in registered Australian shipyards for use in Australian waters or as an Australian vessel for use in overseas trade.[168] A better example still is the Canadian Government Purchasing Scheme under which government contracts have generally been restricted to Canadian Shipyards and, since 1965, have been awarded to the lowest qualified bidder – an exception was a submarine built abroad.[169] More and more maritime nations now adopt this form of intervention. A fairly recent example arose in 1976, when the South Korean government proclaimed that, where possible, all new ships for the South Korean merchant fleet should be built at the country's own yards with the government undertaking, as usual, to subsidize owners and yards.[170]

However, by far the most elaborate scheme is that operated by the Peruvian government. The *Law of January 9, 1962,* authorised the establishment of a naval construction industry providing for 5% state participation. The cost is provided by the revenue from export and import trades.[171] After the government has fulfilled its obligations to this industry, the remainder of the money goes to the CPV for the purchase of ships or for their construction in Peru.[172] Secondly, by the *Ministerial Resolution of June 12, 1972,* no more purchases are allowed in Peru of foreign vessels similar to those built in Peru until the National Industry Commission (NIC), formed earlier in the same month for this purpose, has presented its recommendations to the government on the effect of such requests upon the development of the naval industry.[173]

Finally, all Peruvian flag vessels must be repaired only by Peruvian shipyards or drydocks, unless the owners can show that the national shipyards do not have the capacity for a specific job. Repairs abroad may be made only in case of emergency.[174] In addition to such legislation, another statutory requirement[175] restricting the construction of national flag-ships to domestic shipyards for operation in a nation's foreign and domestic trade, specifies that materials and component parts for the construction of ships and their maintenance and repair, as well as for food, stores and supplies, be purchased domestically.[176] These aid requirements are no different from any of the interventionist schemes discussed above. The objectives remain the establishment and/or expansion of the national fleet.

The fourth major form of state intervention, for the same purpose is, state aid to oceanborne trade.[177]

4. State aid to oceanborne trade

The establishment and/or development of a national fleet would be meaningless unless matched by demand for transportation of the nation's oceanborne trade. Where such trade is non-existent, or in its infancy, governments have sought to create and sustain it through the same mechanisms.[178] This has been done through export promotion, import restrictions, and manipulation of exchange control regulations.

4.1 Export inducements and incentives

No other mode of transportation has had an equivalent effect upon the exchange of goods and services, of all types, between different countries as has merchant shipping.[179] Business firms from the TMNS sell machinery and equipment to DMNS, which in turn sell raw materials to firms in the former.[180] The growth of oceanborne trade has been greatly helped by modern techniques of merchant shipping transportation and communications.[181] These relatively new merchant marine developments have brought countries closer together than they had ever been in the past and have made the conduct of oceanborne trade easier.[182]

More up to date and complete international economic information, too, has made the consignor and consignee more knowledgeable regarding available products and markets.[183] It is the realisation of these potentials, and the desire to tap these resources, that has led various states to actively assist the foreign-trade-promoting aspects of their national merchant marines.[184] One of the most effective ways of achieving this objective has been through incentives and/or inducements. This has been made possible due to the close relations between merchant marine transportation, oceanborne trade and international trade.[185] This is now a common practice among states, TMNS and DMNS.

Take, for example, the case of the Philippines. The *Presidential Decree 806* of October 3, 1975,[186] states that the government will take all steps necessary, including the provision of direct incentives to Philippino flag-vessels and national shipping lines, to enable them to carry a substantial and increasing share of the cargo generated by Philippine foreign trade.[187] The same legislation also states that Philippine flag-vessels and those which are owned, controlled, or chartered by Philippine nationals, shall carry at least an equal share of cargo as that carried by vessels of the other country in trade between the countries.[188] Furthermore, exporters will be able to deduct from their taxable incomes an amount equivalent to 150% of overseas freight expenses and charges in Philippine ports incurred in shipping export products, provided they are Philippine-flag carriers.

So, often, the aid to oceanborne trade is operated together, and simultaneously, with that to international trade. In the Philippine example, enterprises registered with the Board of Investments will also be allowed to deduct from their taxable income, 200% of shipment costs incurred in the transport of their raw materials and products to and from foreign ports, provided the shipments are on Philippino flag vessels.[189] Similar inducements, of a subsidy nature, are provided for in the general export promotion exercises.[190]

4.2 Export promotion

This scheme relates to the export of actual goods, commodities or services shipped from one country or area to another, in the conduct of foreign trade, and operates on the same principles and criteria as the inducements and incentives above.[191] Again, in South Korea such a scheme is operated under four main categories according to the *Law of February 28, 1967*, *viz*.:[192]

(a) The government may give encouragement subsidies to maritime transportation businessmen operating or utilising Korean flag ships in international trade, which contribute towards earning or conserving foreign currencies;[193]

(b) The government shall assist and foster a maritime transportation organisation whose objective is to enhance the status of and to encourage international activities of maritime transportation businessmen;[194]

(c) When a maritime transportation businessman operates his ship on regular international routes for the promotion of foreign trade and to earn foreign currency, the government may subsidize any loss he sustains, as prescribed by the said Presidential Decree;[195]

(d) The government may order any maritime transportation businessman receiving subsidy or loan under applicable law to operate his ship on a specific domestic or international route for a fixed period. Any loss from this service will be compensated in a manner prescribed by Presidential Decree;[196]

(e) The government or any individual shall, for transport of cargo by ship, use a Korean flag ship or ship chartered by a Korean national where available or not in violation of international agreements.[197]

That the requirement be in accordance with international agreements probably refers to the rule against discrimination and equality in the GATT and other international conventions to which South Korea is a signatory or which it has ratified.[198] This provision marks a departure from the practices of other countries. Nevertheless, these and other measures are aimed at export promotion in the national flag vessels. However, besides these measures, there are also measures aimed specifically at the export of the vessels themselves, equipment and parts thereon, as well as of technical know-how.[199] These too operate by way of subsidies. One of these schemes involves ship export credits.

4.3 Ship export credits

So often we forget that ships and aircraft, besides being carriers of physical goods and services, are at the same time themselves subjects of international trade, and perhaps more lucrative ones at that. Ship export, as in shipbuilding, is still largely a monopoly of the TMNS. Take, for example, three leading TMNS.[200] First, West Germany: in order to reduce the cost of export credits for ships, the government has made available ERP loans and interest subsidies, since 1961, to bring credit terms in relation to ship exports approximately to the internationally prevailing level.[201] The reduction of the interest rate applies solely to that portion of the purchasing price for which payment is deferred.

The amount of the reduction of interest rate is dependent on the current interest rates of the capital market; it must not exceed 12%.[202] Needless to say, assistance will be given in accordance with the Understanding on *Export Credit for Ships* in its most recent valid version. At present the 9th Shipbuilding Assistance Programme for ship exports in the period 1979–1982 is being finalised in its implementation.[203] Transactions not financed by a shipyard or its bank are granted to the shipyards in the form of loans by the Combined Export-Import Bank of Japan.[204]

The Japanese Export-Import Bank is the equivalent of the US EXIMBANK and is supported by the government. However, the EXIMBANK loans are supplemented by those of the private banks which cover at most 60% of the total ships' price.[205] Present conditions for the said loans are normally as follows:

1. EXIMBANK loans cover 55% of the combined loans (i.e. 33% of the total price). The term of an EXIMBANK loan is seven years after completion of the ship;[206]
2. Private banks will finance the shipyard with the remainder of the combined loans (i.e. 27% of the total price).[207]

The financing terms of the EXIMBANK are also decided in order that the combined loans meet the *OECD Understanding on Export Credits for Ships.*[208] However, the shipyard which enjoys these credits will grant a deferred payment to the shipowners abroad on the same conditions as the combined loans. These include payment spread over seven years, at approximately 5% interest rate, and a down payment of at least 30% of the price by delivery time.[209] These credits are mainly directed at expansion of shipbuilding and, through it, ship exports. They may have no direct relation to the expansion of the national fleet itself. The latter objective may be achieved through the manipulation of foreign exchange regulations, e.g. exemptions.[210]

4.4 Foreign exchange exemptions

In an economic context, foreign exchange is, of course, the system whereby one currency is exchanged for (or converted into) another, though sometimes the term is used as if it were synonymous with the exchange itself.[211] The three main types of foreign exchange systems are:

(i) The gold standard in its various forms;
(ii) Freely fluctuating exchange rates;
(iii) Several varieties of exchange control.[212]

The fact that each country has its own monetary system is one of the principal complications of international trade. The use of foreign exchange is a country's principal means of selling its transactions and controlling its foreign trade with other countries.[213] Thus, a country's demand for foreign exchange depends on the amount of goods that it wants to import, while the supply of foreign exchange available to it depends on the amount of goods and services it can export. When a nation imports[214] a greater amount of goods and services than it exports, so that foreign exchange expenditure exceeds foreign exchange receipts, the nation is said to have a balance of payments' deficit, which it must finance either from borrowing or reserves of foreign exchange accumulated in the past. Alternatively, that country will impose exchange restrictions.[215]

Occasionally, however, governments do the opposite (exempt certain sectors) to achieve various objectives in international trade generally, and the merchant marine industry in particular.[216] This is because the merchant marine industry, both in its physical exports as well as in export of services in the form of carriage of goods, is regarded as one of the major earners of foreign exchange. This correlation between foreign exchange and merchant shipping has been utilized by many nations. One country which manipulates foreign exchange is Greece.[217] We have already noted that Greek seamen and workers abroad are permitted to open deposits in convertible foreign currencies with the Greek Commercial Banks, the Agricultural Bank, the National Mortgage Bank, and the Posts and Savings Bank. The interest rates on such deposits are as follows: savings deposits 6.25%, time deposits 6.75–8% depending on the duration of the deposits, and sight deposits 3%.[218]

The curious thing to note is that these interest rates are higher than normal. Secondly, these deposits including accrued interest, are regarded as convertible currencies and not as deposits in local currency. The convertibility of such deposits is valid for the entire time of the depositor's stay abroad.[219] As regards seamen, this privilege is extended for a further 3-year period from the date of the retirement, while for other workers for 3 years after final repatriation.[220] It will be apparent by now that this measure, and the one noted earlier on subsidies, which also offers a higher yield than corresponding deposits in local currency, was adopted in order to attract part of the large overseas deposits by Greek workers, especially seamen, abroad.[221] It is, of couse, part of the general drive by the Greek government to attract foreign flags to the Greek flag and also her own vessels currently operating in open registry or under flags of convenience.[222] It is hoped that such moves may rejuvenate the dwindling and ageing Greek fleet as well as improve the country's balance of payments and, consequently, its international trade position. Foreign exchange manipulation has both exemptive and restrictive aims.[223]

4.5 Foreign exchange restrictions

However, the Greek case is a peculiar example and there is no evidence that the overall experiment is working. On the contrary, most countries prefer to restrict foreign exchange dealings[224] to try and improve their international trade positions.[225] In this latter policy the lead is given by Chile where, for instance, on the basis of *Decree No. 179* of February 19, 1968, the Chilean line receives a 20% advantage upon liquidation of foreign currency received from incomes in the transport of cargo and passengers to and from Chile and between foreign ports.[226] In Pakistan, on the other hand, shipping companies receive a 30% bonus on foreign exchange turned into the government for rupees.

However, a fine example from the TMNS, albeit rather an old one,[227] is that of Spain. Prior to 1958 the Spanish government had imposed foreign exchange restrictions on the convertibility of Spanish *pesetas* to dollars.[228] These restrictions made it difficult for US flag operators, among others, to solicit for cargo. An additional regulation published by the Spanish government in 1957 made it mandatory for Spanish importers, before the importers would be allowed to utilize US flag or any foreign flags to lift cargo, to certify that no Spanish ship was available to carry the material.[229] These two sets of regulations were no doubt part of the state intervention to aid the merchant marine in particular and international trade generally.

The combination of the two sets of regulations, however, proved a great handicap for attracting foreign operators, especially American, into the Spanish foreign trade.[230] In 1958, therefore, the US government refused to grant waivers of *Public Resolution 17* to Spain on the grounds that the Spanish actions were discriminatory against US shipping.[231] This was the origin of and justification for countervailing or retaliatory flag discrimination that we shall refer to shortly. The Spanish government subsequently revoked the discriminatory regulations. US and other foreign operators were now considered to have an adequate opportunity for soliciting cargoes in Spanish foreign trade and waivers were granted accordingly[232] allowing Spanish flag vessels to participate in EXIMBANK financed cargoes.

This serves to illustrate the kind of international effects and, therefore, reactions that can follow from a country's unilateral intervention to try to improve her foreign shipping trade.[233] The point to be made is that this was a genuine attempt to use restrictive regulations on foreign currency for the promotion of the national fleet and foreign trade. Sometimes a ban is imposed on physical goods instead.

Import restrictions provide another example of such measures.[234]

4.6 Import restrictions

In ordinary circumstances imports are goods or services received by the country from a foreign country or area, in the course of foreign trade, imported either in response to direct orders or on consignment.[235] In this case, however, the term 'import' means, and includes, goods and services and also the importation of vessels, maritime equipment, spare parts, shipping services and insurance.[236] In an effort to establish and develop merchant marines of their own, as well as to improve their foreign trade position, many countries impose restrictions on both sets of imports.[237] These imports from abroad are, therefore, restricted by:

(1) Tariffs;
(2) Import quotas;
(3) Restrictions of foreign exchange to importers, who do not use national flag (as in the previous paragraph);
(4) Direct prohibitions.[238]

The aim of such an exercise is either to protect domestic shipping, or manufactures, or to try to correct an adverse balance of payments or, indeed to prohibit goods harmful to health or morals.[239] However, as indicated by the Spanish-US example above, restrictions on foreign currency and/or imports on a large scale, generally leads to a fall in exports, since it reduces other countries' earnings of foreign currency. Thus, in contrast to the original objective, reduced foreign trade would lead to reduced national fleets.[240] As intimated earlier, the import licence is yet another weapon in the arsenal of state intervention. Despite the 1958 incident in Spain, imports of ships from all countries are subjected to prior procurement of an import licence; one would expect Spain to have learnt her lesson.[241]

Under some systems of foreign exchange control, again in Spain, shipping merchants are only permitted foreign exchange to pay for ship imports sanctioned by the maritime authorities. In such cases licences have to be obtained before the vessels can be imported.[242] Similarly, where imports of vessels are subjected to quotas, as demanded, for instance, by the Canadian Maritime Transport Ministry, oceangoing vessels can be imported only by shipowners who have obtained the necessary licence.[243] Quotas are, of course, the other alternative to tariffs and licences, as a means of restricting imports. The number of vessels to be imported during a period is first determined, and then licences are issued to the shipbuilding (supplying) countries, assigning a quota to each.[244]

These mechanisms are not restricted only to state intervention in the merchant marine; rather, they are universally recognised, though not acceptable, as a means of state regulation of her foreign trade or protection of domestic industry.[245] Most other maritime nations, especially the DMNS, use import duties (i.e. taxes) imposed on the equipment and services of vessels entering the country, the purpose being either to increase a state's revenue or to protect home shipowners and shipbuilders by making the imported vessels more expensive.[246] This is imposed in addition to the customs, taxes and excise exemptions which should have been imposed on home operators, but from which they are exempted. For example, all imports to Argentina consigned to the federal, provincial or municipal governments, which have entered the country on a foreign flag vessel, will only be cleared after the presentation at the Custom House Offices and/or reception offices of *Certificate of Cargo Loaded on Foreign Flag Vessel – Law No. 18 250.*[247]

In order to obtain this certificate, the importer must submit an application in triplicate to the National Administration of Maritime Interests 30 days before the cargo-loading date. This application must contain a description of the type of cargo, its weight and/or volume, the type of cargo packing, the measure unit and quantity, the country of foreign loading port,[248] the loading date, and the name and nationality of the shipping line and the unloading port. Thus, by setting up almost insurmountable obstacles for the shippers who would otherwise have chosen foreign flags, the idea is to discourage use of foreign flags in favour of national fleets.[249]

The list of mechanisms for state intervention could be endless. We shall, however, simply summarise the others.

5. Other mechanisms of state intervention

Below there follows a series of other measures, some of which may not have a direct bearing on the establishment and/or expansion of national fleets, but which may nevertheless assist the state concerned in assessing the overall view of its national fleet.[250]

5.1 Domestic ship registry

State regulation of shipping through registration, though operating like state intervention through a licensing system, is not a unilateral act but a right granted by an international convention because:

> 'Each state whether coastal or not has a right to sail ships under its own flags on the high seas.'[251]

This privilege includes the right to stipulate the conditions for such registration and the rights of national jurisdiction over such vessels:

> 'Each state shall fix the conditions for the grant of its nationality to ships for the registration of ships in its territory . . . , in particular the state must effectively exercise its jurisdiction and control in administrative, financial and social matters on ships flying its flag . . . '[252]

However, various countries have exercised these rights to enable them to intervene in and control the merchant marine industry in their territory in different ways and in circumstances that could not have been intended by the Convention. One of these adverse uses is discriminating against foreign flags with the ultimate aim of aiding the establishment and/or expansion of the domestic fleet.[253] As we have discussed, the stringency of these registration requirements varies from country to country. The common, immediate, objective of all countries is to have a rough idea of the strength of the merchant marine force and to ensure that shipping falls within the planning requirements of the national economy.[254] Of couse, there is some revenue to be raised from the registration fees but this is a very minor benefit. There do not seem to be major problems caused by stringent national requirements for registration. Even where these are discriminatory, they may be protected by principle sovereignty.[255]

A trend which is causing grave concern is the registration of vessels under so-called 'flags of convenience'. This is, of course, quite a different problem from that of flag discrimination or state intervention. The latter practices stand condemned because[256] interference by governments with the free competition of shipping services, in international trade, is inimical to the interests of all trading nations, whether maritime or not. On the other hand, resort to flags of convenience may not be directly instigated by governments though their actions, particularly in the field of taxation, may indirectly create conditions in which the practice presents attractions to shipowners.[257] How far these attractions are real and permanent may be open to question, but there is no doubt that they can easily bring about conditions which sooner or later provoke counter-measures. Of significance, however, is that of late countries have resorted to actively encouraging foreign registry as a way of aiding their merchant shipping.[258]

5.2 Foreign ship registry

Whether there are already grounds for action by governments and, if so, what lines such action should take or whether the remedy lies in the shipowners' hands are matters requiring the most careful study.[259] Alternatively known as open registry or flags of convenience, foreign registry is the national flag flown by a merchant ship that has been registered in a country other than that of its owners in order to escape higher domestic wages and taxes. There is no exhaustive definition of flags of convenience, as such, which would effectively encompass their significance and characteristics.[260] In 1958, however, the Maritime Transport Committee of the OEEC (now OECD) defined them as:

> 'The flags of such countries as Panama, Liberia, Honduras and Costa Rica whose laws allow and, indeed, make it easy for ships owned by foreign nationals or companies to fly these flags. This is in contrast to the practice in the maritime countries (and in many others) where the right to fly the

national flag is subject to stringent conditions and involves far-reaching obligations.'[261]

The origins of foreign registry are as old as those of flag discrimination and maritime subsidies.

The reasons for the spread of the concept, however, are to be found in the reconstruction efforts following the Second World War with its ensuing recession and soaring costs.[262] The principal sources of open registry are the US, Greece, Italy, UK, Scandinavia, Japan and Western Europe; while the principal destinations are Liberia, Panama, Singapore, Cyprus, Lebanon, Somalia, Honduras, Costa Rica, etc.[263] The disadvantages of open registry (e.g., poor safety records and pollution) far outweigh its advantages, such as the said easing of competition, reductions in running costs, low taxation (in the tax havens), and relaxed regulations, etc. A detailed study of open registry, including the current international efforts to gradually phase it out, is beyond the scope of this chapter.[264]

The relevance, and the point to be made here, is that the named TMNS use open registry as a means of solving their maritime problems and promoting their foreign trade.[265] Let us look at a few examples. About 40% of Dutch-owned shipping tonnage is registered under foreign flags. The Royal Netherlands Shipowners Association attributes this fact to the absence of adequate fiscal measures in the Netherlands.[266] Secondly, since late 1975 the Norwegian government has granted permission for Norwegian shipowners and operators to register some of their tonnage in foreign countries under certain circumstances, e.g., where running costs were too high on a particular type of vessel, or as a way of accommodating the cargo preference rules of other countries.[267]

Finally, since early 1977, Swedish shipowners have received permission to register older, less sophisticated, vessels under third flags provided a special allowance is granted and a new Swedish vessel is taken into service. This is the nearest Swedish equivalent to the American trade-in trade-out scheme though so many of the US vessels have found their way to foreign registry.[268]

6. Advantages of and rationale for state intervention

The advantages of state intervention, if any, are as for an infant industry. The basis for the argument is that a country might have a potential comparative cost advantage[269] in the development of a certain industry. Simply because of an earlier start the industry might have been developed in another country to a point where it would be impossible for a newly established industry to compete with it. Protective policies are often adopted in the DMNS to support not only the merchant marine industry, but also a general policy of industrialisation.[270] 'Infant industry' is thus an economic term employed in seeking protective measures to advance and expand the industries of newly sovereign states or cushion newly established domestic industries in western industrialised countries against foreign competition during their growth to maturity. The DMNS have taken up this argument to justify the establishment and/or development of their own merchant marines.[271]

These countries then go on to argue that their newly established merchant marines remain the most vulnerable of their industrial achievements needing subsidies and protection. These arguments are not without justification.[272] It is generally believed that a newly established merchant marine fleet service is likely to have high costs and, if it is a liner service, it will have excess capacity. A true infant merchant marine industry, that is, one which will eventually be able to stand on its own feet in the foreseeable future, is best helped by maritime subsidies, and state intervention of the kind we have discussed, during the initial dependent period.[273] If the merchant marine is a tramping industry maritime subsidies are only required if the productivity of seamen of all grades is low in relation to their wages which are determined by the need to attract labour from shore-based industries.[274]

Unless the productivity of the sea-faring labour can rise sufficiently in the long run, in the strict economic context, the industry is not an infant industry deserving subsidies and protection.[275] Where the shore-based industries, with which the merchant marine industry has to compete for labour, are protected, say, by tariffs, then the chance of the productivity of seagoing labour rising sufficiently is remote. Compensatory assistance may then be needed in addition to infant industry measures;[276] hence some of the measures advanced herein, i.e. monetary fiscal policies, etc. In the case of liner services these are additional factors to be taken into consideration. Costs are raised by the need for sufficient tonnage to provide a regular service and for a share organisation which initially operates below capacity.[277]

This situation can be met by an operating subsidy, although discrimination devices may be adopted to secure the necessary cargoes. If conferences refuse to admit new member lines, as was often the case with applicants from developing merchant marines, then cargo preference and flag discrimination may be the only alternatives to still-birth.[278] In addition, flag preference and flag discrimination may also be needed to overcome the discriminations implicit in the practice of maritime nations selling exports on CIF terms and buying imports on FOB terms.[279]

For both liners and tramps, however, the necessity to import ships' stores may raise costs and this source of high costs together with higher costs arising from the lack of repairing facilities, may continue well after the productivity of seagoing labour has been raised.[280] The infant merchant marine industry may, therefore, have to be considered as a complex system and assistance continued after the purely merchant marine part of the complex has begun operating economically.[281]

Notes

1. OECD *Maritime Transport,* 1956, para 82, p. 63.
2. See case of *Trust Co. of New Jersey* v *Greenwood Cemetry,* 21 N.J. Misc. 169, 32 A. 2d, 519, at 523.
3. Also the case of *State* v *First State Bank of Ind.* 52 N.D, 231, 202 N.W. 391 at 402.
4. Meaning to save the situation from getting out of hand; towards or back to the normal course.
5. Simply called *encroachment* among the TMNS.
6. For details see Piffer, L. E., *The Choosing of the Public Domain,* Stamford University Press, California, 1951.

7. See also the origin of maritime subsidies in previous chapter.
8. And the section on the justification for maritime subsidies, *ibid.*
9. *Rochdale Report,* Chapter 22, 'Role of Government Shipping Policy', para 1417, p. 375.
10. See also Clawson, M. and Held, B., *The Federal Lands: The Use and Management,* The Hopkins Press, Baltimore, 1957.
11. For comparison see Sorrell, L. C., *Government Ownership and Operations of Railways for the United States,* Prentice-Hall, Inc., Englewoods Cliffs, NJ, 1939.
12. See also 'The nationalisation of British industries', *Law & Contemp. Prob.,* Vol. XVI, No. 4.
13. Even shipping, which had always been conservative, could not ignore technological change, for instance.
14. Attributed to the fact that now three times as many nations own merchant marines than was the case before the war.
15. See earlier chapter on flag preference; the *Rochdale Report,* Appendix 4, pp. 437–40.
16. Brazilian National Shipping Policy, *op. cit,* p. 19.
17. Brown, T., *Transportation and the Economic Integration of Latin America, op. cit,* p. 105.
18. See also Lawrence, T., *Liner Conferences and the Developing Countries, op. cit.* p. 181–89.
19. Bakke, K. E., 'US regulation of international internodal ocean cargo movements', *International Container Industry Conference Proceedings,* November 1977, pp. 23–27.
20. Bors, 'Regulatory and political restraints and their effects on liner shipping', *ibid.,* pp. 17–22.
21. Young, R. T., Chairman, American Bureau of Shipping, in his Address to the Conference on 'The United States and international shipping: the economic Future', published by *Lloyd's Shipping Economist,* 1980, pp. 1–5.
22. Ratcliffe, M., 'The economics of international shipping – the world trade cycle and its long-term effect on shipping markets, politics and their short-term disruptions to markets', *ibid.,* pp. 1–9.
23. Levy, H., 'United States liner shipping policy: a call to reason', *International Container Conference Proceedings, op. cit.,* pp. 80–81.
24. Von Misco, L., *Socialism, an Economic and Social Analysis,* The Macmillan Co., NY, 1936.
25. Pigou, A. C., *Socialism and Capitalism,* The Macmillan Co. London, 1937; Schumpeter, J. A., *Capitalism, Socialism and Democracy,* Harper & Row, Publishers Inc., NY, 1942.
26. But see Sweezy, P. M., *Socialism,* McGraw-Hill Book Co. NY, 1949.
27. See also 'Maritime agreements with state traders', *op. cit.* p. 27.
28. Bayley, G., 'Problems ahead with Soviet tanker surplus', *Fairplay,* Vol. 265, No. 4927, 9th Feb. 1978, pp. 7–8
29. Sager, K. H., 'Russia has signed the UNCTAD (Liner) Code, but will she ratify?', *Norwegian News,* No. 17, 1st Sept., 1978, pp. 8–11.
30. Landawer, C., *The Theory of National Economic Planning,* 2nd edn., University of California Press, Berkeley, California, 1947.
31. For some of these positive aspects see material under 'Advantages of flag preference' in Chapter 3.
32. Both world wars marked the starting point for many changes in the national and international shipping.
33. However, the overriding concern for all these changes is that of maintaining shipping on a commercial and profitable basis.
34. The breaking point came when it was no longer possible to achieve these objectives under the said prevailing conditions.
35. This, then, is when governments came up with what is popularly known as *state intervention.*
36. Harris, S. E., *Economic Planning,* Alfred Knopf, Inc., NY, 1949.
37. Meade, J. E., *Planning and the Price Mechanism: The Liberal-Socialist Solution,* The Macmillan Co., NY, 1948.

38. Packard, V., *The Waste Makers,* David McKay Co. Inc., NY, 1960.
39. Britt, S. H., *The Spenders,* McGraw-Hill Book Co. NY, 1960.
40. See the case *State* v *Manning,* 220 Iowa 525, 259 N.W. 213.
41. They are prepared to accept the FMC.
42. 'Far-Eastern report' (shipping, shipbuilding, shipbreaking, liner trade, Hong Kong), *Fairplay,* Vol. 270, pp. 42–52.
43. Smith, A. M., 'Taiwan's restraint is unleashed' (container shipping), *Containerisation,* Vol. 13, No. 5, May 1979, pp. 17–20.
44. See the case of *Kemp* v *Stanley,* 204 La., 110 15 SO., 2nd. 1, at 11.
45. 'China: trade explosion boosted by boom in bulkers', *Lloyd's Shipp. Econ.,* Vol. 1, No. 1, Feb. 1979, pp. 8–11.
46. 'Japan dazzled by prospects of China's surge forward' (shipping), *Zosen,* Vol. 23, No. 9, Dec. 1978, pp. 22–24.
47. No other DMNS' practice is comparable to that of Taiwan.
48. For *approval* see case of *Rooney* v *South Sioux City,* 111, Feb. 1 1955, N.W. 474, at 475.
49. See also *State* v *Duckett,* 133 S.C.85, 130 SE 340, at 342.
50. And *McCarten* v *Sanderson,* 111 Mont. 407, 109P, 2nd. 1108, at 1112, A.I.R. 1229.
51. It is, therefore, fair to assume state intervention has become common and acceptable.
52. See again case of *Rooney* v *South Sioux City, op. cit.,* at 478.
53. And *State* v *Duckett, op. cit.,* at 345.
54. Provision of employment is predominantly an economic consideration for state intervention.
55. Wasserman, U. in 'Key issues in developments: interview with UNCTAD secretary general', *J.W.T.L.* Vol. 10, No. 1, Jan–Feb. 1976, pp. 17.
56. For detente see *State* v *Oregon-Washington R & Nav.* Co., 128 Wash. 365, 223P. 600, at 608.
57. 'Israeli shipping, 1976', *Sapanut,* Vol. 7, No. 3, Dec. 1977, pp. 1–2.
58. *Ibid.,* p. 11.
59. *Ibid.,* p. 12.
60. Gal-Edd, I., *'Israeli foreign trade', J.W.T.L.* Vol. 3, No. 1, Jan–Feb. 1969, p. 1.
61. Intervention aims to stop, limit or minimise foreign flags from utilising/benefitting from subsidies to national flags.
62. Hazard, J. L., *Transportation; Management Economies; Policy,* Cambridge, Md., Cornell Maritime Press, 1977.
63. 'Growth and future plans for Korean shipbuilding industry', *Asian Shipp.,* May 1978, pp. 30–32.
64. Law of February 28, 1967.
65. Gomer, H., 'Tanker scrapping – a small contribution to a big problem', *Seatrade,* Vol. 17, No. 12, Dec. 1977, pp. 41 & 43.
66. 'Korea shipbuilding complete second of parcel tanker series', *Asian Shipp.,* No. 5, Sept. 1978, pp. 17–18.
67. Article 4 *Geneva Convention on the Law of the Sea* (High Seas).
68. *Ibid.,* Article 5 (1).
69. See *Graves* v *People of State of New York, ex rel.* O'Keefe, NY, 306 US.466, 59, S.Ct. 595, at 597, 83L. Ed. 927, 120 ALR 1466.
70. Sampson, R. J. in the *Proceedings of the Colloquium Series on Transportation 1967–68 Winnipeg,* Centre for Transportation Studies, University of Manitoba, 1968.
71. But the nerve centre of British shipping is regulated by the Board of Trade under the Ministry of Industry.
72. See again Bakke, K. E, 'US regulation of internodal ocean cargo movements', *op. cit.,* pp. 23–27.
73. Phillips, A. (ed.), *Promoting Competition in Regulated Markets,* Washington DC, Brookings Institution, 1975.
74. Kryvoruka, K. J., 'American ocean shipping and the anti-trust laws revised', *J. Marit. Law & Commer.,* pp. 67–107.
75. *Ibid.,* at p. 107.

76. MaGuire, C. J. and McDaniel, R. E., 'Conquering the maze: a proposed reorganisation of the US shipping laws', *Proceedings of the Maritime Safety Council*, Vol. 38, No. 4, June 1981, pp. 93–99.
77. Mason, G. W., 'Regulation, public policy and efficient provision of freight transportation', *Trans. J.* Fall 1975.
78. Lansing, J., *Transportation and Economic Policy*, NY Free Press, 1966.
79. See also Munby, D., *Transport: Selected Readings*, Baltimore, Penguin Books 1968.
80. Middleton, I. and Renouf, A., 'Washington doors close' (US Maritime Policy), *Seatrade*, Vol. 10, No. 10, Nov. 1979, pp. 691–701.
81. Bush, W. L., 'Steamship conference contract rate agreement and the dual rate system', *ICC Practitioner's Journal*, Nov.–Dec. 1972.
82. Gray, M., 'United States: the building of a maritime policy', *Fairplay*, Vol. 272, No. 4015, 11 October 1979, pp. 6–11.
83. Chiarbas, J., 'Murphy's second law' (US maritime proposals), *Seatrade*, Vol. 9, No. 7, July 1979, pp. 3–5.
84. Anonymous, 'US edges slowly towards stricter liner control', *Seatrade*, Vol. 8, No. 3, March 1978, pp. 19 & 21.
85. See *Securities and Exchange Commission* v *Wickham*, D. C. Minn. 1gF. Supp. 245, at 247.
86. See also *Drake* v *Crane, 127 No. 85, 29SW 990, 27.* L.R.A. 653.
87. Kust, M. J., *Foreign Enterprise in India: Law & Policies.* Chapel Hill, University of Carolina Press, 1964.
88. McDougal, M. S. and others 'Maintenance of public order at sea and the nationality of ships', 1960, *AJIL*, Vol. 54, pp. 25–116.
89. Tinbergen, J., *Shaping the World Economy*, NY, Twentieth Century Fwd, 1962.
90. Oliver, C., 'The American foreign investment code', *AJIL*, Vol. 60, pp. 763–84.
91. Hyde, J. N., 'Economic development agreements', *Hague Recuel*, Vol. 105, 1962, pp. 267–374.
92. See also *Stramann* v *Scheefen*, 7 Colo., App. 42 p. 191; *Una* v *Dodd*, 39 N.J. Eq. 186.
93. Phillips, D. M., 'Restraints on foreign investments in the merchant marine – an asset or liability to the US interest?', *Cornell Int. L.J.*, Vol. 11, No. 1, Winter 1978, pp. 1–49.
94. 46 USC para 883 (Suppl. V, 1975).
95. Hanson, D. P., 'Regulation of the shipping industry: an economic analysis of the need for reform' *Law & Pol. Int. Bus.*, Vol. 12, No. 4, 1980, pp. 973–1001.
96. 46 USC para 883, 1970.
97. 7 US Dept. of Commerce, *Foreign Direct Investment in the US*, App. K, 1976, at K. 65.
98. Jantscher, G., *Bread upon the waters: federal aid to the maritime industries* 80, 1975 – note 28 at 51.
99. 46 USC para 802(a) (1970). But see Anon, 'The rising tide of reverse flow', *Mich. L. Rev.*, Vol. 72, 1974, pp. 551–591.
100. *Ibid.;* also Barnes, L. B., 'State regulation of foreign investment', *Cornell Int. L.J.*, Vol. 9, No. 1, Winter 1975, pp. 82–100.
101. 46 USC para 802 (C), 1970.
102. 46 USC para 883–1, 1970.
103. 46 USC para 835, 1970.
104. See generally S. Rep., No. 2145, 85 Cong. 2d Sess., 1958; reprinted in US Code Cong. & Ad. News 5190, 1958.
105. See also Act of July 14 1956, *Pub. Law. No. 8474*, para 1 70 Stat. 544.
106. Vagts, D. F., 'The corporate alien: definitional quations in federal restraint on foreign enterprise', *Harv. L. Rev.*, Vol. 74, 1960–61, pp. 1489–551.
107. *Ibid.*
108. Blackwell, R. J., 'Implementation of the Merchant Marine Act of 1970', *J. Marit. & Law & Comm.*, Jan. 1974.
109. Berglund, A., *Ocean Transportation*, NY Longmans, Green & Co., 1931.
110. *Lobsitz* v *E. Lissberger Co. 168 App. Div. 840*, 154, N.Y.S. 556 at 557.
111. *Preston* v *State Industrial Accident Commission* 174 Ov. 553, 149 P., 2d 957, at 961 & 962.

112. Bonneville, J. H., *et al., Organising and Financing Business,* Prentice-Hall, Inc., Englewood Cliffs NJ, 1959.
113. Friedman, W. G. and Kalmanoff, G., *Joint Internation Ventures,* Columbia University Press, NY, 1961.
114. Gorton, L., 'Joint ventures in shipping law', *J. Bus. Law,* 1978 July, pp 238–44.
115. Keith, L. A. and Gubellin, C. E., *Introduction to Business Enterprise,* McGraw-Hill Book Co., NY, 1962.
116. Whebie, B. S, 'Co-operation through trade facilitation', *ICC International Shipping Conference,* May 1977, pp. 89–96.
117. Upolla, G. H., 'IMCO: an all effort in Latin American', *Latin American Shipping,* 1979, pp. 61–63.
118. Clement, A. G., 'A promising future for owners and builders', *Latin American Shipping,* 1979, p. 13.
119. Egypt (investments, ports, Suez Canal), *Shipbroker,* Vol. 6, No. 2, Feb. 1980, pp. 21–27.
120. 'South Korea, shipping and shipbuilding' (special report), *Lloyd's List,* 11 January, 1979, pp. 4–6.
121. Naess, E. D., 'Liberian flag shipping, the industry's perspective', pp. 117–26.
122. The LSC was created by The Act of April 18, 1961.
123. 'Malaysia shipyard and engineering pulling out of the recession', *Norwegian Shipping News,* Vol. 37, No. 6, May 1981, pp. 23–26.
124. State control is not an end in itself but a means to an end – the establishment and development of national fleets.
125. Nationalisation originates from Spanish or Mexican Law Nationalization Hall, Mexican Law, paras. 749.
126. Domke, M., 'Foreign nationalisations', *AJIL,* Vol. 55, 1961, pp. 585–616.
127. Miller, R. S. and Strangler, R. J. in *Essays on Expropriations,* Columbus, Ohio State University Press, p. 165.
128. Knudsen, O., *The Politics of International Shipping: Conflict and Interaction in a Transitional Issue-Area,* 1946–1948, Lexington Books Mass., Ch. 3 in 2.
129. Lewis, B. W., *British Planning and Nationalisation,* The Twentieth Century Fund, NY 1952.
130. 'The nationalisation of british industries', *Law & Contemp. Prob.,* Autumn 1951.
131. *Rochdale Report,* para 637, p. 776.
132. *Ibid.,* paras 274–280, pp. 77–79.
133. 'Portugal: special report' (shipping ports, shipbuilding, etc.), *Lloyds List,* 18 March, 1980, pp. 5–15.
134. Portugal (survey – shipping and ports), *Shipbroker,* Vol. 6, No. 3, March 1980, pp. 23–28.
135. The other TMNS with nationalised sectors are Australia, Canada, Finland, France, Ireland, Italy, Netherlands, New Zealand, Norway, Spain, Sweden, etc.
136. See again Lewis, C. S., *Government Ownership and Operation of Railways for the US, op. cit.*
137. And 'The nationalisation of british industries', *Law & Contemp. Prob., op. cit.*
138. US Dept of Commerce, *Survey of Current Business: National Income Supplements,* July Issues.
139. Prichett, H. C. *The American Constitution,* McGraw-Hill Book Co., NY, 1959, Cap. 36 for comparison of state ownership, nationalisation and eminent domain.
140. See again Piffer, L. C., *The Closing of the Public Domain, op. cit.*
141. *Beekman* v *Saratoga & S. R. Co. 3 Paige,* N.Y. 45, 73 Am. Cas. 1914C, at 1266.
142. Ireland (survey of shipping, ports, etc.), *Lloyd's List,* 14 March 1978, pp. 9–10.
143. See also Irishman (tug), *Fairplay,* Vol. 265, No. 4940, May 4th 1978, pp. 26–27.
144. FINMARI is a public holding; cf. *Harrison* v *Big Four Bus Lines,* 217.
145. 'Italian marine industries' (survey), *Fairplay,* Vol. 265, no. 4938, April 20th, 1978, pp. 41–57.
146. Almost all the leading DMNS operate from state ownership with exception, perhaps of Cyprus, Saudi Arabia and the UAE.
147. Bross, S., *Ocean Shipping Cambridge,* Md. Mass., Cornell Maritime Press, 1956.

148. Abrahamson, B. J. and Singer, M. A., 'A shipping research program with particular reference to smaller nations', *J. Israel Shipp.* RI April 1972.
149. Fayle, C. E., *A Short History of the World's Shipping Industry,* London Allen & Unwin, 1933.
150. *Oklahoma City* v *Board of Education of Oklahoma City,* 181 Okl, 539, 75P 2d 201.
151. Irving, *The Purchasing Power of Money,* The Macmillan Co., NY, 1912.
152. US Dept. of Commerce, Maritime Administration, *Maritime Subsidies,* 1978, p. 67.
153. *Emergency Law No. 465* Amending and Supplementing Certain Provisions of *Law No. 1880/1951* Concerning Government Purchases of Ships.
154. *Ibid.,* published July 9, 1968; became effective Jan. 1, 1968.
155. On 17 April 1970 *Legislative Decree No. 509* was enacted to extend the purchasing powers of *Law No. 465.*
156. Provided by Legislation governing taxation of ships of all types and/as codified under *Royal Decree No. 800* of Dec. 1, 1970.
157. *Ibid.,* applicable only to flags owned by Greeks.
158. The law provides for two categories of vessels herein designated as (a) and (b).
159. This condition applies to both categories with each category further subdivided into 4 sub-categories, a–d.
160. See laws No. *465/68* and *509/70* as codified by *Law No. 800.*
161. See also Alexanderson, G. and Norstrom, G., *World Shipping,* John Wiley and Sons, NY, 1963.
162. Frankel E. and Marens, H. S., *Ocean Transportation,* Cambridge Mass. MIT Press, 1972.
163. Kendall, L. C., *The Business of Shipping,* Cambridge, Md. Cornell Maritime Press, 1973.
164. Sturmey, S. G., *British Shipping and World Competition,* Athlon Press, 1962, p. 104.
165. *Ibid.,* p. 105, N.1; US Maritime Commission, *Economic Survey of the American Merchant Marine* (Kennedy report), 1937, p. 58.
166. Wettery, D., *High Speed Surface,* Craft Vol. 19, Nos. 9 & 10, June–July 1980 p. 24.
167. 'Newbuilding finance: no abatement in the subsidy scramble', *Fairplay,* Vol. 273, No. 5034, 21 Feb. 1980, pp. 25–27.
168. Phillips, F., 'The innovative line' (Australian national line), *Containerisation,* Vol. 14, No. 3, March 1980, pp. 26–30.
169. Black, R. A., 'The Australian shipper – his shipping needs', *Australian Symposium on Shipping and Management* (conference proceedings), Nov. 1977, Vol. 1, pp. 17–22; Vol. 11, pp. 1–2.
170. South Korea: growth and future plans for Korean shipbuilding industry, *Asian Shipp.,* No. 3, May, 1978, pp. 30–32.
171. Done under *Decree Law of January 9, 1962.*
172. Authorised under *Decree Law No. 20759 of October 15, 1974.*
173. See also *Supreme Decree,* effective March 26, 1976.
174. *Decree Law No. 22067* of January 11, 1978.
175. Decree dated December 30, 1969.
176. The law of February 8, 1957.
177. The other TMNS that practice this are Canada, Iceland, the Scandinavian countries, Spain and the US; the majority of the other DMNS do.
178. Lawrence, S. A., *US Merchant Shipping Policies and Politics,* Washington DC, Brookings Institution, 1966.
179. See *Tennessee Oil Co.* v *McCanless, 178 Tenn.* 683, 157 S.W. 2d 267, at 272.
180. See also *An Introduction to Doing Import and Export Business,* Chamber of Shipping of the US, Washington DC, 1962.
181. Pratt, E. E., *Modern International Commerce,* Allynand & Bacon Inc., Boston, 1956.
182. For *inducement* see *State* v *Stratford, 55 Idaho* 65, 37P. 2d 681, at 682.
183. See also Clark, J. M., 'Business accelerations and the laws of demand: the technical factor in economic cycles', reprinted in *Readings in Business Cycle Theory,* McGraw-Hill Book Co., NY, 1964.
184. And Hamburg, D. and Schultze, C. L., 'Autonomous investment *v* induced investment', *Economic Journal,* Royal Economic Society, London, March 1961.

185. Ackley, G., *Macro-economic Theory,* The Macmillan Co. NY, 1961, pp. 485–93, 518–29.
186. 'Marcos manoevres Phillipine flag' (shipping), *Containerisation,* Vol. 13, No. 3, March 1979, pp. 49–51.
187. Tanesco, G. F., 'The ambitious achievements and developments of the Phillipine shipping industry', *Seatrade,* Hong Kong Conference, Nov. 1978, pp. 31–41.
188. See also the *Phillipines Overseas Shipping Act of 1975.*
189. The Development Bank of the Phillipines authorised to do so by *Presidential Decree Order No. 37* and *Presidential Decree 806* of October 3rd, 1975.
190. The other TMNS doing this are Canada, Denmark, Finland, France, Germany (FRG), Greece, Japan, Spain and Sweden; most DMNS do.
191. See *US* v *Hill,* C.C.A., N.Y., 34F 2d. 133, at 135.
192. Commonly known as *The Shipping Promotion Law* enacted by the Republic of Korea on February 28, 1967.
193. *Ibid.,* para D; also Smith, A. M., 'Korea mixes its Pacific presence' (profile of 3 container shipping co.'s), *Containerisation,* Vol. 15, No. 6, June 1981, pp. 32–36.
194. *Ibid.,* para E; see also 'South Korea's high-riding yards strive to achieve a balance', *Seatrade,* Vol. 11, No. 6, June 1981, pp. 21–23.
195. *Ibid.,* para F; ASEAN (Malaysia, Singapore, Thailand, Phillipines, Indonesia) *Lloyd's List,* Special Report, 7 August 1980, pp. 5–12.
196. *Ibid.,* para G; Featherstone, J. M., 'Through transport and the total export concept', *Conference on Maritime Commercial Practices,* Nov. 1978, pp. 1–8.
197. *Ibid.,* para F; also 'The shipbuilding industry in South Korea and its development', *Schiff und Haven Komm.,* No. 4, April 1979, pp. 271–73.
198. See also *Colins* v *Harris,* 130 Wash. 394, 227P 508, at 509.
199. Thus the above law covers (1) importation, (2) improvements (3) repairs and (4) chartering of a ship on condition the ship will take the Republic of Korea nationality.
200. Maruno, Y. O., *Practice and Law of International Ship Finance* (Ph.D. Thesis, Southampton University, 1978).
201. Ramsay, R. A., 'World trade versus the supply of shipping and ships', *Marine Policy,* Vol. 4, No. 1, Jan. 1980, pp. 63–67.
202. Cassing, J. A., 'Trade pattern productions and resource allocation in a model with jointly supplied international transport services', *Transportation Economics,* Vol. 6, No. 3, Dec. 1979, pp. 293–309.
203. See 'German shipping industries determinedly optimistic despite difficulties', *Asian Shipp.,* No. 22, October 1980, pp. 19–23.
204. Finance (shipping investment, second-hand market), *Marine Week,* Vol. 6, No. 5, 21 Dec. 1979, pp. 27–30.
205. 'Policy amendments to boost shipping industry' (Japan), *Zosen,* Vol. 24, No. 5, Aug. 1979, pp. 14–16.
206. See also 'Japanese shipping activities last year', *Norwegian News,* No. 2, 26 Jan. 1979, pp. 23–28.
207. Yuchi, W., 'Close relationships between shipbuilding industry in Japan and shipowners in Greece', *Zosen,* Vol. 25, No. 3, June 1980, pp. 36–39.
208. 'IBJ surveys Japanese shipping and shipbuilding industry', *Zosen,* Vol. 24, No. 3, June 1979, pp. 14–16.
209. Luthwaite, J. J. R., 'The Japanese problem – bankers opt for prudence as small and medium sized (ships) builders crumble', *Fairplay,* Vol. 265, No. 4938, 20 April 1979, pp. 21 & 23.
210. *OECD European Conference of Ministers of Transport Report of the International Symposium on Theory and Practice in Transportation Economics,* 1964–65, Paris.
211. Mikesell, R., *Foreign Exchange in the Post World War* Twentieth Century Find, NY, 1954.
212. See also Southard, F. Jr., *Foreign Exchange Practice and Policy,* McGraw-Hill Book Co., NY, 1940.
213. Machlup, F., 'The theory of foreign exchanges', in Ellis, H. and Metzler, L. A., *Readings in the Theory of International Trade,* McGraw-Hill Book Co., NY, 1949, C5.

214. See 'Strong D. M. threat to German shipping', *Norwegian News,* No. 17, 1 Sept. 1978, pp. 5–7.
215. Adams, R., 'Pricing in foreign currencies: financing international trade' (conference proceedings), Nov. 1977, p. 4.
216. Williams, H., 'Impact of exchange rates, charges on shipping costs and revenues', *Norwegian News,* Vol. 37, No. 7, May 1981, pp. 23–26; also reported in *Asian Shipp.* April 1981, pp. 58–59.
217. *Continental Grain Export Corporation (US)* v *STM Grain Ltd* (Charles E Ford Ltd), 1979, 2 Lloyds L. R., p. 64.
218. *Law No. 465,* published September, 1968.
219. See also 'Greece adjusts to new realities', *Seatrade,* Vol. 8, No. 6, June 1978, pp. 3–4.
220. And *Legislative Decree No. 509,* April 17, 1970; Ratcliffe, M., 'Greek shipping – going bust waiting for methavrio (the day after tomorrow), *Tanker Bulker, International,* Vol. 4, No. 5, May 1978, pp. 5 & 7.
221. Under the *Royal Decree No. 800;* also 'Greek marine' (safety, casualties, shipping), *Nautical Review,* Vol. 3, No. 8, Aug. 1979, pp. 32–40.
222. *Laws 465/68 & 509/70,* codified by *Law 800.*
223. *Article 23 Greek Constitution 1968;* Cf. *Law 465/1968*
224. Governed by *Laws 1880/60 & 3415/55* as amended by *Legislative Decree 4094/60* and *4419/64.*
225. See *An Introduction to Doing Import and Export Business, op. cit.;* and Humfrey, D. D., *American Imports.*
226. See *Cunard Steamship Co* v *Melton, 43 S.Ct.* 504, 26 US, 100, 67 L. Ed. 894, 2 A.L.R. 1306.
227. *The Conqueror* 49, Fed. 99.
228. Kellough, H. B. & Kellough, L. M., *Economics of International Trade,* McGraw-Hill Book Co., NY, 1948.
229. Ellsworth, P. T., *The International Economy,* The Macmillan Co., NY, 1958.
230. Kindleberger, C. P., *International Economics,* Richard D. Irwin Inc., Homewood, Ill., 1958.
231. Brock, C., *The Control of Restrictive Practices from 1956,* McGraw-Hill Book Co., NY, 1966.
232. Heydon, *The Restraint of Trade Doctrine,* Butterworths, London, 1971.
233. Korah, V., *Competition Law of Britain and the Common Market,* Penguin Books, London, 1968.
234. *OECD Guide to Legislations on Restrictive Business Practices in Europe and North America,* Paris, 1964.
235. For GATT see Peck, A. H., *International Economics,* Thomas Y. Crowell Co., NY, 1957 C.11.
236. See again *Cunard Steamship* v *Mellon* (note 226 above).
237. See also Kellough, H. B. & Kellough, L. M., *Economics of International Trade, op. cit.*
238. Kindleberger, C. P., *International Economics, op. cit.*
239. Ellsworth, P. T., *The International Economy, op. cit.*
240. Brock, C., *The Control of Ristrictive Practices from 1956, op. cit.*
241. Heydon, *The Restraint of Trade Doctine, op. cit.*
242. Korah, V., *Competition Law of Britain and the Common Market, op. cit.*
243. Peck, A. H., *International Economics op. cit.*
244. *OECD Guide to Legislations, op. cit.*
245. *Income Tax Act;* see also 'Canada' (shipowners, shipbuilding, arctic ports), *Marine Week,* Vol. 6, No. 44, 9 Nov. 1979, pp. 18–23.
246. Hayman, C., 'Canadian shipowners make their feelings known', *Seatrade,* Vol. 8, No. 7, July 1978, p. 15.
247. Shaw, J. L., 'Europressor Lineas Maritinas Argentinas SA. Co. profile', *Asian Shipp.,* May 1981, pp. 7–9.
248. *Ibid.;* see also 'Argentina: cargo reservation threat grows', *Lloyds Shipp. Econ.,* Vol. 1, No. 5, June 1979, pp. 11–14.
249. See also 'Back from the brink (UNCTAD Code)', *Seatrade,* Vol. 8, No. 11, Nov. 1978, pp. 3–4.

250. See, for instance, 'Canada, shipping and shipbuilding', *Marine Week,* Vol. 5, No. 8, Aug. 1979, pp. 65–67.
251. Act 4 *Geneva Convention – Law of the Sea – High Seas.*
252. *Ibid.,* Act 5 (1).
253. *Rochdale Report,* paras. 824–825, 1530, 84, 89–90, 101.
254. US Department of Commerce, MARAD, *Maritime Subsidies,* 1978, p. 104.
255. See also Article 5 (2), *Geneva Convention on the High Seas.*
256. OECD *Maritime Transport.*
257. Rodney, C., *Sovereignty for Sale,* Naval Institute Press, Annapolis, Maryland, 1981.
258. Darling, H. J., 'The elements of an international shipping policy for Canada', *Transport Canada Marine,* 1974.
259. American Committee for Flags of Necessity. *The Role of Flags of Necessity,* NY, 1962.
260. Grundley, K., 'Flags of convenience in 1978', *PCL,* Nov. 1978, pp. 1–3.
261. *Rochdale Report,* para 183, p. 51.
262. Yang, P., 'The ITFW disputes over flags of convenience', *Asian Shipp.* Nov. 1980, pp. 46–48.
263. 'Open for compromise (likely outcome of UNCTAD'S Committee on Shipping Meeting on Open Registry)', *Seatrade,* Vol. 11, No. 4, April 1980, pp. 13–15.
264. 'Exposed: how flags of convenience shipping threatens to hand down the red duster', *The Seaman,* July 1981, Supp. 11 pp.
265. US Dept. of Commerce, MARAD, *Maritime Subsidies,* 1978, pp. 113–15, at 113.
266. *Ibid.,* pp. 119–23; also 'Basic industries also in the future' (Norwegian shipping), *Norwegian News,* No. 1, 25 Jan. 1980, pp. 68–70.
267. *Ibid.,* pp. 153–56, at 156; also Parton, D., Swedish yards on the brink -- but where there is life . . . ', *Seatrade,* Vol. 10, No. 2, Feb. 1980, pp. 65–67.
268. *Ibid.,* pp. 168–76; Grundey, K., 'Research into flags of convenience at the PCL', *Pynda Leader,* Winter 1979, pp. 21–24.
269. Ricardo, D., *Principles of Political Economy and Taxation,* Everyman's Library, NY, 1917, Chap. 7.
270. Habebler, G., *The Theory of International Trade,* The Macmillan Co., NY, 1950.
271. Hamilton, A., *Report of Manufacturers, op. cit.*
272. Taussig, F. W., *Some Aspects of the Tariff Question,* Harvard University Press, Cambridge, Mass., 1931.
273. Goss, R. O., *et al. Advances in Maritime Economics,* CUP, pp. 38–39.
274. Knudsen, O., *The Politics of International Shipping, op. cit.,* pp. 38 & 76.
275. Viner, J., *Studies in the Theory of International Trade,* London, Allen & Unwin, 1937.
276. Harrod, R. F., *International Economics,* CUP, 1960, (reprint).
277. Harris, S. E., *International and Interregional Economics,* NY, McGraw-Hill, 1957 (esp. Chaps. 1–7).
278. Gorden, W. M., 'The structure of a tariff system and the effective protective rate', *J. Polit. Econ.,* Vol. 54, June 1966.
279. See also 'The effective protective rate, the uniform tariff equivalent and the average tariff', *Economic Record,* Vol. 42, June 1966, pp. 200–16.
280. Balassa, 'Tariff protection in industrial countries: an evaluation', *J. Polit. Econ.,* Vol. 63, Dec. 1965.
281. Johnson, H. G., 'Trade preferences and developing countries', *Lloyd's Bank Review,* April 1966.

Part Four

Problems caused by and/or arising from the use of the traditional methods of establishing and developing national fleets

Introduction to Part Four

In Parts II and III the *traditional* methods of establishing and developing national fleets were examined. But these methods have caused problems in international economic relations. The consequences of the use of the said methods are varied, but I intend to concentrate here on the legal and economic ones. In the first place, these induce a chain of retaliations, and counter-retaliations, which in the end are neither in the interests of the discriminators or the discriminated. Secondly, they are a breach of international law; causing a conflict of law situation not easily resolvable. Economically, they cause a disruption of international commerce.

It is maintained that the use of these methods constitutes a contravention of customary international law which has for long been a guiding principle in international commercial relations. Customary international law in this context means the body of laws largely uncodified, as opposed to the codified and treaty laws, which have long been observed by states. One of these principles is that of *equality of treatment* – both material and formal. The other two relate to the requirement of *minimum standard treatment* and finally *the freedom of the high seas*. The principle of minimum standards presupposes MFN treatment, national treatment, the equality of flags and the consequences regarding unilateral counter-measures. The freedom of the high seas involves, as a prerequisite, the freedoms of maritime transport, innocent passage for merchant ships, the treatment of vessels of landlocked and geographically disadvantaged states and the freedom of transit passage.

There has been a great deal of criticism of the principle of freedom of the high seas. It is inevitably linked to the liberal principles of *laissez-faire* or free trade – a principle opposed by those countries which use the said methods. The other main criticisms levelled against customary international law are that it is archaic and that the current DMNS were neither state entities, at that time, nor did they participate in the formulation of such principles. In short, they resent being bound by laws to which they were not parties. They, therefore, feel vindicated in resorting to methods that are counter to these principles of customary international law. On the basis of this argument one would expect these countries to respect those conventions which codified the said principles of customary international law. But this is not the case.

Secondly, the use of traditional methods to establish national fleets is a contravention of international economic laws. The term 'international economic laws' is used here to describe that branch of international law which is codified, and made up of conventions, treaties and codes. One of these in the regime regarding international ports, including the *Ports Convention* of 1923, and the position regarding the rights of entry into maritime ports in international law. The other is the regime of IMO Spirit, including the position of the 1948 Convention establishing IMO and its attitude towards discrimination and the establishment of national fleets by traditional means. Related to that is the *IMO Convention* of 1965 concerning the facilitation of maritime transport.

Similar situations could be foreseen when considering the legal regime of international waterways, i.e. the conventions on navigable waterways, international straits and international canals. Most of these fall within the national jurisdiction of one or two sovereign states. It would not be mere speculation to envisage the use of traditional methods posing threats to foreign merchant flags navigating through these waters. This is so because of the threat posed by the extension of the principle of sovereignty, and because these waters basically fall into the sphere of cabotage and national jurisdictions. The international community foresaw these dangers when they came up for consideration as early as a century and a half ago. These dangers are more real now.

With regard to treaties and conventions, those which specifically prohibit the use of the traditional methods are the general principles of GATT, especially its Article 12, on non-discrimination. We also note the ambiguities caused by the exceptions in GATT, especially Article 18, on STNS, and the section relating to the special needs of the DMNS. Secondly, the use of traditional methods is an affront to the spirit of the OECD, especially the efforts of its Maritime Transport Committee, and the *OECD Code for the Liberalisation of Current Invisible Transactions.* It is also necessary to consider the position of the *Treaty of Rome* with regard to the use of traditional methods. Although the OECD and EEC guidelines have no legal binding force, since they are particularly designed for and directed towards the member states, yet they have direct consequences to non-member states. The GATT principles, however, have a wider application and bind users of the traditional methods.

The latest proposed multilateral code directed against the use of traditional methods in the *UN Code on Restrictive Trade Practices (RBPS).* If and when it is ratified it will have universal application binding all the UN member states, including the STNS and DMNS, which have hitherto resorted to the use of traditional methods in order to establish and/or develop their own national fleets. In this respect, we note the exceptions to the abolition of the RBPS in the proposed UN Code. Interestingly, these are similar to those of GATT.

Besides customary and international economic legal problems, the other major consequences of the use of traditional methods are economic. The use of traditional methods can only be justified on political and security grounds often in total disregard of commercial or sound economic principles. This is so despite the enormous economic problems facing the DMNS, such as scarcity of resources, lack of trained and skilled manpower and the inadequacy or absence of the necessary infrastructure for the development of healthy national fleets. To these countries, therefore, priority in establishing and or developing national fleets, particularly through the traditional means, would require a reallocation of scarce and badly needed resources towards this end.

To the international community it would mean disruption of international shipping and, therefore, international commerce; the two being interrelated. The use of the traditional methods is basically uneconomic. It would lead to inefficiency and overtonnaging in international shipping. A combination of these factors is bound to lead to high costs for both the means of transportation and the transported goods. These costs would be transferred to the consumers in both the discriminating and the discriminated countries. An efficient and cheap transportation system is in the best interests of both the international community and the users of traditional methods.

Because of the inherent low levels of development in transport and the means of distribution in the DMNS there is reason to believe that if the worst came to the worst the users of the traditional methods would, probably, have to bear the brunt of the economic consequences. The TMNS and the other economically advanced nations would be able to absorb the hardships. During the period of economic difficulty which is currently prevalent in the world economic climate, the temptation to use discriminations is great. But it is best remembered that discriminations are only short term, rather than long term, solutions and that in the end they are likely to rebound on those who resorted to them in the first place.

These are the main problems and consequences of traditional methods. A comprehensive approach to all aspects and similarities of these methods would be an insurmountable task and could not be adequately dealt with in this survey. The salient features will be looked at in the following three chapters.

CHAPTER 7

Problems relating to customary international law

1. Introduction

The use of national merchant marines for political and security reasons is probably understandable though not necessarily justifiable. So is the rationale for each nation owning its own merchant marine.[1] However, the use of discriminatory means and state intervention as methods of establishing and/or developing national merchant marine fleets may be contrary to established principles of customary international law.[2] It has been established how both mechanisms invite, in turn, counter-discriminations. One of these principles is that of equality of treatment.

2. Equality of treatment

It will be remembered that for centuries equal treatment in foreign commerce has been the aim of the foreign policy of the TMNS and, particularly, of commercial treaties and agreements. For this purpose international treaty practice had, over the years, developed a procedure which was known as the *standard of commercial treatment*.[3] Its object was not to grant any specific material rights, but merely to establish a pattern from which material rights could be achieved. The rights involved were those contained in the laws of the contracting states at any given time.[4] By this method, the national jurisdiction of states on matters of foreign commerce remained untouched, which, of course, greatly facilitated the conclusion of treaties. The standard method was the formal concept of reaching equality of treatment.[5]

It will also be remembered that the various standards of commercial treatment commonly accepted in practice were the following. Firstly, the *standard of reciprocity*, which meant that each party accords to the other exactly the same rights and advantages that the other accords in return.[6] Secondly, the *standard of the most favoured nation*, which means that the granting state extends all rights and advantages which it concedes to any other third state, also to the receiving state,[7] so that the latter will never be in a position inferior to any other third state. Finally, the *standard of national treatment*, which means that the parties accord the nationals of each other the same treatment as they accord their own nationals.[8] This principle has been dealt with briefly before, and will be returned to again. Suffice it to point out that any discrimination in shipping could be an infringment of this customary law doctrine of equality of treatment.[9]

It is apparent from the discussion in the previous two sections that almost every country has departed in practice, in one way or another, from the doctrine which was once the corner-stone of international trade relations. Ironically, the TMNS seem to hold the DMNS to blame for the breakdown and departures from the doctrine.[10] Even if this attitude was justified, which is doubtful, the latter could claim with some justification that these were merely some of the practices established before their emergence as independent nations; that they (the DMNS) were not party to the promulgation of these customary law principles; and, further, that in any case these customs are part of the old economic and legal world order that needs to be dismantled.[11] This argument is strengthened by the fact that the TMNS are equally to blame for the breakdown. Be that as it may, in terms of these commercial standards of customary international law, discrimination and state intervention appear to be the direct antithesis of national treatment.[12]

It was noted earlier that discrimination does create inequality, not necessarily in relation to any third party flag but with respect to the discriminating state itself; in that discrimination is a violation not of *foreign parity* but of the *inland parity*.[13] This cannot be stressed strongly enough because in the common language of international law, discrimination denotes a status inferior to that of a third party.[14] Giving the benefit of the doubt to the critics, discrimination as a denial of inland parity status constitutes a discrimination of its own kind which infringes the international trade relations doctrine of equality of treatment.[15]

Closely linked with the doctrine of equality of treatment is the material concept of flag equality.[16]

2.1 Material concept of flag equality

Flag equality is the maritime arm of equality of treatment. The conclusions that might be reached with regard to both the formal and the material concept for the equality of flags seem to deserve some further consideration as regards the relationship of the concepts to each other.[17] The *formal* concept envisages a treatment of foreign flags that is exactly the same. It will be apparent that the greater the number of states which enjoy national treatment, the greater the equalizing effect. The fact that this effect is achieved, not how it is reached, is the *material* concept of flag equality.[18] Because the means to be employed are not the concern of this concept, it follows that equality can be achieved not only without but also with state intervention.[19] This is the crucial concept of equality of flags. Various illustrations could be given to show that equality of flags has been achieved as effectively by liberalising trade as by planned maritime transport[20] and, indeed, all the bilateral agreements have been made with this aim in mind.[21]

Several instances could also be cited in which aid-receiving countries, having been requested to refrain from discriminations, have, in turn, offered the aid-granting country a fair share of the merchant marine trade,[22] without excluding third-flag participation. Finally, in this context, the practice of the US may be mentioned again, which reserves 50% of AID cargoes to their own flag and leaves the rest to the receiving country.[23] It is probably true to say that as much as all these practices may be covered by the formal concept of flag equality, they cannot be reconciled with the material concept of flag equality, at least, not with the OECD concept (post).[24] The OECD, therefore, has always protested against these practices and has made it clear that, for its members, the formal concept can only be applied in so far as it achieves the implementation of its own material concept.[25] It is ironic, though, that the US, a leading member of the OECD, is also the world's leading practitioner of discriminations. It has been found, therefore, that the application of national treatment finds its natural limit in the material concept of flag equality.[26] If the material concept of flag equality cannot be achieved in that way, it now finds additional restrictions in the rules set forth for the formal concept. This underlines the view expressed earlier that the scope for the application of the formal standards of national treatment ends exactly where the need for it is the greatest.[27]

2.2 Formal concept of flag equality

We have noted that the material concept developed by the OECD seems to have set the target as high as possible. This appears from the fact that not only would all forms of state intervention, with maritime transport, have to be abolished, but also that all maritime transport services would have to be liberalised in so far as they are offered by nationals of the member states.[28] And, as will be apparent shortly, the OECD went so far as to reinforce this position by passing a resolution recommending that governments of member countries rendering financial assistance to non-member countries should refrain from imposing restrictive or discriminative shipping clauses.[29] This would be particularly relevant in connection with the shipment of commodities to be financed by state assistance and in relation to such clauses which the receiving countries themselves might request in a bilateral trade agreement.[30]

In this respect the US requirement regarding cargo reservation of AID cargoes in a violation of this OECD understanding. Because of the high standards set and the wide scope of application called for by the OECD the rules do not have the full force of binding law.[31] It is well known that the OECD granted certain reservations to some countries, particularly Turkey, relieving them in part or in whole from the application of the *Code of Liberalisation for Maritime Transport* (post).[32] It appears also that some state control measures are applied and tolerated by the OECD.[33] It has also been hinted to the OECD that some of the DMNS which are anxious to engage in maritime transport might feel that this requirement would cause great difficulties and thereby compel them to take discriminatory measures.[34]

Such measures would be based on Article XVIII of the GATT Convention which creates a rather large obstacle to the realisation of the OECD goals.[35] On the other hand it is part of the nature of all material concepts aiming at equality that they provide exceptions. Exceptions are, and will be, necessary if a material concept containing detailed rules is to find the widest possible approval.[36] But the granting of exceptions means that the states benefitting from them may, for their own flags, claim a material position more favourable than that of other states. The result is that, on account of the exceptions granted, it may become impossible to persuade the state benefitting from them to agree to national treatment. It seems, therefore, that once again the material concept is not compatible with the formal concept.[37] Both concepts have, as has been seen, their weaknesses, not only within themselves but also in relation to each other.[38]

In a way one could perhaps observe that the strength of the one is the weakness of the other. Unfortunately, both concepts work as alternatives and do not complement each other.[39] The formal concept could also hold good in the developed world, in which the material concepts of the TMNS have been based, at least, on similar principles, leaving the door open to trade with each other on equal basis.[40] In the modern world, however, particularly in the era of the *New Order,* the views differ widely and are often set forth in hard and fast rules. For this reason it appears that any solution can only be a material one.[41] There is, however, a link between the *OECD Code of Liberalisation on Maritime Transport* and both the formal material and concepts of equality of flags, particularly that relating to the requirement of the minimum standard[42] principle of customary international law.

3. Minimum standard and flag equality

The existence of both material and formal concepts of flag equality means that a combination of two standards is sought that are quite different, which amounts to a contradiction in terms.[43] If a combination of such a type could be held valid at all it would import a mere agreement on material reciprocity.[44] If, however, the situation cannot be facilitated it may well be aggravated by the operation of the MFN treatment, outlined earlier; for as soon as state A grants national treatment to state B, and grants MFN treatment to state C, the latter can claim to be treated the same as state B, i.e. on inland parity basis. Theoretically, there would be no justification to deny state C that claim apart from it being blatant discrimination.[45] This means that if a state only once grants national treatment it confers this treatment to all states which enjoy MFN status.

3.1 Most favoured nation treatment

A widespread use of the MFN treatment sets a further limit on the application of national treatment.[46] This becomes crucial to merchant marine practices for it is at the ports of entry and departure that all these trade practices and theories are tested. Thus, for reasons of its inherent nature and of the interdependence of the network of commercial practices, the scope of application of national treatment is limited in international trade generally and maritime transport in particular.[47] It now turns out that the natural limits set for the use of national treatment have a particular bearing for its application to maritime transport.[48]

It is certainly true that the formal quality of this standard had proved to be of great advantage because the differences in the material status of the parties were and could be accepted automatically.[49] But those were the old days, when about half of the world was still under the colonial rule of the other half. In modern times, however, these differences have grown so great that they have developed into complete contradictions leading to discriminations and state intervention. This is particularly true now.[50] A country that pledges itself to the freedom of maritime transport (post) cannot subject its nationals to a cargo preference system and vice versa, the latter system would sacrifice the meaning of national flag protection if it were to allow a third flag to be put on an inland parity basis.[51]

This demonstrates that the formal concept of national treatment, because of its lack of any material meaning, provides no solution to the severest problems of maritime transport in modern times.[52] Of course, a great many trade relations still remain in which national treatment, because of less important differences in the commercial principles ruling in the participating countries, can usually be employed.[53] But where the differences consist in free oceanborne trade on the one hand, and STNS on the other hand, it cannot be overcome by the formal concept of national treatment.[54] Thus, only the doctrines of equality of flags, national treatment and MFN would remain as stumbling blocks for discrimination and vice versa. If the situation cannot be achieved thus, it is aggravated by the operation of the national treatment principle itself.

3.2 National treatment and equality of flags

All the above international trade law doctrines are linked with the doctrine of national treatment,[55] which has been dealt with in detail above. It will only be referred to here in so far as discrimination and state intervention are a direct contravention of it.

It will again be recalled that national treatment has been the standard predominantly applied to international shipping since the beginning of the free trade era.[56] The authoritative pattern was set by the *Cobden Treaty* of 1860,[57] concluded between France and Great Britain, which in general provides for a MFN treatment but with respect to shipping granted national treatment.[58] The example set by the *Cobden Treaty* was followed by a great number of commercial treaties of this period, among the TMNS.[59]

The view that national treatment was the most suitable standard for maritime transport had been accepted not only on a bilateral but also on a multilateral basis.[60] It has long been accepted, in the TMNS, that national treatment represents the highest standard that can be granted because it can be assumed that no state treats its own nationals on a less favourable basis than foreigners.[61] If this standard were to be maintained on the basis of reciprocal agreements, the state granting this standard might be expected to ask what it would gain in return for its own nationals,[62] which should be the status enjoyed by the nationals of that state. It would appear that the current maritime practice of most states is a departure from this doctrine.

Notwithstanding, certain differences in the material status of the nationals of any two states will always be found.[63] But if these differences exceed a certain measure it is likely that the agreement on national treatment would create unwarranted restrictions, for the nationals of other states.[64] There is, therefore, a natural limit to the application of inland parity. An attempt has been made to add an agreement on national treatment a clause providing that neither party could claim inland parity in order to receive rights in excess of those it is granting its own nationals.[65] This means that a combination of two standards is sought which are quite different, and which amount to a *contradictio in adjecto*.[66] If a combination of such types could be held valid at all, it would import a mere agreement on material reciprocity.

The other customary international law principle, infringed on by restrictive oceanborne trade practices, is the doctrine of the minimum standard itself.[67]

3.3 Minimum standard and equality of flags

One of the obstacles that discrimination and state intervention would have to overcome is basically that arising from customary international law. This is a different perspective of the minimum standard.[68] The minimum standard as applied in international treaty practice had been developed as a formula to replace the standard of national treatment, when it became clear that, with respect to the STNS, national treatment was not a suitable means to secure traditional individual rights.[69] It was thought that this could be achieved, at least, partially by an agreement containing a minimum set of material rights. Minimum standards have been applied in agreements affecting the life and liberty of nationals of the contracting states and have, most recently,[70] been employed in treaties for the protection of capital investments in foreign countries.

Even though the minimum standard formula does not lend itself to application to all international relationships, it can still serve to bridge quite a number of differences in the commercial and legal fields.[71] It can most certainly have this effect in the sphere of maritime transport and/or oceanborne commerce. This, then, would be the relevance of the minimum standards to merchant marine treatment. It seems arguable whether a minimum standard for the equality of flags could, and should be developed. It must be understood from the outset, of course, that any minimum standard[72] doctrine could only be based on the principle of free maritime transport as outlined above.

How far this freedom should remain untouched, and how far concessions would have to be made to state intervention, is, of course, an open question. Some hints will be contained in the *Ports Convention*[73] with respect to the coasting trade and the transport of emigrants. Further hints may be taken from the views expressed by the *International Chamber of Shipping* according to which the discriminatory effects of a cargo allocation system can be removed by opening the shares to all flags serving the trade.[74] And last, but not least, it may be observed that the *General Council of British Shipping* appears to be prepared to make some concessions to US flag preference with regard to AID cargoes. Whether or not the hints could give some guidance cannot be decided yet.[75] But it should be noted that whatever concessions are made, the material nature of this concept would allow for their gradual removal. At any rate, it seems to be worthwhile to devote some further thought to the definition of the minimum standard if only in respect of the transformation fo the OEEC into the OECD.[76]

As yet the positions taken by the former OEEC countries on the one hand and the US on the other hand are irreconcilable. Coupled with that is the worst that everybody feared and wished would not happen, that is, the backlash which ensued.[77] With the present state of affairs and the various international methods having largely failed to combat discrimination and state intervention effectively, it is only natural that states consider taking unilateral action. This, indeed, is one of the approaches to the problem adopted by the General Council of British Shipping in a past memorandum[78] which was strongly supported. Among the TMNS, excluding the US, it was pointed out that the forms which counter-measures should take must depend on individual circumstances, but that, in the first instance, it is necessary that each government should equip itself with the general powers needed.[79]

Such powers were given, in the case of the West German Government, by S18 of the *Statute of Foreign Commerce* which reads as follows:

> 'Provided the international flow of shipping is interferred with by measures which restrict the participation on a commercial basis[80] of the German merchant fleet in the contracts of affreightment of foreign flag ships and the chartering of such ships by persons resident in the Federal Republic of Germany such persons may be subject to restrictions in order to prevent substantially detrimental effects to the economic position of the German merchant fleet'.[81]

Such counter-measures have, in themselves, crystallized into a category of flag discrimination. Further examples of the German and Italian approaches were noted earlier.[82] Also the Government of the US, by virtue of Section 19 of the *Merchant Marine Act 1920, inter alia,* can dispose of such general powers. The British example of the Protection of *Trading Interests Act 1980,* The Japanese *Countervailing Act,* etc, are also cases in point.[83]

3.4 The problem of unilateral counter-measures

As regards the US, it was well known that in the case of discriminatory consular fees charged by Ecuador, for instance, it has made use of these powers with the result that Ecuador abandoned the said discriminatory charges.[84] It was expected that other TMNS would follow this example and also acquire powers for unilateral counter-measures. Assuming discrimination is already a problem in itself, then counter-measures might equally pose problems.[85] For such measures, inevitably, involve state intervention in maritime transport and, as we have maintained, an infringment of the Code of Liberalisation (post) As early as 1954, the then *OEEC Maritime Transport Committee* had already been faced with the problem of unilateral counter-measures[86] and had expressed the view that whereas each participating country was free to use its own discretion with respect to such measures yet the insertion of a rule to that effect would be tantamount to a formal antithesis.

There can be no doubt that even the OECD can make use of retaliatory measures as far as they find recognition by customary international law.[87] Unilateral measures to counter discrimination always mean acts of *deliberalisation* for which reason their use can only be advocated as a very last resort. They should be applied only if unilateral alternatives to reach equality have been exhausted.[88] It means, however, that although international actions have largely failed to have the desired effects the multilateral possibilities have not yet been fully exploited. So far, the OECD has confined itself to raising protests with the discriminating countries and has neither applied nor even explored the possibilities of common commercial pressure against such countries.[89] In a fight as close as that between so-called free-shipping and state intervention in international maritime transport, it cannot be expected that any measures short of collectively agreed and effected actions can succeed.

This means that all countries believing in the principle of free maritime transport should assist each other by all means in the negotiation of commercial treaties with third countries.[90] It further means that corporate bodies established for the pursuance of commercial and political aims such as the EEC and the various international institutions for granting aid to developing countries should not take any commercial measures unless the freedom of maritime transport is guaranteed.[91] It finally means that counter-measures should be employed for the protection not only of their own but also of all other flags which are operating according to liberal principles.[92] Only within common decisive actions does it seem possible to provide an efficient alternative to unilateral measures. On the grounds of past experience, however, it is rather doubtful whether common actions of the kind indicated can stand any real chance of success especially in the near future.[93]

Already the US and the rest of the OECD do not agree on cargo preferences, with the former for and the latter against.[94] Secondly, even the EEC took a long time to adopt a common approach in response to the *UN Code of Conduct's Cargo Preference* provisions, and this was despite the stipulated requirements in the *Rome Treaty.*[95] Thus, on the part of the nations believing in free maritime transport a much greater degree of solidarity than has been displayed in the past would have to be achieved.[96] And on the part of the nations believing in flag protectionism, a marked change of attitude would be required. There is no likelihood of such changes taking place now or in the near future.[97] On the contrary there is every indication that flag discrimination, cargo preferences and state intervention are not only on the upsurge, but are actually being institutionalised by practice.

Such practices are not difficult to find; they range from bilateralism, to unilateralism as well as in the *UNCTAD Code of Conduct for Liner Conferences.*[98] In short, protectionist measures for the establishment and/or development of national fleets are not only here with use now, but are probably here to stay. Thus, if the solution is to be a material one, it must be asked whether widespread international approval could be secured for some alternative *material* concept which, while based on the principle of free shipping, would not set the target as high as the OECD Code.[99] This infringment is perhaps much clearer in regard to the freedom of the high seas.

4. Protectionism and the freedom of the high seas

From the kind of actions that protectionism involves it is not disputed that it is an infringement of the *freedom of navigation* – an essential requirement of customary international law. Nor is it disputed that flag discrimination is contrary to the general princple of the freedom of the high seas.[100] Indeed, the *Geneva Convention on the High Seas* presupposes, *inter alia*, that the high seas are open to all nations and that no state may validly purport to subject any part of them to its Sovereignty.[101] Secondly, that the freedom shall be exercised under the conditions laid down by the articles of the convention, and, above all, by the other rules of international law, presumably meaning other conventions and customary international law.[102] Most noticeable among the said articles would be those relating to the freedom of navigation. If there is no formal concept generally available to be set against protectionism, it may be asked whether the material concept exists which could be invoked for the sake of equality of flags.[103]

This view is based on the idea that the freedom of the high seas can be put into effect only if it finds its compliment in the freedom of maritime transport.[104] The fundamental doctrine of this freedom is often thought to encompass within itself liberalism in commercial relations, so that any departure from commercial liberalism is a breach of the doctrine of the freedom.[105] Thus, the real freedom of the seas is the right of all commercial vessels, pursuing their lawful and peaceful endeavours, to sail the high seas and to enter territorial waters without let or hindrance and to find a safe harbour in case of trouble.[106] Of the four components of the freedom it is the freedom of navigation which most concerns merchant shipping. The 'high seas', in this context, of course means all parts of the sea that are not included in the territorial sea or in the internal waters of a state.

4.1 Freedom of maritime transport

Freedom of navigation is further divided into innocent passage, rights of landlocked states, transit passage and maritime transport. But first the freedom of maritime transport.[107] Although protectionism militates against the freedom of maritime transport it must be doubted, however, whether this view can really be upheld. Whereas the freedom of the high seas has been accepted for centuries as a rule of customary international law by the TMNS there are ample examples for the opposite view that this freedom has been contested by a large number of DMNS and STNS.[108] In this context it might be recalled that *Cromwell's Navigation Act 1651* was effective up to the middle of the last century and that similar rules have existed for quite sometime in Spain, France and the Scandinavian countries.[109] Whilst today most of the TMNS try to adhere to the concept of the freedom of maritime transport some of them, together with the DMNS and the STNS, have put the doctrine under increasing pressure by their protectionism.[110]

These measures have never been the subject of litigation before the international courts. Some have no lead to follow in that direction except to note that it is a violation.[111] Indeed, it can be doubted whether they would ever fall within the court's jurisdiction or if they should not rather be regarded as an exercise of national sovereignty in the sphere of foreign commerce.[112] It is, in fact, in this latter context that the approach is presupposed in our study. The position of the interventionists is that no rule of international customary law exists which provides explicitly for the freedom of maritime transport and that the most that could be said is that the existence of such a rule would be desirable.[113] Thus, as is apparent in the discussion ahead, we are left with the awkward situation of having to infer the existence of the principle of the freedom of maritime transport from the rules relating to the freedom of the high seas, generally, and the freedom of navigation in particular.[114]

In fact, the countries which oppose this view, particularly the STNS and DMNS, contest the principle of the freedom of the high seas itself.[115] They contest that during the mercanitilist period the TMNS established such a strength in shipping and trade that the continued adherence to the doctrine which gave them strength would have limited their further growth, whereas the doctrine of free trade and freedom of the seas, which Grotius enunciated opened the prospects of continuous growth if the same doctrine could be sold to their competitors, whose growth it would surely stunt.[116] And that at that time Holland (like the TMNS now) was ready to preach the doctrine of the freedom of the seas and to put the principles into practice because the Dutch had the most powerful merchant fleet in the world.[117]

The protectionists would also point out that, on the contrary, the British would have none of such a doctrine at the time. From the last years of the sixteenth century she rigorously applied a protectionist policy to shipping which guarded the commerce of the Empire strictly for the British ships, while trade with foreign countries was divided between British ships and those of the trading partners.[118] By the mid-century, however, with 52% of the world commercial tonnage, Britain was in a strong position to abandon protectionism and expand liberty. There is a case in this argument that the fundamental doctrine of the freedom of the seas is often thought of as encompassing within itself also liberalism in commercial relations.[119] We need to pause for a moment to examine the relationship between the freedom of the seas and *laissez-faire* and, indeed, its other facets like the doctrine of innocent passage.

4.2 Innocent passage and protectionism

The freedom of the seas in this post-mercantilist sense is one facet of the doctrine of free trade. It is a commercial doctrine and its application produces satisfactory results for all parties only to the extent that the buyers and the sellers in the market have roughly equal bargaining power.[120] This, the DMNS and STNS claim, is totally lacking. In their opinion, therefore, the doctrine was developed by the strong in buying and selling, to whom the advantages of free trade were overwhelming.[121] To these countries, therefore, to talk of freedom of the high seas when one section of the world (TMNS) own all the fleets of the world and the others (DMNS) own nothing, is absurd. This accounts for the rush, on the part of the DMNS, to establish and/or develop merchant marines of their own by whatever means necessary (i.e. discriminations and state intervention). For then, in the political sense, the doctrine of the freedom of the seas means something different.[122]

Freedom of the seas, in their view, is a political concept and is related to questions fundamental to the rights of man and the sovereignty of all nations (not just the TMNS), whereas the use of the same expression in the commercial sphere is a mere statement in a maritime context of the economic doctrine of *laissez-faire.*[123] In short, politically, the freedom of the seas is a real freedom;

commercially it is nothing more than the freedom to exploit. Nowhere is this more explicit than in the doctrine of *innocent passage.* By and large this doctrine is more appropriate to warships.[124] Unless otherwise stated, merchant marine passage should normally be *innocent* and in relation to commercial interests. The provisions relating to innocent passage generally are to be found in Section 111 of the *Geneva Convention on Territorial Seas and Contiguous Zones, 1958.*[125] And the provision relating to what constitutes innocent passage is to be found in Article 14 therein.[126]

> '. . . Ships of all states, whether coastal or not, shall enjoy the right of innocent passage through the territorial sea'.[127]

The major concern of this study, however, is the regulation relating to merchant shipping with the discriminatory implications that it may entail.[128] Subsection B provides rules applicable to merchant ships, the relevant articles being 18 and 20 relating to discriminatory charges and dues:[129]

> 'No charge may be levied upon foreign ships by reason only or their passage through the territorial sea'[130]

or

> 'Charges may be levied upon the foreign ships passing through the Territorial Sea as a payment only for specific services rendered to the ship. *These charges should be levied without discrimination*'.[131]

From the examples given of charges levied on foreign ships in ports it is clear they are discriminatory and in contravention of this convention.

However, the interventionists argue that innocent passage is more relevant to warships and has nothing to do with a nation using traditional methods to establish and develop its national fleet.[132] Even if that were not the case it is not clear whether the right of innocent passage in Article 14 is similar in scope to that applied by the ICJ in the *Corfu Channel Case.*[133] Were the British warships that swept the Corfu Channel for mines on November 13, 1946, engaged in *passage* in the sense of Article 14? Were the other ships that went through the channel earlier on October 22, 1946, not doing so to test the Albanian reaction?[134] If, in this case, they were (as was admitted) was the passage *innocent* according to Article 14?

Would it also have been innocent if they had been taking arms to a state which was then at war with Albania? This is not a remote possibility considering the current role of merchant marines in war.[135] Note that the draft proposed by the International Law Commission, for which Article 14(4) was substituted read:

> 'Passage is innocent so long as a ship does not use the territorial sea for committing any act prejudicial to the security of the coastal state'.[136]

Suppose a merchant ship of State A wishes to pass through the territorial sea of State B at a time when the nationals of State B might be inclined to demonstrate (which is probable these days) against State A for whatever reason. Could State B exclude the merchant ship if it feared demonstrations against it and could not guarantee its safety and the safety of its crew and officers?[137] And if it did exclude it on these grounds would that constitute discrimination or state intervention? Would it be relevant whether the captain of the merchant vessel knew that demonstrations were likely to occur or intended to provoke them?[138]

Be that as it may, it would appear that passage is only innocent if the first sentence of Article (14(4) is complied with. Conduct contrary to the second sentence would probably be illegal but not non-innocent;[139] consequently, the sanction of exclusion from the territorial sea (Article 16(1)) does not apply and would not, therefore, be discriminatory. This is not always true of fishing vessels, under Article 14(5);[140] if they, for example, fail to stow their gear away according to the Coastal States Law their passage is non-innocent. Otherwise for all intents and purposes this study treats fishing vessels as part of the merchant marine.[141]

The third facet of the freedom of the high seas relates to the treatment of landlocked states most of whom are the DMNS.

4.3 Treatment of landlocked states

Nowhere would restrictive shipping practices be more harmful than when related to the treatment, by coastal states, of the landlocked states, especially those of the DMNS.[142] The Geneva Convention which codifies the customary international law on this subject states quite explicitly:

> '1. In order to enjoy the freedom of the high seas on equal terms with coastal states, states having no sea-coast should have free access to the sea. To this end a state having no sea-coast shall by common agreement with the latter and in conformity with existing international conventions accord[143]
>
> (a) to the state having no sea-coast, on a basis of reciprocity, free transit through their territory, and[144]
>
> (b) to ships flying the flag of that state treatment equal to that accorded to their own ships, or to the ships of any other states, as regards access to seaports and the use of such ports[145]
>
> 2. A state situated between the sea and the state having no sea-coast shall settle, by mutual agreement with the latter, and taking into account the rights of the coastal state or state of transit and the special conditions of the state having no sea coast,[146] all matters relating to freedom of transit and equal treatment in ports, in case such states are not already parties to existing international conventions'.[147]

Article 3 of the Geneva Convention was merely a codification of an earlier *Declaration Recognising the Right of Flag of States having no Sea Coast,* an understanding reached in Barcelona, on April 20, 1921.[148] Before World War I, states without a sea coast could not claim a maritime flag. However, as every vessel must, in the interest of the maintenance of law and order on the open sea, sail under the flag of a state,[149] customary international law eventually recognised the rights of these states to fly maritime flags.[150] As of now the said restrictive shipping practices are a threat to the later rights of transit passage accorded these countries.

Freedom of transit passage is, therefore, the fourth and final facet of the freedom of the high seas. Freedom of transit results from transit passage.

4.4 Freedom of transit passage

Discriminations and state intervention are also a contravention of the freedom of transit contained in the *Convention and Statements on Freedom of*

Transit of Barcelona, April 20, 1921.[151] The items scheduled are persons, baggage, goods, vessels, coaching, goods, stock and other means of transport. 'Transit' means and includes the movement of the said items across a sovereign territory with or without transhipments, warehousing,[152] etc., when such movement is only a portion of a complete journey beginning and terminating beyond the frontiers of such sovereign state. Whatever measures and regulations the state takes to forward traffic, it should facilitate the transit and not discriminate on the basis of the nationality of flag, etc.:[153]

> 'No distinction shall be made which is based on the nationality of persons, the flag of the vessels, the place of origin, departure, entry, exit or destination, or any circumstances relating to the ownership of goods or of vessels'.[154]

Instances are foreseen when the transit state incurs costs for the purposes of facilitating such transit passage. It would be unreasonable not to expect some means being provided of balancing the books by the transit state. What is discouraged, however, is that it should be a charge[155] right across the board; and further that it should be done discriminatively:

> 'Traffic in transit shall not be subject to any special dues in respect of transit (including entry and exit). Nevertheless, on such traffic in transit there may be levied dues intended solely to defray expenses of supervision and administration entailed by such transit.[156] The rate of any such dues must correspond as nearly as possible with the expenses which they are intended to cover, and the dues must be imposed under the conditions of equality laid down in the preceding Article, except on certain routes, such dues may be reduced or even abolished on account of differences in the cost of supervision.'[157]

Finally, it is normal to apply tariffs to goods going in and out of the country or merely passing through. Transit is no exception. But again, these tariffs should not be as discriminative as some of the restrictive practices. Accordingly, under the convention, such transit tariffs should be applied, but only in such a way that they:[158]

> '[have] regard to the conditions of traffic and to considerations of commercial competition between routes, are reasonable as regards both their rates and the method of their application. These tariffs should be so fixed as to facilitate international traffic as much as possible.[159] No cargoes, facilities or restrictions shall depend directly or indirectly, on the nationality or ownership of the vessel or other means of transport. . .'[160]

Notes

1. These are economic, political, security, etc.
2. The principle of equal treatment unless otherwise stated.
3. Condliffe, J. B., *The Commerce of Nations*, N. Y., 1950.
4. See the case of *Commerce* v *Housatomic* R. Co. 143 Mass. 264 9NE 547.
5. See also *Forster* v *New Orleans* 94 US 246, 24 L. Ed. 122.
6. See the UK Chamber of Shipping, *Annual Report* 1960/61.
7. *Fairplay*, 1961, p. 39.
8. See also Heck, H., *Foreign Commerce*, N. Y., 1953.
9. See the case of *Louiseville & N. R. Co.* v *Commonwealth* 60 Ky. 769, 170 SW 162 Ann. Cas. 1916A, 405.

10. For instance the *US Reciprocal Trade Agreement Act of 1934*.
11. For additional details on history and results see US Tariff Commission.
12. See also operation of *The Trade Agreement Programme*, periodically.
13. Viner, J., *International Economics,* N.Y., 1951.
14. International Chamber of Shipping Resolution of May 13, 1960.
15. *Ibid*.; see also *Shipping Gazette*, June 1, 1960, p. 519.
16. See the case of *Whitney* v *Robertson*, 124 US 190 8 Oct. 456, 31 L. Ed. 380.
17. The formal is the intended.
18. The material is the practically achievable.
19. For state intervention see Chapter 6.
20. For planned maritime transport see texts under Nationalised Shipping or State Ownership in Chapter 4.
21. For bilateralism see Chapter 3.
22. Luding, E., 'Most favoured nation clause', 3 *AJIL*, p. 57.
23. See Chapter 3.4, for the details.
24. That envisaged by the OECD Code of Liveralisation (treatment ahead).
25. Only if it can be practically realised.
26. E.g., the Indian Reservation to the Resolution of the I.C.C. mentioned earlier on.
27. See Herod, *MFN Treatment*, 1950.
28. See also 3 *AJIL* p. 395.
29. Patton, J. *et al*., 'Cargo preference and Flag discrimination', *Geo. Wash. L. Rev*., Dec. 1965, pp. 257–87.
30. Jahnkel, L. G., 'The economic community and the MFNC', *Can. YBIL*, Vol. 1, 1963 pp. 252–71.
31. Hence countries like the US can get away with violations.
32. See text under *International Economic Laws* (ahead).
33. The US is the case in point.
34. OECD *Maritime Transport*, 1964, para 106, at p. 38.
35. This is the exceptions in favour of the DMNS.
36. Para 8C of *Protocol to French/German Commercial Treaty* of October 27 1956.
37. See *In re Kelly's Estate*, 153 Misc. 445, 274 NYS 488.
38. That is both the strength and the weakness.
39. See Exceptions to the Rule of Non-discrimination, Article XIV of the *Final Act of GATT*.
40. OECD *Maritime Transport* 1965 Part I para 17 p. 10.
41. *Ibid*., para 16, p. 9.
42. See next paragraph for details.
43. *US–Argentine Treaty of Navigation* (Article III of F.C.N. Treaty) TS 4; 10 Stat. 1005 (1854).
45. *US Treaty with Bolivia* (Article 2 of FCN Treaty) TS. 32; 12 Stat. 1003 (1862).
46. Hyde, *International Law*, Vol. 2, paras 536–37.
47. *Ibid*., p. 536.
48. *US–Costa Rica Treaty* (Article III of F.C.N. Treaty) TS. 62; 10 Stat. 916 (1852).
49. *US–Kingdom of Yemen Treaty* (Article IV of FCN Treaty) TIAS 1535; 60 Stat. 1782 (1946).
50. Despitch, N. S., *Transport Policies in Developing Countries*, pp. 31–42.
51. Hackworth, *International Law*, 272 1943.
52. *Ibid*.
53. See *Minerva Case* 96F. 2D 836 at 839.
54. Catwdal, 'The MFNC and the courts', *AJIL*, Vol. 35, 1941, p. 41.
55. Sturmey 'Dirigism and the new international maritime order', *European Shipping and Shipping and Shipbuilding*, 1978.
56. See the ICJ Reports 1952, p. 176.
57. See also *Kolovrat* v *Oregon*, Supreme Court of the US (1961) 366 US. 187.
58. *Treaty of 1881 between US and Serbia* (159 C.T.S. 115).
59. *Declaration of 1923* (appended to the *Anglo-Greek Treaty of Commerce and Navigation* of that date).

60. ICJ Reports, 1953, p. 10, interpreting an earlier *Anglo-Greek Commercial Treaty of 1866*.
61. Article XII *Treaty of Commerce and Navigation between the US and Belgium* 1876 (19 Stat. 628, 1 Molly Treaties 10).
62. *Treaty of Commerce and Navigation Between the US and Belgium* (Art. 13(2) of FCN Treaty) 14 UST. 1284; TIAS 543 (1962).
63. See also *Treaty of Commerce and Navigation between the US and China* (Article XXII(1) of FCN Treaty TIAS 1871; 63 St. 1299 (1948).
64. *US–Denmark Treaty* (Article XIX(4) of FCN Treaty) T.S. 60; 8 Stat. 340 (1962).
65. *US–Ethiopia Treaty* (Article XIV(2) of FCN Treaty) 4 UST 2134; TIAS 2864.
66. *US–FRG Treaty* (Article XX(2) of FCN Treaty) TS 725; 44 Stat. 2132 (1925).
67. Field, J. on the American case of *Whitney* v *Robertson* 124 US 190, 1888.
68. Sinclair, I. M., 'Nationality claims: British practice', *BYBIL*, 1950, pp. 134–137.
69. *Nottebohm Case* (2nd phase) ICJ Reports, 1955, p. 4.
70. *Ambatiole Case*, ICJ Reports, 1953, p. 10.
71. For Minimum Standard Treaty Provisions relating to Third Flag States, see 1965 *AJIL*, Vol. 59, p. 209.
72. *Ibid*., pp. 724–758.
73. See *Ports Convention* 1923 (ahead).
74. See also 1962 *AJIL*, Vol. 56, pp. 215–18, at 217 & 218.
75. And 1970 *AJIL*, Vol. 64(1), pp. 770–771.
76. OECD *Maritime Transport*, 1961, Chap. 1, para 6–7, pp. 7–8.
77. *Ibid*.
78. *Ibid*., para 69 seq.
79. For the US practice see Countervailing or Retaliatory Discrimination.
80. Keyword *commercial basis* would imply negation of political and other considerations giving rise to discriminations.
81. *Sect. 18 Statute of Foreign Commerce of the FRG*.
82. See text under *Countervailing discriminations*.
83. For UK see *Protection of Trading Interest Act 1980*, and the *Shipping and Commercial Documents Act 1964*, as well as the *Merchant Shipping Act 1974*.
84. These powers are provided for under Sect. 19 of the *Merchant Marine Act 1920*.
85. The Latin Americans claim that their flag discrimination is a response to US Cargo Preferences actions and vice-versa.
86. OEEC *Maritime Transport*, 1954, para 70, p. 54.
87. See also US Code Title 46, Sect. 146 as amended 1930.
88. See e.g. FMB (later FMC), dockets nos. 855 & 856 of June 29, 1959.
89. OEEC *Maritime Transport*, 1954, para 69, p. 54.
90. *Ibid*.
91. 1961 *OECD Maritime Transport* (Trends in Economic Sectors) p. 51.
92. *Ibid*., para 132, p. 39.
93. *Ibid*., para 133, p. 39.
94. OEEC *Maritime Transport*, 1954, paras 66–69, pp. 53–54.
95. Lopatin, A. G., 'UNCTAD code', 1980, *Harv. I. L. J.*, Vol. 22, No. 2, Spring, pp. 355–377.
96. Lawn, *op. cit*. pp. 13, 14.
97. E.g. Ecuador & India, cited by OEEC Report of July 23, 1959.
98. Note 95, *supra*.
99. See Annex I, note 1 to Annex of *Code of Liberalisation of Current Invisibles Operations* (adopted by the Council of 12th Dec., 1961).
100. Burke, W. T., 'Contemporary law of the Sea', *Yale Studies in World Political Order* 1, 1976, Vol. 2, pp. 183–283.
101. *Geneva Convention on the High Seas*, Article 2.
102. *Ibid*.
103. Bissell, W. K., 'Intervention on the high seas', *JMLC*, Vol. 4, pp. 718–735.
104. Klein, W., 'Imposition of taxes and levies in international waters', 1976, *Intertax*, Vol. 4, pp. 137–43 (in French and German)

105. Cobanu, D., 'The flag law revisited', *The Heleanna Case* Rev. Belge de Droit Internat. 12, 1976, pp. 166–71.
106. *Ibid.*
107. *Geneva Convention on High Seas*, Article 2.
108. Schwazenberg, V. A., 'Interference with ships in the high seas', 1961, *CLQ*, Vol. 10, pp. 785–817.
109. Eujio, I., 'The thought of Hugo Grotius on the freedom of the sea and after his *Mare Liberum Seinam*,' Vol. 10, 1978, pp. 2–4 & 127–54.
110. Cryer, H. L., 'Legal aspects of the Joanna v and Mamela incidents, April 1966', 1966 *Aust. YBIL*.
111. Akinsanya, A., 'The Pueblo affair and international law', *Ind. L. J.*, Vol. 15, 1975, pp. 485–505.
112. Thommen, T. K., *Legal Status of Government Merchant Ships in International Law*, The Hague, Nijhoff, 1962, p. 177.
113. Simmonds, K. R., 'The limits of sovereignty', 1965, *MCG L. J.* Vol. II, pp. 291–309.
114. Fortmin, H., 'Two questions concerning freedom of navigation on international rivers', 1969, *Neth. Int. L. Rev.*, Vol. 16, pp. 257–81.
115. On the basis herein stated below.
116. See further arguments in Chapter 1.
117. *Ibid.*
118. Now the EEC & OECD.
119. They should be different faces of the same coin.
120. Samuelson, P., *Economics*, 5th ed., N.Y. 1961, Chapter 24.
121. *Ibid.*, Chapter 25.
122. Machlup, F., *The Economics of Sellers' Competition*, Baltimore 1952.
123. Chamberlain, E. H., *The Theory of Monopolistic Competition*, Harvard U. P., 1931.
124. Clark, J. M., *Competition as a Dynamic Process*, The Brookings Institution, Washington DC, 1961.
125. Text as adopted by the Conference at its 20th Plenary Meeting UN. Doc. No. A/Conf. 13/L. 52, April 28, 1958.
126. Bowett, D. W., 'The second UN conference on the law of the sea', 1960, *In. & Con. L. Q.*, Vol. 9, pp. 415–35.
127. Article 14(1) *Geneva Convention on Territorial Sea*, Sect. 111.
128. Article 14(2), *ibid.*
129. Article 14(3), *ibid.*
130. Article 18(1).
131. Article 18(2).
132. Slonim, S., 'The right of innocent passage and the 1958 Geneva conference on the law of the sea', 1966, *Col. J. Trans. L.*, Vol. 5, pp. 96–127.
133. Corfu Channel Case (Merit), *I.C.J. Reports*, 1949, p. 4.
134. Green, L. C., *International Law Through Cases*, 4th ed., Chapter 12, pp. 228–37.
135. *The Times*, July 31, 1946.
136. Article 14 of the Convention.
137. The Corfu Channel Case (Preliminary Objections), *I. C. J. Reports*, 1948, p. 15.
138. The Corfu Channel Case (Assessment of Compensation) (1949), *I.C.J. Reports*, 1949, p. 244.
139. Lee, L. T., 'Justification over foreign merchant ships in the territorial sea', *AJIL*, 1961, Vol. 55, pp. 72–96.
140. Article 16(1) reads 'The coastal slate may take the necessary steps in its territorial sea to prevent passage through which is not innocent'.
141. Butler, W. E., 'Soviet concepts of innocent passage', 1965–66, *Harv. Int. L. J.*, Vol. 66, pp. 113–30.
142. Fried, J. H. E., 'The 1965 convention on transit trade of land-locked state' *Ind. J. Int. L.*, 1966, Vol. 6, pp. 9–30.
143. Article 3(1) *Geneva Convention on High Seas*.
144. Article 2(1)(a).

145. Article 3(1)(b).
146. Glassner, M. J., (ed.) *Access to the Sea for DMNS,* The Hague, Nijhoff, 1970.
147. Article 3(2).
148. Great Britain *Treaty Series* No. 29, 1923. CMND 1994/1923.
149. Article 4.
150. *Treaty of Varsailles*, 1919.
151. Great Britain, *Treaty Series*, No. 27, 1923. CMND. 1992/1923.
152. Article 1 *Statute on Freedom of Transit, op. cit.*
153. *Ibid.*
154. *Ibid.*, Article 2; Glassner, M. J., 'The status of developing land-locked states since 1965', *Lawyer of the Americas*, Vol. 5, pp. 480–98.
155. Govidarat, V. C., 'Landlocked states and their right of access to the sea', *Ind. J. Int. Law.*, 1974, Vol. 14, pp. 190–216.
156. Cf. Articles listed in Chapters 3–4.
157. Article 3, Transit Statute.
158. Article 3, Transit Statute.
159. Frank, T. M., *et al.*, 'The new poor: landlocked, shelf locked, and other geographically disadvantaged states', *N.U.J.I.L. & P.*, 1974, Vol. 7, pp. 33–57.
160. Article 4, Transit Statute.

CHAPTER 8

Problems relating to international economic laws

1. Introduction

There is a tendency among states that resort to traditional means of establishing and developing national fleets, to disregard the rules of customary international law. It is an obvious reflection of the radically different character and methods of international relations in our time that custom can no longer be as predominant or important a source of law, as it was in the formative period of international law.[1] The interventionists argue that custom is too clumsy and slow-moving a criterion to accommodate the evolution of international law in our time, and that the difficulties are increased as the number of subjects of the law of nations swells from a small club of western TMNS to 155 or more sovereign states. More importantly, custom is thought to be an unsuitable vehicle for international 'welfare' or 'cooperative' law.[2]

The latter demands the positive regulation of economic, social, cultural and administrative matters; regulation that can only be effective by specific formulation and enactment. Even in some of the domains of classical international law, as in the various aspects of the law of the sea, multilateral conventions arising out of preparatory work by international legal bodies and international conferences tend to codify and displace customs.[3] These conventions and treaties, too, are prohibitive of discriminations and state intervention. Even if they were not original parties therein, it would be difficult for the interventionists to disregard these conventions and treaties relating to international economic laws generally and oceanborne commerce in particular.[4] Therein lies the second set of legal problems relating to the traditional methods of establishing and developing national fleets. In this section we concentrate on some of these conventions and treaties.[5]

2. The legal regime of maritime ports

It would be beneficial to start with maritime ports – the first point where maritime intercourse takes place. Before the establishment of the *League of Nations' Transit Organisation,* the work of preparing a draft regime for maritime ports was first undertaken by the Ports, Waterways and Railways Commission of the Peace Conference and was subsequently continued by the *Commission of Enquiry on Freedom of Communications and Transit.*[6] The commission, after prolonged deliberations, came to the conclusion that a convention was not necessary and it, therefore, drafted a resolution on ports, placed under an international regime.[7] This resolution was discussed by the Barcelona Conference of 1921, and it ultimately appeared in the form of a recommendation.

It was, therefore, left to the Transit Committee of the League of Nations to draft a convention on maritime ports, which was finally adopted by the Second General Conference on Communications and Transit held in Geneva in 1923.[8] What emerged was the *Convention and Statute on the International Regime of Maritime Ports, December 9, 1923.*[9] This statute constitutes an important charter of freedom of the seas and non-discrimination in shipping.[10]

2.1 The Convention on Maritime Ports, 1923

This convention is not favoured by the interventionists for it explicitly forbids such practices. Article 2 of the statute states that:

> 'Subject to the principle of reciprocity and to the reservation set out in the first paragraph of Article 8, every contracting state undertakes to grant the vessel of every other contracting state equality of treatment with its own vessels, or those of any other state whatsoever,[11] in the maritime ports situated under its sovereignty or authority, as regards freedom of access to the port, the use of the port and the full enjoyment of the benefits as regards navigation and commercial operations which it affords other vessels, their cargoes and passengers.[12]
>
> The Equality of treatment thus established shall cover facilities, as well as dues and charges of all kinds levied in the name or for the account of the Government, public authorities, concessionairies or undertakings of any kind.[13]

Clearly, most of the restrictive methods we have enumerated are contrary to this provision. The convention goes on to require that dues charged shall be published and open to inspection.[14] And that, in making such assessment, the flag of the vessel must not be taken into account; accordingly, no distinction whatsoever may be made to the detriment of the flag of any contracting state as between that flag and the flag of the state under whose sovereignty or authority the port is situated or the flag of any other state whatsoever.[15] This is to be the guideline in assessing and applying customs and other analogous duties, local *octoi* or consumption duties, or incidental charges, levied on the importation or export of goods through the maritime ports situated under the sovereignty or authority of the contracting state.[16] Finally, and in explicit terms, the convention states:

> 'In order that the principle of equal treatment in maritime ports laid down in Article 2 may not be rendered ineffective in practice by the adoption of other *methods of discrimination*[17] against a vessel of a contracting state each undertakes to apply the provisions of Articles 4, 20, 21 and 22 of the Statute annexed to the International Regime of Railways, signed at Geneva, on December 9, 1923,[18] so far as they are applicable to traffic to and from a maritime port, whether or not such contracting state is a party to the said convention on the International Regime of Railways[19] . . . .'

An opportunity arose for an international arbitration involving this and other relevant provisions of the convention. The issue related to the rights of entry into maritime ports in international law. Sometimes it is asserted that, as a matter of customary international law, a right of entry exists for foreign merchant ships into a state's maritime ports. The authority for this is thought to be the Tribunal in the Arbitration between the Saudi Arabian government and ARAMCO[20] in which it was stated that:

> 'According to a great principle of public international law, the ports of every state must be open to foreign merchant vessels and can only be closed when the vital interests of the state so require'.[21]

It is submitted that this statement does not appear to represent the law and even if it did, it would be outside the scope of this inquiry to go into such details.[21] The three authorities cited to support this statement are Guggenheim,[22] Gidel[23] and Ralston.[24] These authorities are rather old and do not seem to agree.[25] Thus, if such rights existed then these are certainly not the proper authority.[26] However, cited as the fourth authority, and of relevance to us, is the *Geneva Convention and the Statute on the Regime of Maritime Ports, 1923.*[27]

2.2 Rights of entry into maritime ports

The right of entry and the rule of non-discrimination are said to be provided by Articles 2–7. However, Article 16 which the ARAMCO Tribunal cited as authority, does not deal with a right of entry. Rather, it deals with the right of parties to close their ports, possibly discriminatively, against certain foreign flags:[28]

> 'Measures of a general or particular character which a contracting state is obliged to take in case of an emergency affecting the safety of the state or the vital interests of the country may, in exceptional cases and for as short a period as possible, involve a deviation from the provisions of Article 2 to 7 inclusive, it being understood that the principles of the present statute must be observed to the most possible extent'.[29]

The use of discriminations for the purposes of establishing national fleets can hardly be called an emergency affecting the safety of state. Neither can it be said that the provisions of Articles 2–7 are necessarily authority for non-discrimination. However, there are still other loopholes that can be used by a state seeking to discriminate in order to establish its own national fleets. Authority for this view is found in the exceptions provided within the convention:

> 'The provisions of the preceding article in no way restrict the liberty of the competent port authorities to take measures as they may deem expedient for the proper conduct of the business of the port provided that these measures comply with the principle of equality of treatment as defined in the said article'.[30]

Giving preferences to national fleets and discriminating against foreign fleets can hardly be described as measures expedient for the proper conduct of the port. Even if they were to be, they could hardly comply with the principle of equality of treatment as defined in the said article.[31] It is true that the rule of non-discrimination may be read in Article 7 but then this privilege seems to be withdrawn immediately by the following Article 8:

> 'Each of the contracting states reserves the power, after giving notice through diplomatic channels, of suspending the benefit of equality of treatment from any vessel of a state which does not effectively apply[32] in any maritime port situated under its sovereignty or authority, the provisions of this statute to the said vessels of the said contracting state, their cargoes and passengers'.[33]

Finally, the statute does not prohibit flag discrimination in the coastal trade[34] and in relation to fishing vessels.[35]

Be that as it may, we are more concerned with discriminations for purposes of establishing national fleets rather than total exclusion from foreign ports. However, the purpose of the Geneva Convention may have been to secure equality of treatment for flag vessels in foreign ports but it did not seek to establish a general right of entry.[35A] In other words, the convention regulated the conditions of entry rather than the rights of entry. And it is these conditions which are threatened by the traditional methods of establishing national fleets. It might still be argued that the limitations on the closure of ports expressed in Article 16 implied a general right of access. However, such rights would be binding only upon parties to the convention. The majority of the STNS and DMNS (interventionists) claim not to be parties or signatories.[36]

In order to bind non-signatories, a right of entry would also have to be a part of customary international law.[37] This situation could only occur if the convention had codified the existing right of entry or had generated a right of entry which later passed into customary international law.[38] The tribunal did not produce evidence that there was a pre-existing rule. Even if it had, this would not bind the interventionists, the majority of whom doubt the continued validity of customary law. In fact Gidel's comments above and the evidence of state practice suggest that no such rule existed.[39] Similarly, no evidence was proffered to show that the rule had passed into customary international law. Indeed, it is doubtful whether such a rule could pass into customary international law.[40]

In view of the exceptions in Articles 3, 8, 9 and 14 it is questionable if the provision had the fundamental norm-creating character to form the basis of a general rule of law. In the *North Sea Continental Shelf Cases,* the ICJ deemed this characteristic a prerequisite for the transformation of conventional rules into customary law.[41] Neither the Geneva Statute of 1923 nor the other authorities cited by the ARAMCO Tribunal support the existence of a rule of customary international law giving merchant ships a right of access to foreign maritime ports. Thus, the Tribunal could not properly assert that a great principle of public international law existed which provided for the right of entry. A much more modern convention that the interventionists are bound to contend with is IMO (formerly IMCO).

3. The legal regime of IMO

IMO was the 12th specialised agency of the UN. The interventionists' argument against the previous convention can hardly be maintained against this one, the signatories of which include not only the TMNS but also the STNS and

DMNS.[42] It was the first intergovernmental body to deal solely with maritime affairs, since its *raison d'etre* is merchant marines engaged in international commerce – a most important field since more passengers and a greater tonnage of goods are still carried in ships than by other means of transport.[43] There are three major functions of IMO. The first objective is to facilitate cooperation among governments in technical matters of all kinds affecting shipping.

In this respect, its aim is to achieve the highest practical standards of maritime safety and efficient navigation.[44] It has a special responsibility for the safety of life at sea. It also provides for the wide exchange of information between nations on all technical maritime subjects. The second aim of IMO is to give advice to other international bodies involved in shipping matters, including agencies of the UN, and to coordinate its activities with those of the other UN agencies dealing with labour questions, telecommunications, meteorology, aviation, atomic energy and health.[45] Other responsibilities of the organisation include such matters as the prevention of pollution of the sea by oil, and the implication of regulations for the tonnage measurement of ships.[46]

3.1 The Convention of IMO, 1948

However, the third, and final function of IMO is what is of major concern to us. This is to discourage discriminatory, unfair and restrictive practices affecting the merchant marines in international trade, so as to promote the freest possible availability of merchant marine services to meet the needs of the world for overseas transport.[47] The use of the traditional restrictive methods for establishing and/or developing national fleets, then, clearly contravenes the spirit of this convention. This function is enshrined in Article 1(b) of the convention, i.e.:

> 'to encourage the removal of discriminatory action and unnecessary restrictions by Governments affecting shipping engaged in international trade so as to promote the availability of shipping services to the commerce of the world without discrimination . . . '.[48]

The convention has been ratified by about 100 states, some 75 of whom are interventionists (STNS and DMNS) so there cannot be any excuse. Nor can the restrictive traditional methods of establishing and/or developing national fleets, or the existence of an emergency, be a reason for departure. Consequently, contravention for such national needs and emergencies were foreseen at the negotiations and taken into consideration thus:[49]

> '. . . assistance and encouragement given by a Government for the development of its national shipping and for purposes of security does not itself constitute discrimination, provided that such a assistance and encouragement is not based on measures designed to restrict the freedom of shipping of all flags to take part in international trade'.[50]

Although this is a self-explanatory provision it does not mean that the opponents of the use of the traditional restrictive methods, for establishing and/or developing national fleets, are home and dry. There is another side of the argument which supports the interventionists within the Convention.

3.2 IMO and the establishment of national fleets

Although the IMO rules call for the removal of discriminatory action and unnecessary restrictions, they do not expressly prohibit flag discrimination nor do they even clarify sufficiently what, by international standards of law, should be regarded as flag discrimination.[51] It can only be assumed that financial measures in favour of the national flag do not, in themselves, constitute 'assistance and encouragement not based on measures designed to restrict the freedom of shipping of all flags to take part in international shipping'. It remains open, however, where the dividing line runs between discriminatory actions, on the one hand, and assistance and encouragement, on the other.[52]

This is the reason why it has been possible for quite a number of those states which have become members of IMO to make reservations just with respect to this provision.[53] The purpose of these reservations invariably is to ensure that measures taken by the reserving states in order to promote the establishment and/or development of national shipping and even cargo allocation are consistent with Article 1 of the convention.[54] There are also a number of the TMNS, among them the Scandinavian countries, which ratified subject to the reservation that IMO would not extend its activities to matters of a purely commercial or economic nature.[55]

These reservations are understandable since the countries involved, including Britain, are mainly cross-traders whose livelihood would be threatened by any attempt to redress the imbalance pertaining to international trade between the TMNS and the DMNS.[56] For the same reason these countries did not welcome the establishment of the UNCTAD sub-committee on shipping (Committee 4) which, to them, appears to lean towards the aspirations of the DMNS in international shipping.[57] Thus, these reservations are surely motivated not by any tendency in favour of flag protection but, on the contrary, by the fear that IMO might feel inclined to go too far in tolerating the protectionist measures used to establish and develop the merchant marines of the DMNS. In short it was fear of possible competition from the mushrooming national fleets of the DMNS. In this respect they could contain IMO but not UNCTAD.[58]

It follows that despite these steps, taken to provide some conventional rule for flag equality, however fragile, it cannot claim to have acquired general acceptance.[59] It was precisely this handicap on the part of IMO that led to the creation of UNCTAD, designed to deal specifically with policy, economics, and trade issues in international shipping.[60] Ever since that time IMO has directed its energy mainly in the technical, pollution and safety aspects of merchant shipping. Even then that was not to be the last we heard of IMO in the non-technical aspects of international shipping.[61]

3.3 IMO Convention on the Facilitation of Maritime Traffic, 1965

Notable among these reminders was the conclusion of the *Convention on the Facilitation of International Maritime Traffic, London 1965.*[62] This convention is an important addition to the achievements of IMO at whose invitation a conference was held in London from March 24 to April 9, 1965 to draw up a convention to facilitate international maritime traffic. No doubt, the rationale behind this convention was the fact that the said restrictive practices had become unbearable to the extent of hindering the smooth flow of maritime traffic.[63] Thus, the convention, which was signed in London on April 9, 1965 marks the first attempt made in recent years towards international deregulation of this vital aspect of maritime activity.[64]

The convention came into force on March 5, 1967 and is deposited with the Secretary General of IMO in accordance with Article XV of the convention. An amendment to the Annex concerning the facilitation of cruise ships,[65] for instance, was circulated to contracting governments by the depository in accordance with Article VII, paragraph 2(b) of the convention, and entered into force on August 12, 1971 in accordance with Article VII (2) (d).[66] The relevant provision is to be found in Annex A, Article II.

> '1. The Contracting Governments undertake to co-operate in accordance with the provisions of the present convention, in the formulation and application of measures for the facilitation, of arrival, stay and departures of ships. Such measures shall be, to the fullest extent practicable, not less favourable than measures applied in respect of other means of international transport . . .'[67]

These provisions seem to be directed against port and berth discriminations and other delay tactics. The convention provides for equality of flags of both landlocked and coastal states:

> '2. The measures for the facilitation of international maritime traffic provided for under the present Convention and its Annex apply equally to the ships of coastal and non-coastal states . . . '[68]

At first these objectives may appear trivial but they are aimed at the elimination of restrictive shipping practices.[69]

4. International waterways

In view of what was laid down in Article 23 of the *Covenant of the League of Nations,* restrictive shipping practices, for the purposes of establishing and/or developing national fleets, are a contravention of the requirements pertaining to international waterways.[70] The said Article states:

> 'Subject to and in accordance with the provisions of international conventions existing or hereafter to be agreed upon, the members of the League will make a provision to secure and maintain freedom of communication and of transit and equitable treatment for the commerce of all the members of the League'.[71]

As in all the other cases a conference was accordingly convened by the League of Nations at Barcelona in 1921 to examine all matters of international concern connected with the freedom of transit and the regime of navigable waterways.[72]

The conference of representatives of member states of the League succeeded in drafting two important international conventions which established freedom of communication by the free exercise of navigation on navigable waterways without discriminations, or restrictions.[73] The League also set up an international organisation for communications and transit with a view to enforcing the principle of free navigation in relation to rivers of international concern. The first convention related to the transit passage rights of landlocked states; the second one was the *International Convention and Statute Concerning the Regime of Navigable Waterways of International Concern, Barcelona, April 20, 1921.*[74] Both conventions prohibit restrictive practices, the kind traditionally employed for the purposes of establishing national fleets.

4.1 Convention on the Regime of Navigable Waterways

The convention refers to navigable rivers and discourages discriminations in favour of equality of flag treatment.[75] The non-discriminatory provision is provided for in Article 4:

> 'In the exercise of navigation referred to above, the nationals, property and flags of all countries shall be treated in all respects on a footing of perfect equality. No distinctions shall be made between the nationals, the property and the flags of the different riparian states including the riparian state exercising sovereignty or authority over the portion of the navigable waterways in question. Similarly no distinction shall be made between the nationals, the property and the flags of riparian and non-riparian states . . . '[76]

But the convention is not watertight against discriminations, as had been suggested; for instance, it permits the riparian state cabotage rights which include the right to practice cargo preference in the coastal waters affected.[77]

> 'A riparian state has the right of reserving for its own flag the transport of passengers and goods loaded at one port situated under its sovereignty or authority and unloaded at another port also situated under its sovereignty or authority. A state which does not reserve the abovementioned transport to its own flag may, nevertheless, refuse the benefits of equality of treatment with regard to such transport to a co-riparian state which does reserve it . . . '[78]

It is clear, therefore, that a state's sovereign right to discriminate against foreign flags, in certain circumstances and for whatever reasons, was recognised by international conventions as early as 1921.[79] Secondly, this convention confers exclusive rights on the riparian state, particularly when the passengers and/or cargo in question are connected with national, regional or interstate trade rather than international trade.[80]

> ' . . . on the Navigable Waterways referred to in Article 2, the Act of Navigation shall only allow the riparian states the right of reserving the local transport of passengers or of goods which are of national origin or nationalised. In every case, however, in which greater freedom of navigation may have been already established, in a previous act of navigation, this freedom shall not be reduced'.[81]

Thirdly, we noted earlier that one of the many types of flag discrimination employed is to charge favourable and discriminatory rates accordingly. This kind of unfair advantage, too, is discouraged by the convention. However, reasonable levies are permissible:[82]

> 'No dues of any kind may be levied anywhere in the course or at the mouth of navigable waterways of international concern, other than dues in the nature of the payment for services rendered solely to cover in an

equitable manner the expenses of maintaining and improving the navigability of the waterway and its approaches, or to meet expenditures incurred in the interests of navigation. These dues shall be in accordance with such expenses and the tariff of the dues shall be posted in the ports . . .'[83]

Finally, although the riparian state is permitted to suspend such freedom of navigation and equal treatment in case of national emergency, this shall be a short temporary measure.[84] Otherwise the normal rule remains that:

'. . . the nationals, property and flags of the contracting states shall, in all ports situated on the navigable waterway of international concern, enjoy, in all that concerns the use of the port, including port dues and charges a treatment equal to that accorded to the nationals, property and flag of the riparian state under whose sovereignty or authority the port is situated . . .'[85]

In conclusion, therefore, apart from a few exceptions, this is yet another international convention that comes down firmly against discrimination for whatever objectives. The same principles apply to international straits.

4.2 The position regarding international straits

With regard to straits, international law recognises two basic principles which have been incorporated into international conventions as well as upheld by the decisions of the ICJ.[86] First, if any strait, even though territorial in character, is known to connect two parts of the open sea and the waters are used for international traffic, the rule is that a foreign merchant vessel cannot be discriminated against or excluded. And, as supported by the ICJ in the *Corfu Channel Case,*[87] this principle extends to military vessels as well. It may be asked whether the test is to be found in the volume of traffic passing through the straits or in the greater or lesser importance for international navigation. But in the opinion of the ICJ the decisive criterion is rather the strait's geographical situation as connecting two parts of the high seas and the fact of its being used for international navigation.[88] Nor can it be decisive that this strait is not a necessary route between two parts of the high seas, but only an alternative passage as, for example, between the Aegean and the Adriatic Seas.[89]

Secondly, the rule is that foreign merchant vessels must be allowed innocent passage through territorial straits, let alone international ones, without any dues and tolls whatsoever.[90] No discriminatory taxes or dues are to be levied except those representing expenses incurred by the riparian state for buoying and dredging, for maintaining lighthouses and for supervising pilotage through the Straits in the interests of general navigation. What is more, this levy shall be without discrimination between flags.[91] With the recognition of the principle of free navigation on the sea, all dues connected with straits became no longer admissible. The problem caused by discriminations for development purposes is not new.

The inconsistency between the collection of such tolls or dues and the freedom of navigation was reconciled once and for all. This was achieved by the *Treaty of Copenhagen of March 14, 1857*[92] which decided in favour of the doctrine of freedom of navigation and all that it stands for. It is said that from time imemorial the TMNS had behaved like the DMNS do now, by charging what are known as 'sound dues' from all foreign merchant vessels seeking passage through the two Belts and Sand, a narrow strait which divides Denmark from Sweden and connects the Kattegat with the Baltic.[93] However, subsequently, and after protests from the US and other TMNS, she agreed in 1857 to discontinue the levy of these tolls in future in consideration of the payment of an indemnity of £300 000, to be apportioned between the contracting states according to the importance of their navigation.[94] The *Treaty of Copenhagen* thus put an end to the collection of tolls as such for innocent use of the Straits. The position is not different in international canals.

4.3 International canals

International canals are international highways that must be kept open in war as well as in peace to merchant ships of all flags.[95] As regards the Suez Canal, for example, Article 14 of the *Firman Concession* of January 5, 1956 embodies this principle:

> 'The canal and the ports dependent on it should be forever open, as neutral passages, to all merchant ships crossing from one sea to the other, without distinction, exclusion or preference of persons or nationalities, on payment of the dues and observance of the regulations established by the Company'.[96]

In fact, in an earlier convention the parties, by application of the principle of equality as regards the free use of the Canal, undertook that none of them should endeavour to obtain with respect to the Canal territorial or commercial advantages or privileges in any international arrangements which may be concluded.[97]

The Egyptian government itself guaranteed the observance of this principle in a later declaration. However, an interesting position was posed by the Kiel Canal whose treaty contains among the stated Articles 360–386 one specifically prohibiting preferential treatment and/or discrimination in Article 380,[98] and particularly 381:

> 'The nationals, property and vessels of all powers, shall in respect of changes, facilities, and in all other respects be treated on a footing of perfect equality in the use of the canal, no distinction being made to the detriment of nations, property and vessels of any power between them and the nationals, property and vessels of Germany or of the most favoured nation.'[99]

Similar situations exist in the Panama and all the other important international canals.[100] Thus, apart from limited exceptions, all the international waterways are uniform in prohibiting the kind of discriminations that are practised by some states for aiding the establishment and/or development of their own national fleets.[101]

Finally, let us address our attention to the situation regarding international economic treaties.

5. International treaties

By international treaties we mean agreements creating institutions like the OECD, EEC, the UN and GATT. The outstanding example is GATT, which consists of an international code of tariffs and trade rules, signed in 1947 by 23 states, including the US, and which became effective on January 1, 1948.[102] The spirit of GATT aims to eliminate the kinds of restrictive shipping practices that we have outlined. The agreement was the culmination of an American-led drive for freer trade after World War II.[103] It was originally intended to be a temporary provision to handle tariff and trade questions along multilateral lines until the *Charter of ITO* was established, but in 1950 the US Senate rejected the ITO Charter and GATT became effective.[104] Since then, it has been renewed and amended many times.

GATT is dedicated to three main principles:

1. Equal, non-discriminatory treatment for all trading nations;
2. Reduction of tariffs by negotiations; and
3. Elimination of import quotas.[105]

These objectives are directly opposed to the interventionists' approach. GATT has eliminated or negotiated reductions in binding tariffs, quantitative reductions, and discriminations, permitting the freer movement of international trade.[106] For instance, about 55 000 tariff concessions were involved in the first three major rounds of tariff reductions concluded in the agreement. The latest challenge facing GATT is the conclusion of an agreement with the EEC and the state interventionists in shipping.[107] GATT would like to make sure that the two agreements do not result in higher barriers to trade than had existed previously.

5.1 GATT Convention and restrictive shipping

It remains to be seen whether the GATT concept will develop so much strength as to achieve a world-wide scope of application with the interventionists in shipping. So far it has not.[108] Against this concept stands the growing number of states, notably the STNS and, to some extent, the DMNS which follow the principle of state planning and intervention in the fields of economics generally and maritime transport in particular.[109] We are not alone in pointing out that the state interventionists contravene the spirit of GATT. A report submitted to the *Inter-American Bar Association,* suggests that any restrictive flag quota violates Article XI of GATT as well as the spirit of many bilateral treaties of friendship, commerce and navigation.[110] Article XI could not have been more explicit:

> 'No prohibitions or restrictions other than duties, taxes or other charges, whether made effective through quotas, import licences or other measures, shall be instituted or maintained by any contracting party on the importation of any product of the territory of any contracting party or on the exportation or sale for export of any product destined for the territory of any contracting party'.[111]

Yet despite this fine start, the rest of the *GATT Convention* is riddled with exceptions to accommodate, for example, any balance of payments crisis, state traders and the special requirements of the developing countries, to mention but a few.[112] It may be presumed that the emergence of the STNS marked the beginning of the decline of the concept of free trade[113] in maritime transport and all the ingredients of the freedom of the high seas.[114] GATT permitted the

STNS' exception, but could not guarantee strict observance of its application to non-discrimination.[115] All it could say is that:

> '(a) Each contracting party undertakes that it establishes or maintains a state enterprise, wherever located, or grants to any enterprise . . . exclusive special privileges, such enterprise shall . . . in a manner consistent with the general principles of non-discriminatory treatment'.[116]

Thus, the STNS have seized on this exception as a licence to discriminate in their shipping relations with other countries.[117] Similarly, the opportunity that the DMNS have seized, to use discriminatory means in aiding the establishment and/or development of their own national fleets, is also to be seen in the loophole provided by yet another GATT exception.[118]

> '1. The contracting parties recognise that special governmental assistance may be required to promote the establishment, development or reconstruction of particular industries . . . and that in appropriate circumstances the granting of such assistance in the form of protective measures is justified.'[119]

It will be remembered that this constituted the rationale for the establishment and/or development of merchant marines by the DMNS. Unfortunately this open licence, combined with their nationalism, meant that these states would not:[120]

> 'recognise that an unwise use of such measures would impose undue burdens on their own economies and unwarranted restrictions on international trade and might increase unnecessarily the difficulties of adjustment for the economies of other countries.'[121]

Thus both the TMN free traders and the state traders with the DMN in between, find ammunition for their cause in the same GATT convention.[122] But a body that leans more towards free shipping, and which has done a lot to help in that direction is the OECD.

5.2 The OECD and international shipping

The OECD was set up under a convention signed in Paris on December 14, 1960,[123] which provides that the OECD shall promote policies designed:

1. To achieve the highest sustainable economic growth and employment and a rising standard of living in member countries, while maintaining financial stability, and thus to constitute to the development of the world economy.[124]
2. To contribute to sound economic expansion in member as well as non-member countries in the process of economic development.[125]
3. To contribute to the expansion of world trade on a multilateral, non-discriminatory basis in accordance with international obligations.[126]

Most significant is the *Maritime Transport Committee* which made its origin as one of the committees set up by the OEEC for the preparation of the programme report for the *Marshall Plan* 1947.[127] The section of this report prepared by the committee included a statement of shipping policy which read as follows:

> 'The shipping practice of the participating countries is based on the free circulation of shipping in international trade, in free and fair competition. Any interference with this free circulation is liable to reduce the efficiency

> of the total shipping available and hence to increase the cost of shipping services'.[128]

This subsequently became the basis of the shipping policy of the *Maritime Transport Committee* of the OEEC and inspired the interpretative note in the *Code of Liberalisation* dealing with member countries' obligations in connection with maritime transport.[129]

When the OECD succeeded the OEEC on the ratification of the OECD Convention on 30th September 1961, the OECD Council retained and widened these policies and functions of the Maritime Committee. The committee has met regularly, and produced annual reports since 1948 in order to deal with questions concerning shipping which are of economic interest to the members.[130] Such questions include problems arising from restrictive practices and flag discrimination. The committee is the sole inter-governmental body that meets regularly to handle problems of international shipping policy. Its members continue to give special consideration to the problems created by flag discrimination by governments, and also keep a close watch on the situation resulting from the policy of creating or developing national merchant fleets without economic justification.[131]

In the general framework of European cooperation the committee constitutes a forum for discussion of all shipping problems, not only between the participating countries but also in relation to other countries. The OECD concerns itself with the seventeen or so member states (except notably the US) with the result that the national laws of these states have been adapted to its material concept.[132] The particular concept for merchant marine practices is embodied in *Note 1 to Annex B* of the Code and bears the following features:

> 'The nationals of each member state shall have the unrestricted right to make use of all the services in the field of maritime transport which are offered by the nationals of each member state.'[133]

Secondly, and more to the point:

> 'Because the shipping policy of the member states is based on the principle of free and fair competition the freedom of shipping shall not be hampered by means of currency control measures, legal provisions in favour of the national flag, similar measures by governmental or semi-governmental bodies, import and export licences, restraining the choice of the flag, privileges in commercial treaties reserved by the national flag, discriminatory taxes and port charges.'[134]

It will be remembered that this list of prohibited acts covers all the traditional methods used to establish and/or develop national fleets. And, as expected only a sound economic rationale is acceptable:

> 'Only commercial considerations should govern decisions relating to the means of transport and the flag of the ship.'[135]

Thus, the concept does not leave any room whatsoever for state intervention, and appears to be the most far-reaching provision that can be achieved in that direction.[141] In that respect it marks the extreme opposite position to the cargo reservation requirements of the *Code of Conduct for Liner Conferences.*[136] For this reason the *Code of Liberalisation of Maritime Transport* has found very few friends outside the OECD; it strikes at the very basis of the traditional restrictive STNS and DMNS.[137] By the very fact that shipping is more of an international service, the Committee finds that its functions inevitably extend beyond the OECD sphere. It takes account of all restrictive shipping practices wherever these occur throughout the world and it advises the Council, in all appropriate cases, of action which might suitably be taken by the OECD governments to combat these practices.[138] It has found it hard to discourage the state interventionists. Nevertheless, the committee firmly believes that in positive achievement and in preventing the further spread of discriminatory practices it is performing an essential task. The basis of that task is the *Code of Liberalisation.*[139]

5.3 OECD Code of Liberalisation and shipping

The states' use of discriminatory and restrictive practices for the purposes of establishing and/or developing their national fleets is contrary to the *OECD Code of Liberalisation of Current Invisible Transactions.*[140] From the above analysis, it would appear, therefore, that the only material concept creating complete freedom of maritime transport has been developed by the OECD. The concept is contained in the Code which was intended to remove natural trade barriers and restrictive shipping practices.[141] It should be noted, however, that the rules of the Code do not have the legal force often binding on states, as for instance the rules of the Ports Convention. They are mere directives for the economic policy of the member states and, as far as the merchant marine is concerned, their validity extends only from one year to another unless extended.[142] This accounts for why the STNS and DMNS have always disregarded the Code in their bid to establish and/or develop merchant marines of their own. However, the directives are being followed by the majority of the methods of establishing and/or developing national fleets. Even within the OECD some states, notably the US, have up to now not adhered to all its principles.[143] Apart from lacking the force of law, it can fairly be stated, however, that the TMNS in the OECD have brought about a concept which substantially excludes flag discrimination.[144]

The *OECD Code of Liberalisation,* intended as a guideline for the member states, could not of course, bind non-members, even if it were otherwise legally binding.[145] Nevertheless, it makes an impact on international maritime law and trade practices in such an important region of the world that the flag discriminating nations would, no doubt, have to take account of.[146] The same shortcomings can be found in the provisions of the *EEC Treaty* which, although, they have the binding force of law, are restricted in application to member states.

5.4 The Treaty of Rome and restrictive shipping

The provisions relating specifically to transport in the *EEC Treaty* are Articles 61 and Title IV of Part Two of the Treaty, i.e. policy of the Community entitled *Transport* (Articles 74–84).[147] Of specific relevance to our analysis is Article 76. This prohibits member states from making their national transport legislation more restrictive vis-à-vis carriers from other member states, pending the introduction of common rules, unless such measures are unanimously approved by the Council.[148] It states that:

'Until the provisions referred to in Article 75(1) have been determined, no Member State may, without the Council's unanimous approval, make less favourable in their direct or indirect effect on carriers of other Member States as compared with Carriers that are its nationals, the various provisions governing the matter which are in operation when this Treaty comes into force.'[149]

However, the Article does not forbid member states from continuing discriminatory practices existing on 1 January, 1958, but merely forbids their increase in any way.[150] Secondly, Article 79 is designed to eliminate discriminations, which take the form of carriers charging different rates and imposing different conditions for the carriage of the same goods over the same transport, on grounds of the country of origin or of the destination of the goods in question. This section may be considered one of the special provisions mentioned by Article 79 (the general rule against discrimination)[151] The exact wording of Article 79(1) is as follows:

'In the case of traffic within the Community discrimination which takes the form of carriers charging different rates and imposing different conditions for transporting the same goods on the same routes, because of the country of origin or of destination of the goods in question, shall be abolished at the latest, before the end of the second stage.'[152]

This means that prior to the creation of the EEC, discrimination existed among the European nations despite the *OECD Code of Liberalisation.* However, since Article 79(1) only mentions carriage of goods, Article 7 must be held to apply to any discrimination relating to carriage of persons. These conditions were to be eliminated by the end of the second stage. Article 79(3) required the council to lay down rules for the implementation of Article 79(1) within two years of the entry into force of the Treaty.[153] This was done by Regulation 11 of 1960, J.O. 1121, which obliges member states to notify the Commission of any tariffs or agreements on transport rates or conditions which discriminate in terms of the country of origin or destination of the goods concerned (Rule 5).[154] These discriminations are further prohibited by Rule 4, which reiterates Article 79.

However, the Regulation excludes from its ambit private law contracts, i.e. individual agreements between trader and carrier. These may continue to be administered even though discriminative in rates and conditions.[155] Under Article 79(4), the Commission is empowered by Rule 14 of the Regulation, to exercise power of scrutiny and control over compliance with the Regulation, although it is in the first place the member states who are responsible for ensuring such compliance.[156] The scope of the Regulation is not perhaps very wide. Article 79(1) of the Treaty, re-enacted by Rule 4(1) of the Regulation, only proscribes discrimination in the carriage of the same goods over the same transport links which narrows the scope of the prohibition.[157]

There is also the application of the special provisions of the Treaty, particularly on discrimination, aids and ententes. For instance, Article 80 prohibits member states from setting rates and conditions involving any elements of support or protection in the interests of one or more particular undertaking or industries, unless authorised by the Commission.[158] Article 81 requires member states to endeavour to reduce the costs of charges or dues in respect of frontier crossings on a progressive basis. Finally the *Treaty of Rome,*[159] in Article 77, enunciates the principle of non-discrimination in transport tariffs and dues in keeping with the minimalist philosophy of the Treaty as a whole.

The other applicable provision of the Regulation is Rule 4(b),[160] which prohibits measures or practices which discriminate between producers, purchasers or consumers especially in prices and delivery terms or transport rates and conditions. This is all part and parcel of the *EEC Common Shipping Policy.*[161] This is all well and good for the EEC, but the problem is not confined to EEC countries. It is the STNS and DMNS who, unlike the EEC, do not have national fleets, or where they do exist, not well established ones. It is not the question of controlling discrimination within the EEC and OECD but in a world that includes the discriminated and the discriminators.[162] Perhaps something with a wider scope like the *UN Code of Restrictive Business Practices* might be more appropriate.

5.5 UN Code of Restrictive Business Practices (RBP)

As a background, the basis of the RBP was formulated at UNCTAD IV, 1976, Nairobi. The *ad hoc* group and conference drafted, and agreed on, a Code that could help developing countries in achieving improved control over RBP's at national level.[163] The purposes of the model law would be to improve control of RBP'S affecting the trade and development of the DMNS. Briefly then, the model law sets out in alternative form the objectives of the law. The first form is a statement that the objective is to prevent, eliminate or control RBP'S which may adversely affect the trade and development of states.[164] The second form contains, in detail, the considerations regarded as relevant by the experts from the DMNS. Although the Code is largely aimed at MNC's, like the liner conferences and MSE's, yet it has the potential to contain and eliminate the traditional RBP's as are used to establish and/or develop national fleets. And, unlike the EEC and OECD Codes, this would be legally binding on all the UN member states, once ratified.[165]

On the actual control of the RBP's, it is laid down that any act or behaviour of any one or more enterprises which, by agreement or arrangement, or through the abuse of or acquisition of a dominant position, is likely to limit access to markets, unduly restrain competition, or result in adverse effects on the consumers, shall be subject to control.[166] This is both specific and wide enough to cover the types of shipping RBP's in point. So do the provisions on restrictive agreements, dealt with by two alternative articles. The first provides that any agreements having certain restrictive effects (such as price fixing, market sharing, etc., which are set out) shall be notified, and that the Commission shall have power to decide whether the agreement is to be prohibited, permitted, or permitted subject to certain conditions and obligations being fulfilled.[167] The alternative provides that the same agreements shall be prohibited unless the parties are able to prove, to the administering authority or the appropriate judicial authority, that such agreements are beneficial to trade or development.[168]

A similar approach is adopted towards acts performed by enterprises in a position of dominant market power. These acts likely to produce abusive behaviour (such as predatory pricing, bilateralism in shipping or tying agreements) are set out, and either the Commission has the power to declare them illegal,[169] or the acts are prohibited unless the enterprise can show that in all circumstances they are beneficial to trade and development. The kinds of shipping RBP's in point can hardly fulfil the conditions for exemptions.[170] A further provision gives the Commission power to call upon enterprises to notify details of their conduct when it is considered that they are in a position of dominant market power. This is exactly the position that shipping RBP's has given the said national fleets.[171]

The procedure suggested recognises that not all agreements or acts restricting competition are bad, but that it is necessary to distinguish between those having an adverse effect and those whose effect is beneficial.[172] As it is virtually impossible to provide any fixed rules for deciding which are good and which are bad, there must always be a discretion in the deciding authority to examine the effect of the restriction on the economy and to determine in the light of wide-ranging criteria whether it is on the whole beneficial or whether it constitutes an abuse.[173] Unfortunately, the doctrine of sovereignty, which would probably protect all the state-run national fleets so set up, would remove them from the abusive to the beneficial category, especially those set up under the said GATT exceptions.[174]

Similarly, in this proposed code there are certain exemptions made to the application of the model law. The first relates to any agreement or act to which the government is a party, or any act necessary for the operation of activities especially authorised under other legislations, e.g. the GATT.[175] At a stroke this amounts to a blanket protection for the said national fleets. There is also provision for exemption for any act of an enterprise wholly or partially owned by the state, which may be limited to the acts necessary for the fulfilment of its functions.[176] This is to enable certain sectors, as is common, to be dealt with by special legislation and also to provide for the operation of cooperatives and the organisation of the market in the case of a single crop country, where these activities are carried out largely under government control.[177]

A further provision, however, excludes export control, or requires registration for them, but the extent of this exemption will depend on the 'principles and rules' formulated in the main discussions.[178] Were it not for these exemptions many types of national fleet would probably be outlawed as RBP's. Thus, apart from the UNCTAD Committee on Shipping, the UNCTAD Code of Conduct for liner shippings' cargo sharing provisions and the GATT exceptions, no other international treaties, conventions and bodies support RBP's as a means of establishing and/or developing national fleets.[179] Even if the STNS and DMNS could get around these legal issues, they would not solve the economic problems. This is the subject of our next chapter.[180]

Notes

1. Friedman, W., *The Changing Structure of International Law,* Chapter 5.
2. Harris, D. J., *Cases and Materials in International Law* p. 2.
3. Friedman, *supra,* Chapter 8.
4. *Ibid.,* Chapter 15.

5. Haas, R., 'Regime internationale des zones franches dans les ports maritimas', *Academe Droit Internationale Recueil Cours,* Vol. 21, 1928, pp. 375–427.
6. Laun, R., *Le regime internationale des ports Academe Droit Internationale Reenel Cours,* Vol. 15, 1926, pp. 1–143.
7. See also Lowe, A. V., 'The right of entry into maritime ports in international law', 1977, *San Diego L. Rev.,* Vol. 14, pp. 597–625.
8. See notes 9 and 10, *post.*
9. For the text of the convention see Great Britain *Treaty Series,* No. 24, 1925, CMND 2419 of 1925.
10. See also League of Nations, *Treaty Series,* No. 1379 and Hudson, *International Legislation,* No. 107.
11. The material concept of flag equality seems to have its roots in this provision.
12. Article 2 of the statute.
13. This is the most general it can be.
14. ARAMCO Arbitration, 27 *ILR* 117, 212.
15. *Ibid.*
16. See also International Labour Organisation Administrative Tribunal, 1958.
17. Guggenheim, P., *Traite de Droit International Public,* 1953, p. 414.
18. 2 Gidel *Le Droit International Public de la Mer,* 1932, p. 39.
19. Raldston, J. H., *The Law and Procedure of International Tribunals,* 1926, p. 305.
20. Footnote 174, *supra.*
21. *Ibid.*
22. *Ibid.,* note 2, at p. 12.
23. Footnote 177, *supra.*
24. Footnote 178, *supra.*
25. Footnote 179, *supra.*
26. Fananchille's note on the Portendick incidence of the 19th Century.
27. 28 L.N.T. S.115; note that the US is not a party.
28. E.g. in ORINOCO Case.
29. Article 16 of the statute.
30. Article 3, *ibid.*
31. *Ibid.*
32. This looks like a licence to revenge; i.e., countervailing flag discrimination.
33. Article 8, *ibid.*
34. Article 9, *ibid.*
35. Article 14, *ibid.*
35A. See judgment of Duffeld in the *Faber case.*
36. Article 16(1) *Convention on High Seas.*
37. E.g. Azuni Imda, *Droit Maritime de Li Europe,* 1805, p. 286.
38. *Ibid.*
39. See notes 40 and 41, *post.*
40. See ORINOCO Arbitration; Ralston, *supra,* p. 305.
41. ICJ Reports, 1969, pp. 41–43.
42. Hence the argument that they were not party to it would not be obtainable to the DMNS.
43. For the 1970 period of IMCO see Johnson, *ibid.,* pp. 39–42.
44. Article 1(9) of the convention.
45. Otherwise, who is the UN body to deal with in health matters?
46. Simmonds, K. R., 'The constitution of IMCO', *ICLQ* Vol. 12, pp. 56–87.
47. Final Acts and Related Documents of the UN Maritime Conference, 1948, VIII 2.
48. Article 1(b).
49. These issues surfaced at the 1948 Conference.
50. Johnson, *supra,* p. 40.
51. Compare Articles 101, 1(b) and 1(c).
52. Hence the various exceptions.
53. E.g. the Mexican Reservation of March 6, 1948.
54. See the US acceptance of August 17, 1950.
55. Kerno's Article in *AJIL,* 1959, Vol. 53, pp. 516–31.

56. US Dept. of State *Treaties and other International* Acts Series, No. 4044.
57. P. W., 'UNCTAD success in shipping', 1970, *JWTL* Vol. 4, July/August No. 4, pp. 586–89.
58. *Ibid.*, UNCTAD. 'Cargo reservation and developing countries', pp. 590–604.
59. 'UNCTAD committee on shipping', Geneva, 9–25 April, 1969, 1969 *JWTL* Vol. 3, No. 4 July–August pp. 420–22.
60. See UNCTAD: 'Policy crisis among traditional maritime nations', 1970, *JWTL, supra.*
61. Schachter, O., 'The question of treaty reservation at 1959 General Assembly', *AJIL*, 1966, Vol. 52, pp. 372–79.
62. Alexandrowicz, G. H., (Article) *ICLQ*, 1969, Vol. 15, pp. 621–59.
63. FAL/E.G.111/3, 2/2 1963 IMCO.
64. Roullier, J., 'A breakthrough in international maritime traffic' *UN Monthly Bulletin*, Vol. 2, (No. 2 Feb) pp. 58–62.
65. Article 1 of Agrt. on the *Importation of Educational, Scientific and Cultural Materials* 1950 (UNESCO).
66. Council XIV/35, 6/5, 1965. E. IMCO.
67. Machesney, B., 'Interpretation of the convention for establishment of IMCO' *AJIL*, 1960, Vol. 54 pp. 884–894.
68. Annex A Article 11(2); *ICJ Reports*, 1960, p. 250.
69. Article 1 (a–c); *AJIL*, 1959, Vol. 53, pp. 516–35.
70. Preamble to *Convention and Statute to Freedom of Transit* Barcelona April 20, 1921.
71. *Ibid.*; Hudson, *International Legislation*, Nos. 41, 41A.
72. *Proceedings of the American Society of International Law*, 1960, Vol. 54, pp. 120–52.
73. Fortuin, H., 'The regime of navigable waterways . . . ' *Neth. Int. L. Rev.*, 1960, Vol. 7, pp. 125–43.
74. League of Nations *Treaty Series*, Vol. 7, p. 35.
75. See Fortuin in *Neth. Int. L. Rev.*, 1969, Vol. 16, pp. 257–81.
76. Article 4 of the convention.
77. Hudson, *International Legislation*, No. 42.
78. Article 5(1).
79. See Case of *HVLTV Webber*, 252 Mich. 198 N.W. 159, 168, 71 ALR 1238.
80. *Bathgate* v *Irvine*, 126 Cal. 135, 58P, 442, 77 Am.St. Rep. 158.
81. Article 5(2).
82. Vitanyi, B., 'The regime of navigation in international waterways', *Neth. Y. B. Int. L.*, 1974, Vol. 5, pp. 111–16 (pt. 1).
83. Article 7.
84. Article 9.
85. *Ibid.*
86. Green, L. C., *International Law Through Cases* (4th ed.) 1978, Chap. 12, pp. 228–81, at 229.
87. *ICJ Reports*, 1949, p. 4; Colombos, *International Law of the Sea*, 3rd ed., p. 149.
88. *ICJ Reports*, 1948 p. 15.
89. Moser, M. B., *Israel Law Rev.*, 1968, Vol. 3, pp. 50–66.
90. Sect. 111(A), *Convention on Territorial Sea.*
91. *Ibid.*, Articles 14–17.
92. Oppenheim, *International Law* (8th ed) pp. 511–12.
93. *Indian Journal of International Law*, 1974, Vol. 14, pp. 169–89.
94. Shaw, K. E., in *Japanese Annual of International Law*, 1970, Vol. 14, pp. 34–47.
95. Baxter, R. R., *The Law of International Waterways*, p. 371.
96. Article 14 *Firman Concession* of January 5, 1956.
97.
98. About the Kiel Canal.
99. Section VI, Article 381, *ibid.*
100. Section 382.
101. *Ibid.*
102. *International Trade 1960 Contracting Parties to GATT*, Geneva, 1961.
103. *Operation of the Trade Agreements Programme*, US, 1961.
104. 13th Report July 1959–June 1960 (GPO) Washington DC, 1962.
105. *Report on Law of the Flag and Labour Relations* (US) 1960, p. 9.

106. Article XI of GATT, 61 Stat. pt. 5.
107. *Ibid.*, p. 11; A32–A33, 1947, TIAS no. 1700.
108. Dam, K. W., *GATT, Law and International Economic Organisation*, Chicago, 1970, p. 480.
109. Svendsen, A. S., 'Shipping in the countries of the Eastern bloc', *Norwegian News*, no. 2, 1962, pp. 52–61.
110. Note 267, *supra.*
111. Article XI, *GATT Agreement.*
112. Article XII.
113. Pound, R., 'Liberty of contract', *Yale Law Journal*, Vol. XVIII, 1908–1909, pp. 454–87.
114. Crichton, G. H., 'Grotius on the freedom of the seas', *Juridicial Review*, 1941, Vol. 53, p. 226.
115. Article XVII of GATT.
116. Article XVII (1) (a).
117. Article XVII.
118. Article XVIII.
119. Article XVIII (1), beginning.
120. UNCTAD, Establishment and Development of National Fleets, *supra.*
121. Article XVIII (1), end.
122. See also Part IV of GATT.
123. For the Membership of the OECD see Annex.
124. Annex.
125. Note application to non-member states.
126. Note the word *non-discriminatory basis.*
127. The OEEC had its roots in the Marshall Plan.
128. OECD *Maritime Transport*, this is aimed at the case of flag discrimination.
129. For this code see next paragraph.
130. *Ibid.*
131. Harris, S. E., *The European Recovery Program*, Harvard, 1948.
132. *Ibid.*, Chapter 5.
133. Ellis, H. S., *The Economics of Freedom*, NY, 1980, p. 100.
134. See also Diebold, Jr. W., *Trade and Payments in Western Europe*, 1952.
135. And Price, H. B., *The Marshall Plan and its Meaning*, NY, 1955.
136. Convention on European Economic Cooperation of April 16, 1948.
137. OEEC *Maritime Transport*, Sept. 1954, Part III, pp. 51–56.
138. See (post) the *Italian Law* of March 1963 and the *German Law* of Sept. 1961.
139. OEEC *Maritime Transport*, Sept 1954, p. 52.
140. Cf. para 63(b).
141. *Ibid.*, para 63(c).
142. *Ibid.*, para 63(d).
143. See US: *European Shipowners*, Memo on European Ministers, March 1963, Resolution 1964 H. R., p. 77.
144. MARAD, DOT, *Subsidies in Shipping* by eleven countries, pp. 11 & 14.
145. See also 'Minister's des Travaux Publico et des Transports, Decret No. 65–612 du 22 Juillet 1965, *Journal Officiel du 28 Juillet 1965*, p. 6601.
146. OEEC *Code of Liberalisation*, Annex B, Chap. I, 1/A.
147. Bender, M., *EEC Law*, Chapter 27, pp. 259–74.
148. Collinson, W. S., 'Economic regulation of transportation under the common transport policy of the European communities', *Stan. L. Rev.*, 1972, Vol. 24, pp. 221–346.
149. Article 76 of the *Treaty of Rome.*
150. Stabenow, W. W., 'Opportunity for an external policy of the EEC in the field of transport', *Com. Mark. L. Rev.*, 1966, Vol. 4, pp. 32–50.
151. Bredimas, A. E., 'The common shipping policy of the European Economic Community', *Com. Mark. L. Rev.*, 1981, Vol. 18, No. 1, Feb., pp. 9–30.
152. Couper, A. D., 'Common shipping policies of the EEC', *Marit. Pol. and Man.*, 1979, Vol. 4, No. 6, (editorial).

153. Seward, N., 'Owners fear EEC competition laws within two years', *Seatrade,* 1979, Vol. 9, No. 8, pp. 27–35.
154. Anguilo *et al.,* 'An inquiry into the economic philosophy . . . ', Vir. J. Int. L., 1964, Vol. 4, pp. 139–74.
155. Deringer, A., *Competition Law of the EEC,* Chicago, 1968, p. 100.
156. McIntosh, A. C. B., 'Antitrust implications of liner conferences', *L.M.C.L.Q.,* 1980, Vol. 1 (May), pp. 139–53.
157. McLachlan, D. L. *et al., Competition Policy in the EEC,* Toronto, 1967.
158. Mork, M. R., 'The cartel policy of the EEC, 1962–1967', *Com. Mark. L. Rev.,* 1968, pp. 67–103.
159. Dashwood, A., 'Control of state aids in the EEC . . . ', *Com. Mark. L. Rev.,* 1975, Vol. 1, pp. 43–58.
160. See 1975 *Tex. Int. L. J.,* Vol. 1, pp. 185–92.
161. Thompson, D., 'The competition policy of the EEC', *JWTL,* 1975, Vol. 10, No. 1, pp. 79–88.
162. Shermers, H. G., 'Community law and international law' *Com. Mark. L. Rev.,* 1975, Vol. 1, pp. 79–90.
163. UNCTAD, Resolution 96 (IV), Section III, para 3.
164. Report of the Second ad hoc Group of Experts on Restrictive Business Practices.
165. *Ibid.;* UNCTAD, Doc. TD/B/600, paras 57–68.
166. UNCTAD first draft of the model law or laws on RBPS to assist developing countries in devising appropriation legislation UN.
167. UNCTAD, Doc. No. TD/RBPS/CONF./1 UN, 1979.
168. Cf. Paranjape, H. Inida, 'Review of the monopoly and RBPS Act' 14 *JWTL,* 1979, p. 68.
169. UNCTAD, Doc. No. TD/50 of 7 May, 1979.
170. UNCTAD, Resolution 103(V) of 30 May 1979.
171. *Ibid.,* Resolution 33/153.
172. *Ibid.,* Doc. No. TD/250.
173. See also Greenhill, C. R., 'UNCTAD control of RBPS', 12 *JWTL,* 1978, p. 67.
174. UNCTAD, Doc. No. TD/RBPS/CONF.10 of May 2, 1980.
175. Krishnamurti, R., 'UNCTAD group of experts on RBPS', *JWTL,* 1973, Vol. 7, No. 6 Nov–Dec, p. 711.
176. Scokoczy-Syllaba, A., 'Restrictive business practices', *JWTL,* 1969, Vol. 3, No. 3 May–June, p. 332.
177. 'UNCTAD restrictive business practices conference', *JWTL,* 1980, Vol. 14, No. 2 March–April, p. 172.
178. 'UNCTAD restrictive business practices, model law on', 14 *JWTL,* Vol. 14, No. 2 March–April, p. 444.
179. Murray, T. *et al.,* 'Quantitative restrictions, developing countries and GATT', *JWTL,* 1967, Vol. 11, No. 5 Sept–Oct, p. 391.
180. Rom, M., 'Restrictive business in EEC agreements with less developed countries', *JWTL,* 1978, Vol. 12, No. 1 Jan–Feb, p. 36.

CHAPTER 9

Consequences to the domestic and foreign groups and economies

1. Introduction

The remainder of this section will be concerned with the economic consequences of the traditional methods for establishing and developing national fleets. Foremost of the restrictive practices that the section concentrate on are cargo reservation and maritime subsidies.[1] But first let us discuss the cost of these two methods to the country using them and to the international economy in general.

2. The cost of restrictive practices and state aid

This is not easy to ascertain as the costs of cargo reservation are difficult to assess since it includes not only the direct effect of an increase in freight rates (if ever such an increase takes place), but also the effects on the quality and regularity of the service.[2] The comparison of costs has also to take into consideration the extent to which cargo would have been carried in national flag ships in the absence of cargo reservation. Since information on this subject appears to be scarce, it may be useful to describe here the major elements relevant in the comparison.[3]

The first probable consequence is *resource allocation.* Both maritime subsidies and cargo reservation affect resource allocation in the country adapting such measures internationally.[4] Within a country these measures tend to cause resources to flow into shipping rather than into other industries or activities which might have been developed on the basis of free competition. From the DMNS' point of view it usually means transfer from the most deserving areas.[5] In many instances, the choice may be between assistance to the merchant marine industry and some other infant industry. Internationally, the resources may flow into the merchant marine industry of countries comparatively ill-equipped, at the time, for the development of merchant shipping, though in this regard account should be taken of the infant industry argument,[6] and the possible correction of the existing inequalities noted earlier, as well as of the desirability of a dynamic rather than a static international division of labour.

The second consequence is the *disruption of services.*[7] Cargo reservation might interfere directly with the choice of a particular ship. The economics of international shipping services, however, depend on the balancing of peaks and troughs in certain trades.[8] The use of cargo reservation cuts across this flexibility. Two points are worth considering in this respect. First, the effect of cargo reservation is more disruptive for cargo liners than for tramps which, by their nature, would readily adjust to the volume of cargo that remains available on a competitive basis after cargo reservation.[9] Secondly, there is a limit up to which subsidies would not directly affect the choice of ships. For example, subsidies to offset higher operating costs, as in the case of the US, do not necessarily directly affect the freedom which ships of other nations have to participate in the carriage of cargo.[10] Subsidies could, however, be raised to a level at which they would prevent effective competition from non-subsidized fleets of countries which could not match the subsidies.

The third probable consequence is *overtonnaging.*[11] Both maritime subsidies and cargo reservation are likely to cause overtonnaging particularly during a recession as is the case at the moment. Ships which could not be put into service under conditions of free competition, or which would have to be laid up, are put into service or continue to sail.[12] It is worth noting, in this context, that in a situation of expanding world trade, and hence of expanding world fleets, the risk of overtonnaging is considerably smaller than in a situation of slack trade.[13] In the short run certain trades or routes may become overtonnaged, but in the long run the expansion of trade and demand for shipping services should rectify this initial dislocation.

Fourth, is the effect on *freight rates.*[14] A direct short run consequence of cargo reservation might be an increase in the load factor of non-national lines if the number of sailings and the size of ships in service are not adjusted to the changing circumstances.[15] A similar effect is likely to occur if a new national line joins a conference or is able to secure a larger share in the carriage of cargo in a conference to which it already belongs. It is not unlikely that, in spite of the preference for the national line, its load factor may continue to be low for it would probably be serving only a part of the total route.[16] In either case, it may well be that demands will be made for higher freight rates to cover the costs of the general over-capacity of the tonnage available. Exactly who bears the costs of this overtonnaging depends very much on the elasticity of demand for the shipping service on the route and on the subsequent evolution of freight rates, but the chances are that the exporting country has to bear the bulk of the additional cost.[17] For a general overview of freight indices see Table 30.

2.1 The question of efficiency

The economic consequence of these policies on freight rates is inevitably linked with the question of efficiency.[18] The effect of subsidies on the general increase in world tonnage is different. Subsidies enable some countries to put ships into service which would otherwise never have been added to the world fleet. Also ships which might, but for the subsidies, have had to be laid up[19] or operate inefficiently at higher costs, continue to sail and offer their services. Whereas one might expect such conditions to bring down freight rates, no such decrease in fact takes place, particularly in the liner trade, owing to the

Table 30. Maritime research general freight index, November 1982–July 1983 (Jan–Dec 1972 = 100).

Week ending	General freight index	Time charter index 1–2 months	2–3 months	over 6 months	Grain freight index	Misc. freight index	No. of weekly fixtures
November 1982							
6	203.0	168.3	144.7	192.4	195.7	218.5	181
13	203.4	170.2	134.5	190.8	196.3	218.6	222
20	208.9	171.3	141.8	194.1	204.9	217.3	202
27	206.7	167.1	148.7	200.7	201.5	217.7	205
December 1982							
4	207.1	173.6	149.5	200.7	202.4	217.1	191
11	204.4	168.5	145.3	191.4	199.0	215.9	220
18	204.5	171.9	140.0	196.4	198.8	216.7	232
25	204.9	174.7	138.7	198.0	199.1	217.5	163
January 1983							
1	205.3	173.9	140.8	198.0	199.4	217.9	96
8	207.5	166.9	139.5	194.7	201.9	219.5	172
15	212.6	179.5	141.6	194.7	206.2	226.1	232
22	214.5	182.3	142.1	208.6	208.6	227.1	231
29	215.2	182.6	145.8	198.0	209.6	227.3	170
February 1983							
5	217.5	165.7	137.4	202.0	210.4	232.8	206
12	220.8	179.2	146.8	204.6	213.3	236.8	182
19	219.0	168.0	138.9	206.6	210.5	237.2	187
26	219.8	171.3	142.5	206.6	211.6	237.5	163
March 1983							
5	220.8	185.4	149.5	203.3	212.8	237.9	198
12	224.7	179.8	144.7	207.3	217.9	239.3	192
19	228.9	186.8	163.2	205.9	223.1	241.4	228
26	231.4	182.6	151.3	205.0	226.3	242.4	250
April 1983							
2	231.5	181.7	148.7	205.0	226.5	242.1	153
9	230.4	177.2	147.6	205.0	224.9	242.2	192
16	235.0	184.0	152.9	209.6	226.5	253.4	237
23	239.3	186.5	145.0	208.3	232.4	255.8	238
30	239.1	188.5	151.1	209.6	232.5	254.9	212
May 1983							
7	241.4	182.9	147.6	211.2	233.6	258.3	159
14	242.7	186.8	157.9	213.9	235.2	258.7	227
21	243.2	192.4	165.3	216.8	236.2	258.2	221
28	240.5	185.4	161.6	218.8	231.9	258.8	212
June 1983							
4	231.2	179.8	164.2	217.8	224.2	246.0	199
11	227.4	173.6	157.6	216.5	220.2	242.8	230
18	218.7	177.2	150.3	215.5	209.5	238.5	222
25	217.4	171.9	158.4	212.2	208.3	237.1	195
July 1983							
2	211.1	164.6	138.9	207.9	203.1	228.3	201
9	208.4	163.2	131.1	207.9	199.8	227.1	173
16	211.4	154.8	129.2	(207.9)	202.1	231.3	171

Source: Shipping Statistics, Institute of Shipping Economics. August 1983, p. 33.

organisation of the industry into conferences which limit competition.[20] It would seem, therefore, that the very subsidization of liners and liner companies with higher running costs has, *inter alia,* helped to strengthen the interest of liner companies in reaching agreement among themselves.

This is contrary to what the DMNS would have liked. In the same way inefficiency which raises freight rates was neither desired by, nor was it in the interests of, the DMNS, TMNS, or oceanborne trade in general. Yet these traditional methods achieve these undesired results, first through encouragement to run superfluous tonnage,[21] secondly, because shipping companies with high running costs may not wish to waste their subsidies in a freight rate war; and lastly, because unsubsidized companies do not care to put their financial resources against the wealth of other (subsidized) countries.[22] On the other hand, preventing competition between national flag and foreign flag ships, causes the former to be less efficiently operated than they would otherwise be if exposed to full competition, assuming that they could survive at all in the absence of cargo reservation.[23] Subsidies, beyond a certain point, could have precisely the same effect. The phenomenon of limitation of competition leading to inefficiency is also a feature of conferences, especially these with pooling arrangements.[24]

Both cargo reservation and maritime subsidies, once granted, are difficult to withdraw, although exceptions do exist, such as during the period 1964–1969 in Japan, where subsidy schemes contained a provision for an annual reduction.[25] Such a scheme could also provide for a gradual reduction and eventual elimination of cargo reservation. Although in an entirely different context, Japan, upon its admission to the OECD in 1962, set a timetable for the gradual reduction of cargo reservation in certain trades.[26] In cases where cargo reservation is used for obtaining admission to liner conferences, it will be eliminated as and when the national line is admitted to the conference and allowed an appropriate share in the carriage of cargoes.[27] It is to be noted, however, that the cost of subsidy can specifically and quantitatively be identified, whereas that of cargo reservation cannot. It is, therefore, likely that the gradual reduction of subsidies may be an easier task than that of cargo reservation.

Both cargo reservation and maritime subsidies could take the form of a countervailing action.[28] In cases where the national line is refused entry into the appropriate conferences, or though admitted is not given an appropriate share of cargo, and where methods such as deferred rebate systems are used to prevent the entry of non-conference ships into the trade, there may remain no effective alternative but cargo reservation to fight against the conference practice of excluding outside competition.[29] It needs to be emphasized that conferences themselves have used cargo reservation through agreements or understandings with governements for the carriage of a certain proportion of a country's trade to the exclusion of other conferences and independent lines.[30] A more subtle form of cargo reservation is practised by the conferences through pooling arrangements that result in the sharing of the cargo of a country whose ships are not in the conference.

It is this situation which seems to have led some DMNS to raise the question of cargo reservation and participation in conferences and the carriage of an appropriate share of cargoes by their national flag lines.[31] Finally, cargo reservation

Table 31. Norwegian shipping news' freight indices.

1. Dry cargo

Month	Time Charter (1971 = 100) 1980	1981	1982	1983	Trip Charter (July 1965–June 1966 = 100) 1980	1981	1982	1983
January	335.8	392.6	231.8	190.0	193.8	225.5	165.5	154.6
February	327.3	390.6	215.6	177.9	209.8	219.8	165.8	163.3
March	373.3	377.3	235.4	203.3	209.3	214.8	169.2	166.7
April	400.1	381.4	262.3	210.7	216.7	204.1	176.8	168.5
May	418.0	372.4	257.4	210.8	220.9	199.8	172.8	177.7
June	420.6	374.7	214.3	194.9	226.1	202.3	158.7	176.8
July	405.1	333.4	173.4		207.7	201.3	147.0	
August	385.9	299.6	156.5		206.7	177.0	145.1	
September	381.4	285.4	165.8		201.1	178.7	149.6	
October	366.9	260.5	176.3		204.0	176.7	151.5	
November	371.0	269.5	172.2		227.3	177.7	153.0	
December	392.9	267.4	192.5		241.3	168.8	152.2	
Average	381.5	333.7	204.4		213.3	195.5	158.9	

2. Tanker market (worldscale)

Year/ Month	VLCC/ULCC 150 000 dwt & above	Medium crude carriers (60 000–150 000 dwt)	Small crude & product carriers (30 000–60 000 dwt)	Handy-sized (30 000 dwt & less) dirty	clean
Average 1978	29.1	64.1	108.0	152.2	162.4
Average 1979	47.5	117.8	216.7	331.8	337.5
Average 1980	47.0	89.9	145.8	231.9	237.2
Average 1981	27.9	55.7	88.7	145.0	148.5
Average 1982	26.3	49.4	78.0	129.4	125.5
1982					
January	22.1	50.8	78.8	139.6	133.5
February	20.4	44.8	77.6	128.6	125.4
March	20.4	46.2	73.9	129.0	134.4
April	21.7	47.0	72.6	123.4	134.6
May	24.5	50.1	82.1	134.7	136.5
June	23.1	50.0	77.6	129.8	129.5
July	24.0	52.2	74.0	127.4	122.6
August	31.9	47.9	73.4	117.4	119.5
September	46.3	49.3	76.1	133.8	125.2
October	28.2	52.8	87.5	122.2	121.7
November	27.7	52.5	87.6	133.8	98.6
December	25.5	49.6	74.7	133.6	124.2
1983					
January	25.4	51.6	86.2	134.0	118.7
February	25.5	47.9	75.1	118.9	120.6
March	27.2	47.7	84.7	125.8	114.2
April	21.9	47.6	81.3	132.6	114.0
May	24.4	52.9	86.7	119.1	110.0
June	22.8	50.3	75.3	109.7	105.7

Source: Shipping Statistics, Institute of Shipping Economics, Bremen, August 1983, p. 26.

may be practised by the DMNS to counteract a situation in which precisely the same objective is achieved when the importers in the DMNS, importing on a CIF basis, select ships from a small group of countries.[32] The methods of assistance that a particular country might find suitable depend naturally on its economic situation. For countries with merchant fleets established primarily as an export industry, i.e. operating in the cross-trade, cargo reservation is of a limited significance, as is the case with the TMNS.[33]

2.2 Administrative restraints

For national fleets already carrying a substantial proportion of their own countries' trade, (which appears to be the case with the majority of the TMNS), cargo reservation is unnecessary.[34] However, countries entering the shipping market and having a substantial trade of their own which was previously either not being carried, or only to an insignificant extent, in national flag ships, are in a different situation.[35] Some of them may assist their national fleets by granting maritime subsidies, others by cargo reservation, and still others by both. These are the countries seeking to establish or maintain national fleets as a form of import substitution. For this purpose, and with the objective of establishing a variety of industries, in many countries both tariff and non-tariff measures of protection are often used.[36] Such developments may be forestalled, as far as liner shipping is concerned, by the admission of a national line into the appropriate conferences, and way-port conferences, and ensuring in the conference the allocation of an appropriate share of cargo for them.[37]

Although both the alternatives of subsidy and reservation are open to a particular country desiring to assist its national fleet, for some countries it is easier, because of budgetry constraints and lack of flexibility in financial structure, to use reservation rather than subsidies.[38] Initially, the shipper bears the cost of protection accorded to the national fleet, but eventually it is shifted to the consumers in the case of imports and to producers in the case of exports.[39] This is basically a question concerning a country's internal income distribution and it is quite likely that the incidence in both cases may fall on the same population group given the preponderance of indirect taxes in most of the DMNS and the generally low tax base.[40] The administration of a subsidy programme may become quite elaborate in the case of certain types of subsidies, whereas cargo reservation could be operated without a large administrative machinery.

Both reservation and subsidies are open to retaliation. It is probable that they would be more effective if no retaliation took place.[41] However, if other countries do so, the effect of the assistance granted is reduced. The DMNS have such a small share of the world tonnage, that the economic effect on the rest of the world as a whole of any assistance they give to their national fleets would be minimal.[42] Hence, there should be no risk of retaliation. Unless it was intended to defend the principle of free trade in shipping, a principle which, as we have noted, has been honoured more in the breach than the observance.[43] The same does not apply to liner shipping. In-so-far as assistance is granted to liners, which is often the case, the impact on a particular trade and on the foreign vessels securing the trade, which is usually organised in conferences, may be very serious.[44] It is this specific impact which is more likely to provoke retaliation, rather than the negligible general impact on world shipping.

Counter-measures could take a variety of forms, ranging from trade sanctions to measures aimed directly at the national fleet of the countries giving the subsidies or adopting cargo-reservation.[45] A general embargo on imports from the discriminating country, or an embargo limited to imports carried in that country's national flag ships, penal tariff rates and excessive taxes on imports, are examples of trade sanctions and, therefore, the probable economic consequences of the traditional restrictive approach to establishing national fleets.[46] Among the other measures employed are denial of the use of ports to ships of the discriminating flags or barring of these ships from the carriage of exports and penal port or other dues.[47] Otherwise the shipping conferences can do very little by way of retaliation and all these measures can be imposed only through government intervention in favour of their own national fleet.

The following example illustrates this point and provides further examples of retaliation. In 1959 the FMC (then the FMB) imposed an equalising fee on all goods shipped from the US to Ecuador in Ecuadorian vessels, in order to counter the discriminatory consular fees charged by Ecuador on foreign ships.[48] Furthermore, where the ships of aid-receiving countries world, under US practice, have been entitled to carry 50% of the cargoes concerned, permission to carry this percentage was refused in the case where the aid-receiving countries practised flag discrimination on US and other foreign flags.[49] It is worth noting here that retaliation, as used in this context, is not necessarily the same as an *embargo*. The former, as an economic consequence of the use of the traditional restrictive measures, is a unilateral act by a state for commercial reasons, whereas the latter may involve a group of countries with the aim of achieving a political objective.[50]

2.3 Wider economic consequence of aiding national fleets

A report submitted for the Board of the Royal Netherlands Shipowners Association (RNSA) does not exclude the possibility of the use of cargo preferances even by the TMNS.[51] Flag discrimination, as already indicated, dates from the end of World War II, but since then it has continually taken more serious forms.[52] It will, with conditions remaining as they are, not only be applied in the near future by more countries, which will probably include the so-called TMNS, but also by groups of other countries.[53] We noted that cargo reservation is most effectively directed against those countries whose national fleets already carry a large proportion of their trade[54] and which largely operate in cross trades. These countries consist mainly of the TMNS.[55] The use of cargo reservation by some DMNS for purposes of establishing and expanding their national fleets is but one manifestation of a larger problem – how to protect and promote a particular economic activity in which the countries concerned are not able to compete on a free trade basis.[56]

The favoured or protected activity varies from country to country; it may be shipping in some DMNS, textiles in the UK, or agriculture in the US.[57] This failure to relate shipping policies to the general corpus of economic policy enables the British to be free traders in the shipping industry but not in agriculture or a wide range of manufactured goods.[58] A possible connection between the protection to the British cotton industry and India's desire to

Table 32. Tonnage laid-up[a]–mid July 1983 (Merchant ships of 300 grt & dwt, and over).

1. By months (1982 and 1983)

	1982			1983		
Mid	No.	grt	dwt	No.	grt	dwt
January	353	14 111 351	26 391 431	1 292	40 657 444	77 168 000
February	370	14 467 304	26 847 600	1 372	41 403 068	78 302 700
March	417	16 312 474	30 636 213	1 460	43 273 474	81 621 037
April	449	18 581 489	35 181 484	1 460	43 858 328	82 908 948
May	515	20 754 534	39 399 195	1 430	44 377 782	84 116 633
June	568	24 120 134	46 387 205	1 416	44 605 895	84 832 726
July	624	25 437 346	49 122 489	1 403	45 092 581	85 754 693
August	757	29 103 939	56 172 954			
September	887	32 041 906	61 506 369			
October	1 071	35 292 715	67 260 123			
November	1 184	37 545 656	71 485 992			
December	1 247	38 815 178	73 792 737			

2. By flag and ship type

	Total			Liners[b]		Passenger vessels		Ref. vessels	
Flag	No.	grt	dwt	No.	grt	No.	grt	No.	grt
1 Liberia	186	13 135 284	27 401 908	5	34 609	–	–	4	17 939
2 Greece	581	10 604 407	19 474 185	117	888 305	5	39 252	17	90 137
3 Norway	67	5 103 201	9 936 929	3	9 925	2	9 154	–	–
4 UK	61	3 208 970	5 947 856	14	121 136	–	–	–	–
5 Italy	45	1 719 971	3 092 645	14	118 460	2	56 221	1	5 496

Flag	Total			Liners[b]		Passenger vessels		Ref. vessels	
	No.	grt	dwt	No.	grt	No.	grt	No.	grt
6 US	73	1 659 415	2 456 413	43	544 810	1	14 812	–	–
7 Panama	103	1 609 216	2 774 131	21	138 680	6	91 897	6	15 809
8 Denmark	19	1 150 132	2 315 188	2	19 246	–	–	–	–
9 France	12	1 139 602	2 130 460	3	21 836	–	–	–	–
10 Spain	27	774 010	1 469 544	10	34 498	–	–	2	3 245
11 Japan	11	634 924	1 203 081	–	–	–	–	2	3 709
12 Saudi Arabia	4	471 182	945 848	1	9 481	–	–	–	–
13 Iraq	4	371 270	736 314	2	19 837	–	–	–	–
14 FR of Germany	6	355 255	607 759	1	25 558	–	–	–	–
15 Netherlands	15	335 440	652 330	2	13 294	–	–	–	–
16 Kuwait	7	313 589	575 789	4	32 889	1	6 471	–	–
17 Others	182	2 506 713	4 034 313	79	622 877	2	8 405	10	62 783
Total									
July 1983	1 403	45 092 581	85 754 693	321	2 655 441	19	226 212	42	199 118
				(dwt	3 508 198)	(dwt	105 138)	(dwt	231 602)
June 1983	1 416	44 605 895	84 932 726	337	2 766 992	19	248 038	28	97 578
				(dwt	3 660 831)	(dwt	113 896)	(dwt	109 758)
July 1982	624	25 437 346	49 122 489	135	948 188	21	249 056	11	49 216
				(dwt	1 278 258)	(dwt	119 547)	(dwt	60 539)

[a] Sea-going cargo and/or passenger carrying vessels only.
[b] Including container ships and ro-ro vessels.

Source: Shipping Statistics, Institute of Shipping Economics, Bremen, August 1983, p. 16.

establish a national maritime fleet was not perceived. A generic analysis might reveal that discrimination in favour of India's shipping has the same effect as a retaliatory tariff in putting India onto a higher community indifference cuve than that to which British import quotas on cotton goods consigned her.[59] In the field of primary commodities and manufactures, tariff and non-tariff barriers and other restrictions of various kinds constitute obstacles to exports from the DMNS.[60]

The general tendency among industrialised TMNS is to protect the domestic production of textile fabrics. The textile industry has long been the sick man of the manufacturing sector in many of these countries. At the same time its flexible character, the relative simplicity of the technological process, and the labour intensiveness of its manufacture make the textile industry a candidate for becoming the first manufacturing export industry in many DMNS.[61] Correspondingly, the main effect of the all-round protection of textile fabrics in the TMNS is to retard the expansion of exports from the DMNS. In many discussions of the protective effect of tariffs, it is not only the nominal rate of duty which is relevant. The appropriate basis for assessing the restrictive effect of a tariff structure on trade is provided by the effective rate of protection of the productive process, i.e. of values added, in the process.[62]

The economic effect of restrictive shipping practices is the same as that of tariffs generally. The distinction between the nominal protection and effective protection assumes a greater significance in view of the fact that the typical tariff of the TMNS escalates by each stage of production, i.e. the rate of duty rises from raw materials to semi-manufacture and from semi-manufactures to finished goods.[63] There is a correlation between the tariffs of the TMNS and the RSPS of the DMNS. These tariff structures consequently impose especially heavy barriers on the relatively low cost labour intensive goods that the DMNS are most likely to export, i.e. goods in the production of which many DMNS have a comparative advantage.[64] In these circumstances, therefore, some DMNS adversely affected by the tariff and non-tariff restrictions, which prevent them from specialising in what would have been their best economic activity under a free-trade system, took recourse to other activities, notably shipping.[65]

For this purpose they resorted to restrictive practices and state aid of a similar kind to those by which the TMNS had denied to them their best form of activity. This has, however, not been the DMNS' sole motivation.[66] The rationale for assistance by the DMNS to national fleets, was also to lessen the distortion caused by protection for other industries, in the TMNS. In other words, it is in addition to and not as a substitute for their basic *infant industry* argument.[67] Shipping, unlike other industries, does not require any specific natural resource endowment, and some DMNS, in the long run, may have a comparative advantage in this field and may develop it as a viable industry, particularly as a major earner of foreign exchange, as did some of the TMNS in the past.[68]

3. Effects of discriminations on various groups and nations

The broad implications of the two principal forms of assistance – subsidies and reservations – have their advantages and disadvantages. The specific application of these two methods of support seems to depend on the economic circumstances prevailing in a particular country at a given time.[69] Many of the present established large national fleets of the TMNS have benefitted from the two principal types of assistance at one stage or another. Admittedly, to a certain extent, subsidies result in fewer distortions than does reservation, but it does not necessarily follow that only subsidies should be used as the method of assistance.[70] Given the budgetory and administrative constraints, a DMN seeking to establish a national fleet on the basis of subsidies may find it difficult, if not impossible, to raise enough additional revenue for subsidies. Whereas through reservation the cost is dispersed over the economy as a whole, without any need to collect additional taxes, or to forego existing public expenditures.[71]

The use of subsidies as a method of assistance in some major TMNS is attributable partly to the developed nature of the economy and to a flexible fiscal and administrative system, and partly to the nature of their shipping industry, which is export biased rather than based on import substitution.[72] Perhaps it was the recognition of some of these economic realities in the DMNS which led to the following observations.[73] In the above RNSA report, it is stated that:

> 'Reasonable aspirations with regard to shipping cannot be denied the developing countries . . . If the right could be acknowledged for developing countries to reserve a certain percentage of the cargo volume for the national flag[74] these countries could undertake to stop discrimination or, if applicable, to withhold no more of their cargo volume from the free market than has been agreed upon.'[75]

Let us, return to the economic consequences, on states and social groups, of subsidies and reservation.[76] These types of discrimination do not necessarily lead to measures that are either price-raising or cost-reducing for the country's own national fleets.[77] They have been introduced to maintain or develop the national fleet. This should, in practice, presuppose that the national fleet is not in need of a large income or a smaller expenditure. The larger gross profit that may be obtained through such assistance is a consequence of the monopolistic position the home shipowners may have acquired, which has granted them the right to take higher freights, doubtless with the unofficial approval of their governments,[78] when the shipowners in this way gain a monopolistic protection, it is possible that they are not as cost-conscious as before and consequently their efficiency may be less as their costs rise.

Expenditure is naturally connected with the full use of capacity.[79] During a boom period, for instance, the home flag ships would probably be well used, and protectionist measures by the state would, therefore, not be very important, if of any value at all. In times of depression on the other hand, such measures can be of very considerable importance because the shipowners will obtain greater incomes than they would otherwise.[80] In reality these large receipts can be decisive for the continued existence of the national fleet. According to these basic rules one would imagine such growth of income could support the national fleet in the discriminating country.[81] The national fleets of the foreign nations, which operate in the market in question, fare otherwise. As a result of their exclusion from that part of the market which has been taken over by the discriminating country, competition will become more severe in the remaining part of the market, and also in the world market.[82]

Table 33. Tonnage broken-up[a]–June 1983 (merchant ships of 300 grt & dwt and over).

1. By months (1982 and 1983)

	1982			1983		
Month	No.	grt	dwt	No.	grt	dwt
January	96	1 183 903	2 153 942	115	1 356 609	2 354 003
February	77	2 149 462	4 180 965	117	1 918 721	3 500 180
March	78	1 216 603	2 229 737	108	1 912 889	3 709 113
April	117	2 263 664	4 228 111	135	2 510 394	4 727 076
May	93	981 647	1 765 078	111	1 970 175	3 724 802
June	94	1 310 800	2 421 509	123	1 145 765	1 997 653
July	71	1 568 737	2 907 638			
August	48	1 158 855	2 177 464			
September	111	970 144	1 610 760			
October	113	2 150 980	4 016 293			
November	87	1 766 451	3 231 659			
December	97	964 245	1 666 557			

2. By flag and ship type[b]

	Total			Liners[c]		Passenger vessels		Refridgerated vessels[d]	
Flag	No.	grt	dwt	No.	grt	No.	grt	No.	grt
1 Panama	25	173 161	298 080	9	61 685	–	–	–	–
2 Netherlands	1	127 502	253 411	–	–	–	–	–	–
3 South Korea	2	107 894	214 941	–	–	–	–	–	–
4 Greece	12	107 877	194 892	2	18 965	1	3 743	1	3 104
5 Liberia	4	99 231	1 187 181	1	7 392	–	–	–	–

Flag	Total			Liners[c]		Passenger vessels		Refridgerated vessels[d]	
	No.	grt	dwt	No.	grt	No.	grt	No.	grt
6 Italy	4	78 285	122 343	–	–	1	8 604	–	–
7 Mexico	2	68 119	–	–	–	–	–	–	–
8 US	5	61 009	105 272	–	–	–	–	–	–
9 Brazil	1	58 610	107 254	–	–	–	–	–	–
10 Japan	8	47 485	70 264	–	–	–	–	1	7 520
11 Indonesia	19	34 611	49 533	1	8 775	–	–	–	–
12 USSR	6	26 486	33 093	1	8 590	–	–	1	1 676
13 Saudi Arabia	3	25 959	39 985	2	17 343	–	–	–	–
14 Cyprus	4	19 191	29 223	–	–	–	–	–	–
15 Taiwan	2	14 099	20 629	1	9 489	–	–	1	4 610
16 Peru	1	12 649	19 653	–	–	–	–	–	–
17 Others	24	83 597	112 416	11	61 179	–	–	1	3 739
Total									
June 1983	123	1 145 765	1 997 653	28	193 418	2	12 347	5	20 649
				(dwt	269 167)	(dwt	9 206)	(dwt	22 540)
May 1983	111	1 970 175	3 724 802	30	195 408	–	–	4	30 659
				(dwt	272 052)	–	–	(dwt	41 288)
June 1982	94	1 310 800	2 421 509	30	191 311	1	6 807	–	–
				(dwt	264 209)	(dwt	1 228)	–	–

[a] Sea-going cargo and/or passenger carrying vessels only.
[b] Excluding combined carriers, including LNG/LPG and chemical tankers.
[c] Including container ships and ro-ro vessels.
[d] Including tramps.

Note: Including ship sales for breaking and ship losses

Source: Shipping Statistics, Institute of Shipping Economics, Bremen, August 1983, p. 18.

If a market trade boom prevails within a given trading area, the reduced income effect should not be very great for the foreign national fleets concerned.[83] On the other hand, it can happen during a market slump period, that not even a market reduction in the freight rate brings about any noticeable increase of cargo.[84] To the extent that the working costs cannot be expected to be covered within a fairly short time, the foreign national fleets that are affected by the discrimination face the possibility of having to take their ships out of traffic.[85] The restrictive practices therefore, make the market situation akin to monopolistic or imperfect competition, i.e. the condition prevailing in a market in which one or more buyers or sellers are large enough to affect the price of goods and services traded.

3.1 Increase in domestic gross profit

Discriminatory measures also have the tendency to increase the gross profit of the shipowners in the home as against foreign markets. The traffic which, by reason of this discrimination, has been reserved for the country's own national fleets, will form a market where competition is conceivable, but probably at a higher price level than in the rest of the freight market.[86] If we continue to look at the consequences for other groups of the community involved, it is evident that seamen – the word being taken in its widest sense – in the discriminating country have better prospects of higher wages.[87] This would probably be noticeable in the freights that one quoted. The consumers in the discriminating country would finally have to bear these increased expenses.[88]

For the maritime nations that are subject to the discrimination, the reverse is to be expected. During times of depression the shippers would pay smaller freights and the crews would have a smaller chance of a rise in wages, while at the same time consumers would have lower prices to the extent that the lower freights are passed on.[89] Nations that have no national fleets that are directly affected by the trade that is subjected to the discrimination, would thus be able to pay for the transport of their goods on a market that is more competitive in principle and would consequently pay lower freights.[90] On the other hand, there are discriminatory measures that increase the gross profits of the shipowners in the home country at the expense of the foreign shipowners. Some of the discriminatory measures dealt with in Part III are based on decreases which are intended to influence the gross profits of the shipowners, even though they may do so.[91]

The measures of discrimination dealt with in Part II were intended to change the relation between home and foreign ships which ply a certain trade.[92] The alteration is made by way of a change in the relative gross profits of home and foreign national fleets. Just to remind ourselves these measures can be divided into the following groups.[93]

(a) Expenditure that affects foreign vessels;
(b) Expenditure that affects cargo that is carried by foreign vessels; and
(c) Subsidies to the country's own national fleets.[94]

As indicated in Part II of this survey, included in the expenditures that affects foreign vessels are, the treatment of ships in port, which involves discrimination: in tonnage measurement, in consular fees, in light-house dues, in pilot fees and taxes on freight incomes of foreign national fleets, to mention but a few.

Table 34. Shipping and seaborne trade: World casualty returns (ships of 500 tons gross & over).

1. Reported total losses by months (1982 and 1983)

	1982			1983		
Month	No.	grt	1000[a] dwt	No.	grt	1000[a] dwt
January	18	132 134	199	23	174 791	310
February	16	69 984	99	16	94 273	152
March	21	187 303	333	24	162 894	275
April	22	138 719	215	23	91 979	130
May	20	109 063	191	12	116 967	195
June	17	58 645	84			
July	26	99 036	128			
August	23	201 862	357			
September	16	46 871	73			
October	21	207 595	316			
November	21	110 900	182			
December	15	98 100	166			
Jan.–Dec.	236	1 460 212	2343			

2. Total losses by nature of casualty

Nature of casualty	October	November	December	January	February	March	April	May
Weather damage	2	2	2	5	3	6	6	3
Founderings & abandonments	3	5	5	7	2	3	3	–
Strandings	6	5	3	3	4	1	4	2
Collisions	1	1	1	–	–	1	1	1
Contact damage	–	2	–	1	3	–	1	–
Fires and explosions	9	3	3	6	3	9	8	6
Missing	–	–	–	–	–	–	–	–
Damage to machinery etc.	–	2	1	–	–	1	–	–
Other casualties	–	1	–	1	1	3	–	–
Total	21	21	15	23	16	24	23	12

[a] Dwt partly calculated by Institute of Shipping Economics, Bremen.
Source: Shipping Statistics, Institute of Shipping Economics, Bremen, August 1983, p. 20.

Included in expenditure that affects cargo carried by foreign vessels are discrimination on railway tariff rates and concerning duties.[95] And, finally, under subsidies to the country's own national fleets are included building subsidies, operating subsidies, low interest loans, ship discarding subsidies, mortgage guarantees, state charters, duty free foreign purchase, free writing-off of ships, postal contracts and admiralty contracts.[96] Closely associated with these are the economic consequences for countries and sections of the country, and the national economy in general.[97] Although aimed against foreign nationals, discrimination can, and does, affect various sections of the community as well as the national economy of the discriminating home country.[98]

3.2 Effects on sections of the economy of the country

The factors that should be observed in dealing with the economic consequences of flag discrimination are four-fold.[99] First, whether it is expenditure-reducing and consequently income-increasing for the home country,[100] or whether it is expenditure-increasing and consequently income-reducing for other countries; here it is a question of reversed conditions between the two groups.[101] Secondly, whether the costs affected are fixed[102] or variable.[103] Thirdly, whether the economic situation is good or bad.[104] Fourthly, and lastly, whether the groups that are affected through the shipowners by the flag discrimination are shipowners,[105] crews,[106] consumers,[107] municipalities or states.[108] Normally the municipalities and states are treated as one group (the community) as reactions by these institutions finally influence consumers.[109]

The effects on the shipowners and consumers, will be dealt with in detail below. The discussion which follows on the economic consequences to the states themselves, and sections of the community in these countries, is based on the following diagram (Figure 3), referring to the home country's economy.[110] The economy of foreign countries is on the whole a reverse of this picture. In order not to complicate the diagram, and thereby reduce its clarity, the fluctuating items, i.e. fixed or variable costs,[111] and a good or bad economic situation, have not been included. Furthermore, the conditions applicable to the diagram are: a given demand, and competition between home and foreign ships.[112] With the diagram, it will be easier to explain the connection between the different units in the following paragraph.

It will be apparent from the diagram and the foregoing paragraph[113] that, for the sake of simplicity, one can count on a single (average) freight level for the traffic to and from the discriminating country.[114] The conclusions to be drawn are, first, that the incomes per unit performed tend to be the same in a maket where there is competition.[115] Gross profit is the difference between the total revenues and expenditures of a ship.[116] Secondly, the gross profits of the home ships increase by reason of the freight level rising for transport to and from the country, by the home shipowners being given incomes over and above the freight itself, or by the expenditures of the country's own shipowners being reduced.[117] Owing to the varying gross profits the proportion between home and foreign ships in traffic to and from the home country is altered.[118]

Thirdly, direct and indirect measures concerning ships of foreign countries and ships of the home country refer to both sides of what is in principle the same matter. These component groups are, therefore, identical, with the exception, of course, of income-increasing, or price-reducing items of a subventional character, which are only to be found under the heading: ships of own country.[119] Fourthly, and lastly, other variables of the shipping companies, i.e. fixed and variable costs, are not included in the diagram, nor is the distinction between good and bad economic situations.[120] These two variable units will be included in the following discussions on the economic consequences to the shipowners, the community and consumers.

3.3 The economic consequences to shipowners

It is also apparent from the diagram that when the government of a country wishes to increase the possibilities of employment[121] for its national fleet in a

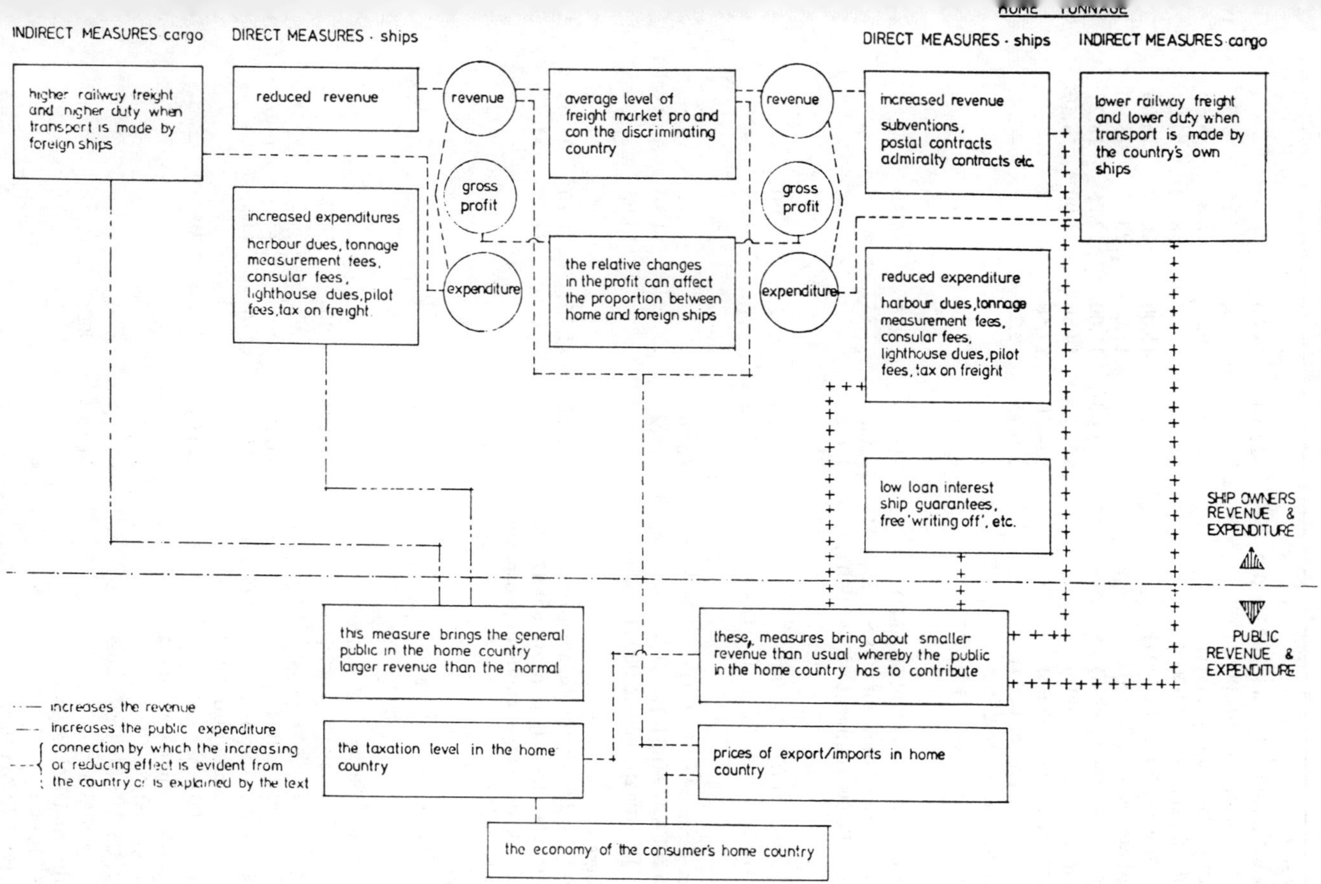

INDIRECT MEASURES cargo
DIRECT MEASURES · ships
DIRECT MEASURES · ships
INDIRECT MEASURES cargo
higher railway freight and higher duty when transport is made by foreign ships
reduced revenue
increased expenditures
harbour dues, tonnage measurement fees, consular fees, lighthouse dues, pilot fees, tax on freight.
revenue
gross profit
expenditure
average level of freight market pro and con the discriminating country
the relative changes in the profit can affect the proportion between home and foreign ships
revenue
gross profit
expenditure
increased revenue
subventions, postal contracts admiralty contracts etc.
reduced expenditure
harbour dues, tonnage measurement fees, consular fees, lighthouse dues, pilot fees, tax on freight
low loan interest ship guarantees, free 'writing off', etc.
lower railway freight and lower duty when transport is made by the country's own ships
SHIP OWNERS REVENUE & EXPENDITURE
PUBLIC REVENUE & EXPENDITURE
this measure brings the general public in the home country larger revenue than the normal
these measures bring about smaller revenue than usual whereby the public in the home country has to contribute
the taxation level in the home country
prices of export/imports in home country
the economy of the consumer's home country
increases the revenue
increases the public expenditure
connection by which the increasing or reducing effect is evident from the country or is explained by the text

Figure 3.

Table 35. Freight rate comparison in leading trades, 2nd quarter 1982 and 1983.

	2nd quarter 1982		2nd quarter 1983	
	Highest	Lowest	Highest	Lowest
Heavy grain				
Gt Lakes-Holland/Belgium (abt 25 000 t)	$22.50	18.00	–	–
US Gulf-Holland (abt 40 000 t)	$–	–	7.75	7.75
US Gulf-Holland (abt 60 000 t)	$12.00	8.00	8.85	8.50
US Gulf-Holland (70–75 000 t)	$12.25	6.00	8.50	7.00
US Gulf-Denmark (abt 14 000 t)	$20.25	15.00	16.50	15.00
US Gulf-Mexico (abt 20 000 t)	$–	15.05	23.00	18.00
US Gulf-Japan (abt 30 000 t)	$24.00	17.00	22.25	18.25
US Gulf-Japan (abt 50 000 t)	$21.75	14.50	21.00	14.50
US Gulf-China (abt 30 000 t)	$34.50	27.50	–	–
N Pacific-Japan (abt 50 000 t)	$10.75	9.25	–	–
N Pacific-S Korea (abt 25 000 t)	$–	–	–	–
S Africa-three Japan (abt 14 000 t)	$20.75	18.25	–	–
Coal				
Hampton Roads-Japan (abt 50 000 t)	$19.60	12.75	17.50	12.35
Hampton Roads-Continent (abt 50–55 000 t)	$10.50	7.85	–	–
Hampton Roads-Continent (80–85 000 t)	$ 6.25	–	–	–
Ore				
Brazil-Continent (60–80 000 t)	$ 6.80	6.36	6.00	–
Monrovia-Continent (60–80 000 t)	$ 5.75	4.30	4.65	–
Sugar				
Durban-Japan (abt 15 000 t)	$22.00	–	–	–
Mauritius-UK (29 ft 3 in)	£14.25	–	14.50	13.65
Maceio-US Atlantic (abt 15 000 t)	$–	–	14.95	–
Fertilisers				
Aqaba-WC India (phosphate, abt 10 000 t)	$12.25	11.25	11.10	11.00
Casablanca-WC India (phospahte, abt 12 000 t)	–	–	24.75	–
US Gulf-WC India (di-ammonium phosphate, abt 14 000 t)	$–	–	–	–
Cement				
N Korea-EC India (abt 13 000 t)	$24.75	–	–	–
Time charter				
UK/Cont, trip Persian Gulf/Red Sea (15–16 000 t, 14–15 knots, daily rate)	$5600	4300	5825	–
UK/Cont, trip Persian Gulf/Red Sea (25–27 000 t, geared)	$8250	–	–	–
Europe, Great Lakes round, (26–27 000 t)	$6500	4750	4400	–
Europe, US Atlantic/Gulf round, (25–30 000 t)	$4750	–	–	–
Europe, US Atlantic/Gulf round, (35–40 000 t)	$6.33	–	–	–
Europe, US Atlantic/Gulf round, (50–60 000 t)	$4.19	3.82	–	–
US Gulf, trip UK/Cont/Med, (25–30 000 t)	$–	–	–	–
Brazil, trip UK/Cont/Med, (15–25 000 t)	$4900	4200	–	–
Japan, Pacific/Australia round, (27–33 000 t)	$4750	–	4750	3700

Table 35. (Cont.)

	2nd quarter 1982		2nd quarter 1983	
	Highest	Lowest	Highest	Lowest
Japan, Pacific/Australia round, (57–63 000 t)	$2.97	–	2.28	–
Far East, trip UK/Cont/Med, (25–30 000 t)	$6.25	4.75	3.40	–
Far East, trip UK/Cont/Med, (70 000 t)	$1.72	–	–	–
Twelve mths' tdg (25–30 000 t)	$–	–	–	–
Twelve mths' tdg (35–40 000 t)	$–	–	–	–
Twelve mths' tdg (50–60 000 t)	$–	–	–	–

Source: Shipping Statistics, Institute of Shipping Economics, Bremen, August 1983, p. 34.

short space of time, it can, in principle, proceed, first, by taking steps to make it possible for home ships to receive higher freights than those of other countries. This can be achieved, for instance, by allowing a lower railway freight on goods carried by home tonnage or by conceding it a lower duty.[122] Secondly, the government can take measures to give the ships of the home country revenues in addition to the freight itself. This can be done, for instance, by operating subsidies and economically advantageous mail-carrying contracts.[123] Thirdly, the discriminating government can take steps to reduce the expenditure of its own ships, for instance, by manipulating the tariffs for tonnage measurements and consular fees. The effect is achieved if the charges for foreign ships are increased to a level higher than for the home ships.[124]

Fourth, and lastly, if the home government manipulates the tariffs for tonnage measurement, consular fees, etc., foreign ships will be placed in an inferior position as regards the variable costs.[125] In a trade boom the demand is so great that the freight which the freight rates would generate would more than cover the difference in charges. In a trade slump, on the other hand, the difference in these charges can have the effect of foreign shipping companies being unable to cover their variable costs.[126] Foreign ships would thereby be induced to leave the particular market in question, as bad economic conditions have a tendency to spread on such an international market as shipping.[127] The prospects are poor even within the sphere of other transport, which as a consequence enhances the risk of selling tonnage or laying up. Nevertheless, it would be the oldest ships having the most unfavourable operation costs that would run the greatest risks.[128]

It should be emphasized that one can thus distinguish between two main types of discriminatory measures by dividing them into variable costs and fixed costs; that is, those measures that directly influence employment during a trade slump, and those long-term measures which only give support without in any way affecting employment in times of trade slump.[129] Far-sighted supporting measures are those which only affect the capital costs of the ships.[130] They cannot be expected to affect the employment of the country's ships in the short term, but in the long term they can render support and help to develop the national fleet.[131] Examples of such measures are low-rates of interest, guarantees for loans, free writing off, admiralty contracts and ship subsidies of an initial nature. When the income of the national fleets is increased by such measures, or its costs are reduced, it is the fixed costs and the fixed incomes that are affected.[132]

Foreign ships that compete on the market will be placed in a worse situation in this respect. On the other hand, the connection between running costs and running incomes for home and foreign ships does not change.[133] The connection between gross profits is unaltered within the period of time during which the calculation only includes running incomes and expenditures.[134] These long-running supporting measures act in such a way that during good as well as bad times, the national fleet has larger incomes or lower expenditures than corresponding foreign ships.[135] Viewed in the long term the profitability becomes greater, which stimulates the procuring of ships. This is also promoted through the financing being made easier.[136] On the other hand, they do not lead to the country's ships being better employed during a trade slump than they would otherwise have been. The same argument can be extended to the economic consequences to the community and consumers.[137]

3.4 Economic consequences to the community and consumers

In Figure 3 a line reference has been made between expenditure and revenue. This reference is applicable when the revenue of the national fleet increases through the subsidies, and, therefore, its employees will draw attention to the increased scope for higher wages.[138] Correspondingly, the employees in the discriminated country may consider that there is reduced scope for higher wages even if they do not consider a reduction in wages to be necessary.[139] It appears from what has been said that foreign ships are affected less by supporting measures that do not concern variable incomes and expenses.[140] Their competitive powers are certainly reduced, but this happens slowly and is not very apparent. Measures of a discriminatory nature that affect variable expenses and incomes can, on the other hand, be very severe during a trade slump. The affected shipowners, therefore strongly oppose this type of discrimination.[141]

In connection with the traditional subventions made to the national fleet, such as guarantees of ship mortgages, the community has to shoulder increased expenditure which in the end has to be borne by the consumers in the form of taxes.[142] When it comes to discrimination against foreign ships in the form of high railway tariffs, duties, harbour dues, etc., the general public benefits by the corresponding income and this has a reducing effect on taxes.[143] At the same time, however, the consumers will, through the increased prices of goods, have to carry the increased freights that are the result of the subventions.[144] From the consumers' point of view the expenditure on transport which affects them will remain unchanged. This applies to transportations that are made by foreign ships.[145] The national fleet will be able to increase their freights to a little below or to the same level as these of the competing foreign flags. This portion is carried by the consumers, via the goods. The consumers will, in the end, have to pay the increased revenue that benefits the national fleet.[146]

And, finally, the discriminating country should, of course, try to carry through its measures in such a way as to make them as effective as possible. The costs of the discriminating organisation should also be absorbed. In endeavouring to further the interests of the national fleet in the long run[147] there are measures that do not at the same time affect employment during a trade slump and measures that have this effect.[148] Measures that only further the development in the long run without any effect on employment naturally involve a direct rise in prices for the economy of the country, since the same transportations could otherwise have been carried out more cheaply by foreign ships.[149]

It is possible that by some measures a country can build up a national maritime fleet of its own which, after some time, can exist without support.[150] There are two principal ways of financing the discriminations. On the other hand, the costs can be borne by the tax payers[151] of the country with an unaltered low transport charge, and on the other hand, the costs can be paid by the community through higher transport charges, whereby sometimes the state can also benefit by way of tax revenues.[152]

Notes

1. We do not go into statistical details which are best left to maritime and transport economists.
2. Alson, T. F., 'Cargo preference and the American merchant marine', *Law & Contemp. Prob.,* 1968, Vol. 25, pp. 82–105.
3. Patton, J. *et al.*, 'Cargo preferences and flag discrimination in international shipping', *Geo. Wash L. Rev.,* 1965, Dec., pp. 257–87.
4. Mund, V., *Government and Business,* NY, 1950.
5. Cf. opportunity or alternative cost (note 7 below).
6. In the *Report of Manufactures,* Alexander Hamilton stated that such industries should be protected by tariff until they have had a chance to grow.
7. Fellner, W., *Modern Economic Analysis,* NY, 1960, pp. 105–05.
8. Taussig, F. W., *Some Aspects of the Tariff Question,* HUF, 1931, pp. 100–101.
9. For definition of tramps see the Glossary at the end.
10. Subsidies are not discriminations and are therefore, acceptable.
11. For definition of overtonnaging see Glossary.
12. As in a slump or recession; see also *National Bureau of Economic Research.*
13. Moore, G. H., (ed.) *Business Cycle Indicators,* Princeton, NY, p. 85.
14. See Hanson, D. P., 'Regulation of shipping industry: an economic analysis of need for reform', *Law & Pol in Inter. Bus.,* 1980, Vol. 12, No. 4, pp. 973–80.
15. US Staff Joint Econ. Comm. 89th Cong., 2nd Sess. *Report on Discriminatory Ocean Freight Rates and the Balance of Payments* 2–3 (Comm. Print 1966).
16. Cf. *Monopoly Problems in Regulated Industries: Hearings Before the Subcommittee on Antitrust of the House Committee on the Judiciary,* 86th Cong., 1st Sess., pt. 1, v., at 4930, 1959.
17. See also *Steamship Conference Study: Hearings Before the Special Subcommittee on Steamship Conferences of the House Committee on Merchant Marines and Fisheries, ibid,* pt. 2, at 465.
18. Knudsen, O., *Issues in International Shipping,* pp. 73–705.
19. Bennathan E. & Walter, *Revenue Pooling Cartels,* Oxford Economic Papers, 1969.
20. Chinitz, B., 'An analysis of ocean liner freight rates', *Econometrica,* 1956, p. 351.
21. Brown, R. T., *Transport and the Economic Integration of South America, supra.*
22. Chinitz, B., *Rate Discrimination in Ocean Transportation,* Ph.D. Dissertation, Harvard University, April 1956.
23. OEEC *Maritime Transport,* 1954, para. 60, p. 51.
24. *Ibid.*, para. 61.
25. *Zosen,* 1979, Vol. 24, No. 3, June pp. 14–15.
26. OECD *Maritime Transport,* 1963, para. 124, p. 42.

27. OEEC *Maritime Transport,* 1956, para. 83, p. 63.
28. Barcello, J. J., 'Subsidies and countervailing duties analysis and proposal', *Law & Pol Inter Bus.,* 1977, Vol. 9, pp. 779–853.
29. OEEC *Maritime Transport,* 1956, para. 84, pp. 63–64.
30. Deakin, B., (ed.) 'Ocean shipping and freight rates and developing countries', *Proceedings of UNCTAD,* Geneva, March 23–June 16, 1964, Vol. V, NY.
31. Zamora, S., 'Rate regulation in ocean transport, developing countries confront liner conferences', *Cal L Rev.,* 1971, Vol. 59, pp. 1299–1332.
32. Lebluhm, D. J., 'Practising CIF & FOB today', *Eur. Tran. Law.* Vol. 16, No. 1, pp. 24–35.
33. UNCTAD *Reprive for Cross-Traders, a Note.*
34. Glower, R. W. & Harris, J. R., *Puerto Rican Shipping and the US Maritime Laws,* 1965, p. 74–77.
35. Deakin, B., *supra.*
36. Escarpenter, C., *The Economics of International Ocean Transport,* 1965. p. 61.
37. UNCTAD, Doc. No. TD/B/C.4/36.
38. Ferguson, A. R. *et al., The Economic Value of the US Merchant Marine,* 1961, p. 103.
39. UNCTAD, Doc. No. TD/B/C.4/42.
40. UNCTAD, Doc. No. TD/B/C.4/79.
41. Gorter, W., *US Shipping Policy,* NY, 1956, p. 192.
42. UNCTAD, Doc. No. TD/B/C.4/75.
43. Viner, J., *International Trade & Economic Development,* OUP, 1953.
44. Allen, W. R. & Allen, C. L., *Foreign Trade and Finance,* 1959, p. 100.
45. *Covenant of the League of Nations,* Art. 16; *UN Charter,* Art. 41.
46. Bonsal, *OAS Recommends Further Economic Action Regarding Dominican Republic,* Dept. of State Bulletin, Feb. 20, 1961, pp. 273–76.
47. See also texts to *Sanctions Flag Discriminations.*
48. Patton, J. R. & Schornhorst, *supra,* at 280.
49. *Ibid.,* at pp. 262, 285–286 for the types of cargoes in question.
50. *Ibid.,* pp. 268–270.
51. UNCTAD, Doc. No. TD/B/C.4/78.
52. OEEC *Maritime Transport,* 1954, Part VII, para 82, at p. 63.
53. *Ibid.,* pp. 53–54.
54. *Ibid.,* paras. 65–69.
55. For definition of cross-trading, see Glossary.
56. OECD *Maritime Transport,* 196, para. 130, p. 39.
57. Ellsworth, P. T., *The International Economy,* NY, 1958, p. 88.
58. Kindleberger, C. P., *International Economics,* 1958.
59. Kellough, H. B. & Kellough, L. M., *Economics of International Trade,* 1948, NY, p. 5.
60. US Tariff Commission, *US Import Duties.*
61. Grossman, W. L., *Ocean Freight Rates,* NY, 1956.
62. Wasserman, U., 'Synthetics the challenge of: V. Lawrie Oils', *JWTL,* 1973, Jan–Feb, Vol. 7, No. 1, p. 64.
63. Rom, M., 'Tariff quota, the', *op. cit.,* No. 4, July–Aug. p. 421.
64. Ricardo, D., *Principles of Political Economy and Taxation,* NY, 1917, Chap. 7.
65. Haberler, G., *The Theory of International Trade,* NY, 1950.
66. Marx, D., *International Shipping Cartels, supra.*
67. Vanagas, A. H., pp. 37–64 of Gross, *Advances in Maritime Economics.*
68. Cf. *Journal of Industrial Economics,* Vol. XIII, No. 2, March 1965.
69. Kopanitsas, D. E. in *Journal of the Royal Statistical Society* Series A, Vol. 121, 1958.
70. Cargo preference and flag discrimination are alternatives.
71. Wijkham, P. M., 'Effects of cargo reservation: a review of UNCTAD'S code', *Marine Policy,* Vol. 4, No. 4, Oct. 1980, pp. 271–90.
72. US Chamber of Commerce, *An Introduction to Doing Import and Export Business,* Washington DC, 1962.
73. Supposedly the basis of the UNCTAD Code for Liners Article 2(4).
74. See also Note 78 *Harv. L. Rev.* 635, at 636–637, 1965.

75. Henell, O., *Flag Discrimination, Purposes, Motives and Economic Consequences,* p. 41.
76. Lund, B., *Cargo Preference Systems and International Shipping & Trade,* 1955, p. 17.
77. OECD *Maritime Transport,* 1961, p. 60.
78. Hegh, L., *Discriminations in International Shipping,* 1955, p. 6.
79. OECD *Maritime Transport* 1961, *supra.*
80. See Part III of this Study for details.
81. *Ibid.*
82. See also Part II.
83. *Ibid.*
84. *Ibid.*
85. Goss, R. O., 'The regulation of international transport by sea', *The World Today,* October 1965.
86. Lewis, W. A., 'Notes on the economics of loyalty', *Econometrica,* Feb. 1942.
87. Marshall, A., *Industry and Trade,* London, 1966, pp. 55.
88. Sturmey, S. G., *British Shipping and World Trade, supra,* pp. 202–3.
89. Goss, R. O., 'US legislation and the foreign shipowners', *Journal of Industrial Economics,* Nov. 1963.
90. Hyde, F. E. *et al., Shipping Enterprise and Management,* 1830–1939.
91. Cf. McLachlan, D. L., *Yorkshire Bulletin of Economics and Social Research,* June 1980.
92. US Congress, *Discriminatory Ocean Freight Rates & BOP, supra.*
93. Sturmey, S. G., *National Shipping Policies, supra.*
94. HMSO Imperial Shipping Committee, *British Shipping in the Orient, op. cit.*
95. Hyde, F. E., *Blue Funnel,* Liverpool, 1957.
96. McLachlan, D. L., *Scottish Bulletin of Political Economy,* Dec. 1963.
97. Sturmey on the *Pricing of Tramp Ships Freight Service,* Bergen, 1965.
98. UN, *Study of Latin American Trade,* NY, 1957, Chap. VI.
99. US Congress, *Discriminatory Ocean Freight Rates and the BOP, supra.*
100. Frankel, A. J., 'Impact of cargo sharing on US trade', *Marine Policy,* Vol. 5, No. 1, Jan. 1981, pp. 23–39.
101. Stigler, G. J., *The Theory of Price,* NY, 1952.
102. National Bureau of Economic Research, *Cost Behaviour and Price,* NY, 1943.
103. Clark, J. B., *The Distribution of Wealth,* NY, 1889.
104. Moore, *Business Cycle Indicators, supra.*
105. Rochdale Report, paras. 390–400, pp. 114–16.
106. *Ibid.,* Chapter 13, paras. 780–883, pp. 212–39.
107. Katona, G., *The Powerful Consumer,* NY, 1960.
108. Keynes, J. M., *The General Theory of Employment, Interest and Money,* NY, 1936, Chapters 8, 9 and 10.
109. Friedman, M., *A Theory of the Consumption Function,* National Bureau of Economic Research, NY, 1955.
110. FMC, *Effectiveness of Steamship Conference Organisation.*
111. Robinson, J., *The Economics of Imperfect Competition,* London, 1933.
112. Marx, D., *supra.*
113. US Dept. of Labour, *Monthly Labour Review.*
114. US Congress, *Bonner Committee,* Washington DC, (GPO), 1959.
115. Groves, H., *Financing Government,* NY, 1954, Chaps. 7–9.
116. Backer, M., (ed.) *Handbook of Modern Accounting Theory,* NY, 1955, pp. 437–40, 443–46.
117. US Fed. Trade Comm., *Quarterly Financial Report for Manufacturers.*
118. Bodenborn, D., *Intermediate Price Theory,* 1961, NY, Chap. 9.
119. Cf. Corden, W. M., 'The maximisation of profit', *Review of Economic Studies,* Vol. XX, No. 3, pp. 181–90.
120. Robinson, C., *Understanding Profits,* NJ, 1961.
121. Larner, A. P., *Economics of Employment,* NY, 1951.
122. Ellsworth, P. T., *The International Economy,* NY, 1958; Kindleberger, *supra.*
123. Koch, G. M., *Current Pricing Behaviour in Liner Shipping,* Bergen, 1968.
124. HMSO, *Royal Commission on Shipping Rings,* CMND, 4668.

125. Thornburn, T., *Supply and Demand of Water Transport,* 1961.
126. Metaxas, B. N., *The Economics of Tramp Shipping,* Chap. 9, pp. 200–28.
127. Lemms, W. A., *Overhead Costs,* London, 1949.
128. Orr, D. & Macavoy, P. M., 'Price strategies to promote cartel stability', *Econometrica,* May 1965.
129. Robertson, D. H., *Economic Fragments,* London, 1931.
130. US Joint Econ. Committee, *Subsidy and Subsidylike Programmes,* 1960.
131. HMSO, *Report on the Freight Rate in the UK-New Zealand Trade,* 1935.
132. Keynes, J. M., *The General Theory of Employment, supra.*
133. Fisher, I. *The Theory of Interest* N.Y. 1950 p. 100.
134. Mennis, E. A., 'Different measures of corporate profits', *Financial Analysis Journal,* Sept.–Oct. 1962.
135. Goode, R., *The Corporation Income Tax,* NY, 1951.
136. Groves, H., *Postwar Taxation and Economic Progress,* NY, 1946.
137. HMSO, *Final Report on the Deferred Rebates System,* CMND. 1802, 1923.
138. Smith, R. C. & Murphy, M. J., *Job Evaluation and Employee Rating,* 1946.
139. Lowden, J. K., *Wage Incentives,* HUP, 1960.
140. Sanklecha, S. N., *Tramp Shipping in India,* Bombay, 1960.
141. E.g., US Anti-trust like the *Sherman Act, Clayton Act,* etc.
142. Samuelson, P. A., *Economics,* 1961, Chaps. 24 & 25.
143. Gordon, M. S., *Barriers to World Trade,* NY, 1941.
144. Heuser, H., *Control of International Trade, supra.*
145. Mikesell, R. F., *Freight Exchange in the Postwar World,* NY, 1954.
146. Taylor, P. E., *The Economics of Public Finance,* NY, 1953, Chap. 20.
147. Groves, H., *Financing Government,* Supra, 1954, Chap. 11.
148. Buehler, A. G., *General Sales Taxation,* NY, 1932.
149. Machlup, F., *The Economics of Sellers' Competition,* 1952.
150. Chamberlain, E. H., *The Theory of Monopolistic Competition,* HUP, 1931.
151. Clark, J. M., *Competition as a Dynamic Process,* 1961.
152. Galbraith, J. K., *American Capitalism: The Theory of Countervailing Power,* Boston, 1962.

Part Five

Resolving the problem: Recommendations

CHAPTER 10

Future prospects for national and international shipping

1. Introduction

The likely outcome of the traditional methods of establishing and developing national fleets would be disastrous for both national and international fleets. First, they raise a conflict of laws situation with countervailing and retaliatory discriminations in international trade.[1] Secondly, the ensuing inefficiency would make maritime transport very expensive – which would be counterproductive – and would not be in the interests of either the TMNS or the DMNS. The initial aims for establishing and/or developing national maritime fleets would, therefore, not have been achieved.[2] Thirdly, this result is bound to disrupt international trade, and international systems, both so interlinked and so dependent on international shipping for their carriage and facilitation respectively. All nations depend on international exchange for their development, some for their very survival.[3]

The fourth, and perhaps the most far reaching and also disastrous consequence would be the total disintegration of international and national fleets as we know them today. This part of the survey concentrates on these likely consequences. A few recommendations as to more rational ways of establishing and/or developing national fleets are introduced.[4] The way things are developing, unless some kind of cooperation between the TMNS and the DMNS can be arranged, on a regional and interregional basis, it appears inconceivable for the foreseeable future that the latter states will be able to acquire a significant stake in the higher technology sectors of the merchant marine industry. The introduction of high technology has added an extra dimension to the already complex and volatile situation.[5]

But this is not to say that the plans of the DMNS for expanding their merchant marines will necessarily be on the whole ineffective. The reason being that the very size and complexity of the new ships, together with the massive investments required in providing adequate port facilities for them, virtually ensures that the proposed superliners of the future will probably not be calling at every port.[6] In fact, it has been estimated that the port facilities which are required to adequately serve the new large ships are such that an optimal number of such ports in the entire world would be somewhere in the region of eight or nine.[7] Such developments are likely to make the drive for national fleets redundant, with the general trend reverting towards international fleets.

In the light of these considerations, what might occur in the merchant marine industry could be the evolution of a two-tier world: a *big league,*[8] consisting of the long distance, capital intensive, high volume traffic moving about the network of superports and controlled by tight-knit multi-national consortia; and the *little league,*[9] designed to take care of the transverse trade between the superports and the countries of ultimate destination of the cargoes. The supertanker world already presents a similar picture. Whether the DMNS will be happy with this kind of second class status in the industry remains to be seen.[10] They would probably feel betrayed and short-circuited by the TMNS since their preference for national rather than international fleets was designed to enable them to escape from such a second class status.

However, this time round they might not have much choice in the matter. It should be noted, though, that it is not only the DMNS which will be members of this *little league.* Some STNS as well as former TMNS may also find themselves placed there if they choose (whether expressly or by default) not to make the massive investments required by the new technology.[11] It would, therefore, be best to regard the approaching bifurcation of the merchant marine industry (if indeed it occurs) in a positive light and view it as a step towards a rational way of organising the merchant marine industry.[12] Future prospects for national fleets might then look different. There might be some truth in the argument that there might not be any need for every state to build its own national fleet of superships, for instance, just as there might be no need for every nation to produce steel or petrochemicals for export, or for every state to embark on a space programme.[13]

There might be nothing sacrosanct about national fleets just as there is, or should be, nothing so extraordinary about an ultra modern merchant marine industry that a state should consider itself deprived of its birthright by virtue of not possessing one.[14] After all, advanced shipping, like all technological advancements, is a threat to jobs as the TMNS have painfully discovered. It was concluded above that the cargo-sharing provisions contained in the *Code of Conduct for Liner Conferences* are justified on the basis that they will function, *de facto*, as aid measures for the DMNS but not on the basis that they will promote an economically optimal international merchant marine world.[15] And that goal should still be achieved in the hypothetical bifurcated merchant marine industry of the future.

It seems a likely outcome that the TMNS, by virtue of advanced technology, will continue to dominate the transoceanic routes.[16] While the DMNS and other maritime nations, by virtue of their juridical regimes set up by the UNCTAD Convention, will have the transverse trades reserved for them in substantial part.[17] The DMNS should remain free, of course, to make the substantial commitments needed to place them in the *big league* of the merchant marine world if they so choose. Such a division of labour is, perhaps, not ideal from the standpoint of either the TMNS, which will suffer the loss of cross-trading opportunities,[18] or the DMNS, who will find themselves still unable to become substantial maritime powers. But in the light of the many prevailing constraints – political, economic and technological – the compromise would seem to be an eminently fair one. Otherwise, perhaps the DMNS should consider other alternatives.[19]

2. Earlier attempts to deal with the problem of national fleets

There have been numerous attempts by the TMNS, both governmental and non-governmental, to deal with the problems caused by the use of traditional methods to establish and/or develop national fleets. These attempts have been both fundamental, administrative and legislative.[20] An example of the administrative approach is that of the Maritime Transport Committee of the OECD which has put on record its belief in the urgent necessity for co-operation between all governments to secure the removal of discriminatory governmental practices and unnecessary governmental restrictions affecting shipping engaged in international trade in order to allow the free and unrestricted interplay of shipping services in the commerce of the world.[21]

2.1 Administrative approach

Recognising the detrimental effect of restrictive practices of these kinds on the provision of international shipping services at economic levels, the OECD countries resolved to avoid them to the fullest possible extent among themselves. As early as 1950 the then-OEEC resolved that governments should refrain from influencing the terms adopted for the sale or purchase of goods in such a way as to affect the method and flag of shipping.[22] Instead normal commercial practices and procedures should be followed and normal commercial considerations should alone determine the method and flag of shipment. Already mentioned is the *OECD Code of Liberalisation for Invisible Transactions* where these principles were enshrined. To give effect to these principles, for example, at their meeting in July 1954, the then-OEEC Maritime Committee expressed its view that the *Saudi Arabian/Onassis Agreement*[23] constituted a flagrant case of flag discrimination, in that it sought by government action to force purchasers of oil from Saudi Arabia to use tankers of a particular flag contrary to accepted international shipping practice. The Committee deplored such interference by a government with the shippers' freedom of choice and agreed that the delegates of the countries represented on the Committee should report these views to their governments in order that they could consider what action should be taken in the matter.[24] A similar approach to the US government was not successful. With the council's approval an unofficial mission to Washington endeavoured to arrange a conference. It transpired, however, that although this idea was acceptable in principle to the US government, they considered that from the political standpoint it was unacceptable.[25] Many other intergovernmental, and non-governmental bodies have attempted in vain to outlaw this practice.

Whilst the Maritime Transport Committee of the OECD was the only intergovernmental body, at the time, which took action in this field, the *International Chamber of Commerce,* working at commercial level and, through its Commission on Sea Transport adopted a resolution (78th Session on 24th and 25th February, 1953), urging all countries to reaffirm by positive action their belief in the principle of the freedom of the seas and their determination to secure the removal of all acts of flag discrimination of whatever kind.[26] We have seen how the efforts of even the UN bodies like GATT and IMCO were fruitless. The same fate seems to have affected the other conventions on Maritime

Transport. Only the OECD seem initially to have met with some limited success. It would appear that the UN Code on RBP's will meet a similar fate.[27]

Similarly, the governments of the TMNS have tried to tackle problems caused for international trade by the use of traditional methods of establishing and/or developing national fleets. Already mentioned are countervailing actions and retaliatory flag discrimination. Inserting clauses in trade agreements forbidding flag discriminations and diplomatic pressures are other methods.[28] In the case of the *Saudi Arabian/Onassis Agreement,* besides the OECD approach, subsequent protests were made by several of the governments concerned to the Saudi Arabian government, and in particular the UK government made a declaration to Parliament strongly condemning the Agreement. Thus, it needed a combination of the OECD and some diplomatic threats to have any effect. Even then were this to have been merely a state-to-state agreement, none of these approaches would have succeeded.[29]

Government action that has been relatively more successful is exemplied by the US exemption under *Public Resolution 17.*[30] Take the case of Ghana; until the latter part of 1961, Ghanaian-flag vessels, favoured by government direction of cargo, were carrying the greater share of cocoa exports from Ghana to the US. When the American government was discussing waivers of *Public Resolution 17* on Eximbank-Financed material for projects with Ghana, the unsatisfactory situation in the cocoa trade was called to the attention of the Government. It was made clear that waivers of *Public Resolution 17* would be considered in the context of a larger participation by US flag carriers in the cocoa trade.[31] The Ghanaian government accordingly revised its cocoa export shipping policy to the satisfaction of the US carriers. Waivers of *Public Resolution 17* were then granted. The US has taken similar action with all her discriminating partners. The success of this procedure is attributed to US influence, commercial and political power, rather than anything else.[32] Ironically, the US is also the major practitioner of flag preferences and all approaches from the OECD major trading partners have been to no avail. More recent, and of direct relevance to the establishment and/or development of national fleets, are two representations made by the TMNS.[33] The first recommendation is the *Alternative Investments* option. While the other is an almost identical *Scheme for the DMNS.* These two proposals are worth discussing in some detail for the light they throw on the nature of the problem.

2.2 The legislative approach: the Brussels Package

The TMNS seem to have reacted more determinedly in their response to the cargo-sharing provisions of the *UN Code of Conduct for Liner Conferences.* The kinds of practices envisaged by Article 2 of the Code would, therefore, be contrary to the *EEC Rules of Competition*[33A] which prohibit cargo-sharing, flag discrimination, maritime subsidies and other related restrictive shipping practices. All that was left was for the Council to act, since it has power to decide by a unanimous decision, whether, to what extent and by what procedure appropriate provisions could be made in respect of sea transport.[34] When it became clear that continued opposition to the Code would be futile the whole club decided to formulate a common approach, in line with the *Treaty of Rome* which calls upon Member States to approach transport policies within the framework of the *Common Transport Policy.*[35]

Hence the *Brussels Package.* To avoid an apparent division among the member countries on their response to the Code, the EEC formulated this common policy, embodied in a *Council Regulation.*[36] The Regulation is directed to securing that there is no discrimination between shipping lines of the EEC or of the OECD which do not themselves practice such, as Australia, Canada, etc.[37] It cannot be said that the EEC-OECD accepted the Code willingly. It appears that two other factors caused the TMNS to look again at the Code:

(a) The realisation that in the absence of the Code, an increasing number of the DMNS would seek to take even more damaging unilateral action to reserve cargoes for their own ships;[38] and
(b) Certain EEC member states were adamant that they intended to ratify the Convention, whatever the views of their partners.[39]

It appears, however, that the EEC in accepting the Code was more conscious of its value in combating the incursions of Soviet tonnage into Common Market trades, often operating outside the conferences, than of contributing to the realisation of the legitimate aspirations of the DMNS.[40] The sum-total of the *Brussels Package* is that the objectionable parts (I–V) of the Code, especially Article 2(4) (a) and (b) will fall under reservations and will operate as between the DMNS and STNS (or SCS) on the one hand, and the EEC-OECD on the other, but not within the EEC and OECD member states themselves.[41] The instrument of ratification or accession, by the EEC–OECD will be accompanied by the reservations set out in *Annex 1 of the Council Regulation.* According to the EEC-OECD, therefore, the purpose of the *Brussels Package* is to reduce to a minimum the damage to international trade caused by the Code's cargo-sharing provisions.[42]

This purpose would be achieved by implementing them only in so far as it is necessary to meet the rights which the Code gives the DMNS, who are those who conceived the idea.[43] The idea is that assuming all the EEC-OECD countries continue to renounce cargo-sharing favouring their own lines, government-imposed cargo reservation would be avoided in all intra-OECD Conference trades.[44] In trades between OECD signatories to the Code and Codist-DMNS, the latter would reserve cargo allocated to them under the Code rules but the share that would otherwise fall to OECD lines will be aggregated and redistributed by them on a commercial basis.[45] It is hoped, by this, that this pattern of DMN protectionism, together with renewed commitment on the part of the EEC-OECD, to commercial trading principles, would be the way forward for the development of world liner trades.[46]

Another effect of the Package is to save cross-traders (especially the UK) by displacing cargo-sharing from among the TMNS. Were this not to be the case it would have placed British Shipping, for instance, in an invidious situation and effectively cut her out of much of the European cross-trades.[47] It was with this situation in mind, and largely on the initiative of the UK government, that the Package was negotiated providing a regime for the disapplication of the Code's cargo-sharing provisions in the intra-OECD trades.[48] The result of the Package is that so long as all the OECD countries acceding to the Code disapply its cargo-sharing provisions in this, 75% of the world's liner conference trades will remain free of cargo reservation.[49] This also means that on a route between an EEC member and a third country Conference lines from all member states will compete on the same footing.[50]

This effectively disarms the Code and deprives it of its most important provision.[51] As a result of this fundamental modification of the Codes provisions, calculations suggest that the Code's cargo-sharing provisions will apply in practice to only about 25% of the world's liner conference trades.[52] The other 75% will be free of the Code's cargo-reservation provisions because they will either not be applicable in intra-OECD trades, and they will be substantially modified in trades between the OECD and the DMNS, or because of the intention of the other OECD countries such as the US and Australia not to accede.[53] If liner trades constitute about 20% of world shipping it follows that only 5% (i.e. a quarter) will be subject to the Code's cargo-sharing.

The other function of the *Brussels Package* was to sound a warning to the adversaries that the TMNS will not tolerate cargo-sharing in the proposed *UNCTAD Code of Conduct in the Bulk Trade.*[54] But generally the function of the Package was an attempt to reverse regulatory aspects in shipping. The interests of the TMNS would seem to coincide in opposing these manifestations of protectionism.[55] It is inevitably a complex problem to regulate world shipping, as it is to regulate world aviation. The TMNS maintain that when governments begin to tamper and to intrude into commercial arrangements, on these occasions, profitability goes out through the window.[56] These governments also maintain that the legal privileges under which shipping trades require the discipline of exposure to competition of these are to remain acceptable.[57]

If, therefore, the TMNS find competition eliminated from their trade routes by other governments, whether or not they pray the Code in aid, they will continue to make clear to the governments concerned that this is unacceptable.[58] and that the TMNS stand by to use the very considerable powers which the EEC, OECD and their parliaments[59] provide to counter acts which damage their shipping. Finally, the *Brussels Package* was drawn up to allay the US fears that the EEC ratifications were neither acceptance of protectionism nor intended to leave the rest of the OECD in the cold.[60]

2.3 Alternative investments for developing maritime nations

Despite the foreign currency payments required to support national maritime fleets and the foreign receipts sacrificed because of the merchant marine development programme, a national fleet may not earn revenue sufficient to cause even a slight net improvement in the balance of payments,[61] as any moderately sensible economic investment is likely to do. It was noted earlier that, in the case of Britain, investment in the merchant marine industry was the better alternative. But that did not mean that the other alternatives were to be neglected.[62] Besides, what is true for Britain, or indeed any other TMN, might not necessarily be true for the DMNS.[63] A complete balance of payments' analysis, however, must consider whether investments involving similar amounts of capital might yield a higher return of foreign capital.[64] The opportunity cost of an investment with this purpose is the highest return of foreign currency foregone by the decision to so allocate.[65]

It must be said likewise that political considerations form the opportunity cost foregone by establishing and/or developing national fleets for political prestige using (non-economic) traditional methods. A nation desiring to maximise improvements in its balance of payments will eliminate opportunity costs by investing in the project that yields the greatest flow of foreign currency over its life.[66] Ideally, a separate calculation should be made for every possible investment. However, the predicted rates of return on the capital investments in various enterprises can be used for comparative purposes as surrogates for their relative impact on the balance of payments' position of a country.[67] In certain cases the relatively low rates of return on capital invested in the merchant marine industry might suggest that other investments would probably make greater improvements in a nation's balance of payments.[68]

Though the exact statistics may not be readily available, this is especially true in the DMNS where returns on investments are typically higher for labour-intensive industries such as agriculture than for capital-intensive industries such as cargo-shipping.[69] For the DMNS, the options have to be weighed against the economic effects of the probable inefficiencies that are bound to be caused by state intervention in, and aid to the merchant marine industry generally.[70] The alleged economic benefits of the protectionist approach to merchant shipping, have been widely discussed by the DMNS, but their economic costs are generally overlooked.[71] This has been examined exhaustively.

Needless to say, perhaps, that by failing to consider the probable economic costs of implementing state aid and restrictive practices, the DMNS overlook the shortcomings of their ambitious plans and hence overvalue the ultimate benefits of the merchant marine investment in the national fleets.[72] But, since, as has been reiterated, economics is but one of the factors taken into consideration, the idea of abandoning the establishment and development of the merchant marine industry in favour of alternative investments might be a non-starter as far as these countries are concerned.[73] Especially where that proposal originates from the TMNS.

The desire of the DMNS to establish and/or develop their own national fleets at all costs has caused such confrontation and suspicion on the part of the TMNS that both camps more or less think nothing good of the other. The argument might be a plot by their former colonial masters, and now rivals, to keep their participation out of this vital area, and therefore to keep them perpetually subjugated.[74] Their suspicions are further reinforced by the fact that (and it is hardly surprising) the idea was first floated by the TMNS. The TMNS, on their part, suffer from the suspicion that the DMNS, like the STNS, must have a long-term ulterior motive to commit almost all their available resources to establishing and developing national fleets when such a policy has no economic justification.[75] Such initial distrust unfortunately, tends to cloud what would otherwise be reasonable proposals, such as, for example, the *Scheme for the DMNS.*

2.4 A scheme for the developing maritime nations

Another idea floated by the TMNS, which again, was not popular with or well received by the DMNS is the so-called Scheme for the DMNS.[76] This is really a natural development from the *Alternative Investment Scheme.* In a nutshell, the idea is to apply the cargo-sharing provisions of the *Convention on the Code of Conduct for Liner Conferences* in a rather different fashion from what the drafters of the Code had contemplated.[77] Instead of expecting the DMNS to establish and/or develop their own national fleets for the carriage of their reserved cargoes, it might make some sense for cargoes to be physically carried by container vessels built by the TMNS which presently have the necessary technology and the capital required.[78] And then a *share of the revenues* from this trade would be allocated to the DMNS involved in each relevant trading route, presumably after deducting some proportion of the capital costs and operating expenses involved.[79]

Further, the DMNS might even be allowed to provide part of the crew of the vessels, though a significant number of recruits would not be involved in view of the low-labour requirements of the new ships.[80] It was hoped that such a scheme would help to avoid the dire consequences of over-tonnaging, while at the same time providing for a flow of resources to the DMNS.[81] The effect of such a scheme would be to convert the convention, *inter alia*, from a *magna carta* for Third World national merchant fleets into a sort of specific taxation regime involving levies upon the merchant marine consortia for the benefit of the DMNS, which they serve.[82] In principle such a plan might be acceptable to the DMNS provided the burdens on the one hand and the benefits on the other are not greater or less (respectively) than would be acceptable to these countries.[83] But this too overlooks the fundamental rationale involved in the establishment and/or development of national fleets by the DMNS.

Otherwise this suggested plan is not so radical as the hypothetical aid optimal solution mentioned in the previous alternative for the assistance of the DMNS; that plan entailed the setting up of a regular mechanism for the systematic collection of assistance money from the wealthier TMNS for the benefit of the DMNS.[84] This plan is more modest. It would be merely the implementation of the principle of cargo-sharing in a way which might be more convenient for all parties concerned.[85] For the TMNS because they can afford to pay their dues, as it were, to the DMNS in the form of cash (which they might persuade their governments to reimburse) rather than in kind (in the form of suffering from overtonnaging);[86] for the DMNS, since they will be faced with the relatively easy dilemma of deciding whether (or to what extent) to reimburse their national merchant marines for payments made instead of facing the more difficult problems arising from the unemployment that would accompany the overtonnaging in the national merchant marine industry.[87]

It would be equally beneficial for shippers since they would still be able to reap the benefits of low freight rates which the new technology promises; and finally to the DMNS, which would receive assistance in the form of cash grants from the merchant marines instead of payments in kind in the form of enhanced opportunities for national merchant marines.[88] This last point, however, is the one on which the plan is likely to founder. The one losing party in the complicated arrangement would be the newly established national maritime fleets of the DMNS.[89] They would benefit from the system only if their governments chose to expand the aid resources received by them. Yet it would be most likely that the TMNS would make an end to such aid as a condition for the programme.

In so far as the major justification for the convention is as an aid measure, this point should be of no great importance.[90] But in so far as the Convention is regarded as the mechanism for the promotion of the DMNS national merchant fleets such a taxation system as the one proposed here would be the very negation of the Convention's principle.[91] It was concluded in the previous section that the justification for the Code from the standpoint of the international community as a whole lay in its role as an aid measure. It is quite likely, however, that the DMNS would see differently and consider the fostering of national merchant marines to be an essential, and not merely a peripheral element of the Code.[92]

The fact that the DMNS wish to establish and/or develop national maritime fleets more for political, than economic reasons would seem to eliminate the feasibility of this solution. It would need bigger concessions from the TMNS to silence the nationalism of the DMNS.[93] To the DMNS, the flag of the ship assumes the role of identity of economic nationhood, emulation of power and independence and a symbolic value of industrial competence. The national maritime fleet, therefore, serves as a psychological satisfaction.[94] Thus, nationalism emerges as the most powerful driving force for the DMNS to establish and/or develop their own national fleets. The use of these restrictive traditional practices as a method of achieving this goal is no more than a symptom of this force. This reveals the weaknesses in the administrative and legislative approaches outlined.[95]

The shortcoming of the OECD approach is that it is artificial and aims to treat only the symptoms rather than tackle the fundamental problems underlying these symptoms.[96] On the other hand, the approach by the TMNS suffers from the same inadequacy in that it merely leads to further confrontation in an area needing consultation and compromise. One is, of course, referring to countervailing actions and retaliatory discriminations. By resorting to these rather crude methods, the TMNS fall into the same trap as did the DMNS in resorting to flag preference and discriminations.[97] The other recommendations for alternative investments and the scheme for the DMNS would satisfy the economic but not the political aspirations of the DMNS. But to the DMNS, political aspirations have the upper hand.[98]

The latter two methods were a genuine attempt to get at the fundamental problems but they, too, faltered for the reasons outlined. One appreciates the aspirations of the DMNS to establish and develop national fleets of their own. But in resorting to the use of the non-economic traditional methods they have adopted the wrong tactics.[99] In other words, while one can in principle be in sympathy with their desires, it is their methods to achieve them that are in question. What is required is compromise and consultation between the TMNS and the DMNS; cooperation on the part of the TMNS and reason on the part of the DMNS. In our view, therefore, the best policy for the DMNS is to adopt a more rational approach.[100] Joint ventures and cooperation in shipping between all parties concerned would best serve their respective interests and save international shipping from disintegration. One feels this is the best way forward for the future prospects of national fleets.

3. Cooperation and joint ventures

Cooperation, joint ventures and consultation might solve most of the problems and satisfy the conflicting interests raised by this study.[101] The proposed reforms would solve the abuses of the liner conference and flags of convenience systems and, therefore, answer some of the many criticisms of these systems by the DMNS. The economic problems might be solved by the ensuing reduced costs.[102] The conflict of law problems might also be reduced. There might be no need or cause for flag discrimination as problems of availability of cargoes might consequently vanish. The DMNS might, hopefully, have acquired their own national fleets and solved their other problems such as their lack of capital, skilled labour and technology.[103]

The TMNS will not have lost much ground in international shipping. Above all, they will not have lost much face either; pride plays an important part in shipping. All these conflicting interests and objectives might be achieved with minimal damage to international shipping and with no major disruption to international trade and relations.[104] Therein lies the alternative and, perhaps, the better approach to accommodating both the emerging national maritime fleets as well as preserving international shipping and oceanborne trade intact. The rest of the survey is, therefore, devoted to the broad outline of this alternative approach to the future prospects of the national maritime fleets.[105]

3.1 Regional cooperation between the DMNS

With regard to the scheme for the DMNS, and especially its relation to the *Convention on the Code of Conduct for Liner Conferences,* it will be recalled that one of the Resolutions adopted at UNCTAD V in Manilla[106] reaffirmed that:

> 'The aim of the developing countries to establish and expand their liner fleets in accordance with the provisions of the Convention . . . '[107]

It appears likely, therefore, that the DMNS will insist on applying Article 2(4) in all its rigour to physical cargoes, though the Article refers to the sharing of the freight and volume of traffic.[108] What effect might such a stance by the DMNS have on the future of the merchant marine industry?

Perhaps, rather than look to the TMNS for confrontation and/or support, the DMNS had better look to themselves first.[109] There could be two methods of achieving this objective. The first is to set up regional *shipping corporations* by themselves; South-to-South rather than the traditional North-to-South. Structures for such ventures are not unknown to them. Probably the best example is provided by the *Water Transport Aims* of the LAFTA Conventions.[110] Considering the increasingly powerful position of some of the LAFTA member countries, such as Brazil, Venezuela and Argentina, such a regional approach would provide them with a good bargaining position with the Europeans and North Americans.[111] Other outstanding examples of regional approaches among the DMNS are the former Eastern African National Shipping Lines (EANSL), the shipping wing of the now defunct East African Community (EAC).[112]

The EANSL was probably the model approach to maritime transport by the DMNS. Unfortunately, the only such example of shipping cooperation, still in operation, is the *Maritime Transport Charter for West and Central Africa:*[113] the *Ministerial Conference of the West and Central African States* established in May 1975 and based in Abidjan in the Ivory Coast.[114] Of course the regional approach would be only a substitute for the national approach. Currently, only a handful of the DMNS can afford to establish and run a commercially viable national maritime fleet.[115] The others, who may at this time be unable to do so, might perhaps consider regionalism. The position is much clearer in Latin America than in South-east Asia or Africa. Even then, regionalism should try as much as possible to encompass compatibility.[116]

In addition to regionalism, the other alternative is a *joint venture* involving the DMNS along similar lines.[116A] There are already encouraging developments in this direction. Since 1977, several new joint ventures involving the DMNS have been reported: between Nigerian and Indian interests, resulting in the establishment in Nigeria of Equatorial Carriers Limited;[117] between Seatrains Incorporated; and Trinidad and Tobago resulting in the formation of the Shipping Corporation of Trinidad and Tobago.[118] There are in existence, similar joint ventures between Tanzania an the Peoples Republic of China on the one hand, and Tanzania and Mozambique on the other.[119]

What one is talking of here are circumstances in which a DMN, especially one which might be among both the least developed and landlocked, considering the establishment and/or development of its own national maritime fleet, might find it economically preferable to act jointly with other DMNS in a similar position;[120] or in which a DMN that already possesses a national maritime fleet might decide, on the basis of economic considerations, to integrate the whole or part of its fleet with those of other countries. The whole process might be repeated on a larger scale when similar relationships might be extended to cover the whole of the international shipping field, i.e. between the TMNS and the DMNS.[121]

3.2 Joint ventures between the TMNS and DMNS: multinational shipping enterprises (MSE) or consortia

Thus, what might turn out to be the only rational solution to current problems, is the recommendation for cooperation and joint ventures.[122] It is our view that such a solution might bypass the current nationalism in the industry and render restrictive maritime practices quite unnecessary. Again, as in the case of regional cooperation, there are already indications of these taking off too. UNCTAD reported that, as of 1977, the Saudi Arabian Triad Group on the one hand, and Finlines and Valmet of Finland, on the other hand, had established a Saudi International Shipping Company;[123] Indonesian and Swedish interests formed P.T. Indonesian Tankers; Moroccan, British and Belgian interests formed the Societé Marocaine de Navigation SA.[124]

At this stage we should, perhaps, point out that the kind of joint ventures we have in mind would differ, both quantitatively and qualitatively, from the existing liner conferences and other Western-oriented (and based) Transnational Shipping Corporations.[125] In this context, a 'multinational shipping enterprise' is any joint venture undertaken by interests in two or more DMNS, (with a possible participation of interests in the TMNS provided the interests in the

DMNS maintain effective control) which provides for transport of goods (including live-stock) and/or passengers by sea.[126] As will be apparent shortly, *control* by the DMNS is essential in order to avoid a repetition of the kind of abuses that drove these countries to opt for the establishment or development of their national fleets in the first place.

By definition, therefore, a MSE differs fundamentally from a Multinational Corporation or Liner Conference[127] in the sense that the former does not involve, as the latter is usually understood to, direct foreign investment by a foreign company establishing a wholly or partly-owned subsidiary abroad.[128] Also, a greater degree of public ownership and participation is implied in the former as opposed to private enterprise in the latter.[129] Some kind of government participation might satisfy the DMNS and at the same time serve to guarantee the participation of foreign interests. The most important criterion here is *ownership* and not *management*.[130] The main reason for using the criterion of ownership (joint capital investment) is that, since in the DMNS managerial skills are scarce, management of the new MSE may be contracted to foreign shipping firms in the initial periods.[131]

The alternative would be to include joint ventures between interests from the DMNS on the one hand and from the TMNS on the other.[132] A qualification must, however, be added: only enterprises where interests from the DMNS hold more than 50% rights or can exercise a veto power, or where interests from the TMNS hold less than 50% of the equity, should be permitted[132A] in respect of the basic decisions of the enterprise. It should be apparent that the purpose of these, somewhat arbitrary, conditions is to exclude from the scope of the recommended joint venture arrangements cases where the TMNS, having effective control, use the MSE as a device to take advantage of the DMNS in various respects.[133]

At the same time the TMNS should not be allowed to use the MSE in order to enjoy fiscal privileges granted by the DMNS to vessels flying their own flag, as is the case, for example, with companies set up in order to take advantage of a so-called flag of convenience.[134] Secondly, the TMNS should not be able to benefit from favourable credit facilities, ship-building facilities, depreciation allowances and other concessions offered by the DMNS to such merchant marine fleets,[135] or to exploit the possibilities open to the MSE of operating from several countries, and thus having multiple sources of cargo.[136] Finally, the TMNS should not use the joint ventures in the MSE simply to take advantage of flag preferences and flag discriminations operated by the respective DMNS.[137]

Coupled with these possible abuses is the possibility of the TMNS increasing, indirectly, through their participation in the MSE, their total cargo share in a conference of which they are already members,[138] and generally furthering their interests without specific concern for these of the DMNS.[139] Otherwise with careful planning designed to protect sufficiently the interests of the DMNS, the MSE, as compared to national shipping can enjoy a number of benefits in different fields and provide a bright future for national and international shipping.[140] More specifically they would assist the DMNS to overcome the basic fundamental problems associated with underdevelopment.[141]

3.3 Joint ventures and national shipping contrasted

In the first place, the MSE would solve the problem of the *availability of capital.* This is the problem that in the first instance drove the DMNS to prefer the non-economic restrictive measures involved in establishing national fleets.[142] To get around this problem the MSE would have access to finance or guarantees for investments from several countries, hence the ability to obtain capital more readily than national fleets.[143] It would have greater advantages in respect of maritime subsidies, the advantage which stems from the obviously greater capacity of several DMNS acting together than each acting individually. The MSE may obtain preferential terms for loans from international institutions such as the regional development banks, terms which may not be available to national shipping lines.[144]

Finally, the availability of credit may be greater if the governments of several DMNS participate as shareholders in the MSE and *share investments.*[145] The same advantages would apply, even if the purchase of new vessels is made with a down payment of, say, only 20% with the balance on credit, since the initial capital outlay would be a substantial burden on the resources of a great number of the DMNS, especially the least developed and geographically disadvantaged ones.[146] No doubt, these financial benefits would extend to improvements in the balance of payments. Shipping is often cited as a major earner of foreign currency, although this may well be counterbalanced by the need to obtain hard currency loans for the initial fleet acquisition programme.[147] The MSE would take care of the balance of payments' problems of the DMNS which had been their major rationale for establishing their own national fleets.

It has also been mentioned that national fleets would lead to high operating costs, inefficiencies and overtonnaging. In the first place, the MSE would take care of the *operating costs* and thereby solve the DMNS' major handicap, namely, the lack of the large financial outlay required by the merchant marine industry.[148] The MSE would get around the problem of overtonnaging by avoiding excess capacity and inefficiency which would normally occur if a number of neighbouring DMNS each operated their own national fleet services between the ports and given destinations.[148A] In these circumstances the MSE could operate more efficiently and reduce or eliminate excess capacity, while offering an equally satisfactory service with a smaller number of vessels.[149] Joint ventures also have the advantage of *sharing commercial risks* instead of these being borne entirely (normally with dire consequences) by a single country. These risks are associated principally with reduction of demand for merchant marine services and the pressure of competition.[150]

The third advantage of the joint venture over national fleets concerns *availability of personnel.* One of the major problems facing the DMNS – lack of manpower – could be solved by recruitment of seagoing and managerial personnel from a wider source. The MSE can draw on the manpower resources of all the participating countries for managerial, clerical and seagoing personnel, a highly important advantage,[151] since together with the scarcity of capital, the shortage of skilled manpower including officers and managerial personnel, is the principal obstacle to the establishment and development of national fleets in the DMNS.[152] The need to use expatriate seagoing personnel or of contracting management to foreign firms which normally confronts the DMNS, would be reduced to the advantage of both the joint venture and the participants.[153]

The fourth advantage of the venture relates to *sources of cargo.* It is this factor which gave rise to flag preferences and flag discrimination. The venture would also solve this problem which, in turn, would harmonise the issue of cargo-reservation and ease international tension for cooperation.[154] Unlike the national fleet, which may be restricted to the carriage of the trade of its home country, the joint venture of the lines of neighbouring DMNS can serve the trades of the various participants, tap several sources of demand for maritime transport and thus achieve economies of scale.[155] For the smaller DMNS, this is likely to be the only means whereby they can participate economically in the liner shipping conferences, owing to indivisibility of vessels and the possibly smaller volumes of their oceanborne trade.[156]

The joint venture might be the solution to the problems of the landlocked DMN whose oceanborne trade is limited or which, in order to avoid dependence on a single neighbour, channels its trade through the ports of more than one transit country, thereby reducing the concentration of shipments.[157] The joint venture would also *increase the competitiveness of the DMNS' merchant marines,* within the conferences or in third countries. Or, for various reasons, several DMNS in the same area may prefer to operate lines outside the liner conferences and adopt independent freight rate policies.[158] While each of these lines might not individually be able to stand up to the opposition of the conferences, the joint venture would be in a better position to do so, because of the economic benefits it can enjoy, including the wider market for cargoes and the support of the governments of the participants.[159]

3.4 ICC joint venture project for the DMNS

In pursuit of this objective, maritime experts from the EEC-TMNS have started fact-finding studies in 8 DMNS on prospects for successful joint ventures in shipping.[160] The individuals concerned, all of whom were senior executives of large shipping companies, visited the ASEAN countries, India, Mexico and Brazil. A principal move by the shipping industry in the TMNS is to convince the DMNS that shipping operations should be based on free-market principles[161] rather than government intervention or protectionism. The project was launched by the Sea Transport Commission of the International Chamber of Commerce (ICC) under the terms of the *Caracas Declaration* of September 1981.[162]

Against a background of increasing politicisation, both national and international, which it believed to be in restraint of trade, the ICC held its Fourth Shipping Conference in Caracas, Venezuela, in September 1981.[163] The mood was that the world business community should give the lead in trying to find a new approach. Delegates felt that the governments of the developing nations did not reflect the views of the shipping industry and were only concerned with the politics of the industry.[164] It was also believed that the Regional Grouping System (A, B, C and D) practised in UNCTAD only served to intensify confrontation.[165]

It seemed there must be a better way. At the end of the conference the participants codified their beliefs in the *Caracas Declaration,* which sought to find it.[166] Thus, the Conference mapped out a programme for mutually beneficial cooperation with the DMNS in developing and operating their fleets.[167] Its elements were:

(a) A full examination of the conditions necessary for successful joint ventures;[168]
(b) A detailed consideration of the most appropriate methods for the transfer of shipping technology including the enhancement of technical and managerial skills;[169]
(c) Sustained activity to ensure the existance of viable national maritime codes[170] and supporting legal, tax and labour regimes; and
(d) A serious search for innovative financial mechanisms for fleet development.[171]

3.5 The elements of the Caracas Declaration

The heart of the Declaration is joint ventures. The concept is not one of charity, developed to developing, but of mutual self-help, business to business, in the absence of government regulation or pressure.[172] It is a term which implies a risk element and covers any mutually beneficial sea-transport-related activity which can be developed on a commercial basis.[173] According to the ICC Sea Transport Commission,[174] the main criteria for successful ventures (which are by no means new – there are a number of successful ones) are:

(a) The element of risk – the parties must recognise their mutual interdependence and that there are no short cuts to success;[175]
(b) There must be a suitable environment which facilitates joint ventures – this covers, *inter alia*, the political and legal areas;[176]
(c) The parties must know their business, but this does not inevitably mean that the developed partner should guard all his expertise.[177] He must be prepared to pass it on;
(d) The input and interests of the parties must be essentially complementary. Ventures must not be one-sided, with one party doing all the work;[178]
(e) There must be mutual trust between the parties; and
(f) There must be a clear centre for decision-making and vessel management.[179]

The other important aspects are:

(a) Transfer of technology, part of the on-going UN efforts involving sending experts to the DMNS, training schemes (in the TMNS and DMNS) and, particularly important, on-the-job training for personnel from the DMNS in successful shipping vnetures wherever situated;[180]
(b) Viable national maritime codes; these are essential to provide a framework for the operations, including the financing/mortgage arrangements which may be applicable;[181] and
(c) Innovative financial mechanisms to break the lack of cargo/finance vicious circle which in practice generates pressures for cargo reservation in order to provide that firm base.[182]

Finally, there is the follow-up. Of particular interests to the DMNS and the joint venture would be:

(a) The subsequent establishment of a Project Office with a full programme of work;[183]
(b) The development of a programme of exploratory field work by experts visiting a cross-section of the DMNS;
(c) An investigation (consulting with UNCTAD officials) into possibilities of the 'on-the-job' training for the DMNS' candidates;[184]
(d) The establishment of a high level expert group to consider new ways of approaching ship finance in order to break the vicious circle already referred to;
(e) A preliminary investigation into the need for an ICC Information and Advisory Service[185] to facilitate the further establishment of joint venture companies; and
(f) A positive approach to requests for information or assistance from entrepreneurs whether in the TMNS or DMNS.[186]

The studies now in progress are part of the joint EEC/ICC effort. The EEC plans to arrange for more industry experts to get out latter this year to other DMNS in Latin America and Africa.[187] The Project Chairman is of the view that joint ventures between shipping interests in the DMNS and TMNS could cover the whole field of activities relating to sea transport.[188] This could include the formation of new shipping companies, the improvement of existing concerns and the development of port facilities.[189] The studies would help to define the services which the planned ICC Maritime Information and Advisory Centre could provide. The Caracas Project team had already handled inquiries from both the DMNS and TMNS.[190]

3.6 The Japanese program for the DMNS

The Maritime International Cooperation Centre of Japan (MICCJ) established on March 1, 1982, has the same aims and ambitions as the one set up by the ICC. The former has also launched services offered to the DMNS and drawn up a program of research studies to be undertaken in the first year of operations.[191] Established with the authorisation of the Japanese Ministry of Transport, the MICCJ was incorporated to provide assistance and advice for the DMNS in all respects of maritime affairs.[192] Its main function, therefore, consists of research and study for upgrading maritime industries in any DMN and the dispatching of specialists and engineers to give advice and guidance for undertaking development projects. Training and orientation will also be provided for personnel (such as seafarers or port operations people) from the DMNS, or those to be sent there for consultancy work.[193]

For each specific project or research undertaking, specialists will be seconded from member companies/organisations.[194] Since every major shipping line in Japan, as well as most Japanese maritime/shipbuilding/shipping associations and institutes are represented on the board of the organisation, it has a vast pool from which to draw staff. Moreover, the Centre can also call upon outside consultants and university personnel in the country and can even recruit non-Japanese specialists in certain fields.[195] Although the MICCJ is a non-profit-making organisation, it is funded by three main bodies: the Japan Maritime Development Association (JANDA), the Japan Maritime Foundation (JMF), and the Japanese Shipowners Association (JSA).[196]

Although much of the work to be undertaken in the fields of ports, shipbuilding and shipping operations, will overlap work performed by bodies like UNCTAD, ICC and ESCAP, the MICCJ[197] hopes to keep close contact with especially ESCAP and others, and will avoid acting against their guidelines, or duplicating any of their work, but hopes to work independently with the same spirit. The spirit of the organisation is captured in its document outlining the duties to be performed which are aimed at fostering international friendship[198] and understanding with the DMNS and their peoples. However, some of the Centre's activities (i.e. the promotion and assistance of the DMN's fleets) will be directly against the interests of the TMNS and especially of the Japanese shipping lines involved in the MICCJ work.[199]

Though in some cases in the short-term some (Japanese) lines may suffer to a certain degree due to her assistance in a DMN, the MICCJ remains philosophical that in the long-run it would be an inducement to healthy international cooperation and development, and will produce long-term benefits.[200] One danger confronting such international (ICC) and national (MICCJ) advisory bodies is the accusation that in return for consultation and advisory aid, the DMNS will subsequently be subjected to pressure form the aid giving nation to order equipment and services from that country only.[201] But be that as it may, after only a month in being, the MICCJ had already received some three requests for assistance in the form of research and advice coming from the Philippines, Malaysia and Guinea (West Africa).[202]

Although the MICCJ believes that most requests are expected to emanate from the SEA, it is hopeful that it will find work in East and West Africa and Latin America.[203] In this context the introduction of containerisation to various parts of the DMNS will be reflected significantly in the Centre's work schedule,[204] though it will take some time for containerisation to become firmly established in the DMNS.[205]

3.7 Advantages and disadvantages of joint shipping

The joint ventures need not be confined exclusively between the DMNS. Where a TMN is involved, one may repeat that it would be desirable that the DMNS keep effective control of the MSE in their own hands through, say a majority holding or special voting rights.[206] The combination of interests from the DMNS and TMNS would help overcome many of the difficulties facing national fleets and international shipping. It would also overcome most of the problems which the DMNS (and in particular the least developed and geographically disadvantaged ones among them) face when developing merchant marines, especially in the initial stages.[207] Thus, the participation of capital from the TMNS would bring in foreign currency for the financing of investments, while the wider distribution of the equity would spread the risks of the venture more widely.[208]

Banks and other credit institutions may provide loans, and perhaps on easier terms, to projects to which the TMNS are parties.[209] Again, with respect to manpower shortages in the DMNS, the TMNS could provide all the managerial and technical personnel until such time as there would be persons from the DMNS able to take part in the management.[210] The MSE is also likely to gain a greater volume of business due to the commercial contacts, business know-how, experience and research of the partners from the TMNS.[211] Furthermore, the DMNS would have the advantage of the established contacts of their partners from the TMNS with shipyards, supplies, bankers and ship-chandlers.[212] In some cases, the assistance may be temporary and the DMNS consequently may purchase the holding of their partners from the TMNS in accordance with the original agreement, while in other cases the arrangements may be permanent.[213]

A stronger case for the joint ventures which include participation of interests from the TMNS appears to exist in the case of the systems of unit load transport, wherever the adoption of high capital intensive systems of unitization in the DMNS is economically preferable to conventional break-bulk shipping.[214] In this way the DMNS would sidetrack the problems of the need to transfer technology, resources and technical assistance from the TMNS to themselves. The partners from the TMNS, too, would benefit.[215] The high capital cost of containerisation has led some operators from the TMNS to combine their resources through the creation of consortia, the formation of subsidiaries or by operating in other ways to eliminate or reduce competition in the container trades.[216] In the more probable event that a DMN cannot afford, on its own, to acquire any container vessels it will thus need to establish with other DMNS or with the TMNS a MSE joint venture to purchase the vessels and operate them jointly with other lines or within the venture.[217]

Similarly, an integrated approach is desirable among the DMNS, and between the DMNS and the TMNS, in using barge carrying vessels. In fact, with this form of unitization, the inducement is even greater, because the capital cost per unit of freight of such vessels is even higher than that of container vessels.[218]

So much for the advantages; this proposal has its disadvantages as well. Indeed, it would be misleading to present too rosy a picture. Of course, the establishment of the proposed MSE raises enormous problems; probably as many as the benefits. But most of the problems are little different from those encountered by national fleets.[219] There are, however, certain areas where special problems or difficulties may arise through the very fact that a MSE has participants from several countries. This is particularly the case where the governments of these countries do not sufficiently harmonise their policies towards the merchant marine industry, or towards foreign trade.[220]

Thus, special problems may arise concerning the policies and objectives of the enterprise, particularly regarding conflicting national maritime legislation, and the choice of location of incorporation and registration of the enterprise. As was the case with national fleets there could also be problems of registration (cf. flags of convenience) of the vessels[221] fiscal regulations and foreign exchange control. Although we have dwelt at length on the advantages of the availability of manpower, there could be problems as to where the recruitment of personnel is to take place as well as problems involving national quotas or equitable representation from all the participating countries.[222] Another factor that had earlier bedevilled the national fleets is the conflict of national interests such as national sovereignty and national defence.[223]

The protection of minority interests has already been mentioned. There may well be many more such problems, but at least one would expect these not to be as insurmountable as those emanating from restrictive shipping practices, preferences and discriminations.[224] All in all the advantages of joint ventures seem to outweigh the disadvantages. From the foregoing discussion, it is apparent that a joint approach to the establishment of the MSE is particularly attractive for the DMNS participating in schemes of economic integration. Such as customs and/or monetary unions or looser forms of economic cooperation.[225]

Likewise, such cooperation can more easily be extended to merchant marines in the case of countries having, for historical or other reasons, a tradition of economic and political cooperation and countries sharing a common legal system, even if there are no formal institutional arrangements.[226] For example, if the countries belong to the same currency area or are linked in a monetary union, there would be no problems of foreign exchange transfers from one country to another, and if there is a common fiscal system many problems of taxation would be avoided.[227] These and others are the kinds of problems that have threatened to wreck both national and international shipping. Similarly, in the absence of any restrictions on the movement of labour among participating countries, the MSE would have a wider scope than would national fleets for attracting managerial and seagoing personnel.[228] Finally, if there is already cooperation among the countries, especially in the fields of joint ventures in other related transport services, the experience gained can be put to use in operating the MSE.[229]

Nothing in the foregoing, however, should be construed as implying that integration in merchant marines through the MSE is feasible only as part of other schemes of cooperation.[230] A joint approach among the DMNS towards the establishment or expansion of their merchant marine industry is advisable in any event, not only because the venture is likely to be more profitable than national fleets and better able to serve the national interests of the countries concerned, but also because, if successful, it can stimulate cooperation in other fields related to merchant shipping.[231]

This is particularly so because involvement in shipping broadens the industrial base of the participants with various spin-off advantages. Although cooperation in these other fields is not conditional upon the existence of a joint MSE, nevertheless, it is more easily achieved, and in fact becomes inevitable, when there is already cooperation through the existence of related joint ventures.[232] The areas to be highlighted for cooperation in the case of the MSE are to be found in general merchant marine policies. These outlined proposals coupled with consultation machinery, concentration of cargoes and the establishment of freight booking centres, or freight bureaus would be the rational alternatives to the individual national fleets.[233] In addition, these developments should result in an overall improvement in the shipping infrastructure such as inland transport, and the development of ports.

Coupled with the improvement in the necessary infrastructures are improvements in ship repairing, ship building and salvage operations. The MSE should also focus attention on the training of managers and seagoing personnel as well as safety and manning regulations. There should also be developed a code specifying minimum requirements of competence for seagoing personnel and conditions of employment and welfare of seamen.[234] And finally, the MSE should not lose sight of pollution control. In one's view, if implemented properly, these alternative recommendations would provide better prospects for the future of national maritime fleets. These developments might also lead to the formulation of an international shipping authority.

4. The case for an international shipping authority

The transformation from international shipping led to the demand for national maritime fleets. One has endeavoured to prophecy that due to its external and internal contradictions such a policy would probably be self-destroying.[235] However, with some guidance along the lines recommended above, national fleets would give way to joint ventures in the form of the MSE. The MSE is indeed a kind of international shipping but of a different type from its predecessors.[236] The new form of international shipping would be the result of *cooperation*, *compromise*, *consultation* and *wider participation* as opposed to the former type which was characterised by a *monopoly* of a few TMNS, *inequality* and *confrontation* with the DMNS.[237]

It is forecast that if successful, the MSE's would not be an end in themselves but a means to an end; in other words, a truly integrated and international shipping regime would be the natural development from the MSE.[238] Such a regime could be administered by, say, an *international shipping authority.* It would have as its central element, an *international shipping registry,* which would be in line with the NIEO and NIMO.[239] But before this could be established, there would have to be a reform of the shipping multinationals (TSC's) and the liner conference systems together with the phasing out of flags of convenience.

4.1 NIMO and reforming transnational shipping corporations

It will be remembered that through the *Declaration of the Establishment of a New International Economic Order,* the membership of the UN expressed its desire to progress towards a new world economic order. It has also been mentined that NIMO is part and parcel of that new order.[240] Expanding industrialisation and new industrial logistics are important components of the new emerging regimes. No doubt, the growth and restructuring of the transport infrastructure between nations was the central aim of the economic development efforts intended to have been pursued during the First and Second UN Development Decades and in the *UN Development Strategy.*[241] The Third UN Development Decade is no doubt more associated with NIEO and NIMO.

The movement of cargoes across national boundaries and over the seas is a major concern for transportation interests generally and maritime transportation in particular. The declared aim of the UN is the internationalisation of merchant shipping activities, not only to increase international trade but also to broaden the participation in merchant shipping activities of many nations who now have only a minor or secondary role.[242] Besides the crucial issues of dealing with liner conferences, flags of conveniences, etc., the importance of the present and future roles of the TSCS needs to be examined in order to provide more information that will be helpful in maximizing the mutual benefits generated by the TSCS and to assure the appropriate distribution of these benefits among the participants in international shipping.[243]

Figure 5 indicates how the problem of the transnational shipping corporations fits into the general question of transportation, NIEO, NIMO and the MSE with which one has proposed to reform and replace it.[244] Needless to say, the failure to implement such a policy would leave the DMNS with no alternative but to implement cargo-reservation rules, a privilege which, it is admitted, can hardly be denied to any country.[245] They would then allocate cargoes to their own national fleets up to the maximum practical carrying capacities and only give other TSCS a part of their merchant marine business when additional carrying capacity was needed. Figure 4 depicts the cargo allocation process between a national fleet and the TSCS under a system of cargo-reservation.

It indicates that occasionally demands fall below the carrying capacity of the national fleets.[246] At other times demand may substantially exceed average levels and only then would the services of the TSCS be employed. Figure 4, however, is only a policy model. On this model cargoes are assigned:

(1) According to a policy decision (not economic principles) to use domestically based national and international merchant marine capacity; and
(2) According to the need for use of foreign-based TSCS.[247]

4.2 The case for an international shipping registry: transformation of liner conferences and phasing out of flags of convenience

Coupled with the above-enumerated advantages, joint ventures in the form of the MSE may in fact supplement the *Convention on the Code of Conduct for Liner Conferences'* recommendations for the reform of the system.[248] Through the support of the governments concerned, the MSE may succeed in obtaining better terms of admission in respect of sailing rights, cargo quotas (in absence of reservation), or ports to be served.[249] It could carry larger shares

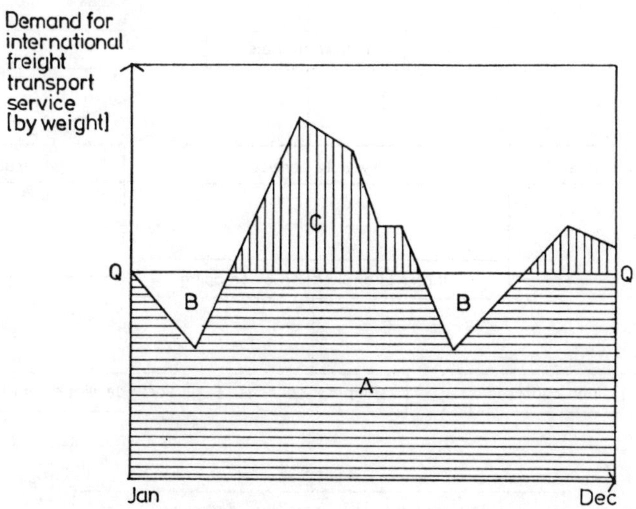

Figure 4. Allocation of cargoes between national flags and TSCS. A: Tonnage carried by national flag; B: excess capacity of national flag; C: tonnage carried by TSCS; D: average capacity of national flag.

of conference cargoes than could individual national fleets. By the same token, and by speaking in the Conference with a single voice on behalf of the several countries participating, the joint venture would be able to exert a greater influence on Conference decisions on crucial matters,[250] such as freight rates (including promotional freight rates for non-traditional exports of the DMN member states) and the adequacy of services affecting the participating DMNS, than could separate national fleets.

By becoming full members, with full rights, the joint ventures would overcome the obstacles raised by the conferences to the participation of fleets from

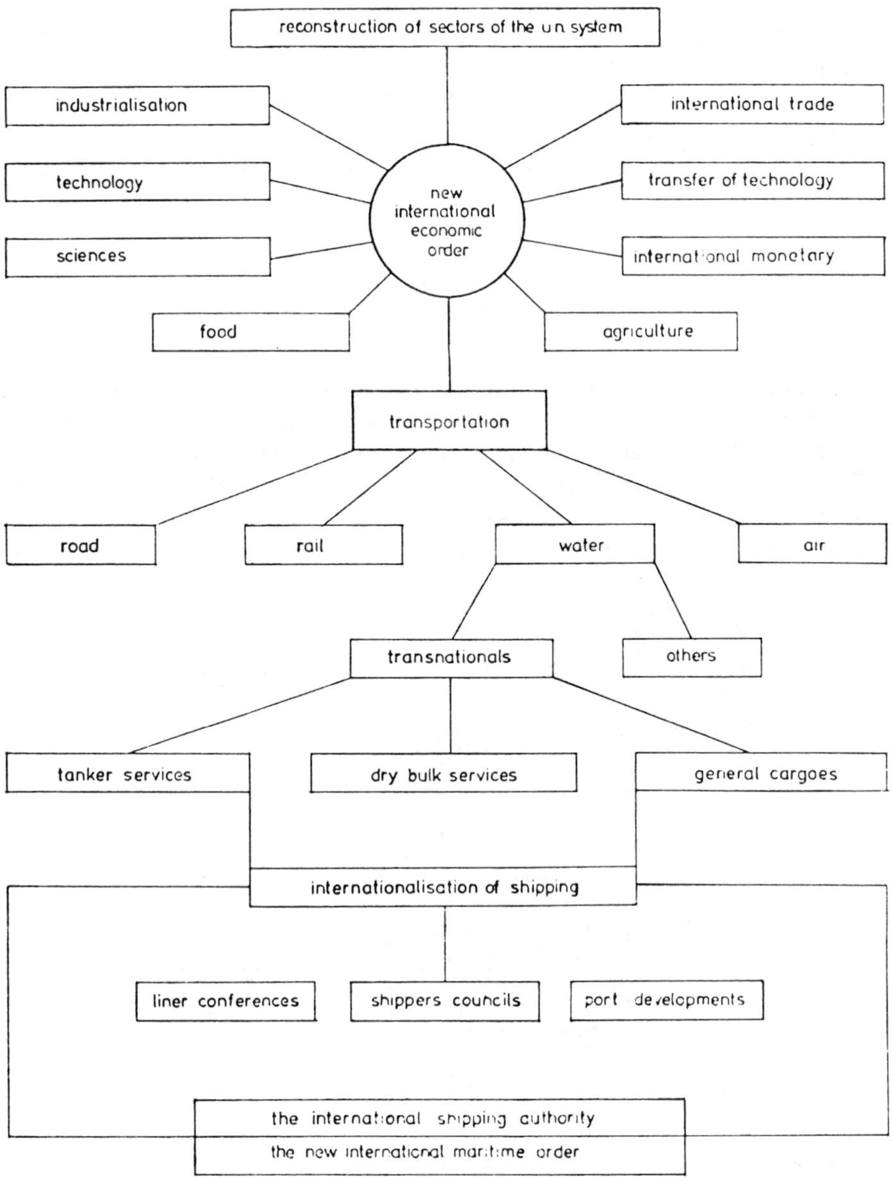

Figure 5. Transnational shipping corporations and the new international economic order.

the DMNS as third-flag-carriers.[251] One other object which the joint venture might achieve – which has always eluded international shipping – is the phasing out of the flags of convenience.[252] Particularly in joint ventures involving both TMNS and DMNS, a compromise could be worked out whereby ships currently sailing under flags of convenience could be transferred to the various joint ventures. This could be done to the benefit of all and without any particular party losing face or gaining unduly at the others' expense.[253] The joint ventures would have, hopefully, eliminated the fears and suspicions which are the basic cause for the existence of flags of convenience.[254]

Coupled with the other advantages mentioned earlier, such a compromise would also have solved the problem of the DMNS' lack of capital to purchase even second-hand ships of their own.[255] The former flags of convenience would then belong to neither the TMNS the DMNS but to the joint ventures in the form of the MSE.[256] Perhaps international shipping would benefit from the absence of flags of convenience, on the one hand, and the relatively reformed liner conference system on the other.[257] The DMNS would have satisfied their national ego in possessing national fleets of their own albeit as part of a joint venture.[258] Later perhaps, those who are able to do so, could negotiate to buy off the shares of the TMNS in these ventures.

They will not have acquired at least merchant marines that are truly their own, but they would have achieved participation of a kind. This result would have been achieved smoothly without dislocating their national economies or disrupting international shipping.[259] They would also have, to a restricted extent, gained possession of national fleets of their own. The experience acquired during the initial periods of the joint ventures will also have gained these countries managerial skills, expertise and technical know-how.[260] But above all the joint ventures will have avoided what the TMNS had feared all along – the temptations to the DMNS to otherwise effect full-scale nationalisation of the merchant marine interests based in or serving their foreign trade.[261]

4.3 The case for an international shipping authority

What has been advocated in these pages is a truly international shipping industry with the emphasis on consultation and cooperation, not mistrust, which presently seems to be the order of the day.[262] Every maritime interest and nation should benefit and feel needed, which can only be possible through a mechanism that regulates and protects everybody's interests.[263] All these recommendations lead to one conclusion. It would not be over-ambitious, or idealistic, to recommend the creation of an *international shipping authority,*[264] in the form of an International Merchant Marine Authority [IMMA?] along similar lines as the proposed International Seabed Authority. As was the case with UNCLOSS, or any other previous similar institution,[265] the formation of IMMA could be achieved through a resolution of UNGA calling on the UN Secretary General to commission a committee of experts to work on consultations and a draft convention.[266]

Then at an agreed date and venue a conference of plenipotentiaries could be convened to debate and approve a UN convention on IMMA.[267] All nations, governmental and non-governmental bodies, specialised agencies and other interested parties concerned with the merchant marine would be consulted and invited to comment and attend.[268] Such an international shipping authority is necessary because of the importance of international shipping to international trade and to international relations. It would influence and harmonise the future prospects for a national fleet. Above all, maritime transport is still largely responsible for the carriage of international trade from ports of origin to ports of destination.[269]

The authority would enable most parties involved to have a say in this crucial activity, and influence the future development of what affects their very existence and livelihood. It is probable that the reason there has not been peace and harmony in international shipping is largely due to lack of coordinated regulation[270] by an international authority such as the one proposed. For some time international shipping has been left in the hands of a few nations and private interests to the detriment of the majority of other nations.[271] It needs scrutiny. Another strong case for the authority is the fact that merchant shipping issues have been largely neglected by the Law of the Sea Conference,[272] although it would probably be too late to start a wholesale revision of the *UNCLOSS III Draft Convention* to include provision for such an authority.

In any case, such an approach would treat merchant shipping as a mere side issue and not accord it the importance it deserves.[273] Only a conference and convention devoted exclusively to merchant marine issues would be appropriate. It will be interesting to note that at the discussion leading to the *Convention on the Code of Conduct for Liner Conferences,* the DMNS had in mind such an international shipping authority but were argued out of it by the TMNS[274] on the pretext that it would be bureaucratic and only a duplication of the already existing organisations dealing with merchant shipping matters. However, the proposed authority would incorporate all existing international organisations concerned with merchant shipping.[275]

4.4 The structure of the proposed international shipping authority

The detailed structure of the proposed authority is given in Fig. 6, and consists of the General Assembly,[275A] the Secretariat, the Council, the Bureaux, the Enterprise, the Judicial bodies and the Commissions in that order of hierarchy, with the respective duties and functions described herein. Under the umbrella of *UNGA*, the Convention would set up the authority answerable directly to it, as is the case with UNCTAD, which would put it above most of the other UN specialised agencies.[276] That means, *inter alia*, that the draft convention would have to be ratified by resolution at a special session of UNGA. Immediately below the Assembly in the structure would be the *International Admiralty Court* (IDC),[277] the maritime equivalent of the ICJ, but subordinate to the latter. Appeals would come from the judicial bodies and go to the ICJ. The IDC would be desirable as a specialist maritime appeals court.[278]

The *Secretariat,* on the other hand, would perform all the necessary duties and functions of an administrative nature. Answerable to the Assembly, would be a *Secretary General* who would be the Chief Administrative Executive,[279] answerable to the IMMA membership through the UN Secretary General. He/She should preferably come from among the DMNS but be assisted by experts drawn

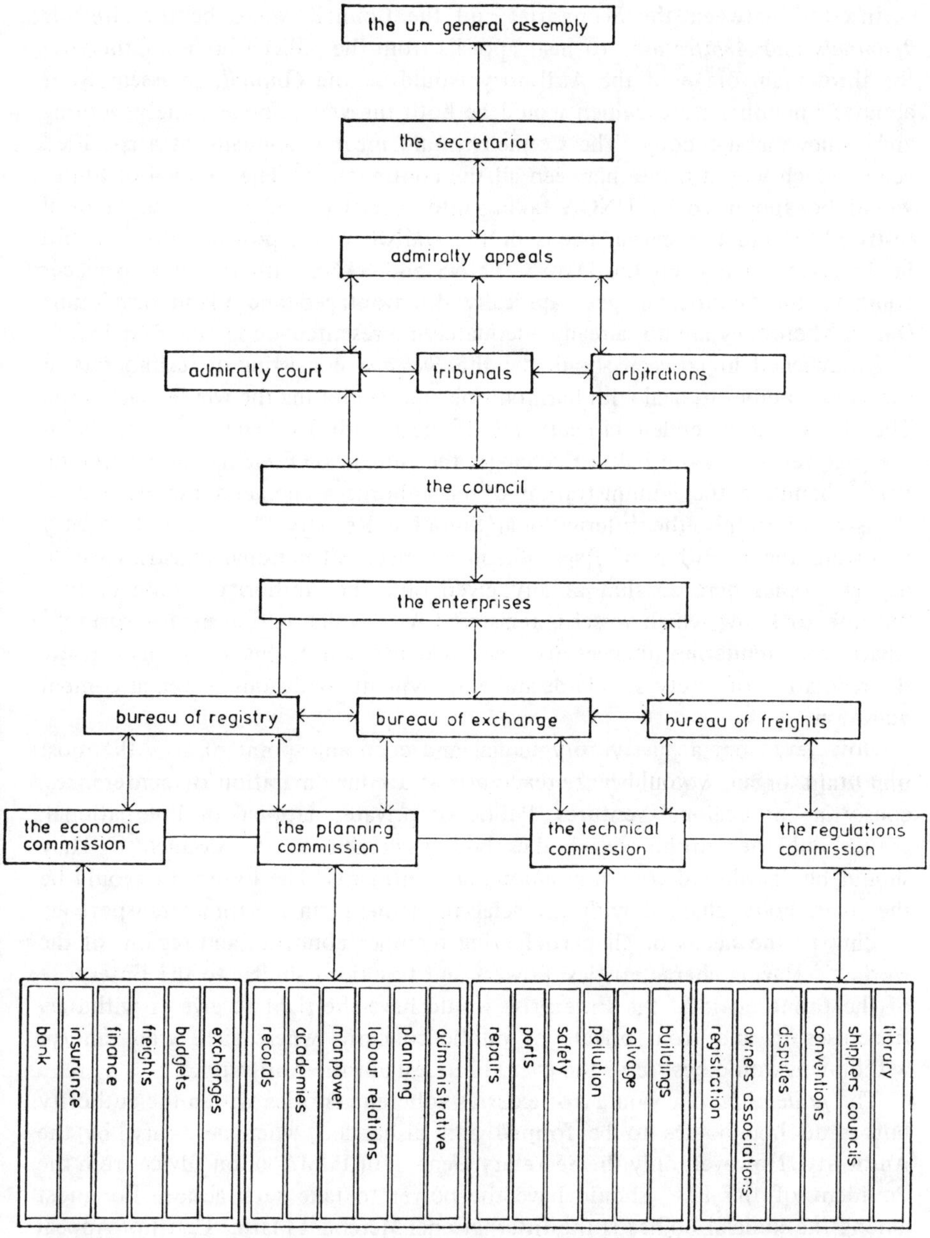

Figure 6. Proposed international shipping authority – the international merchant marine authority (IMMA).

equitably from the participating UN member states, taking into consideration geographical distribution and the special interests of the DMNS.[280] The Secretariat should be based at a central and neutral location. Malta, due to its central situation between America, Asia, Africa and Europe could be ideal for the headquarters of the Secretariat. Its strategic position in the Mediterranean on the main East/West route would merit added consideration.[281]

Inserted between the Secretariat and the Council would be the *Appeals Tribunals* and *Arbitrations* to hear appeals from the judicial bodies. Otherwise the third main organ of the Authority would be the *Council*, an assembly of about 50 member states which would be both the watchdog and the governing and policy-making body. The Council should meet bi-annually at a specified venue which would rotate between all the continents.[282] The Council of States would be appointed by UNGA taking into special consideration geographical distribution and the special needs of the DMNS. Where possible, there should be 15 states each from the DMNS, TMNS and STNS with the other 5 places going to the landlocked, geographically disadvantaged and island developing DMNS where they are not already adequately represented among the first 15.[283]

Sandwiched in-between should be the *Bureaux* consisting of technocrats or specialised bodies to deal with harmonising and facilitating the whole machinery. The three recommended bureaux are to deal with Exchange,[284] – an international version of the Baltic Exchange; the Bureau of Freights and Commodities[285] handling the administration of oceanborne trade, and the Bureau of Registry or simply the International Shipping Registry,[286] a central registry following the abolition of flags of convenience. All national registries would deposit copies here so that at any given time the Authority should be in a position to know which vessel is registered with which nation in the world.[287] Apart from rendering unnecessary flags of convenience, this would also ensure the regulation of safety standards and employment conditions as well as combat pollution.

However, from a purely commercial and economic point of v the most important organ would be the *Enterprises*; a conglomeration of conferences, consortia and regional ventures. Public or private, national or international, they should be autonomous bodies but answerable to the Council.[288] They should be distributed equitably among all continents. The Enterprise would be the main body charged with financial investments in maritime transport according to the needs of all participating member countries and regions of the world.[289] Having characteristics, powers and functions similar to the Enterprise of the proposed ISA, the Enterprise would have the right to give or withdraw franchises to and from private or public concerns where such grant and/or withdrawn, would best serve the overall interests of the Authority.[290]

The *judicial bodies* would not exist as coherent entities within the authority but as ad hoc bodies to be formed and disbanded, when necessary, by the Authority. However, only the Secretary General of IMMA, upon advice from the President of the IAC, should have the power to take such action. Foremost among the judicial bodies is the International Merchant Marine Court of Appeal (the IAC),[291] hearing appeals from all the appeals tribunals, arbitrations, dispute settlement and disciplinary bodies including any Commissions of Inquiries that may be set up from time to time. From here the appeals may go straight to the ICJ. The IAC may also advise the main organs of the Authority where litigation may not be the best course of action or would be prejudicial to the interests of the Authority.[292]

To assist the Enterprise with its day to day running of the Authority's business would be a group of *specialist commisions,* four in number, in liaison with the Bureaux but answerable mainly to the Enterprise.[293] Being located in proximity to the main operations of the Enterprise, the commisions would be staffed by highly skilled and qualified civil-servant-like types of decision implementors. The *Planning Commission* would be responsible for the general planning of the Enterprises investments.[294] Under its mandate would come responsibility for research and the administration of the maritime academies; recruitment, training and disciplining personnel; manpower, labour relations and general administrative planning.[295] The International Seamen's Union, the ILO, etc., would probably also come within its jurisdiction.

As the name would suggest, the *Economic Commission* would deal with and handle the Authority's finances, revenues, and budgetory issues; the main source of the Authority's revenues would come from the UN to cover the costs of administration.[296] This should not be confused with the source of revenue of the Enterprises, entirely for investment purposes which would come from a special UN fund, to be established for the purpose.[297] The main features of the Economic Commission would be the International Merchant Marine Bank (IMMB), a central Marine Insurance (a kind of international Lloyds), and a Central Pension and General Purposes Scheme.[298]

The *Technical Commission*, on the other hand, would handle matters relating to ports and inland water transport;[299] the technical aspects of safety, pollution prevention and environmental protection; shipbuilding, repairs, salvage and bunkering operations, etc. Falling under its jurisdiction would be the already existing frameworks, such as the IM and UNEP.[300] Working closely with the Technical Commission would be the *Regulations Commission,* a kind of legal office and/or drafting facet of the judicial bodies to handle matters relating to the Central Registry,[301] Shipper's Councils and Shipowners' Associations, initial dispute settlements, legislative drafting, conventions and liaison or public relations office.[302]

5. Conclusion

The approach previously adopted by the TMNS was bound to fail in the long run though it might solve short-term problems. This was because it viewed the problem only from the standpoint and interests of the TMNS. Such one-sided solutions were bound to fail. They not only overlooked the fundamental issues but also aggravated the situation in some respects. Thus, the administrative and legislative approaches did not get the backing of even the major members of the TMNS, such as the US. Similarly, the alternative investment approach might as well have been designed to shelve the problem rather than to face it. The same can be said of the scheme for the DMNS. These developments, however, were a step in the right direction and formed a basis upon which improvements could later be made.

At the same time it is rather ironic to recommend joint ventures and multinational shipping enterprises at a time when there is growing concern by the developing countries towards the alleged abuses of the multinational corporations. The present proposal, however, is rather different. In the first place, it would involve participation by the DMNS as joint and equal partners as far as possible. They would have the opportunity to consult and be consulted and be part of the decision-making process to influence the venture. It would take into consideration their interests and serve them. Although the proposed cooperation would raise problems of its own, it would solve the fundamental problems of which the restrictive practices are but symptoms. By avoiding inefficiency, inequality, duplication and bifurcation of the shipping industry, it would reap the benefits of economies of scale. Above all it would eliminate the reasons that gave rise to the demand for national fleets.

Similarly, the International Shipping Authority would eliminate the remaining grievances of the DMNS and chart a brighter future for national fleets. The foregoing recommendations for the authority aim to eradicate the problems raised in the introduction – why create national fleets? Regulation of the liner conference system, the phasing out of flags of convenience, and the control of multinational shipping corporations are the basic essentials for cooperation and joint ventures in international shipping. They would be in line with the general aims of the UN system and especially the demand for the *New International Economic Order* generally and the *New International Maritime Order* in particular. From the foregoing analysis it is clear that previous attempts by both the TMNS and DMNS fell far short of an acceptable solution to the question of national fleets. These said attempts are diametrically opposed to each other and in no way provide the compromise which is the only viable solution to the problems raised by national fleets.

Notes

1. As well as flag discrimination.
2. Caused by inefficiency.
3. See the diagram ahead.
4. See Strange, S., 'Who runs shipping', *International Affairs,* 1976, p. 346, at 364.
5. See also 'Fairer shares?', *Fairplay,* 1979, 23rd Aug., p. 3.
6. Chrzanowski, I., 'Current aspects of international shipping policy', *Marit. Pol. & Man.,* Vol. 5, No. 4, Oct. 1978, pp. 289–495, at 291.
7. See Neef, S. C., 'The UN code of conduct for liner conferences' *JWTL,* Vol. 00, No. 00, pp. 398–423, at 416.
8. See Chrzanowski, I., 'Manilla, a chance to deal the cards again', *Fairplay,* 17th May 1979, p. 7.
9. UNCTAD, Doc. No. TD/CODE/1/Rev. 1 & Corr. 1, 1974; reprinted in 13 *ILM* 912.
10. Zamora, S., 'UNCTAD II – the question of shipping', *JWTL,* 1973, Vol. 7, No. 1, Jan–Feb. issue, p. 91.
11. Bosles, W. & Green, W., 'The liner conference convention: launching an international regulatory regime', *Law. & Pol. Int. Bus.,* 1974, Vol. 6, p. 533.
12. Bennathan, E. & Walters, A. 'Conferences: an economic analysis', *J. Marit. L. & Comm.,* 1973, Vol. 4, p. 93.
13. Sturmey, S. G., 'Economics and international liner conferences, *J. Trans. L. Pol.,* 1967, Vol. 1, p. 190.
14. Marx, D., 'Regulation of international liner shipping and freedom of the seas', *I. Incl. Econ.,* 1967, Vol. 16, p. 46.
15. Marx, D., *International Shipping Cartels: A Study of Industrial Self-Regulation by Shipping Conferences,* 1953.
16. UNCTAD, Doc. No. TD/B/C.4/62/Rev. 1, 1970; liner conference system.
17. Ellsworth, R., 'Competition of rationalisation in the liner industry?', *J. Man. L. Comm.,* 1979, Vol. 10, p. 497.

18. Lawrence, S. A., *International Sea Transport: The Years Ahead,* 1972, p. 153; Strange, S., *op. cit.* p. 354.
19. Agman., 'Competition, rationalization and US shipping policy', *J. Marit. L. Comm.,* 1976, Vol. 8, p. 1, at pp. 13–14.
20. Note, these are problems of the use of the traditional methods and not the national fleets themselves.
21. See also OEEC *Maritime Transport,* 1954, p. 53.
22. Note that the OEEC was the forerunner of the OECD.
23. See also 'Rights of entry into maritime ports in international law', *op. cit.*
24. See also the tribunals' findings in the above arbitration.
25. Ever since, the US and her major trading partners have drifted further apart on shipping policy.
26. See also *The Randals Commission* that was sent to the US from Europe in 1954.
27. See also the representation of the General Council of British Shipping to the American Federal Maritime Commission.
28. Diplomatic pressures seem to achieve a little bit more than mere legislative approaches.
29. However, none of these approaches aim at tackling the fundamental problems.
30. See also texts under the paragraph countervailing flag discriminations in Chapter 2 of this study.
31. *Ibid.;* and also retaliatory flag discriminations in Chapter 3, *ibid.*
32. See also the Spanish dilemma discussed earlier in connection with this in Chapter 2.
33. Cf. the Indian experience of September 1st, 1964, in relation to the American waivers.
33A. *EEC Treaty,* Part 3, Chapter 1, Section 1, Articles 85–94; Howard Smith, 'New calls for EEC shipping policy', *Lloyd's List,* No. 52383, of Tuesday 7th June 1983, p. 2.
34. *Ibid.,* Article 84; see again Howard Smith, 'EEC may seek ship deal with Japan', *Lloyd's List,* No. 52352, of 29th April 1983, Friday – front page.
35. *Ibid.* Article 74; and Bridget Hogan, 'Industry views are canvassed on liner code', *Lloyd's List,* No. 52352, of Friday 29th April 1983 – front page.
36. Council Regulation (EEC) No. 954/79 of May 15, 1979; but see 'EEC lashed over transport policy failure', *Lloyd's List,* No. 52312, of Friday 11th March 1983 – front page.
37. For the text of the package see *Lloyd's List,* No. 52408, of Wednesday July 6 1983, p. 6.
38. Hansard (House of Lords) 29th June 1982, Cols. 163–166 during the debate on the *Merchant Shipping (Liner Conferences) Act 1982.*
39. *Ibid.;* see also David Mott 'UK cargo on foreign ships grave threat', *Lloyd's List,* No. 52351, of 28th April 1983, Thursday – front page.
40. *Ibid.;* see also Hansard (House of Commons) Vol. 21, Col. 708; and Ian Gronback, 'British waterways board warns on consequences of UK fleet neglect', *Lloyd's List,* No. 52348, of Monday 28th April 1983, p. 3.
41. Article 4(1) of the *Brussels Package;* and Bridget Hogan 'General council of British shipping report backs freedom to flag out', *Lloyd's List,* No. 52372, of 24th May 1983 – front page.
42. *Ibid.;* but see 'EEC faces criticism over shipping', in *Lloyd's List,* No. 52275, of Thursday 27th January 1983 – front page.
43. For details see 'Impasse over UNCTAD cargo code checks trade for expanding fleet', *Lloyd's List,* No. 52292, of Wednesday 16th February 1983, p. 7.
44. Article 4(2) of the *Brussels Package;* Cf. 'The UNCTAD code, what is it?', *Norwegian Shipping News,* Vol. 38, No. 9, of 27th August 1982, p. 3.
45. *Ibid.,* Article 4(3); Cf. Val Preston, 'EEC package expected for shipbuilders', *Lloyd's List,* No. 52293, of Thursday 17th February 1983, p. 3.
46. *Ibid.,* Article 4(4). See, however, 'The case for the defence', (the failure of the EEC's Council of Ministers to formulate a Common Transport Policy) *Cargo Systems International,* Vol. 10, No. 5, May 1983, pp. 73–75.
47. Lisa Buckingham, 'UK under pressure on liner code', *Lloyd's List,* No. 52403, of Thursday June 30 1983 – front page; see also pp. 3 and 10.
48. Bridget Hogan, 'Countdown to vital talks on cargo sharing', *Lloyd's List,* No. 52415, Thursday July 14 1983 – front page.

49. Seventy-five per cent of world liner trade is owned by or is between the TMNS whilst only 25% is between the DMNS and STNS codists.
50. Article 4(5) of the Brussels package; but see 'US wheat deal may revive trade war with the EEC', *Lloyd's List,* No. 52272, of Monday 24th January 1983 – back page.
51. See the author's views on 'How the Brussels package will effectively undermine liner code', *Lloyd's List,* No. 52434, of Friday August 5 1983, p. 4.
52. Note 49 *supra;* and 'European shippers council warning over the UN code', *Lloyd's List,* No. 52342, of 18th April 1983 – front page.
53. See, for instance, Vanya Walker-Leigh, 'US opposed to UNCTAD shipping probe demand', *Lloyd's List,* No. 52406, of Monday July 4 1983, p. 3.
54. Since the Code on Liner Conferences (1974) the idea has been to extend the Code to bulk carriage. Support for this started at UNCTAD V (Manilla 1979). See also Vanya Walker-Leigh (reporting from UNCTAD VI in Belgrade), 'Concept of bulk sharing backed by Third World', in *Lloyd's List,* No. 52404 of July 1 1983, p.2.
55. See, for instance, Howard Smith, 'EEC warns against curbs on shipping', *Lloyd's List,* No. 52410, of Friday July 8 1983, p. 3.
56. See views expressed by delegates at the Lloyd's Shipping Economist Conference, 'UNCTAD liner code: the new order', held on 4–5 at the Royal Lancaster Hotel, London.
57. But see Dr. H. B. Desai, 'Outdated clauses mean fresh legislation', and Lisa Buckingham (ed.), 'Perplexed lawyers try to make sense of 'hotchpotch' UN code', *Lloyd's List,* No. 52416, of July 15 1983, p. 4.
58. See, for example David Mott, 'NUS attacks UK's 'free trade' policy', *Lloyd's List,* No. 52408, of July 6 1983 – front page.
59. See, for example, the British *Merchant Shipping (Liner Conferences) Act 1982,* the *Protection of Trading Interests Act 1980* in which the UK legislature sought to use these powers.
60. Note 53, *supra;* see also Lisa Buckingham (ed.) 'Japanese decision on UNCTAD code will be critical to FEFC', *Lloyd's List,* No. 52422, of Friday July 22 1983, p. 4.
61. Note 'Rate regulation in ocean shipping', *Harv. L. Rev.,* 1965, p. 635; Bennathan & Walters, *op. cit.,* p. 93.
62. Brown, R., *Transport and Economic Integration of South America, 1966,* pp. 145–49.
63. *Ibid.,* pp. 96–97.
64. Jantscher, G., *Bread upon the Waters: Federal Aids to Maritime Industries,* 1975, pp. 76 and 104.
65. *Economist,* October 16, 1976, p. 21.
66. *Ibid.* p. 23.
67. Goss, R., *Studies in Maritime Economics,* 1970, p. 46.
68. *Economist, op. cit.* p. 21.
69. UNCTAD, Doc. No. TD/26/Rev. 1, at pp. 7–8, 1968.
70. Goss, *Supra,* p. 54.
71. *Ibid.*
72. UNCTAD on the Establishment of Merchant Marines, (Note 42 above) p. 31.
73. *Ibid.,* 32–33.
74. *Ibid.* pp. 35, 57–63.
75. Goss, *supra,* at 49–51.
76. *Rochdale Report,* paras. 85–90.
77. Alexander Report (US), 1914.
78. UNCTAD, Doc. No. E/CONF. 46/133, 1964.
79. Herman, L., 'Code of conduct for liner conferences: frustration on the road to Utopia', 1966, *Cam. Yearbook IL,* Vol. 14, p. 157.
80. Rodiere, R., 'Code de conduite des conference maritimes' *Journal de Droit International,* 1976, Vol. 103, p. 335.
81. Holderness, C., 'Economic analysis of the UN code of conduct for liner conferences', *Stan. L. Rev.,* 1977, Vol. 29, p. 853.
82. Shah, M., 'Implementation of the UN code', *J. Mar. L. Com.,* 1979, Vol. 9, p. 79.
83. Grossman, W., *Oceanfreight Rates,* 1956.

84. Bevier. 'Ratemaking in international shipping conferences', *Stan. T.I.E.S.*, 1969, Vol. 4, p. 84.
85. Heaver, 'The structure of liner conference rates', *J. Indus. Econ.* 1973, Vol. 21, p. 251.
86. Note, 'Rate regulation in ocean transport: developing countries confront the liner conference system', *Cal. L. Rev.*, 1971, Vol. 59, p. 1299.
87. Deakins, *supra*, p. 70–112.
88. UNCTAD Doc. No. TD/B/C.4/128, 1975.
89. UNCTAD Doc. No. TD/B/C.4/61/Rev. 1, 1970.
90. UN Doc. No. E/CN.12/812, 1969.
91. Evans & Benham, 'A fork tariff system for liner freight rates', *J. Trans. Econ. Pol.*, 1978, Vol. 9, p. 62.
92. UNCTAD Doc. No. TD/B/C.4/31, 1967.
93. Patton, J. R. & Schornhorst, T. F., 'Cargo preference and flag discriminations', *Geo. Wash. L. Rev.*, 1965, pp. 257–87.
94. *House Hearings* Doc. No. 805, 63rd Cong., 2nd Sess., 1914.
95. UNCTAD Liner Conference System, *op. cit.* pp. 24–41.
96. Koch, A. G. M., *Current Pricing Behaviour in Liner Shipping*, Bergen 1968.
97. Bennathan & Walters, *supra*, p. 100.
98. US House Committee on Merchant Marine & Fisheries: *Report on Steamship Agreements and Applications in American, Foreign and Domestic Trade.*
99. UNCTAD Secretariet, Report by, Freight Rates: Costs and Freight Rates in Liner Trades, p. 105.
100. Heaver, 'Trans-pacific trade liner shipping, and conference rates', *Logistic and Transport Review*, Spring 1972.
101. Even UNCTAD favours consultation in shipping.
102. High costs are no doubt one of the major objections arising from the use of traditional methods to establish national fleets.
103. See also the problems we raised in Chapter II of this study.
104. Disruptions of international shipping is one of the major consequences of protectionism.
105. Some of this may not be alternative as have been tried.
106. Kirkpatrick, C. H., 'UNCTAD V issues and prospects 1979', *J.W.T.L.*, Vol. 13, No. 3, May–June Issue, p. 279.
107. Kirkpatrick & Jeokes, S., 'UNCTAD V. The results of 1979', *J.W.T.L.*, Vol. 13, No. 6, Nov.–Dec. Issue p. 535.
108. UNCTAD Doc. No. TD/B/C.4/20/Rev. 1, 1970.
109. UNCTAD Doc. No. TD/B/108/Supp. 1/Rev. 1.
110. Valente, R., 'The participation of developing countries in shipping', *International Conciliation*, Vol. 582, p. 27, at 56.
111. Simmonds, K. R., 'The central American Common Market: an experiment in regional integration', *I. & C.L.Q.*, 1967.
112. *Ibid.*, Vol. 16, pp. 911–45.
113. Johnson, M. D., *East African Shipping Trade and Development*, 1970.
114. *Norwegian News*, No. 21, 1976, p. 22.
115. Tanoe Echimane, 'The Ivorien maritime strategy and NIMO', *UWIST Diploma Dissertation*, UWIST 1981.
116. US Douglas Report, p. 8; also 1964 *House Hearings.*
116A. Ibid.
117. Note, *Harv. L. Rev.*, 1965, p. 635, at 636–37.
118. *Pakistan Times*, July 19, 1965, p. 1, Col. 7.
119. Reported from interviews with MARAD officials in London, Washington D.C., October 1965.
120. Ever since there has been cooperation in many other fields in the Caribean.
121. Sino-Tanzania venture is 'Friendship' and Mozambique is 'Urafiki' which means the same.
122. UNCTAD Trade & Development Board – Official Records – Third Sess., Suppl. No. 2 Annex 1(a), para 11 & 12.
123. *Ibid.*, Tenth Sess. Suppl. No. 5 Annex 1.

124. UNCTAD Doc. No. TD/B/C.4/178/Rev. 1.
125. *Ibid.*, Section B Joint Ventures involving DMNS, para. 98 pp. 34–35, at 35.
126. UNCTAD *Review of Maritime Transport,* 1977.
127. UNCTAD Doc. No. TD/108/Supp. 1/Rev. 1.
128. *Ibid.*, UN New York: UN Sales No. E:72:11:D:17.
129. UNCTAD, *National Shipping Enterprises,* Chapter VII.
130. Vagts, D. F., 'The multinational enterprises: a new challenge', *Harv. L. Rev.,* 1969–70, Vol. 83, pp. 739–92.
131. *In re-Huggins Estate,* 96 N.J. Eq. 275, 125, A27, 30.
132. *Halferty* v *Karr,* 188 MO.App.241, 175 Sw. 145, 147.
132A. *Ibid.*
133. Behrmann, J. N., *National Interests,* 1961, p. 100.
134. Rubin, S. J., 'Multinational enterprises and national sovereignty', *L. Pol. Int. Bus.,* 1971, Vol. 3, pp. 1–41.
135. Gower, *Basic Principles of Company Law,* 4th ed., p. 81.
136. UNCTAD: Establishment and/or Development of National Fleets.
137. Grundy, K., 'Flags of Convenience', *P.C.L.,* 1978.
138. UNCTAD Doc. No. TD/B/C.4/59/Corr. 1.
139. UNCTAD Secretariat, Report by, *The Nature and Extent of Cargo Reservation.*
140. UNCTAD Secretariat, Report by, *Unitization of Cargo Sales,* No.E.71.11. D.2., part 1, note 2, para. 147.
141. *Ibid., The Liner Conference System.*
142. See the example of *Flota Mercante Grancolombiana.*
143. For example, the Inter-American Development Bank willingness to advance loans to *Flota.*
144. See para 3 of Resolution DE-92/66. of the Board of Executive Directors of the above bank.
145. *Ibid.;* reproduced in the *Inter-American Institute of Legal Studies,* instruments relating to the economic integration of Latin America (Dobbs Ferry, NY, Oceana Publications, 1968) pp. 367–69.
146. See also article 2 of the agreement establishing the African Development Bank, signed in Khartoum on August 4, 1963; for text see UN Treaty Series Vol. 510, 1964, p. 46.
147. See also African Development Bank. Loans and Investments – Statements of Policy and Procedure. (Abidjan, 1969).
148. UNCTAD, *Financing for the purchase of new and second-hand flags by the developing countries.*
148A. *Ibid.*
149. *Ibid.;* Doc. No. TD/B/C.4/58 and Corr. I and Add. 1, Appendix III.
150. UNCTAD, *Action taken by the OECD in connection with the Understanding on Export Credits for Ships.*
151. *Ibid.*, Doc. No. TD/B/C.4/L.71.
152. See also the *OECD Understanding on the Export Credits for Ships* concluded in May 1969.
153. And UNCTAD, *Report of the group of exports on problems involved in the trade and economic development of the landlocked developing countries.*
154. *Ibid.;* also, *Official Report of the Trade and Development Board,* Tenth Session, first series parts, Annex, Agenda Item 13.
155. See also US *Congressional Hearings* (Washington DC) Vol. 73, No. 206, 27 October.
156. See Chapter V of UNCTAD Report, *Expansion and development of merchant marines in developing countries, supra.*
157. Cf. UNCTAD Report, *Manpower requirements and training facilities for the establishment or expansion of merchant marines in developing countries.*
158. *Ibid.*, Doc. No. TD/B/C.4/65, and Corr.1–2.
159. Official records of the Trade and Development Boards, Ninth Session, Third Part, Annex, Agenda item 15.
160. The International Chamber of Commerce was founded in June 1920, Paris, following a decision taken at the International Trade Conference of 1919, Atlantic City, to

establish a permanent organisation of world business. Registered by *French Ministeral Decree,* 24 January 1949, Paris.

161. See also Ronald Swayne, 'Shipping – some political and economic consequences of changes in technology and ownership', *Transport Review,* Vol. 3, No. 2, April/June 1983, p. 139.
162. The ICC Sea Transport Commission is one of the many under the Transport Policy Board of the Transport and Trade faciliation Secretariat.
163. See again Note 160 *infra;* and 'FMC warns on protectionism', *Lloyd's List* No. 52322 of Wednesday 23rd March 1983, p. 3.
164. A view gathered, by the author, after scanning through the conference reports and press releases; see also 'Third world drops finance demands', *Lloyd's List* No. 52395 of Tuesday 21st June 1983 – front page.
165. For further classification of countries by the UNCTAD Committee on Shipping see Appendix I, pp. 17–19.
166. For details of the ICC Project and the Caracas Declaration see 'EEC joint venture project underway', repoted in *Fairplay International Shipping Weekly,* Vol. 286, No. 5205 of 9th June 1983 p. 10.
167. *Ibid.*
168. See also Bridget Hogan, 'Experts urge joint shipping ventures', reporting the efforts of the ICC project, in *Lloyd's List* No. 52352 of Friday 29th April 1983, p. 3.
169. See, for example, UNCTAD Document No. TD/B/C.4/230, 'Report on availability of technical assistance . . . '.
170. On the model of the ESCAFE Regional Maritime Code.
171. See UNCTAD Document No. TD/B/C.4/229 'Review of the studies and activities of other international organisations concerning technical assistance and international financing and aid . . . '.
172. Cf. conditions for joint ventures outlined at the beginning of this section.
173. For further comparison see 'European consortium goes into joint operation with Malaysian line', *Fairplay International Shipping Weekly,* Vol. 285, No. 5189 of 17th February 1983, p. 7.
174. The commission provides the widest possible forum for suppliers and users of maritime and intermodal transport, and for other commercial interests concerned. It promotes general freedom from governmental intervention in the commercial aspects of maritime and intermodal operation.
175. 'Container link forged between Europe and Angola', Note 172, *infra,* p. 7.
176. Cf. 'Another joint venture bids for Chinese offshore supply now', *ibid.*
177. See also 'Joint venture set up in vegetable oil trade', *Lloyd's List* No. 52390 of Wednesday 15th June 1983, p. 5.
178. 'ICC to report on joint venture shipping firms', *Lloyd's List* No. 52362 of Thursday 12th May 1983, p. 4.
179. Mutual trust can only be gained by practice. It may be prudent to cite the centre for decision-making and vessel management somewhere in the DMNS.
180. Note 168, *infra;* see also UNCTAD Document No. TD/B/C.4/189 Maritime Management Training in the Developing Countries.
181. Note 169, *infra;* see also UNCTAD Document No. TD/B/C.4/196 Directory of Services for technical assistance in shipping and ports to developing countries.
182. Note 153, *infra;* see also 'Latin American warning on cargo-reservation' *Lloyd's List* No. 52362 of Thursday 12th May 1983, p. 4.
183. Though the ICC is based in Paris, the temporary Project Office is based at the Atlantic Container Line House (ACL) Herbert Walker Avenue, Western Docks, Port of Southampton in England.
184. Note 179, *infra;* the recently established World Maritime University (under IMO) in Malmo might also be useful.
185. See again notes 165 and 177, *infra;* and UNCTAD Document No. TD/B/C.4/241 'Technical assistance and training: directory on shipassist'.
186. Information obtained from an interview between the author and Mr. Angus Nicholson, the Project Consultant at the Southampton office.

187. Interview with the Chairman of the Caracas Steering Committee, Mr. Muller, the vice-chairman of Van Ommeren Shipping Company of Rotterdam.
188. Note that the ICC's current working programme aims basically at supporting all policies favouring expansion of international trade and at examining jointly with the major IGO's all measures which might help the liberalization of international trade and promote world trade. Particular attention is at present being given to the special needs of the developing countries.
189. This would be more appropriate with the aims of the ICC which is to represent all the economic factors of international business including commerce, industry, transportation and finance; ascertain and express the considered judgement of those interested in international business; secure effective and consistent action for improvement of business conditions between nations and for the solution of international economic problems; encourage intercourse and better understanding between businessmen and business organisations of the various countries; and thereby promote peace and cordial relations among nations.
190. For details see Alan M. Smith, 'Maritime international cooperation centre of Japan's (MICCJ) link with the developing nations', *Containerisation International,* Vol. 16, No. 7 July 1982, p. 41.
191. *Ibid.;* see also 'Japanese report: consensus for change? . . . ', *Seatrade,* Vol. 13, No. 7, July, 1983, pp. 97–119.
192. *Ibid.;* and 'Japanese shipbuilding and allied industries', (Special Supplement), Supplement to Motor Ship, July 1983, pp. 22.
193. *Ibid.;* see also *Lloyd's List,* 30 June 1983, p. 4.
194. See, for example, 'Japanese develop high speed ship propelled by electromagnets', *Fairplay International Shipping Weekly,* Vol. 285, No. 5192, 10th March 1983, p. 29.
195. The JSA (for example) alone has a membership of just over 200 companies of which approximately 80 trade internationally and, therefore, with the DMNS; 'JAMDA conducts research on wind pressure resistance of ship's superstructure', *Zosen,* Vol. 28, No. 3 June 1983, pp. 24–30.
196. Note 190, *infra.*
197. The MICCJ is also backed by the Ministry of Transport, which is responsible for Japan's maritime industries, each sector being controlled by a separate bureau. These include the Bureau of Shipping, the Ship Bureau, Bureau of Seafarers, Bureau of Ports and Harbours and the Maritime Safety Agency. It also controls a number of research institutes, training establishments and port construction organisations.
198. 'Japanese ship management – a survey', *Lloyd's List Manager,* Vol. 3, No. 9, December 1982, pp. 13–17.
199. See also 'Japan: meeting new challenges – special report', *Lloyd's List,* No. 52425 of Tuesday 26th July 1983, pp. 5–19.
200. See also 'Japanese ratification of UN Liner Code could isolate US', *Lloyd's List,* No. 52366 of Tuesday 17th May 1983 – front page.
201. Lundberg, K. & Malaguerra, H., 'West Africa RO–RO come to stay', *RO–RO 81 International Conference,* pp. 323–29.
202. See 'Containerisation – special report', *Lloyd's List,* 23 June 1983, p. 5–12.
203. 'Kawasaki completes containerisation and LPG tanker for K line (the "Richmond Bridge")', *Asian Shipping,* May 1983, pp. 31–33.
204. Smith, A., 'Containerisation report', *Seatrade,* Vol. 13 No. 4 April 1983, pp. 97–119; 'The containership fleet increases its threat to refer tramp operators', *Containerisation International,* Vol. 17, No. 8, August 1983, pp. 34–36.
205. 'Liner shipping and the developing countries', *Norwegian Shipping News,* Vol. 39, No. 7, 3rd June 1983, pp. 79–84.
206. *Ibid.,* Doc. No. TD/B/288, para 5(b).
207. See also UNCTAD Report, *Promotional Freight Rates on non-traditional exports of developing countries.*
208. *Ibid.,* Doc. No. 105 and Corr. 1.
209. *Ibid.;* and Supplement to the report TD/105/Suppl. 1 and Corr. 1.
210. UNCTAD Secretariat Report, *The Economics of Bulk Cargoes.*

211. *Ibid.*, Doc. No. TD/B/C.4/67.
212. See also UNCTAD; *The Maritime transportation of tropical timber.*
213. *Ibid.*, Doc. No. TD/B/C.4/59 and Corr. 1.
214. Ellis, G. B., 'US multinational corporations: the impact of foreign direct investment on US foreign relations', *San Diego L. Rev.*, 1973–74, Vol. II, pp. 1–26.
215. Cf. UNCTAD Report, *The maritime transportation of natural rubber.*
216. *Ibid.*, UN Publication Sales No. E.70. 11.D.11.
217. Reich, R. B., 'Global social responsibility for the multinationals', *Texas I.L.J.*, 1973, Vol. 8, pp. 187–217.
218. UNCTAD Report, *The maritime transportation of jute.*
219. *Ibid.;* Doc. No. TD/B/C.4/85 and Corr. 1.
220. Nehemkis, P., 'Supranational control of the international corporations – a dissenting view', *Cal. W.L.R.*, Vol. 10, pp. 286–324.
221. *Ibid.*
222. See also UNCTAD Report, *Consultation in Shipping,* first report.
223. *Ibid.;* see also second report Doc. No. TD/B/C.4/78.
224. *Ibid.;* see particularly Chapter 1, para. 6.
225. Hahn, M., 'Functional limits of multinational enterprises', *N.Y. U.J. I. L. & Pol.*, 1974, Vol. 7, pp. 475–93.
226. *Far Eastern Economic Review* (Hong Kong), 20 Feb. 1971. p. 24 and 22 May 1971.
227. See the decision by Cameroon in early 1971 to withdraw from the multinational airline Air Afrique (see, for example, *Le Monde,* 21 July 1971).
228. For example, see the structure of Scandinavian Airlines Systems (SAS).
229. SAS involves Denmark, Norway and Sweden.
230. As was the case of the EANSL of the EAC.
231. See, for example, Articles 4 & 6 of the *SAS Consortium Agreement,* Revision 1962.
232. *Ibid.;* see also Justice Henrik Bahr, 'The Scandinavian Airlines System; its origin, present organisation and legal aspects', *Arkiv far Luftrett,* Vol. 1, No. 4, Nov. 1961.
233. For further details see Gorton, L., 'Joint ventures in shipping law', *J. Bus. L.*, 1978, pp. 238–44.
234. *Ibid.;* pp. 240–41.
235. Dawson, F. G. *et al.*, 'Towards a new international economic order', *Virg. J.I.L.*, 1975, Vol. 16, pp. 297–353.
236. Krenin, M. E. & Finger, J. M., 'A critical survey of the New International Economic Order', *J.W.T.L.*, 1976, Vol. 10, pp. 493–512.
237. Pisar, S. *et al.*, 'International trade: the role of multinational companies in the international community', *J.I.L. & Econ.*, 1975, Vol. 10, pp. 267–353.
238. McWhinney, E., 'The international law making process and the New International Economic Order', *Can. Yearbook of I.L.*, 1976, Vol. 14, pp. 57–72.
239. Despicht, M. S., 'European transportation policy as a model for transport in developing countries' (conference proceedings), pp. 31–42.
240. Matthews, H., 'Protectionism in shipping supply is a boomerang', *Norwegian News,* 1980, No. 14, pp. 12–14.
241. Davies, J. E., 'The economics of the open conference system', *Marit. Pol. & Man.*, Vol. 7, No. 2, April 1980, pp. 85–103.
242. Totland, T., 'Protectionism in shipping and some economic effects', *ibid.*, pp. 103–15.
243. *Norwegian News,* Vol. 15 No. 10, Nov. 1980, pp. 88–91.
244. Hareveld, V. M., *National Transport Planning and Coordination in the Developing Countries.*
245. *Ibid.;* 'Transport planning in the developing countries' (conference proceedings) pp. 79–89.
246. See Ewing's article regarding the legal position in Great Britain today, *J. Mon. L. Comm.*, Vol. II, No. 4, July 1980, pp. 804–18.
247. Cf. Rajwar, L. M. S., 'Open registry fleets, the case for a modified approach', *Fairplay,* Vol. 269, No. 4980, Feb. 1979, pp. 13–15.
248. See also Couper, G., 'Leading Liberia's counter-attack', *Seatrade,* Vol. 8, No. 12, Dec. 1978, pp. 24–25.

249. Krem, A. F., 'Financing the fleets of emerging maritime nations', *Asian Shipping,* No. 1, Jan. 1978, pp. 28–29.
250. Metaxas, B. N., 'Flags of convenience and shipping strategies', *Maritime Research, European Shipping and Shipbuilding* (Conference), 1978, pp. 198–220.
251. Grey, M., 'Convenience flags – fewer friends each day', *Fairplay,* Vol. 271 No. 5013, 27 Sept. 1979, p. 7.
252. Boull, D., *A Guide for transport planning for the developing countries,* MOD London, HMSO, 1978.
253. Hawkins, R. C., *Transport in a Developing Country* MSC Thesis, Southampton University, 1974.
254. Hoyle, B. S., *Transport and Development,* Selected Readings, 1973.
255. Haepelle, E. T., *Transport and National Goals,* 1979.
256. Vambery, R. G., 'Commentary: nationalism in shipping', *Mal. Pol. & Man.,* Vol. 3, No. 4, April 1974, pp. 243–47.
257. *Ibid.,* p. 245.
258. *Ibid.,* p. 246.
259. Wheble, B. S., 'Cooperation through trade facilitation', *ICC Journal-International Shipping Conference,* May 1977, pp. 89–96.
260. *Ibid.,* p. 90–93.
261. *Ibid.,* p. 94–96.
262. Note: 'The experience of change in world shipping', *Seaman,* Vol. 37, No. 7, July 1979, pp. 105–09.
263. *Ibid.,* p. 107.
264. *Ibid.,* p. 108.
265. Based on the INCT International Seabed Authority.
266. As was the case with UNCLOSS III which drew up the ISA text.
267. Cf. *UN Conference of Phenipotenitiaries on a Code of Conduct for Liner Conferences,* Vol. I.
268. *Ibid.,* Vol. II.
269. Marlow, P. B., 'The indirect benefits of shipping to a national economy', *Man. Pol. & Man.,* Vol. 6, No. 4, p. 100.
270. As was the case with the Code (Note 197 above).
271. Cf. *Ibid.,* held Geneva from 12 Nov. to 15 Dec. 1973 (2nd part).
272. *Ibid.,* 11 March to 6 April 1974 (2nd part).
273. Just as the UNCLOSS I, II & III deal with it just by way of passing.
274. *UN Conference of Plenipotentories on a Code of Conduct for Liner Conferences, op. cit.*
275. Such as the UNCTAD Committee on Shipping, IMCO, Lloyds, CMI, ILO Committee on Shipping, etc.
275A. The only other UN body directly linked with the UN General Assembly is UNCTAD; this shows the importance we attach to the IMMA.
276. A restructuring of the UN systems generally and the specialised bodies in particular would follow.
277. Apart from national courts, at the moment there is no international appelate court dealing exclusively with Admiralty issues.
278. Schelb, E., 'The process of amending the Statute of the ICJ', *AJIL,* 1970, Vol. 64 pp. 880–91.
279. For the duties of the Secretary General and the functions and nature of the Secretariat see Article 164 of UNCLOSS III, subsection 4, ICNT.
280. *Ibid.,* Article 166 for the staff of the Authority.
281. *Ibid.,* Article 167 for the international character of the Secretariat – it is proposed to base the Seabed Authority in Jamaica.
282. Most other UN bodies are based on this structure, e.g. UNCTAD, IMCO and others dealing with maritime matters.
283. Cf. UNCLOSS III proposals for the ISA–ICNT, Articles 159–161.
284. To be known simply as International Maritime Exchange (IME).
285. For details and relationship with the existing Baltic exchange, see UNCTAD Doc. No. TD/B/C.4/167.

286. Cf. Slater, P., 'An international open registry, one ship, one law, no politics (proposal for reform of registry of shipping)', *Asian Shipping,* No. 14, Feb. 1981, pp. 54–56.
287. Cf. Articles 4–7 Geneva Convention (2 High Seas), or Articles 90–94, UNCLOSS III, ICNT.
288. Cf. UNCLOSS III, ICNT, subsection 5, Article 169 of the ISA.
289. *Ibid.,* Article 151(2)(1), 173(3) & Annex III(10).
290. Note that throughout the special needs of the DMNS are stressed.
291. Gross, L., 'Some observations on the ICJ', *Am. J. Int. L.,* 1962, Vol. 56, pp. 33–62.
292. Dalfen, C. M., 'The world court: reform or reappraisal', *Cam. Yearbook of Int. L.,* 1968, Vol. 6, pp. 212–25.
293. Would be the most organs of the Enterprise, in implementing the decisions of the Authority.
294. See Seymour, E. H., *Economic Planning,* NY, 1949.
295. See also Grayson, H., *Economic Planning under Free Enterprise Public Affairs,* Washington DC, 1954 Cf. Articles 162 (1–3) of UNCLOSS III, ICNT.
296. This would be the International Merchant Marine Bank to finance all the ventures to be undertaken by the Enterprise.
297. Cf. Article 164 (4–7) of UNCLOSS III, ICNT.
298. *Ibid.,* Article 163.
299. *Ibid.*
300. UNEP is the UN body charged with environmental issues.
301. Appeals from here would go to the judicial bodies, then to the ICJ.
302. Cf. UNCLOSS III, Article 164, ICNT.

Part Six

Overall conclusion and bibliography

Concluding remarks

In surveying the emergence of national fleets and the problems caused by the use of traditional methods for their establishment and development, attempts have been made to show that the future prospects for the evolution of national fleets lie in consultation, cooperation and compromise between the interested and participating nations. This approach is also in line with the general trend of world opinion for the discouragement and gradual removal of restrictive business practices (RBPS). In fact, even UNCTAD, suspected of supporting the cause of developing countries, has called for consulatation as the way forward for national fleets. In advocating this policy UNCTAD was only adding support to the position adopted by other national and international organisations such as GATT and the OECD.

A word of caution is, however, necessary. In prescribing this solution there should be no over-emphasis on the conflict-resolving mechanisms herein prescribed. It was necessary to present the problem of the future prospects for national fleets in conflict form between the TMNS and the STNS. That is an economic conflict. Attempts have been made to avoid the TMNS–STNS or East–West model of presentation which would have been more politically tainted. It is true that in the course of this presentation it was found necessary to digress into other fields and disciplines. It could not have been otherwise but to avoid the temptation of getting drawn into the complex area of the East–West political conflict.

There were temptations to draw simplistic conclusions; but it was felt that there are no easy and ready-made solutions to the enormous problems affecting the future prospects for national fleets. On the one hand, we do not think that flags of convenience, and all the disadvantages that go with them, will be phased out overnight. Neither do we think that the liner conference system will be reformed within a short span of time. Nevertheless, it should eventually be reformed along the lines we have suggested. Likewise, we are of the opinion that the *Code of Conduct for Liner Conferences* was long overdue, though a lot more than has been achieved at present needs to be done to it. The same goes for multinational shipping companies.

Perhaps it is not desirable to overemphasize the advantages of cooperation in shipping for fear that the serious problems which might be involved will be overlooked and, therefore, that the disadvantages will be underestimated. It is hoped the impression was not given that there will be drastic changes overnight in the distribution in international shipping between national fleets. A lot of patience will be required from the DMNS. It is true that the emergence of the national fleets of the DMNS has affected the TMNS by virtue of the fact that the latter are and have always been cross-traders, but nobody, least of all the DMNS, is going to deprive any state of its rights in international shipping. To be realistic, and the TMNS should be well aware of this, it will probably take another century before the DMNS pose a realistic threat and an effective challenge to the TMNS' interests in international shipping.

What is taking place in international shipping has already been achieved with respect to international air services. However, in this survey, we did not feel at liberty to discuss this aspect or the situation relating to the regulation of the road and rail industry. Many other factors have led to the emergence of national fleets, such as nationalistic and defence considerations, and other issues like the provision of employment and improving the balance of payments' situation. We have only touched on these in passing, but have not discussed them in detail. Nor was it felt relevant to include the *anti-trust* muddle and the general protective discussions in the survey. The problem of the future prospects for the development of national fleets has been further aggravated by the introduction of new technological innovations, such as containerisation, at a time when this originally conservative industry was having to cope with other problems.

The recommendations herein are more political and economic than legal; since the problem is considered political and economic rather than legal. At any rate, legal demands are only subtle ways of advancing the real, fundamental demands – the political and economic ones.

Certain inescapable conclusions have to be drawn. Despite the conflict of opinion between the parties, what is generally agreed on is that international and national shipping is not free from politics and other external factors. It was also possible to demonstrate that state intervention in, and planning of, national fleets is no longer the monopoly of the STNS or the DMNS. Further, that the role played by governments in this matter is not so bad or restrictive as otherwise portrayed; there must be some measure of state control and regulation of the national fleet. The alternative is chaos. The realisation has dawned that the days of classical liberalism and *laissez-faire* are probably over.

The material conditions in the world have changed to such an extent in the last two decades that the TMNS should accept them as inevitable. Certain principles, doctrines and customs should either be abandoned or modified and new ones accepted. For instance, there has been a shift, though a minor and gradual one, of political and economic influence from the TMNS to the DMNS. The TMNS are in general decline; Britain, for example, is no longer the world's leading maritime nation. The doctrine of the principle of the freedom of the high seas should take on a more political inclination as discussed above. Only then will shipping be truly international as it should be.

What clearly emerges is that all countries need each other; in this complex modern world there are very few, if any, really self-sustaining economies. All nations need international trade and cheaper ways of conveying that trade by sea. One might be led to think that the DMNS are entirely to blame for resorting to the protectionism involved in the traditional methods of establishing and developing national fleets. This survey has shown, to the contrary, that restrictive shipping practices and the desire to possess national fleets is not a monopoly of a few countries but a widespread practice. However, unlike the other industries, shipping, by the nature of its internationality has attracted lots of attention; so have the DMNS due to their vocal demands.

To the DMNS the demand for the establishment and development of their own national fleets has been regarded as some kind of revenge directed at the TMNS; an outlet for frustrations suffered in other areas of international economic relations. The harsh lessons of the oil crisis and the colossal damage to their economies caused by the ensuing world-wide inflation are still fresh in the minds of these countries. This was felt particularly in international shipping which reacts badly to fluctuations in trade. The DMNS' hopes for the *New International Economic Order*, especially in the area of the transfer of resources and technology from the TMNS to them, had been but negligible. The same could be said about the North–South Dialogue, especially the call for the reform of the International Monetary System (IMS), the integrated commodity agreements, etc., by the Brandt Commission. What transpired at the UNCLOSS III held no hopes for the DMNS regarding the call for NIMO.

This is in addition to the fact that the TMNS were resorting to more restrictive practices in international trade because all was not well with them either. There is a natural tendency to reach for the protective lever and to point the accusing finger at others when the going gets tough, which results in both the avoidable and the unavoidable moves becoming muddled. Chapter 2 demonstrated what drove the DMNS' hands towards that lever. Chapters 3 to 6 indicated how that lever was used by the DMNS and counter-used by the TMNS. To succumb to that temptation may be the easy way out, but it is only a short-term solution with possible counter effects in the longer run. To resist that temptation and look for alternatives may be the harder way, but it is the longer-lasting and durable one because it would be difficult to support the methods used by the DMNS though one sympathises with their desire to establish, develop and own their own national fleets.

The crunch of the matter is that, seen from a different global angle, the problem is not the future prospects for the development of national fleets, but the future prospects for the development of an international system. The problem is not confined to national fleets and oceanborne trade nor does it really concern the use of restrictive practices. It is political and economic in context, of which national fleets are but the tip of the iceberg, or the symptom. Not only is the demand for a national fleet one of the arguments the DMNS use to advance their general political and economic desires, but it is one of the highlights of restrictive trade protectionism facing international relations. This viewpoint has been arrived at through the survey of national fleets. It is probably fair to reflect that one could have reached the same conclusion through a survey of similar issues in politics, economics, law or international relations.

To a DMN, the demand for its own national fleet reflects a demand for political and economic independence. It is part of a desire by these countries for the process of industrialisation, and a movement away from their current underdevelopment. There are currently over 150 member states of the UN, most of them yearning for their own national fleets, which is quite a change from when, only about two decades ago, almost all of the world's shipping requirements were monopolised by about 20 or so TMNS. In a nut-shell, the global problem portrayed by the demand for national fleets is the case of expanding participants and, therefore, increasing demand upon either a shrinking or static cake. Put in another context, legal wrangles about flag discrimination or state intervention are only symptoms of the underlying political and economic policies of the actors.

If a solution is to be found it would have to be an economic compromise and involve political goodwill on the part of the actors along the lines herein suggested. It would probably be wiser for the TMNS to cooperate now, and defuse this potentially explosive situation, than face the dire consequences which might be too ghastly to contemplate. The situation equally calls for the DMNS to be flexible. They will probably have discovered, in the two decades that most of them have been independent, that it is not simply by throwing away old traditions or by using the wrong methods that they can achieve the right course. If the TMNS have to accept inevitable changes, the DMNS would have to meet them half way. It is only the spirit of give-and-take that will ensure any prospect of success for the future of national fleets.

The discussions surrounding the *Convention on the Code of Conduct for Liner Conferences* probably took away lots of steam from the would-be direct face-to-face confrontation between the DMNS and TMNS. No-one can deny any nation or group of nations the legitimate right to carry, in their own vessels, cargo generated by their own international trade. The rest of the international shipping community would, therefore, have to come to terms with and accomodate the shipping interestst of the DMNS. The creation of UNCTAD, particularly its sub-committee (4) on shipping, should be seen as a welcome development, and the opportunity should be seized and used as a tool for change. Thus, the present mistrust and hostility should be replaced with dialogue and compromise.

There are a few other aspects about which the DMNS are unhappy. One of these is their resentment at being viewed as 'intruders' or 'maritime lepers' in an industry and a world that belongs to them as much as it does to the TMNS. The other cause for their resentment is the fact that despite the changes that have occurred in the last 3 to 4 decades, the international system should continue to be ruled by norms, customs and doctrines that were formulated 2 to 3 centuries ago. As such they would, no doubt, wish to see a fundamental change in the international economic, political, financial and other systems. More frustrating to them is the fact that these said customs were formulated by their former colonial masters long before their (DMNS) independence. They were not party to these customs.

Much as the use of the traditional restrictive methods, may be objectionable it should be remembered that these constitute one of the few options open to the DMNS in view of their lack of the financial and other resources with which the TMNS are richly endowed. In addition, the forms of state intervention and aid mechanisms operated by the TMNS far outweigh the DMNS' restrictive practices both quantitatively and qualitatively. It has become apparent that the US, in particular, operates more aid and intervention schemes than any other nation in the world, let alone in the DMNS. However, it might be naive to presume that the TMNS are united in their opposition to the use of the traditional restrictive methods to establish and expand national fleets for political reasons, just as it would be naive to assume that the DMNS are in agreement in their approach.

There are two other factors which provide a further stumbling block for the future prospects of national fleets. First, in a world of many countries with varying cultural, political and economic backgrounds there are bound to be conflicting aspirations and interests, particularly when these countries are at different levels of development. Secondly, in a world with such inequality and regional disparity in wealth, the kind of problems symptomized by the demand for national fleets are only to be expected. In the world of the *haves* and the *have-nots*, the latter will not rest till they have made gains from the former. That puts the TMN-*haves* in a defensive position, with the DMNS in the corresponding offensive position. If the DMNS are to realise their aspirations, then the TMNS will have to give some ground, even after taking into consideration expansion in oceanborne trade. There are no indications of a corresponding expansion in world production.

The DMNS are not happy with the little progress they have achieved so far, while the TMNS are resisting any further reform. The emergence of new national fleets is rapid and widespread. There is no corresponding equality of distribution among all the participating nations. Neither is there a systematic increase in world production and, therefore, international trade to match it. In the absence of compromise, the prospects for the future development of national fleets would be very bleak indeed.

Bibliography

1. Glossary

1. *Bulk cargo:* Cargo that can be shipped in complete shiploads without packaging.
2. *Bulk carrier:* Ship assigned to carry a shipload of one particular cargo at a time.
3. *Automation on board:* The process of automating procedures on board a ship, particularly navigation, that were previously controlled manually.
4. *Cargo n.o.s.:* Items that are not listed separately in a freight rate tariff – generally items moving rarely or in small quantities or for the first few times.
5. *Cargo reservation:* State action aimed at reserving a certain portion of exports and/or imports for vessels flying the national flag.
6. *CIF:* 'Cost, Insurance, Freight'. The cif price of goods includes the cost of the goods plus insurance and freight to the named destination and normally also the costs of loading and unloading.
7. *Coastal shipping: (feeder services)* Shipping services connecting a major central port and other minor ports along the coast.
8. *Containerization:* A form of unitization, i.e. the combining of the small components (or units) of a load into a single larger unit. A container is basically a metal box, most commonly 8 × 8 × 20 ft and 8 × 8 × 40 ft.
9. *'Courtier maritime':* French maritime broker based at all the ports with monopoly powers vested in him.
10. *Cross-trade:* Any trade not involving the country of the registration (flag) of the vessel.
11. *Deadweight tonnage (dwt):* The carrying capacity of a ship in tons of 2240 pounds; the difference between a ship's displacement light and her displacement loaded.
12. *Deferred rebate:* A discount (normally 10%) on the freight rate payable to a shipper in arrears who has exclusively shipped by conference vessels during a given time (usually 6 months); it is a method of retaining the loyalty of shippers and of excluding outside competition from conference vessels.
13. *Draft in ports and approaches:* Minimum depth of water in port and in approaches to the port available for ships to navigate in. The maximum may be under greater depending on the extent of tidal variations and seasonal factors.
14. *Dual rate contract:* A method of rewarding shippers who sign a contract undertaking to ship exclusively by conference vessels during a certain period. Shippers who sign such a contract are offered a lower rate than non-signatory shippers. The difference is usually 10–15%.
15. *Elasticity of supply and demand:* The responsiveness of supply and demand to changes in the price of a product. In relation to freight rates, the responsiveness of the supply and demand for shipping services to changes in rates.
16. *Feeder services:* See coastal shipping (feeder) services.
17. *Flag discrimination:* State shipping policy that discriminates between different flags in giving cargoes and/or granting privileges.

18. *Flag preference:* State shipping policy which favours certain flags – generally its own – in giving cargoes and/or granting privileges.
19. *Flag of Convenience:* Flags other than those of the country of the owner, under which a vessel is registered in order to gain fiscal and other advantages. Major flags of convenience are Liberia and Panama.
20. *F.o.b.:* 'Free on Board'. The job price of goods includes all changes until the goods are stowed in a ship at the post of shipment.
21. *Freight financing:* Export credits granted on condition that goods be shipped on vessels flying the flag of the country granting the credit.
22. *Gross-registered tonnage (grt):* The entire internal cubical capacity of a ship in tons of 100 cubic feet.
23. *Industrial carriers:* Vessels (generally carriers and tankers) owned by the exporter or importer of goods carried.
24. *Invisibles:* All exports and imports other than goods; generally services such as shipping, insurance, banking, commerce and tourism.
25. *Landed price:* The price of a good when landed at the destinction, i.e. including freight costs and all other off-loading charges.
26. *Law of comparative advantage:* A country has a comparative advantage *vis-à-vis* a second country in the production of a commodity if it is relatively more efficient in producing that commodity. Thus, if two countries are both producing quantities of the same commodities, the total output of both commodities can always be increased if each country transfers resources into the production of the commodity in which it has a comparative advantage.
27. *Lighter-aboard (LASH) vessels:* A specific type of barge-carrying vessel designed to carry large barges, or lighters (each loaded with 500 to 600 tons of cargo).
28. *Liner:* A ship plying a fixed route or routes, sailing according to a predetermined schedule, which offers cargo and/or passenger space at fixed rates to those who wish to have goods transported or to make journeys.
29. *Liner conferences:* Association of liner owners engaged in a particular trade who have agreed upon uniform freight rates.
30. *Mammoth tankers:* Giant tankers with capacities ranging from anywhere between 150 000 to 500 000 deadweight tons.
31. *Non-bulk cargo:* Cargo which is shipped as individual packages or parcels.
32. *Oil-bulk-ore (OBO) carriers:* Bulk carriers designed to carry ore and bulk commodities such as grain or oil.
33. *Open charter market:* Free competitive market for chartering vessels.
34. *Optimization model:* A mathematical model based on the functional relationship between component parts, which can be used to indicate the optimum utilization of resources, including ships.
35. *Overtonnaging:* Situation in which there is more than adequate shipping capacity (tonnage) available on a route.
36. *Palletization:* Process involving the use of a wooden or metal platform (pallet) on which boxes, bags, or other goods are strapped for transport as a single unit.
37. *Pre-slinging of cargoes:* Combining of cargoes generally bales or bags, into units by means of a continuous sling so that a number of items can be handled as a single unit.
38. *Reservation of national cargo:* See cargo reservation.
39. *Roll on/roll off ships:* Vessels designed so that laden vehicles, including containers, can be driven on and off.
40. *Shipper:* Exporter or importer purchasing shipping services for transport of goods.
41. *Super bulk carriers:* Large bulk carriers up to 200 000 – 250 000 deadweight tons.
42. *Tanker:* A carrier for bulk petroleum and petroleum products.
43. *Tax-free reserve funds:* Fiscal provision under which a shipowner can transfer part of his profits – untaxed – into a reserve fund to be used solely for improving or enlarging his fleet.
44. *Tramp market:* The international market in which charters for tramp ships are arranged. The voyage charter-market includes the tramp market, but also embraces the chartering of, for example, tankers.

45. *Tramp shipping:* Ocean transport by tramp ship, i.e. ships that are available on the open market for charter (for a single voyage or for longer periods) to carry any available cargo.
46. *Turn-around time:* Time spent by a ship in a port.
47. *Unit-load services:* Shipping services based on unitization.
48. *US Reserve Fleet:* That part of the US fleet, mainly wartime structures, which has been inactivated due to high operation costs. The fleet is fast diminishing and in 1970 was 6.3 in grt.
49. *Unitization:* The combination of the small components (or units) of a load into a single larger unit.
50. *Visible exports:* Exports of physical goods (exports excluding invesibles).
51. *Voyage charter rate:* The price fixed directly by an agreement between the charterer and the shipowner, for hiring a vessel for a pre-specified journey, expressed as a cost per deadweight ton.
52. *Wayport conference:* A conference covering a liner trade (serving way ports) which forms part of the longer liner trade.

2. Selected list of international and maritime journal abbreviations

Akron L Rev	Akron Law Review
Albany L Rev	Albany Law Review
Alberta L Rev	Alberta Law Review
Am J Int L	American Journal of International Law
Am J Juris	American Journal of Jurisprudence
Am UL Rev	American University Law Review
Anglo-Am L Rev	Anglo-American Law Review
Archiv des Volk	Archiv des Volkerrechts
Ariz L Rev	Arizona Law Review
Aust Yearbook Int L	Australian Yearbook of International Law
Boston UL Rev	Boston University Law Review
Brit Yearbook Int L	British Yearbook of International Law
Brooklyn J Int L	Booklyn Journal of International Law
Brooklyn L Rev	Brooklyn Law Review
Buffalo L Rev	Buffalow Law Review
C de D	Les Cahiers de Droit
Calif L Rev	California Law Review
Calif Western Int LJ	California Western International Law Journal
Camb LJ	Cambridge Law Journal
Can Bar Rev	Canadian Bar Review
Can Yearbook Int L	Canadian Yearbook of International Law
Case W Res J Int L	Case Western Reserve Journal of International Law
Catholic UL Rev	Catholic University Law Review
Chi-Kent L Rev	Chicago-Kent Law Review
Column JL & Soc Prob	Columbia Journal of Law and Social Problems
Colum J Transnat L	Columbia Journal of Transnational Law
Column L Rev	Columbia Law Review
Comp & Int LJ Southern Africa	Comparative and International Law Journal of Southern Africa
Cornell Int LJ	Cornell International Law Journal
Current Legal Prob	Current Legal Problems
Denver J Int L & Pol	Denver Journal of International Law and Policy
De Paul L Rev	De Paul Law Review
Duke L J	Duke Law Journal
East African LJ	East African Law Journal

Eastern Africa L Rev	Eastern Africa Law Review
Ecology LQ	Ecology Law Quarterly
Environ Aff	Environmental Affairs
Fla L Rev	Florida Law Review
Fordham L Rev	Fordham Law Review
Ga J Int & Comp L	Georgia Journal of International and Comparative Law
Ga L Rev	Georgia Law Review
Geo LJ	Georgetown Law Journal
Geo Wash L Rev	George Washington Law Review
Hague Recueil	Hague Academy of International Law, Recueil des Cours
Harv Int LJ	Harvard International Law Journal
Harv L Rev	Harvard Law Review
Hastings Const LQ	Hastings Constitutional Law Quarterly
Hastings Int & Comp L Rev	Hastings International and Comparative Law Review
Hastings LJ	Hastings Law Journal
Houston L Rev	Houston Law Review
How LJ	Howard Law Journal
Human Rights J	Human Rights Journal (Revue des Drroits de L'homme)
Ind J Int L	Indian Journal of International Law
Ind LJ	Indiana Law Journal
Int & Comp LQ	International and Comparative Law Quarterly
Int Law	The International Lawyer
Int Org	International Organisation
Iowa L Rev	Iowa Law Review
Irish Jur	The Irish Jurist
Israel L Rev	Israel Law Review
J Air L	Journal of Air Law and Commerce
Jap Ann Int L	Japanese Annual of International Law
J Int Law & Econ	Journal of International Law and Economics
J Legal Ed	Journal of Legal Education
J Maritime L	Journal of Maritime Law and Commerce
J Soc Pub TL	Journal of the Society of Public Teachers of Law
J Space L	Journal of Space Law
J World Trade L	Journal of World Trade Law
Kan L Rev	University of Kansas Law Review
LQ Rev	Law Quarterly Review
La L Rev	Louisiana Law Review
Law Am	Lawyer of the Americas
Law & Contemp Prob	Law and Contemporary Problems
Law & Pol Int Bus	Law and Policy in International Business
Loyola L Rev	Loyola Law Review
Malaya L Rev	Malaya Law Review
McGill LJ	McGill Law Journal
Md L Rev	Maryland Law Review
Mercer L Rev	Mercer Law Review
Mich L Rev	Michigan Law Review
Miss LJ	Mississippi Law Journal
Modern L Rev	Modern Law Review
Natural Resources J	Natural Resources Journal
Natural Resources Law	Natural Resources Lawyer
NC L Rev	North Carolina Law Review
Neth Int L Rev	Netherlands International Law Review (Nederlands Tijdschrift voor Internationaal Recht)

Neth Yearbook Int L	Netherlands Yearbook of International Law
New England L Rev	New England Law Review
No Ire LQ	Northern Ireland Legal Quarterly
Nordisk Tid Int Ret	Nordisk Tidsskrift for International Ret
Notre Dame Law	Notre Dame Lawyer
Nw UL Rev	Northwestern University Law Review
NYLF	New York Law Forum
NYUJ Int & Politics	New York University Journal of International Law and Politics
Ocean Devel & Int L	Ocean Development and International Law
Ore L Rev	Oregon Law Review
Osgoode Hall LJ	Osgoode Hall Law Journal
Ottawa L Rev	Ottawa Law Review
Philip Int LJ	Philippine International Law Journal
Philip LJ	Philippine Law Journal
Philip Yearbook Int L	Philippine Yearbook of International Law
Proc Am Soc Int L	Proceedings of the American Society of International Law
Rev Belge Droit Int	Revue Belge de Droit International
Rev Droit Int	Revue de Droit International
Rev Egypt Droit Int	Revue Egyptienne de Droit International
Rev Hell Droit Int	Revue Hellenique de Droit International
Riv Diritto Int	Rivista di Diritto Internazionale
Rutgers Camden LJ	Rutgers Camden Law Journal
S African Yearbook Int L	South African Yearbook of International Law
San Diego L Rev	San Diego Law Review
Scand Studies in L	Scandinavian Studies in Law
SC L Rev	South Carolina Law Review
SD L Rev	South Dakota Law Review
So Ill ULJ	Southern Illinois University Law Journal
St Louis ULJ	St Louis University Law Journal
Stan J Int Studies	Stanford Journal of International Studies
Stan L Rev	Stanford Law Review
Sw LJ	Southwestern Law Journal
Sydney L Rev	Sydney Law Review
Syracuse L Rev	Syracuse Law Review
Syr L Int L & Com	Syracuse Journal of International Law and Commerce
Temp LQ	Temple Law Quarterly
Texas Int LF	Texas International Law Forum
Texas Int LJ	Texas International Law Journal
Texas L Rev	Texas Law Review
Tul L Rev	Tulane Law Review
U Chi L Rev	University of Chicago Law Review
U Colo L Rev	University of Colorado Law Review
U Fla L Rev	University of Florida Law Review
U Ill LF	University of Illinois Law Forum
U Miami L Rev	University of Miami Law Review
U Mich JL Ref	University of Michigan Journal of Law Reform
UP	University Press
U Pa L Rev	University of Pennsylvania Law Review
U Pitt L Rev	University of Pittsburgh Law Review
Utah L Rev	Utah Law Review
U Tol L Rev	University of Toledo Law Review
U Toronto LJ	University of Toronto Law Journal
Vand Int	The Vanderbilt International [sic]

Vand J Transnat L	Venderbilt Journal of Transnational Law
Vill L Rev	Villanova Law Review
Virg J Int L	Virginia Journal of International Law
Virg L Rev	Virginia Law Review
W & M L Rev	William and Mary Law Review
Wash & Lee L Rev	Washington and Lee Law Review
Wayne L Rev	Wayne Law Review
Wis L Rev	Wisconsin Law Review
Yale LJ	Yale Law Journal
Yearbook of WA	Yearbook of World Affairs
Zao RV	Zeitschrift fur Auslandisches Offentliches Recht und Volkerrecht

3. List of selected maritime and transportation journal abbreviations

Asian Shipp	Asian Shipping
Cargo Syst Inc	Cargo Systems International
Commer Fish	Commercial Fishing
Containerisation Int	Containerisation International
Containers	Containers
Cock & Harbour Auth	Dock and Harbour Authority
Docks	Docks
Eur Transp Law	European Transport Law
Fairplay Int Shipp Weekly	Fairplay International Shipping Weekly
Hazardous Cargo Bull	Hazardous Cargo Bulletin
Hinterland	Hinterland
IMCO News	IMCO News
Int Freighting Manage	International Freighting Management
Int J Phys Distrib	International Journal of Physical Distribution and Materials Management
Int J Transp Econ	International Journal of Transport Economics
Int Shipbuild Prog	International Shipbuilding Progress
J Bus Law	Journal of Business Law
J Commer	Journal of Commerce
J Mar Res	Journal of Marine Research
J Marit Law & Commer	Journal of Maritime Law and Commerce
J Navig	Journal of Navigation
J Ship Res	Journal of Ship Research
J Arab Marit Transp Acad	Journal of the Arab Maritime Transport Academy
J Transp Econ & Policy	Journal of Transport Economics and Policy
J Transp Hist	Journal of Transport History
Lloyds Law Rep	Lloyds Law Reports
Lloyds List	Lloyds List
Lloyds Marit & Commer Law Q	Lloyds Maritime and Commercial Law Quarterly
Lloyds Ship Manager	Lloyds Ship Manager
Lloyds Ship Econ	Lloyds Shipping Economist
Mar Obs	Marine Observer
Mar Policy	Marine Policy
Mar Pollut Bull	Marine Pollution Bulletin
Mariner	Mariner
Marit Policy & Manage	Maritime Policy and Management
Maritimes	Maritimes
Mot Ship	Motor Ship
Navigation	Navigation

Navy Int	Navy International
Noroil	Noroil
Norw Shipp News	Norwegian Shipping News
Ocean Ind	Ocean Industry
Ocean Manage	Ocean Management
Offshore	Offshore
Offshore Oil Weekly	Offshore Oil Weekly
Offshore Res Focus	Offshore Research Focus
Offshore Sev	Offshore Services
Pet Econ	Petroleum Economist
Port Balt Bull	Port of Baltimore Bulletin
Port Clevel	Port of Cleveland
Port Houst Mag	Port of Houston Magazine
Port Lond	Port of London
Port Toron News	Port of Toronto News
Pynda Leader	Pynda Leader
Railway Gaz Int	Railway Gazette International
Reeds Spec. Ships	Reeds Special Ships
Res Transp Econ	Research on Transport Economics
Rotter Europoort Delta	Rotterdam-Europoort-Delta
Saf Sea	Safety at Sea
Sea Breezes	Sea Breezes
Seafarer	Seafarer
Seaman	Seaman
Seatrade	Seatrade
Seaways	Seaways
Shipbroker	Shipbroker
Shipcare & Marit Manage	Shipcare and Maritime Management
Shipp World & Shipbuild	Shipping World and Shipbuilder
Ships Monthly	Ships Monthly
Telegraph	Telegraph
Trans. North East Coast Inst Eng & Shipbuild	Transactions of the North East Coast Institution of Engineers and Shipbuilders
Transport	Transport
Transp Hist	Transport History
Transp Manage	Transport Management
Transportation	Transportation
Transp J	Transportation Journal
Transp Plann & Technol	Transportation Planning and Technology
Transp Res News	Transportation Research News
Via Port NY	Via Port of New York
World Fish	World Fishing
World Oil	World Oil
Yachting World	Yachting World
Zosen	Zosen
100 Al	100 Al

4. UNCTAD shipping documents

TD/B/C.4/188	Formation and strengthening of shippers commodity groups
TD/B/C.4/187	Merchant ship development (shipment of bulk cargo between developing countries
TD/B/C.4/186	Merchant ship development: guidelines for developing countries

TD/B/C.4/185	Proposed programme of work of the Committee on shipping in the field of multimodal transport and containerisation
TD/B/C.4/182/Add.1	Review of Maritime Transport, 1978
TD/B/C.4/182	Review of Maritime Transport, 1978
TD/B/C.4/181	Follow-up report on aspects of economic and social implications of international multimodal transport in Developing countries
TD/B/C.4/180	Relationship between shippers at both ends of the trade
TD/B/C.4/179	Report of the group of experts on improved methods of financing ship acquisition by developing countries, 21st August 1980
TD/B/C.4/178	Review of Maritime Transport, 1977
TD/B/C.4/178/Add.1	Review of Maritime Transport, 1977 (Addendum)
TD/B/C.4/177	Report of the Ad Hoc Intergovernmental
TD/B/C.4/177/AC.1/3	Working Group on the economic consequences of the existence or lack of a genuine link between vessel and flag registry
TD/B/C.4/174	Appraisal of port investments
TD/B/C.4/169	World developments in shipping, ports and multimodal transport
TD/B/C.4/168/Add.1	Economic consequences of the existence or lack of a genuine link between vessel and flag registry (Addendum)
TD/B/C.4/168	Economic consequences of the existence or lack of a genuine link between vessel and flag registry
TD/B/C.4/167/Supp.1	Report problems: The extent and causes of port cost increases
TD/B/C.4/167	Report problems: Causes of increases in port costs and their impact
TD/B/C.4/166	Report problems: Benefits from port improvements
TD/B/C.4/165	Institutional arrangements for work in transport questions
TD/B/C.4/164	Technical and financial assistance in shipping and ports
TD/B/C.4/163	Technical and financial assistance in shipping and ports
TD/B/C.4/162/Add.1	Status of the Convention on a Code of Conduct for Liner Conferences (Addendum)
TD/B/C.4/6	Report of the Committee on Shipping on 1st session (also TD/B/36)
TD/B/C.4/7	Terms and rules of (reference) the Committee on Shipping
TD/B/C.4/8	Provisional agenda of the Committee on Shipping
TD/B/C.4/9	Level and structure of freight rates, conference practices and adequacy of shipping services
TD/B/C.4/10	Incidence of freight rates on trade in manufactures and services
TD/B/C.4/11	(same) S.G. Sturmey – on ocean freight rates and economic research
TD/B/C.4/12	(same) Note by Secretary General of UNCTAD
TD/B/C.4/13	Agenda for Committee on Shipping meeting 18/7/66
TD/B/C.4/4/14	Statement by Raul Prebish – Secretary General of UNCTAD
TD/B/C.4/15	Report of the Bureau of the Committee on Shipping on credentials
TD/B/C.4/16	(TD/B/83) Report of the Committee of Shipping on its special session
TD/B/C.4/17	Shipping and the world economy: Report of the session on shipping economics
TD/B/C.4/18	(TD/B/C2/6) Provisional outline for a maritime transport on timber

TD/B/C.4/19	Provisional Agenda for second session.
TD/B/C.4/20	Consultation in shipping: Establishment of national and regional shippers bodies, consultation and negotiation between Shippers and shipowners
TD/B/C.4/21	Provisional outline for a maritime transport study of timber. Suggestions of the Ad Hoc Joint UNCTAD/FAO Working Party on forests and timber products
TD/B/C.4/22	Progress report on the work programme in the field of shipping
TD/B/C.3/23	Development of ports; progress reports by the Secretariat 19/12/66
TD/B/C.4/24	Outlines of reviews of current and long term aspects of maritime transport
TD/B/C.4/25	Reviews of developments in shipping
TD/B/C.4/26	Review of Studies and activities in the field of shipping and ports
TD/B/C.4/33	(TD/B/141) Action taken by ECOSOC relevant to UNCTAD activities in shipping
TD/B/C.4/34	Basic economies of containerisation and unitization in ocean shipping
TD/B/C.4/31	Liner shipping in India's overseas trade, by T.K. Savere, Nov. 1967
TD/B/C.4/162	Status of the Convention on a Code of Conduct for Liner Conferences
TD/B/C.4/161	Technical and financial assistance in shipping and ports
TD/B/C.4/160	International shipping legislation
TD/B/C.4/159	Promotion of maritime transport
TD/B/C.4/158/Corr.1	Economic cooperation in merchant shipping, 14th January 1977.
TD/B/C.4/158	Economic cooperation in merchant shipping (main document)
TD/B/C.4/157	The maritime transport of cotton
TD/B/C.4/173	Report of the Committee on Shipping on its 5th session
TD/B/C.4/27	Activities of UNCTAD in the field of shipping (including ports)
TD/B/C.4/28	Agenda for committee meeting on 1/2/67
TD/B/C.4/29	Report of the Bureau on Credentials
TD/B/C.4/30	Report of the Committee on Shipping on its 2nd session
TD/B/C.4/126	Institutional arrangements for work on transport questions
TD/B/C.4/127	Draft report of the Committee on Shipping on its 8th session
TD/B/C.4/128	Draft resolution on landlocked developing countries by Mexico for Latin America
TD/B/C.4/129	World developments in shipping, ports and multimodal transport
TD/B/C.4/130	Effectiveness of consultation machinery – freight rates
TD/B/C.4/131	Report of the Sessional Committee of Shipping
TD/B/C.4/132	Port problems
TD/B/C.4/133	Draft resolution on landlocked developing countries
TD/B/C.4/134	Technical and financial assistance in shipping and ports
TD/B/C.4/135	Economic consequences of the existence or lack of flag discriminations
TD/B/C.4/135/Add.7	Statements of financial implications submitted by the Secretariat
TD/B/C.4/136	Institutional arrangements for work on transport questions
TD/B/C.4/1	Provisional arrangements for first ever meeting of Committee on Shipping, 29/9/65
TD/B/C.4/2	Consideration and adoption of the programme of work

TD/B/C.4/3	Relationship between IMCO and UNCTAD
TD/B/C.4/4	Agenda for Committee on Shipping meeting 9/11/65
TD/B/C.4/5	Report of the Bureau of the Committee on Credentials
TD/B/C.4/32	The West African shipping range, by Dag Trescott of Bergen (Norway)
TD/B/C.4/36	Level & structure. . .: Terms of Shipment 13/12/68.
TD/B/C.4/37	Level & structure. . .: Indices of freight rates of special interests to developing countries
TD/B/C.4/38	Level. . .: Freight markets and the level and structure of freight rates
TD/B/C.4/208/Add.1	Follow-up report on containerisation of fibres, particularly jute
TD/B/C.4/217	Annotated agenda to third special session of the Committee on Shipping
TD/B/C.4/218	Beneficial ownership of open registry fleets, 1980
TD/B/C.4/219	Report of the Working Group on International Shipping Legislation on its 7th session
TD/B/C.4/220	Open-registry fleets
TD/B/C.4/221	Report of the group of experts on problems faced by the developing countries in the carriage of bulk cargoes
TD/B/C.4/222	Review of Maritime Transport, 1980
TD/B/C.4/229	Review of the Studies and activities of other international organisations concerning technical assistance and international financing and aid in the field of multimodal transport and containerisation
TD/B/C.4/230	Report on availability of technical assistance
TD/B/C.4/231	Beneficial ownership of open-registry fleets, 1981
TD/B/C.4/251	Review of Maritime Transport, 1981
TD/B/C.4/255	Beneficial ownership of open-registry fleets, 1982
TD/B/C.4/175	Port Development – Handbook for planners in developing countries
TD/B/C.4/176	Protection of shippers' interests: Guidelines for developing countries
TD/B/C.4/189	Maritime management training in developing countries.
TD/B/C.4/190	Report on financing of ships and ports
TD/B/C.4/192	A summary of the work carried out under the Ports Project 1969–1979, and new project proposals
TD/B/C.4/193	A note on the manual on a uniform system of port statistics and performance indicators developed for the port management association of West and Central Africa (see also UNCTAD/SHIP/185)
TD/B/C.4/194	Promotion of shipping
TD/B/C.4/196	Directory of services for technical assistance in shipping and ports to developing countries
TD/B/C.4/197	Seaborne trade statistics
TD/B/C.4/199	Action taken with repsect to port congestion task forces. A progress report
TD/B/C.4/202	The rationalisation of port congestion surcharges. A progress report
TD/B/C.4/203	Control by transnational corporations over dry bulk cargo movements
TD/B/C.4/204	Technical assistance and training in shipping and ports
TD/B/C.4/207	Liner conference container rules
TD/B/C.4/208	Containerization of Abaca on the Philippines/Japan route and its possible implications for the shipment of other fibres, particularly jute
TD/B/C.4/239	Protection of shipper interests: Outstanding issues

TD/B/C.4/241	Technical assistance and training: Directory on SHIP-ASSIST.
TD/B/C.4/242	Practices of liner conferences in relation to container tariff rules and the feasibility of preparing model container tariff rules
TD/B/C.4/245	Establishment of an enquiry service
TD/B/C.4/246	Action taken to implement resolution 35(IX) of the Committee on Shipping
TD/B/C.4/247	Port congestion surcharges: Follow-up
TD/B/C.4/248	Ports and economic development: policy issues
TD/B/C.4/249	Status of the United Nations Convention on the Carriage of Goods by Sea
TD/B/C.4/206	Status of the Convention of a Code of Conduct for Liner Conferences
TD/B/C.4/240	Status of the Convention on a Code of Conduct for Liner Conferences
TD/B/C.4/183	Establishment of the multimodal transport operators in developing countries
TD/B/C.4/233	Multimodal air cargo movements as a means of facilitating the export of goods by air from developing countries and of increasing the air transport fleets of developing countries
TD/B/C.4/235	Report of developments in standardization of containers and related activities
TD/B/C.4/236	Status of the Convention on International Multimodal Transport of Goods
TD/B/C.4/238	Guidelines on the introduction of containerisation and multimodal transport and the modernization and improvements of the infrastructure of developing countries (also Supp. 1 and Corr. 1, Supp. 2 and Corr. 1, Supp. 3 and Supp. 4)
TD/B/C.4/243	The relationship among interested parties in multimodal transport
TD/B/C.4/250	Palletization and containerisation of bananas (also TD/B/C.4/IPC/Bananas/8)
TD/B/C.4/195	Container standards for international multimodal transport
TD/B/C.4/256	Report of the Working Group on International Shipping Legislation on its session
TD/B/C.4/255	Beneficial ownership of open registry fleets 1982; report by the UNCTAD Secretariat
TD/B/C.4/257	Report of the group of experts on international sea transport of liquid hydrocarbons in bulk on its 1st session

5. Selected articles

1. Abrahamson, B. J., 'Liner and tramp rates', *Journal of Israeli Shipping Research Institute*, Winter 1972.
2. Abrahamson, B. J., 'A shipping research program with particular reference to smaller nations' (*ibid*.).
3. Adler, 'British and American shipping policies', 59 *Political Science Quarterly*, 193.
4. Agman, 'Competition, rationalization and US shipping policy', 8 *J. Mar. L. & Com*., 1976, p. 1.
5. Al-Jadir, A., 'Developing a fairer share', *Seatrade* 9, Sept. 1980, p. 152.
6. Baker, 'Flags of refuge for shipping industry', 13 *Tax L. Rev*., 1958, p. 137.

7. Baker, 'US federal income taxation of foreign flag shipping earnings', 26 *Nat. Tax. J.*, 1973, p. 537.
8. Barcello III, J. J., 'Subsidies and countervailing duties – analysis and proposal', *Law & Pol. I. A. Bus.*, Vol. 9, 1977, p. 779–853.
9. Bar-Lev, 'UNCTAD Code of Practice for the Regulation of Liner Conferences', 3 *J. Mar. L. & Com.*, 1972, p. 783.
10. Barry, B., 'Maritime Issues in North-East Asia: their impact on regional politics', *Marine Policy*, Vol. 3, No. 3, 1979, pp. 190–200.
11. Bauer, M. J., 'Ratemaking in international shipping conferences', *Stan. J. Int. Studies*, Vol. IV, June 1969, pp. 84–115.
12. Bennathan *et al.*, 'Shipping conferences: an economic analysis', 4 *J. Mar. L. & Com.*, 1972, p. 93.
13. Bennathan, 'Revenue Pooling in cartels', *Oxford Economic Papers*, 1969.
14. Benham, A., 'Political factors and the envolution of national fleets in developing countries', *Man. St. & Man.*, Vol. 3, 1976, pp. 131–40.
15. Berghoff, 'Ocean shipping conferences', 33 *ABA Antitrust L.* 3, 1967, p. 57.
16. Bertram, S., 'The internationality of shipping', *Institute of Transport Journal*', May 1969, pp. 140–47.
17. Beth, H. L., 'Fluctuations of exchange rates – their impact on shipping', Bremen Institute of shipping, No. 26.
18. Blackwell, R. J., 'Implementation of the Merchant Marine Act of 1970', *J. Man. L. & Com.*, Jan. 1974.
19. Bowman, 'The Merchant Marine Act of 1970', 5 *J. Mar. L. & Com.*, 1974, p. 167.
20. Borgese, E. M., 'The new international economic order and the law of the sea', *San Diego L. Rev.*, Vol. 14, 1977, pp. 584–96.
21. Boxer, B., *Ocean Shipping in the Evolution of Hong Kong*, Chicago 1961.
22. Breuer, 'Code of conduct, Legal aspects of Hamburg', *Ministry of Transport Journal*.
23. Breton, A., 'The economics of nationalism', *J. Pol. Econ.*, Vol. 66, 1964, pp. 376–86.
24. Bredimas, A. E., 'The common shipping policy of the EEC', *Com. Mark. L. Rev.*, Vol. 18, 1981, No. 1, Feb., pp. 9–29.
25. Brian, M., 'UNCTAD and ocean influence and organization', *Marine Policy,* Vol. 5, 1981, pp. 152–54.
26. Bush, W. L., 'Steamship conference contract rate agreements and the dual rate system', 40 *ICC Prac. J*, 1972, p. 14.
27. Button, K. J., 'The application of 'Andrew's Theory' to shipping conferences', *Man. Pol. & Man.*, 1980, Vol. 7, No. 1 pp. 17–20.
28. Bryan, I. A., 'The effect of ocean transport costs and the demand for some Canadian exports', *Weltwirtschaftliches Archiv*. No. 4, 1974.
29. Bryan, I. A. *et al.*, 'Shipping conferences in Canada', *Res. Memo.*, No. 2, 1978.
30. Cadwallader, F. J. J., 'Flag discrimination or something more', *Curr. Leg. Rob.*, 1976, pp. 99–111.
31. Cadwallader, F. J. J., 'Uniformity in the regulation of combined transport', *J. Bus. L.*, 1974.
32. Calmus, T. W., 'Full cost versus incremental cost again', *Transportation Journal*, Winter 1969.
33. Campbell, T. C., 'Transport and its impact on developing countries', *Transportation Journal*, Fall 1972.
34. Canadian T. Commission. *Study of Economic Implications of the International Convention on a Code of Conduct for Liner Conferences*. ESAB 76–13, Ottowa, Feb. 1976.
35. Capone, R. A., 'US laws and the Convention on a Code of Conduct for Liner Conferences: a catalogue of conflicts and dilemmas', *Virg. J. Int. L.*, Vol. 15, No. 2, Winter 1975.
36. Carlisle, R., 'The American century implemented: Stethinisus and the Liberian flag of convenience', *Bus. Hist. Rev. Vol. Liv.*, No. 2, Summer 1980, pp. 175–91.
37. Cassing, J., 'Shipping Innovation in the pure theory of international trade', *Int. J. Tran. Econ.*, Vol. VII, No. 3, Dec. 1980, pp. 301–26.

38. Cates, 'United Nations maritime conference', 18 *Dept. St. Bull.* 1948, p. 495.
39. Chiang, 'Characterisation of a vessel as a common or private carrier', 48 *Tul. L. Rev.*, 299 1974.
40. Chintz, B., 'An analysis of ocean liner freight rates', *Econometrica*, 1976, p. 351.
41. Chinkin, 'Trading activities by foreign sovereign states and the law of sovereign immunity', 39 *Mod. L. Rev.*, 1976, p. 597.
42. Chrzanowski, I., 'Governments and shipping', *Fairplay,* Vol. 274, No. 5050, 12th June 1980, p. 18.
43. Chrzanowski, I., 'Current Aspects of International Shipping', *Mar. Pol. & Man.*, No. 3, 1976, pp. 289–95.
44. Chrzanowski, I., 'Shipping in the 1980's – a future with uncertainty', *Mar. Pol. & Man.*, Vol. 7, No. 1, 1980, pp. 1–8 (editorial).
45. Cohen, D., *et al.* 'The domestic resource costs of establishing/expanding a national fleet', *Mar. Stu. & Man.*, Vol. 3, 1976, pp. 221–36.
46. Comite Maritime International, International Conventions on Maritime Law, Secretariat, Belgium.
47. *Container News*, 'National reservation proves a resilient principle – special report', May 1977, Vol. 12, No. 5, pp. 46–57.
48. *Containerization International*, 'The Code makes for Ivory Coast', Vol. 14, No. 5, May 1980, pp. 24, 25, 27, 29.
49. Cook, 'Government assistance in financing Title XI federal guarantees', 47 *Tul. L. Rev.* 653, 1973.
50. Cook, *et al.*, 'Shipping and fishing industries are affected by Tax Reform Act of 1976', 46 *J. Tax. 88*, 1977.
51. Couper, A. D., 'Shipping Policies of the EEC' (editorial), *Mar. Pol. & Man.*
52. Cragg, C., 'Beneficial commodity deal for Third World countries', *Seatrade,* Vol. 10, No. 7, July 1980, pp. 43–47.
53. Cummins, P., 'Asian pacific and European shippers agree to cooperate', *Asian Shipp.*, June 1980, pp. 36–39.
54. Cundick, 'High seas intervention: parameters of unilateral action', 10 *San Diego L. Rev.* 514, 1973.
55. Currie, 'Flags of convenience, American Labour and the conflict of laws' *Sup. Ct. Rev.* 34, 1963.
56. Dabrowski, K., 'International and External Shipping Measures'.
57. Danaher, M. J., 'Anti-trust law: the drawback and other features of the UK protection of trading interest Act 1980', *Law. & Bus. Int. Bus.*, Vol. 12, No. 4, 1980, pp. 947–71.
58. Davies, J. E., 'The economics of the open conference system', *Mar. Pol. & Man.,* Vol. 7, No. 2, 1980, pp. 85–102.
59. Davies, J. E., 'The effects of US shipping regulation on specific aspects of liner conference operation', *Man. Pol. & Man.,* Vol. 7, No. 1, 1980, pp. 37–54.
60. Deakin, B. M., 'Ocean shipping and freight rates and developing countries', UNCTAD, Geneva, March 23, 1964–June 16 1964, Vol. V.
61. Deakin, B. M., 'Shipping conferences, some economic aspects of international regulation', *Mar. Stu. & Man.*, July 1974.
62. Devanney, J. W., 'Conference rate making and the West Coast of South America', *J. Trans. Econ. & Pol.*, May 1975, 154.
63. Diebold, 'Shipping in the intermediate postwar years', 53 *J. Pol. Econ.*, 15, 1945.
64. Doganis *et al.*, 'The impact of flags of convenience', *P.C.L.*, No. 3, Sept. 1976, London.
65. Douglas, P. S., 'Financing new and used liner tonnage for developing countries – problems & solutions'.
66. Downs, A., 'An economic theory of political action in a democracy', *J. Pol. Econ.*, Vol. 56, 1957) pp. 35–50.
67. Dreschel, K., 'The shipping Act of 1916 and the dual rate amendment. A problem of Enforcement'. 4 *Na. J. Int. L.* 215, 1964.
68. Drewery, H. P., 'West African liner shipping', No. 75 in Series Research Division, Drewery Shipping Consultants.

69. Drewery, H. P., 'The rise of national fleets', No. 16, in a series.
70. Drewery, H. P., 'Organisation and structure of the dry bulk shipping industry', Study No. 63, London 1978.
71. Drewery, H. P., 'Ports and terminals for barge bulk carriers'.
72. Erler, 'New convention on facilitation of international maritime traffic', 13 *McGill L. J. 323*, 1967.
73. Fairhall, D., 'Soviet merchant marine', *Brassey's Annual*.
74. Faust, M. P., 'Barge carrier supply-demand analysis', Pamphlet No. 22, Bremen Series, 1979.
75. Fearnley, *et al.*, 'World bulk trades' (Annual), *Oslo Review*.
76. Fitzpatrick, P. B., 'Soviet-American trade 1972–74', *Va. J. Int. L.*, Vol. 15, No. 1, 1974, pp. 39–71.
77. Frankel, E. G. *et al.*, 'Impact of cargo sharing on US liner trade', *Marine Policy*, Jan. 1981, pp. 23–39.
78. Frankel, E. G., 'Shipping policy under conditions of a new world economic and political environment', *Mar. Pol. & Man.*, 1980, Vol. 7, No. 1, pp. 21–36.
79. Fridlund, 'Tax problems in allocation & subsidies. . .', 7 Jan. Tax. 304, 1957.
80. Fuotts, J, *The Shipping Industry in Canada*, ILO Research Series No. 2, 1976.
81. Gallagher, 'Maritime tax: The Capital Construction Fund of the Merchant Marine Act 1970', 6 *J. Mar. L. & Com.* 105, 1974.
82. Galland, 'Steamship tariffs in foreign commerce', 35 *Tul. L. Rev.* 141, 1960.
83. Gardner, 'Steamship conferences and the Shipping Act, 1916', 35 *Tul. L. Rev.* 129, 1960.
84. Georgandopoulos, E. L. A., *Shipping in Developing Countries*, Problems and Prospects Pamphlet No. 20, Bremen Series.
85. Georgandopoulos, E. L. A., *The Dry Bulk Cargo Markets*, Pamphlet No. 21, Bremen Series.
86. Geren, P. S., *Diplomatic Adjustment by the Maritime Nations*, Dept. of State Bull., Vol. LIV, No. 1386, Publications 8018, Jan. 17 1966.
87. Gibney, J. C., 'Plenty of port traffic but little shipboard action for third world', *Containerisation International*, Vol. 14, No. 10, Oct. 1980, pp. 51–55.
88. Gifford, W. C., 'Permanent establishment under the non-discrimination clause in income tax treaties', *Cornell I. L. J.*, Vol. 11, No. 1, Winter 1978, pp. 51–71.
89. Gilman, S., 'Optimal shipping technologies for routes to developing countries', *J. Trans. Econ. & Pol.*, Jan. 1977.
89A Gold, E., 'New directions in maritime international law'.
90. Goldie, 'Recognition & dual nationality. A problem of flags of convenience', 39 *BYBIL* 220, 1963.
91. Gordon, J. S., 'Shipping regulation and FMC', 37 *U. Ch. L. Rev.* 90, 1969.
92. Gorman, 'Shipping conferences and the Bonner Act 1961', *J. Bus. L.* 24, 1962.
93. Gorton, L., 'Joint ventures in shipping law', *J. Bus. L.*, July 1978, pp. 238–44.
94. Goss, R. O., 'Investment in shipping and balance of payments'. *J. Ind. Econ.*, March 1965, pp. 103–15.
95. Goss, R. O., 'US legislation and the foreign shipowner – a critique', *J. ind. Econ.*, Nov. 1963, pp. 1–19.
96. Goss, R. O., 'The regulation of international transport', *The World Today*, Oct. 1965.
97. Grammenos, C., 'Bank finance for ship purchase', *Bangor Occassional Papers, Economics*, No. 16.
98. Grundey, K., *Flags of Convenience in 1978*, Paper No. 8, PCL Transport Studies Group.
99. Gulland, J., 'Developing countries and the new law of the sea', *Oceans*, Vol. 22, No. 1, Spring 1979, pp. 37–42.
100. Haji, I., 'UNCTAD and shipping', *JWTL*, pp. 59–119.
101. Hanson, D. P., 'The rise of Soviet merchant marine', *The World Today*, Vol. 26, No. 3, March 1970, pp. 130–37.
102. Hanson, D. P., 'Regulation of the shipping industry: an economic analysis of the need for reform', *Law & Pol. Int. Bus.*, Vol. 12, No. 4, 1980.

103. *Hawkins*, R. *et al*., 'UNCTAD: reprieve for cross-traders', *Seatrade*, May 1972, p. 1.
104. Hawkins, R., 'Tropical and special features: the conference system under attack', *Seatrade*, Jan. 1972, pp. 10–11.
105. Hearn, G. H., 'Cargo preference and control', *J. Mar. L. & Com*., Vol. 2, No. 3, April 1971, pp. 481–98.
106. Hearn, G. H., 'Problems and prospects in international maritime regulation', 4 *Sw. UL Rev*., 157, 1978.
107. Heaver, T. D., 'Trans pacific trade liner shipping and conference rates', *Trans. Leg. Rev*., Spring 1972.
108. Heaver, T. D., 'A theory of shipping conferences pricing and policies', *Mar. St. & Man*., No. 1, 1973.
109. Heaver, T. D., 'The structure of liner conference rates', *J. Ind. Econ*., 1973.
110. Hedlin, 'Canadian merchant marine-analysis of economic potential', *Canadian Transport Commission*, Dec. 1970.
111. Hellawell, 'Less developed countries and developed country law: problems from the law of admiralty', 7 *Col. J. Trans.* L. 203.
112. Hickey, 'Legal problems relating to combined transport and barge carrying vessels', 45 *Tul. L. Rev.* 863, 1971.
113. Hill-Norton, 'World shipping at risk: the looming threat to the lifeline', *Conflict Studies*.
114. Holderness, C. G., 'Economic analysis of the UN code of conduct for liner conferences, *Stan. L. Rev.*, Vol. 29, April 1977, pp. 853–77.
115. Horn, J., 'Economics of shipping and shipping policy: nationalism *vs* internationalism'. *J. Trans. Econ. & Pol.*, Sept. 1969, pp. 245–50.
116. Huntley, K. A., 'The Protection of Trading Interest Act 1980: some juridicial aspects of enforcement of antitrust laws', 1 *CLQ*, Vol. 30, Jan. 1981, pp. 213–33.
117. HMSO. British Shipping in the Orient, 38th Report 1939.
118. HMSO. Final Report on the Deferred Rebate System, CMND 1802, 1923.
119. HMSO. Report of Rates Freight in the Trade from the UK to New Zealand, 1935.
120. James, L. G., 'Some current development in US control of international shipping', *International Lawyer*, Vol. 7, No. 7, pp. 541–59.
121. Jenkis, 'Nationality, the flag and registration as criteria for demarcating the scope of maritime convention', 19 *J. Comp. Leg.* (3rd Ser) 19, 1937.
122. Johnson, H. G., 'A theoretical model of economic nationalism in new and developing states', *Pol. Sc. Q*., Vol. 70, No. 2, June 1965.
123. Johnson, H. G., 'IMCO: the First Four Years (1959–1962)', 12 *Int. & Comp. LQ* 31, 1963.
124. Johnson, H. G., 'The Baltic conventions', 25 *Int. Comp. LQ*., 1976.
125. Jones, 'Admission to Steamship Conferences', 9 *Geo. Wash. L. Rev*. 93, 1940.
126. Kilgour, J. C. E., 'The energy transportation security act of 1974', *J. Mar. L. & Com*., Vol. 7, No. 4, July 1976.
127. Kilgour, J. C. E., 'Double subsidy issue in shipping', 6 *J. Mar. L. & Com*. 395, 1975.
128. Kilgour, J. C. E., 'Effective US control', 8 *J. Mar. & Com.* 337, 1977.
129. Kominers, 'Federal government aids to merchant shipping', 47 *Tul. L. Rev.* 691, 1973.
130. Kopanitsas, D. E., 'Differential prices for the services of ships belonging to the same general class: a case of oligopoly', *J. Ray. Stat. Seociety*, Vol. 121, 1958.
131. Krzyzanowski, M., 'Socialist countries planning and programming of liner shipping', Bremen Series.
132. Lays, 'New directions in the law of the sea', *Oceana*, 1973.
133. Laing, E. T., 'Shipping freight rates for developing countries – who ultimately pays?', *J. Trans. Econ. & Pel*., Sept. 1977, pp. 262–76.
134. Laing, E. T., 'The rationality of conference pricing and output policies', *Mar. Stu. & Man*., No. 3, Part 1 & Part II, 1976.
135. Law, 'Title XI of the merchant marine act 1936: proposals for its amendment', 2 *J. Mar. L. & Com.* 63, 1970.
136. Lebluhm, 'Practising CIF and FOB today', *Eu. Trans. Law,* Vol. 16, No. 1 pp. 24–35.

137. Lewis. W. A., 'Notes on the economics of loyality', *Econometrica*, Feb. 1942.
138. Lopatin, A. G., 'The UNCTAD code of conduct for liner conferences: time for a United States response', *Harv. L. J.,* Vol. 22, No. 2, Spring 1981, pp. 355–77.
139. Lowe, A. V., 'The right of entry into maritime ports in international law', *San Diego L. Rev.*, Vol. 14 No. 3, April 1977, pp. 597–621.
140. Lowenfeld, 'To have one's cake – the FMC and the conferences' 1 *J. Mar. L. & Com. LQ* 31, 1963.
141. Llorca, 'Antitrust exemption of shipping conferences', 6 *J. Mar. L. & Com.* 287, 175.
142. Lloyds, 'The world and shipping', *Lloyds Ship. Econ.*, Vol. 2, No. 4, April 1980, pp. 6–7.
143. Lloyds, 'West Africa: special supplement'. *Lloyds List*, Thursday 29 Nov., 1979, p. 5.
144. Lloyds, 'Developed nations falling into a political trap on cargo sharing', *Lloyds List*, Thursday 24 April, 1980.
145. Lloyds, 'A convenient solution to the trade shuttle', *Lloyds List*, Thursday 8 Feb., 1979.
146. Lloyds, 'An end to convenience flags?', *Lloyds List*, Tuesday 6 Feb., 1979, p. 4.
147. Lloyds, 'All eyes turning to UNCTAD V', *Lloyds List*, Tuesday 2 Feb., 1979.
148. Lloyds, 'Africans told to stop fronting for foreigners', *Lloyds List*, Jan. 25, 1980, front page.
149. Lloyds, 'Safety, labour, both key UNCTAD issues flags of convenience', *Lloyds List*, 25 Jan., 1980, p. 2.
150. Lloyds, 'Africans urged to set up joint local shipyards', *Lloyds List*, Thursday Jan. 24, 1980, p. 2.
151. Lloyds, 'Finance threat to developing countries fleets: banker warns third world of economic reality'.
152. Maccio, M. E., 'Extent of shipping fleets', Pamphlet No. 24, of the Bremen Series.
153. Maddy, 'Acquisition and ownership of vessels', 47 *Tul. L. Rev.* 489, 1973.
154. Magnusson, 'Shipping conferences dual rate contract arrangments, as a competitive weapon', 38 *St. John's L. Rev.* 221, 1964.
155. Magnusson, 'Maritime agreement with state traders' 46 *St. John's L. Rev.* 48, 1971.
156. Mahal, 'Some problems in vessel financing – a lender's lawyer's view', 47 *Tul. L. Rev.* 629, 1973.
157. Malinowski, W. R., 'Toward a change in international distribution of shipping activity – shipping and the developing countries. Malinowski, W. R, 'Shipping and the third world intereconomics', No. 1, Jan. 1971, pp. 6–10.
158. Mankabady, 'International and national organisation concerned with shipping'.
159. Maritime Research, 'The world liner tramp fleets', Special Supplement, May 1972.
160. Marx, D. Jr., 'Regulation of international liner shipping and freedom of the seas', *J. Ind. Econ.* XVI, No. 1, Nov. 1967.
161. Marx, D. Jr., 'International organisation of shipping', 55 *Yale L. J.* 1214, 1946.
162. May, 'The status of FMC shipping regulation under principles of international law', 54 *Geog. L. J.* 794 1966.
163. Mayer, H. M., 'Some geographic aspects of technological change in maritime transportation', *Economic Geography*, April 1973.
164. Macdonald, 'Documentation and transfer of vessels; transfer of US vessels to aliens', 47 *Tul. L. Rev.* 511, 1973.
165. Macdonald, 'A world maritime organisation', 18 *Dept St. Bull* 99, 1948.
166. McDonell, 'Unilateral regulation of international trade, US-Brazil coffee trade example', 3 *J. Mar. L. & Com.* 793, 1973.
167. McIhiney, P. T., 'Transportation: a developing profession, *Transportation Journal*, Fall 1964.
168. McGee, 'Ocean freight rate conferences and the American merchant marine', 27 *U. Ch. L. Rev.* 191 1960.
169. McIntosh A. C. B., 'Antitrust implications of liner conferences alternatives to the regulation of liner trades with emphasis on European approach' 2 *LMCLQ* (1980) May 1980, pp. 139–56.

171. McLachlan, D. L., 'The price policy of liner conferences', *Scottish J. Pol. Econ.*, Vol. X., Nov 1963 pp. 322–35.
172. McLachlan, D. L., 'Index numbers of liner freight rates in UK trades 1946–1957', *Yorkshire Bull. Pol. Econ.*, Dec. 1963.
173. Metaxas, B. N., 'Notes on the Internationalisation process in the maritime sectors', *Mar. Pol. & Man.* Jan. 1978.
174. Moore, J. N., 'Law and foreign policy of the oceans', *Cal. W. I. L. J.*, Vol. 5, Nol 9, 1979, pp. 522–39.
175. Morse, 'Study of American merchant marine legislation', 25 *Law & Conte Prob.* 57, 1960.
176. Morse. 'A review of the assistance provided to the American merchant marine and their administration by the FMB and the MARAD', 18 Feb., *B. J.* 354, 1958.
177. Moyer, C., 'A critique of the rational for present US maritime programs', *Transportation Journal*, Winter 1974.
178. Mundell, R. A., 'Transport costs in international trade, *Can. J. Econ. & Pol. Sci.*, Vol. 21, Aug. 1957, pp. 331–48.
179. Neef, S. C., 'The UN Code of Conduct for Liner Conferences', *JWTL*.
180. Newsome, 'US merchant marine policy examined', 19 *Jag. J.* 95, 1968.
181. Neto, J. M. P., 'The emergence of new manufacturing nations, *Shipping 2000*.
182. Non-aligned countries, Charter of Algiers – Ministerial Conference of 77 Developing Counties, 24/10/67 7 *ILM* 1977.
183. Non-Aligned countries. Manilla Declaration and Programme of Action for Commodities, 15 *ILM* pp. 414–452.
184. Northwestern, 'In search of a rational line shipping policy', *Northwestern University Transportation Centre*, 1978.
185. *Norwegian News*, 'West and Central African cooperation in maritime transport' No. 21, 1976, p. 22.
186. *Norwegian News*, 'Who will run shipping?', No. 9, 14 May, 1976, p. 5.
187. *Norwegian News*, 'COMECON and the liner trade', No. 10, 1975, p. 5.
188. *Norwegian News*, 'Planned or free market economy?', No. 6, 1975, p. 5.
189. *Norwegian News*, 'The French merchant fleet', No. 19, 1975 pp. 10–13.
190. Note. 'UNCTAD Flags of Convenience', *J. W. T. L.*
191. Note. 'UNCTAD V: shipping resolutions pushed through the dock and harbour authority'.
192. Note. 'The Code of Conduct for Liner Conferences: frustrations on the road to Utopia', *Can. YBIL*, 1976, pp. 257–69.
193. Note. 'UNCTAD restrictive business practices Conference', *JWTL*, pp. 172–79.
194. Note. 'UNCTAD model law on restrictive business practices', *JWTL*, pp. 444–50.
195. OECD, 'OECD study on flags of convenience', *J. Mar. L. & Com.*, Vol. 4, No. 2, Jan. 73, pp. 231–54.
196. OECD, *OECD Code of Liberalisation of Current Invisible Operations*, OECD Paris.
197. Olson, T. F., 'Cargo preference and the American merchant marine', *Law & Cont. Prob.*, Vol. 25, pp. 82–105.
198. Oribe, S. J. E., 'Flag preference in Latin America', *J. Mar. L. & Com.*, Vol. 10, No. 1, Oct. 1978.
199. Orr, D., 'Price strategies to promote cartel stabilization', *Econometrica*, May 1965.
200. Osieke, E., 'Flags of convenience vessels: recent developments', *AJIL*, Vol. 73, 1979, pp. 604–27.
201. Oyevaar, 'Flag discrimination: a manifesto absurdity', OECD 1961.
202. Oyevaar, *Technological change and the Future of Shipping in Developing Countries, Shipping and Developing Countries*. Chapter 3, pp. 44–66.
203. Padwa, D. J., 'The curriculum of IMCO', *International Organisation*, Vol. XIV No. 4,, Autumn 1960.
204. van Panhuys, 'The genuine link doctrine and flags of convenience', *AJIL* Vol. 62, 1968, pp. 942–43.
205. Patton, J. R. *et al.*, 'Cargo preference and flag discrimination in international shipping – actions and reactions', *Geo. Wash. L. Rev.*, 1965, pp. 257–87.

206. Pawson, E., 'Transport and development: perspectives from historical geography', *Int. J. Tran. Econ.* Vol. 6, No. 2, 1979, pp. 125–37.
207. Payne, J. G., 'The Soviet presence: the prospect for 2000', *Shipping 2000*.
208. Pearce, J., 'Maritime policy: will the seas be free of containerisation?', *Trans. Law J.*, Vol. 5, No. 1, Jan. 1973, pp. 23–43.
209. Phillips, 'Restraint on foreign investments in the merchant marine – an asset or liability to US interest?', 11 *Cornell Int. L. J.*, 1, 1978.
210. Prebisch, P., 'A new strategy for development', *J. Econ. Studies*, Vol. 3, No. 1, pp. 3–14.
211. Rajwar, L. M. S., 'Trade and shipping needs of developing countries'. *Shipping and Developing Countries, supra*, pp. 7–27.
212. Ramsey, R. A., 'The flag of convenience debate in UNCTAD', *Seaways*, July 1982, pp. 5–6.
213. Remond, Y. P., 'The land–sea interchange: transport development in the next decades', *Shipping 2000*.
214. *Report*. Shipbuilding in Sweden.
215. Restrictive TPC (Canada). Shipping Conferences, Arrangements and Practices, Ottowa, 1966.
216. Richards, P. J., 'Shipping problems of underdeveloped countries', *Bull. Ox. Inst. Econ. & Stat.*, Aug. 1967, pp. 265–80.
217. Richardson, 'Capital construction funds under the merchant marine act', 29 *Tex. L. Rev*. 751, 1974.
218. *Rochdale Report*. The Committee of Inquiry into Shipping. HMSO. *CMND* 4337 1970.
219. Rohreke, H. G., 'The formula and material concept of flag equality', Pamphlet No. 4/1961.
220. Romans, T. J., *The American Merchant Marine – flags of Convenience and International Law*, Vol. 3, pp. 121–52.
221. Rothschild, K. W., 'Price Theory and Oligopoly', *Economic Journal* 57, 1947.
222. Royal Commission. Royal Commission on Shipping Rings, *CMND* 4668, HMSO 1909.
223. Rozental, A., 'The charter of economic rights and duties and the NIEO', *Na. J. I. L.*, Vol. 16, 1966 No. 2 pp. 309–22.
224. Ryver, J., 'The criteria for shipyard subsidies must be altered', *Norwegian News*, Vol. 15, No. 10, Sept. 1980, pp. 26–29.
225. Salen, S. H., 'Protection and development – cross currents in shipping', *J. C. I. T.* July 1979, pp. 311–25.
226. Sampson, R. J., 'The pricing of transportation services', *Centre for Transportation* 1967–1968.
227. Samuelson, P. A., 'Transfer problems and transport costs, Part I: The terms of trade when impediments are absent', *Economic Journal*, Vol. LXII, June 1952, pp. 278–304. Samuelson P. A., 'Part II: Analysis of the effects on trade impediments', *Economic Journal*, Vol. 64, June 1954, pp. 264–89.
228. Sandberg, M. G. R., Financing in the Future: Ships and Trade, *Shipping 2000*.
229. Saraiva, C. O., Brazilian International Shipping Policy, *Lawyer of Americas* pp. 28–43.
230. Sager, K. H., Cargo Sharing and Liner Shipping The Future of Liner Shipping, Bremen, Sept. (1975) pp. 97–110.
231. Schmeltzer, *et al*. 'Container feeder system' 4 *J. Mar. L. & Com*. 215, 1973.
232. Schmidt, L. *et al*. 'The UNCTAD Code of Conduct for Liner Conferences – an analysis and evaluation of its application in the US foreign line trades', *Hapag Lloyds*, April 1979.
233. Schmidt, L., 'The international shipping policy issues at UNCTAD V, Manila, May 1979', *Mar. Pol. & Man.*, 1979, Vol. 6, No. 4, pp. 269–76.
234. Schneerson, D., 'The structure of liner freight rates', *J. Trans. Econ. & Pol.*, Jan. 1976.
235. Schneerson, D., 'The rationality of conference pricing and output policies', *Mar. Stu. & Man.*, No. 3, 1976.

236. Seaward, N., 'Owners fear EEC competition rule within two years', *Seatrade*, Aug. 1979, pp. 27–35.
237. Servais, 'Title XI federal ship mortgage and loan insurance – a new concept of ship financing', 18 *Fed. B. J.* 388, 1958.
238. Shadburne, 'Coastwise and intercoastal shipping II', *ICC Proc. J.* 189, 1943.
239. Sher, 'The FMC and labour related matters', 3 *J. Man. L. & Com.* 677, 1972.
240. Shils, 'Flags of convenience, flags of necessity or runaway ships', 13 *Lab. L. J.* 1009, 1967.
241. Shils, 'Industrial unrest in the nations maritime industry', 15 *Lab. L. J.* 337, 1964.
242. Shimojo, T, 'Charter base and case, their origins, logistics, and applications', Bremen Series.
243. Shimojo, T., 'Analysis of shipping Costs as Criteria for Decision Making – Bremen Series.
244. Shimojo, T, 'Cost analysis and shipping stumulation for shipping decision making – Japanese traditions', Bremen Series, Pamphlet No. 18/19.
245. Shipping Conferences. 'Shipping Conferences Rate Policy and Developing Countries', *Hamburg Institute for International Economics*, 1973.
246. Shipping Statistics. *Shipping Statistics Yearbook* (Annual), Bremen Institute of Shipping Economics.
247. Shorter Articles. 'Impact of cargo sharing proposals in the dry bulk trades', *Asian Shipp.*, May 1980, p. 60.
248. Shorter Articles. 'UNCTAD success in shipping: political crisis among the TMNS', *JWTL*, pp. 586–90.
249. Shorter Articles. 'Cargo reservation and developing countries', *JWTL*, pp. 590–604.
280. Shorter Articles. 'UNCTAD: control of restrictive business practices', *JWTL*, pp. 67–74.
251. Silberman, R. M., 'Cargo preference: the US and future regulation of international shipping', *Va. JIL*, Vol. 16, No. 4, Summer 1976, pp. 865–901.
252. Silvestein, 'Technological politics & maritime affairs – comparative participation in IMCO', *F. J. Mar. L. & Com.* 367, 1976.
252. Simmonds, 'Constitution of the maritime safety committee of IMCO', 12 *Int. & Contemp. L. Q.* 56, 1963.
253. Smith, J. R., 'Ocean freight rates', *Political Science Quarterly*, No. 2, 1906.
254. Sorenson, 'The ITF view of flags of convenience', *Asian Shipp.*, Nov. 1980, pp. 122–24.
255. Steiner, H. M., 'Social benefit cost anslysis of transport proposals', *Transportation Research Forum* 14, 1973.
256. Strahm, D., 'Research vessels and exploration of marine resources', Pamphlet No. 25, Bremen Series.
257. Stuchten, R., 'Port planning in developing countries – a case description', Pamphlet No. 17, Bremen Series.
258. Sturmey, S. G., 'Liberalism, divigism and the new international maritime order', *European shipping and Shipbuilding*, 1978, pp. 169–90.
259. Sturmey, S. G., 'National shipping policies', *J. Ind. Econ.*, 1965, pp. 14–29.
260. Sturmey, S. G., *Shipping in the 1960's*, Institute of Shipping Research, Bergen.
261. Sturmey, S. G., 'Economic consequences of the code of conduct'.
262. Sturmey, S. G., 'The development of the code of conduct for liner conferences', *Marine Policy*, Vol. 3, No. 2 April 1979, pp. 133–48.
263. Sturmey, S. G., 'Economics of international liner services', *J. Trans. Econ. & Pol.*, Vol. 1, No. 1 May 1967, pp. 190–203.
264. Svendsen, A. S., *Trends in World Seaborne Shipping*, Pamphlet of the Bergen Series.
265. Svendsen, A. S., 'Shipping in the countries of the Eastern Bloc', *Norwegian News*, No. 2, 1962, pp. 52–62.
266. Takyiwaa, M., 'Shipping and the new international economic order', Faculty of Law, University of Dar es Salaam.
267. Thompson, J. M., 'Some reflections on transport research in europe', *Canadian Transport Commission*, Ottowa 1978.

268. Totland, T., 'Protectionism in international shipping and some economic effects', *Mar. Pol. & Man.*, Vol. 7, No. 2, 1980, pp. 103–14.
269. Tozzoli, A., 'Containerisation and its impact on port development', *J. Waterways*, Aug. 1972.
270. Troxell, 'Reorganisation of the US FMC', 17 *J. B. A. Dist. Colum.* 502, 1980.
271. Ullman, 'Ocean freight rate forwarders in the US', 7 *J. Mar. L. & Com.* 708, 1976.
272. Ullman, 'The role of the american ocean freight forwarders in intermodal containerised transportation', 2 *J. Mar. L. & Com.* 625, 1971.
273. UN (See list of UNCTAD Documents).
274. UNCTAD (iden).
275. US. Index of Current Regulations of MARAD, Dept. of Trade.
276. US. US and International Shipping: Economic Future 1972.
277. US. US Shipping Subsidies and National Treatment Treaty Provisions (MARAD).
278. US. US. Shipping Restrictions on Grain Sales 5 LIM, pp. 42–50.
279. Vallega, A., 'International relations and maritime dependence'.
280. Valente, M. G., 'The participation of developing countries in shipping', *Shipping and the Developing Countries*, Chapter 2, pp. 27–44.
281. Vamberly, R. G., 'Mechanism for the control of transnational shipping corporations', *Man. Pol. & Man.*
282. Vellenga, *et al.* 'Technological transfer in transportation: problems & research questions', *Trans. Research Forum*, 16/1975.
283. Walden, 'Dual rate movatorium – end of the Isbrandtsen odyssey', 10 *J. Pub. L.* 78, 1961.
284. Walgreen, J. A., 'Liner nationality and steamship conference rate making', *J. Ind. Econ.* July 1969, pp. 205–09.
285. Wijkham, M., 'Effects of cargo reservation: a review of UNCTAD's code of conduct for liner conferences', *Marine Policy*, Oct. 1980, pp. 271–89.
286. William, H., 'Regulation public policy and efficient provision of freight transportation', *Trans. J.*, Fall 1975.
287. William, H., 'The impact of exchange rate changes on shipping costs and revenues', *Norwegian News*, No. 7, May 1981, pp. 23–25.
288. Wilson, G. W., 'UNCTAD's plan for transforming world shipping', *Financial Times*, Friday Jan. 18, 1980.
289. Yang, 'Shipping practice', *Asian Shipp.*, Dec. 1980, pp. 60–62.
291. Ying, C. A., 'Australia, overseas cargo shipping Part X – Trade Practices Act 1974', *Aust. Bus. L. Rev.*, Vol. 9, pp. 72–73.
292. Young, W., 'UK maritime policy – coordination at government level', *Marine Policy*, Oct. 1980, pp. 322–25.
293. Zamora, S., 'Rate regulation in ocean transport: developing countries confront the liner conference system', *Cal. L. Rev.*, Vol. 59, pp. 1299–1332.
294. Zamora, S, 'UNCTAD III – the question of shipping', *JWTL*, pp. 91–115.
295. Zannetos, Z., 'Persistent economic misconceptions in the transportation of oil by sea', *Mar. Stu. & Man.*, No. 1 1973.
296. Zerby, J. A., 'On the practicality of the UNCTAD 40–20–40 Code for Liner Conferences', *Mar. Pol. & Man.* 1979, Vol. 6, No. 4, pp. 241–51.

6. Selected books

1. Adler, H. A., *Economic Appraisal of Transport*, Indiana, 1971.
2. Agrawal, N. M., *Merchant Shipping Legislation in India and U.K.*, Bombay UP, 1973.
3. Aldcroft, D. H., *Studies in British Transport History*, London, 1974.
4. Alexanderson, G. *et al.*, *World Shipping*, N.Y., 1963.
5. Allum, D. N., *Marine Transport: A Guide to Libraries and Sources of Information in the U.K.*, 1974.

6. Altiag, A. M., *The Lome Convention and a New International Economic Order*, Leyden, 1977.
7. Anand, R., *Legal Regime of Seabed of the Developing Countries*, Leyden, 1976.
8. Anderson, R. E., *The Merchant Marine and World Frontiers*, Cornell, N.Y., 1945.
9. Athay, R. E., *The Economics of Soviet Merchant Shipping Policy*, OUP, 1972.
10. Atiyah, P. S., *The Sale of Goods*, 2nd ed., London, 1971.
11. Bally, B., *Massachusetts Shipping 1697–1914*, Harvard, 1959.
12. Bamford, C. G., *The Geography of Transport*, Plymouth, 1978.
13. Barker, *et al., The US Merchant Marine in National Perspective*, Lexington Mass., 1970.
14. Bartle, R. D., *Introduction to Shipping Law*, London, 1958.
15. Berlund, A., *Ocean Transportation*, N.Y., 1931.
16. Behnam, A.Y., *A Study of the Value of National Fleets and Shipping Policies in Developing Countries*, Cardiff MSc Thesis.
17. Behrens, C. B. A., *Merchant Shipping and the Demands of War*, HMSO, 1955.
18. Becker, G. S., *The Economics of Discrimination*, UCP.
19. Benavea, M. R., *The Economics of Transport*, CUP, 1958.
20. Bennathan, E., *The Economics of Ocean Freight Rates*, N.Y., 1969.
21. Bennathan, E. *et al., Port Pricing and Investment Policy for Developing Countries*, OUP, 1979.
22. Bennathan, E., *Revenue Pooling and Cartels*, 1969.
23. Biden, C., *The Present Condition of the Merchant Service*, Madras, 1835.
24. Bes, J., *Chartering and Shipping Terms*, Vols. 1–3, N.Y., 1975.
25. Bes, J., *Bulk Carriers*, N.Y., 1975.
26. Blake, G., *Lloyds Register of Shipping 1760–1960*.
27. Boczek, B. A., *Flags of Convenience: An International Legal Study, Mass.,* 1962.
28. Bonavia, M. R., *The Economics of Transport*, CUP, 1958(r).
29. Boul, D., *A Guide for Transport Planning for Developing Countries*. London, HMSO, 1978.
30. Boxer, B., *Ocean Shipping in the Evolution of Hong Kong*, Chung UP, 1961.
31. Buchanan, D. S., *Merchant Shipping, A Guide to Government Publications*, HMSO, London.
32. Burke, W. T., *Contemporary Law of the Sea, Transportation, Communication and Flight*, Rhode Island, 1975.
33. Burley, K., *British Shipping and Australia 1920–1939*.
34. Burwash, D., *English Merchant Shipping 1960–1540*, 1947.
35. Branch, A. E., *The Elements of Shipping*, London.
36. Branch, A. E., *Dictionary of Shipping/International Trade Terms and Appreciation*, London, 1976.
37. Branch, A. E., *The Elements of Shipping*, 4th ed, London, 1977.
38. Bremen. *The Future of Liner Shipping*, Bremen, 1975.
39. Bremen. *Liner Shipping in the Eighties*, Bremen, 1980.
40. Bridges, R., *Cronen's World Directory of Freight Conferences*, 1965.
41. Brock, C., *The Control of Restrictive Practices from 1956*.
42. Bross, S., *Ocean Shipping*, Cambridge Mass., 1956.
43. Brown, R. T., *Transport and the Economic Integration of South America*, Brookings, 1966.
44. Cair, M. L., *Economics of Transportation in the US*, 1950.
45. Carlisle, R., *Sovereignty for Sale*, Maryland, 1980.
46. Carver, T. G., *A Treaties on the Law Related to Carriage of Goods by Sea*, London, 1971.
47. Chinitz, B., *Rate Discrimination in Ocean Transportation*, Harvard, 1956.
48. Chisholm, M., *Freight Flows and Spatial Aspects of the British Economy*, CUP, 1973.
49. Chorley, R. S. T., *Shipping Law*, London, 1963.
50. Chrzanowski, I. H., *Concentration and Centralisation of Capital in Shipping*, Farnborough, 1975.
51. Churchill, R. *et al., New Directions in the Law of the Sea*, 1973.

52. Clower, R. W. *et al., Puerto Rican Shipping and the US Maritime Laws, An Economic Appraisal*, 1965.
53. Constant, B., *The Law Relating to the Mortgage of Ships*, London, 1920.
54. Cotton, E., *East India Co's Maritime Service*, London, 1949.
55. Couper, *The Geography of Sea Transport.*
56. Cufley, C. F. H., *Ocean Freight Rates and Chartering,* London, 1974.
57. Currie, A. W., *Economics of Canadian Transportation* Toronto, 1954.
58. Darling, A. J., *The Elements of International Shipping Policy for Canada*, Ottowa, 1974.
59. Davis, R., *The Rise of the English Shipping Industry*, London, 1962.
60. Day, *International Trade in a Nutshell*, London, 1980.
61. Deakin, B. M., *Shipping Conferences: A Study of their Origins*, Development and Economic Practices, CUP.
62. Dearing, C. L., *National Transportation Policy*, 1979.
63. Denison, *America's Maritime History*, 1944.
64. Despicht, *Policies for Transport in the Common Market*, 1964.
65. Devanny, J. W., *Marine Decisions under Uncertainty,* Cambridge Mass., 1971.
66. De Verchove R., *International Maritime Dictionary*, 2nd ed., Princeton, 1961.
67. Dover, V., *The Shipping Industry: Its Constitution and Price*, London.
68. Drummond, S. H., *The Maritime Trade of North-Western Europe*, 1973.
69. Duff, P., *British Ships and Shipping*, 1949.
70. Dupuit, J., *Public Works and the Consumer in Transport*, 1968.
71. E.E.C., *Round Table on Transport Economics*, Paris, 1979.
72. E.E.C., *Options in Transport, Tariff Policy*, Brussels, 1965.
73. Elden, R. M., *Ships Management: Study in Definition and Measurements*, Cambridge Mass., 1962.
74. Escarpenter, C., *The Economics of International Ocean Transport*, Milwaukee, 1965.
75. Evans, A. A., *Technical and Social Changes in the World Ports*, Geneva, ILO, 1969.
76. Evans, A. A., *Transport: Its History and Economics*, 1946.
77. Evershein, F., *Effects of Shipping Subsidization*, Bremen, 1962.
78. Exton, J., *The Maritime Dicaelogie*, London, 1946.
79. Fair, M. L. *et al., Economics of Transportation and Logistics*, Dallas, 1973.
80. Faulks, R. W., *Elements of Transport*, London, 1965.
81. Fayle, C. E., *A Short History of the World's Shipping Industry*, London, 1933.
82. Fearnley, *et al. Trades of World Bulk Carriers.* Oslo.
83. Fearnley, *et al. World Carriers,* Oslo.
84. Fellner, W. J., *Competition Among the Few*, N.Y., 1960.
85. Ferguson, A. R., *The Economic Value of the US Merchant Marine*, Evanston, 1961.
86. Flere, W. A., *Port Economics*, London, 1967.
87. Frankel, E. *et al., Ocean Transportation*, Mass., 1972.
88. Frantzeskakis, J. M. *et al., Fifth International Symposium on the Theory and Practice of Transport Economics*, Athens, 1973.
89. Frederick, J. H., *Commercial Air Transportation*, 5th ed, Homewood, 1961.
90. Friedman, *The Future of the Oceans*, London, 1972.
91. Gandhi, D. S., *Shipowners, Mariners and the New Law of the Sea*, Fairplay 1977.
92. G. B. Agri., *Highlands Transport Board*, Edinburgh, 1967.
93. G. B. Econ., *Transport Policy in Consultative Document*, London, 1976.
94. G. B. Inf., *The British Shipping Industry Today*, London, 1947.
95. George, H., *Cost Benefit Analysis and Public Investment in Transport,* London, 1973.
96. Gilmore, H., *Transportation and the Growth of Cities*, Glencoe, 1953.
97. Glazebrook, G. P. I., *A History of Transportation in Canada*, 1964.
98. Glulliam, K. N., *Transport and Public Policy.*
99. Gold, E., *New Directions in Maritime Law*, Halifax, 1978.
100. Gorter, W., *The US Shipping Policy*, N.Y.
101. Gorton, *The Concept of Common Carrier*, 1971.
102. Goss, R. O., *Studies in Maritime Economics*, CUP, 1968.

103. Goss, R. O., *Advances in Maritime Economics*, CUP, 1977.
104. Grime, R. P., *Shipping Law*, London, 1978.
105. Gripaios, *Tramp Shipping*, 1959.
106. Grossman, W. L., *Ocean Freight Rates*, Cambridge, 1956.
107. Grundey, K., *Flags of Convenience*, London, 1978.
108. Gunston, B., *Transport Problems and Prospects*, London, 1972.
109. Haefele, E. T., *Transport and National Goals*, Brookings, 1909.
110. Hardy, A. C., *Seaways and Seatrade*, 1927.
111. Hargrove, J., *Who Protects the Oceans?*, 1975.
112. Harper, L. A., *The English Navigation Laws*, London, 1939.
113. Harrison, A. J., *The Economics of Transport Appraisal*, London, 1974.
114. Hawkins, R. C., *Transport in a Developing Country*, Southampton, 1978.
115. Hay, A., *Transport for the Space Economy*, London, 1973.
116. Hazard, J. L., *Transportation, Management, Economics, Policy*, Cambridge Mass. 1977.
117. Henly, O., *Flag Discrimination, Purposes, Motives and Consequences*, Gothenburg, 1960.
118. H.M.S.O., *British Shipping Industry Today*, London, 1966.
119. Heydon, *The Restraint of Trade Doctrine*, London, 1971.
120. Hillie, S. J. *et al.*, *Transportation Principles and Perspectives*, Danville, 1974.
121. Hodgson, A. J., *Shipping Documents*, London, 1929.
122. Honett, B. O., *Ocean Traffic and Trade*, 1970.
123. Hope, *Introduction to the Merchant Navy*, 1967.
124. Hoyle, B. S., *Transport and Development*, London, 1973.
125. Hoyle, B. S., *Seaports and Developments in Tropical Africa*, London, 1970.
126. Hubbard, M., *The Economics of Transporting Oil to and within Europe*, London, 1967.
127. Hutchison, J. G. B., *The American Maritime Industry's and Public Policy 1794–1914*, Harvard, 1941.
128. Hutchison, J. G. B., *The American Maritime Industry and Public Policy*, Harvard, 1950.
129. Hurd, S. W. A., *The Shipping World and Shipbuilding.*
130. Hyde, F. E., *Shipping Enterprises and Management 1830–1939*, Liverpool, 1967.
131. IBG, *Transport and Public Policy*, Aston Villa, 1977.
132. IMCO, *International Conference on Space requirements for Special Trade Ships*, London, 1973.
133. Insead, *The Regeneration of an Industry; British Shipping 1969–73*, London, 1976.
134. Johnson, K. M., *The Economics of Containerisation*, London, 1971.
135. Jones, C. W., *British Merchant Shipping*, London, 1923.
136. Kendal, L. C., *The Business of Shipping*, Cambridge, 1973.
137. Kilgour, J. G., *The US Merchant Marine; National Maritime Policy*, N.Y., 1978.
138. King, T. A., *Criticisms and Accuracies of Transportation Models*, Southampton, 1979.
139. Kirkaldy, A. W. *et al.*, *The History and Economics of Transport.*
140. Kneafsey, J. T., *Transportation Economic Analysis*, Lexington, 1975.
141. Knudsen, *Politics of International Shipping 1973*, Lexington, 1973.
142. Koch, A. G. M., *Current Pricing Behaviourism in Liner Shipping*, Bergen, 1968.
143. Korah, V., *Competition Law of Britain and the Common Market*, London, 1968.
144. Lane, R., *Analytical Transport Planning*, London, 1971.
145. Langford, J., *Transport in Transition*, Montreal, 1976. Lansing J. *Transportation and Economic Policy*, N.Y., 1968.
146. Larner, R., *Public Policy in Ocean Freight Industry*, Brookings, 1978.
147. Lassas, A. K., *An Approach to Maritime Transport Planning in Algeria*, Southampton, 1980.
148. Lawrence, S. A., *International Sea Transport: The Years Ahead*, Lexington, 1972.
149. Lawrence, S. A., *US Merchant Shipping Policies and Politics*, Brookings, 1966.
150. Leighton, A. C., *Transport and Communication in Early Medieval Europe*, London, 1972.

151. Lewa, E. J., *Transport in a Developing Country*, Southampton, 1976.
152. Lewis, W. A., *Overhead Costs,* London, 1949.
153. Lewis, C. B., *Survey of Canadian Activity in Transportation*, Ottowa, 1971.
154. Lindsay, W. S., *History of Merchant Shipping and Ancient Commerce, 4 Vols*, London, 1874.
155. Locklin, P. D., *Economics of Transportation*, Homewood, 1972.
156. Lynch, T. D., *Policy Analysis in Public Policy-Making*, Lexington, 1972.
157. Madigan, *Taxation of the Shipbuilding Industry*, 1971.
158. Mance, O., *International Seaport*, OUP, 1945.
159. Mance, O., *International Sea Transport*, OUP, 1945.
160. Manga, P., *International Maritime Law*, Antwerp, 1973.
161. Marcus, H. A., *Planning Ship Replacement in the Containerisation Era*, Lexington, 1974.
162. Marlowe, J., *The Making of the Suez Canal*, London, 1964.
163. Marx, D., *International Shipping Cartels*, Princeton, 1953.
164. Maruno, Y. O., *Practice and Law of International Ship Finance*, Southampton, 1978.
165. McCulloch, J. R., *A Dictionary of Practical, Theoretical and History of Commerce and Navigation*, London, 1882.
183. McDougal, M. S., *The Public Order of the Oceans*, YUP, 1962.
184. McDowell & Gibbs., *Ocean Transportation*, 1954.
185. McFairland, M. E., *Ships Business*, 1944.
186. McMaster, D. N., *Transport in Africa*, Edinburgh, 1970.
187. Mertins, H., *National Transportation Policy in Transition*, Lexington, 1972.
188. Merrills, J. G., *Current Bibliography of International Law*, London, 1978.
189. Metaxas, B. N., *The Economics of Tramp Shipping*, London, 1971.
190. Meyers, B. H., *The Nationality of Ships,* The Hague, 1967.
191. Meyers, B. H., *History of Transportation in the US before 1860*, The Hague, 1948.
192. Millan, T. S., *The Early History of the Don Navigation*, MNP, 1965.
193. Milson, C. H., *Guide to Merchant Navigation*, 1968.
194. Moresby, D., *The Human Element in Shipping*, London, 1975.
195. Morris, M. A., *International Politics and the Sea*, 1979.
196. MOT, *Highland Transport Enquiry*, HMSO, 1963.
197. Munby, D., *Transport,* London, 1968.
198. Munro-Smith, R., *Merchant Ship Types*, London, 1975.
199. Naess, E. D., *The Great Panlibho Controversy*, Farnborough, 1958.
200. Nash, C., *A Public versus Private Transport*, London, 1971.
201. National Academy of Sciences, *Maritime Information*. Sources: *A Guide to Current Statistical Data*.
202. National Academy of Sciences, *Legal Impediments to International Intermodal Transportation*, 1971.
203. Norton, H. S., *Modern Transportation Economics*, Ohio, 1971.
204. Nuffield Foundation, *A Policy for Transport*, London, 1977.
205. OECD, *Guide to Legislation on Restrictive Business Practices in Europe and North America*, Paris, 1964.
206. OECD, *Maritime Transport* (Annual), Paris.
207. OECD, *Export Cartels*, Paris, 1974.
208. OECD, *Ocean Freight Rates as Part of Total Transport Costs*, Paris, 1967.
209. OECD, *Developments and Problems of Seaborne Container Transport*, Paris, 1971.
210. OECD, *Transport of the Future*, 1964–1965.
211. OCL. *A Merchant's Guide to Liabilities and Problems*, 1979.
112. Ogley, R., *Whose Common Heritage*?, London, 1973.
213. Oglivie, P. M., *International Waterways*, 1920.
214. Okolie, C. C., *International Law Perspectives of the Developing Countries*, N.Y. 1978.
215. O'Loughlin, C., *The Economics of Sea Transport*, London.
216. Otterson, J. E., *Foreign Trade and Shipping*, 1st ed, London, 1945.

217. Owen, W., *Strategy for Mobility*, Washington, D.C. 1970.
218. Padelford, N. J., *The Panamal Canal*, 1943.
219. Parsons, T., *A Treatise on Maritime Law,* Boston, 1859.
220. Pegrum, D. F., *Transportation: Economics and Public Policy*, Homewood, 1973.
221. Philips, A., *Promoting Competition in Regulated Markets,* Washington D.C. 1970.
222. Pigou, A. C., *The Economics of Welfare,* London, 1952.
223. Piggot, F. T., *The Free Seas in War,* London, 1918.
224. Potter, M. A., *The Freedom of the Seas in Industry, Law and Politics*, 1974.
225. Pozen, R. C., *Legal Chances for State Enterprises in the Third World*, N.Y., UP, 1976.
226. Prescott, J. R. V., *The Political Geography of Oceans*, Vancouver, 1975.
227. Prest, A. R., *Transport Economics in Developing Countries*, London.
228. Quskill, S. W., *A Merchant Fleet in War,* London, 1962.
229. Ram, M. S., *Shipping*, London.
230. Reader, E. R., *The British Coasting Trade*, London, 1937.
231. Reese, *Merchant Marine Policy*, 1963.
232. Reliff, *The US and the Treaty Law of the Seas*, 1958.
233. Richardson, J. J., *The Policy-Making Process*, London, 1969.
234. Rinman, T., *et al., Shipping, How it Works*, Gothenburg, 1978.
235. Robertson, J. M., *Shipping after the War*, London, 1916.
236. Robertson, D. H., *Economic Fragments,* London, 1931.
237. Robinson, J., *The Economics of Imperfect Competition,* London, 1933.
238. Sampson, R. J., *et al., Domestic Transportation*, Hongton, 1979.
239. Sanjeeva, R. T. S., *A Short History of Modern Indian Shipping,* Bombay.
240. Sanklecha, S. N., *Tramp Shipping in India,* Bombay, 1966.
241. Sarnder, A., *Maritime Law*, London, 1901.
242. Savage, C. F., *An Economic History of Transport*, London, 1966.
243. Schadee, H., *Transport,* The Netherlands, 1974.
244. Schenker, E., *et al., Port Planning and Development*, Cornell, 1974.
245. Schymer, C. A., *The Problem of Transport*, 1968.
246. Schwartenberger, G., *Economic World Order,* MUP, 1978.
247. Sharp, C. H., *Transport Economics,* London, 1973.
248. Sharp, C. H., *The Problems of Transport*, OUP, 1965.
249. Singh, N., *International Conventions on Merchant Shipping*, London, 1973.
250. Singh, N., *et al., Shipowners,* London, 1967.
251. Singh, N., *The Legal Regime of Merchant Shipping,* Bombay, 1969.
252. Skeins, W. I., *Transport in the Highlands and Islands*, Glasgow, 1962.
253. Smith, J. R., *The Ocean Carrier*, 1908.
254. Smith, M. R. L., *An Examination of the Economic Benefits of the Establishment of a Merchant Marine*, UWIST, 1973.
255. Smykay, E. W., *Physical Distribution Management*, N.Y. 1973.
256. Society, *et al., Transport 69,* London, 1909.
257. Starkie, D. N. M., *Transport Planning Policy and Analysis*, Ox., 1976.
258. Stevens, E. F., *Dictionary of Shipping Terms and Phrases*, London, 1947.
259. Stevens, E. F., *Shipping Practice*, London, 1947.
260. Sturmey, S. G., *On the Pricing of Tramp Ship Freight Services,* Bergen, 1965.
261. Sturmey, S. G., *Shipping in the 1960's*, Bergen, 1965.
262. Sturmey, S. G., *Shipping Economics*, London, 1975.
263. Sturmey, S. G., *British Shipping and World Competition*, London, 1962.
264. Svendsen, A. S., *Trends in World Seaborne Trade*, Bergen, 1905.
270. Taff, C. A., *Management of Physical Distribution and Transportation*, Homewood, 1978.
271. Taylor, L. G., *Seaports: An Introduction to Their Place and Purpose*, Glasgow, 1974.
272. Temperly, R., *Merchant Shipping Acts, 1954*, 1976.
273. Tenter, C. Cab. *A Treatise of the Law relating to Merchants, Ships, Seamen and Ports,* 1846.

274. Tharper, L. A., *The English Navigation Laws*, N. Y. 1939.
275. Thommen., *International Legislation on Shipping*, UNCTAD, 1969.
276. Thompson, A. W. J., *The Nationalised Transport Industries*, London, 1973.
277. Thornburn, T., *The Supply and Demand of Water Transport*, Stockholm, 1960.
278. Thornton, R. H., *British Shipping*, CUP, 1939.
279. Tressel, D., *The Controversy over the Division of Labour in International Seaborne Transport*, Bergen.
280. Ullman., *The Ocean Freight Forwarders,* 1967.
281. Van Den Burg. *Containerisation: A Modern Transport System*, London, 1969.
282. Walters, A. A., *The Economics of Road User Charges,* Baltimore, 1968.
283. Woodward, J., *Systems Analysis in Marine Transport,* N.Y. 1968.
284. Wronski, M., *FOF and CIF Contracts in the Container Age*, Southampton, 1972.
286. Zannetos., *The Theory of Oil Tankship Rates*, MIT, 1966.
285. Zeiss., *American Shipping Policy*, 1938.

7. Selected legislations

Argentina	Law No. 20447, May 22, 1973
	Income Tax Act
	Law No. 18250
Australia	The Ship Construction Bounty Act, June 1975
	Income Tax Act
	Australian Navigation Act
Belgium	Income Tax Act
	The Act of August 23, 1948
Brazil	Decree Law No. 60679, May 3, 1967
	Law No. 4, 622, May 3, 1965
	Income Tax Act
	Decree Law No. 666, July 2, 1969
Canada	The British North America Act (UK) Victoria C.3 (1967)
	The Ferries' Act 30–31 (1970) (RS Nfld. C.128)
	National Transportation Act 1970
	Department of Transport Act 1970
	The Pilotage Act 1970–71–72. S.C. C.52
	The St. Lawrence Seaway Authority Act 1970 RSC C.S-1
	Canada Ports Act (1970) (RSC C.N-8)
	National Harbours Board Act (1970 RSC C.H.1)
	The Harbour Commission Act (1970 – SC. C.61)
	The Carriage of Goods Act 1910
	Statute of Westminster (UK 1931) 22 Geo. V C.4
	The Coasting Trade Act
	Combines Investigation Act RSC 1970 C.23
	Carriage of Goods by Water Act
	The Colonial Laws Validity Act (UK 1865) 28–29 VIC. C.63
	The Income Tax Act
	Shipping Act 1970 RSC S-9, C.1
	Transport Act 1972
	Inland Water Freight Rate Act 1970
	Maritime Code Act
	Foreign Investment Review Act
	Shipping Conferences Exemption Act, 27 Elizabeth II, 1978
	Business Records Protection Act 1947, Ont. Stat. C.10
	Business Concerns Record Act (1957–58) Que. Stat. C.42
Chile	Decree of 1974
	Decree Law of 23 December, 1975
	Income Tax Act

Colombia	Law 10 of 1946
	Decree No. 1208, July, 1969
	Decree No. 994, 1966
	Decree 616 of 1972
	Income Tax Act
	Decree No. 2349 of 1971
Cyprus	Law No. 47 June 25, 1963
	Income Tax Act
Denmark	Act No. 557, November 17, 1976
	Act No. 469, September 17, 1977
	Act No. 604, November 14, 1977.
	Income Tax Act.
Ecuador	Law of Cargo Reservation 1970
	Decree No. 416, May 31, 1972
	Income Tax Act
Egypt	Ministerial Decree 221, 1974
	Law No. 433
	Income Tax Act
Finland	The Act of Allowances for the Promotion of Production and Exports of Shipbuilding and other Metal Industries 1956
	The Act of Allowance for the Promotion of Production and Exports of Shipbuilding and other Metal Industries, Amendment 1970
	Income Tax Act
France	Law of December 28, 1959
	Decree of April 1931
	Law of 30 October 1935
	Decree of February 26, 1974
	Decree of 27 October, 1960
	The Law of 1953
	Ordinance of September 28, 1967
	Law of July 19, 1977
	Law of January 24, 1961
	Law of 30 December, 1968
	Law of July 16, 1976
	Income Tax Act
	Law of July 29, 1881
	Law of April 17, 1967
	Law of May 20, 1967
Gabon	Decree of 7th September, 1978
	Income Tax Act
FRG (West Germany)	Income Tax Act
	Measures Against Detrimental Shipping Policies of Foreign Countries
Greece	Emergency Law No. 465, July 9, 1968
	Law No. 1880 of 1951
	Law Concerning Taxation of Ships
	Law No. 378 of 1968
	Law No. 89 of 1967
	Legislative Decree No. 509, April 17, 1970
	Royal Decree No. 800, December 1, 1970
	Greek Constitution 1968, Article 23
	Legislative Decree 3415 of 1955
	Legislative Decree 4094 of 1960
	Legislative Decree 4419 of 1964
	Legislative Decree 1084 of 1971, Article 3
Iran	Decree No. 35510 of 23 August 1976
	Income Tax Act
Israel	Merchant Shipping (Vessels) Act 1960
	Income Tax Act

Italy	Law 684, December 20, 1974
	Law of January 4, 1968
	Law 878 of 27 December 1975
	Law No. 231, 25th May 1978
	Law No. 622 of July 24, 1959
	Law No. 720 of 23 December, 1975
	Law No. 26 of February 2, 1974
	Law No. 234, 25 May, 1978
	Law of March 1979
Japan	Maritime Transport Act, June 1, 1949
	Maritime Transport Act, June 1, 1951
	Maritime Transport Act, June 1, 1957
	Japanese Seamans Law No. 149, 1951
	Ships' Safety Law, No. 11, of 1933
	Law on Special Measures against Unfavourable Treatment to Japanese Ocean-going Ship Operators by Foreign Government and Others, 20 July 1977
	Export Society Law, No. 27 of 1925
	Import Export Commodities Industrial Society Law, No. 28 of 1925
	Law Concerning the Prohibition of Private Monopolies and the Maintenance of Fair Trade (The Antimonopoly Act), Law No. 54, 1947
	The Business Organisation Law, No. 191 of 1948
	Marine Transportation Act, Law No. 187 of 1949
Korea (South) Republic of	Shipping Promotion Law, February 28, 1967
	Presidential Decree
	Income Tax Act
Liberia	Shipping Act April 18, 1961
Mexico	Decree of April 28, 1966
	Decree of January 30, 1967
	Decree of January 18, 1963
	Decree of January 1, 1966
Panama	Fiscal Code – Article 708
	Cabinet Decree No. 15 of January 27, 1972
Peru	Law of January 9, 1964
	Ministerial Resolution of June 12, 1972
	Decree Law No. 20759 of October 15, 1974
	Supreme Decree, March 26, 1976
	Decree 22067, January 11, 1978
	Decree of December 30, 1969
	Law of February 8, 1957
Philippines	Overseas Shipping Act, 1955
	Presidential Order No. 37
	Presidential Decree 806, October 3, 1975
	Presidential Decree 894, February 26, 1976
	Presidential Decree No. 1466, June 11, 1978
	Presidential Decree No. 900, March 1976
Portugal	Law Decree 770 of 25 October, 1976
	Decree Law 205-C of 1975, April 16, 1975
	Decree Law 205-D of 1975, April 16, 1975
	Resolution No. 153 of May 5, 1977
	Law Decree of November 16, 1977
Saudi Arabia	Royal Decree
	(Another Law?)
South Africa	Act 58 of 1962
Spain	Law of May 12, 1956
	Royal Decree June 1976
Sweden	Shipbuilding Act, November 2, 1978

UK	Highlands and Islands Shipping Act 1960
	The Industry Act 1972
	The Industry Act 1975
	Trade Restrictions Act 1980
	Transport Act 1962
	Transport Act 1968
	Restrictive Trade Practices Act 1976
	Shipping Contracts and Commercial Documents Act 1964. Shipping Contracts and Commercial Documents Act 1974, C.87
	Industrial Development Act 1966
	Industrial Development (Ships) Act 1970
	Merchant Shipping Act 1894
	Cromwell's Navigation Acts 1690
	Merchant Shipping Act 1970
	Finance Act 1971
	Fair Trading Act 1973, Para. 83
	Protection of Trading Interests Act 1980
Uruguay	Law No. 14, 650
USA	The Merchant Marine Act 1936, 49 Stat 1985 46 USC
	The Merchant Marine Act 1970
	Public Law 90–341
	Public Law 911
	Public Law 480
	Public Law 664 (1954)
	Public Resolution No. 17, 1934
	The 1904
	Federal Ship Financing Act 1972
	Ocean Mail Act 1891
	Shipping Act 1916, 39 Stat. 728, 46 USC
	Railroad Revitalisation and Regulatory Reform Act 1976, Pub. L. 94–210, 90 Stat. 31
	Tax Reduction Act 1975
	Tax Reform Act 1976
	Act of October 3, 1961
	Act of July 20, 1789
	Act of March 1, 1817
	Jones Act of July 17, 1952
	Clayton Act 1970
	Energy Policy and Conservation Act
	Webb-Pomerave Export Trade Act 1970
	McArron-Ferguson Act 1970
	Sports Broadcasting Act 1961 (93–107, 47 USC).
	Sports Broadcasting Act (amended) 1966
	Kennedy Common Airline Regulatory Act
	Sherman Antitrust Act 15 USC
	Interstate Commerce Act 1887, 24 Stat. 379
	Ports and Waterways Safety Act
	Energy Transportation Act 1974
	Energy Transportation Security Act 1974
	Foreign Investment Code
	Federal Trade Commission Act 38 Stat. 717 (1914)
	Transportation Act 1920 41 Stat
	Merchant Marine Act 1920, 46 USC
	Emergency Railroad Transportation Act 1933
	Intercoastal Shipping Act (1933)
	Federal Communications Act (1934) 47 USC
	Motor Carrier Act of 1935

	Civil Aeronautics Act 1938, 52 Stat. 973, 49 USC
	National Transportation Policy Act 1940. 54 Stat. 899
	The Reed-Bulwinkle Act, 62 Stat. 472 (1948) 49 USC
	Celler-Kefauver Act 1950, 38 Stat. 731
	Federal Aviation Act 1958, 72 Stat. 731, 49 USC
	Antitrust Civil Process Act 1962, 15 USC
	Antitrust Procedures and Penalties Act 1974, 15 USC
	Hart-Scott-Rodino Antitrust Improvements Act 1974, 28 USC
	Foreign Sovereign Immunities Act 1976, 90 Stat. 28 USC
	Air Cargo Deregulation Act 1977, Pub. L. 95-163
	Airline Deregulation Act. Pub. L. 95-504, 92 St. (1978)
	Ocean Shipping Act 1978, Pub. L. 95-483
	International Air Transportation Competition Act 1979 Pub. L. 96-192
	Staggers Rail Act, Pub. L. 96-448
	Motor Carrier Act 1980, Pub. L. 96-296
	Cargo Preference Act 1954
	Economic Co-operation Act 1948
	Agricultural Trade Development and Assistance Act
	Defence Production Act 1970
	Mutual Security Act 1951
	Mutual Security Act 1954
	Mutual Defence Assistance Act, 1949
	Cargo Preference Act 1974
USSR	Merchant Shipping Code
	Act of September 26, 1950
Venezuela	The Law for the Protection and Development of the National Merchant Marine
	The Pilotage Law of August 6, 1971
Zaire	Law No. 74-014

7.1. Selected byelaws

Canada	Coasting Trade Exemptions Regulations SOR/77-49
	Ship Construction Drawback Regulations SOR/63-294
	Shipping (Customs) Regulations SOR/63-270
	Ship Subsidy Regulations SOT/66-297
	Shipbuilding Temporary Assistance Program Regulations, SOR/71-7
	The Shipbuilding Industry Assistance Regulations SOR/76-329
France	Regulation of February 17, 1968
	Regulation of July 22, 1965
	Regulation of March 27, 1977
	Regulation of July 28, 1969
	Regulation of July 20, 1972
	Regulation of July 10, 1975
	Regulation of February 18, 1977

8. Cases referred to

International Cases

Corfu Channel Case ICJ Reports 1949, p. 4
North Sea Continental Shelf Cases ICJ Reports
ARAMCO Arbitrations ICJ Reports

The Nottebhom ICJ Reports
ORINOCO Case ICJ Reports
The Constitution of IMCO ICJ Reports
English cases
Re-Keighley Maxtteel, 1894, 70 LT 155
In *Wimble* v *Rosenberg*., 1913, 3 KB 743
Renter v *Sala*, 1979, 4 CPD 239
Biddel Bros N E Clements Horst Co, 1911, IKB 214 at 220
Wilson Holgate Co v *Belgian Grain Produce Co* 1920, 2 KB 1
Diamond Alkali v *Burgeors*, 1921, 3 KB 443
Weis v *Produce Brokers' Co*, 1921, 7 LLLR 211
Oliaria Tirvena v *Algenieene Oliehdele*, 1972, 1 LLR 341
The Julia, 1949, AC 293 at 309
Rio Tinto Zinc v *Westinghouse*, 1978, AC 547 at 617
U Baltic Corp v *Burgett*, 1921, 8 LLR 190
American and other cases
Alcoa SS Co. v *Cia Anonima Venezuela de Navegacio*, 1962, 7 FMC 345, 737
Alcoa Co v *FMC*, 321F, 2d 756 (DC Cir 1963)
John T Bill Co v *US*, 104 F. 2d 67 (CCPA 1939)
US Federal Maritime Commission Docket No. 65-34
US Federal Maritime Commission Docket No. 65-45
US Federal Maritime Commission Docket No. 66-49
NY Life Insurance Co v *Anderson CCA NY*, 263F, 527 at 529
Boston & AR. Co v *NY Central RI*, 256 Mass 600, 166 Wis 163, NW 652 at 655
People ex rel Adwondack Power & Light Co v *Public Service Co*, 193 NYS 186, 191, 200 AD 268
Southern Bell Tel Co v *Rail Commissioner of South Carolina*, DCSC 5F 2d, 77 at 96
In re Lallar's Estate, 362, Ill 621 IN E 2d 50, 53
McLondon v *Johnson*, 71 GA App 424, 31E, 2d 89 at 92
Securities & Exch Comm v *Wickham*, DC Min 12F, Supp 245
Moore v *Sampson Country*, 220, NC 232, 17 SE 2d 22 at 23
US v *Marine Co* CCA Ill 90F, 2Nd 549 at 551
US v *Fischo DC Wash*, 262F 1001, at 1005
Strusman v *Des Meins City RI*, 180 Iowa, 524, 163 NW 580 at 585
Trust Co v *Greenwood Cemetry*, 21 NJ Misc 169, 32A 2d, 519 at 523
State v *First State Bank of Ind*, 52 ND 231, 202 NW, 391 at 402
State v *Manning*, 220 Iowa, 525, 259 NW 213
Kemp v *Stanley*, 204 La 110 15 50 2d, 1 at 11
State v *Duckett*, 133 SC 85, 130 SE 340 at 342
Rooney v *South Sioux City*, 111 Feb 1, 1955, NW 474 at 475
McCarten v *Sanderson*, 111 Mont 407 109P, 2d 1108 at 1112 A1 R 1229
Graves v *People of State of NY*, 306 US 466, 59 SCL 595 at 597
Drake v *Crane*, 127 No 85, 29 SW 990, 27 LRA 653
Lobsitz v *Lissberger*, 168 App. Div. 840, 154 N.Y.S. 556 at 557
Preston v *State Industrial Acc Comm*, 174 OV 553, 149P 2d 957
Beckman v *Saratoga*, 3 Paige NY 45, 73 Am Cas 1914 C at 1266
Harrison v *Big Four Bus Lines*, 217
Oklahoma City v *Board of Education*, 181 OKI 539, 75P 2d 201
Tennessee Oil v *McCanless*, 178 Tenn 683, 157 SW 2d 267 at 272
State v *Stratford*, 55 Idaho 65, 37P 2d 681, at 682
US v *Hill CCA NY*, 34F 2d 133, at 135
Colins v *Harris*, 130 Wash 394 227P, 508 at 509
Continental Grains v *STM Grain*, 1972, 2 Lloyds LR 64
The H Webber, 252 Mich, 198 NW, 159, 168, 71 ALR 1238
Bathgate v *Irvine*, 126 Cal 135, 58P. 442, 77 Am St Rep 158
In re Huggins Estate, 96 NJ Eq 275, 125, A27, 30
Halferty v *Karr*, 188 Mo App 241, 175 SW 146, at 147

9. Selected conventions

Geneva Convention on the Territorial Sea and Contiguous Zone 1958, UN Doc. No. A/Conf. 13/L.52, April 28, 1958

Geneva Convention on the High Seas, UN Doc. No. A/Conf.13/L.13. and Corr. 1

Convention Regarding the Regime of the Straits of Montreux, July 20, 1936, League of Nations *Treaty Series*, Vol. 28, p. 115

Firman Concession of January 5, 1856 (Suez Canal)

Imperial Firman of March 19, 1866 (Suez Canal)

Convention Respecting the Free Navigation of the Suez Maritime Canal, signed at Constantinopole, October 29, 1888

Declaration of the Government of Egypt on the Suez Canal and the agreements for its operation, April 24, 1957

Declaration by the Government of Egypt in respect of the jurisdiction of the International Court of Justice, July 18, 1957

Declaration Recognising Flag of States Having No Sea Coast, Barcelona, April 20, 1921. (Great Britain *Treaty Series*, No. 29, 1923, Cmd 1994/1923)

Convention and Statute on the International Regime of Maritime Ports, Geneva, December 9, 1923 (League of Nations *Treaty Series*, No. 1379)

Convention and Statute on Freedom of Transit, Barcelona, April 20, 1921 (Great Britain *Treaty Series*, No. 27, CMD 1992/1923.

International Convention and Statute Concerning the Regime of Navigable Waterways of International Convern, Barcelona, April 20, 1921 (League of Nations *Treaty Series*, Vol. 7, p. 35)

Additional Protocol to the Convention on the Regime of Navigable Waterways of International Concern, Barcelona, April 20, 1921

Convention on the Inter-Governmental Maritime Consultative Organisation. (UN Pub. Sales No. 1948)

Convention on Facilitation of International Maritime Traffic, London, 1965

Inter-American Convention on Facilitation of International Waterborne Transportation (Convention of Mar Del Plata) June 7, 1973

United Nations Convention on Code of Conduct for Liner Conferences, Geneva, April 1974

United Nations Convention on Multimodal Transport

Loam Convention (between the EEC and the ACP countries)

9.1. Treaties and agreements

Anglo-French Agreement of April 8, 1904 (Suez Canal)

Treaties connected with the peace settlements after the First World War

Anglo-Egyptian Agreement of August 26, 1936 (Suez Canal)

Treaty of Peace between the allied and associated powers and Germany, signed at Versailles, June 28, 1919 (Kiel Canal)

Hay-Pauncefote Treaty between Great Britain and the United States of America, Washington, November 18, 1901 (US *Treaty Series* 401) (Panama Canal)

Hay-Bunan Vaxilla Treaty between Panama and the United States of America, Washington, November 18, 1903 (US *Treaty Series* 431)

General Treaty between the United States of America and Panama, signed at Washington, March 2, 1936 (US *Treaty Series* 945)

Treaty of mutual understanding and cooperation between the United states of America and Panama, signed at Panama on January 25, 1955 (US *Treaty Series* 3297)

Agreement between the United States of America and the Union of Soviet Socialist Republics regarding certain maritime matters, Washington, October 1972 (23 UST 3576; TIAS 7513)

Agreement between the United States of America and the Peoples Republic of China on maritime transport, Washington, September 17, 1980

Agreement between the United States of America and the Socialist Republic of Romania on maritime transport, Washington, June 4, 1976 (27 UST 1416; TIAS 8254)

Agreement between the United States of America and the Socialist Peoples' Republic, amending and extending the prior agreement on August 30, 1979

Agreement Between the United States of America and the Peoples' Republic of Bulgaria, Sofia, February 19, 1981

Agreement Between the Polish Peoples' Republic and the United States of America on maritime matters: port access procedure, Warsaw, September 27, 1973 (24 UST 2271; TIAS 7748; UNTS No. 13325)

Panama Canal Treaty between the United States of America and the Republic of Panama, Washington, September 7, 1977

Agreement between Mexico and the United States of America concerning maritime boundaries, Mexico City, November 24, 1976 (29 UST 196; TIAS 8805)

Agreement between Denmark and the United States of America concerning the Jurisdiction over vessels in the United States deep water ports. Washington, August 22, 1978 (30 UST. 1702; TIAS. 9278)

Agreement between the United States of America and Liberia, Washington, January 15, 1979 (30 UST 1706; TIAS 9279)

Agreement between the United States of America and Norway concerning jurisdiction over vessels in the United States deep water ports, Washington, July 11, 1978 (30 UST 1671; TIAS. 9275)

Agreement between the United States of America and Portugal concerning jurisdiction over vessels in the United States deep water ports, Washington, July 11, 1979 (TIAS. 9526)

Agreement between the United States of America and Sweden concerning the jurisdiction over Vessels in the United States Deep Water Ports, Washington, August 22, 1978 (30 UST 1998; TIAS. 9297)

Agreement between the United States of America and the United Kingdom concerning the jurisdiction over vessels in the United States deep water ports, Washington, May 25, 1979 (TIAS 9525)

Memorandum of Understanding between Argentina and the United States concerning maritime matters, Buenos Aires, March 31, 1978 (30 UST. 1054; TIAS 9239)

Agreement between Brazil and the United States of America concerning equal access to government controlled cargoes, Washington 17, 1977 (29 UST 2860; TIAS 8981)

Cobden Treaty, 1860

Treaty for European Economic Cooperation (Treaty of Rome)

The Commonwealth Shipping Agreement

9.2. Reports

A. *USA government official reports*

House of Representatives. Committee on Merchant Marine and Fisheries. *Steamship Conference Study*, GPO, Washington DC, 1959 (The Bonner Committee)

House of Representatives. Committee on Merchant Marine and Fisheries. *Steamship Agreements and Affiliations in the American Foreign and Domestic Trade*, GPO, Washington DC, 1914 (The Alexander Committee)

House of Representatives. Committee on the Judiciary, Antitrust Sub-Committee. *Ocean Freight Rate*, GPO, Washington DC, 1962 (The Celler Committee)

House of Representatives. Committee on Merchant Marine and Fisheries. *Third Flag*, GPO, Washington DC, 1977

House of Representatives, Joint Economic Committee. *Discriminatory Ocean Freight Rates and the Balance of Payments*, GPO, Washington DC, 1965

Congress. Senate. Eommittee on Commerce, Science, and Transportation. *Illegal Rebating in the US Ocean Commerce*, GPO, Washington DC, 1977

Department of Commerce (DOC), Maritime Administration (MARAD) Annual Reports of Marad, *Maritime Subsidies*, GPO, Washington DC

Department of Commerce, (DOC), Maritime Administration, (MARAD) GPO, Washington DC, *A Statistical Analysis of the World's Merchant Fleet*, Annual Reports of MARAD

Department of Commerce, (DOC), Maritime Administration (MARAD), GPO, Washington, DC, *Effective US Control of Merchant Ships*, A Statistical Study

Department of Commerce, (DOC), Maritime Administration (MARAD), GPO, Washington DC, *Foreign Flag Ships Owned by US Parent Companies*, MARAD Annual Report

Department of Justice, Antitrust Division, GPO, Washington DC, *The Regulated Ocean Shipping Industry*, 1977

Department of Commerce (DOC), Maritime Administration (MARAD), GPO, Washington DC. Bread upon the Waters; Federal Aid to the Maritime Industries 1975

B. *UK government official publications*

Department of Education and Science (DESS). *Scientific Research in British Universities and Colleges*. HMSO, London, (Published Annually, from 1966–67 in 3 volumes. Prepared jointly with the British Council)

Economic Development Committee for the Movement of Exports *Exports by Air*; a report by a working party. HMSO, London 1967

Economic Development Committee for the Development of Exports. *Through Transport to Europe*. HMSO, London, 1966

Financial Advisory Panel on Exports. *Britain's Invisible Earnings*: The report of the Committee on invisible exports. British National Export Council, 1967

Imperial Shipping Committee. *British Shipping in the Orient*. HMSO, London, 1939

Imperial Shipping Committee. *Final Report. . . on the Deferred Rebate Scheme*. HMSO, London, 1923 CMND 1802

Ministry of Labour. *Final report of the Court of Inquiry into certain matters concerning the Shipping Industry*. HMSO, London 1967 (CMND 3211) (Chairman of the Court: Lord Pearson)

Ministry of Labour. *First report of the Court of Inquiry into certain matters concerning the Shipping Industry.* HMSO, London, 1966 (CMND 3025) (Chairman of the Court: Lord Pearson)

Ministry of Transport. *Proposed fixed channel link*. HMSO, London, 1963 (CMND 2137)

Ministry of Transport. *Report of the Committee of Inquiry into the Major Ports of Great Britain*. HMSO, 1962 (CMND 1824) (Chairman of the Committee: Viscount Rochdale)

Ministry of Transport. *Reorganisation of the ports*. HMSO, London 1969 (CMND 3903)

Ministry of Transport and Civil Aviation. *Seafarers and their Ships: Story of a century of progress in the Safety of Ships and the Well-being of Seamen*. HMSO, London 1955

Royal Commission on Shipping Rings. *Report of . . . Commission* HMSO, London, 1909 (CMND 4668) (Chairman of the Commission: A. Cohen)

Working Group on Marine Reactor Research. *Nuclear Power for Ship Propulsion*: Report of the Working Group. HMSO, London 1964 (CMND 2358) (Chairman: Sir Thomas Padmore)

Board of Trade. *Committee of Inquiry into Shipping*. Report of the Working Party. HMSO, London, 1970 (CMND 4337). (Chairman: Viscount Rochdale) (The Rochdale Report)

C. *General reports*

Behrens, C. B. A., *Merchant Shipping and the Demands of War*. HMSO and Longmans. London, 1955 (History of the Second World War; United Kingdom Civil Series)

British Shipping Federation, *Passport to Adventure*, 1969

British Shipping Federation, *Work Study and the Seafarer*, 1968. (Issued jointly with the Chamber of Shipping of the United Kingdom).

Canada, Restrictive Trade Practices Commission, *Shipping Conference Arragements and Practices*. Ottowa: Queen's Printer, 1965.

Chamber of Shipping of the United Kingdom. Annual Reports.

Container and Cargo Handling Committee. *New Zealand Overseas Trade*: A report by the. . . Committee: Wellington: 1967 (Chairman of the Committee: W. Molyneux. Report made on behalf of the New Zealand Shipping Company Limited; Shaw Savil and Albion Company Limited, Ports Line Limited, and Blue Star Limited)

General Council of British Shipping. *Survey of British Shipping with Recommendations and Policy*, 1960

Hampshire Technical Research Industrial Commercial Services (HATRICS). *Containerisation, a Bibliography*. 2nd edition. Southampton: Central Public Library, 1969

Producer Boards' Shipping Utilisation Committee. *New Zealand. Overseas Trade*: Report on Shipping, Ports, Transport and other services. New Zealand Tonnage Committee, 1964. (Prepared jointly with the New Zealand Streamlining Committee)

Royal Institution of Naval Architects. *The Higher Education and Training of Naval Architects*: report of a Committee (Chairman of Committee: J. H. B. Chapman), 1966

Shell Briefing Service. *Trends in Tanker transportation*. 1967. (Prepared as a management information brief for the Staff of the companies of the Royal Dutch/Shell Group. Study Group with Representatives from the British Ship Research Association, Docks and Harbour Authorities' Association, Ministry of Technology, Naitonal Physical Laboratory and the Naitonal Ports' Council

Timber Research and Development Association. *Softwood handling project*: final report, 1968

University of Lancaster. Department of Operation Research. UK deep sea trade routes; the potential of container services based on physical cargo characteristics. Lancaster: 1968. (Report of a Study carried out for the Naitonal Ports Council)

D. *Other reports*

Bremen Institute of Shipping Economics (Occasional)

Drewery Shipping Consultants (Occasional)

EEC Transport Ministerial Conference (Occasional)

International Chamber of Commerce (Occasional)

International Chamber of Shipping (Occasional)

Committee Maritime International (Occasional)

OEEC *Maritime Transport* (Annual till 1960)

OECD *Maritime Transport* (Annual since 1961)

Lloyds (various journals, reports etc.) (Annual and occasional).

Seatrade Ship Research (Occasional)

Seatrade Academy (Annual)

Annexes

ANNEX 1

List of signatory nations which have adopted the UNCTAD liner code in order of accession as of July 1, 1983

Ghana	Iraq
Chile	Costa Rica
Pakistan	Peru
Gambia	Egypt
Sri Lanka	Tunisia
Venezuela	Korea
Bangladesh	Czechoslovakia
Nigeria	Honduras
Benin	USSR
Tanzania	East Germany
Niger	Sierra Leone
Philippines	Uruguay
Guatemala	Bulgaria
Mexico	Guyana
Cameroon	Morocco
Cuba	Jordan
Indonesia	Yugoslavia
Ivory Coast	Guinea
Central African Republic	Mauritius
Senegal	China
Zaire	Barbacos
Madagascar	Romania
Togo	Jamaica
Cape Verde	Congo
India	West Germany*
Kenya	Netherlands*
Mali	Malaysia
Sudan	Trinidad and Tobago
Gabon	
Ethiopia	

Source: Lloyds List, July 1, 1983.
*Also applying the Brussels Package for trade between the EEC-DECD.
Note: Signatories pending include the UK which plans to introduce legislation later this year.

ANNEX 2

The Brussels Package

COUNCIL REGULATION (EEC) No. 954/79 of 15 May 1979 concerning the ratification by Member States of, or their accession to, the United Nations Convention on a Code of Conduct of Liner Conferences.

The Council of the European Communities
Having regard to the Treaty establishing the European Economic Community, and in particular Article 84 (2) thereof, having regard to the draft Regulation submitted by the Commission, having regard to the opinion of the European Parliament, having regard to the opinion of the Economic and Social Committee.

Whereas a Convention on a Code of Conduct for Liner Conferences has been drawn up by a Conference convened under the auspices of the United Nations Conference on Trade and Development and is open for ratification or accession;

Whereas the questions covered by the Code of Conduct are of importance not only to the Member States but also to the Community, in particular from the shipping and trading viewpoints, and it is therefore important that a common position should be adoted in relation to this Code;

Whereas this common position should respect the principles and objectives of the Treaty and make a major contribution to meeting the aspirations of developing countries in the field of shipping while at the same time pursuing the objective of the continuing application in this field of the commercial principles applied by shipping lines of the OECD countries;

Whereas to secure observance of these principles and objectives, since the Code of Conduct contains no provision allowing the accession of the Community as such, it is important that Member States ratify or accede to the arrangements provided for in this Regulation;

Whereas the stabilising role of conferences in ensuring reliable services to shippers is recognised, but it is nevertheless necessary to avoid possible breaches by conferences of the rules of competition laid down in the Treaty; whereas the Commission will accordingly forward to the Council a proposal for a Regulation concerning the application of those rules to sea transport.

has adopted this regulation:

Article 1

1. When ratifying the United Nations Convention on a Code of Conduct for Liner Conferences, or when acceding thereto, Member States shall inform the Secretary-General of the United Nations in writing that such ratification or accession has taken place in accordance with this Regulation.

2. The instrument of ratification or accession shall be accompanied by the reservations set out in Annex 1.

Article 2

1. In the case of an existing conference, each group of shipping lines of the same nationality which are members thereof shall determine by commercial negotiations with another shipping line of that nationality whether the later may participate as a national shipping line in the said conference.

If a new conference is created, the shipping lines of the same nationality shall determine by commercial negotiations which of them may participate as a national shipping line in the future conference.

2. Where the negotiations referred to in paragraph 1 fail to result in agreement, each Member State may, at the request of one of the lines concerned and after hearing all of them, take the necessary steps to settle the dispute.

3. Each Member State shall ensure that all vessel-operating shipping lines established on its territory under the Treaty establishing the European Economic Community are treated in the same way as lines which have their management head office on its territory and the effective control of which is exercised there.

Article 3

1. Where a liner conference operates a pool or a berthing, sailing and/or any other form of cargo allocation agreement in accordance with Article 2 of the Code of Conduct, the volume of cargo to which the group of national shipping lines of each Member State participating in that trade or the shipping lines of the Member States participating in that trade as third-country shipping lines are entitled under the Code shall be redistributed, unless a decision is taken to the contrary by all the lines which are members of the Conference and parties to the present redistribution rules. This redistribution of cargo shares shall be carried out on the basis of a unanimous decision by those shipping lines which are members of the conference and participate in the redistribution, with a view to all those lines carrying a fair share of the conference trade.

2. The share finally allocated to each participant shall be determined by the application of commercial principles, taking account in particular of:

(a) the volume of cargo carried by the conference and generated by the Member States whose trade is served by it;

(b) past performance of the shipping lines in the trade covered by the pool;

(c) the volume of cargo carried by the conference and shipped through the ports of the Member States;

(d) the needs of the shippers whose cargoes are carried by the conference.

3. If no agreement is reached on the redistribution of cargoes referred to in paragraph 1, the matter shall, at the request of one of the parties, be referred to conciliation in accordance with the procedure set out in Annex II. Any dispute not settled by the conciliation procedure may, with the agreement of the parties, be referred to arbitration. In that event, the award of the arbitrator shall be binding.

4. At intervals to be laid down in advance, shares associated in accordance with paragraphs 1, 2 and 3 shall be regularly reviewed, taking into account the criteria set out in paragraph 2 and in particular from the viewpoint of providing adequate and efficient services to shippers.

Article 4

1. In a conference trade between a Member State of the Community and a State which is a party to the Code of Conduct and not an OECD country, a shipping line of another Member State of the OECD wishing to participate in the redistribution provided for in Article 3 of this Regulation may do so subject to reciprocity defined at governmental or ship-owners' level.

2. Without prejudice to paragraph 3 of this Article, Article 2 of the Code of Conduct shall not be applied in conference traded between Member States or, on a reciprocal basis, between such States and the other OECD countries which are parties to the Code.

3. Paragraph 2 of this Article shall not affect the opportunities for participation as third country shipping lines in such trades, in accordance with the principles reflected in Article 2 of the Code of Conduct, of the shipping lines of a developing country which are recognised as national shipping lines under the Code and which are:

(a) already members of a conference serving these trades; or

(b) admitted to such a conference under Article 1 (3) of the Code.

4. Articles 3 and 14 (9) of the Code of Conduct shall not be applied in conference trades between Member States or, on a reciprocal basis, between such States and other OECD countries which are parties to the code.

5. In conference trades between Member States and between these States and other OECD countries which are parties to the Code of Conduct, the shippers and ship-owners of Member States shall not insist on applying the procedures for settling disputes provided for in Chapter VI of the Code in their mutual relationships or, on a reciprocal basis, in relation to shippers and ship-owners of other OECD countries where other procedures for settling disputes have been agreed between them. They shall in particular take full advantage of the possibilities provided by Article 25 (1) and (2) of the Code for resolving disputes by means of procedures other than those laid down in Chapter VI of the Code.

Article 5

For adoption of decisions relating to matters defined in the conference agreement concerning the trade of a Member State, other than those referred to in Article 3 of this Regulation, the national shipping lines of such State shall consult all the other Community lines which are members of the conference before giving or witholding their assent.

Article 6
Member States shall, in due course, and after consulting the Commission, adopt the laws, regulations or administrative provisions necessary for the implementation of this Regulation.

This Regulation shall be binding in its entirety and directly applicable in all Member States.

Done at Brussels, 15 May 1979.

For the Council
The President
R. Boulin

Annex I: Reservations
When ratifying the Convention or when acceding thereto, Member States shall enter the following three reservations and interpretative reservation:

1. For the purposes of the Code of Conduct, the term 'national shipping line' may, in the case of a Member State of the Community, include any vessel-operating shipping line established on the territory of such Member State in accordance with the EEC Treaty.

2. (a) Without prejudice to paragraph (b) of this reservation, Article 2 of the Code of Conduct shall not be applied in conference trades between the Member States of the Community or, on a reciprocal basis, between such States and other IECD countries which are parties to the Code.

(b) Point (a) shall not affect the opportunities for participation of third country shipping lines in such trades, in accordance with the principles reflected in Article 2 of the Code, of the shipping lines of a developing country which are recognised as national shipping lines under the Code and which are:

(i) already member of a conference serving these trades;

or

(ii) admitted to such a conference under Article 1 (3) of the Code.

3. Articles 3 and 14 (9) of the Code of Conduct shall not be applied in conference trades between the Member States of the Community or, on a reciprocal basis, between such States and the other OECD countries which are parties to the Code.

4. In trades to which Article 3 of the Code of Conduct applies, the last sentence of that Article is interpreted as meaning that:

(a) Without groups of national shipping lines will coordinate their positions before voting on matters concerning the trade between their two countries;

(b) This sentence applies solely to matters which the conference agreement identifies as requiring the assent of both groups of national shipping lines concerned, and not to all matters covered by the conference agreement.

Annex II: Conciliation referred to in Article 3 (3)
The parties to the dispute shall designate one or more consiliators.

Should they fail to agree on the matter, each of the parties to the dispute shall designate a conciliator and the consiliators thus designated shall co-opt another consiliator to act as chairman. Should a party fail to designate a conciliator or the consiliators designated by the parties fail to reach agreement on the chairman, the President of the International Chamber of Commerce shall, at the request of one of the parties, make the necessary designations.

The conciliators shall make every endeavour to settle the dispute. They shall decide on the procedure to be followed. The fees shall be paid by the parties to the dispute.

Non-EEC member of OECD
Australia, Austria, Canada, Finland, Greece, Iceland, Japan, New Zealand, Norway, Portugal, Spain, Sweden, Switzerland, Turkey, United States.

ANNEX 3

Agreement between Brazil and the United States concerning equal access to government-controlled cargoes (29 UST 2860; TIAS 8981 – Washington, November 17, 1977).

I would like to clarify our understanding of the mechanisms to be employed to continue ensuring that Brazilian-flag ships obtain 'equal access' to United States government-controlled cargoes in accordance with principles established in the Memorandum of Consultation, dated March 7, 1970,* which continues to be in full force and effect.

Any and all government-controlled cargo shall be divided in accordance with the pooling agreements in the trades between the two countries. Based on this understanding, we are agreeable to affording Brazilian-flag ships equal access to United States government-controlled cargoes.

In order to implement the equal access provided for in the preceding paragraph, it has been proposed that a blanket waiver be granted by the Maritime Administration for a three (3) year period ending December 31, 1980, which would permit vessels of Brazilian flag to participate to the extent of fifty percent (50%) in the movement of all government-controlled cargoes between our two countries, subject to each of the approved pooling agreements.

The Maritime Administration is agreeable to granting a blanket waiver of the requirements of Public Resolution 17 covering Export-Import Bank loans as proposed under the following terms and conditions:

1) Ships of Brazilian flag would participate to the extent of fifty percent (50%) and ships of United States would participate to the extent of fifty percent (50%) of the United States government-controlled cargoes within the scope of Public Resolution 17 moving under each of the respective pooling agreements;

2) Freight revenues would be the main criterion for determining flag participation. In this regard consideration may also be given to cargo valuation, freight tons, payable tons, etc. Accordingly, with respect to cargoes moving under Public Resolution 17, throughout the term of each respective pooling agreement, United States-flag vessels would receive fifty percent (50%) of the freight revenues. An overearning on government-controlled cargoes up to ten percent (10%) is to be tolerated in a semiannual period, but it shall be compensated and adjusted in the following semiannual period. When Brazilian-flag vessels are in the overearners, the Maritime Administration shall instruct all shippers to use United States-flag vessels until the required participation has been achieved and shall advise SUNAMAM of such action;

3) When the deviation from the stated percentages becomes too large or too persistent, the Maritime Administration may suspend the blanket waiver in order to restore the United States flag participation to the required level;

4) The term of the waiver would be effective for a period of three (3) years, but the waiver would terminate simultaneously with the cancellation of any of the respective pooling requirements within that three (3) years and would require explicit and formal written approval to be applicable to any extension of the pooling agreements beyond the three (3) year period;

5) Equal access to government-controlled cargoes shall be determined and administered under each pooling agreement rather than on a nationwide basis;

6) Representatives of the Maritime Administration shall confer regularly with SUNAMAM to ensure that equal access is being maintained. The Maritime Administration shall furnish the SUNAMAM with copies of the records of cargo movements which the Administration receives in accordance with the requirement in each Export-Import Bank loan agreement.

In regard to shipments by all other government agencies, particularly AID and Agriculture, which are covered by Public Law 83–664,** only fifty percent (50%) is reserved for the United States flag. Part of this Public Law 83–664 coverage concerns certain relief cargoes moving under Title II of the Public Law 83–480*** for which freight charges are paid by the United States Government only when the cargoes are carried on United States flag

* Not printed.
** 68 Stat.832; 46 U.S.C. para. 1241.
*** 68 Stat.457; 7 U.S.C. para. 1721 *et seq.*

vessels. However, even these are available to Brazilian-flag vessels provided the Brazilian Government is agreeable to paying the freight charges and it is our understanding that the Brazilian Government has so agreed, by SUNAB (Ministry of Agriculture) letter of January 3, 1972, to AID (Administration for International Development). Thus, existing procedures offer adequate assurances that Brazilian-flag vessels will be given equal access under Public Law 83–664.

The accountant for the carriers in the pool agreements will submit to the Maritime Administration as well as SUNAMAM copies of reports reflecting the carriage of Government controlled cargoes by the national flag vessels of Brazil and United States. The borrowers will report monthly to the Maritime Administration all shipments under Public Resolution 17.****

The Maritime Administration believes the procedures outlined above foster attainment of the desirable goal of equal access to the trade by national flag vessels. However, these procedures by the United States will not be implemented unless Brazil agrees to reciprocate by providing equal access to Brazilian government-controlled cargoes which would necessarily include the same treatment for United States-flag vessels carrying cargoes between the two countries as is received by Brazilian-flag vessels.

The Brazilian National Superintendent, Merchant Marine, to the Assistant Secretary of Commerce for Maritime Affairs

In acknowledgement of the undertaking of 'equal access' to United States government-controlled cargoes in your letter dated November 17, 1977, we are agreeing also that any an all Brazilian government-controlled cargoes included in pooling agreements are afforded equal access to United States flag ships of lines participating in pool agreements in the trade between the two countries for a period of three years ending December 31, 1980.

Insofar as the waiver requirements are concerned, the Superintendencia Nacional de Marinha Mercante is also agreeable to issuing a blanket waiver in order to ensure an equal division of the aforementioned government-controlled cargoes, during the term of the duration of the respective pooling agreements, with the provisions as follows:

a) The waiver of the Brazilian government-controlled cargoes will be assured for the duration of the pooling agreements, unless extended and except if suspended or cancelled as provided; it is understood, however, that the Government of the United States and the Government of Brazil will consult with each other before either government terminates the equal access provision which have been put into effect.

In case of a temporary suspension of the pooling agreements and any extension beyond the three year period ending December 31, 1980, that also would require an explicit and formal written consultation between the government authorities concerned in order to acknowledge and approve.

b) Considering that the pooling agreements specify that all cargo carried by the parties to the pooling agreements, including any and all government-controlled cargoes shipped from ports of the United States of America and destined to ports of Brazil, are to be divided between the national flag lines of the two countries, it is understood that the Brazilian flag vessels will participate to the extent of fifty percent (50%), and vessels of United States-flag will participate to the extent of fifty percent (50%) of all Brazilian government-controlled cargoes carried by the parties under each pooling agreement.

c) The division of cargoes will be made on a freight revenue basis, in this regard consideration may also be given to cargo valuation, freight tons, payable tons, etc., in order to achieve an equal and equitable division of cargoes; an overearning on government-controlled cargoes up to ten percent (10%) is to be tolerated in a semiannual period but shall be compensated and adjusted in a following semiannual period. If the compensation of the tolerance is not complied with as has been established or the ten percent limit connected with revenue been surpassed by United States-flag vessels, then SUNAMAM may suspend its respective blanket waiver until the minimum requirement of fifty percent (50%0 has been restored to the Brazilian-flag vessels and shall advise MARAD of such action.

**** 48 Stat.500; 15 U.S.C. 616a.

d) The Brazilian Government will assure that Brazilian import licenses and other contracting documents covering the abovementioned government-controlled cargoes are stamped, 'Ship via Brazilian Lines (names of lines to be inserted) or U.S. Lines (names of lines to be inserted)', when transportation is by ocean-going vessels.

e) It is understood that any and all United States government-controlled cargoes, existing in reason of Public Resolutions and Public Laws, and others which related to liner cargoes covered by the pooling agreements that can be created during the time of duration of the pooling agreements, are to be included in this understanding of equal access statement, and given adequate assurances that Brazilian-flag vessels will participate equally, as provided herein.

f) Considering that the movement of bulk cargoes under the P.L. 83–480 is outside the scope of the pooling agreements, and is already subjected to a division of fifty percent (50%) for each national flag carrier, it is stated that actual procedures of division of such cargoes transported by the national flag lines are maintained and therefore are not affected by the present understanding for equal access.

g) It is our intention that the 50% of cargoes covered by P.L. 83–664, not reserved for the U.S.-flag vessels, will be carried by Brazilian-flag vessels.

h) The accountant for the carriers in the pool agreements will submit to SUNAMAM as well as to MARAD copies of reports reflecting the carriage of government-controlled cargoes by the national flag vessels of Brazil and the United States. The borrowers will report monthly to the Maritime Administration all shipments under Public Resolution 17.

i) The MARAD will forward to SUNAMAM copy of the borrower's monthly report under Public Resolution 17.

j) Equal access to all government-controlled cargoes shall be determined and administered under each pooling agreement rather than on a nationwide basis.

k) In the eventuality that the ships of the two national flags are not able or in a position to carry some portion of the government-controlled cargoes then SUNAMAM and MARAD with indispensable consultation with each other, will take the proper steps to issue the necessary waivers for ships of third flag in order that no difficulties should arise for the loading of the cargo at port of embarkation nor difficulties for customs release of the stated cargo at destination in Brazil.

l) The term ships of Brazilian-flag shall be extended to include ships operating under Brazilian control whether of Brazilian registry or charter substituting tonnage in construction under a shipbuilding program, hereinafter referred to as Brazilian-flag ships.

m) In keeping with the objectives set forth in the March 7, 1970 Memorandum of Consultation pooling agreement membership requirements as well as accounting procedures may be established in a manner which will properly serve the interests of the pools and may, if approved by appropriate agencies of the two countries, provide for accounting by commodity category or character of service.

As we indicated to you during our meetings which we concluded today, it is our belief that with your cooperation the procedures outlined above are consistent with the promotion of a reasonable equilibrium in the balance of payments of freights, the goal of fair cooperation, and the guidelines established in the Memorandum of Consultation of March 7, 1970. These procedures provide for reciprocal treatment for United States and Brazilian-flag vessels in the transportation of the cargoes between the United States and Brazil and for the equal division of revenue of government-controlled cargoes, considering cargo valuation, freight tons, payable tons, etc. by the national flag lines of our two countries.

ANNEX 4

CONVENTION ON A CODE OF CONDUCT FOR LINER CONFERENCES: OBJECTIVES AND PRINCIPLES

The Contracting Parties to the present Convention,

Desiring to improve the liner conference system,

Recognising the need for a universally acceptable code of conduct for liner conferences,

Taking into account the special needs and problems of the developing countries with respect to the activities of liner conferences serving their foreign trade,

Agreeing to reflect in the Code the following fundamental objectives and basic principles:

(*a*) The objective to facilitate the orderly expansion of world sea-born trade;

(*b*) The objective to stimulate the development of regular and efficient liner services adequate to the requirement of the trade concerned;

(*c*) The objective to ensure a balance of interests between suppliers and users of liner shipping services;

(*d*) The principle that conference practices should not involve any discrimination against the shipowners, shippers or the foreign trade of any country;

(*e*) The principle that conferences hold meaningful consultations with shippers' organisations, shippers' representatives and shippers on matters of common interest, with, upon request, the participation of appropriate authorities;

(*f*) The principle that conferences should make available to interested parties pertinent information about their activities which are relevant to those parties and should publish meaningful information on their activities,

Have agreed as follows:

PART ONE
CHAPTER I: DEFINITIONS

Liner conference or conference

A group of two or more vessel-operating carriers which provides international liner services for the carriage of cargo on a particular route or routes within specified geographical limits and which has an agreement or arrangement, whatever its nature, within the framework of which they operate under uniform or common freight rates and any other agreed conditions with respect to the provision of liner services.

National shipping line

A national shipping line of any given country is a vessel-operating carrier which has its head office of management and its effective control in that country and is recognized as such by an appropriate authority of that country or under the law of that country.

Lines belonging to and operated by a joint venture involving two or more countries and in whose equity the national interests, public and/or private, of these countries have a substantial share and whose head office of management and whose effective control is in one of those countries can be recognized as a national line by the appropriate authorities of those countries.

Third-country shipping line

A vessel-operating carrier in its operations between two countries of which it is not a national shipping line.

Shipper

A person or entity who has entered into, or who demonstrates an intention to enter into, a contractual or other arrangement with a conference or shipping line for the shipment of goods in which he has a beneficial interest.

Shippers' organisation

An association or equivalent body which promotes, represents and protects the interests of shippers and, if those authorities so desire, is recognized in that capacity by the appropriate authority or authorities of the country whose shippers it represents.

Goods carried by the conference

Cargo transported by shipping lines members of a conference in accordance with the conference agreement.

Appropriate authority

Either a government or a body designated by a government or by national legislation to perform any of the functions ascribed to such authority by the provisions of this Code.

Promotional freight rate

A rate instituted for promoting the carriage of non-traditional exports of the country concerned.

Special freight rate

A preferential freight rate, other than a promotional freight rate, which may be negotiated between the parties concerned.

CHAPTER II: RELATIONS AMONG MEMBER LINES

Article 1

MEMBERSHIP

1. Any national shipping line shall have the right to be a full member of a conference which serves the foreign trade of its country, subject to the criteria set out in article 1, paragraph 2. Shipping lines which are not national lines in any trade of a conference shall have the right to become full members of that conference, subject to the criteria set out in article 1, paragraphs 2 and 3, and to the provisions regarding the share of trade as set out in article 2 as regards third-country shipping lines.

2. A shipping line applying for membership of a conference shall furnish evidence of its ability and intention, which may include the use of chartered tonnage, provided the criteria of this paragraph are met, to operate a regular, adequate and efficient service on a long-term basis as defined in the conference agreement within the framework of the conference, shall undertake to abide by all the terms and conditions of the conference agreement, and shall deposit a financial guarantee to cover any outstanding financial obligation in the event of subsequent withdrawal, suspension or expulsion from membership, if so required under the conference agreement.

3. In considering an application for membership by a shipping line which is not a national line in any trade of the conference concerned, in addition to the provisions of article 1, paragraph 2, the following criteria, *inter alia*, should be taken into account:

(*a*) The existing volume of the trade on the route or routes served by the conference and prospects for its growth;

(*b*) The adequacy of shipping space for the existing and prospective volume of trade on the route or routes served by the conference;

(*c*) The probable effect of admission of the shipping line to the conference on the efficiency and quality of the conference service;

(*d*) The current participation of the shipping line in trade on the same route or routes outside the framework of a conference; and

(*e*) The current participation of the shipping line on the same route or routes within the framework of another conference.

The above criteria shall not be applied so as to subvert the implementation of the provisions relating to participation in trade set out in article 2.

4. An application for admission or readmission to membership shall be promptly decided upon and the decision communicated by a conference to an applicant promptly, and in no case later than six months from the date of application. When a shipping line is refused admission or readmission the conference shall, at the same time, give in writing the grounds for such refusal.

5. When considering applications for admission, a conference shall take into account the views put forward by shippers and shippers' organizations of the countries whose trade is carried by the conference, as well as the views of appropriate authorities if they so request.

6. In addition to the criteria for admission set out in article 1, paragraph 2, a shipping line applying for re-admission shall also give evidence of having fulfilled its obligations in accordance with article 4, paragraphs 1 and 4. The conference may give special scrutiny to the circumstances under which the line left the conference.

Article 2

PARTICIPATION IN TRADE

1. Any shipping line admitted to membership of a conference shall have sailing and loading rights in the trades covered by that conference.

2. When a conference operates a pool, all shipping lines members of the conference serving the trade covered by the pool shall have the right to participate in the pool for that trade.

3. For the purpose of determining the share of trade which member lines shall have the right to acquire, the national shipping lines of each country, irrespective of the number of lines, shall be regarded as a single group of shipping lines for that country.

4. When determining a share of trade within a pool of individual member lines and/or groups of national shipping lines in accordance with article 2, paragraph 2, the following principles regarding their right to participation in the trade carried by the conference shall be observed, unless otherwise mutually agreed:

(*a*) The group of national shipping lines of each of two countries the foreign trade between which is carried by the conference shall have equal rights to participate in the freight and volume of traffic generated by their mutual foreign trade and carried by the conference;

(*b*) Third-country shipping lines, if any, shall have the right to acquire a significant part, such as 20 percent, in the freight and volume of traffic generated by that trade.

5. If, for any one of the countries whose trade is carried by a conference, there are no national shipping lines participating in the carriage of that trade, the share of the trade to which national shipping lines of that country would be entitled under article 2, paragraph 4 shall be distributed among the individual member lines participating in the trade in proportion to their respective share.

6. If the national shipping lines of one country decide not to carry their full share of the trade, that portion of their share of the trade which they do not carry shall be distributed among the individual member lines participating in the trade in proportion to their respective shares.

7. If the national shipping lines of the countries concerned do not participate in the trade between those countries covered by a conference, the shares of trade carried by the conference between those countries shall be allocated between the participating member lines of third countries by commercial negotiations between those lines.

8. The national shipping lines of a region, members of a conference, at one end of the trade covered by the conference, may redistribute amongst themselves by mutual agreement the shares in trades allocated to them, in accordance with article 2, paragraphs 4 to 7 inclusive.

9. Subject to the provisions of article 2, paragraphs 4 to 8 inclusive regarding shares of trade among individual shipping lines or groups of shipping lines, pooling or trade-sharing agreements shall be reviewed by the conference periodically, at intervals to be stipulated in those agreements and in accordance with criteria to be specified in the conference agreement.

10. The application of the present article shall commence as soon as possible after entry into force of the present Convention and shall be completed within a transition period which in no case shall be longer than two years, taking into account the specific situation in each of the trades concerned.

11. Shipping lines members of a conference shall be entitled to operate chartered ships to fulful their conference obligations.

12. The criteria for sharing and the revision of shares as set out in article 2, paragraphs 1 to 11 inclusive shall apply when, in the absence of a pool, there exists berthing, sailing and/or any other form of cargo allocation agreement.

13. Where no pooling, berthing, sailing or other trade participation agreements exist in a conference, either group of national shipping lines, members of the conference, may require that pooling arrangements be introduced, in respect of the trade between their countries carried by the conference, in conformity with the provisions of article 2, paragraph 4; or alternatively they may require that the sailings be so adjusted as to provide an opportunity to these lines to enjoy substantially the same rights to participate in the trade between those two countries carried by the conference as they would have enjoyed under the provisions of article 2, paragraph 4. Any such request shall be considered and decided by the conference. If there is no agreement to institute such a pool or adjustment of sailings among the members of the conference, the groups of national shipping lines of the countries

at both ends of the trade shall have a majority vote in deciding to establish such a pool or adjustment of sailings. The matter shall be decided upon within a period not exceeding six months from the receipt of the request.

14. In the event of a disagreement between the national shipping lines of the countries at either end whose trade is served by the conference with regard to whether or not pooling shall be introduced, they may require that within the conference sailings be so adjusted as to provide an opportunity to these lines to enjoy substantially the same rights to participate in the trade between those two countries carried by the conference as they would have enjoyed under the provisions of article 2, paragraph 4. In the event that there are no national shipping lines in one of the countries whose trade is served by the conference, the national shipping line or lines of the other country may make the same request. The conference shall use its best endeavours to meet this request. If, however, this request is not met, the appropriate authorities of the countries at both ends of the trade may take up the matter if they so wish and make their views known to the parties concerned for their consideration. If no agreement is reached, the dispute shall be dealt with in accordance with the procedures established in this Code.

15. Other shipping lines, members of a conference, may also request that pooling or sailing agreements be introduced, and the request shall be considered by the conference in accordance with the relevant provisions of this Code.

16. A conference shall provide for appropriate measures in any conference pooling agreement to cover cases where the cargo has been shut out by a member line for any reason excepting late presentation by the shipper. Such agreement shall provide that a vessel with unbooked space, capable of being used, be allowed to lift the cargo, even in excess of the pool share of the line in the trade, if otherwise the cargo would be shut out and dealyed beyond a period set by the conference.

17. The provisions of article 2, paragraphs 1 to 16 inclusive concern all goods regardless of their opinion, their destination or to use for which they are intended, with the exception of military equipment for national defence purposes.

Article 3

DECISION-MAKING PROCEDURES

The decision-making procedures embodied in a conference agreement shall be based on the equality of all the full member lines; these procedures shall ensure that the voting rules do not hinder the proper work of the conference and the service of the trade and shall define the matters on which decisions will be made by unanimity. However, a decision cannot be taken in respect of matters defined in a conference agreement relating to the trade between two countries without the consent of the national shipping lines of those two countries.

Article 4

SANCTIONS

1. A shipping line member of a conference shall be entitled, subject to the provisions regarding withdrawal which are embodied in pool schemes and/or cargo-sharing arrangements, to secure its release, without penalty, from the terms of the conference agreement after giving three months' notic, unless the conference agreement provides for a different time period, although it shall be required to fulfil its obligations as a member of the conference up to the date of its release.

2. A conference may, upon notice to be specified in the conference agreement, suspend or expel a member for significant failure to abide by the terms and conditions of the conference agreement.

3. No expulsion or suspension shall become effective until a statement in writing of the reasons therefore has been given and until any dispute has been settled as provided in chapter VI.

4. Upon withdrawal or expulsion, the line concerned shall be required to pay its share of the outstanding financial obligations of the conference, up to the date of its withdrawal or expulsion. In cases of withdrawal, suspension or expulsion, the line shall not be relieved of

its own financial obligations under the conference agreement or of any of its obligations towards shippers.

Article 5

SELF-POLICING

1. A conference shall adopt and keep up to date an illustrative list, which shall be as comprehensive as possible, of practices which are regarded as malpractices and/or breaches of the conference agreement and shall provide effective self-policing machinery to deal with them, with specific provisions requiring:

(*a*) The fixing of penalties or a range of penalties for malpractices or breaches, to be commensurate with their seriousness;

(*b*) The examination and impartial review of an adjudication of complaints, and/or decisions taken on complaints, against malpractices or breaches, by a person or body unconnected with any of the shipping lines members of the conference or their affiliates, on request by the conference or any other party concerned;

(*c*) The reporting, on request, on the action taken in connection with complaints against malpractices and/or breaches, and on a basis of anonymity for the parties concerned, to the appropriate authorities of the countries whose trade is served by the conference and of the countries whose shipping lines are members of the conference.

(2) Shipping lines and conferences are entitled to the full co-operation of shippers and shippers' organizations in the endeavour to combat malpractices and breaches.

Article 6

CONFERENCE AGREEMENTS

All conference agreements, pooling, berthing and sailing rights agreements and amendments or other documents directly related to, and which affect, such agreements shall be made available on request to the appropriate authorities of the countries whose trade is served by the conference and of the countries whose shipping lines are members of the conference.

CHAPTER III: RELATIONS WITH SHIPPERS

Article 7

LOYALTY ARRANGEMENTS

1. The shipping lines members of a conference are entitled to institute and maintain loyalty arrangements with shippers, the form and terms of which are matters for consultation between the conference and shippers' organizations or representatives of shippers. These loyalty arrangements shall provide safeguards making explicit the rights of shippers and conference members. These arrangements shall be based on the contract system or any other system which is also lawful.

2. Whatever loyalty arrangements are made, the freight rate applicable to loyal shippers shall be determined within a fixed range of percentages of the freight rate applicable to other shippers. Where a change in the differential causes an increase in the rates charged to shippers, the change can be implemented only after 150 days' notice to those shippers or according to regional practice and/or agreement. Disputes in connexion with a change of the differential shall be settled as provided in the loyalty agreement.

3. The terms of loyalty arrangements shall provide safeguards making explicit the rights and obligations of shippers and of shipping lines members of the conference in accordance with the following provisions, *inter alia*:

(*a*) The shipper shall be bound in respect of cargo whose shipment is controlled by him or his affiliated or subsidiary company or his forwarding agent in accordance with the contract of sale of the goods concerned, provided that the shipper shall not, by evasion, subterfuge, or intermediary, attempt to divert cargo in violation of his loyalty commitment;

(*b*) Where there is a loyalty contract, the extent of actual or liquidated damages and/or penalty shall be specified in the contract. The member lines of the conference may, however, decide to assess lower liquidated damages or to waive the claim to liquidated damages. In any event, the liquidated damages under the contract to be paid to the shipper shall not exceed the freight charges on the particular shipment, computed at the rate provided under the contract;

(*c*) The shipper shall be entitled to resume full loyalty status, subject to the fulfilment of conditions established by the conference which shall be specified in the loyalty arrangement;

(*d*) The loyalty arrangement shall set out:

(i) A list of cargo, which may include bulk cargo shipped without mark or count, which is specifically excluded from the scope of the loyalty arrangement;

(ii) A definition of the circumstances in which cargo other than cargo covered by (i) above is considered to be excluded from the scope of the loyalty arrangement;

(iii) The method of settlement of disputes arising under the loyalty arrangement;

(iv) Provision for termination of the loyalty arrangement on request by either a shipper or a conference without penalty, after expiry of a stipulated period of notice, such notice to be given in writing; and

(v) The terms for granting dispensation.

4. If there is a dispute between a conference and a shippers' organization, representatives of shippers and/or shippers about the form or terms of a proposed loyalty arrangement, either party may refer the matter for resolution under appropriate procedures as set out in this Code.

Article 8

DISPENSATION

1. Conferences shall provide, within the terms of the loyalty arrangements, that requests by shippers for dispensation shall be examined and a decision given quickly and, if requested, the reasons given in writing where dispensation is withheld. Should a conference fail to confirm, within a period specified in the loyalty arrangement, sufficient space to accommodate a shipper's cargo within a period also specified in the loyalty arrangement, the shipper shall have the right, without being penalized, to utilize any vessel for the cargo in question.

2. In ports where conference services are arranged subject to the availability of a specified minimum of cargo (i.e. on inducement), but either the shipping line does not call, despite due notice by shippers, or the shipping line does not reply within an agreed time to the notice given by shippers, shippers shall automatically have the right, without prejudicing their loyalty status, to use any available vessel for the carriage of their cargo.

Article 9

AVAILABILITY OF TARIFFS AND RELATED CONDITIONS AND/OR REGULATIONS

Tariffs, related conditions, regulations, and any amendments thereto shall be made available on request to shippers, shippers' organizations and other parties concerned at reasonable cost, and they shall be available for examination at offices of shipping lines and their agents. They shall spell out all conditions concerning the application of freight rates and the carriage of any cargo covered by them.

Article 10

ANNUAL REPORTS

Conferences shall provide annually to shippers' organizations, or to representatives of shippers, reports on their activities designed to provide general information of interest to them, including relevant information about consultations held with shippers and shippers' organizations, action taken regarding complaints, changes in membership, and significant changes in service, tariffs and conditions of carriage. Such annual reports shall be submitted, on request, to the appropriate authorities of the countries whose trade is served by the conference concerned.

Article 11

CONSULTATION MACHINERY

1. There shall be consultations on matters of common interest between a conference, shippers' organizations, representatives of shippers and, where practicable, shippers, which may be designated for that purpose by the appropriate authority if it so desires. These consultations shall take place whenever requested by any of the above-mentioned parties. Appropriate authorities shall have the right, upon request, to participate fully in the consultations, but this does not mean that they play a decision-making role.

2. The following matters, *inter alia*, may be the subject of consultation:

(*a*) Changes in general tariff conditions and related regulations;
(*b*) Changes in the general level of tariff rates and rates for major commodities;
(*c*) Promotional and/or special freight rates;
(*d*) Imposition of, and related changes in, surcharges;
(*e*) Loyalty arrangements, their establishment or changes in their form and general conditions;
(*f*) Changes in the tariff classification of ports;
(*g*) Procedure for the supply of necessary information by shippers concerning the expected volume and nature of their cargoes: and
(*h*) Presentation of cargo for shipment and the requirements regarding notice of cargo availability.

3. To the extent that they fall within the scope of activity of a conference, the following matters may also be the subject of consultation:

(*a*) Operation of cargo inspection services;
(*b*) Changes in the pattern of services;
(*c*) Effects of the introduction of new technology in the carriage of cargo, in unitization, with consequent reduction of conventional service or loss of direct services; and
(*d*) Adequacy and quality of shipping services, including the impact of pooling, berthing or sailing arrangements on the availability of shipping services and freight rates at which shipping services are provided; changes in the areas served and in the regularity of calls by conference vessels.

4. Consultations shall be held before final decisions are taken, unless otherwise provided in this Code. Advance notice shall be given of the intention to take decisions on matters referred to in article 11, paragraphs 2 and 3; Where this is impossible, urgent decisions may be taken pending the holding of consultations.

5. Consultations shall begin without undue delay and in any event within a maximum period specified in the conference agreement, or in the absence of such a provision in the agreement, not later than 30 days after receipt of the proposal for consultations, unless different periods of time are provided in this Code.

6. When holding consultations, the parties shall use their best efforts to provide relevant information, to hold timely discussions and to clarify matters for the purpose of seeking solutions of the issues concerned. The parties involved shall take account of each other's views and problems and strive to reach agreement consistent with their commercial viability.

CHAPTER IV: FREIGHT RATES

Article 12

CRITERIA FOR FREIGHT-RATE DETERMINATION

In arriving at a decision on questions of tariff policy in all cases mentioned in this Code, the following points shall, unless otherwise provided, be taken into account:

(*a*) Freight rates shall be fixed at as low a level as is feasible from the commercial point of view and shall permit a reasonable profit for shipowners;
(*b*) The cost of operations of conferences shall, as a rule, be evaluated for the round voyage of ships, with the outward and inward directions considered as a single whole. Where applicable, the outward and inward voyage should be considered

nature of cargoes, the interrelation between weight and cargo measurement, as well as the value of cargoes;

(*c*) In fixing promotional freight rates and/or special freight rates for specific goods, the conditions of trade for these goods of the countries served by the conference particularly of developing and land-locked countries, shall be taken into account.

Article 13

CONFERENCE TARIFFS AND CLASSIFICATION OF TARIFF RATES

1. Conference tariffs shall not unfairly differentiate between shippers similarly situated. Shipping lines members of a conference shall adhere strictly to the rates, rules and terms shown in the tariffs and other currently valid published documents of the conference and to any special arrangements permitted under this Code.

2. Conference tariffs should be drawn up simply and clearly, containing as few classes/categories as possible, depending on the commodity and, where appropriate, for each class/category; this should also indicate, wherever practicable, in order to facilitate statistical compilation and analysis, the corresponding appropriate code number of the item in accordance with the Standard International Trade Classification, the Brussels Tariff Nomenclature or any other nomenclature that may be internationally adopted; the classification of commodities in the tariffs should, as far as practicable, be prepared in co-operation with shippers' organizations and other national and international organizations concerned.

Article 14

GENERAL FREIGHT-RATE INCREASES

1. A conference shall give notice of not less than 150 days, or according to regional practice and/or agreement, to shippers' organizations or representatives of shippers and/or shippers and, where so required, to appropriate authorities of the countries whose trade is served by the conference, of its intention to effect a general increase in freight rates, an indication of its extent, the date of effect and the reasons supporting the proposed increase.

2. At the request of any of the parties prescribed for this purpose in this Code, to be made within an agreed period of time after the receipt of the notice, consultations shall commence, in accordance with the relevant provisions of this Code, within a stipulated period not exceeding 30 days or as previously agreed between the parties concerned; the consultations shall be held in respect of the bases and maounts of the proposed increase and the date from which it is to be given effect.

3. A conference, in an effort to expedite consultations, may or upon the request of any of the parties prescribed in this Code as entitled to participate in consultations on general freight-rate increases shall, where practicable, reasonably before the consultations, submit to the participating parties a report from independent accountants of repute, including, where the requesting parties accept it as one of the bases of consultations, an aggregated analysis of data regarding relevant costs and revenues which in the opinion of the conference necessitate an increase in freight rates.

4. If agreement is reached as a result of the consultations, the freight-rate increase shall take effect from the date indicated in the notice served in accordance with article 14, paragraph 1, unless a later date is agreed upon between the parties concerned.

5. If no agreement is reached within 30 days of the giving of notice in accordance with article 14, paragraph 1, and subject to procedures prescribed in this Code, the matter shall be submitted immediately to international mandatory conciliation, in accordance with chapter VI. The recommendation of the conciliators, if accepted by the parties concerned, shall be binding upon them and shall be implemented, subject to the provisions of this article 14, paragraph 9, with effect from the date mentioned in the conciliators' recommendation.

6. Subject to the provisions of article 14, paragraph 9, a general freight-rate increase may be implemented by a conference pending the conciliators' recommendation. When making their recommendation, the conciliators should take into account the extent of the above-mentioned increase made by the conference and the period for which it has been in force. In the event that the conference rejects the recommendation of the conciliators, shippers

and/or shippers' organizations shall have the right to consider themselves not bound, after appropriate notice, by any arrangement or other contract with that conference which may prevent them from using non-conference shipping lines. Where a loyalty arrangement exists, shippers and/or shippers' organizations shall give notice within a period of 30 days to the effect that they no longer consider themselves bound by that arrangement, which notice shall apply from the date mentioned therein, and a period of not less than 30 days and not more than 90 days shall be provided in the loyalty arrangement for this purpose.

7. A defered rebate which is due to the shipper and which has already been accumulated by the conference shall not be withheld by, or forfeited to, the conference as a result of action by the shipper under article 14, paragraph 6.

8. If the trade of a country carried by shipping lines members of a conference on a particular route consists largely of one or few basic commodities, any increase in the freight rate on one or more of those commodities shall be treated as a general freight-rate increase, and the appropriate provisions of this Code shall apply.

9. Conferences should institute any general freight-rate increase effective in accordance with this Code for a period of a stated minimum duration, subject always to the rules regarding surcharges and regarding adjustment in freight rates consequent upon fluctuations in foreign exchange rates. The period over which a general freight-rate increase is to apply is an appropriate matter to be considered during consultations conducted in accordance with article 14, paragraph 2, but unless otherwise agreed between the parties concerned during the consultations, the minimum period of time between the date when one general freight-rate increase becomes effective and the date of the notice for the next general freight-rate increase given in accordance with article 14, paragraph 1 shall not be less than 10 months.

Article 15

PROMOTIONAL FREIGHT RATES

1. Promotional freight rates for non-traditional exports should be instituted by conferences.

2. All necessary and reasonable information justifying the ned for a promotional freight rate shall be submitted to a conference by the shippers, shippers' organizations or representatives of shippers concerned.

3. Special procedures shall be instituted providing for a decision within 30 days from the date of receipt of that inforamtion, unless mutually agreed otherwise, on application for promotional freight rates. A clear distinction shall be made between these and general procedures for considering the possibility of reducing freight rates for other commodities or of exempting them from increases.

4. Information regarding the procedures for considering applications for promotional freight rates shall be made available by the conference to shippers and/or shippers' organizations and, on request, to the Governments and/or other appropriate authorities of the contries whose trade is served by the conference.

5. A promotional freight rate shall be established normally for a period of 12 months, unless otherwise mutually agreed between the parties concerned. Prior to the expiry of the period, the promotional freight rate shall be reviewed, on request by the shipper and/or shippers' organization concerned, when it shall be a matter for the shipper and/or shippers' organization, at the request of the conference, to show that the continuation of the rate is justified beyond the initial period.

6. When examining a request for a promotional freight rate, the conference may take into account that, while the rate should promote the export of the non-traditional product for which it is sought, it is not likely to create substantial competitive distortions in the export of a similar product from another country served by the conference.

7. Promotional freight rates are not excluded from the imposition of a surcharge or a currency adjustment factor in accordance with articles 16 and 17.

8. Each shipping line member of a conference serving the relevant ports of a conference trade shall accept, and not unreasonably refuse, a fair share of cargo for which a promotional freight rate has been established by the conference.

Article 16

SURCHARGES

1. Surcharges imposed by a conference to cover sudden or extraordinary increases in costs or losses of revenue shall be regarded as temporary. They shall be reduced in accordance with improvements in the situation or circumstances which they were imposed to meet and shall be cancelled, subject to article 16, paragraph 6, as soon as the situation or circumstances which prompted their imposition cease to prevail. This shall be indicated at the moment of their imposition, together, as far as possible, with a description of the change in the situation of circumstances which will bring about their increase, reduction or cancellation.

2. Surcharges imposed on cargo moving to or from a particular port shall likewise be regarded as temporary and likewise shall be increased, reduced or cancelled, subject to article 16, paragraph 6, when the situation in that port changes.

Before any surcharge is imposed, whether general or covering only a specific port, notice should be given and there shall be consultation, upon request, in accordance with the procedures of this Code, between the conference concerned and other parties directly affected by the surcharge and prescribed in this Code as entitled to participate in such consultations, save in those exceptional circumstances which warrant immediate imposition of the surcharge. In cases where a surcharge has been imposed without prior consultation, consultations, upon request, shall be held as soon as possible thereafter. Prior to such consultations, conferences shall furnish data which in their opinion justify the imposition of the surcharge.

4. Unless the parties agree otherwise, within a period of 15 days after the receipt of a notice given in accordance with article 16, paragraph 3, if there is no agreement on the question of the surcharge between the parties concerned referred to in that article, the relevant provisions for settlement of disputes provided in this Code shall prevail. Unless the parties concerned agree otherwise, the surcharge may, however, be imposed pending resolution of the dispute, if the dispute still remains unresolved at the end of a period of 30 days after the receipt of the above-mentioned notice.

5. In the event of a surcharge being imposed, in exceptional circumstances, without prior consultation as provided in article 16, paragraph 3, if no agreement is reached through subsequent consultations, the relevant provisions for settlement of disputes provided in this Code shall prevail.

6. Financial loss incurred by the shipping lines members of a conference as a result of any delay on account of consultations and/or other proceedings for resolving disputes regarding imposition of surcharges in accordance with the provisions of this Code, as compared to the date from which the surcharge was to be imposed in terms of the notice given in accordance with article 16, paragraph 3, may be compensated by an equivalent prolongation of the surcharge before its removal. Conversely, for any surcharge imposed by the conference and subsequently determined and agreed to be unjustified or excessive as a result of consultations or other procedures prescribed in this Code, the amounts so collected or the excess thereof as determined hereinabove, unless otherwise agreed shall be refunded to the parties concerned, if claimed by them within a period of 30 days of such claim.

Article 17

CURRENCY CHANGES

1. Exchange rate changes, including formal devaluation or revaluation, which lead to changes in the aggregate operational costs and/or revenues of the shipping lines members of a conference relating to their operations within the conference provide a valid reason for the introduction of a currency adjustment factor or for a change in the freight rates. The adjustment or change shall be such that in the aggregate the member lines concerned neither gain nor lose, as far as possible, as a result of the adjustment or change. The adjustment or change may take the form of currency surcharges or discounts or of increases or decreases in the freight rates.

2. Such adjustments or changes shall be subject to notice, which should be arranged in accordance with regional practice. where such practice exists, and there shall be consultations in accordance with the provisions of this Code between the conference concerned

and the other parties directly affected and prescribed in this Code as entitled to participate in consultations, save in those exceptional circumstances which warrant immediate imposition of the currency adjustment factor or freight-rate change. In the event that this has been done without prior consultations, consultations shall be held as soon as possible thereafter. The consultations should be on the application, size and date of implementation of the currency adjustment factor or freight-rate change, and the same procedures shall be followed for this purpose as are prescribed in article 16, paragraphs 4 and 5, in respect of surcharges. Such consultations should take place and be completed within a period not exceeding 15 days from the date when the intention to apply a currency surcharge or to effect a freight-rate change is announced.

3. If no agreement is reached within 15 days through consultations, the relevant provisions for settlement of disputes provided in this Code shall prevail.

4. The provisions of article 16, paragraph 6 shall apply, adapted as necessary to currency adjustment factors and freight-rate changes dealt with in the present article.

CHAPTER V: OTHER MATTERS

Article 18

FIGHTING SHIPS

Members of a conference shall not use fighting ships in the conference trade for the purpose of excluding, preventing or reducing competition by driving a shipping line not a member of the conference out of the said trade.

Article 19

ADEQUACY OF SERVICE

1. Conferences should take necessary and appropriate measures to ensure that their member lines provide regular, adequate and efficient service of the required frequency on the routes they serve and shall arrange such services so as to avoid as far as possible bunching and gapping of sailings. Conferences should also take into consideration any special measures necessary in arranging services to handle seasonal variations on cargo volumes.

2. Conferences and other parties prescribed in this Code as entitled to participate in consultations, including appropriate authorities if they so deisre, should keep under review, and should maintain close co-operation regarding the demand for shipping space, the adequacy and suitability of service, and in particular the possibilities for rationalization and for increasing the efficiency of services. Benefits identified as accruing from rationalization of services shall be fairly reflected in the level of freight rates.

3. In respect of any port for which conference services are supplied only subject to the availability of a specified minimum of cargo, that minimum shall be specified in the tariff. Shippers should give adequate notice of the availability of such cargo.

Article 20

HEAD OFFICE OF A CONFERENCE

A conference shall as a rule establish its head office in a country whose trade is served by that conference, unless agreed otherwise by the shipping lines members of that conference.

Article 21

REPRESENTATION

Conferences shall establish local representation in all countries served, except that where there are practical reasons to the contrary the representation may be on a regional basis. The names and addresses of representatives shall be readily available, and these representatives shall ensure that the views of shippers and conferences are made rapidly known to each other with a view to expediting prompt decisions. When a conference considers it suitable, it shall provide for adequate delegation of powers of decision to its representatives.

Article 22

CONTENTS OF CONFERENCE AGREEMENTS, TRADE PARTICIPATION AGREEMENTS AND LOYALTY ARRANGEMENTS

Conference agreements, trade participation agreements and loyalty arrangements shall conform to the applicable requirements of this Code and amy include such other provisions as may be agreed which are not inconsistent with this Code.

PART TWO

CHAPTER VI: PROVISIONS AND MACHINERY FOR SETTLEMENT OF DISPUTES

A. GENERAL PROVISIONS

Article 23

1. The provisions of this chapter shall apply whenever there is a dispute relating to the application or operation of the provisions of this Code between the following parties:

(*a*) A conference and a shipping line;
(*b*) The shipping lines members of a conference;
(*c*) A conference or a shipping line member thereof and a shipper's organization or representatives of shippers or shippers; and
(*d*) Two or more conferences.

For the purposes of this chapter the term 'party' means the original parties to the dispute as well as third parties which have joined the proceedings in accordance with (*a*) of article 34.

2. Disputes between shipping lines of the same flag, as well as those between organizations belonging to the same country, shall be settled within the framework of the national jurisdiction of that country, unless this creates serious difficulties in the fulfilment of the provisions of this Code.

3. The parties to a dispute shall first attempt to settle it by an exchange of views or direct negotiations with the intention of finding a mutually satisfactory solution.

4. Disputes between the parties referred to in article 23, paragraph 1 relating to:

(*a*) Refusal of admission of a national shipping line to a conference serving the foreign trade of the country of that shipping line;
(*b*) Refusal of admission of a third-country shipping line to a conference;
(*c*) Expulsion from a conference;
(*d*) Inconsistency of a conference agreement with this Code;
(*e*) A general freight-rate increase;
(*f*) Surcharges;
(*g*) Changes in freight rates or the imposition of a currency adjustment factor due to exchange rate changes;
(*h*) Participation in trade; and
(*i*) The form and terms of proposed loyalty arrangements

which have not been resolved through an exchange of views or direct negotiations shall, at the request of any of the parties to the dispute, be referred to international mandatory conciliation in accordance with the provision of this chapter.

Article 24

1. The conciliation procedure is initiated at the request of one of the parties to the dispute.

2. The request shall be made:

(*a*) In disputes relating to membership of conferences: not later than 60 days from the date of receipt by the applicant of the conference decision, including the reasons therefor, in accordance with article 1, paragraph 4 and article 4, paragraph 3;
(*b*) In disputes relating to general freight-rate increases: not later than the date of expiry of the period of notice specified in article 14, paragraph 1;
(*c*) In disputes relating to surcharges: not later than the date of expiry of the

30-day period specified in article 16, paragraph 4 or, where no notice has been given, not later than 15 days from the date when the surcharge was put into effect; and

(*d*) In disputes relating to changes in freight rates or the imposition of a currency adjustment factor due to exchange rate changes: not later than five days after the date of expiry of the period specified in article 17, paragraph 3.

3. The provisions of article 24, paragraph 2 shall not apply to a dispute which is referred to international mandatory conciliation in accordance with article 25, paragraph 3.

4. Requests for conciliation in disputes other than those referred to in article 24, paragraph 2, may be made at any time.

5. The time-limits specified in article 24, paragraph 2 may be extended by agreement between the parties.

6. A request for conciliation shall be considered to have been duly made if it is proved that the request has been sent to the other party by registered letter, telegram or teleprinter or has been served on it within the time-limits specified in article 24, paragraphs 2 or 5.

7. Where no request has been made within the time-limits specified in article 24, paragraphs 2 or 5, the decision of the conference shall be final and no proceedings under this chapter may be brought by any party to the dispute to challenge that decision.

Article 25

1. Where the parties have agreed that disputes referred to in article 23, paragraph 4(*a*), (*b*), (*c*), (*d*), (*h*) and (*i*) shall be resolved through procedures other than those established in that article, or agree on procedures to resolve a particular dispute that has arisen between them, such disputes shall, at the request of any of the parties to the dispute, be resolved as provided for in their agreement.

2. The provisions of article 25, paragraph 1 apply also to the disputes referred to in article 23, paragraph 4(*e*), (*f*) and (*g*), unless national legislation, rules or regulations prevent shippers from having this freedom of choice.

3. Where conciliation proceedings have been initiated, such proceedings shall have precedence over remedies available under national law. If a party seeks remedies under national law in respect of a dispute to which this chapter applies without invoking the procedures provided for in this chapter, then, upon the request of a respondent to those proceedings, they shall be stayed and the dispute shall be referred to the procedures defined in this chapter by the court or other authority where the national remedies are sought.

Article 26

1. The Contracting Parties shall confer upon conferences and shippers' organizations such capacity as is necessary for the application of the provisions of this chapter. In particular:

(*a*) A conference or a shippers' organization may institute proceedings as a party or be named as a party to proceedings in its collective capacity;

(*b*) Any notification to a conference or shippers' organization in its collective capacity shall also constitute a notification to each member of such conference or shippers' organization;

(*c*) A notification to a conference or shippers' organization shall be transmitted to the address of the head office of the conference or shippers' organization. Each conference or shippers' organization shall register the address of its head office with the Registrar appointed in accordance with article 46, paragraph 1. In the event that a conference or a shippers' organization fails to register or has no head office, a notification to any member in the neame of the conference or shippers' organization shall be deemed to be a notification to such conference or organization.

2. Acceptance or rejection by a conference or shippers' organization of a recommendation by conciliators shall be deemed to be acceptance or rejection of such a recommendation by each member thereof.

Article 27

Unless the parties agree otherwise, the conciliators may decide to make a recommendation on the basis of written submissions without oral proceedings.

B. INTERNATIONAL MANDATORY CONCILIATION

Article 28

In international mandatory conciliation the appropriate authorities of a Contracting Party shall, if they so request, participate in the conciliation proceedings in support of a party being a national of that Contracting Party, or in support of a party having a dispute arising in the context of the foreign trade of that Contracting Party. The appropriate authority may alternatively act as an observer in such conciliation proceedings.

Article 29

1. In international mandatory conciliation the proceedings shall be held in the place unanimously agreed to by the parties or, failing such agreement, in the place decided upon by the conciliators.

2. In determining the place of conciliation proceedings the parties and the conciliators shall take into account, *inter alia*, countries which are closely connected with the dispute, bearing in mind the country of the shipping line concerned and, especially when the dispute is related to cargo, the country where the cargo originates.

Article 30

1. For the purposes of this chapter an international panel of conciliators shall be established, consisting of experts of high repute or experience in the fields of law, economics of sea transport, or foreign trade and finance, as determined by the Contracting Parties selecting them, who shall serve in an independent capacity.

2. Each Contracting Party may at any time nominate members of the panel up to a total of 12, and shall communicate their names to the Registrar. The nominations shall be for periods of six years each and may be renewed. In the event of the death, incapacity or resignation of a member of the panel, the Contracting Party which nominated such person shall nominate a replacement for the remainder of his term of office. A nomination takes effect from the date on which the communication of the nomination is received by the Registrar.

3. The Registrar shall maintain the panel list and shall regularly inform the Contracting Parties of the composition of the panel.

Article 31

1. The purpose of conciliation is to reach an amicable settlement of the dispute through recommendations formulated by independent conciliators.

2. The conciliators shall identify and clarify the issues in dispute, seek for this purpose any information from the parties, and on the basis thereof, submit to the parties a recommendation for the settlement of the dispute.

3. The parties shall co-operate in good faith with the conciliators in order to enable them to carry out their functions.

4. Subject to the provisions of article 25, paragraph 2, the parties to the dispute may at any time during the conciliation proceedings decide in agreement to have recourse to a different procedure for the settlement of their dispute. The parties to a dispute which has been made subject to proceedings other than those provided for in this chapter may decide by mutual agreement to have recourse to international mandatory conciliation.

Article 32

1. The conciliation proceeding shall be conducted either by one conciliator or by an uneven number of conciliators agreed upon or designated by the parties.

2. Where the parties cannot agree on the number of the appointment of the conciliators as provided in article 32, paragraph 1, the conciliation proceedings shall be conducted by three conciliators, one appointed by each party in the statement(s) of claim and reply respectively, and the third by the two conciliators thus appointed, who shall act as chairman.

3. If the reply does not name a conciliator to be appointed in cases where article 32, paragraph 2 would apply, the second conciliator shall, within 30 days following the receipt of the statement of claim, be chosen by lot by the conciliator appointed in the statement of claim from among the members of the panel nominated by the Contracting Party or Parties of which the respondent(s) is (are) a national(s).

4. Where the conciliators appointed in accordance with article 32, paragraphs 2 or 3 cannot agree on the appointment of the third conciliator within 15 days following the date of the appointment of the second conciliator, he shall, within the following 5 days, be chosen by lot by the appointed conciliators. Prior to the drawing by lot:

(*a*) No member of the panel of conciliators having the same nationality as either of the two appointed conciliators shall be eligible for selection by lot;

(*b*) Each of the two appointed conciliators may exclude from the list of the panel of conciliators an equal number of them subject to the requirement that at least 30 members of the panel shall remain eligible for selection by lot.

Article 33

1. Where several parties request conciliation with the same respondent in respect of the same issue, or of issues which are closely connected, that respondent may request the consolidation of those cases.

2. The request for consolidation shall be considered and decided upon by majority vote by the chairmen of the conciliators so far chosen. If such request is allowed, the chairmen will designate the conciliators to consider the consolidated cases from among the conciliators so far appointed or chosen, provided that an uneven number of conciliators is chosen and that the conciliator first appointed by each party shall be one of the conciliators considering the consolidated cases.

Article 34

Any party, other than an appropriate authority referred to in article 28, if conciliation has been initiated, may join in the proceedings:

either

(*a*) As a party, in case of a direct economic interest;

or

(*b*) As a supporting party to one of the original parties, in case of an indirect economic interest,

unless either of the original parties objects to such joinder.

Article 35

1. The recommendations of the conciliators shall be made in accordance with the provisions of this Code.

2. When the Code is silent upon any point, the conciliators shall apply the law which the parties agree at the time the conciliation proceedings commence or thereafter, but not later than the time of submission of evidence to the conciliators. Failing such agreement, the law which in the opinion of the conciliators is most closely connected with the dispute shall be applicable.

3. The conciliators shall not decide *ex aequo et bono* upon the dispute unless the parties so agree after the dispute has arisen.

4. The conciliators shall not bring a finding of *non liquet* on the ground of obscurity of the law.

5. The conciliators may recommend those remedies and reliefs which are provided in the law applicable to the dispute.

Article 36

The recommendations of the conciliators shall include reasons.

Article 37

1. Unless the parties have agreed before, during or after the conciliation procedure that the recommendation of the conciliators shall be binding, the recommendation shall become binding by acceptance by the parties. A recommendation which has been accepted by some parties to a dispute shall be binding as between those parties only.

2. Acceptance of the recommendation must be communicated by the parties to the conciliators, at an address specified by them, not later than 30 days after receipt of the notification of the recommendation; otherwise, it shall be considered that the recommendation has not been accepted.

3. Any party which does not accept the recommendation shall notify the conciliators and the other parties, within 30 days following the period specified in article 37, paragraph 2 of its grounds for rejection of the recommendation, comprehensively and in writing.

4. When the recommendation has been accepted by the parties, the conciliators shall immediately draw up and sign a record of settlement, at which time the recommendation shall become binding upon those parties. If the recommendation has not been accepted by all parties, the conciliators shall draw up a report with respect to those parties rejecting the recommendation, noting the dispute and the failure of those parties to settle the dispute.

5. A recommendation which has become binding upon the parties shall be implemented by them immediately or at such later time as is specified in the recommendation.

6. Any party may make its acceptance conditional upon acceptance by all or any of the other parties to the dispute.

Article 38

1. A recommendation shall constitute a final determination of a dispute as between the parties which accept it, except to the extent that the recommendation is not recognized and enforced in accordance with the provisions of article 39.

2. 'Recommendation' includes an interpretation, clarification or revision of the recommendation made by the conciliators before the recommendation has been accepted.

Article 39

1. Each Contracting Pary shall recognize a recommendation as binding between the parties which have accepted it and shall, subject to the provisions of article 39, paragraphs 2 and 3, enforce, at the request of any such party, all obligations imposed by the recommendation as if it were a final judgment of a court of that Contracting Party.

2. A recommendation shall not be recognized and enforced at the request of a party referred to in article 39, paragraph 1 only if the court or other competent authority of the country where recognition and enforcement is sought is satisfied that:

(*a*) Any party which accepted the recommendation was, under the law applicable to it, under some legal incapacity at the time of acceptance;

(*b*) Fraud or coercion has been used in the making of the recommendations;

(*c*) The recommendation is contrary to public policy (*ordre public*) in the country of enforcement; or

(*d*) The composition of the conciliators, or the conciliation procedure, was not in accordance with the provisions of this Code.

3. Any part of the recommendation shall not be enforced and recognized if the court or other competent authority is satisfied that such part comes within any of the subparagraphs of article 39, paragraph 2 and can be separated from other parts of the recommendation. If such part cannot be separated, the entire recommendation shall not be enforced and recognized.

Article 40

1. Where the recommendation has been accepted by all the parties, the recommendation and the reasons therefor may be published with the consent of all the parties.

2. Where the recommendation has been rejected by one or more of the parties but has been accepted by one or more of the parties:

(*a*) The party or parties rejecting the recommendation shall publish its or their grounds for rejection, given pursuant to article 37, paragraph 3, and may at the same time publish the recommendation and the reasons therefor;

(*b*) A party which has accepted the recommendation may publish the recommendation and the reasons therefor; it may also publish the grounds for rejection given by any other party unless such other party has already published its rejection and the grounds therefor in accordance with article 40, paragraph 2(*a*).

3. Where the recommendation has not been accepted by any of the parties, each party may publish the recommendation and the reasons therefor and also its own rejection and the grounds therefor.

Article 41

1. Documents and statements containing factual information supplied by any party to the conciliators shall be made public unless that party or a majority of the conciliators agrees otherwise.

2. Such documents and statements supplied by a party may be tendered by that party in support of its case in subsequent proceedings arising from the same dispute and between the same parties.

Article 42

Where the recommendation has not become binding upon the parties, no views expressed or reasons given by the conciliators, or concessions or offers made by the parties for the purpose of the conciliation procedures, shall affect the legal rights and obligations of any of the parties.

Article 43

1. (*a*) The costs of the conciliators and all costs of the administration of the conciliation proceedings shall be borne equally by the parties to the proceedings, unless they agree otherwise.

(*b*) When the conciliation proceedings have been initiated, the conciliators shall be entitled to require an advance or security for the costs referred to in article 43, paragraph 1(*a*).

2. Each party shall bear all expenses it incurs in connexion with the proceedings, unless the parties agree otherwise.

3. Notwithstanding the provisions of article 43, paragraphs 1 and 2, the conciliators may, having decided unanimously that a party has brought a claim vexatiously or frivolously, assess against that party any or of all the costs of other parties to the proceedings. Such decision shall be final and binding on all the parties.

Article 44

1. Failure of a party to appear or to present its case at any stage of the proceedings shall not be deemed an admission of the other party's assertions. In that event, the other party may, at its choice, request the conciliators to close the proceedings or to deal with the questions presented to them and submit a recommendation in accordance with the provisions for making recommendations set out in this Code.

2. Before closing the proceedings, the conciliators shall grant the party failing to appear or to present its case a period of grace, not exceeding 10 days, unless they are satisfied that the party does not intend to appear or to present its case.

3. Failure to observe procedural time-limits laid down in this Code or determined by the

conciliators, in particular time-limits relating to the submission of statements or information, shall be considered a failure to appear in the proceedings.

4. Where the proceedings have been closed owing to one party's failure to appear or to present its case, the conciliators shall draw up a report noting that party's failure.

Article 45

1. The conciliators shall follow the procedures stipulated in this Code.

2. The rules of procedure annexed to the present Convention shall be considered as model rules for the guidance of conciliators. The conciliators may, by mutual consent, use, supplement or amend the rules contained in the annex or formulate their own rules of procedure to the extent that such supplementary, amended or other rules are not inconsistent with the provisions of this Code.

3. If the parties agree that it may be in the interest of achieving an expeditious and inexpensive solution of the conciliation proceedings, they may mutually agree to rules of procedure which are not inconsistent with the provisions of this Code.

4. The conciliators shall formulate their recommendation by consensus or failing that shall decide by majority vote.

5. The conciliation proceedings shall finish and the recommendation of the conciliators shall be delivered not later than six months from the date on which the conciliators are appointed, except in the cases referred to in article 23, paragraph 4(*e*), (*f*), and (*g*), for which the time limits in article 14, paragraph 1 and article 16, paragraph 4 shall be valid. The period of six months may be extended by agreement of the parties.

C. INSTITUTIONAL MACHINERY

Article 46

1. Six months before the entry into force of the present Convention, the Secretary-General of the United Nations shall, subject to the approval of the General Assembly of the United Nations, and taking into account the views expressed by the Contracting Parties, appoint a Registrar, who may be assisted by such additional staff as may be necessary for the performance of the functions listed in article 46, paragraph 2. Administrative services for the Registrar and his assistants shall be provided by the United Nations Office at Geneva.

2. The Registrar shall perform the following functions in consultation with the Contracting Parties as appropriate:

(*a*) Maintain the list of conciliators of the international panel of conciliators and regularly inform the Contracting Parties of the composition of the panel;

(*b*) Provide the names and addresses of the conciliators to the parties concerned on request;

(*c*) Receive and maintain copies of requests for conciliation, replies, recommendation, acceptances, or rejections, including reasons therefor;

(*d*) Furnish on request, and at their cost, copies of recommendations and reasons for rejection the shippers' organizations, conferences and Governments, subjects to the provisions of article 40;

(*e*) Make available information of a non-confidential nature on completed conciliation cases, and without attribution to the parties concerned, for the purposes of preparation of material for the Review Conference referred to in article 52; and

(*f*) The other functions prescribed for the Registrar in article 26, paragraph 1(*c*) and article 30, paragraphs 2 and 3.

CHAPTER VII: FINAL CLAUSES

Article 47

IMPLEMENTATION

1. Each Contracting Party shall take such legislative or other measures as may be necessary to implement the present Convention.

2. Each Contracting Party shall communicate to the Secretary-General of the United Nations, who shall be the depositary, the text of the legislative or other measures which it has taken in order to implement the present Convention.

Article 48

SIGNATURE, RATIFICATION, ACCEPTANCE, APPROVAL AND ACCESSION

1. The present Convention shall remain open for signature as from 1 July 1974 until and including 30 June 1975 at United Nations Headquarters and shall thereafter remain open for accession.

2. All States are entitled to become Contracting Parties to the present Convention by:

(*a*) Signature subject to an followed by ratification, acceptance or approval; or

(*b*) Signature without reservation as to ratification, acceptance or approval; or

(*c*) Accession.

3. Ratification, acceptance, approval or accession shall be effected by the deposit of an instrument to this effect with the depositary.

Article 49

ENTRY INTO FORCE

1. The present Convention shall enter into force six months after the date on which not less than 24 States, the combined tonnage of which amounts to at least 25 per cent of world tonnage, have become Contracting Parties to it in accordance with article 48. For the purpose of the present article the tonnage shall be deemed to be that contained in *Lloyd's Register of Shipping–Statistical Tables 1973*, table 2 'World Fleets–Analysis by Principal Types', in respect to general cargo (including passenger/cargo) ships and container (fully cellular) ships, exclusive of the United States reserve fleet and the American and Canadian Great Lakes fleets.

2. For each State which thereafter ratifies, accepts, approves or accedes to it, the present Convention shall come into force six months after deposit by such State of the appropriate instrument.

3. Any State which becomes a Contracting Party to the present Convention after the entry into force of an amendment shall, failing an expression of a different intention by that State:

(*a*) Be considered as a Party to the present Convention as amended; and

(*b*) Be considered as a Party to the unamended Convetion in relation to any Party to the present Convention not bound by the amendment.

Article 50

DENUNCIATION

1. The present Convention may be denounced by any Contracting Party at any time after the expiration of a period of two years from the date on which the Convention has entered into force.

2. Denunciation shall be notified to the depositary in writing, and shall take effect one year, or such longer period as may be specified in the instrument of denunciation, after the date of receipt by the depository.

Article 51

AMENDMENTS

1. Any Contracting Pary may propose one or more amendments to the present Convention by communicating the amendments to the depositary. The depositary shall circulate such amendments among the Contracting Parties, for their acceptance, and among States entitled to become Contracting Parties to the present Convention which are not Contracting Parties, for their information.

2. Each proposed amendment circulated in accordance with article 51, paragraph 1 shall be deemed to have been accepted if no Contracting Party communicates an objection thereto to the depository within 12 months following the date of its circulation by the depositary. If a Contracting Party communicates an objection to the proposed amendment, such amendment shall not be considered as accepted and shall not be put into effect.

3. If no objection has been communicated, the amendment shall enter into force for all Contracting Parties six months after the expiry date of the period of 12 months referred to in article 51, paragraph 2.

Article 52

REVIEW CONFERENCES

1. A Review Conference shall be convened by the depositary five years from the date on which the present Convention comes into force to review the working of the Convention, with particular reference to its implementation, and to consider and adopt appropriate amendments.

2. The depository shall, four years from the date on which the present Convention comes into force, seek the views of all States entitled to attend the Review Conference and shall, on the basis of the views received, prepare and circulate a draft agenda as well as amendments proposed for consideration by the Conference.

3. Further review conferences shall be similarly convened every five years, or at any time after the first Review Conference, at the request of one-third of the Contracting Parties to the present Convention, unless the first Review Conference decides otherwise.

4. Notwithstanding the provisions of article 52, paragraph 1, if the present Convention has not entered into force five years from the date of the adoption of the Final Act of the United Nations Conference of Plenipotentiaries on a Code of Conduct for Liner Conferences, a Review Conference shall, at the request of one-third of the States entitled to become Contracting Parties to the present Convention, be convened by the Secretary-General of the United Nations, subject to the approval of the General Assembly, in order to review the provisions of the Convention and its annex and to consider and adopt appropriate amendments.

Article 53

FUNCTIONS OF THE DEPOSITORY

1. The depository shall notify the signatory and acceding States of:

(*a*) Signatures, ratifications, acceptances, approvals and accessions in accordance with article 48;

(*b*) The date on which the present Convention enters into force in accordance with article 49;

(*c*) Denunciations of the present Convention in accordance with article 50;

(*d*) Reservations to the present Convention and the withdrawal of reservations;

(*e*) The text of the legislative or other measures which each Contracting Party has taken in order to implement the present Convention in accordance with article 47;

(*f*) Proposed amendments and objections to proposed amendments in accordance with article 51; and

(*g*) Entry into force of amendments in accordance with article 51, paragraph 3.

2. The depository shall also undertake such actions as are necessary under article 52.

Article 54

AUTHENTIC TEXTS–DEPOSIT

The original of the present Convention, of which the Chinese, English, French, Russian and Spanish texts are equally authentic, will be deposited with the Secretary-General of the United Nations.

IN WITNESS WHEREOF the undersigned, have been duly authorized to this effect by their respective Governments, have signed the present Convention, on the dates appearing opposite their signatures.

ANNEX TO THE CONVENTION: MODEL RULES OF PROCEDURE FOR INTERNATIONAL MANDATORY CONCILIATION

Rule 1

1. Any party wishing to institute conciliation proceedings under the Code shall address a request to that effect in writing, accompanied by a statement of claim to the other party, and copied to the Registrar.

2. The statement of claim shall:

(*a*) Designate precisely each party to the dispute and state the address of each;

(*b*) Contain a summary statement of pertinent facts, the issues in dispute and the claimant's proposal for the settlement of the dispute;

(*c*) State whether an oral hearing is desired and, if so, and to the extent then known, the names and addresses of persons to give evidence, including experts' evidence, for the claimant;

(*d*) Be accompanied by such supporting documentation and relevant agreements and arrangements entered into by the parties as the claimant may consider necessary at the time of making the claim;

(*e*) Indicate the number of conciliators required, any proposal concerning the appointment of conciliators, or the name of the conciliator appointed by the claimant in accordance with article 32, paragraph 2; and

(*f*) Contain proposals, if any, regarding rules of procedure.

3. The statement of claim shall be dated and shall be signed by the party.

Rule 2

1. If the respondent decides to reply the claim, he shall, within 30 days following the date of his receipt of the statement of claim, transmit a reply to the other party and copied to the Registrar.

2. The reply shall:

(*a*) Contain a summary statement of pertinent facts opposed to the contentions in the statement of claim, the respondent's proposal, if any, for the settlement of the dispute and any remedy claimed by him with a view to the settlement of the dispute;

(*b*) State whether an oral hearing is desired and, if so, and to the extent then known, the names and addresses of persons to give evidence, including experts' evidence, for the respondent;

(*c*) Be accompanied by such supporting documentation and relevant agreements and arrangements entered into by the parties as the respondent may consider necessary at the time of making the reply;

(*d*) Indicate the number of conciliators required, any proposal concerning the appointment of conciliators, or the name of the conciliator appointed by the respondent in accordance with article 32, paragraph 2; and

(*e*) Contain proposals, if any, regarding rules of procedure.

3. The reply shall be dated and shall be signed by the party.

Rule 3

1. Any person or other interest desiring to participate in conciliation proceedings under article 34 shall transmit a written request to the parties to the dispute, with a copy to the Registrar.

2. If participation in accordance with (*a*) of article 34 is desired, the request shall set forth the grounds therefor, including the information required under rule 1, paragraph 2(*a*), (*b*) and (*d*).

3. If participation in accordance with (*b*) of article 34 is desired, the request shall state the ground therefor and which of the original parties would be supported.

4. Any objection to a request for joinder by such a party shall be sent by the objecting party, with a copy to the other party, within seven days of receipt of the request.

5. In the event that two or more proceedings are consolidated, subsequent requests for

third-party participation shall be transmitted to all parties concerned, each of which may object in accordance with the present rule.

Rule 4

By agreement between the parties to the dispute, on motion by either party, and after affording the parties an opportunity of being heard, the conciliators may order the consolidation or separation of all or any claims then pending between the same parties.

Rule 5

1. Any party may challenge a conciliator where circumstances exist that cause justifiable doubts as to his independence.

2. Notice of challenge, stating reasons therefor, should be made prior to the date of the closing of the proceedings, before the conciliators have rendered their recommendation. Any such challenge shall be heard promptly and shall be determined by majority vote of the conciliators in the first instance, as a preliminary point, in cases where more than one conciliator has been appointed. The decision in such cases shall be final.

3. A conciliator who has died, resigned, become incapacitated or disqualified shall be replaced promptly.

4. Proceedings interrupted in this way shall continue from the point where they were interrupted, unless it is agreed by the parties or ordered by the conciliators that a review or rehearing of any oral testimony take place.

Rule 6

The conciliators shall be judges of their own jurisdiction and/or competence within the provisions of the Code.

Rule 7

1. The conciliators shall receive and consider all written statements, documents affidavits, publications or any other evidence, including oral evidence, which may be submitted to them by or on behalf of any of the parties, and shall give such weight thereto as in their judgement such evidence merits.

2. (*a*) Each party may submit to the conciliators any material it considers relevant, and at the time of such submission shall deliver certified copies to any other party to the proceedings, which party shall be given a reasonable opportunity to reply thereto;

(*b*) The conciliators shall be the sole judges of the relevance and materiality of the evidence submitted to them by the parties;

(*c*) The conciliators may ask the parties to produce such additional evidence as they may deem necessary to an understanding and determination of the dispute, provided that, if additional evidence is produced, the other parties to the proceeding shall have a reasonable opportunity to comment thereon.

Rule 8

1. Whenever a period of days for the doing of any act is provided for in the Code or in these rules, the day from which the period begins to run shall not be counted, and the last day of the period shall be counted, except where that last day is a Saturday, Sunday or a public holiday at the place of conciliation, in which case the last day shall be the next business day.

2. When the time provided for is less than seven days, intermediate Saturdays, Sundays and public holidays shall be excluded from the computation.

Rule 9

Subject to the provisions relating to procedural time-limits in the Code, the conciliators may, on a motion by one of the parties or pursuant to agreement between them, extend any such time-limit which has been fixed by the conciliators.

Rule 10

1. The conciliators shall fix the order of business and, unless otherwise agreed, the date and hour of each session.

2. Unless the parties otherwise agree, the proceedings shall take place in private.

3. The conciliators shall specifically inquire of all the parties whether they have any further evidence to submit before declaring the proceedings closed, and a noting thereof shall be recorded.

Rule 11

Conciliators' recommendations shall be in writing and shall include:

(*a*) The precise designation and address of each party;
(*b*) A description of the method of appointing conciliators, including their names;
(*c*) The dates and place of the conciliation proceedings;
(*d*) A summary of the conciliation proceedings, as the conciliators deem appropriate;
(*e*) A summary statement of the facts found by the conciliators;
(*f*) A summary of the submissions of the parties;
(*g*) Pronouncements on the issues in dispute, together with the reasons therefor;
(*h*) The signatures of the conciliators and the date of each signature; and
(*i*) An address for the communication of the acceptance or rejection of the recommendation.

Rule 12

The recommendation shall, so far as possible, contain a pronouncement on costs in accordance with the provisions of the Code. If the recommendation does not contain a full pronouncement on costs, the conciliators shall, as soon as possible after the recommendation, and in any event not later than 60 days thereafter, make a pronouncement in writing regarding costs as provided in the Code.

Rule 13

Conciliator's recommendations shall also take into account previous and similar cases whenever this would facilitate a more uniform implementation of the Code and observance of conciliators' recommendations.

ANNEX 5

Extracts from 'International Development Strategy, for the Second United Nations Development Decade', adopted by UNGA resolution 2626 (XXV) of 24 October 1970

4 Invisibles including shipping

(53) The objective is to promote, by national and international action, the earnings of developing countries from invisible trade and to minimize the net outflow of foreign exchange from these countries arising from invisible transactions, including shipping. In pursuance of the objective, action held shall be taken, inter alia, in the following areas, by Governments and International Organisation and, where necessary, appropriately, involving Liner Conferences, Shippers' Councils and other relevant bodies:

(a) The principle that the national shipping lines of developing countries should be admitted as full members of liner conferences operating in their national maritime trade and have an increasing and substantial participation in the carriage of cargoes generated by their foreign trade should be implemented in the Decade;

(b) Further, Governments should invite liner conferences to consider favourably, fairly and on equal terms application of the national shipping lines, in particular of developing countries, for admission as full members to way-port trades related to these countries' foreign trades, subject to the rights and obligations of conference membership, as provided in paragraph 4, Section II of resolution 12(IV) of 4 May 1970 adopted by the Committee on Shipping;

(c) In order that the developing countries have an increasing and substantial participation in the carriage of maritime cargoes, and recognizing the need to reverse the existing trade whereby the shares of the developing countries in the world merchant fleet has been declining instead of increasing developing countries should be enabled to expand their national and multinational merchant marines through the adoption of such measures as may be appropriate to permit their shipowners to compete in the international freight market and thus contribute to a sound development of shipping;

(d) It is also necessary that further improvements be made in the liner conference system, and all unfair practices and discrimination where such exist in liner conference practices should be eliminated;

(e) In the determination and adjustment of liner freight rates, due consideration should be given, as is commercially possible and/or appropriate to

(1) The needs of the developing countries, in particular their efforts to promote non-traditional exports;
(2) The special problems of the least developed among the developing countries, in order to encourage and promote the import and export interests in these countries;
(3) Port improvements leading to a reduction of the cost of shipping operations in ports;
(4) Technological developments in maritime transport; and
(5) Improvements in the organization of trade.

(f) Governments of developed countries members of the United Nations Conference on Trade and Development should, upon request made by developing countries within the framework of their overall development priorities, duly consider extending, directly or through international institutions, financial and technical assistance, including training, to developing countries to establish and expand their national and multinational merchant marines, including tanker and bulk carrier fleets, and to develop and improve their port facilities. Within assistance programmes, special attention should be paid to projects, including training projects, for developing the shipping and ports of the least developed among the developing countries and for reducing their maritime transport costs;

(g) The terms and conditions on which bilateral aid and commercial credit are available for purchase of ships by developing countries should be kept under review in the light of relevant resolutions of the United Nations Conference on Trade and Development, namely, Conference Resolution 12(II) of 24 March 1968, and resolution 9(IV) of 4 May 1970 adopted by the Committee on Shipping.

(h) Freight rates, conference practices, adequacy of shipping services and other matters of common interest to shippers and shipowners should be the subject of consultation between liner conferences and shippers and, where appropriate, shippers' councils or equivalent bodies and interested public authorities. Every effort should be made to encourage the institution and operation of shippers' councils, where appropriate, or equivalent bodies and the establishment of effective consultation machinery. Such machinery should provide for consultation by Liner Conferences well before publicly announcing changes in freight rates;

(i) In view of the common interest of member countries of the United Nations Conference on Trade and Development, Shippers and Shipowners in improving imports, thus covering the cost of maritime transport and permitting reductions in freight rates, a concerted national and international effort should be evolved in the course of the Decade to promote the development and improvement of port facilities of developing countries;

(j) Maritime transport costs, the level and structure of freight rates, conference practices, adequacy of shipping services and related matters should continue to be kept under review within the United Nations Conference on Trade and Development, and additional measures to attain the objectives set out in this field should be considered within the whole programme of the permanent machinery of the Conference'.

ANNEX 6

Example of shipping cooperation: Ministerial Conference of West and Central African States on Maritime Transports – Abidjan, 5–6–7 May, 1975

Maritime Transport Charter for West And Central Africa

'*Preamble*

The States of West and Central Africa,

- Recognising their economic development as a first priority,
- Recognising the impact of maritime transport on their respective economies,
- Considering the arbitrary decisions made by the Maritime Conferences particularly in the field of freight rate increases,
- Considering the favourable dispositions of the Code of Conduct of the Maritime Conferences for the development of the merchant fleets of developing countries, notably for the sharing out of cargoes on a 40–40–20 basis.

decide:

A. Maritime affairs

(1) To set up a permanent coordinating body on maritime transport and particularly to institutionalise the ministerial conference;

(2) To create Shippers' Councils or similar bodies in those countries where they do not already exist in such a way that they become operational by the end of next year;

(3) To group these various councils within the framework of a cooperating body. To this effect an ad hoc Committee, whose mission is to study the form and functioning of this grouping, is to be set up by the Conference.

(4) To set up FAL national and regional Committees for the facilitation of Administrative formalities concerning international maritime trade;

(5) To organise the effective intervention of the States concerned in the activities of auxiliary maritime transport services (transit, lighterage, stevedoring, etc.);

(6) To create freight grouping bodies in order to help shipping companies in the region and to this effect to recommend the gradual transformation of the labelling of purchase contracts from CIF to FOB for imports and FOB to CIF for exports;

(7) To create national marine insurance bodies in order to obtain better protection of the interests of Shippers and of shipping companies in the region.

B. Development of Shipping Companies

(8) To unite their efforts with a view to assuring maritime transport coming from or going to their countries under the most advantageous conditions for their economy;

(9) To create and develop their merchant fleets;

(10) To coordinate the action of national shipping companies in order to make the best use of transporting capacity through a very close organisation of lines and agencies with a view to exploitation in a pool system.

(11) To urge those countries who wish to establish shipping lines in partnership with foreign countries to control the majority of the shares;

(12) To set up an African Maritime Conference for West and Central Africa;

(13) To ensure the rapid Africanisation of the representatives in Africa of foreign maritime conferences serving the coasts of the region;

(14) To make application to African financing bodies and other international bodies to enable the purchase on favourable terms of the ships necessary for the development of merchant fleets, especially in view of the restrictive measures imposed on export credits by resolution C7488 – final of the OECD Countries dated 18 July 1974;

(15) To undertake a study on the feasibility of setting up multinational shipping companies.

C. Ports

(16) a. To set up the necessary to ensure traffic flow.

b. To organise the best possible use of port installation by setting up the appropriate management structures and by ensuring economic utilization of port labour forces;

c. To give the ports a wider management autonomy in order to obtain higher efficiency;

(17) To encourage management association of the ports of West and Central Africa in the setting up of cooperation and information bodies.

(18) To undertake long-term port development studies to accommodate bulk cargo and container vessels.

D. Landlocked countries

(19) To institutionalise the participation of landlocked countries in the management of the ports on which they depend and to encourage them to participate in the capital of the shipping companies of countries on the coast;

(20) To give preferential treatment to goods coming from or going to landlocked countries, with the agreement of coastal countries.

E. Training and information

(21) To set up with the help of the specialised bodies of the United Nations regional training and information centres to train both seagoing and shore staff as soon as possible'.

ANNEX 7

Aims and objectives of the OECD

The Organisation for Economic Cooperation and Development was set up under a Convention signed in Paris on 14th December 1960 by the member countries of the Organisation for European Economic Cooperation and by Canada and the United States. This Convention provides that the OECD shall promote policies designed:

- To achieve the highest sustainable economic growth and employment and a rising standard of living in member countries, while maintaining financial stability, and thus to contribute to the development of the world economy;
- To contribute to sound economic expansion in member as well as non-member countries in the process of economic development;
- To contribute to the expansion of world trade on a multilateral, non-discriminatory basis in accordance with international obligations.

The legal personality possessed by the Organisation for European Economic Cooperation continues in the OECD, which came into being on 30th September 1961.

The members of OECD are: Austria, Belgium, Canada, Denmark, France, the Federal Republic of Germany, Greece, Iceland, Ireland, Italy, Luxembourg, the Netherlands, Norway, Portugal, Spain, Sweden, Switzerland, Turkey, the United Kingdom and the United States.

ANNEX 8

Note 1 to Annex A of the Code of Liberalisation of Current Invisible Operations (adopted by the Council on 12th December, 1961)

Note 1

The provisions of C/1 'Maritime freights, including chartering, harbour expenses, disbursements for fishing vessels, etc.', of C/5, first sub-paragraph. 'For all means of maritime transport; harbour services (including bunkering and provisioning, maintenance, repairs, expenses for crews, etc.)', and of the other items that have a direct or indirect bearing on international maritime transport, are intended to give residents of one member state the unrestricted opportunity to avail themselves of, and pay for, all services in connection with international maritime transport which are offered by residents of any other member state. As the shipping policy of the governments of the members is based on the principle of free circulation of shipping in international trade in free and fair competition, it follows that the freedom of transactions and transfers in connection with maritime transport should not be hampered by measures in the field of exchange control, by legislative provisions in favour of the national flag, by arrangements made by governmental or semi-governmental organisations giving preferential treatment to national flag ships, by preferential shipping clauses in trade agreements, by the operation of import and export licensing systems so as to influence the flag of the carrying ship, or by discriminatory port regulations or taxation measures – the aim always being that liberal and competitive commercial and shipping practices and procedures should be followed in international trade and normal commercial considerations should alone determine the method and flag of shipment.

The second sentence of this Note does not apply to the United States.

ANNEX 9

Articles 1 to 3 of the Convention on the Organisation for Economic Cooperation and Development

Article 1

The aims of the Organisation for Economic Cooperation and Development (hereinafter called the 'Organisation') shall be to promote policies designed:

(a) To achieve the highest sustainable economic growth and employment and a rising standard of living in member countries, while maintaining financial stability, and thus to contribute to the development of the world economy;

(b) To contribute to sound economic expansion in member as well as non-member contries in the process of economic development; and

(c) To contribute to the expansion of world trade on a multi-lateral, non-discriminatory basis in accordance with international obligations.

Article 2

In the pursuit of these aims, the members agree that they will, both individually and jointly:

(a) Promote the efficient use of their economic resources;

(b) In the scientific and technological field, promote the development of their resources, encourage research and promote vocational training;

(c) Pursue policies designed to achieve economic growth and internal and external financial stability and to avoid developments which might endanger their economies or those of other countries;

(d) Pursue their efforts to reduce or abolish obstacles to the exchange of goods and services and current payments and maintain and extend the liberalisation of capital movements; and

(e) Contribute to the economic development of both member and non-member countries in the process of economic development by appropriate means and, in particular, by the flow of capital to those countries, having regard to the importance to their economies of receiving technical assistance and of securing expanding export markets.

Article 3

With a view to achieving the aims set out in Article 1 and to fulfilling the undertakings contained in Article 2, the Members agree that they will:

(a) Keep each other informed and furnish the Organisation with the information necessary for the accomplishment of its task;

(b) Consult together on a continuing basis, carry out studies and participate in agreed projects; and

(c) Cooperate closely and where appropriate take coordinated action.

ANNEX 10

Note of understanding (reached between European Conference Lines and European Shippers, following European Ministers' March 1963 Resolution)

In view of their mutual interest in the implementation of the Ministers' March 1963 Resolution, the European Shippers' Councils (representative of both European exporters and importers) and European shipowners decided to exchange views, particularly in relation to Clause 4 and Clause 5, sub-paragraphs b) and c) of that Resolution. As a result, discussions have taken place between representatives of the European Conference Lines nominated by the National Shipowners' Associations in the ten countries and representatives of the Shippers' Councils in all of these countries except Denmark and Greece where no such Councils presently exist. As a result of these talks, the following understanding has been reached between European Conference Lines and the European Shippers' Councils –

1. Both parties note with satisfaction the endorsement given in the Resolution to the Conference system and agree as to the importance of means existing to ensure fair practices and the discussion of grievances as between shippers and conferences.

2. The parties agree adn desire to stress that, in the commercial operation of the conference system which is designed to meet the requirements of the trading interests, it is essential that the machinery suitable for the maintenance of fair practices and for the discussion of matters of mutual interest – and these are far wider in scope than the strict interpretation of 'grievances' – should and can be provided satisfactorily by agreement between carriers and users and be operated by them. Consistent with these views they have further agreed as follows:

3. Their representatives should meet at regular intervals to discuss matters of principle and broad issues of mutual interest.

4. Insofar as differences may arise in the detailed day-to-day operations of individual conferences, every endeavour should be made to continue and improve the normal machinery for resolving such differences through discussions between the trade organisation representing shippers and that conference.

5. Failing agreement through these normal discussions between shipper and conference, the following procedure should apply:

a) The matter in dispute would be referred either by the shipper or shippers concerned (or by the trade organisation) or by the shipowner or conference to the appropriate Shippers' Council. If this Council is satisfied that the matter in dispute has substance, it will endeavour to reach an understanding with the conference. Should the matter in dispute effect traders in a number of countries, there would be consultation between the Shippers' Councils in those several countries.

b) In those cases where the procedure outlined above does not lead to a mutually-satisfactory understanding, the matter would be referred to an 'Independent Panel', this Panel to consist of three representatives nominated by European shipowners and three representatives nominated by the European Shippers' Councils. The representatives so nominated would be of the highest standing and, so far as possible, would not be intimately concerned with the matter in dispute. The nominating bodies would be left to vary the selection of their representatives as suitable in each particular investigation. It would be the function of the Panel to find a fair and equitable solution of the matter in dispute and its recommendation would then be considered by the interests concerned in a spirit of mutual acceptance.

If in any particular case the shipowner and shipper representatives on the Panel feel that it would help them to resolve the matter in dispute, they shall be free to co-opt an independent Chairman who shall be a person of high commercial or professional standing.

6. Both parties desire to emphasise the importance of disputes regarding freight rate questions being determined by direct negotiation between the parties concerned in a particular trade. It would be quite impracticable for the assessment and adjustment of individual rates to be subject to the machinery agreed. On the other hand, they are agreed that some freight rate issues raise matters of general principle which go beyond the considerations applying to individual rates and that, in such circumstances, these issues may be discussed and investigated under the procedure of paragraph 5.

7. Finally, it must be recognised that European Conference Lines serve shippers and consignees in many parts of the world and that, in the procedures, detailed above, due regard must be given to these third-party interests.

ANNEX 11

U.S. Shipping Act 1916 (and flag discrimination)

Note: The U.S. Shipping Act 1916, with appropriate editorial adjustments, is found in the various editions of the U.S. Code, commencing in 1926, in Title 46, sections 801–842. Section 14 of the statute as enacted is found in U.S. Code Title 46, section 812; the following sections follow in sequence.

Rebates; discrimination; 'fighting ships'

Section 14. That no common carrier by water shall, directly or indirectly, in respect to the transportation by water of passengers or property between a port of a State, Territory, District, or possession of the United States and any other such port or a port of a foreign country,

First. Pay, or allow, or enter into any combination, agreement, or understanding, express or implied, to pay or allow, a deferred rebate to any shipper. The term 'deferred rebate' in this Act means a return of any portion of the freight money by a carrier to any shipper as a consideration for the giving of all or any portion of his shipments to the same or any other carrier, or for any other purpose, the payment of which is deferred beyond the completion of the service for which it is paid, and is made only if, during both the period for which computed and the period of deferment, the shipper has complied with the terms of the rebate agreement or arrangement.

Second. Use a fighting ship either separately or in conjunction with any other carrier through agreement or otherwise. The term 'fighting ship' in this Act means a vessel used in a particular trade by a carrier or group of carriers for the purpose of excluding, preventing or reducing competition by driving another carrier out of the said trade.

Third. Retaliate against any shipper by refusing, or threatening to refuse, space accommodations when such are available, or resort to other discriminating or unfair method, because such shipper has patronized nay other carrier or has filed a complaint charging unfair treatment, or for any other reason.

Fourth. Make any unfair or unjustly discriminatory contract with any shipper based on the volume of freight offered, or unfairly treat or unjustly discriminate against any shipper in the matter of (a) cargo space accommodations or other facilities, due regard being had for the proper loading of the vessel and the available tonnage; (b) the loading and landing of freight in proper conditions; or (c) the adjustment and settlement of claims.

Any carrier who violates any provision of this section shall be guilty of a misdemeanor punishable by a fine of not more that 25 000 dollars for each offense. (Septermber 7, 1916).

Sanction – exclusion from U.S.A. ports (1920)

Section 14a. The board upon its own initiative may, or upon complaint shall, after due notice to all parties in interest and hearing, determine whether any person, not a citizen of the United States and engaged in transportation by water of passengers or property,

(1) Has violated any provision of section 14, or

(2) Is a party to any combination, agreement, or understanding, express or implied, that involves in respect to transportation of passengers or property between foreign ports, deferred rebates or any other unfair practice designated in Section 14, and that excludes from admission upon equal terms with all other parties thereto, a common carrier by water which is a citizen of the United States and which has applied for such admission.

If the board determines that nay such person has violated any such provision or is a party to any such combination, agreement, or understanding, the board shall thereupon certify such fact to the Secretary of Commerce. The Secretary shall thereafter refuse such person the right of entry for any ship owned or operated by him or by any carrier directly or indirectely controlled by him, into any port of the United States, or any Territory, District, or possession thereof, until the board certifies that the violation has ceased or such combination, agreement, or understanding has been terminated. (Section 14-1 was added, June 5, 1920.)

Contracts between carriers to be filed – approval, disapproval

Section 15. That every common carrier by water, or other person* subject to this Act,

* The question, Who is 'another person' subject to the regulatory provisions of the Act? is reviewed from time to time by the Federal Maritime Board. Proceedings have been conducted in respect of Brokers. Marine Terminals.

shall file immediately with the board a true copy, or, if oral, a true and complete memorandum, of every agreement with another such carrier or other person subject to this Act, or modification or cancellation thereof, to which it may be a party or conform in whole or in part, fixing or regulating transportation rates or fares; giving or receiving special rates, accommodations, or other special privileges or advantages; controlling, regulating, preventing, or destroying competition; pooling or apportioning earnings, losses, or traffic; allotting ports or restricting or otherwise regulating the number and character of sailings between ports; limiting or regulating in any way the volume or character of freight or passenger traffic to be carried; or in any manner providing for an exclusive, preferential, or cooperative working arrangement. The term 'agreement' in this section includes understandings, conferences, and other arrangements.

The board may by order disapprove, cancel, or modify any agreement, or any modification or cancellation thereof, whether or not previously approved by it, that it finds to be unjustly discriminatory or unfair as between carriers, shippers, exporters, importers, or ports, or between exporters from the United States and their foreign competitors, or to operate to the detriment of the commerce of the United States, or to be in violation of this Act, and shall approve all other agreements, modifications, or cancellations.

Agreements existing at the time of the organization of the board shall be lawful until disapproval by the board. It shall be unlawful to carry out any agreement or any portion thereof disapproved by the board.

All agreements, modifications, or cancellations made after the organization of the board shall be lawful only when and as long as approved by the board, and before approval or after disapproval it shall be unlawful to carry out in whole or in part, directly or indirectly, any such agreement, modification, or cancellation.

Every agreement, modification, or cancellation lawful under this section shall be excepted from the provisions of the Act approved July second, eighteen hundred and ninety, entitled 'An Act to protect trade and commerce against unlawful restraints and monopolies',** and amendments and Acts supplementary thereto, and the provisions of sections seventy-three to seventy-seven, both inclusive, of the Act approved August twenty-seventh, eighteen hundred and ninety-four, entitled 'An Act to reduce taxation, to provide revenue for the Government, and for other purposes', and amendments and Acts supplementary thereto.

Whoever violates any provision of this section shall be liable to a penalty of 1000 dollars for each day such violation continues, to be recovered by the United States in a civil action. (Sept. 7, 1916)

Discriminatory Acts prohibited; false billing

Section 16. That it shall be unlawful for any shipper, consignor, consignee, forwarder, broker, or other person, or any officer, agent, or employee thereof, knowingly and willfully, directly or indirectly, by means of false billing, false classification, false weighing, false report of weight, or by any other unjust or unfair device or means to obtain or attempt to obtain transportation by water for property at less than the rates or charges which would otherwise be applicable.

Discrimination by carrier prohibited

That it shall be unlawful for any common carrier by water, or other person subject to this Act, either alone or in conjunction with any other person, directly or indirectly,

First. To make or give any undue or unreasonable preference or advantage to any particular person, locality, or description of traffic in any respect whatsoever, or to subject any particular person, locality, or description of traffic to any undue or unreasonable prejudice or disadvantage in any respect whatsoever.

Second. To allow any person to obtain transportation for property at less than the regular rates or charges then established and enforced on the line of such carrier by means of false billing, false classification, false weighing, false report of weight, or by any other unjust or unfair device or means.

** Known as the Sherman Anti-Trust Act, 1890.

Discrimination by insurer prohibited

Third. To induce, persuade, or otherwise influence any marine insurance company or underwriter, or agent thereof, not to give a competing carrier by water as favorable a rate of insurance on vessel or cargo, having due regard to the class of vessel or cargo, as is granted to such carrier or other person subject to this Act.

Whoever violates any provision of this section shall be guilty of a misdemeanor punishable by a fine of not more than 5000 dollars for each offence (Sept. 7, 1916; June 16, 1936).

Discriminatory rates prohibited

Section 17. That no common carrier by water in foreign commerce shall demand, charge, or collect any rate, fare, or charge which is unjustly discriminatory between shippers or ports, or unjustly prejudicial to exporters of the United States as compared with their foreign competitors. Whenever the board finds that any such rate, fare, or charge is demanded, charged, or collected it may alter the same to the extent necessary to correct such unjust discrimination or prejudice and make an order that the carrier shall discontinue demanding, charging, or collecting any such unjustly discriminatory or prejudicial rate, fare, or charge.

Every such carrier and every other person subject to this Act shall establish, observe, and enforce just and reasonable regulations and practices relating to or connected with the receiving, handling, storing, or delivering of property. Whenever the board finds that any such regulation or practice is unjust or unreasonable it may determine, prescribe, and order enforced a just and reasonable regulation or practice (Sept. 7, 1916).

ANNEX 12

Foreign reaction to U.S. promotional policies (subsidy and cargo preference)

Foreign governments and foreign shipowners have learned to live with the U.S. subsidy system. They recognize the military justification and the broad political justification for the existence of the U.S. merchant marine. They also recognize its inability to compete with foreign-flag shipping without assistance and accept the direct subsidy system as a necessary evil.

The maritime nations, however, continue to be strongly opposed to cargo preference policies (except for military cargo). They maintain that certain of the cargoes, for example those financed by the Export-Import Bank, are essentially commercial in character and should be made available to ships of all flags on a competitive basis. Most importantly, they maintain that the cargo preference system sets a bad example for the developing nations and encourages the latter to adopt their own cargo preference systems, in most cases applicable to commercial cargoes rather than, as in the case of the United States, confined to 'government-sponsored' cargoes.

The Department of State has consistently supported the development of a modern and efficient U.S. merchant marine. The Department has considered that the basic promotional legislation embodied in the *Merchant Marine Act* of 1936 has been essential to the maintenance of an American merchant marine posture, and has defended other legislation, including *Public Resolution 17* and *Section 901 (b) of the Merchant Marine Act (50–50 law)*. The Department has on many occasions, both in bilateral and multilateral negotiations with foreign governments, defended the U.S. cargo preference system on the grounds that the system allocates to American-flag shipping only those cargoes in which the United States has a proprietary interest, or which otherwise may be considered a 'government-sponsored'. The Department has reiterated on many occasions its opposition to the allocation by foreign governments of commercial cargoes to national-flag vessels and has equally consistently opposed the actions of certain foreign governments which have tended to artificially cloak commercial cargoes under the colors of government cargoes.

Any move in the direction of extending U.S.-flag preference into the commercial area would be certain to bring forth a violent foreign reaction, and would rightly be recognized as constituting a major reversal in American foreign policy. Our friendship, commerce, and navigation treaties with over 30 nations contain nondiscriminatory shipping clauses. Any decision to extend discrimination to commercial cargoes would place us in violation of all of these treaties. The FCN treaties are, of course, of basic importance to our commercial policy and our commercial relations.

ANNEX 13

Foreign reactions to U.S. regulatory policies

The Federal Maritime Commission (FMC) is the independent agency responsible for the administration of those provisions of the shipping statutes relating to the regulation of common carriers engaged in U.S. oceanborn commerce. In recent years the Commission has been vigorous in its regulatory activities and the measures taken have given rise to numerous complaints by the maritime countries, largely on the grounds of jurisdiction. Efforts by the Commission to secure documents from abroad in connection with studies of freight rate disparities have met with a particularly adverse reaction and 14 of the maritime countries have concerted to dispute what they allege is a gross invasion of their jurisdictions. Under State Department auspices a long series of discussions, consultations, and negotiations has been held with the 14 countries as a group in an effort to seek an understanding of our regulatory philosophy and cooperation in carrying out the statutory responsibilities of the FMC in a way acceptable to the group. This effort has achieved considerable success.

The method of discussion and conciliation also brought acceptance by the foreign-domiciled shipping conferences of the FMC-prescribed dual-rate shipping contract, to which the 14 governments had also objected as an invasion of their sovereignty. These are but two – the most important in the recent period – instances of U.S. regulatory activities in international shipping that have given concern to foreign countries and resulted in the introduction of irritants in U.S. relations with other governments. As in all the numerous other instances, the Department and the FMC have worked closely together in pursuing the objectives of U.S. law and have tried to minimize conflict with friendly maritime powers.

ANNEX 14

Countervailing flag discrimination

Generally, these aspects of foreign maritime policies which have an unfavourable impact on U.S. shipping and consequently are opposed by the U.S. Government are related to cargo discrimination in favor of national ships.

With the exception of France, the major maritime nations have no overt cargo preference or subsidy support systems based on law or regulation. France, and to a lesser extent Italy, make significant financial contributions to their merchant marine similar to those of the United States through what are, in effect, construction and operating subsidies.

Among the developing countries there is a marked tendency to 'nationalize' cargo in one fashion or another, and in many cases to flatly reserve a proportion of all ocean commerce, whether commercial or governmental, to the national flag. Hence, for the most part, the current efforts of the U.S. Government to secure equal treatment for U.S. vessels in the face of foreign discriminatory governmental actions are directed at the 'developing' countries.

Listed below, by country, are specific examples of actions deemed to be discriminatory against American-flag shipping and American-flag shipping policy which have been the subject of action by the Department of State. It should be emphasized that the Department has at all times worked in the closest liaison with other agencies of the Government, particularly the Maritime Administration, in developing policies and procedures to deal with foreign discrimination against U.S. shipping.

Argentina. During the Peron regime, a centralized Argentina trading agency controlled cargo routings and directed a preponderant share to Argentina-flag vessels. In addition, the Central Bank of Argentina directed cargo to Argentine ships through import licensing and preferential exchange rates for payment of freight if such cargoes moved on Argentine-flag vessels. After the fall of the Peron government Argentina received a series of Export-Import Bank loans totalling about 180 million dollars. Since the discriminatory policies mentioned above had not been rescinded, waivers of Public Resolution 17 were denied. In 1958 the Argentine Government asked for discussions of the shipping problems with the Department of State and the Maritime Administration. The Argentine Embassy subsequently gave assurances to the U.S. Government that the pertinent decrees had been withdrawn, and, as a result, waivers of Public Resolution 17 have been granted to Argentina.

Chile. Several years ago Chile enacted a law, the intent of which was to reserve 50% of all Chilean oceanborne commerce to national-flag vessels. The U.S. Government made strenuous representations to Chile. While the Chilean legislation was not repealed, a pooling arrangement had been set up between the American-flag and Chilean-flag lines placing the American carrier in the same position as the Chilean line with respect to Chilean ocean trade.

Columbia. The Government of Columbia gives preference to national-flag carriers in the transportation of government cargoes. An increase in the volume of government cargoes, now amounting to some 40 percent of all imports and exports, has been caused by the creation of additional governmental and semigovernmental entities handling Columbian national trade and by a loose interpretation of the term 'government cargo'. Discussions with the Columbia Government have not been successful in obtaining satisfactory treatment for U.S. vessels, and consequently, the U.S. Government has declined in recent years to authorize waivers of the shipping provisions of Public Resolution 17 to Columbia, thereby reserving 100% of cargoes generated under Eximbank loans to American-flag vessels.

Ecuador. In the immediate postwar period the Government of Ecuador instituted a differential in consular invoice fees for imports into Ecuador which favored national-flag ships. This differential in some cases actually amounted to more that the freight on the material shipped, and the result was the virtual elimination of U.S.-flag services in the import trade of Ecuador. The U.S. Government protested but to no avail, and eventually Ecuador was warned that unless the differential was eliminated the United States would take countercailing action against *Ecuadorian vessels under section 19 of the Merchant Marine Act of 1920.* Ecuador subsequently abolished the differential, and American-flag participation in Ecuadorian imports reverted to its former satisfactory level.

Ghana. Until the latter part of 1961, Ghanaian-flag vessels, favored by Government direction of cargo, were carrying the greater share of cocoa exports from Ghana to the United States. When the Ghanaian Government was discussing waivers of *Public Resolution 17 on Eximbank* financed material for projects within Ghana, the unsatisfactory situation in the cocoa trade was called to the attention of the Government. It was made clear that waivers of *Public Resolution 17* would be considered in the context of a larger participation by U.S.-flag carriers in the cocoa trade. The Ghanian Government accordingly revised its cocoa export shipping policy to the satisfaction of the American carriers. Waivers of Public Resolution 17 were then granted.

India. On *September 1, 1964 the Ministry of Commerce of the Government of India* issued a circular letter to various chambers of commerce in India urging that a particular foreign-flag nonconference line be utilized by shippers in the trade from the west coast of India to the United States. Representatives of the Indian Government were promptly informed that the U.S. Government considered this action discriminatory against American-flag shipping in that trade and that it could lead to a revocation of current Public Resolution 17 waivers and to a denial of future request for waivers. The Government of India promptly rescinded its action by circulating a second letter to the original addressees canceling the first.

Certain questions regarding the effect on American carriers of the recent Indian-United Arab Republic shipping agreement remain unresolved. The United States Government is continuing negotiations with the Indian Government in pursuit of the interests of the

American lines and, in the meantime, is withholding action on current requests for *Public Resolution 17 waivers.*

Spain. Prior to 1958 the Spanish Government had placed in effect foreign exchange restrictions which restricted the convertibility of Spanish pesetas to dollars. These restrictions made it difficult for U.S.-flag operators to solicit cargo. An additional regulation published by the Spanish Government in 1957 made it mandatory on Spanish importers, before the importer would be allowed to utilize U.S.-flag vessels to lift cargo, to certify that no Spanish ship was available to carry the material. The combination of the two sets of regulations proved a great handicap to the solicitation efforts of American operators in the Spanish trade. In 1958 the U.S. Government refused to grant waivers of PR-17 to Spain on the grounds that the Spanish actions were discriminatory against U.S. shipping. The Spanish Government subsequently revoked the discriminatory regulations. U.S. operators are now considered to have an adequate opportunity for soliciting Spanish cargoes and waivers accordingly have been granted allowing Spanish-flag vessels to participate in Eximbank financed cargoes.

Uruguay. In *July 1963 the Government of Uruguay*, in an effort to promote the national shipping interests, issued certain regulations which made it far less expensive for Uruguayan importers to utilize national-flag vessels. Prolonged discussions between the U.S. Government and the Government of Uruguay have resulted in agreement on the part of the Uruguayan Government that the discriminatory regulations of 1963 will be supplanted by new promotional shipping legislation of a nondiscriminatory character. While at one point it appeared that it would be necessary to invoke countervailing measures under section 19 of the Merchant Marine Act, 1920, currently American shipping interests are not being adversely affected and the effective date of the countervailing action has been postponed pending the enactment of the nondiscriminatory legislation by Uruguay.

Venezuela. Venezuelan Decree No. 331 reserves to national-flag vessels all cargo which is exonerated from the payment of import duties. This cargo represents an important part of Venezuelan imports. Waivers of PR-17 were denied to Venezuela until the primary U.S.-flag carrier in the Venezuelan trade was able to work out a pooling agreement with the Venezuelan line which gave the U.S. carrier the same privileges as to exonerated cargoes as were enjoyed by the Venezuelan carrier. Other U.S. carriers in the Venezuelan trade are currently engated in conversations with the Venezuelan Government in the hope that they will be granted equivalent status with the U.S.-flag member of the existing pooling agreement. Since these carriers contend that they are discriminated against by the Government of Venezuela under the terms of decree 331, waivers of PR-17 have been withheld from Venezuela since mid-1964.

ANNEX 15

National treatment – flag preference

Belgium (Art. 13(2) of FCN Treaty) 14 UST 1284; TIAS 5432 (1962). Vessels of either Party en route to or from the territories of the other Party shall be accorded national treatment and most-favored-nation treatment with respect to the right to carry all cargo that may be carried by vessel.

China (Art. XXII(1) of FCN Treaty) TIAS 1871; 63 Stat. 1299 (1948). The vessels and cargoes of either High Contracting Party shall, within the ports, places and waters of the other High Contracting Party, in all respect be accorded treatment no less favourable than the treatment accorded to the vessels and cargoes of such other High Contracting Party, irrespective of the port of departure or the port of destination of the vessel, and irrespective of the origin or destination of the cargo.

Denmark (Art. XIX(4) of FCN Treaty) TS 60; 8 Stat. 340 (1926). Vessels of either Party shall be accorded national treatment and most-favored-nation treatment by the other Pary with respect to the right to carry all articles that may be carried by vessel to or from the territories of such other party.

Ethiopia (Art. XIV(2) of FCN Treaty) 4 UST 2134; TIAS 2864 (1953). Commercial vessels lawfully under the flag of either High Contracting Party may come with their cargoes to all ports, places and waters of the other High Contracting Party open to foreign commerce and navigation, and shall therein be accorded in all respects treatment no less favorable than that accorded vessels of such other High Contracting Party or of any third country.

Germany (Art. XX(2) of FCN Treaty) TS 725; 44 Stat. 2132 (1925). Vessels of either Party shall be accorded national treatment and most-favored-nation treatment with respect to the right to carry all cargo that may be carried by vessel to or from the territories of the other Party.

Greece (Art. XXL(5) of FCN Treaty) 5 UST 1829; TIAS 3057 (1954). Vessels of either Party shall be accorded by the other Party national treatment and shall enjoy most-favored-nation treatment with respect to the right to carry any articles, capable of being carried by sea, to or from the territories of such other Party.

Iran (Art. X(4) of FCN Treaty) 8 UST 899; TIAS 3953 (1957). Vessels of either High Contracting Party shall be accorded national treatment and most-favored-nation treatment by the other High Contracting Party with respect to the right to carry all products that may be carried by vessel to or from the territories of such other High Contracting Party.

Iraq (Art. III of FCN Treaty) TS 960; 54 Stat. 1790 (1940). Vessels of the United States of America will enjoy in Iraq and Iraqui vessels will enjoy in the United States of America treatment not less favorable than that accorded to national vessels or vessels of the most favored nation.

Ireland (Art. XVIII(4) of FCN Treaty) 1 UST 765; TIAS 2155 (1950). Vessels of either Party shall be accorded national and most-favored-nation treatment by the other Party with respect to the right to carry all articles that may be carried by vessel to or from the territories of such other Party.

Israel (Art. XIX(4) of FCN Treaty) 5 UST 550; TIAS 2948 (1964). Vessels of either party shall be accorded national treatment and most-favored-nation treatment by the other Party with respect to the right to carry all articles that may be carried by vessel to or from the territories of such other party.

Italy (Art. XX(1) of FCN Treaty) TIAS 1965; 63 Stat. 2255 (1949). The vessels and cargoes of either High Contracting Party shall within the ports, places and water of the other High Contracting Party, in all respects be accorded treatment no less favorable than the treatment accorded to the vessels and cargoes of such other High Contracting Party irrespective of the port of departure or the port of destination of the vessel, and irrespective of the origin or destination of the cargo.

Japan (Art. XIX(4) of FCN Treaty) 4 UST 2063; TIAS 2863 (1953). Vessels of either Party shall be accorded national treatment and most-favored-nation treatment with respect to the right to carry all products that may be carried by vessel to or from the territories of such other Party.

Korea (Art. XIX(4) of FCN Treaty) 8 UST 2217; TIAS 3947 (1957). Vessels of either Party shall be accorded national treatment and most-favored-nation treatment by the other Party with respect to the right to carry all products that may be carried by vessel to or from the territories of such other Party.

Liberia (Art. XIV of FCN Treaty) TS 956; 54 Stat. 1739 (1939). The merchant or other private vessels and cargoes of one of the High Contracting Parties shall, within the territorial waters and harbors of the other Party in all respects and unconditionally be accorded the same treatment as the vessels and cargoes of that Party, irrespective of the port of departure of the vessel, or the port of destination, and irrespective of the origin of the destination of the cargo.

Luxemburg (Art. XIII(2) of FCN Treaty) 14 UST 251; TIAS 5306 (1963). (2) Vessels of either Party shall be accorded national treatment and most-favored-nation treatment by the other Party with respect to the right to carry all products that may be carried by vessel to or from the territories of such other Party.

Muscat (Art. X(4) of FCN Treaty) 11 UST 1835; TIAS 4530 (1960). Vessels of either Party shall be accorded national treatment and most-favored-nation treatment by the other Party with respect to the right to carry all products that may be carried by vessel to and from the territory of such other Party.

Netherlands (Art. XIX(3) of FCN Treaty) 8 UST 2043; TIAS 3942 (1957). Vessels of either Party shall be accorded national treatment and most-favored-nation treatment with respect to the right to carry all cargo that may be carried by vessel to or from the territories of the other Party.

Nicaragua (Art. XIX(4) of FCN Treaty) 9 UST 449; TIAS 4024 (1958). Vessels of either Party shall be accorded national treatment and most-favored-nation treatment by the other Party with respect to the right to carry all products that may be carried by vessel to or from the territories of such other Party.

Turkey (Art. III of FCN Treaty) TS 819; 46 Stat. 2743 (1930).
(a) Vessels of the United States of America will enjoy in Turkey and Turkish vessels will enjoy in the United States of America the same treatment as national vessels.
(b) (Exceptions not relevant)
(c) All other exceptions not included in those mentioned above shall be subject to most-favored-nation treatment.

Viet-Nam (Art. XI(4) of FCN Treaty) 12 UST 1703; TIAS 4890 (1961). Vessels of either Party shall be accorded national treatment and most-favored-nation treatment by the other Party with respect to the right to carry all products that may be carried by vessel to or from the territories of such other Party.

ANNEX 16

Most-favoured-nation treatment – flag preference

Argentina (Art. III of FCN Treaty TS 4; 10 Stat. 1005 (1854) The two High Contracting Parties agree that any favor, exemption, privilege or immunity whatever, in matters of commerce or navigation, which either of them has actually granted, or may hereafter grant, to the citizens or subjects of any other government, nation, or state, shall extend, in identity of cases and circumstances to the citizens of the other Contracting Party, gratuitously, if the concession in favor of that other government, nation, or state shall have been gratuitous – or, in return for an equivalent compensation, if the concession shall have been conditional.

Bolivia (Art. 2 of FCN Treaty) TS 32; 12 Stat. 1003 (1862). If either party shall, hereafter, grant to any other nation, its citizens or subjects, any particular favor in navigation or commerce, it shall, immediately, become common to the other party, freely, when freely granted to such other nation, or as yielding the same compensation when the grant is conditional.

Columbia (Art. II of FCN Treaty) TS 54; 9 Stat. 881 (1848). The United States of America and the Republic of New Granada, desiring to live in peace and harmony with all the nations of the earth, by means of a policy frank and equally friendly with all, engage mutually not to grant any particular favor to other nations, in respect of commerce and navigation, which shall not immediately become common to the other party, who shall enjoy the same freely, if the concession was freely made, or on allowing the same compensation, if the concession was conditional.

Costa Rica (Art. III of FCN Treaty) TS 62; 10 Stat. 916 (1852). It being the intention of the two High Contracting Parties to bind themselves by the preceding Articles to treat each other on the footing of the most favored nation, it is hereby agreed between them, that any favor, privilege, or immunity whatever, in matters of commerce and navigation which either Contracting Party has actually granted or may hereafter grant, to the subjects of any other State, shall be extended to the subjects or citizens of the other High Contracting Party, gratuitously, if the concessions in favor of that other nation shall have been gratuitous, or in return for compensation as nearly as possible of proportionate value and effort, to be adjusted by mutual agreement, if the concession shall have been conditional.

Nepal (Art. 7 of FCN Treaty) TIAS 1585; 61 Stat. 2566 (1947). Any advantage, favor, privilege or immunity with respect to any duty, charge or regulation affecting commerce or navigation now or hereafter accorded by the United States of American or by the Kingdom of Nepal to any third country shall be accorded immediately and unconditionally to the commerce and navigation of the Kingdom of Nepal and of the United States of America, respectively.

Paraquay (Art. III of FCN Treaty) TS 272; 12 Stat. 1091 (1860). The two High Contracting Parties hereby agree that any favor, privilege, or immunity whatever, in matters of commerce or navigation which either Contracting Party has actually granted, or may hereafter grant to the citizens or subjects of any other State shall extend in identity of cases and circumstances, to the citizens of the other Contracting Party gratuitously, if the concession in favor of that other State shall have been gratuitous, or in return for an equivalent compensation, if the concession shall have been conditional.

Thailand (Art. 7 of FCN Treaty) TS 940; 53 Stat. 1731 (1938). No duties of tonnage, harbor, pilotage, lighthouse, quarantine or other similar corresponding duties or charges of whatever nature or of whatever denomination levied in the name or for the profit of the Government, public functionaires, private individuals, corporations or establishments of any kind shall be imposed in the ports of the territories or territorial waters of either country upon the vessels of the other country, which shall not equally and under the same conditions be imposed in the like cases on national vessels. Such equality of treatment shall apply reciprocally to the respective vessels, from whatever port or place they may arrive and whatever may be their place of destination. In no case shall the treatment accorded to the vessels and cargoes of one of the Parties be less favorable than that accorded to the vessels and cargoes of any third State.

Yemen (Art. IV of FCN Treaty) TIAS 1535; 60 Stat. 1782 (1946). Any advantage, favor, privilege or immunity with respect to any duty, charge or regulation affecting commerce or navigation now or herafter accorded by the United States of America or by the Kingdom of Yemen to any third country will be accorded immediately and unconditionally to the commerce and navigation of the Kingdom of Yemen and of the United States of America, respectively.

Yugoslavia (Art. XIII of FCN Treaty) TS 319; 22 Stat. 963 (1982). Ships of the United States and their cargoes shall in Serbia, and Serbian ships and their cargoes shall in the United States, from whatsoever place arriving, and whatever may be the place of origin or destination of their cargoes, be treated in every respect as the ships and cargoes of the most favored state. The preceding stipulation applies to local treatment, dues and charges in the ports, basins, docks, roadsteads, harbors and rivers of the two countries, pilotage, and generally to all matters connected with navigation.

Every favor or exemption in these respects, or any other privilege in matters of navigation which either of the contracting parties shall grant to a third power shall be extended immediately and unconditionally to the other party.

ANNEX 17

Miscellaneous preferences and discriminations

Austria (Art. VII of FCN Treaty) TS 838; 47 Stat. 1876 (1931). All articles which are or may be legally imported from foreign countries into ports of the United States or are or may be legally exported therefrom in vessels or the United States may likewise be imported into these ports or exported therefrom in Australian vessels without being liable to any other or higher duties or charges whatsoever than if such articles were imported or exported in vessels of the United States.

Honduras (Art. VII of FCN Treaty) TS 764; 45 Stat. 2618 (1928). All articles which are or may be legally imported from foreign countries into ports of the United States or are or into these ports or exported therefrom in Honduran vessels without being liable to any other or higher duties or charges whatsoever than if such articles were imported in vessels of the United States.

Finland (Art. XII of FCN Treaty) TS 868; 49 Stat. 2659 (1934). All articles which are or may be legally imported from foreign countries into ports of the territory of the United States or are or may be legally exported therefrom in vessels of the United States may likewise be imported into these ports or exported therefrom in Finnish vessels without being liable to any other or higher duties or charges whatsoever than if such articles were imported or exported in vessels of the United States.

Norway (Art. VII of FCN Treaty) TS 348; 8 Stat. 346 (1828). All Articles which are or may be legally imported from foreign countries into ports of the United States or are or may be legally exported therefrom in vessels of the United State may likewise be imported into those ports or exported therefrom in Norwegian vessel, without being liable to any other or higher duties whatsoever than if such articles were imported or exported in vessels of the United States.

About the author

Dr. Ademuni-Odeke, who lives and works in the United Kingdom, was born on the 22nd of May, 1950 in the eastern Ugandan town of Tororo. He was educated there and at King's College Budo and Makerere University, Kampala, before being forced into exile, by the former Amin dictatorship. He lived briefly in East and Central Africa and obtained a bachelor's degree in law (LLB) with honours in Legal Aspects of International Trade and Investments from the Faculty of Law, University of Dar es Salaam-Tanzania. He later obtained a Master's degree (LLM) in Maritime Law from the Faculty of Law of Southampton University, and a Doctorate (PhD) in International Shipping at the Institute of Maritime Law of the same University. Professionally, he is a fall Corporate Member of the British Institute of Management (MBIM); and a Companion of the Nautical Institute.

He has had a varied career ranging from a Mining Engineer (Trainee) at a Copper Mining concern, in Uganda, to a National Organising Secretary of an International Charity and Coordinator of the World Council of Churches' (WCC) Economic Feasibility Studies of the Anglican Provinces of the Churches of Uganda, Ruanda, Burundi and Zaire. He later became a State Attorney at the Ministry of Justice and Attorney General's Chamber, United Republic of Tanzania, and Legal/Deputy Corporation Secretary of an International Investment Bank in the same country. In this latter aspect Dr. Ademuni-Odeke's experience involved handling the purchase of second hand ships for the defunct Eastern African National Shipping Line.

After several years at the Institute of Maritime Law, Southampton University, he spent some time on consultancy with the Southampton based International Chamber of Commerce Project looking into possibilities of joint Shipping Ventures between the Advanced and Developing Countries. He is currently a Lecturer in Maritime Law and Legal Aspects of International Trade, at the Department of Private Law of the University of Aberdeen Scotland. He is also a free-lance Maritime Consultant as well as being on the list of experts with the UNCTAD Shipping Committee, the International Maritime Organisation (IMO), Commonwealth Development Corporation, International Labour Organisation (ILO), etc.

His research and publication interests are the legal, economic and political aspects of International Shipping, especially the New International Maritime Order, Developing Country Shipping, Flag Discriminations, Flag Discriminations, Flag Preferences, Cargo Reservations, Cabotage Restrictions, State Interventions, Maritime Subsidies, Bilateralism, and other Restrictive Shipping Practices. He has written on the UN Code of Conduct for Liner Conferences. He is a member of several professional and International Maritime Organisations including the International Commission of Jurists (Justice-British Section), Junior Chambers International (Aberdeen Branch), The Scottish Group of International Lawyers, The Society of Public Law Teachers, The International Bar Association, Third World Foundation (founder member), the National Maritime Economists' Conferences, and International Chamber of Commerce.

Index